Fodor's

THE BEST OF
ITALY

Welcome to Italy

Rome, Florence, and Venice are home to awe-inspiring art and architecture, iconic museums, and stunning historical ruins—as well as some of the world's best food, wine, and shopping. Also beckoning are the sun-kissed olive groves and vineyards, charming hill towns, and atmospheric castles, monasteries, and farmhouses of the Tuscan and Umbrian countryside. As you plan your travels to Italy, please confirm that places are still open and let us know when we need to make updates by writing to us at: editors@fodors.com.

TOP REASONS TO GO

★ **Food:** Italy is a pasta lover's paradise, but don't forget the pizza and the gelato.

★ **Romance:** Whether you're strolling atmospheric Venice or sipping wine, Italy enchants.

★ **History:** The ruins of ancient Rome and the leaning tower of Pisa breathe antiquity.

★ **Art:** The big hitters—Botticelli, Michelangelo, Raphael, Caravaggio, and more.

★ **Shopping:** Few things say quality or style like "made in Italy."

★ **Stunning landscapes:** Tuscany, Umbria, the Cinque Terre, to name just a few.

Contents

MAPS

Fodor's Features

EXPERIENCE THE BEST OF ITALY

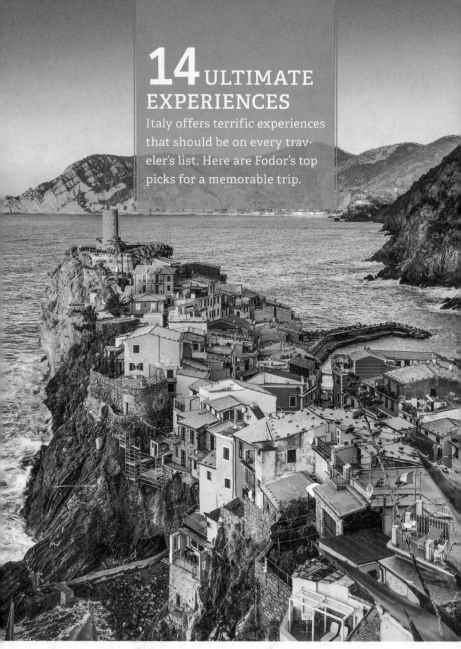

14 ULTIMATE EXPERIENCES

Italy offers terrific experiences that should be on every traveler's list. Here are Fodor's top picks for a memorable trip.

1 Hike the Cinque Terre

Walk the scenic footpaths that connect the five former fishing villages that make up the Cinque Terre; each one appears to hang off the cliffs, allowing for absolutely stunning views of the vineyards above and blue waters below. (Ch. 5)

2 People-Watch in Venice

Venice's Piazza San Marco (St. Mark's Square), flanked by the gorgeous Basilica di San Marco, is certainly one of the world's loveliest squares for people-watching. (Ch. 4)

3 Shop in Milan

In Italy's fashion capital of Milan, you'll find the highest of high-end designers in the Quadrilatero della Moda district, north of the Duomo. (Ch. 5)

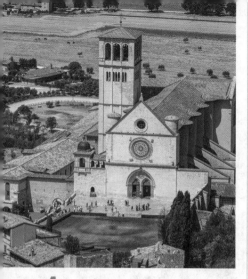

4 See Assisi's Frescos

The peaceful medieval town of Assisi is home to enormous Basilica di San Francesco, which includes 28 frescoes showing the life of St. Francis. (Ch. 7)

5 Marvel at Mosaics

Some of the greatest Byzantine mosaics can be found in the unassuming city of Ravenna. You can view the most elaborate ones in the 5th-century Mausoleo di Galla Placidia. (Ch. 5)

6 Ponder *The Last Supper*

Restoration work has returned *The Last Supper* to its original glory, so the painting is amazingly clear and luminous. (Ch. 5)

7 See a Medieval City

Perhaps Italy's best-preserved medieval city, Siena's narrow streets are fun to explore. The Piazza del Campo is one of the most beautiful squares in the country. (Ch. 7)

8 Toss a Coin in Trevi

The can't-miss-Instagramming Trevi Fountain, in Rome, is a Baroque fantasy of sea beasts, seashells, and mermaids in front of a triumphal arch. (Ch. 3)

9 Rent a Villa in Tuscany

One of the supreme pleasures of a visit to the countryside of Tuscany is the chance to stay in a villa—preferably one with a swimming pool and vineyard views. (Ch. 7)

10 The Vatican Museums

As the home base for the Catholic Church and the papacy, the Vatican sees millions of visitors each year, who come to explore its museums and Michelangelo's Sistine Chapel. (Ch. 3)

11 Taste Wine in Chianti

With 17,000 acres of vineyards, sipping your way through Chianti is a fine way to spend a day. (Ch. 7)

12 Walk Along Lucca's Walls

This elevated walkway is the site of what for some is a daily ritual of *passeggiata delle mura* (walk along the walls). (Ch. 7)

13 See Michelangelo's *David*

David, 17 feet of Carrara marble carved by Michelangelo in the 1500s, could be the most famous man in the world. (Ch. 6)

14 Stand in Awe

Dominating Florence's skyline, the magnificent Duomo is an architectural marvel that took almost 600 years to complete. (Ch. 6)

WHAT'S WHERE

1 Rome. Italy's capital is one of the greatest cities in Europe. It's a large, busy metropolis that lives in the here and now, yet there's no other place on earth where you'll encounter such powerful evocations of a storied and spectacular past, from the Colosseum to St. Peter's.

2 Venice. One of the world's most unusual cities, Venice has canals instead of streets, along with an atmosphere of faded splendor. It's also a major international cultural center.

3 Northern Italy. In the Veneto region of Italy, the green plains stretching west of Venice hold three of northern Italy's most artistically significant midsize cities: Padua, Vicenza, and Verona. To the west is Milan, Italy's second-largest city and its business capital. It holds Italy's most renowned opera house, and as the hub of Italian fashion and design, it's a shopper's paradise. Northern Italy's attractive coastline runs along the Italian Riviera and includes Cinque Terre and its famous hiking trails and villages. Many of Italy's signature foods come from the Emilia-Romagna region, where Bologna is a significant cultural center and the mosaics of Ravenna are glittering Byzantine treasures.

4 Florence. In the 15th century, Florence was at the center of an artistic revolution, later labeled the Renaissance, which changed the way people saw the world. Five hundred years later the Renaissance remains the reason people visit Florence.

5 Tuscany and Umbria. Outside of Florence, the town of Lucca is laid-back yet elegant while Pisa is still famous for its leaning tower. The hills spreading south of Florence make up Chianti, a region of sublime wine. South of Chianti, hillside towns like Arezzo and Cortona offer gorgeous views of the countryside. In Tuscany, Siena remains one of Italy's most appealing medieval towns. Umbria, north of Rome, is a region of beautiful rolling hills topped by towns full of history, like Orvieto, Spoleto, Perugia, and Assisi, the birthplace of Saint Francis.

Elevation

feet	meters
15,577	4,748
10,825	3,300
9,840	3,000
8,860	2,700
7,875	2,400
6,900	2,100
5,900	1,800
4,920	1,500
3,940	1,200
2,920	900
1,970	600
980	300
490	150
250	75
100	30

Best Ancient Sites in Rome

COLOSSEUM

Perhaps the monument most symbolic of ancient Rome, the Colosseum is one of the city's most fascinating—and popular—tourist attractions. It officially opened in AD 80 with 100 days of games, including wild-animal fights and gladiatorial combat.

FORO DI TRAIANO

Trajan's Forum was the last of imperial Rome's forums—and the grandest. Comprising a basilica, two libraries, and a colonnade surrounding a piazza, it's connected to a market that once bustled with commercial activity.

PANTHEON

Built as a pagan temple to the gods, the Pantheon is Rome's best-preserved ancient site, perhaps because it was later consecrated as a church. Step inside and you'll be amazed at its perfect proportions and the sunlight streaming in from the 30-foot-wide oculus. It's truly a wonder of ancient engineering.

ROMAN FORUM

One of the Eternal City's most emblematic sites, the Roman Forum stretches out between the Capitoline and Palatine Hills. This vast area filled with crumbling columns and the ruins of temples, palaces, and shops was once the hub of the ancient world and the center of political, commercial, and religious life in the city.

CIRCUS MAXIMUS

It might be hard to imagine now, but the grassy area between the Palatine and Aventine Hills was once the site of the largest hippodrome in the Roman Empire. The huge oval course was rebuilt under Julius Caesar and later enlarged by subsequent emperors. During its heyday, it hosted epic chariot races and competitions that sometimes lasted as long as 15 days.

BOCCA DELLA VERITÀ

Legend has it the mouth in this ancient stone face will bite off the hand of a liar, and tourists line up to stick their hand inside the mouth and put it to the test. (Gregory Peck's character tricks Audrey Hepburn's Princess Ann into thinking he lost a hand inside it in a scene from *Roman Holiday*.) You'll find the enigmatic face in the portico of the Church of Santa Maria in Cosmedin, near the Circus Maximus.

The Roman Forum

TEATRO MARCELLO
It may look a bit like a smaller version of the Colosseum, but the Teatro Marcello was once ancient Rome's largest and most important theater. Julius Caesar ordered the land for the theater to be cleared, but he was murdered before it was built. It was inaugurated in AD 12 by Augustus and hosted performances of drama and song. It's kept that purpose even today, at least during the summer, when it hosts concerts.

APPIA ANTICA
Head to the southeastern edge of the city to Appia Antica Park and you can walk on the same stones that ancient Roman soldiers and citizens once trod—which are incredibly well-preserved. This ancient thoroughfare once stretched all the way to Brindisi, some 300 miles away on the Adriatic Coast. Today, the first 10 miles are part of a regional park, and it's a perfect spot for bike rides and picnics in the grass under the shadow of Rome's emblematic umbrella pines.

ARA PACIS AUGUSTAE
Now housed in a modern glass-and-travertine building designed by renowned American architect Richard Meier, the Ara Pacis Augustae has some of the most incredible reliefs you'll see on any ancient monument. It was commissioned to celebrate the Emperor Augustus's victories in battle and the Pax Romana, a peaceful period that followed. It's centrally located on the Tiber River and definitely worth a visit.

BATHS OF CARACALLA
A testament to ancient Rome's bathing culture, this site was essentially a massive spa, with saunas, baths, what would be an Olympic-size pool, and two gymnasiums for boxing, weightlifting, and wrestling.

Best Museums in Rome

MAXXI

Tucked away in the quiet Flaminio neighborhood, the Museo Nazionale delle Arti del XXI Secolo (National Museum of 21st Century Arts)—or MAXXI, for short—proves that there's more to Rome than ancient and Baroque art.

CAPITOLINE MUSEUMS

Second in size only to the Vatican Museums, the Capitoline Museums were the world's first public art museums. The two buildings on Michelangelo's famous piazza house a collection spanning from Ancient Rome to the Baroque era, with masterpieces including Caravaggio's *The Fortune Teller* and *St. John the Baptist*.

GALLERIA NAZIONALE D'ARTE MODERNA E CONTEMPORANEA

Located within Villa Borghese, this art museum in a huge white Beaux Arts building hosts one of Italy's most important collections of 19th- and 20th-century art. You'll find works by Degas, Monet, Courbet, Cézanne, and Van Gogh, but the emphasis is on understanding Italian Modernism through a historical lens.

GALLERIA BORGHESE

It would be hard to find a more beautiful villa filled with a must-see collection of masterpieces by Bernini, Caravaggio, Raphael, Rubens, and Titian. Cardinal Scipione Borghese had the gorgeous Renaissance villa built in 1612 to display his collection, though it has undergone many changes since.

MUSEO NAZIONALE ETRUSCO DI VILLA GIULIA

The pre-Roman civilization known as the Etruscans appeared in Italy around 2,000 BC, though no one knows exactly where they originated. To learn more about them, plan a visit to this museum in Villa Giulia, which was built for Pope Julius III in the mid-1500s.

PALAZZO DORIA PAMPHILJ

For a glimpse into aristocratic Rome, it's hard to beat this museum in the 15th century palazzo of the Doria Pamphilj family. Wander through the Hall of Mirrors—fashioned after the one at Versailles, naturally—but don't miss the Old Master paintings.

VATICAN MUSEUMS
One of the largest museum complexes in the world, the Vatican palaces and museums comprise some 1,400 rooms, galleries, and chapels. By far the most famous is the Sistine Chapel painted by Michelangelo and a team of other painters, but the Raphael Rooms come in a close second when it comes to must-see works.

MACRO
Housed in the former Peroni brewery, this modern and contemporary art museum focuses on Italian art from the 1960s through the present. The building, with its striking red structure and glass walkways, was designed by French architect Odile Decq and is worth a visit in and of itself.

CENTRALE MONTEMARTINI
Nowhere else is the theme of gods and machines more apparent than at this museum. Rome's first power plant now houses the runoff from the Capitoline Museums' collection; the sculptures of men in togas and women in dresses form a poignant contrast to the machinery.

Architectural Wonders in Venice

PONTE DI RIALTO
The iconic Ponte di Rialto was completed in 1591. Its generous arch, central portal, and Renaissance arcade make it appear so beautifully balanced that Palladio himself would surely have approved.

SAN FRANCESCO DELLA VIGNA
The harmonious combination of architectural designs by two Renaissance maestri and the tranquil neighborhood setting make this church a wonderful place to escape the crowds.

MOLINO STUCKY
This behemoth, neo-Gothic warehouse-like building, formerly a flour mill and pasta factory, on the western end of the Giudecca certainly stands out on the Venetian skyline.

SANTA MARIA DELLA SALUTE
One of the city's most beloved and iconic churches, La Salute was built to mark the end of the 1630 plague that took almost 50,000 Venetian lives.

PUNTA DELLA DOGANA
There has been a Punta della Dogana (Sea Customs House) situated between the Grand and Giudecca Canals since the 15th century, although the building you see today was designed in the 1860s. Above the entrance tower, two Atlases lift a bronze sphere topped by the figure of Fortune.

ARSENALE
For centuries, the colossal Arsenale complex of shipyards, warehouses, and armories was Europe's largest military-industrial compound. Although many areas are still cordoned off as military zones, the southern side is open to the public during the Biennale di Arte.

JEWISH GHETTO
Originally the site of a foundry (*geto* in the local dialect), both the atmosphere and the architecture set the Jewish Ghetto apart: *palazzi* and *case* are taller here than elsewhere, with story upon story piled on high in an effort to make the best use of limited space.

Palazzo Ducale

PALAZZO DUCALE

Adorned with a series of soaring Gothic arches topped by an ornately columned arcade, the labyrinthine Palazzo Ducale has a wedding-cake-like delicacy when viewed from the Piazza San Marco or the waterside Bacino di San Marco.

MADONNA DELL'ORTO

An alluring, redbrick Gothic church with ornate marble decoration, it was dedicated to St. Christopher, the patron saint of travelers, until a Madonna statue was found in a nearby *orto* (kitchen vegetable garden).

CA' DA MOSTO

As you drift along the Grand Canal, you'll see palazzi far more eye-catching than the Ca' da Mosto, but none more enduring—the crumbling Byzantine-style palace has been here since the 13th century. The ground and first floors are an example of a *casa-fondaco*.

10 Best Museums in Florence

PALAZZO PITTI
Florence's rich and powerful all walked down the halls of Palazzo Pitti. In its current museum status, its gallery rooms and royal apartments are lavishly decorated as a palace should be. With more than 500 paintings (mostly Renaissance-era) including works by Raphael and Titian.

BARGELLO
The fortress-like Bargello has had many incarnations—family palace, Florentine government building, prison, and the site of executions on its patio. As a nod to its conflicted past, it also houses a collection of weapons, armor, and medals from the powerful Medici family. The real draw though is Donatello's bronze *David* standing victorious over the head of Goliath, Michelangelo's marble *Bacchus*, and a collection from major Renaissance sculptors.

GALLERIA DEGLI UFFIZI
It's one of the most visited museums in Florence, Italy, and the world, for a reason. Head to the former offices of Florentine magistrates to see a wow-worthy collection of art. In one room, gaze at Sandro Botticelli's *Birth of Venus* and *Primavera*, and in another, Leonardo da Vinci's *Annunciation*. Works by Michelangelo, Raphael, Giotto, and Caravaggio are also here and museum aficionados may want to spend several hours exploring. Avoid the lines by booking tickets in advance on the Uffizi Gallery website.

GALLERIA DELL'ACCADEMIA
Come for *David*, stay to see everything else. There's no doubt that the line running down Via Ricasoli to enter a seemingly nondescript building is for Michelangelo's most famous man in the world—*Il Davide*. There is something marvelous about seeing his 17 feet of artfully carved Carrara marble "in the flesh," poised before his battle with Goliath. After you've caught your breath, check out the museum's early- to late-Renaissance works by Sandro Botticelli, and Andrea del Sarto; Florentine Gothic paintings; and collection of musical instruments.

MUSEO DELL'OPERA DEL DUOMO
When Santa Maria del Fiore—also known as Florence cathedral, or Il Duomo—was completed in the late 1400s along with its baptistery and bell tower, it was the largest church in Europe, and was decorated by some of Italy's most celebrated artists. But those master works that you see on the cathedral today, like Lorenzo Ghiberti's famous doors, or Gates of Paradise, which took him 27 years to finish, are fake, to save the original bronze from the elements. The doors and some of the other decorations and sculptures that once adorned the church are now housed in the Museo dell'Opera del Duomo.

MUSEO SALVATORE FERRAGAMO

You may think that you've died and gone to shoe heaven at this museum in a former palazzo that has been the former southern Italian–born shoe designer's workshop since 1938. The permanent collection from the brand's archives includes a Technicolor-and-gold wedge sandal that looks like it was designed with a Judy Garland "Somewhere Over the Rainbow" theme in mind for her in 1938, and a cross-strap ballet flat created for Audrey Hepburn's slim feet in the 1950s (which became one of the designer's signature styles and is still made today). Because of Ferragamo's status as a "creator to the stars," the museum often runs temporary exhibits that merge history, film, art, and culture, with fashion history.

PALAZZO STROZZI

Unlike city-run museums in Florence (such as Galleria degli Uffizi), Palazzo Strozzi is an independent foundation, meaning the exhibits here range from classic to avant-garde. On show could be a retrospective of cinquecento art in Florence, a 65-foot spiral tunnel for visitors called The Florence Experiment, or controversial performance artist Marina Abramovic's *The Cleaner*, featuring live nude actors. There is also a permanent collection about the history of the palace, which was built for prominent Florentine banker, Filippo Strozzi, who died before it was completed.

PALAZZO VECCHIO

Also called Palazzo della Signoria, the monumental building surrounded by one of Italy's most famous piazzas has been home to Florence's city government since the Renaissance. Walk past a copy of Michelangelo's *David* at the entrance, and up opulent marble staircases to see expansive gold-highlighted and frescoed ceilings and walls. The Salone dei Cinquecento is one of the most grand, designed and painted by celebrated art historian (and artist in his own right), Giorgio Vasari.

SANTA CROCE

In Florence, churches are museums, too. At Santa Croce—considered the largest Franciscan church in the world (and said to be founded by St. Francis of Assisi)—you'll find 16 chapels that were once frequented by significant Florentine families who funded their decoration. There are frescoes by Renaissance master Giotto in the Bardi and Peruzzi chapels, and a terracotta altarpiece by another quattrocento heavy hitter, Andrea Della Robbia. If the art isn't enough of a draw to visit one of Florence's most significant churches, the basilica also holds the tombs of Michelangelo, Galileo, and Machiavelli.

Santa Croce

SANTA MARIA NOVELLA

Dominican monks founded the basilica of Santa Maria Novella in the 13th century, making it one of the most religiously significant churches in Florence—and it still is. The facade is a beauty, with green and white marble inlay work by Genoa-born Leon Battista Alberti. Inside are some of the world's finest examples of Renaissance art. Masaccio's *Trinita* fresco, painted in the 1400s (which was covered and rediscovered in the 1800s), is on the main altar and is considered one of the earliest examples of perspective during the Renaissance. Giotto's *Crucifix* is another master work that was likely painted in the late 1200s. In the basilica's largest chapel, Tornabuoni, Ghirlandaio painted frescoes about the Virgin Mary's life (to whom the church is dedicated) in the late 1400s.

Best Hilltop Villages in Tuscany and Umbria

MONTEFOLLONICO, SIENA

Montefollonico's name alludes to textile workers, likely honoring the wool-working monks who settled the village in the Middle Ages, though the area has been inhabited for at least 60,000 years, from the time Neanderthals left behind artifacts that have been more recently uncovered.

ASSISI, UMBRIA

Assisi claims history as ancient as 1000 BC and is probably best known for its most famous resident, St. Francis, whose 13th-century basilica is now a UNESCO World Heritage Site. In fact, the entire village itself is, too. Plenty of other impressive churches, Roman ruins, and not one but two castles top the extensive list of architectural offerings of this ancient town. From ceramics to medieval weaponry, Assisi's artisan history remains strong. Cured meats and chocolate are popular here, so grab a snack between sword fights, and refuel on the Assisi ribbon-type pasta *stringozzi*, often served with Norcia black truffles, asparagus, or *piccante* (spicy) tomato sauce.

ORVIETO, UMBRIA

A quintessential medieval Italian village so evocative that dozens of Italian TV shows and movies have been filmed there, Orvieto is also a foodie's dream. Famous for both white and red wines, Orvieto's culinary classics run the gamut from boar and dove to pastas and pastries that will keep you eating around the clock. Above all, olive oil reigns supreme in this Umbrian village, which is probably the reason why Orvieto's culinary specialty seems to be . . . everything. While architectural wonders adorn the village (including the massive 13th-century Duomo), what's underground may be even more fascinating: a series of more than 1,000 tunnels forms a labyrinth under Orvieto, and much of it is now open to the public for exploration.

PITIGLIANO, TUSCANY

While most Italian villages are overflowing with impressive churches, Pitigliano may be most famous for its synagogue, drawing attention to its rich history of Jewish settlement and giving the old town its nickname of Little Jerusalem. Of course, countless churches dot the rest of this Tuscan village, as do a smattering of museums and other historic gems like the Palazzo Orsini, a Renaissance palace built on the ruins of medieval fortresses and containing both art and archaeological museums of its own.

SAN GIMIGNANO, TUSCANY

While most medieval towers have given way to war and erosion through the centuries, San Gimignano retains so many that it has been dubbed the Town of Fine Towers and its historic center is a UNESCO World Heritage Site. While packed with immaculate examples of medieval architecture, this village is among the more tourist-minded, with contemporary events like music festivals and art exhibitions, and plenty of modern conveniences and services for travelers. San Gimignano even has its own app.

SORANO, TUSCANY

Ham it up in Sorano, where the local ham is so revered they hold a festival for it every August. If you don't eat pork, don't worry; there are plenty of other local specialties highlighted in this festival, particularly dairy products including sheep's milk ricotta cheese and fruits, such as oranges—not to mention the ever-popular Italian liqueur, limoncello. Don't miss the Masso Leopoldina (sometimes called the Rocca Vecchia), which was once central to the defense of the town but is now a fabulous terrace for panoramic views of Tuscany (and a great place to swig another limoncello).

VOLTERRA, UMBRIA

Twelve miles from the better-known village of San Gimignano is the less visited (less crowded) Volterra. While there are some serious medieval remnants in this village, especially its narrow streets in the town center, it's much more famous for the historical periods before and after. Some of its ancient Etruscan fortification walls still surround Roman ruins, including an impressive amphitheater worth exploring (there are also remains of ancient Roman baths and a forum). The Florentine influence of the Medici family left behind some dazzling Renaissance art and architecture throughout the once bustling mercantile village. The alabaster trade remains strong today and provides beautiful souvenirs from this Tuscan treasure.

TODI, UMBRIA

Compact and ancient Todi is a hilltop citadel town with a strong whiff of a real-life fairytale medieval castle complex. Todi's beautiful patchwork architecture interweaves three sturdy walls, begun by the 3rd-century Etruscans followed by Romans and medieval dynasties. Starting at the café-community hub Piazza del Popolo, with an imposing 12th-century Romanesque-Gothic Duomo built upon a Roman temple, a maze of cobbled lanes and steep staircases fan out, inviting leisurely exploration. For grandstand views over roofs and the Umbrian hills beyond, climb the campanile of San Fortunato, and leafy walks abound in the Parco della Rocca, the city-wall park.

Italy Today

ENDURING CUISINE

The old joke goes that three-quarters of the food and wine served in Italy is good—and the rest is amazing. In some sense, that's still true, and the "good" 75% has gotten even better. Those pundits would claim that ingredients that in the past were available only to the wealthy can now be found even in the remotest parts of the country at reasonable prices. Dishes originally conceived to make the most of inferior cuts of meat or the least flavorful part of vegetables are now made with the best.

But many Italians would say that the food in Italy is getting worse. There's a proliferation of fast-food establishments, and increasing tourism has allowed many restaurants to lower their standards while raising their prices. This is true not only in Rome, but in most other tourist centers as well. The good news is Italy is home to one of the world's greatest cuisines, and its traditional favorites still put meat on bones and smiles on faces. Italian restaurateurs seem determined to make the most of the country's reputation for good food. Although quaint, family-run trattorias with checkered tablecloths, traditional dishes, and an informal atmosphere are still common if on the decline, nearly every town has a newer eatery with matching flatware, a proper wine list, and an innovative menu.

This also holds for Italian wine. Today, through investment and experimentation, Italy's winemakers are figuring out how to get the most from their gorgeous vineyards. It's fair to say that Italy now produces more types of high-quality wine from more different grape varieties than any other country in the world.

SOCCER RULES

Soccer (or, as the Italians say, *calcio*—which means "kick") stands without rival as the national sport of Italy, though some complain that big-money influence and loose financial regulations are polluting the beautiful game. That aside, Italy did win its fourth World Cup in 2006 giving the country more world titles than any other this side of Brazil. More recently, Italy won the prestigious UEFA Euro 2020 championship (though due to COVID-19 it was played in 2021). Although the game is still played at a high level, its teams have not fared as well in European club competitions recently. More games in the schedule and a dwindling fan base mean fewer people are seen at the stadium. Still, fans can't stop watching the game on television.

AN AGING POPULATION

Italy's population is the oldest in Europe (as percentage of population)—the result of its low birth rate and one of the highest life-expectancy rates in the world. The median age of an Italian in 2015 was 45.9; projections for 2021 are 47.3. Chronic underfunding of the public healthcare system has left older Italians particularly vulnerable to COVID-19.

Italy's famously stable population is now aging and set to contract according to recent estimates, putting a strain on the country's pension system and on families because elderly family members are likely to live with their children or grandchildren in a country where retirement homes are rare.

The trend also has an impact in other areas, including politics (where older politicians are eager to promote policies aimed at older voters), the popular culture (where everything from fashion to television programming takes older consumers into consideration), and a kind of far-reaching nostalgia. Thanks to a long collective memory, it's common to hear even younger Italians celebrate or rue something that happened 50 or 60 years earlier as if it had just taken place.

THE BLACK-MARKET ECONOMY

Nobody knows how big Italy's black-market economy is, though experts all agree it's massive. The presence of the black market isn't obvious to the casual observer, but whenever a customer isn't given a printed receipt in a store or restaurant, tobacco without a tax seal is bought from a street seller, or a product or service is exchanged for another product or service, that means the transaction goes unrecorded, unreported, and untaxed. But that's all penny-ante stuff compared to what many professionals evade by neglecting to declare all they earn.

Austerity measures imposed in 2012 have led to much disgruntlement among the population; now most shopkeepers insist that you take a receipt. If you don't, you could be fined, as could the shopkeeper. These measures remain in place, but the country still struggles to meet the 3% limit to its budget deficit as mandated by European Union (EU) agreements, and it is pretty certain that Italy will continue to struggle to meet it in coming years.

A GROWING PARKS SYSTEM

Italy has 25 national parks covering a total of around 1½ million hectares (5,800 square miles), or about 6% of the entire surface area of the country—more than twice as much as 25 years ago.

Part of the reason for the expansion has been a growing environmental movement in Italy, which has lobbied the government to annex undeveloped land for parks, thus protecting against development. But the trend is a boon for visitors and nature lovers, who can enjoy huge expanses of unspoiled territory.

STAYING HOME IN AUGUST

Italy used to be the best example of Europe's famous August exodus, when city dwellers would spend most of the month at the seaside or in the mountains, leaving the cities nearly deserted. Today the phenomenon is less prevalent, as economic pressures have forced companies to keep operating through August. As a result, vacations are more staggered and more modest.

The loss of shared vacation time for Italian workers means good things for visitors: in August there's a little more room on beaches and mountains; in addition, cities promote events for nonvacationing natives. Summers in Italy now offer a plethora of outdoor concerts and theatrical events, extended museum hours, and local festivals.

MUSEI DIFFUSI

In recent years the idea of promoting tourism away from Italy's increasingly clogged destinations has spurred the idea of Musei Diffusi or "Scattered Museums." COVID regulations and social-distancing measures have only accelerated the need to support local communities and encourage visitors to seek out art and linger in sleepy, overlooked hilltop *borghi* instead of queuing for hours to glimpse Botticelli's *Venus*. The trend has evolved from Strade dei Vini (Wine Roads) and themed itineraries: now grand collections like the Uffizi are launching curator-led online exhibition tours and dusting off artworks in storage destined for display in municipal collections.

What to Watch and Read

ITALIAN FOLKTALES
BY ITALO CALVINO

In 1956 the celebrated, Cuban-born and Liguria-raised, magical realist published this fabulous collection of some 200 traditional folktales from across the archipelago. The prose in the 800-page *Fiabe italiane* tome is simple yet evocative, and the stories appeal to young and old alike. They're largely fantastical morality tales involving love, loss, revenge, and adventure on the part of kings, princesses, saints, and peasants. The book is a fabulous bedtime or beach read.

AMARCORD, DIRECTED
BY FEDERICO FELLINI

Amarcord ("I remember," in the Romagnol dialect) is filled with comic archetypes and dreamlike excursions inspired by Fellini's 1930s adolescence in Rimini. The rosy-cheeked protagonist, Titta, and his pals have humorous encounters with authority figures—pompous schoolteachers, frustrated fathers, cruel Fascist officials—as well as with the buxom hairdresser, Gradisca. The 1973 movie, which won the Oscar for Best Foreign Language Film, offers poignant, entertaining, and often bonkers insight into the Italian psyche, family dynamics, and interwar society. Nino Rota's wistful soundtrack adds to the feeling of nostalgia.

THE ITALIANS BY JOHN HOOPER

In this 2015 book, longtime Rome correspondent John Hooper addresses the complexities of contemporary Italy, attempting to reveal "what makes the Italian tick." Here you'll learn the lexicon needed to negotiate and understand Italian culture. Of course, food, sex, and the weather—among other things—are heartily embraced in everyday life, but there is also an *amaro* (bitter) side.

Hooper illustrates how the power of the *famiglia* (family) and the *chiesa* (church) has produced a society in which *furbizia* (cunning) is rewarded and meritocracy is replaced with *raccomandazioni* (favors) to get ahead in the world.

THE LEOPARD
BY GIUSEPPE TOMASI
DI LAMPEDUSA

Il gattopardo, an Italian literary classic, chronicles the tumultuous, revolutionary years of the Risorgimento (1860s–early 20th century). Lampedusa was the last in a line of minor princes, and the novel, borne of a lengthy depression, was published in 1958, a year after his death. Set in Sicily, the epic story of decay amid a changing society centers on the ebbing influence and power of Don Fabrizio, Prince of Salina, and his family, and hints at the emergence of the Mafia. One particularly insightful quote in the book—spoken by the prince's young nephew, Tancredi—sheds light on how Italy adapts to shifting political forces and class struggle: "For everything to stay the same, everything must change."

COSA NOSTRA
BY JOHN DICKIE

Journalist and academic John Dickie packs a lot of gruesome detail into this fast-paced history of the Mafia. He traces the Cosa Nostra's origins during the Risorgimento years, its infiltration and corruption of the First Republic, and the curious and notorious role of the town of Corleone in its development. Dickie also recounts the organization's birth and rise in America, the Mafia Wars, and the recent crises and tragedies connected to Italy's corrupt political system.

THE CONFORMIST, DIRECTED BY BERNARDO BERTOLUCCI

Il conformista, Bertolucci's stylish psychological thriller set in 1930s Fascist Italy, is considered a postwar cinematic classic. As its name suggests, the 1970 film tackles the issue of conformity through the lens of the cruel, febrile political atmosphere created by Mussolini and his followers. Despite its dark themes, the movie is beautifully lit and shot, filled with vibrant colors, exquisite costuming, and atmospheric locations. It has inspired many directors of the American New Wave and beyond, including Martin Scorsese, Francis Ford Coppola, and the Coen brothers.

DELIZIA! BY JOHN DICKIE

If you think you know all there is to know about Italian food, you'll think again after reading this book. Dickie's gastronomic journey across the regions of Italy through the ages covers everything from *pastasciutta* in 12th-century Palermo to today's Slow Food movement in Turin. Carry this book with you as you travel, so you can compare your menu to, say, that for a 1529 Ferrara banquet, which featured "105 soused sea bream" and "15 large salted eels" for starters, followed by "104 roasted capon livers" and "sweet pastry tarts deep-filled with the spleens of sea bass, trout, pike and other fish." *Che delizia!*

THE GREAT BEAUTY, DIRECTED BY PAOLO SORRENTINO

Although directed by a Neapolitan, this Oscar-winning 2013 film is set in Rome and serves as a kind of contemporary *La Dolce Vita.* The lead character in *La grande bellezza,* Jep Gambardella (Toni Servillo), is an aging hedonistic journalist, who, while pining for his glory days, comes to realize the superficiality of his bourgeois lifestyle. Beset by Roman ennui after his raucous rooftop 65th-birthday bash, Jep goes in search of beauty beyond the vanity of his milieu.

THE NEAPOLITAN NOVELS

Elena Ferrante's novels (2012–15) and the HBO TV series bring multilayered postwar Naples to life, going beyond postcard beauty to portray the grim, savage reality of growing up in a rough *rione* (district). The four books explore the complexities of friendship and Italian society. With vivid depictions—mixing the palatial and the squalid—the pseudonymous author details the lifetime bond and inner lives of Elena and Lila and their interactions with a cast of characters across Italy as well as in Naples.

1992, 1993, AND 1994

The ten-episode television series *1992* and its follow-ups, *1993* and *1994,* (originally aired in 2015, 2017, and 2019, respectively) are political dramas that follow the intertwined lives of six people amid the tumult of early-1990s Italy. Massive cracks appear in the postwar political compromise, with the *Mani Pulite* (Clean Hands) investigation led by prosecutor Antonio Di Pietro initiating the fall of the First Republic. As the country is rocked by the so-called *Tangentopoli* (Bribesville) scandal, marketing man Stefano Accorsi sees an opportunity for an outside figure to seize power. And so up steps media tycoon Silvio Berlusconi and his populist Forza Italia party. Sound familiar?

Making the Most of Your Euros

TRANSPORTATION

Italy's state-sponsored train system has been given a run for its money by a private company. Sadly, the competitor (Italo) only operates major, high-speed connections (such as Rome to Naples, Florence to Venice, Milan to Bologna) and not local routes. Because of the competition, Trenitalia and Italo engage in price wars, which only plays to the consumer's advantage; depending on time of day and how far in advance you purchase the tickets, great bargains can be had.

No such good news exists for the *regionali* trains. These are trains connecting cities, highly frequented by commuters and used often by visitors who want to get to less visible towns. These trains are habitually late and almost always crowded. Patience is a virtue, and much-needed when taking them, particularly during high season.

FOOD AND DRINK

Always remember, when you enter a bar, that there is almost always a two-tier pricing system: one if you stand, and one if you sit. It's always cheaper to stand, but sometimes sitting is not only necessary, but fun: you can relax and watch the world go by.

Italians love a good sandwich for lunch. Seek out popular sandwich shops (long lines signify that the place is worth visiting) or go to a *salumeria* (delicatessen) and have them make a sandwich for you. It will be simple—cheese and/or cold cuts with bread, no trimmings—but it will be made while you wait, fresh, delicious, and inexpensive.

SIGHTS

There are plenty of free wonderful things to see. Visit the Musei Vaticani, the Uffizi, and the Accademia in Florence (book ahead whenever possible), but don't forget that many artistic gems are found in churches, most of which can be visited with no charge (some of Caravaggio's best work can be found in various churches in Rome). Also consider renting audio guides if you want direction to any specific place; if you find the idea of joining an organized tour daunting, most museums sell official guidebooks that can help you target what to see. Walking in *centri storici* (historic centers) is also a joy, and free. Seek out piazzas, climb towers, and look for views.

LODGING

High season in Italy runs from Easter to mid-October. If you want to have Florence practically to yourself, come in November or February (most Italian cities are very crowded during the Christmas holidays, which begin around Christmas and finish on January 6). Many hotels in cities offer bargain rates in July and August because most people are off to the beach or the mountains. Remember to factor in great heat and massive crowds, along with the money you'll save. If you decide to travel then, ensure that you have access to a pool and/or air-conditioning.

A great budget-conscious way to travel is via Airbnb (*www.airbnb.com*). You can sleep on someone's couch, rent a private room in an apartment (sometimes with en suite bathroom), or spread out in an entire apartment or house. One of the best things about Airbnb is that many of these accommodations come with refrigerators and kitchens, which means you don't have to spend all your money eating out.

In general, whatever your lodging choice, book sooner rather than later. You'll often find better deals that way.

Chapter 2

TRAVEL SMART

Updated by
Fergal Kavanagh

★ **CAPITAL:**
Rome

👫 **POPULATION:**
60,396,434

💬 **LANGUAGE:**
Italian

$ **CURRENCY:**
Euro

☎ **COUNTRY CODE:**
39

⚠ **EMERGENCIES:**
112

🚗 **DRIVING:**
On the right

⚡ **ELECTRICITY:**
220v/50 cycles; electrical
plugs have two round prongs

🕒 **TIME:**
6 hours ahead of New York

🌐 **WEB RESOURCES:**
www.italia.it

www.beniculturali.it

Know Before You Go

A TALE OF TWO COUNTRIES

Italy as we know it is just over 160 years old, united by Giuseppe Garibaldi in 1861, and traditions and customs die hard. Differences and rivalries between the wealthier north and the more relaxed south abound, but you will need to spend time in both for the full Italian experience.

DRINK YOUR FILL

Bottled water is available everywhere but often at an inflated price. Carry a refillable bottle and fill up for free at the strategically placed water fountains in cities. In restaurants you can ask for tap water (*acqua del rubinetto*), although you may have to insist.

GO FOOTBALL CRAZY

Soccer—*calcio*—is taken very seriously in Italy, with rivalries running deep. A little knowledge of a local team's performance makes for great conversation. Just avoid wearing your Juventus shirt in Naples if you want to make new friends.

BOOK IN ADVANCE

Avoid waiting in line for hours by buying museum tickets online before your visit. Also, the earlier you buy train tickets, the less expensive they're likely to be. Trenitalia and Italo offer substantial first-come, first-served discounts on high-speed services; check their websites, and prepare to be flexible with your travel times. Discounts aren't offered on regional trains, and neither is seat reservation. Unless bought online, tickets for regional trains must be stamped before boarding.

TAKE THE BACK ROADS

So you've rented a car. Why stick to the highways? Much of Italy's beauty is along winding mountain roads or coastal secondary routes, so take your time and wander a little. Not only will you save on tolls, but you'll save on fuel, too, as gas prices are generally lower than on the *autostrade*. Also, if you're renting a car between November 15 and April 15, remember to ask for snow chains (obligatory on many roads).

EAT FOR (NEARLY) NOTHING

The *aperitivo* is a staple of many areas of the north, where, for little more than the price of a drink, you can partake of a vast buffet to substitute for your evening meal. Bars vie with each other to provide the best array of pasta dishes, *pizzette*, and panini , so check out a few of them before sitting down.

PLAN YOUR DAY

Although breakfast (*la colazione*) is generally served from 7 to 10:30, other mealtimes vary by region. In the north, lunch (*il pranzo*) is noon to 2, whereas restaurants in the south often serve it until 3. You may have difficulty finding dinner (*la cena*) in the north after 9 pm, when most southerners are just sitting down to eat (restaurants there tend not to open until 7:30). And shoppers take note: many stores close from 1 to 4:30.

LACE UP YOUR WALKING SHOES

The best—and often the only—way to see a city is on foot. Public transport works well (albeit generally better in the north), and in recent years many city and town centers have been pedestrianized. Parking costs can add up, so when possible don your most comfortable shoes and prepare to pound the pavement. Fall in with a weekend afternoon *passeggiata* in smaller towns, where Italians stroll up and down the main street dressed in their Sunday best.

DRINK LOCAL

Italy offers a vast array of fine wines, with each region boasting its own appellation. While you may see Chianti on a wine list in Catania, it will probably be no different to what you find at home; for a more authentic taste of the area, try a local Sicilian wine instead.

YOU GET A COFFEE IN A BAR

Coffee culture is different here. Italians take their single-shot espresso standing at a bar—where snacks and alcoholic drinks are also served, and which usually closes in the evening. Pay the cashier, then set your receipt on the counter and place your order. If you choose to sit, there is usually a surcharge, whether there is table service or not. Also, if you order a latte you'll get a glass of milk.

NEVER PASS A RESTROOM

Public restrooms in train stations usually cost €1, and bars frown on the use of theirs without making a purchase, so before you leave the hotel, restaurant, or museum, use the facilities.

DAY TRIPPER

Lodging in tourist hot spots is at a premium during high season, but deals can be found a little farther from the action. Consider booking outside town and taking a local train or bus to see the sights—you might miss the evening atmosphere, but you'll have more to spend on lunch.

TAKE YOUR TIME

The Italian experience differs from region to region. Try to plan an itinerary that leaves time to explore each destination at leisure. Sure, quick in-and-out visits to cities will allow you to see the major sights, but rushing things means missing out on each area's unique atmosphere.

BE ITALIAN

Food is one of Italy's defining features, and locals continue to be horrified by the idea of pineapple on pizza or (heaven forbid!) ketchup on pasta. You don't need a knife to eat spaghetti (although using a spoon to help wind the pasta around a fork is allowed), and it's fine to pick your pizza up. Most restaurants set a per-person fee for *pane e coperto* (bread and cover charge), although waiters also appreciate a tip—which is standard (around 10%) in the south.

BEWARE OF SCAMS

Larger train stations are notorious for porters insisting on carrying your bags, then charging a fee, so be firm if you're not interested. Also, be careful where you store your wallet and valuables and avoid purchasing from illegal street vendors.

LOOK INTO SIGHT PASSES

Many cities and towns sell multiday passes for access to different museums and sites. These offer great savings if you plan to visit several attractions; some include deals on public transport.

LEARN THE LINGO

Most Italians have some command of English, although this isn't a fail-safe rule, particularly in the south. You can get by on hand gestures and pointing, but a *grazie* or *buongiorno* here and there can't hurt.

Getting Here and Around

Air

Most nonstop flights between North America and Italy serve Rome's Aeroporto Internazionale Leonardo da Vinci (FCO), better known as Fiumicino, and Milan's Aeroporto Malpensa (MXP), though the airports in Venice, Pisa, and Naples also accommodate nonstop flights from the United States. Flying time to Milan or Rome is approximately 8–8½ hours from New York, 10–11 hours from Chicago, and 11½ hours from Los Angeles.

Alitalia has direct flights from London to Milan and Rome, while British Airways and smaller budget carriers provide services between Great Britain and other locations in Italy. EasyJet connects London's Gatwick and Stansted Airports with 15 Italian destinations. Ryanair flies from Stansted to 21 airports. Since tickets are frequently sold at discounted prices, investigate the cost of flights within Italy (even one-way) as an alternative to train travel.

You can take the Ferrovie dello Stato Italiane (FS) airport train or bus to Rome's Termini station or to Cadorna or Centrale in Milan; from the latter you can then catch a train to any other location in Italy. It will take about 40 minutes to get from Fiumicino to Roma Termini, less than an hour from Malpensa to Milano Centrale.

A helpful website for information (location, phone numbers, local transportation, etc.) about all of the airports in Italy is *italianairportguide.com*.

Bus

Italy's far-reaching regional bus network, often operated by private companies, isn't as attractive an option as in other European countries, partly due to convenient train travel. Schedules are often drawn up with commuters and students in mind and can be sketchy on weekends. But, car travel aside, regional bus companies often provide the only means of getting to out-of-the-way places. Even when this isn't the case, buses can be faster and more direct than local trains, so it's worth taking time to compare bus and train schedules. Busitalia–Sita Nord covers Tuscany and the Veneto. Sita Sud caters to travelers in Puglia, Basilicata, and Campania. FlixBus offers a low-cost long-distance service.

All buses, even those on long-distance routes, offer a single class of service. Cleanliness and comfort levels are high on private motor coaches, which have plenty of legroom, sizable seats, luggage storage, and usually toilets. Smoking isn't permitted on buses. Private lines usually have a ticket office in town or allow you to pay when you board.

Major Italian cities have inexpensive urban bus service. Although some city buses have ticket machines on board, generally you buy tickets from newsstands or tobacconists and have them validated on board. Buses can get packed during busy travel periods and rush hours.

Car

Italy has an extensive network of *auto-strade* (toll highways), complemented by equally well-maintained but free *super-strade* (expressways). You'll need your autostrada ticket from entry to pay the toll when you exit; on some shorter auto-stradas, you pay the toll when you enter. The condition of provincial roads varies, but maintenance is generally good.

Most gas stations have self-service options. Those on autostradas are open 24 hours; others are generally open Monday through Saturday 7–7, with a break at lunchtime. Automobile Club Italiano offers 24-hour road service. To call the police in an emergency, dial 112.

PARKING
Curbside spaces are marked by blue lines; pay at a nearby *parcometro* machine, and leave the printed ticket on your dashboard. Fines for violations are high, and towing is common. You often need a permit to enter historic centers with a vehicle—violating this strictly enforced rule can also result in hefty fines. It's best to park in designated (preferably attended) lots; even small towns often have them just outside their historic centers.

RULES OF THE ROAD
You can rent a car with a U.S. driver's license, but Italy also requires non-Euro-peans to carry an International Driver's Permit (IDP), available for a nominal fee via the AAA website (*www.aaa.com*). Speed limits are generally 130 kph (80 mph) on autostradas, 90 kph (55 mph) on state roads, and 50 kph (30 mph) in towns; this can drop to 10 kph (6 mph) in congested areas. Exceed the speed limit by more than 60 kph (37 mph), and your license could be confiscated.

Right turns on red lights are forbidden. Headlights must be kept on outside

municipalities, and you must wear seat belts. Fines for using mobile phones while driving can exceed €1,000. The blood alcohol limit is 0.05% (stricter than in the United States).

Train

The fastest trains on the Ferrovie dello Stato Italiane (FS), or Italian State Rail-ways, are the *Frecciarossa*. Their privately owned competitor, Nuovo Trasporto Viaggiatori (NTV), or Italo, also runs high-speed service between all major north-ern cities and as far as Salerno in the south. Seat reservations are mandatory for these bullet trains, just as they are for the Eurostar and slower Intercity (IC) trains; tickets for the latter are about half the price of those for the faster trains.

You can buy your tickets at machines in the station or on *www.trenitalia.com*—consider downloading the Trenitalia app. Reservations are not available on *Regionale* and *Espresso* trains, which are slower, make more stops, and are less expensive. For these trains, you must validate your ticket before boarding by punching it at a wall- or pillar-mounted yellow or green box—if you forget to do this, find a conductor immediately. Fines for attempting to ride a train without a ticket are €200.

TRAIN PASSES
A rail pass can save you money on train travel, but it's good to compare the cost with actual fares to make sure. Generally, the more often you plan to travel long distances on high-speed trains, the more sense a rail pass makes. Keep in mind that even with a rail pass you still need to reserve seats on the trains that require them.

Travel Times by Train and Ferry

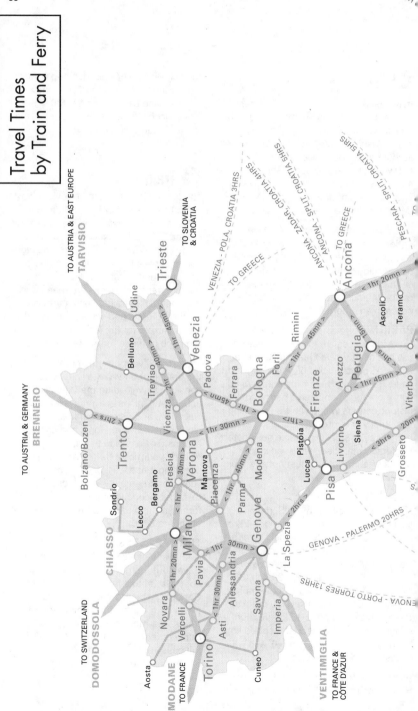

TO GREECE

TO GREECE

BARI - DUBROVNIK

TO GREECE

Lecce

Brindisi

Taranto

Crotone

Bari

Catanzaro

Potenza

Reggio Calabria

< 5hrs 30mn >

Catania

Siracusa

Campobasso

Foggia

Benevento

Messina

Avellino

< 40mn >

NAPOLI - CATANIA 11HRS

< 4hrs 45mn >

Salerno

Enna

< 3hrs >

Isernia

Caserta

NAPOLI - PALERMO 8HRS

Agrigento

< 5hrs >

Napoli

< 1hr 15mn >

CIVITAVECCHIA - PALERMO 13HRS

Palermo

Roma

NAPOLI - OLBIA 12HRS

Trapani

CIVITAVECCHIA - CAGLIARI 15HRS

LIVORNO - OLBIA 5HRS

CIVITAVECCHIA - OLBIA

CAGLIARI - PALERMO 14HRS

Olbia

< 4hrs >

Oristano

Sassari

Cagliari

KEY	
⭘	Major train stations
⊙	National train service
⊙	Regional train service
---	Ferry service
MODANE	Border stations
<time>	Eurostar (shortest) travel time between stations.

Essentials

➕ Health/Safety

EMERGENCIES

No matter where you are in Italy, dial 112 for all emergencies. Key words to remember for emergency situations are aiuto for "help" (pronounced "aye-*you*-toh") and *pronto soccorso*, which means "first aid." When confronted with a health emergency, head straight for the *Pronto Soccorso* department of the nearest hospital or dial 118. To call a Red Cross *ambulanza* (ambulance), dial 800/065510. If you just need a doctor, ask for un medico. Ask the physician for *una fattura* (an invoice) to present to your insurance company for reimbursement.

HEALTH

Smoking is banned inside all public places, so sit indoors (where there's also often air-conditioning) if the smoke in outdoor seating areas bothers you.

It's always best to travel with your own trusted medications. Should you need prescription medication while in Italy, speak with a physician to ensure it's the proper kind. Aspirin (*l'aspirina*) can be purchased at any pharmacy, as can over-the-counter medicines, such as ibuprofen or acetaminophen.

COVID-19

COVID-19 brought travel to a virtual standstill for most of 2020 and into 2021, but vaccinations have made travel possible and more safe. However, each destination (and each business within that destination) may have its own requirements and regulations. Travelers may expect to continue to wear a mask in some places and obey any other rules (and non-vaccinated travelers may face certain restrictions). Given how abruptly travel was curtailed at the onset of the pandemic, it is wise to consider protecting yourself by purchasing a travel insurance policy that will reimburse you for cancellation costs related to COVID-19. Not all travel insurance policies protect against pandemic-related cancellations, so always read the fine print.

🛏 Hotels

Many Italian lodgings, some quite luxurious, are in palazzi, villas, monasteries, and smaller historic buildings that have been restored to blend modern comforts with original atmosphere. Another option is renting a vacation property—although, in addition to budget, you should keep in mind location (street noise and neighborhood ambience in cities and towns, degree of isolation in the countryside), the availability of an elevator or the number of stairs, the utility costs, and what's supplied (furnishings, including pots and linens, as well as sundries like dish detergent).

If you're intrigued by the "locavore" movement, ask local tourism offices about *agriturismo* accommodations. Rural farmstay properties range from luxury villas to farmhouses with basic facilities.

The lodgings we list are the cream of the crop in each price category. Properties are assigned price categories based on the rate for two people sharing a standard double room in high season, including tax and service.

Item	Average Cost
Cup of Coffee	€0.90–€1.50
Soft Drink (glass/can/ bottle)	€2–€3
Glass of Beer	€3–€6
Sandwich	€3–€5.50
2-km (1-mile) Taxi Ride in Rome	€9

$ Money

Of Italy's major cities—where, as in other countries, prices are higher than in the countryside—Milan is by far the most expensive. Resort areas like Capri, Portofino, and Cortina d'Ampezzo cater to wealthy vacationers and also charge top prices. Good value can be found in the scenic Trentino–Alto Adige region of the Dolomites and in Umbria and Le Marche. With a few exceptions, southern Italy and Sicily also offer bargains for those who do their homework before they leave home.

🌐 Passports

A U.S. passport is relatively simple to obtain and is valid for 10 years. You must apply in person if you're getting a passport for the first time; if your previous passport was lost, stolen, or damaged; or if it has expired and was issued more than 15 years ago or when you were under 16. The cost of a new passport is $145 for adults, $115 for children under 16; renewals are $110 for adults, $115 for children under 16. Allow four to six weeks for processing.

■ TIP→ Before your trip, make two copies of your passport's data page (one for someone at home and another for you to carry separately). Alternatively, scan the page and email it to someone at home and/ or yourself.

🍴 Restaurants

Italian cuisine is still largely regional, so try spaghetti *alla carbonara* (with bacon and egg) in Rome, pizza in Naples, *cinghiale* (wild boar) in Tuscany, or truffles in Piedmont. Nowadays, vegetarian and gluten-free options are widely available. Still, if you have dietary restrictions, ask about ingredients; not everything is listed in menu descriptions.

The restaurants we list are the finest in each price category. Unless otherwise noted, they're open for lunch and dinner, closing one or two days a week.

MEALS

Although the distinction has blurred, *ristoranti* tend to be more elegant and expensive than *trattorias* or *osterie*, which serve traditional, home-style fare. Meals generally consist of an *antipasto* (starter) followed by a *primo* (first course), a *secondo* (main course) or *contorno* (vegetable side dish), and *dolce* (dessert). You can, of course, eat less (perhaps just a primo or *secondo* and a *dolce*). Single dishes are more the norm at an *enoteca* or pizzeria, and you can grab affordable snacks at bars, cafés, and spots for pizza *al taglio* (by the slice).

WINES, BEER, AND SPIRITS

The grape has been cultivated here since the time of the Etruscans, with Tuscany, Piedmont, the Veneto, Puglia, Calabria, Sicily, Le Marche, and Umbria among the renowned areas. Beer is readily available, and Italy has some excellent microbreweries, so ask about local brews. In addition, Italians are imaginative with their cocktails, so consider trying the aperitivo della casa (house aperitif). The minimum drinking age in Italy is 16.

Helpful Italian Phrases

BASICS

Yes/no	Sí/No	see/no
Please	Per favore	pear fa-**vo**-ray
Thank you	Grazie	**grah**-tsee-ay
You're welcome	Prego	**pray**-go
I'm sorry (apology)	Mi dispiace	mee dis-pee-**atch**-ay
Excuse me, sorry	Scusi	**skoo**-zee
Good morning/ afternoon	Buongiorno	bwohn-**jor**-no
Good evening	Buona sera	**bwoh**-na **say**-ra
Good-bye	Arrivederci	a-ree-vah-**dare**-chee
Mr. (Sir)	Signore	see-**nyo**-ray
Mrs. (Ma'am)	Signora	see-**nyo**-ra
Miss	Signorina	see-nyo-**ree**-na
Pleased to meet you	Piacere	pee-ah-**chair**-ray
How are you?	Come sta?	**ko**-may-**stah**
Hello (phone)	Pronto?	**proan**-to

NUMBERS

one-half	mezzo	**mets**-zoh
one	uno	**oo**-no
two	due	**doo**-ay
three	tre	Tray
four	quattro	**kwah**-tro
five	cinque	**cheen**-kway
six	sei	Say
seven	sette	**set**-ay
eight	otto	**oh**-to
nine	nove	**no**-vay
ten	dieci	dee-**eh**-chee
eleven	undici	**oon**-dee-chee
twelve	dodici	**doh**-dee-chee
thirteen	tredici	**trey**-dee-chee
fourteen	quattordici	kwah-**tor**-dee-chee
fifteen	quindici	**kwin**-dee-chee
sixteen	sedici	**say**-dee-chee
seventeen	dicissette	dee-chah-**set**-ay
eighteen	diciotto	dee-chee-**oh**-to
nineteen	diciannove	dee-chee-ahn-**no**-vay
twenty	venti	**vain**-tee
twenty-one	ventuno	**vent**-oo-no
thirty	trenta	**train**-ta
forty	quaranta	kwa-**rahn**-ta
fifty	cinquanta	cheen-**kwahn**-ta
sixty	sessanta	seh-**sahn**-ta
seventy	settanta	seh-**tahn**-ta
eighty	ottanta	o-**tahn**-ta
ninety	novanta	no-**vahn**-ta
one hundred	cento	**chen**-to
one thousand	mille	**mee**-lay
one million	un milione	oon **mill**-oo-nay

COLORS

black	Nero	**nair**-ro
blue	Blu	bloo
brown	Marrone	ma-**rohn**-nay
green	Verde	**ver**-day
orange	Arancione	ah-rahn-**cho**-nay
red	Rosso	**rose**-so
white	Bianco	bee-**ahn**-koh
yellow	Giallo	**jaw**-low

DAYS OF THE WEEK

Sunday	Domenica	do-**meh**-nee-ka
Monday	Lunedi	loo-ne-**dee**
Tuesday	Martedi	mar-te-**dee**
Wednesday	Mercoledi	**mer**-ko-le-**dee**
Thursday	Giovedi	jo-ve-**dee**
Friday	Venerdì	ve-ner-**dee**
Saturday	Sabato	**sa**-ba-toh

MONTHS

January	Gennaio	jen-**ay**-o
February	Febbraio	feb-**rah**-yo
March	Marzo	**mart**-so
April	Aprile	a-**pril**-ay
May	Maggio	**mahd**-joe
June	Giugno	**joon**-yo
July	Luglio	**lool**-yo
August	Agosto	a-**gus**-to
September	Settembre	se-**tem**-bre
October	Ottobre	o-**toh**-bre
November	Novembre	no-**vem**-bre
December	Dicembre	di-**chem**-bre

USEFUL WORDS AND PHRASES

Do you speak English?	Parla Inglese?	**par**-la een-**glay**-zay
I don't speak Italian	Non parlo italiano	non **par**-lo ee-tal-**yah**-no
I don't understand	Non capisco	non ka-**peess**-ko
I don't know	Non lo so	non lo **so**
I understand	Capisco	ka-**peess**-ko
I'm American	Sono Americano(a)	**so**-no a-may-ree-**kah**-no(a)
I'm British	Sono inglese	so-no een-**glay**-zay
What's your name?	Come si chiama?	**ko**-may see kee-**ah**-ma
My name is ...	Mi Chiamo...	mee kee-**ah**-mo
What time is it?	Che ore sono?	kay **o**-ray **so**-no
How?	Come?	**ko**-may
When?	Quando?	**kwan**-doe
Yesterday/today/ tomorrow	Ieri/oggi/domani	**yer**-ee/ **o**-jee/ do-**mah**-nee

This morning	Stamattina/Oggi	sta-ma-**tee**-na/ **o**-jee
Afternoon	Pomeriggio	po-mer-**ee**-jo
Tonight	Stasera	sta-**ser**-a
What?	Che cosa?	kay **ko**-za
What is it?	Che cos'è?	kay ko-**zey**
Why?	Perchè?	pear-**kay**
Who?	Chi?	**Kee**
Where is ...	Dov'è...	doe-**veh**
the train station?	la stazione?	la sta-tsee-**oh**-nay
the subway?	la metropolitana?	la may-tro-po-lee-**tah**-na
the bus stop?	la fermata dell'autobus?	la fer-**mah**-ta del-ow-tor-**booss**
the airport	l'aeroporto	la-er-roh-**por**-toh
the post office?	l'ufficio postale	loo-**fee**-cho po-**stah**-lay
the bank?	la banca?	la **bahn**-ka
the hotel?	l'hotel...?	lo-**tel**
the museum?	Il museo	eel moo-**zay**-o
the hospital?	l'ospedale?	lo-spay-**dah**-lay
the elevator?	l'ascensore	la-shen-**so**-ray
the restrooms?	il bango?	eel **bahn**-yo
Here/there	Qui/là	kwee/la
Left/right	A sinistra/a destra	a see-**neess**-tra/a **des**-tra
Is it near/far?	È vicino/lontano?	ay vee-**chee**-no/ lon-**tah**-no
I'd like ...	Vorrei...	vo-**ray**
a room	una camera	**oo**-na **kah**-may-ra
the key	la chiave	la kee-**ah**-vay
a newspaper	un giornale	oon jore-**nah**-vay
a stamp	un francobollo	oon frahn-ko-**bo**-lo
I'd like to buy ...	Vorrei comprare...	vo-**ray** kom-**prah**-ray
a city map	una mappa della città	**oo**-na **mah**-pa **day**-la chee-**tah**
a road map	una carta stradale	**oo**-na **car**-tah stra-**dahl**-lay
a magazine	una revista	**oo**-na ray-**vees**-tah
envelopes	buste	**boos**-tay
writing paper	carta de lettera	**car**-tah dah **leyt**-ter-rah
a postcard	una cartolina	**oo**-na car-tog-**leen**-ah
a ticket	un biglietto	oon bee-**yet**-toh
How much is it?	Quanto costa?	**kwahn**-toe **coast**-a
It's expensive/ cheap	È caro/ economico	ay **car**-o/ ay-ko-**no**-mee-ko
A little/a lot	Poco/tanto	**po**-ko/**tahn**-to
More/less	Più/meno	pee-**oo**/**may**-no
Enough/too (much)	Abbastanza/ troppo	a-bas-**tahn**-sa/tro-po
I am sick	Sto male	sto **mah**-lay
Call a doctor	Chiama un dottore	kee-**ah**-mah-oondoe-**toe**-ray

| Help! | Aituo! | a-**yoo**-to |
| Stop! | Alt! | ahlt |

A bottle of ...	Una bottiglia di...	**oo**-na bo-**tee**-lee-ah dee
A cup of ...	Una tazza di...	**oo**-na **tah**-tsa dee
A glass of ...	Un bicchiere di...	oon bee-key-**air**-ay dee
Beer	La birra	la **beer**-rah
Bill/check	Il conto	eel **cone**-toe
Bread	Il pane	eel **pah**-nay
Breakfast	La prima colazione	la **pree**-ma ko-la-**tsee**-oh-nay
Butter		eel **boor**-roh
Cocktail/aperitif	L'aperitivo	la-pay-ree-**tee**-vo
Dinner	La cena	la **chen**-a
Fixed-price menu	Menù a prezzo fisso	may-**noo** a **pret**-so **fee**-so
Fork	La forchetta	la for-**ket**-a
I am vegetarian	Sono vegetariano(a)	**so**-no vay-jay-ta-ree-**ah**-no/a
I cannot eat ...	Non posso mangiare	non **pose**-so mahn-gee-**are**-ay
I'd like to order	Vorrei ordinare	vo-**ray** or-dee-**nah**-ray
Is service included?	Il servizio è incluso?	eel ser-**vee**-tzee-o ay een-**kloo**-zo
I'm hungry/ thirsty	Ho fame/sede	oh **fah**-meh/**sehd**-ed
It's good/bad	E buono/cattivo	ay **bwo**-bo/ka-**tee**-vo
It's hot/cold	E caldo/freddo	ay **kahl**-doe/**fred**-o
Knife	Il coltello	eel kol-**tel**-o
Lunch	Il pranzo	eel **prahnt**-so
Menu	Il menu	eel may-**noo**
Napkin	Il tovagliolo	eel toe-va-lee-**oh**-lo
Pepper	Il pepe	eel **pep**-peh
Plate	Il piatto	eel pee-**aht**-toe
Please give me ...	Mi dia...	mee **dee**-a
Salt	Il sale	eel **sah**-lay
Spoon	Il cucchiaio	eel koo-kee-ah-yo
Tea	tè	tay
Water	acqua	**awk**-wah
Wine	vino	**vee**-noh

Essentials

💲 Tipping

In restaurants a service charge of 10%– 15% may appear on your check, but it's not a given that your server will receive this; consider leaving a tip of 5%–10% (in cash) for good service. At a hotel bar, tip €1 and up for a round or two of drinks. Taxi drivers also appreciate a euro or two, particularly if they help with luggage.

In hotels, give the *portiere* (concierge) about 10% of the bill for services or €3–€5 for help with dinner reservations and such. In moderately priced hotels, leave chambermaids about €1 per day, and tip a minimum of €1 for valet or room service. In expensive hotels, double these amounts. Sightseeing guides should receive €1.50 per person for a half-day group tour, more if the tour is longer and/or they're especially knowledgeable.

🇺🇸 U.S. Embassy/Consulate

In addition to the embassy in Rome, the United States has consulates general in Florence, Milan, and Naples. (Note: you aren't allowed to bring laptops into any of these facilities.) If you're arrested or detained, ask Italian officials to notify the embassy or nearest consulate immediately. Consider participating in the U.S. Department of State's Smart Traveler Enrollment Program (STEP; *step.state. gov*) to receive alerts and make it easier to locate you in an emergency.

🛂 Visa

When staying for 90 days or less, U.S. citizens aren't required to obtain a visa prior to traveling to Italy. A recent law requires that you fill in a declaration of presence within eight days of your arrival—the stamp from passport control at the airport substitutes for this. If you plan to travel or live in Italy or the European Union for longer than 90 days, you must acquire a valid visa from the Italian consulate serving your state *before you leave the United States.* The process of obtaining a visa will take at least 30 days, and the Italian government doesn't accept applications submitted by visa expediters.

📅 When to Go

High Season: June through September is expensive and busy. In August, most Italians take their own summer holidays; cities are less crowded, but many shops and restaurants close. July and August can be uncomfortably hot.

Low Season: Unless you're skiing, winter offers the least appealing weather, although it's the best time for airfare and hotel deals and to escape the crowds. Temperatures in the south can be mild.

Value Season: By late September, temperate weather, saner airfares, and more cultural events can make for a happier trip. October is also great, but November is often rainy. March and early April weather is changeable. From late April to early May, the masses have not yet arrived.

Great Itineraries

Rome in 3 Days

Rome wasn't built in a day—so don't try to see it all in a day. Three days is a doable, if jam-packed, amount of time to visit the ancient city's major attractions.

Logistics: Much of the city shuts down on Sunday (including the Vatican Museums, except for the last Sunday of the month), and many restaurants and state museums are closed on Monday. To skip lines and better enjoy your experiences, reservations are a good idea at the Colosseum and the Vatican Museums; they're required for the Galleria Borghese.

DAY 1: ANCIENT ROME
Spend your first day in Rome exploring the likes of the **Roman Forum**, **Musei Capitolini**, and the **Colosseum**. This area is pretty compact, but you can easily spend a full morning and afternoon exploring its treasures. It's best to try and beat the crowds at the Colosseum by getting there right when it opens at 8:30 am (advance tickets help, too). A guided tour of the Forum is also a good way to make the most out of your afternoon. After your day of sightseeing, stop for a classic Roman dinner in nearby Monti.

DAY 2: THE VATICAN AND PIAZZA NAVONA
Another full day of sightseeing awaits when you make your way to the city-state known as the **Vatican**. You'll once again want to try and avoid the biggest crowds here, especially for a glimpse of the Sistine Chapel (the best way to do this is to make online reservations for an extra €4 ahead of time). Booking a tour of the **Vatican Museums** is a good way to take full advantage of the site; most tours last two hours. Be sure to stop in and marvel at **St. Peter's Basilica**, too. Stop for lunch in nearby Prati, but after you're done with the Vatican, cross the river to **Piazza**

Navona. Spend some time exploring this glorious piazza and its sculptures, but make sure to stop by the **Pantheon** before heading to Campo de' Fiori for dinner at an outdoor restaurant. Afterward, there are plenty of nearby bars to keep you occupied.

DAY 3: PIAZZA DI SPAGNA, VILLA BORGHESE, AND TRASTEVERE
Start your morning with breakfast near the **Trevi Fountain**, before doing some window-shopping up Via Condotti and along the many surrounding backstreets as you make your way to the **Spanish Steps**. Pose for some postcard-worthy photos there before heading to nearby **Villa Borghese**. If you're sick of museums, feel free to explore Rome's main park and enjoy the great views; if you're up for some more art, the **Galleria Borghese** is one of the city's best art museums. Afterwards, head to trendy Trastevere for dinner, and soak in the cobblestone streets and charming medieval houses as you barhop your last night in town.

IF YOU HAVE MORE TIME
If you want to make the most of your time in the city itself, take your time exploring the many churches and cathedrals, like **Sant'Ignazio** or **San Clemente**. You can also stop by to explore gorgeous palaces, like the **Palazzo Doria Pamphilij**, and check out lesser known but just as impressive museums, like the MAXXI or the MACRO. Visiting the ancient Roman road known as the Via Appia Antica and its spooky yet mesmerizing catacombs is another great way to spend an afternoon immersed in Roman history.

Great Itineraries

Venice, Florence, Rome, and Highlights in Between

Think of this itinerary as a rough draft for you to revise according to your interests and time constraints.

DAY 1: VENICE

Arrive in Venice's Marco Polo Airport, and hop on the bus to the city's main bus station. Check into your hotel, get out, and get lost along the canals for a couple of hours before dinner.

Logistics: At the main bus station, you can immediately transfer to the most delightful "bus" in the world: the vaporetto. Enjoy your first ride up the Grand Canal, and make sure you're paying attention to the *fermata* (stop) where you need to get off.

DAY 2: VENICE

Have coffee at a real Italian coffee shop before taking in the top sights, including the **Basilica di San Marco, Palazzo Ducale,** and **Galleria dell'Accademia**. Don't forget **Piazza San Marco**: the intense anticipation as you near the giant square climaxes in a stunning view of the piazza. Stop for lunch, sampling the traditional Venetian specialty *sarde in saor* (sardines in a mouthwatering sweet-and-sour preparation with onions and raisins), and check out the fish market at the foot of the **Rialto Bridge**; then see the sunset at the **Zattere** before dinner. Later, stop at a bar on the **Campo San Luca** or **Campo Santa Margherita,** where you can toast to being free of automobiles.

Logistics: Venice is best seen on foot, with the occasional vaporetto ride. Always carry a city map: it's very easy to get totally lost here.

Tips

■ The itinerary can also be completed by car on the autostradas. Obviously, it's best to pick up your car on Day 3, when you leave Venice.

■ The sights along this route can be crowded; you'll have a better time if you make the trip outside the busy months of June, July, and August.

DAY 3: FERRARA/BOLOGNA

The ride to **Ferrara,** your first stop in Emilia-Romagna, is about 90 minutes. Visit the **Castello Estense** and **Duomo** before grabbing lunch. Wander Ferrara's cobblestone streets, then hop on the train to **Bologna** (less than an hour away). Check into your hotel, and walk around **Piazza Maggiore** before dinner. Later check out some of Italy's best nightlife.

Logistics: The train station lies a bit outside the center of Ferrara, so you may want to take a taxi or a less expensive city bus into town.

DAY 4: BOLOGNA/FLORENCE

After breakfast, visit some of Bologna's churches and piazzas, and climb the leaning **Torre degli Asinelli** for a red-rooftop-studded panorama. After lunch, take the short train ride to **Florence**. You'll arrive in time for an afternoon siesta and an evening passeggiata.

DAY 5: FLORENCE

Start with the **Uffizi Gallery,** where you'll see Botticelli's *Primavera* and *Birth of Venus,* among other works. Next, walk to **Piazza del Duomo,** site of Brunelleschi's spectacular dome, which you can climb for an equally spectacular view. After a simple trattoria lunch, either devote the afternoon to art or hike up to **Piazzale Michelangelo,** which overlooks the

city. Finish the evening in style with a traditional *bistecca alla fiorentina* (grilled T-bone steak with olive oil).

Logistics: It's best to reserve Uffizi Gallery tickets in advance; you *must* reserve in advance to climb Brunelleschi's dome.

DAY 6: LUCCA/PISA

After breakfast, board a train for a 90-minute ride to the walled medieval city of **Lucca**. Don't miss the Romanesque **Duomo** or a walk along the city's ramparts. Have lunch at a trattoria before continuing on to **Pisa** (30 minutes away) and its **Campo dei Miracoli,** where you'll spend an afternoon seeing the **Leaning Tower,** along with the **Duomo** and **Battistero.** Walk down to the banks of the Arno River and dine at one of the inexpensive local restaurants in the real city center.

Logistics: Lucca's train station is conveniently situated just outside the walled city. Although across town from the Leaning Tower, Pisa's train station isn't far from the city center.

DAY 7: ROME

Take a high-speed train bound for **Rome**, a 90-minute trip from Florence, or 3 hours from Pisa. Although the Eternal City took millennia to build, on this whirlwind trip you'll have just two days to tour it. Make your way to your hotel and relax for a bit before heading to the **Piazza Navona, Campo de' Fiori,** and **Trevi Fountain**—it's best in the evening—and have a stand-up *aperitivo* (Campari and soda is a classic) at an unpretentious local bar. For dinner, you can't go wrong at any of Rome's popular local pizzerias.

DAY 8: ROME

In the morning, head to the **Vatican Museums** to see Michelangelo's glorious frescoes at the **Sistine Chapel.** Visit **St. Peter's Basilica and Square** before heading for lunch near the Pantheon. Next, visit the magnificent **Pantheon,** and then the **Colosseum,** stopping along Via dei Fori Imperiali to check out the **Roman Forum** from above. From the Colosseum, walk or take a taxi to **Piazza di Spagna,** a good place to shop at stylish boutiques.

Logistics: Avoid lines and waits by buying tickets online.

DAY 9: ROME/DEPARTURE

Head by taxi to Termini station and catch the train to Fiumicino airport.

Logistics: For most people, the train from Termini station is preferable to a taxi ride.

On the Calendar

Spring

Carnevale. Venice earned its international reputation as the "city of Carnevale" in the 18th century, when partying would begin several months before Lent and the city seemed to be one continuous masquerade. The celebration was revived for good in the 1970s, and each year over the 15- to 17-day Carnevale period (ending on the Tuesday before Ash Wednesday), more than a half-million people attend concerts, theater and street performances, masquerade balls, historical processions, fashion shows, and contests.

If you're not planning on joining in the revelry, you'd be wise to choose another time to visit Venice. Crowds throng the streets (which become one-way, with police directing foot traffic), bridges are designated "no-stopping" zones to avoid gridlock, and prices skyrocket. *www.carnevale.venezia.it.*

Scoppio del Carro (Explosion of the Cart). On Easter Sunday, Florentines and foreigners alike flock to the Piazza del Duomo to watch as the Scoppio del Carro, a monstrosity of a carriage pulled by two huge oxen decorated for the occasion, makes its way through the city center and ends up in the piazza. Through an elaborate wiring system, an object representing a dove is sent from inside the cathedral to the baptistery across the way. The dove sets off an explosion of fireworks that come streaming from the carriage. You have to see it to believe it.

Vinitaly. This widely attended international wine and spirits event takes place for a few days in April. Recent gatherings have attracted more than 4,000 exhibitors from two dozen countries. The festivities kick off with Opera Wine, a showcase for the top 100 Italian wines as chosen by *Wine Spectator* magazine, which takes place in the Palazzo della Gran Guardia, in Piazza Bra.

Summer

Arena di Verona Opera Festival. Milan's La Scala and Naples' San Carlo offer performances more likely to attract serious opera fans, but neither offers a greater spectacle than the Arena di Verona. During the venue's summer season (June to August), as many as 16,000 attendees sit on the original stone terraces or in modern cushioned stalls. Most of the operas presented are big and splashy, like *Aida* or *Turandot*, demanding huge choruses, lots of color and movement, and, if possible, camels, horses, or elephants. Order tickets by phone or through the arena website: if you book a spot on the cheaper terraces, be sure to take or rent a cushion—four hours on a 2,000-year-old stone bench can be an ordeal (from €27 for general admission). *www.arena.it.*

Festa del Redentore. On the third Sunday in July, crowds cross the Canale della Giudecca by means of a pontoon bridge, built every year to commemorate the doge's annual visit to Palladio's Chiesa del Santissimo Redentore to offer thanks for the end of a 16th-century plague. The evening before, Venetians—accompanied each year by an increasing number of tourists—set up tables and chairs along the canals. As evening falls, practically the whole city takes to the streets and tables, and thousands more take to the water. Boats decorated with colored lanterns (and well provisioned with traditional Redentore meals) jockey for position to watch the grand event. Half an hour before midnight, Venice kicks off a fireworks display over the Bacino, with brilliant reflections on its waters. You'll find good viewing anywhere along the Riva degli Schiavoni; you could also try

Zattere, as close to Punta Dogana as you can get, or on the Zitelle end of the Giudecca. After the fireworks, join the young folks and stay out all night, greeting the sunrise on the Lido beach, or rest up and make the procession to mass on Sunday morning. If you're on a boat, allow a couple of hours to dislodge yourself from the nautical traffic jam when the festivities break up.

Festa di San Giovanni (Feast of St. John the Baptist). On June 24 Florence mostly grinds to a halt to celebrate the Festa di San Giovanni in honor of its patron saint. Many shops and bars close, and at night a fireworks display lights up the Arno and attracts thousands.

Festival dei Due Mondi. Each summer Umbria hosts one of Italy's biggest arts festivals: Spoleto's Festival of the Two Worlds. Starting out as a classical music festival, it has now evolved into one of Italy's brightest gatherings of arts aficionados. Running from late June through mid-July, it features modern and classical music, theater, dance, and opera. Increasingly there are also a number of small cinema producers and their films. *www.festivaldispoleto.com.*

Luminaria. Pisa is at its best during the Luminaria feast day, on June 16. The day honors St. Ranieri, the city's patron saint. Palaces along the Arno are lit with white lights, and there are plenty of fireworks.

Ravenna Festival. Orchestras from all over the world perform in city churches and theaters during this renowned music festival, which takes place in June and July, as well as during a few days at the beginning of November. *www.ravennafestival.org.*

Umbria Jazz Festival. Perugia is hopping for 10 days in July, when more than a million people flock to see famous names in contemporary music perform at the Umbria Jazz Festival. In recent years the stars have included Wynton Marsalis, Sting, Eric Clapton, Lady Gaga, Tony Bennett, and Elton John. There's also a shorter Umbria Jazz Winter Festival from late December to early January. *www.umbriajazz.com.*

Fall

Eurochocolate Festival. If you've got a sweet tooth and are visiting in fall, book early and head to Perugia for the Eurochocolate Festival. This is one of the biggest chocolate festivals in the world, with a million visitors, and is held over a week in late October. *www.eurochocolate.com.*

Sagra Musicale Umbra. Held mid-September, the Sagra Musicale Umbra celebrates sacred music in Perugia and in several towns throughout the region. *www.perugiamusicaclassica.com.*

Contacts

 Air

AIRLINE SECURITY ISSUES Transportation Security Administration. (*TSA*). ☏ *866/289–9673* ⊕ *www.tsa.gov.*

AIRPORT INFORMATION Aeroporto di Bologna. (*BLQ, aka Guglielmo Marconi*). ✉ *6 km (4 miles) northwest of Bologna* ☏ *051/6479615* ⊕ *www.bologna-airport.it.* **Aeroporto di Caglari.** (*CAG, aka Elmas*). ✉ *7 km (4½ miles) from Cagliari, Via dei Trasvolatori, Elmas, Cagliari* ☏ *070/211211* ⊕ *www.sogaer.it.* **Aeroporto di Catania.** (*CTA, aka Fontanarossa*). ✉ *7 km (4½ miles) southwest of Catania* ☏ *095/7239111* ⊕ *www.aeroporto. catania.it.* **Aeroporto di Firenze.** (*FLR, aka Amerigo Vespucci or Peretola*). ✉ *6 km (4 miles) northwest of Florence* ☏ *055/3061830* ⊕ *www.aeroporto.firenze. it.* **Aeroporto di Milan Linate.** (*LIN*). ✉ *8 km (5 miles) southeast of Milan* ☏ *02/232323* ⊕ *www. milanolinate-airport.com.* **Aeroporto di Pisa.** (*PSA, aka Aeroporto Galileo Galilei*). ✉ *2 km (1 mile) south of Pisa, 80 km (50 miles) west of Florence* ☏ *050/849111* ⊕ *www. pisa-airport.com.* **Aeroporto di Roma Ciampino.** (*CIA*). ✉ *15 km (9 miles)*

southwest of Rome ☏ *06/65951* ⊕ *www.adr.it.* **Aeroporto di Venezia.** (*VCE, aka Marco Polo*). ✉ *6 km (4 miles) north of Venice* ☏ *041/2609260* ⊕ *www. veneziaairport.com.* **Aeroporto di Roma Fiumicino.** (*FCO, aka Leonardo da Vinci*). ✉ *35 km (20 miles) southwest of Rome* ☏ *06/65951* ⊕ *www.adr. it.* **Aeroporto Internazionale di Napoli.** (*NAP, aka Capodichino*). ✉ *5 km (3 miles) northeast of Naples* ☏ *081/7896111 weekdays 8–4* ⊕ *www.aeroporto- dinapoli.it.* **Aeroporto di Milano Malpensa.** (*MXP*). ✉ *45 km (28 miles) north of Milan* ☏ *02/232323* ⊕ *www.milanomalpen- sa-airport.com.* **Aeroporto Orio al Serio (BGY).** ✉ *Via Orio al Serio 49/51* ☏ *035/326323* ⊕ *www. milanbergamoairport.it.*

🚌 Bus

ACTV. ☏ *041/2424* ⊕ *actv. avmspa.it.* **ANM.** ✉ *Via G. Marino 1, Naples* ☏ *800/639525 toll-free in Italy* ⊕ *www.anm. it.* **ATAC.** ☏ *06/0606* ⊕ *www.atac.roma.it.* **ATAF.** ✉ *Stazione Centrale di Santa Maria Novella, Florence* ☏ *800/424500, 199/104245 from mobile phone (toll)* ⊕ *www.ataf. net.* **ATM.** ☏ *02/48607607*

⊕ *www.atm.it.* **Busita- lia-Sita Nord.** ✉ *Viale dei Cadorna, 105, Florence* ☏ *80075/373760 toll free* ⊕ *www.fsbusitalia.it.* **Dolomiti Bus.** ✉ *Via Col da Ren 14,* ☏ *0437/217111* ⊕ *www.dolomitibus. it.***FlixBus.** ☏ *02/94759208* ⊕ *www.flixbus.com.* **Mari- no Bus.** ☏ *080/3112335* ⊕ *www.marinobus.it.* **Sita Sud.** ✉ *Via S. Francesco d'Assisi 1,* ☏ *080/5790111* ⊕ *www.sitasudtraspor- ti.it.* **Trasporti Toscani.** ✉ *Via Bellatalla, 1, Pisa* ☏ *050/884111* ⊕ *www. cttnord.it.*

 Train

TRAIN INFORMATION FS-Trenitalia. ☏ *06/68475475 from out- side Italy (English), 892021 in Italy* ⊕ *www.trenitalia. com.* **NTV Italo.** ☏ *06/0708* ⊕ *www.italotreno.it.*

CONTACTS Eurail. ⊕ *www. eurail.com.* **Italia Rail.** ☏ *877/375–7245 in U.S., 06/9763 2451 in Italy* ⊕ *www.italiarail.com.* **Rail Europe.** ⊕ *www. raileurope.com.* **RailPass.** ☏ *877/3757245 toll-free from US* ⊕ *www.railpass. com.*

Chapter 3

ROME

Updated by
Laura Itzkowitz

👁 **Sights**
★★★★★

🍴 **Restaurants**
★★★☆☆

🛏 **Hotels**
★★★★★

🛍 **Shopping**
★★★★☆

🍸 **Nightlife**
★★★★☆

WELCOME TO ROME

TOP REASONS TO GO

★ **The Vatican:** Although its population numbers only in the hundreds, the Vatican makes up for it with the millions who visit each year. Marvel at Michelangelo's Sistine Chapel and St. Peter's Basilica.

★ **The Colosseum:** The largest amphitheater of the Roman world was begun by Emperor Vespasian and inaugurated by his son Titus in AD 80.

★ **Piazza Navona:** You couldn't concoct a more Roman street scene: crowded café tables at street level, wrought-iron balconies above, and, at the center, Bernini's Fountain of the Four Rivers and Borromini's Sant'Agnese.

★ **Roman Forum:** This fabled labyrinth of ruins variously served as a political playground, a center of commerce, and a place where justice was dispensed during the Roman Republic and Empire.

★ **Trastevere:** This neighborhood is a maze of jumbled alleyways, traditional Roman trattorias, cobblestone streets, and medieval houses.

1 Ancient Rome with Monti and Celio. The Forum and Palatine Hill were once the hub of Western civilization.

2 The Vatican with Borgo and Prati. St. Peter's Basilica and the Sistine Chapel draw millions.

3 Piazza Navona, Campo de' Fiori, and the Jewish Ghetto. This is the heart of the historic quarter. The Ghetto still preserves the flavor of Old Rome.

4 Piazza di Spagna. Travel back to the days of the Grand Tour in this area.

5 Repubblica and the Quirinale. These areas house government offices, churches, and sights.

6 Villa Borghese and Around. Rome's most famous park is home to the Galleria Borghese.

7 Trastevere. Rome's left bank has kept its authentic roots.

8 Aventino and Testaccio. Aventino is a posh residential area, and Testaccio is more working class.

9 Esquilino and Via Appia Antica. These neighborhoods have plenty of ancient sights and churches.

FLAMINIO

Viale delle Belle Arti

Villa
Giulia

Viale delle Belle Arti

Giardino
Zoologico

Giardino
D.Lago

Parco
D.Daini

Villa
Strohl
Fern

Galleria Borghese ◆

VILLA
BORGHESE

6

Villa
Borghese

PIAZZA DEL
POPOLO

Villa
Medici

Corso d'Italia

Via Vitt. Veneto

Via Boncompagni

PIAZZA DI
SPAGNA

4

Via Ludovisi

Via Sistina

Via Vitt. Veneto

Via L. Bissolati

Via Barberini

Via del Tritone

Via d. Quattro Fontane

Via XX

REPUBBLICA

QUIRINALE

5

Via del Quirinale

Via Nazionale

ESQUILINO

9

PIAZZA
NAVONA ◆

Piazza
Navona

3

MONTI

Vittorio Emanuele II

V.d. Plebiscito

CAMPO
DE'FIORI

V. delle Sotteghe Oscure

Via G. Lanza

JEWISH
GHETTO

Roman
Forum

1

Via Cavour

ANCIENT
ROME

Colosseum ◆

Palatine Hill ◆

CELIO

Via Labicana

TRASTEVERE

7

Via L. Manara

Porto di Risa

Via del Circo Massimo

Villa
Celimontana

AVENTINO &
TESTACCIO

8

Parco
di Porta
Capena

EAT LIKE A LOCAL IN ROME

In Rome, tradition is the dominant feature of the cuisine, with a focus on freshness and simplicity, so when Romans continue ordering the standbys, it's easy to understand why. That said, Rome is the capital of Italy, and the influx of residents from other regions of the country has yielded many variations on the staples.

ARTICHOKES

There are two well-known preparations of *carciofo,* or artichoke, in Rome. Carciofi *alla romana* are stuffed with wild mint, garlic, and pecorino, then braised in olive oil, white wine, and water. Carciofi *alla giudia* (Jewish-style) are whole artichokes, deep-fried twice, so that they open like a flower, the outer leaves crisp and golden brown, while the heart remains tender. When artichokes are in season—late winter through the spring—they're served everywhere.

BUCATINI ALL'AMATRICIANA

It might look like spaghetti with red sauce, but there's much more to *bucatini all'amatriciana*. It's a spicy, rich, and complex dish that owes its flavor to *guanciale*, or cured pork jowl, as well as tomatoes and crushed red pepper flakes. It's often served over *bucatini*, a hollow, spaghetti-like pasta, and topped with grated pecorino Romano.

CODA ALLA VACCINARA

Rome's largest slaughterhouse in the 1800s was in the Testaccio neighborhood, and that's where you'll find dishes like *coda alla vaccinara*, or "oxtail in the style of the cattle butcher." This dish is made from ox or veal tails stewed with tomatoes, carrots, celery, and wine, and it's usually seasoned with cinnamon. It's simmered for hours and then finished with raisins and pine nuts or bittersweet chocolate.

GELATO

Its consistency is often said to be a cross between regular American ice cream and soft-serve. The best versions of gelato are extremely flavorful, and almost always made fresh daily. When choosing a *gelateria*, watch for signs that say *gelato artigianale* (artisan- or homemade); otherwise, keep an eye out for the real deal by avoiding gelato that looks too bright or fluffy.

PIZZA

There are two kinds of Roman pizza: *al taglio* (by the slice) and *tonda* (round pizza). The former has a thicker, focaccia-like crust and is cut into squares; these are sold by weight and generally available all day. The typical Roman pizza tonda has a very thin crust and is served almost charred. Because they're so hot, the ovens are usually fired up only in the evening, which is why Roman *pizzerie* tend to open for dinner only.

CACIO E PEPE

The name means "cheese and pepper," and this is a simple pasta dish from the *cucina povera*, or rustic cooking, tradition. It's a favorite Roman primo, usually made with *tonnarelli* (fresh egg pasta a bit thicker than spaghetti), which is coated with a pecorino-cheese sauce and lots of freshly ground black pepper. Some restaurants serve the dish in an edible bowl of paper-thin baked cheese.

FRITTI

The classic Roman starter in a trattoria and especially at the pizzeria, is *fritti*: an assortment of fried treats, usually crumbed or in batter. Often, before selecting a pizza, locals will order their fritti: *filetti di baccalà* (salt cod in batter), *fiori di zucca* (zucchini flowers, usually stuffed with anchovy and mozzarella), *supplì* (rice balls stuffed with mozzarella and other ingredients), or *olive ascolane* (stuffed olives).

LA GRICIA

This dish is often referred to as a "white amatriciana" because it's precisely that: pasta (usually spaghetti or rigatoni) served with pecorino cheese and guanciale—thus amatriciana without the tomato sauce. It's a lighter alternative to *carbonara* in that it doesn't contain egg, and its origins date back further than the amatriciana.

The timeless city to which all roads lead, Mamma Roma enthralls visitors today as she has since time immemorial. Here the ancient Romans made us heirs-in-law to what we call Western Civilization; where centuries later Michelangelo painted the Sistine Chapel; and where Gian Lorenzo Bernini's Baroque nymphs and naiads still dance in their marble fountains.

Today the city remains a veritable Grand Canyon of culture. Ancient Rome rubs shoulders with the medieval, the modern runs into the Renaissance, and the result is like nothing so much as an open-air museum.

But always remember: "*Quando a Roma vai, fai come vedrai*" (When in Rome, do as the Romans do). Don't feel intimidated by the press of art and culture. Instead, contemplate the grandeur from a table at a sun-drenched café on Piazza della Rotonda; let Rome's colorful life flow around you without feeling guilty because you haven't seen everything. It can't be done, anyway. There's just so much here that you'll have to come back, so be sure to throw a coin in the Trevi Fountain.

Planning

When to Go

Spring and fall are the best times to visit, with mild temperatures and many sunny days. Summers are often sweltering, so come in July and August if you like, but we advise doing as the Romans do—get up and out early, seek refuge from the afternoon heat, resume activities in early evening, and stay up late to enjoy the nighttime breeze.

Most attractions are closed on major holidays. Come August, many shops and restaurants shutter as locals head out for vacation. Remember that air-conditioning is still a relatively rare phenomenon in this city, so carrying a small paper fan in your bag can work wonders. Roman winters are relatively mild, with persistent rainy spells.

Getting Around

The Metro is the easiest and fastest way to get around Rome. There are stops near most of the main tourist attractions; street entrances are marked with red "M" signs. The Metro has three lines: A and B, which intersect at Termini station, and also C. Linea A (red) runs from the eastern part of the city, with stops at San Giovanni in Laterano, Piazza Barberini, Piazza di Spagna, Piazzale Flaminio (Piazza del Popolo), and Ottaviano/San Pietro, near the Basilica di San Pietro and the Musei Vaticani. Linea B (blue) has stops near the Colosseum, the Circus Maximus, the Pyramid (Ostiense station and trains for Ostia Antica), and the Basilica di San Paolo fuori le Mura. Linea C runs from the eastern outskirts of the city through Pigneto. The Metro opens at 5:30 am, and the last trains leave the last station at either end at 11:30 pm (on Friday and Saturday nights the last trains on the A and B lines leave at 1:30 am).

Although not as fast as the Metro, bus and tram travel is more scenic. With reserved bus lanes and numerous tram lines, surface transportation is surprisingly efficient, given the volume of Roman traffic. At peak times, however, buses can be very crowded. If the distance you have to travel is not too great, walking can be a more comfortable alternative. ATAC city buses are orange, gray-and-red, or blue-and-orange; trams are orange or green. Remember to board at the rear and to exit at the middle: some bus drivers may refuse to let you out the front door, leaving you to scramble through the crowd to exit the middle or rear doors. Don't forget that you must buy your ticket before boarding, and be sure to stamp it in a machine as soon as you enter. The ticket is good for a transfer and one Metro trip within the next 100 minutes. Buses and trams run 5:30 am–midnight, after which time there's an extensive network of night buses with service throughout the city.

The bus system is a bit complicated to navigate due to the number of lines, but ATAC has a website (www.atac.roma.it/en/home) that will help you calculate the number of stops and bus route needed, and even give you a map directing you to the appropriate stops.

Rome's integrated transportation system includes buses and trams (ATAC), the Metropolitana (the subway, or Metro), suburban trains and buses (COTRAL), and commuter rail run by the state railway (Trenitalia). A ticket (BIT), valid for 100 minutes on any combination of buses and trams and one entrance to the Metro, costs €1.50. Tickets are sold at ATAC ticket booths, tobacco shops, newsstands, some coffee bars, and some bus stops, as well as in automatic ticket machines in Metro stations and on some buses. You can purchase individual tickets or buy in quantity. It's always a good idea to have a few tickets handy so you don't have to hunt for a vendor when you need one. All tickets must be validated by time-stamping in the yellow meter boxes aboard buses and in underground stations, immediately prior to boarding. Failure to validate your ticket will result in a fine of €54.90.

A Roma24H ticket, or *biglietto integrato giornaliero* (integrated daily ticket), is valid for 24 hours (from the moment you stamp it) on all public transit and costs €7. You can also purchase a Roma48H (€12.50), a Roma72H (€18), and a CIS (Carta Integrata Settimanale), which is valid for one week (€24). Each option gives unlimited travel on ATAC buses, COTRAL urban bus services, trains for the Lido and Viterbo, and the Metro. There's an ATAC kiosk at the bus terminal in front of Termini station. If you're going farther afield, or planning to spend more than a week in Rome, think about getting a BIRG (daily regional ticket) or a CIRS (weekly regional ticket) from the railway station. These give you unlimited travel on all state transport throughout the region of Lazio. This can take you as far as the Etruscan city of Tarquinia or medieval Viterbo.

Making the Most of Your Time

There's so much to do in Rome that it's hard to fit it all in, no matter how much time you have. If you're a first-time visitor, the Vatican Museums and the remains of ancient Rome are must-sees, but both require at least half a day, so if you only have one day, you're best off picking one or the other. Save time and skip lines by purchasing tickets for the Vatican Museums and the Colosseum (with the Roman Forum and Palatine Hill) online beforehand. If you have more than one day, do one on one morning and the other on the next. If you're planning to visit the Galleria Borghese, tickets can sell out days (or weeks) in advance during high season, so make sure to book early.

Addresses in Rome

In the *centro storico* (old town/historic center), most street names are posted on ceramic-like plaques on the sides of buildings, which can make them hard to see. Addresses are fairly straightforward: the street name is followed by the street number, but it's worth noting that Roman street numbering, even in the newer outskirts of town, can be erratic. Usually numbers are even on one side of the street and odd on the other, but sometimes numbers are in ascending consecutive order on one side of the street and descending order on the other side.

Etiquette

Although you may find Rome much more informal then many other European cities, Romans will nevertheless appreciate attempts to abide by local etiquette. When entering an establishment, the key words to know are: *buongiorno* (good morning), *buona sera* (good evening), and *buon pomeriggio* (good afternoon). These words can also double as a goodbye upon exit. Italians greet friends with a kiss, usually first on the right cheek, and then on the left. When you meet a new person, shake hands and say *piacere* (*pee*-ah-*chair*-ay).

How to Save Money

In addition to single- and multiday transit passes, a three-day Roma Pass (☐ €52) covers unlimited use of buses, trams, and the Metro, plus free admission to two museums or archaeological sites of your choice and discounted entrance to others. A two-day pass is €32 and includes one museum.

Hop-On, Hop-Off

Some might consider them kitsch, but guided bus tours can prove a blissfully easy way to enjoy a quick introduction to the city's top sights—if you don't feel like being on your feet all day. Sitting in a bus, with friendly tour-guide commentary (and even friendlier fellow sightseers from every country under the sun), can make for a fun experience—so give one a whirl even if you're an old Rome hand. Of course, you'll want to savor these incredible sights at your own leisure later on.

The least expensive organized sightseeing tour of Rome is the one run by **CitySightseeing Roma**. Double-decker buses leave from Via Marsala, beside Termini station, but you can pick them up at any of their nine stopping points. A day ticket costs €24 and allows you to get off and on as often as you like. The price includes an audio guide system in six languages. The total tour takes about two hours and covers the Colosseum, Piazza Navona, St. Peter's, the Trevi Fountain, and Via Veneto. Tickets can be bought on board. Two- and three-day tickets are also available. Tours leave from Termini station every 20 minutes 9–7:30.

All operators can provide a luxury car for up to three people, a limousine for up to seven, or a minibus for up to nine, all with an English-speaking driver, but guide service is extra. Almost all operators offer "Rome by Night" tours, with or without dinner and entertainment. You can book tours through travel agents.

Roman Hours

In Italy, almost nothing starts on time except for (sometimes) a theater, opera, or movie showing. Italians even joke about a "15-minute window" before actually being late somewhere. In addition, the day starts a little later than normal here, with many shops not opening until 10 am, lunch never happens before 1 pm, and dinner rarely starts before 8 pm. On Sunday, Rome virtually shuts down, and on Monday, most state museums and exhibition halls, plus many restaurants, are closed. Daily food shop hours generally run 10 am–1 pm and 4 pm–7:30 pm or 8 pm; but other stores in the center usually observe continuous opening hours. Pharmacies tend to close for a lunch break and keep night hours (*ora rio notturno*) in rotation. As for churches, most open at 8 or 9 in the morning, close noon–3 or 4, then reopen until 6:30 or 7. St. Peter's, however, has continuous hours 7 am–7 pm (until 6 pm in the fall and winter); and the Vatican Museums are open Monday but closed Sunday (except for the last Sunday of the month).

Restaurants

In Rome, the Eternal(ly culinarily conservative) City, simple yet traditional cuisine reigns supreme. Most chefs prefer to follow the mantra of freshness over fuss and simplicity of flavor and preparation over complex cooking techniques.

Rome has been known since antiquity for its grand feasts and banquets, and dining out has always been a favorite Roman pastime. Until recently, the city's *buongustai* (gourmands) would have been the first to tell you that Rome is distinguished more by its enthusiasm for eating out than for a multitude of world-class restaurants—but this is changing. There is an ever-growing promotion of Slow Food practices, a focus on sustainably and locally sourced produce. Economic crisis has forced the food industry in Rome to adopt innovative ways to maintain a clientele who are increasingly looking to dine out but want to spend less. The result has been the rise of "street food" restaurants, selling everything from inexpensive and novel takes on classic *supplì* (Roman fried-rice balls) to sandwich shops that use a variety of organic ingredients.

Generally speaking, Romans like Roman food, and that's what you'll find in many of the city's trattorias and wine bars. For the most part, today's chefs cling to the traditional and excel at what has taken hundreds, sometimes thousands, of years to perfect. This is why the basic trattoria menu is more or less the same wherever you go. And it's why even the top Roman chefs feature their versions of simple trattoria classics like carbonara, and why those who attempt to offer it in a "deconstructed" or slightly varied style will often come under criticism. To a great extent, Rome is still a town where the Italian equivalent of "What are you in the mood for?" still gets the answer, "Pizza or pasta."

Hotels

It's the click of your heels on inlaid marble, the whisper of 600-thread-count Frette sheets, the murmured *buongiorno* of a coat-tailed porter bowing low as you pass. It's a rustic attic room with a wood-beam ceiling, a white umbrella on a roof terrace, a 400-year-old palazzo. Maybe it's birdsong pouring into your room as you swing open French windows to a sun-kissed view of the Colosseum, a timeworn piazza, or a flower-filled marketplace.

When it comes to accommodations, Rome offers a wide selection of high-end hotels, bed-and-breakfasts, designer boutique hotels—options that run the gamut from whimsical to luxurious. Whether you want a simple place to rest your head or a complete cache of exclusive amenities, you have plenty to choose from.

Restaurant and hotel reviews have been shortened. For full information, visit Fodors.com.

WHAT IT COSTS in Euros

	$	$$	$$$	$$$$
RESTAURANTS				
	under €15	€15–€24	€25–€35	over €35
HOTELS				
	under €125	€125–€200	€201–€300	over €300

Visitor Information

The Department of Tourism in Rome, called Roma Capitale, staffs green information kiosks (with multilingual personnel) near important sights, as well as at Termini station and Leonardo da Vinci Airport.

Ancient Rome with Monti and Celio

Time has reduced ancient Rome to fields of silent ruins, but the powerful impact of what happened here, of the genius and power that made Rome the center of the Western world, echoes across the millennia. In this one compact area of the city, you can step back into the Rome of Cicero, Julius Caesar, and Virgil. You can walk along the streets they knew, cool off in the shade of the Colosseum that loomed over the city, and see the sculptures poised over their piazzas. Today, this part of Rome, more than any other, is a perfect example of the layering of historic eras, the overlapping of ages, of religions, of a past that is very much a part of the present.

Outside the actual ancient sites, you'll find neighborhoods like Monti and Celio, *riones* that are just as much part of Rome's history as its ruins. These are the city's oldest neighborhoods, and today they are a charming mix of the city's past and present. Once you're done exploring ancient Rome, these are the easiest places to head for a bite to eat or some shopping.

GETTING HERE AND AROUND
The Colosseo Metro station is right across from the Colosseum and a short walk from both the Roman and the Imperial Forums, as well as the Palatine Hill. Walking from the very heart of the historic center will take about 20 minutes, much of it along the wide Via dei Fori Imperiali. The little electric Bus No. 117 from the center or No. 85 from Termini will also deliver you to the Colosseum's doorstep. Any of the following buses will take you to or near the Roman Forum: Nos. 60, 75, 85, and 170.

Sights

Arco di Costantino (*Arch of Constantine*)
RUINS | This majestic arch was erected in AD 315 to commemorate Constantine's victory over Maxentius at the Milvian Bridge. It was just before this battle, in AD 312, that Constantine—the emperor who converted Rome to Christianity—legendarily had a vision of a cross and heard the words, "In this sign thou shalt conquer." Many of the costly marble decorations for the arch were scavenged from earlier monuments, both saving money and placing Constantine in line with the great emperors of the past. It is easy to picture ranks of Roman centurions marching under the great barrel vault. ⊠ *Piazza del Colosseo, Monti* Ⓜ *Colosseo.*

★ **The Campidoglio**
PLAZA/SQUARE | Spectacularly transformed by Michelangelo's late-Renaissance designs, the Campidoglio was once the epicenter of the Roman Empire, the place where the city's first shrines stood, including its most sacred, the Temple of Jupiter. The Capitoline Hill originally

consisted of two peaks: the Capitolium and the Arx (where Santa Maria in Aracoeli now stands). The hollow between them was known as the Asylum. Here, prospective settlers once came to seek the protection of Romulus, legendary first king of Rome—hence the term "asylum." Later, during the Republic, in 78 BC, the Tabularium, or Hall of Records, was erected here. By the Middle Ages, however, the Capitoline had become an unkempt hill strewn with ancient rubble. In preparation for the impending visit of Charles V in 1536, triumphant after the empire's victory over the Moors, his host, Pope Paul III Farnese, decided that the Holy Roman Emperor should follow the route of the emperors, finishing triumphantly at the Campidoglio. The pope was embarrassed by the decrepit goat pasture the hill had become and so commissioned Michelangelo to restore the site to glory. The resulting design added a third palace along with Renaissance-style facades and a grand paved piazza. Newly excavated ancient sculptures, designed to impress the visiting emperor, were installed in the palaces, and the piazza was ornamented with the giant stone figures of the Dioscuri and the ancient Roman equestrian statue of Emperor Marcus Aurelius. A copy of this extraordinary statue is still the piazza's centerpiece (the 2nd-century original has been housed in the neighbouring Musei Capitolini since 1999). While there are great views of the Roman Forum from the terrace balconies to either side of the Palazzo Senatorio, the best view is from the 1st century BC Tabularium, now part of the Musei Capitolini. The museum café is on the Terrazza Caffarelli, with a magical view toward Trastevere and St. Peter's, and is accessible without a museum ticket. ⊠ *Piazza del Campidoglio, including the Palazzo Senatorio and the Musei Capitolini, the Palazzo Nuovo, and the Palazzo dei Conservatori, Piazza Venezia* Ⓜ *Colosseo.*

Circo Massimo (*Circus Maximus*)
RUINS | From the belvedere of the Domus Flavia on the Palatine Hill, you can see the Circus Maximus; there's also a great free view from Piazzale Ugo La Malfa on the Aventine Hill side. The giant space where once 300,000 spectators watched chariot races while the emperor looked on is ancient Rome's oldest and largest racetrack; it lies in a natural hollow between the two hills. The oval course stretches about 650 yards from end to end; on certain occasions, there were as many as 24 chariot races a day and competitions could last for 15 days. The charioteers could amass fortunes rather like the sports stars of today. (The Portuguese Diocles is said to have totted up winnings of 35 million sestertii.) The noise and the excitement of the crowd must have reached astonishing levels as the charioteers competed in teams, each with their own colors—the Reds, the Blues, etc. Betting also provided Rome's majority of unemployed with a potentially lucrative occupation. The central ridge was the site of two Egyptian obelisks (now in Piazza del Popolo and Piazza San Giovanni in Laterano). Picture the great chariot race scene from MGM's *Ben-Hur* and you have an inkling of what this all looked like. ⊠ *Between Palatine and Aventine Hills, Aventino* Ⓜ *Circo Massimo.*

★ **The Colosseum**
RUINS | The most spectacular extant edifice of ancient Rome, the Colosseum has a history that is half gore, half glory. Once able to house 50,000 spectators, it was built to impress Romans with its spectacles involving wild animals and fearsome gladiators from the farthest reaches of the Empire. Senators had marble seats up front and the vestal virgins took the ringside position, while the plebs sat in wooden tiers at the back, then the masses above on the top tier. Looming over all was the amazing velarium, an ingenious system of sail-like awnings rigged on ropes and maneuvered by sailors from

the imperial fleet, who would unfurl them to protect the arena's occupants from sun or rain. From the second floor, you can get a bird's-eye view of the hypogeum: the subterranean passageways that were the architectural engine rooms that made the slaughter above proceed like clockwork. In a scene prefiguring something from Dante's *Inferno*, hundreds of beasts would wait to be eventually launched via a series of slave-powered hoists and lifts into the bloodthirsty sand of the arena above. Designed by order of the emperor Vespasian in AD 72, and completed by his son Titus in AD 80, the arena has a circumference of 573 yards, and its external walls were built with travertine from nearby Tivoli. Its construction was a remarkable feat of engineering, for it stands on marshy terrain reclaimed by draining an artificial lake that formed part of the vast palace of Nero. Originally known as the Flavian amphitheater (Vespasian's and Titus's family name was Flavius), it came to be known as the Colosseum thanks to a colossal gilded bronze statue which once stood nearby. The legend made famous by the Venerable Bede says that as long as the Colosseum stands, Rome will stand; and when Rome falls, so will the world … not that the prophecy deterred medieval and Renaissance princes and popes from using the Colosseum as a quarry. In the 19th century, poets came to view the arena by moonlight; today, mellow golden spotlights make the arena a spectacular sight at night, and evening visits are possible with guided tours from May through October. One way to beat the notoriously long ticket lines is to buy a Roma Pass ticket, which includes the Colosseum. You can also book a timed ticket in advance online for a €2 surcharge. Aim for early or late slots to minimize lines, as even the preferential lanes get busy in the middle of the day. Alternatively you can book a tour online with a company (do your research to make sure it's reputable) that lets you skip the line.

Avoid the tours sold on-the-spot around the Colosseum; although you can skip the lines, the tour guides tend to be dry, the tour groups huge, and the tour itself rushed. ⊠ *Piazza del Colosseo, Monti* ☎ *06/39967700* ⊕ *www.coopculture.it* ⊠ *€16 (combined ticket with the Roman Forum and Palatine Hill, 1 entry for either site if used within 2 days)* Ⓜ *Colosseo.*

Domus Aurea (*Golden House of Nero*)
RUINS | Legend has it that Nero famously fiddled while Rome burned. Fancying himself a great actor and poet, he played, as it turns out, his harp to accompany his recital of "The Destruction of Troy" while gazing at the flames of Rome's catastrophic fire of AD 64. Anti-Neronian historians propagandized that Nero, in fact, had set the Great Fire to clear out a vast tract of the city center to build his new palace. Today's historians discount this as historical folderol (going so far as to point to the fact that there was a full moon on the evening of July 19, hardly the propitious occasion to commit arson). But legend or not, Nero did get to build his new palace, the extravagant Domus Aurea (Golden House)—a vast "suburban villa" that was inspired by the emperor's pleasure palace at Baia on the Bay of Naples. His new digs were huge and sumptuous, with a facade of pure gold; seawater piped into the baths; decorations of mother-of-pearl, fretted ivory, and other precious materials; and vast gardens. It was said that after completing this gigantic house, Nero exclaimed, "Now I can live like a human being!" Note that access to the site is currently only on weekends and exclusively via guided tours that use virtual reality headsets for part of the presentation. Booking ahead is essential. ⊠ *Viale della Domus Aurea 1, Monti* ☎ *06/39967700 booking information* ⊕ *www.coopculture.it* ⊠ *€16 including booking fee and guided visit* ☉ *Closed weekdays* Ⓜ *Colosseo.*

Rome Metro and Suburban Railway

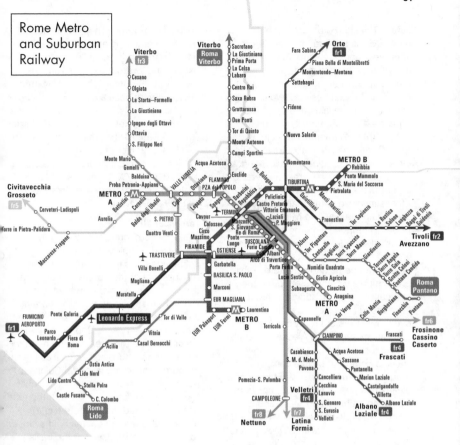

Tickets

A ticket (BIT) valid for 100 minutes on any combination of buses and trams and one entrance to the metro costs €1.50. Tickets are sold at newsstands, some coffee bars, ticket machines in metro stations, and ATAC and COTRAL ticket booths. Time-stamp your ticket when boarding the first vehicle, and stamp it again when boarding for the last time within 75 minutes. You stamp the ticket at Metro sliding electronic doors, and in the little yellow machines on buses and trams.

Fare fees	Price
Single fare	€1.50
Biglietto integrato giornaliero (Integrated Daily Ticket) BIG	€6
Biglietto turistico integrato (Three-Day Pass) BTI	€16.50
Weekly pass	€24
Monthly unlimited pass	€35

Foro di Traiano (*Forum of Trajan*)
RUINS | Of all the Fori Imperiali, Trajan's was the grandest and most imposing, a veritable city unto itself. Designed by architect Apollodorus of Damascus, it comprised a vast basilica, two libraries, and a colonnade laid out around the square—all at one time covered with rich marble ornamentation. Adjoining the forum were the Mercati di Traiano (Trajan's Markets), a huge, multilevel brick complex of shops, taverns, walkways, and terraces, as well as administrative offices involved in the mammoth task of feeding the city. The Museo dei Fori Imperiali (Imperial Forums Museum) takes advantage of the Forum's soaring vaulted spaces to showcase archaeological fragments and sculptures while presenting a video re-creation of the original complex. In addition, the series of terraced rooms offers an impressive overview of the entire forum. A pedestrian walkway, the Via Alessandrina, also allows for an excellent (and free) view of Trajan's Forum. To build a complex of this magnitude, Apollodorus and his patrons clearly had great confidence, not to mention almost unlimited means and cheap labor at their disposal (readily provided by slaves captured in Trajan's Dacian Wars). The complex also contained two semicircular lecture halls, one at either end, which are thought to have been associated with the libraries in Trajan's Forum. The markets' architectural centerpiece is the enormous curved wall, or *exedra*, that shores up the side of the Quirinal Hill excavated by Apollodorus's gangs of laborers. Covered galleries and streets were constructed at various levels, following the exedra's curves and giving the complex a strikingly modern appearance. As you enter the markets, a large, vaulted hall stands in front of you. Two stories of shops and offices rise up on either side. Head for the flight of steps at the far end that leads down to Via Biberatica. (*Bibere* is Latin for "to drink," and the shops that open onto the street are believed to

have been taverns.) Then head back to the three retail and administrative tiers that line the upper levels of the great exedra and look out over the remains of the Forum. Empty and bare today, the cubicles were once ancient Rome's busiest market stalls. Though it seems to be part of the market, the Torre delle Milizie (Tower of the Militia), the tall brick tower that is a prominent feature of Rome's skyline, was actually built in the early 1200s. ⊠ *Via IV Novembre 94, Monti* ☎ *06/0608* ⊕ *www.mercatiditraiano.it* ⊠ *€11.50* Ⓜ *Cavour.*

Fori Imperiali
RUINS | A compound of five grandly conceived complexes flanked with colonnades, the Fori Imperiali contain monuments of triumph, law courts, and temples. The complexes were tacked on to the Roman Forum, from the time of Julius Caesar in the 1st century BC until Trajan in the very early 2nd century AD, to accommodate the ever-growing need for administrative buildings as well as grand monuments. From Piazza del Colosseo, head northwest on Via dei Fori Imperiali toward Piazza Venezia. Now that the road has been closed to private traffic, it's more pleasant for pedestrians (it's closed to all traffic on Sunday). On the walls to your left, maps in marble and bronze, put up by Benito Mussolini, show the extent of the Roman Republic and Empire (at the time of writing, these were partially obstructed by work on Rome's new subway line, Metro C). The dictator's own dreams of empire led him to construct this avenue, cutting brutally through the Fori Imperiali and the medieval and Renaissance buildings that had grown upon the ruins, so that he would have a suitable venue for parades celebrating his expected military triumphs. Among the Fori Imperiali along the avenue, you can see the Foro di Cesare (Forum of Caesar) and the Foro di Augusto (Forum of Augustus). The grandest was the Foro di Traiano (Forum of Trajan), with its huge semicircular Mercati di Traiano and the

Colonna Traiana (Trajan's Column). You can walk through part of Trajan's Markets on the Via Alessandrina and visit the Museo dei Fori Imperiali, which presents the Imperial Forums and shows how they would have been used through ancient fragments, artifacts, and modern multimedia. ⊠ *Via dei Fori Imperiali, Monti* 🕾 *06/0608* ⊕ *www.mercatiditraiano.it* 🖻 *Museum €11.50* Ⓜ *Colosseo*.

★ Musei Capitolini

RUINS | Surpassed in size and richness only by the Musei Vaticani, this immense collection was the world's first public museum. A greatest-hits of Roman art through the ages, from the ancients to the Baroque, it's housed in the Palazzo dei Conservatori and the Palazzo Nuovo, which mirror one another across Michelangelo's famous piazza. The collection was begun by Pope Sixtus IV (the man who built the Sistine Chapel) in 1473, when he donated a room of ancient statuary to the people of the city. This core of the collection includes the She Wolf, which is the symbol of Rome, and the piercing gaze of the Capitoline Brutus. Buy your ticket and enter the Palazzo dei Conservatori where, in the first courtyard, you'll see the giant head, foot, elbow, and imperially raised finger of the fabled seated statue of Constantine, which once dominated the Basilica of Maxentius in the Forum. Upstairs is the resplendent Sala degli Orazi e Curiazi (Hall of the Horatii and Curatii), decorated with a magnificent gilt ceiling, carved wooden doors, and 16th-century frescoes depicting the history of Rome's legendary origins. At each end of the hall are statues of two of the most important popes of the Baroque era, Urban VIII and Innocent X. The heart of the museum is the modern Exedra of Marcus Aurelius (Esedra di Marco Aurelio), which displays the spectacular original bronze statue of the Roman emperor whose copy dominates the piazza outside. To the right, the room segues into the area of the Temple of Jupiter, with the ruins of

part of its vast base rising organically into the museum space. A reconstruction of the temple and the Capitoline Hill from the Bronze Age to the present day makes for a fascinating glimpse through the ages. On the top floor, the museum's *pinacoteca*, or painting gallery, has some noted Baroque masterpieces, including Caravaggio's *The Fortune Teller* and *St. John the Baptist*. To get to the Palazzo Nuovo section of the museum, take the stairs or elevator to the basement of the Palazzo dei Conservatori, where the corridor uniting the two contains the Epigraphic Collection, a poignant assembly of ancient gravestones. Just over halfway along the corridor, and before going up into the Palazzo Nuovo, be sure to take the staircase to the right to the Tabularium gallery and its unparalleled view over the Forum. On the stairs inside the Palazzo Nuovo, you'll be immediately dwarfed by Mars in full military rig and lion-topped sandals. Upstairs is the noted Sala degli Imperatori, lined with busts of Roman emperors, and the Sala dei Filosofi, where busts of philosophers sit in judgment—a fascinating who's who of the ancient world. Within these serried ranks are 48 Roman emperors, ranging from Augustus to Theodosius. Nearby are rooms filled with sculptural masterpieces, including the famed *Dying Gaul*, the *Red Faun* from Hadrian's Villa, and a *Cupid and Psyche*. ⊠ *Piazza del Campidoglio 1, Piazza Venezia* 🕾 *06/0608* ⊕ *www.museicapitolini.org* 🖻 *€11.50 (€15 with exhibitions); €13.50 with access to Centrale Montemartini; audio guide €7* Ⓜ *Colosseo*.

★ Palatine Hill

RUINS | Just beyond the Arco di Tito, the Clivus Palatinus—the road connecting the Forum and the Palatine Hill—gently rises to the heights of the **Colle Palatino** (Palatine Hill), the oldest inhabited site in Rome. Now charmingly bucolic, with pines and olive trees providing shade in summer, this is where Romulus is said to have founded the city that bears his

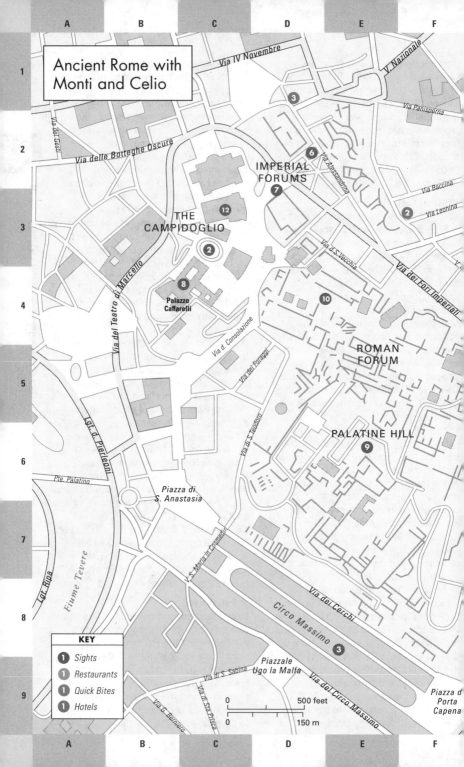

Sights ▼

Restaurants ▼

Quick Bites ▼

Hotels ▼

name, and despite its location overlooking the Forum's traffic and attendant noise, the Palatine was the most coveted address for ancient Rome's rich and famous. During the Roman Republic it was home to wealthy patrician families—Cicero, Catiline, Crassus, and Agrippa all had homes here—and when Augustus (who had himself been born on the hill) came to power, declaring himself to be the new Romulus, it would thereafter become the home of emperors. The Houses of Livia and Augustus (which you can visit with the S.U.P.E.R. ticket, for the same price as the Roman Forum admission) are today the hill's best-preserved structures, replete with fabulous frescoes. If you only have time for one, the House of Augustus is the more spectacular of the two. After Augustus's relatively modest residence, Tiberius extended the palace and other structures followed, notably the gigantic extravaganza constructed for Emperor Domitian which makes up much of what we see today. ✉ *Entrances at Piazza del Colosseo and Via di San Gregorio 30, Monti* ☎ *06/39967700* ⊕ *www.coopculture.it* ✉ *€16 combined ticket, includes single entry to Palatine Hill–Forum site and single entry to Colosseum (if used within 24 hours); S.U.P.E.R. ticket €22 (€24 with online reservation) includes access to the Houses of Augustus and Livia, the Palatine Museum, Aula Isiaca, Santa Maria Antiqua, and Temple of Romulus* Ⓜ *Colosseo.*

★ The Roman Forum

RUINS | Whether it's from the main entrance on Via dei Fori Imperiali or by the entrance at the Arch of Titus, descend into the extraordinary archaeological complex that is the Foro Romano and the Palatine Hill, once the very heart of the Roman world. The Forum began life as a marshy valley between the Capitoline and Palatine Hills—a valley crossed by a mud track and used as a cemetery by Iron Age settlers. Over the years, a market center and some huts were established here, and after the land was drained in the 6th century BC, the site eventually became a political, religious, and commercial center: the Forum. Hundreds of years of plunder reduced the Forum to its current desolate state. But this enormous area was once Rome's pulsating hub, filled with stately and extravagant temples, palaces, and shops and crowded with people from all corners of the empire. Adding to today's confusion is the fact that the Forum developed over many centuries; what you see today are not the ruins from just one period but from a span of almost 900 years, from about 500 BC to AD 400. Nonetheless, the enduring romance of the place, with its lonely columns and great broken fragments of sculpted marble and stone, makes for a quintessential Roman experience. There is always a line at the Colosseum ticket office for the combined Colosseum/Palatine/Forum ticket, but in high season, lines sometimes also form at the Forum and Palatine entrances. Those who don't want to risk waiting in line can book their tickets online in advance, for a €2 surcharge. Choose the print-at-home option (a PDF on a smartphone works, too) and avoid the line to pick up tickets. Your ticket is valid for one entrance to the Roman Forum and the Palatine Hill, which are part of a single continuous complex. Certain sites within the Forum require a S.U.P.E.R. ticket. ✉ *Entrance at Via dei Fori Imperiali, Monti* ☎ *06/39967700* ⊕ *www.coopculture.it* ✉ *€16 (combined ticket with the Colosseum and Palatine Hill, if used within 24 hours); audio guide €5* Ⓜ *Colosseo.*

★ San Clemente

CHURCH | One of the most impressive archaeological sites in Rome, San Clemente is a historical triple-decker. A 12th-century church was built on top of a 4th-century church, which had been built over a 2nd-century pagan temple to the god Mithras and 1st-century Roman apartments. The layers were uncovered in 1857, when a curious prior, Friar Joseph Mullooly, started excavations beneath the present basilica. Today, you can descend to explore all three. The upper church (at street level) is a gem in its own right. In the apse, a glittering 12th-century mosaic shows Jesus on a cross that turns into a living tree. Green acanthus leaves swirl and teem with small scenes of everyday life. Early Christian symbols, including doves, vines, and fish, decorate the 4th-century marble choir screens. In the left nave, the Castiglioni chapel holds frescoes painted around 1400 by the Florentine artist Masolino da Panicale (1383–1440), a key figure in the introduction of realism and one-point perspective into Renaissance painting. Note the large Crucifixion and scenes from the lives of Saints Catherine, Ambrose, and Christopher, plus the Annunciation (over the entrance). To the right of the sacristy (and bookshop), descend the stairs to the 4th-century church, used until 1084, when it was damaged beyond repair during a siege of the area by the Norman prince Robert Guiscard. Still intact are some vibrant 11th-century frescoes depicting stories from the life of St. Clement. Don't miss the last fresco on the left, in what used to be the central nave. It includes a particularly colorful quote—including "Go on, you sons of harlots, pull!"—that's not only unusual for a religious painting, but also one of the earliest examples of written vernacular Italian. Descend an additional set of stairs to the Mithraeum, a shrine dedicated to the god Mithras. His cult spread from Persia and gained a foothold in Rome during the 2nd and 3rd centuries AD. Mithras was believed to have been born in a cave and was thus worshipped in cavernous, underground chambers, where initiates into the all-male cult would share a meal while reclining on stone couches, some visible here along with the altar block. Most such pagan shrines in Rome were destroyed by Christians, who often built churches over their remains, as happened here. ✉ *Via San Giovanni in Laterano 108, Celio* ☎ *06/7740021* ⊕ *www.basilicasanclemente.com* ✉ *Archaeological area €10* Ⓜ *Colosseo.*

Santa Maria di Aracoeli

CHURCH | Sitting atop 124 steps, Santa Maria di Aracoeli perches on the north slope of the Capitoline Hill. The church rests on the site of the temple of Juno Moneta (Admonishing Juno), which also housed the Roman mint (hence the origin of the word "money"). According to legend, it was here that the Sibyl, a prophetess, predicted to Augustus the coming of a Redeemer. He in turn responded by erecting an altar, the Ara Coeli (Altar of Heaven). This was eventually replaced by a Benedictine monastery, and then a church, which was passed in 1250 to the Franciscans, who restored and enlarged it in Romanesque-Gothic style. Today, the Aracoeli is best known for the Santo Bambino, a much-revered olivewood figure of the Christ Child (today a copy of the 15th-century original that was stolen in 1994). At Christmas, everyone pays homage to the "Bambinello" as children recite poems from a miniature pulpit. In true Roman style, the church interior is a historical hodgepodge, with classical columns and large marble fragments from pagan buildings, as well as a 13th-century Cosmatesque pavement. The richly gilded Renaissance ceiling commemorates the naval victory at Lepanto in 1571 over the Turks. The first chapel on the right is noteworthy for Pinturicchio's frescoes of St. Bernardino of Siena (1486). ✉ *Via del Teatro di Marcello, at top of long, steep stairway, Piazza Venezia* ☎ *06/69763839* Ⓜ *Colosseo.*

★ Santa Maria Maggiore

CHURCH | Despite its florid 18th-century facade, Santa Maria Maggiore is one of the oldest churches in Rome, built around 440 by Pope Sixtus III. One of the four great pilgrimage churches of Rome, it's also the city center's best example of an Early Christian basilica—one of the immense, hall-like structures derived from ancient Roman civic buildings and divided into thirds by two great rows of columns marching up the nave. The other three major basilicas in Rome (San Giovanni in Laterano, St. Peter's, and St. Paul Outside the Walls) have been largely rebuilt. Paradoxically, the major reason why this church is such a striking example of Early Christian design is that the same man who built the undulating exteriors circa 1740, Ferdinando Fuga, also conscientiously restored the interior, throwing out later additions and, crucially, replacing a number of the great columns. Precious 5th-century mosaics high on the nave walls and on the triumphal arch in front of the main altar bear splendid testimony to the basilica's venerable age. Those along the nave show 36 scenes from the Old Testament (unfortunately, tough to see clearly without binoculars), and those on the arch illustrate the Annunciation and the Youth of Christ. The resplendent carved-wood ceiling dates to the early 16th century; it's supposed to have been gilded with the first gold brought from the New World. The inlaid marble pavement (called Cosmatesque, after the family of master artisans who developed the technique) in the central nave is even older, dating to the 12th century. The Cappella Sistina (Sistine Chapel), in the right-hand transept, was created by architect Domenico Fontana for Pope Sixtus V in 1585. Elaborately decorated with precious marbles "liberated" from the monuments of ancient Rome, the chapel includes a lower-level museum in which some 13th-century sculptures by Arnolfo da Cambio are all that's left of what was the once richly endowed chapel of the *presepio* (Christmas crèche), looted during the Sack of Rome in 1527. Directly opposite, on the church's other side, stands the Cappella Paolina (Pauline Chapel), a rich Baroque setting for the tombs of the Borghese popes Paul V—who commissioned the chapel in 1611 with the declared intention of outdoing Sixtus's chapel across the nave—and Clement VIII. The Cappella Sforza (Sforza Chapel) next door was designed by Michelangelo and completed by Della Porta. Just right of the altar, next to his father, lies Gian Lorenzo Bernini; his monument is an engraved slab, as humble as the tombs of his patrons are grand. Above the loggia, the outside mosaic of Christ raising his hand in blessing is one of Rome's most beautiful sights, especially when lighted at night. The loggia mosaics can be seen close-up by following a 30-minute guided tour (€5). Tours run roughly every hour, though have no fixed timetable. For information or to join either tour, go through the souvenir shop inside the church on the right and down the stairs to the right to the museum entrance. ✉ *Piazza di Santa Maria Maggiore, Monti* ☎ *06/69886802* 🎫 *Museum tour €4, loggia mosaics tour €5* [M] *Termini.*

🍴 Restaurants

★ Urbana 47

$$$ | MODERN ITALIAN | This restaurant serving breakfast through dinner embodies the *kilometro zero* concept, highlighting hyper-local food from the surrounding Lazio region. The local boho crowd comes in the morning for a continental or "American" breakfast (with free Wi-Fi); lunch means tasty "fast slow-food" options like grain salads and healthy panini, as well as a few more substantial dishes, with a more extensive menu for dinner. **Known for:** hyper-local produce; healthy lunch options; aperitivo and tapas. [$] *Average main: €30* ✉ *Via Urbana 47, Monti* ☎ *06/47884006* 🌐 *www.urbana47.it* 🕓 *Closed Tuesday* [M] *Cavour.*

Coffee and Quick Bites

★ Fatamorgana

$ | ICE CREAM | The emphasis is on all-natural ingredients at this woman-owned gelateria, which has several locations in Rome. Flavors change often, but might include favorites like stracciatella and hazelnut as well as more unusual flavors like matcha. **Known for:** gluten-free with many vegan options; all natural ingredients; unusual flavors. $\boxed{\$}$ *Average main: €3* ✉ *Piazza degli Zingari 5, Monti* ☎ *06/48906955* ⊕ *www.gelateriafatamorgana.com* Ⓜ *Cavour.*

Ⓨ Nightlife

★ Ai Tre Scalini

WINE BARS | An ivy-covered wine bar in the center of Monti, Rome's trendiest 'hood, Ai Tre Scalini has a warm and cozy menu of delicious antipasti and light entrées to go along with its enticing wine list. After about 8 pm, if you haven't booked, be prepared to wait—this is one extremely popular spot with locals. ✉ *Via Panisperna 251, Monti* ☎ *06/48907495* ⊕ *www.aitrescalini.org* Ⓜ *Cavour.*

★ The Court

COCKTAIL LOUNGES | For a winning combination of creative cocktails and incredible views of the Colosseum, this bar in Palazzo Manfredi can't be beat. Bar manager Matteo "Zed" Zamberlan cut his teeth in New York's top bars and here his creativity is on full display. The cocktails are pricey, but they come with a bounty of snacks from the hotel's acclaimed restaurant. ✉ *Via Labicana 125, Colosseo* ☎ *06/77591380* ⊕ *www.palazzomanfredi.com* Ⓜ *Colosseo.*

Shopping

★ Sacripante

WOMEN'S CLOTHING | This tiny Monti art gallery/boutique/bar houses some of the most sophisticated retro-inspired fashion garments around Rome. Its owner, Wilma Silvestri, cleverly combines ethnic and contemporary fabrics for her label Le Gallinelle, evolving them into stylish clothing with a modern edge made for everyday wear. ✉ *Via Panisperna 59, Monti* ☎ *06/48903495* ⊕ *www.sagripantegallery.com* Ⓜ *Cavour.*

The Vatican with Borgo and Prati

Climbing the steps to St. Peter's Basilica feels monumental, like a journey that has reached its climactic end. Suddenly, all is cool and dark … and you are dwarfed by the gargantuan nave and its magnificence. Above is a ceiling so high it must lead to heaven itself. Great, shining marble figures of saints frozen mid-whirl loom from niches and corners. And at the end, a throne for an unseen king whose greatness, it is implied, must mirror the greatness of his palace. For this basilica is a palace, the dazzling center of power for a king and a place of supplication for his subjects. Whether his kingdom is earthly or otherwise may lie in the eye of the beholder.

For good Catholics and sinners alike, the Vatican is an exercise in spirituality, requiring patience but delivering joy. Some come here for a transcendent glimpse of a heavenly Michelangelo fresco; others come in search of a direct connection with the divine. But what all visitors share, for a few hours, is an awe-inspiring landscape that offers a famous sight for every taste: rooms

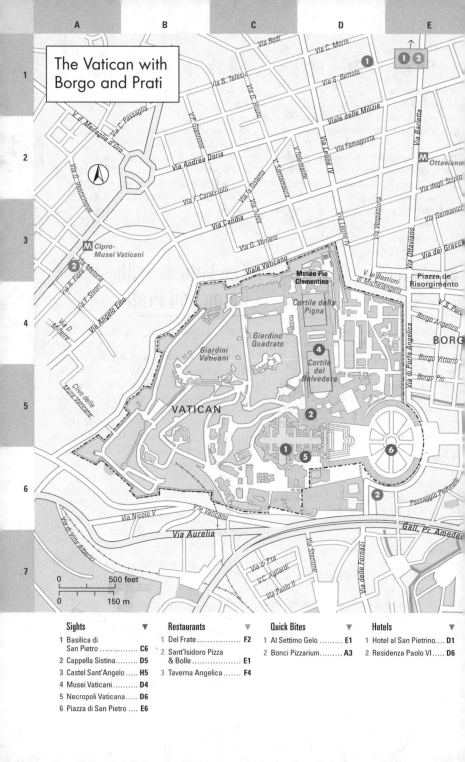

The Vatican with Borgo and Prati

	A	B	C	D	E

Via Rodi
Via C. Morin
Via B. Telesio
Via G. Bettolo
V.d. Medaglie d'Oro
V. C. Passaglia
V.le delle Milizie
V.P. Giannone
Via G. Bruno
Via Famagosta
Via G. Venticinque
Via Andrea Doria
V.le Leone IV
Via Baletta
Ottaviano
Via F. Caracciolo
Via Goletta
Via Tunis
A. Santamaura
Via degli Scipio
Via Candia
Via Germanico
Via R. Fiore
Via Memoria
Via G. Veniero
Viale Vaticano
Via dei Gracc
Via F. Sivori
Cipro-Musei Vaticani
Via Angelo Emo
Via Leone IV
Via Ottaviano
Via Vespasiano
Piazza de Risorgimento
Museo Pio Clementino
V. le Bastioni di Michelangelo
V. S. Port
Via D. Milaitre
Cortile della Pigna
Borgo Angelico
BORG
Giardino Quadrato
Cortile del Belvedere
Via di Porta Angelica
Borgo Vittorio
Giardini Vaticani
Borgo Pio
Clivio delle Mura Vaticane
VATICAN
Passaggio Pedonale
Via di Villa Albetici
Via Nicolo V
Vle Vaticano
Gall. Pr. Amede
Via Aurelia
Via di Pia
Via Stazione
V.C. Agliardi
Via delle Fornaci
Via Paolo II

| 0 | 500 feet |
| 0 | 150 m |

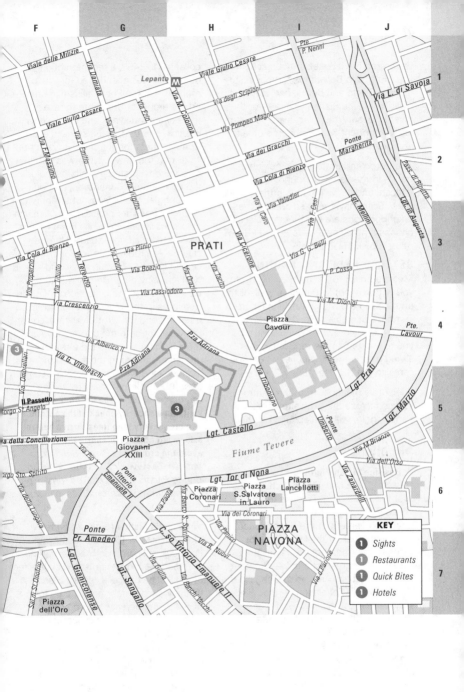

decorated by Raphael, antique sculptures like the Apollo Belvedere, famous paintings by Giotto and Bellini, and, perhaps most of all, the Sistine Chapel—for the lover of beauty, few places are as historically important as this epitome of faith and grandeur.

The Borgo and Prati are the neighborhoods immediately surrounding the Vatican, and it's worth noting that, while the Vatican may well be a priority, these neighborhoods are not the best places to choose a hotel, as they're quite far from other top sights in the city.

GETTING HERE AND AROUND

Metro stop Cipro or Ottaviano will get you within about a 10-minute walk of the entrance to the Musei Vaticani. Or, from Termini station, Bus No. 40 Express or the famously crowded No. 64 will take you to Piazza San Pietro. Both routes swing past Largo Argentina, where you can also get Bus No. 46.

A leisurely meander from the centro storico, across the exquisite Ponte Sant'Angelo, will take about a half hour.

Sights

★ Basilica di San Pietro

CHURCH | The world's largest church, built over the tomb of St. Peter, is the most imposing and breathtaking architectural achievement of the Renaissance (although much of the lavish interior dates to the Baroque). No fewer than five of Italy's greatest artists—Bramante, Raphael, Peruzzi, Antonio da Sangallo the Younger, and Michelangelo—died while striving to erect this new St. Peter's. The history of the original St. Peter's goes back to AD 326, when the emperor Constantine completed a basilica over the site of the tomb of Saint Peter, the Church's first pope. The original church stood for more than 1,000 years, undergoing a number of restorations and alterations, until, toward the middle of the 15th century, it was on the verge of

collapse. In 1452, a reconstruction job began but was abandoned for lack of money. In 1503, Pope Julius II instructed the architect Bramante to raze all the existing buildings and build a new basilica, one that would surpass even Constantine's for grandeur. It wasn't until 1626 that the new basilica was completed and consecrated. Highlights include the Loggia delle Benedizioni (Benediction Loggia), the balcony where newly elected popes are proclaimed; Michelangelo's *Pietà*; and Bernini's great bronze baldacchino, a huge, spiral-columned canopy—at 100,000 pounds, perhaps the largest bronze object in the world—as well as many other Bernini masterpieces. There's also the collection of Vatican treasures in the Museo Storico-Artistico e Tesoro, and the Grotte Vaticane crypt. For views of both the dome above and the piazza below, take the elevator or stairs to the roof; those with more stamina (and without claustrophobia) can then head up more stairs to the apex of the dome. ■ TIP→ **The basilica is free to visit, but a security check at the entrance can create very long lines. Arrive before 8:30 or after 5:30 to minimize the wait and avoid the crowds.** ⊠ *Piazza San Pietro, Vatican* ⊕ *www.vaticanstate.va* ⊙ *Closed during Papal Audience (Wed. until 1 pm) and during other ceremonies in piazza* Ⓜ *Ottaviano.*

★ Cappella Sistina (*Sistine Chapel*)

ART MUSEUM | In 1508, the redoubtable Pope Julius II commissioned Michelangelo to fresco the more than 10,000 square feet of the Sistine Chapel's ceiling. (*Sistine*, by the way, is simply the adjective form of *Sixtus*, in reference to Pope Sixtus IV, who commissioned the chapel itself.) The task took four years, and it's said that, for many years afterward, Michelangelo couldn't read anything without holding it over his head. The result, however, was the greatest artwork of the Renaissance. A pair of binoculars helps greatly, as does a small mirror—hold it facing the ceiling and look down to study the reflection. More than 20 years after his work on the ceiling, Michelangelo was called on again, this time by Pope Paul III, to add to the chapel's decoration by painting the Last Judgment on the wall over the altar. By way of signature on this, his last great fresco, Michelangelo painted his own face on the flayed-off human skin in St. Bartholomew's hand.

■ TIP→ The chapel is entered through the Musei Vaticani, and lines are much shorter after 2:30 (reservations are always advisable)—except free Sundays, which are extremely busy and when admissions close at 12:30. ⊠ Musei Vaticani, Vatican ⊕ www. museivaticani.va 🎟 €17 (part of the Vatican Museums) ⊘ Closed Sun. ⚲ Reservations required Ⓜ Ottaviano.

Castel Sant'Angelo

CASTLE/PALACE | FAMILY | Standing between the Tiber and the Vatican, this circular castle has long been one of Rome's most distinctive landmarks. Opera lovers know it well as the setting for the final scene of Puccini's *Tosca*. Started in AD 135, the structure began as a mausoleum for the emperor Hadrian and was completed by his successor, Antoninus Pius. From the mid-6th century the building became a fortress, a place of refuge for popes during wars and sieges. Its name dates to AD 590, when Pope Gregory the Great, during a procession to plead for the end of a plague, saw an angel standing on the summit of the castle, sheathing his sword. Taking this as a sign that the plague was at an end, the pope built a small chapel at the top, placing a statue next to it to celebrate his vision—thus the name, Castel Sant'Angelo. In the rooms off the Cortile dell'Angelo, look for the Cappella di Papa Leone X (Chapel of Pope Leo X), with a facade by Michelangelo. In the Pope Alexander VI courtyard, a wellhead bears the Borgia coat of arms. The stairs at the far end of the courtyard lead to the open terrace for a view of the Passetto, the fortified corridor connecting Castel Sant'Angelo with the Vatican. In the

appartamento papale (papal apartment), the Sala Paolina (Pauline Room) was decorated in the 16th century by Perino del Vaga and assistants with lavish frescoes of scenes from the Old Testament and the lives of Saint Paul and Alexander the Great. ⊠ *Lungotevere Castello 50, Prati* 🕾 *06/6819111 central line, 06/6896003 tickets* ⊕ *castelsantangelo.beniculturali.it* 🎟 *€15* ⊘ *Closed Mon.* ⚲ *Online reservations recommended* Ⓜ *Lepanto.*

★ **Musei Vaticani** (*Vatican Museums*)
ART MUSEUM | Other than the pope and his papal court, the occupants of the Vatican are some of the most famous artworks in the world. The Vatican Palace, residence of the popes since 1377, consists of an estimated 1,400 rooms, chapels, and galleries. The pope and his household occupy only a small part; most of the rest is given over to the Vatican Library and Museums. Beyond the glories of the Sistine Chapel, the collection is extraordinarily rich: highlights include the great antique sculptures (including the celebrated Apollo Belvedere in the Octagonal Courtyard and the Belvedere Torso in the Hall of the Muses); the Stanze di Raffaello (Raphael Rooms), with their famous gorgeous frescoes; and the Old Master paintings, such as Leonardo da Vinci's beautiful (though unfinished) *St. Jerome in the Wilderness*, some of Raphael's greatest creations, and Caravaggio's gigantic *Deposition in the Pinacoteca* (Picture Gallery). For those interested in guided visits to the Vatican Museums, tours start at €34, including entrance tickets, and can also be booked online. Other offerings include a regular two-hour guided tour of the Vatican gardens; call or check online to confirm. For more information, call 06/69884676 or go to museivaticani.va. For information on tours, call 06/69883145 or 06/69884676; visually impaired visitors can arrange tactile tours by calling 06/69884947. ⊠ *Viale Vaticano, near intersection with*

Continued on page 82

HEAVENS ABOVE:
THE SISTINE CEILING

Forming lines that are probably longer than those waiting to pass through the Pearly Gates, hordes of visitors arrive at the Sistine Chapel daily to view what may be the world's most sublime example of artistry:

Michelangelo: *The Creation of Adam*, Sistine Chapel, The Vatican, circa 1511.

Michelangelo's Sistine Ceiling. To paint this 12,000-square-foot barrel vault, it took four years, 343 frescoed figures, and a titanic battle of wits between the artist and Pope Julius II. While in its typical fashion, Hollywood focused on the element of agony, not ecstasy, involved in the saga of creation, a recently completed restoration of the ceiling has revolutionized our appreciation of

MICHELANGELO'S
MISSION IMPOSSIBLE

Designed to match the proportions of Solomon's Temple described in the Old Testament, the Sistine Chapel is named after Pope Sixtus VI, who commissioned it as a place of worship for himself and as the venue where new popes could be elected. Before Michelangelo, the barrel-vaulted ceiling was an expanse of azure fretted with golden stars. Then, in 1504, an ugly crack appeared. Bramante, the architect, managed do some patchwork using iron rods, but when signs of a fissure remained, the new Pope Julius II summoned Michelangelo to cover it with a fresco 135 feet long and 44 feet wide.

Taking in the entire span of the ceiling, the theme connecting the various participants in this painted universe could be said to be mankind's anguished waiting. The majestic panel depicting the Creation of Adam leads, through the stages of the Fall and the expulsion from Eden, to the tragedy of Noah found naked and mocked by his own sons; throughout all runs the underlying need for man's redemption. Witnessing all from the side and end walls, a chorus of ancient Prophets and Sibyls peer anxiously forward, awaiting the Redeemer who will come to save both the Jews and the Gentiles.

APOCALYPSE NOW

The sweetness and pathos of his *Pietà*, carved by Michelangelo only ten years earlier, have been left behind. The new work foretells an apocalypse, its congregation of doomed sinners facing the wrath of heaven through hanging, beheading, crucifixion, flood, and plague. Michelangelo, by nature a misanthrope, was already filled with visions of doom thanks to the fiery orations of Savonarola, whose thunderous preachments he had heard before leaving his hometown of Florence. Vasari, the 16th-century art historian, coined the word "terrabilità" to describe Michelangelo's tension-ridden style, a rare case of a single word being worth a thousand pictures.

Michelangelo wound up using a Reader's Digest condensed version of the stories from Genesis, with the dramatis personae overseen by a punitive and terrifying God. In real life, poor Michelangelo answered to a flesh-and-blood taskmaster who was almost as vengeful: Pope Julius II. Less vicar of Christ than latter-day Caesar, he was intent on uniting Italy under the power of the Vatican, and was eager to do so by any means, including riding into pitched battle. Yet this "warrior pope" considered his most formidable adversary to be Michelangelo. Applying a form of blackmail, Julius threatened to wage war on Michelangelo's Florence, to which the artist had fled after Julius canceled a commission for a grand papal tomb unless Michelangelo agreed to return to Rome and take up the task of painting the Sistine Chapel ceiling.

MICHELANGELO, SCULPTOR

A sculptor first and foremost, however, Michelangelo considered painting an inferior genre—"for rascals and sissies" as he put it. Second, there was the sheer scope of the task, leading Michelangelo to suspect he'd been set up by a rival, Bramante, chief architect of the new St. Peter's Basilica. As Michelangelo was also a master architect, he regarded this fresco commission as a Renaissance mission-impossible. Pope Julius's powerful will prevailed—and six years later the work of the Sistine Ceiling was complete. Irving Stone's famous novel *The Agony and the Ecstasy*—and the granitic 1965 film that followed—chart this epic battle between artist and pope.

THINGS ARE LOOKING UP

To enhance your viewing of the ceiling, bring along opera-glasses, binoculars, or just a mirror (to prevent your neck from becoming bent like Michelangelo's). Note that no photos are permitted. Insiders know the only time to get the chapel to yourself is during the papal blessings and public audiences held in St. Peter's Square. Failing that, get there during lunch hour. Admission and entry to the Sistine Chapel is only through the Musei Vaticani (Vatican Museums).

SCHEMATIC OF THE SISTINE CEILING

The ceiling's biblical symbols were ideated by three Vatican theologians, Cardinal Alidosi, Egidio da Viterbo, and Giovanni Rafanelli, along with Michelangelo. As for the ceiling's painted framework, this quadratura alludes to Roman triumphal arches because Pope Julius II was fond of mounting "triumphal entries" into his conquered cities (in imitation of Christ's procession into Jerusalem on Palm Sunday).

Prophet turned art-critic or, perhaps doubling as ourselves, the ideal viewer, Jonah the prophet (painted at the altar end) gazes up at the Creation, or Michelangelo's version of it.

1 The first of three scenes taken from the Book of Genesis: God separates Light from Darkness.

2 God creates the sun and a craterless pre-Galilean moon while the panel's other half offers an unprecedented rear view of the Almighty creating the vegetable world.

3 In the panel showing God separating the Waters from the Heavens, the Creator tumbles towards us as in a self-made whirlwind.

4 Pausing for breath, next admire probably Western Art's most famous image—God giving life to Adam.

The Creation of Eve from Adam's rib leads to the sixth panel.

6 In a sort of diptych divided by the trunk of the Tree of Knowledge of Good and Evil, Michelangelo retells the Temptation and the Fall.

Illustrating Man's fallen nature, the last three panels narrate, in un-chronological order, the Flood. In the first Noah offers a pre-Flood sacrifice of thanks.

8 Damaged by an explosion in 1794, next comes Michelangelo's version of Flood itself.

Finally, above the monumental Jonah, you can just make out the small, wretched figure of Noah, lying drunk—in pose, the shrunken anti-type of the majestic Adam five panels down the wall.

THE CREATION OF ADAM

Michelangelo's Adam was partly inspired by the Creation scenes Michelangelo had studied in the sculpted doors of Jacopo della Quercia in Bologna and Lorenzo Ghiberti's Doors of Paradise in Florence. Yet in Michelangelo's version Adam's hand hangs limp, waiting God's touch to impart the spark of life. Facing his Creation, the Creator—looking a bit like the pagan god Jupiter—is for the first time ever depicted as horizontal, mirroring the Biblical "in his own likeness." Decades after its completion, a crack began to appear, amputating Adam's fingertips. Believe it or not, the most famous fingers in Western art are the handiwork, at least in part, of one Domenico Carnevale.

Via Leone IV, Vatican ☎ 06/69883145 🌐 www.museivaticani.va ⏲ Closed Sun. and church holidays ✍ Reservations required 🎫 €17 with online reservations [M] Cipro–Musei Vaticani or Ottaviano–San Pietro; Bus 64 or 40.

Necropoli Vaticana (*Vatican Necropolis*)
CEMETERY | With advance notice you can take a 1½-hour guided tour in English of the Vatican Necropolis, under the Basilica di San Pietro, which gives a rare glimpse of Early Christian Roman burial customs and a closer look at the tomb of St. Peter. Apply via the contact form online, by fax, or in person (the entrance to the office is on the left of the Bernini colonnade), specifying the number of people in the group (all must be age 15 or older), preferred language, preferred time, available dates, and your contact information in Rome. Each group will have about 12 participants. Visits are not recommended for those with mobility issues or who are claustrophobic. ✉ *Ufficio Scavi, Vatican* ☎ *06/69885318, 06/69873017 reservations* 🌐 *www.scavi.va* 🎫 *€13* ⏲ *Closed Sun. and Roman Catholic holidays* ✍ *Reservations required* [M] *Ottaviano.*

★ **Piazza di San Pietro**
PLAZA/SQUARE | Mostly enclosed within high walls that recall the papacy's stormy history, the Vatican opens the spectacular arms of Bernini's colonnade to embrace the world only at St. Peter's Square, scene of the pope's public appearances. One of Bernini's most spectacular masterpieces, the elliptical Piazza di San Pietro was completed in 1667 after only 11 years' work and holds about 100,000 people. Surrounded by a pair of quadruple colonnades, it is gloriously studded with 140 statues of saints and martyrs. At the piazza's center, the 85-foot-high Egyptian obelisk was brought to Rome by Caligula in AD 37 and moved here in 1586 by Pope Sixtus V. The Vatican post offices can be found on both sides of St. Peter's Square and inside the Vatican Museums complex and are open to the public. ■ **TIP→ The main information office is just left of the basilica as you face it.** ✉ *Piazza di San Pietro, Vatican* 🌐 *www.vaticanstate.va* [M] *Ottaviano.*

🍴 Restaurants

★ **Del Frate**
$$ | **MODERN ITALIAN** | This impressive wine bar matches sleek, modern decor with creative cuisine and three dozen wines available by the glass. The house specialty is marinated meat and fish, but you can also get cheeses, smoked meats, and composed salads. **Known for:** wide selection of after-dinner drinks, including mezcal (smoky agave liquor) and amari (bitter cordial); daily aperitivo with a nice selection of wines by the glass; adjacent to one of Rome's noted wine shops. [$] *Average main: €23* ✉ *Via degli Scipioni 118, Prati* ☎ *06/3236437* 🌐 *www.enotecadelfrate.it* ⏲ *Closed Aug.* [M] *Ottaviano.*

Sant'Isidoro Pizza & Bolle
$ | **PIZZA** | Taking the traditional pairing of pizza and beer up a notch, this modern pizzeria on a quiet street pairs its pies with an extensive selection of sparkling wines. More upscale than a typical pizzeria but casual enough for a weeknight, this place serves classic flavor combinations as well as some creative options, like a pizza topped with stracciatella, raw shrimp, lemon peel, and mint. **Known for:** chic modern design; wide selection of sparkling wines; creative pizzas. [$] *Average main: €12* ✉ *Via Oslavia 41, Prati* ☎ *06/89822607* 🌐 *www.pizzaebolle.it* [M] *Lepanto.*

Taverna Angelica
$$ | **MODERN ITALIAN** | The Borgo area near St. Peter's Basilica hasn't been known for culinary excellence, but this is starting to change, and Taverna Angelica was one of the first refined restaurants in this part of town. The dining room is small, which allows the chef to create a menu that's inventive without being pretentious. **Known for:** tiramisu with amaretti biscuits;

eclectic Italian dishes; elegant surroundings. $ *Average main: €22* ✉ *Piazza Amerigo Capponi 6, Borgo* ☎ *06/6874514* ⊕ *www.tavernaangelica.com* ⊘ *Closed Mon.* Ⓜ *Ottaviano.*

Coffee and Quick Bites

Al Settimo Gelo
$ | **ICE CREAM** | The unusual flavors of gelato scooped up here include cinnamon and ginger and fig with cardamom and walnut, but the classics also get rave reviews. Ask for a taste of the *passito* flavor, if it's available; it's inspired by the popular sweet Italian dessert wine. **Known for:** completely gluten-free shop; organic Sicilian lemon sorbetto; homemade whipped cream. $ *Average main: €5* ✉ *Via Vodice 21/a, Prati* ☎ *06/3725567* ⊕ *www.alsettimogelo.it* ⊘ *Closed Mon., and 1 wk in Aug.* Ⓜ *Lepanto.*

Bonci Pizzarium
$ | **PIZZA** | This tiny storefront by famed pizzaiolo Gabriele Bonci is the city's most famous place for pizza *al taglio*. It serves more than a dozen flavors, from the standard margherita to slices piled high with prosciutto and other tasty ingredients. **Known for:** long lines; Rome's best pizza *al taglio*; over a dozen flavors. $ *Average main: €5* ✉ *Via della Meloria 43, Prati* ☎ *06/39745416* ⊕ *www.bonci.it* Ⓜ *Cipro.*

Hotels

Hotel al San Pietrino
$ | **HOTEL** | This simple budget hotel on the third floor of a 19th-century palazzo offers rock-bottom rates at a five-minute walk from the Vatican. **Pros:** air-conditioning and Wi-Fi; free parking; heavenly rates near the Vatican. **Cons:** no bar; flat pillows and basic bedding; a couple of Metro stops from the centro storico. $ *Rooms from: €65* ✉ *Via Giovanni Bettolo 43, Prati* ☎ *06/3700132* ⊕ *www.sanpietrino.it* 🛏 *12 rooms* ⓘ *No Meals* Ⓜ *Ottaviano.*

Residenza Paolo VI
$$ | **HOTEL** | Set in a former monastery—still an extraterritorial part of the Vatican—magnificently abutting Bernini's colonnade of St. Peter's Square, the Paolo VI (pronounced "Sesto," a reference to Pope Paul VI) is unbeatably close to St. Peter's, with comfortable and amazingly quiet guest rooms. **Pros:** direct views of St. Peter's from the rooftop terrace; lovely staff and service; quiet rooms. **Cons:** some rooms are really small; bathrooms are a tight space; far away from Rome's historical attractions. $ *Rooms from: €143* ✉ *Via Paolo VI 29, Borgo* ☎ *06/684870* ⊕ *www.residenzapaolovi.com* 🛏 *35 rooms* ⓘ *Free Breakfast* Ⓜ *Ottaviano.*

Nightlife

Bukowski's Bar
COCKTAIL LOUNGES | This cozy spot outside the Vatican is furnished like a familiar living room with a giant velvet sofa and armchairs, making it easy to meet the people sitting next to you. In addition to a strong cocktail and wine menu, the owners regularly host art, theater, and shopping events. Aperitivo is served every evening, with a selection of drinks and the option of adding a small plate for €5. ✉ *Via Degli Ombrellari 25, Borgo* ☎ *06/64760105* Ⓜ *Ottaviano.*

Emerald's Bar
COCKTAIL LOUNGES | This classy cocktail bar a few blocks from the Vatican makes you feel transported to a cozy salon in New York or London. The bartenders shake up reliably good classics, including an excellent Dirty Martini, and also some original creations. ✉ *Via Crescenzio 91C, Prati* ☎ *06/88654275* ⊕ *www.emeraldsbar.com* ⊘ *Closed Mon.* Ⓜ *Ottaviano.*

⬟ Shopping

★ Castroni

FOOD | Opening its flagship shop near the Vatican in 1932, this gastronomic paradise has long been Rome's port-of-call for decadent delicacies from around the globe; there are now 13 locations throughout the city. Jonesing expats and study-abroad students pop in for local sweets, Twinings teas, and even some good old-fashioned Kraft Macaroni & Cheese. If you're just doing a little window-shopping, be sure to try their in-house roasted espresso, some of the best coffee in Rome. ⊠ *Via Cola di Rienzo 196/198, Prati* ☎ *06/6874383* ⊕ *www.castronicoladirienzo.com* Ⓜ *Lepanto, Ottaviano.*

Savelli Arte e Tradizione

CRAFTS | Here you'll find a fully stocked selection of religious gifts: everything from rosaries and crosses to religious artwork and Pope Francis memorabilia. Founded in 1898, this family business provides a place for pilgrims to pick up a souvenir from the Holy See and also specializes in mosaics. The store has another location at Il Colonnato Self Service Restaurant in Piazza del Sant'Uffizio. ⊠ *Via Paolo VI 27–29, Borgo* ☎ *06/68307017* ⊕ *www.savellireligious.com* Ⓜ *Ottaviano.*

Piazza Navona, Campo de' Fiori, and the Jewish Ghetto

Set between Via del Corso and the Tiber bend, these time-burnished districts are some of the city's most beautiful. They're filled with airy piazzas, half-hidden courtyards, and narrow streets bearing curious names. Some of Rome's most coveted residential addresses are nestled here. So, too, are the ancient Pantheon and the Renaissance square of Campo de' Fiori, but the spectacular, over-the-top Baroque monuments of the 16th and 17th centuries predominate.

The hub of the district is the queen of squares, Piazza Navona—a cityscape adorned with the most jaw-dropping fountain by Gian Lorenzo Bernini, father of the Baroque. Streets running off the square lead to many historic must-sees, including noble churches by Borromini and Caravaggio's greatest paintings at San Luigi dei Francesi. This district has been an integral part of the city since ancient times, and its position between the Vatican and Lateran palaces, both seats of papal rule, put it in the mainstream of Rome's development from the Middle Ages onward. Craftsmen, shopkeepers, and famed artists toiled in the shadow of the huge palaces built to consolidate the power of leading figures in the papal court. Artisans and artists still live here, but their numbers are diminishing as the district becomes increasingly posh and—so critics say—"Disneyfied." But three of the liveliest piazzas in Rome—Piazza Navona, Piazza della Rotonda (home to the Pantheon), and Campo de' Fiori—are lodestars in a constellation of some of the city's finest cafés, stores, and wine bars.

Although today most of Rome's Jews live outside the Ghetto, the area remains the spiritual and cultural home of Jewish Rome, and that heritage permeates its small commercial area of Judaica shops, kosher bakeries, and restaurants. The Jewish Ghetto was established by papal decree in the 16th century. It was by definition a closed community, where Roman Jews lived under lock and key until Italian unification in 1870. In 1943–44, the already small Jewish population there was decimated by deportations. Today there are a few Judaica shops and kosher groceries, bakeries, and restaurants (especially on Via di Portico d'Ottavia), but the neighborhood mansions are now being renovated and much coveted by rich and stylish expats.

GETTING HERE AND AROUND

The Piazza Navona and Campo de' Fiori are an easy walk from the Vatican or Trastevere, or a half-hour stroll from the Spanish Steps. From Termini or the Vatican, take Bus No. 40 Express or the No. 64 to Largo Torre Argentina; then walk 10 minutes to either piazza. Bus No. 62 winds from Piazza Barberini past the Trevi Fountain to Campo de' Fiori.

From the Vatican or the Spanish Steps, it's a 30-minute walk to the Jewish Ghetto, or take the No. 40 Express or the No. 64 bus from Termini station to Largo Torre Argentina.

Sights

Campo de' Fiori

MARKET | A bustling marketplace in the morning (Monday through Saturday from 8 to 2) and a trendy meeting place the rest of the day and night, this piazza has plenty of down-to-earth charm. Just after lunchtime, all the fruit and vegetable vendors disappear, and this so-called *piazza trasformista* takes on another identity, becoming a circus of bars particularly favored by study-abroad students, tourists, and young expats. Brooding over the piazza is a hooded statue of the philosopher Giordano Bruno, who was burned at the stake here in 1600 for heresy, one of many victims of the Roman Inquisition. ⊠ *Intersection of Via dei Baullari, Via Giubbonari, Via del Pellegrino, and Piazza della Cancelleria, Campo de' Fiori.*

★ Crypta Balbi

RUINS | The fourth component of the magnificent collections of the Museo Nazionale Romano, this museum is unusual because it represents several periods of Roman history. The crypt is part of the Balbus Theater complex (13 BC), and other parts of the complex are from the medieval period, up through the 20th century. The written explanations accompanying the well-lit exhibits are excellent, and this museum is a popular field trip for teachers and school groups. ⊠ *Via delle Botteghe Oscure 31, Jewish Ghetto* ☎ *06/39967701* ⊕ *www.coopculture. it* ⊠ *€8 Crypta Balbi only; €10 includes 3 other Museo Nazionale Romano sites over a 1-week period (Palazzo Altemps, Palazzo Massimo, Museo Diocleziano)* Ⓜ *Bus Nos. 64 and 40, Tram No. 8.*

Fontana delle Tartarughe

FOUNTAIN | Designed by Giacomo della Porta in 1581 and sculpted by Taddeo Landini, this fountain, set in pretty Piazza Mattei, is one of Rome's most charming. The focus of the fountain is four bronze boys, each grasping a dolphin spouting water into a marble shell. Bronze turtles held in the boys' hands drink from the upper basin. The turtles were added in the 17th century by Bernini. ⊠ *Piazza Mattei, Jewish Ghetto.*

Il Gesù

CHURCH | The mother church of the Jesuits in Rome is the prototype of all Counter-Reformation churches, and its spectacular interior tells a great deal about an era of religious triumph and turmoil. Its architecture influenced ecclesiastical buildings in Rome for more than a century (the overall design was by Vignola, the facade by della Porta) and was exported by the Jesuits throughout the rest of Europe. Though consecrated in 1584, the interior of the church wasn't fully decorated for another 100 years. It was originally intended that the interior be left plain to the point of austerity— but, when it was finally embellished, the mood had changed and no expense was spared. Its interior drips with gold and lapis lazuli, gold and precious marbles, gold and more gold, all covered by a fantastically painted ceiling. Unfortunately, the church is also one of Rome's most crepuscular, so its visual magnificence is considerably dulled by lack of light. The architectural significance of Il Gesù extends far beyond the splendid interior. As the first of the great Counter-Reformation churches, it was put up

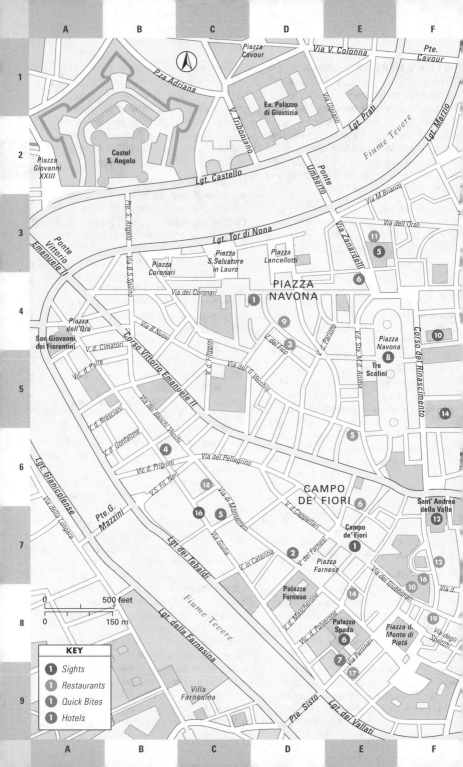

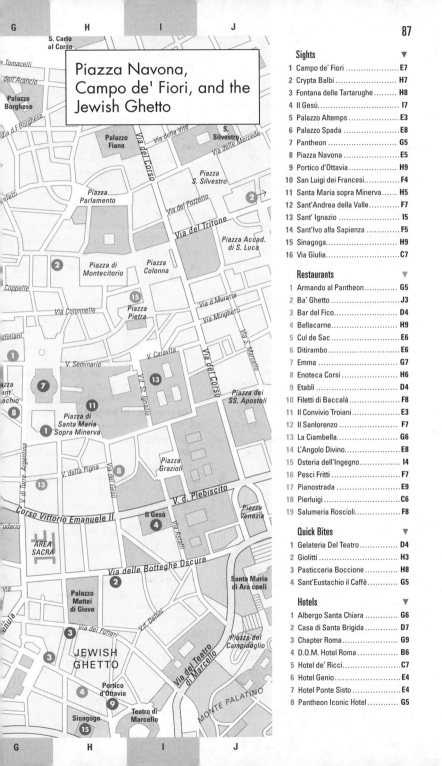

Piazza Navona, Campo de' Fiori, and the Jewish Ghetto

Sights ▼

1	Campo de' Fiori	E7
2	Crypta Balbi	H7
3	Fontana delle Tartarughe	H8
4	Il Gesù	I7
5	Palazzo Altemps	E3
6	Palazzo Spada	E8
7	Pantheon	G5
8	Piazza Navona	E5
9	Portico d'Ottavia	H9
10	San Luigi dei Francesi	F4
11	Santa Maria sopra Minerva	H5
12	Sant'Andrea della Valle	F7
13	Sant' Ignazio	I5
14	Sant'Ivo alla Sapienza	F5
15	Sinagoga	H9
16	Via Giulia	C7

Restaurants ▼

1	Armando al Pantheon	G5
2	Ba' Ghetto	J3
3	Bar del Fico	D4
4	Bellacarne	H9
5	Cul de Sac	E6
6	Ditirambo	E6
7	Emma	G7
8	Enoteca Corsi	H6
9	Etablì	D4
10	Filetti di Baccalà	F8
11	Il Convivio Troiani	E3
12	Il Sanlorenzo	F7
13	La Ciambella	G6
14	L'Angolo Divino	E8
15	Osteria dell'Ingegno	I4
16	Pesci Fritti	F7
17	Pianostrada	E9
18	Pierluigi	C6
19	Salumeria Roscioli	F8

Quick Bites ▼

1	Gelateria Del Teatro	D4
2	Giolitti	H3
3	Pasticceria Boccione	H8
4	Sant'Eustachio il Caffè	G5

Hotels ▼

1	Albergo Santa Chiara	G6
2	Casa di Santa Brigida	D7
3	Chapter Roma	G9
4	D.O.M. Hotel Roma	B6
5	Hotel de' Ricci	C7
6	Hotel Genio	E4
7	Hotel Ponte Sisto	E4
8	Pantheon Iconic Hotel	G5

after the Council of Trent (1545–63) had signaled the determination of the Roman Catholic Church to fight back against the Reformed Protestant heretics of northern Europe. The church decided to do so through the use of overwhelming pomp and majesty, in an effort to woo believers. As a harbinger of ecclesiastical spectacle, Il Gesù spawned imitations throughout Italy and the other Catholic countries of Europe as well as the Americas. The most striking element is the ceiling, which is covered with frescoes that swirl down from on high to merge with painted stucco figures at the base, the illusion of space in the two-dimensional painting becoming the reality of three dimensions in the sculpted figures. Baciccia, their painter, achieved extraordinary effects in these frescoes, especially in the *Triumph of the Holy Name of Jesus*, over the nave. Here, the figures representing evil are cast out of heaven and seem to be hurtling down onto the observer. To appreciate in detail, the spectacle is best viewed through a specially tilted mirror in the nave. The founder of the Jesuit order himself is buried in the Chapel of St. Ignatius, in the left-hand transept. This is surely the most sumptuous Baroque altar in Rome; as is typical, the enormous globe of lapis lazuli that crowns it is really only a shell of lapis over a stucco base—after all, Baroque decoration prides itself on achieving stunning effects and illusions. The heavy, bronze altar rail by architect Carlo Fontana is in keeping with the surrounding opulence. ⊠ *Via degli Astalli 16, Campo de' Fiori* ☎ *06/697001* ⊕ *www.chiesadel-gesu.org.*

★ Palazzo Altemps

CASTLE/PALACE | Containing some of the finest ancient Roman statues in the world, Palazzo Altemps is part of the Museo Nazionale Romano. The palace's sober exterior belies a magnificence that appears as soon as you walk into the majestic courtyard, studded with statues and covered in part by a retractable awning. The restored interior hints at the Roman lifestyle of the 16th–18th centuries while showcasing the most illustrious pieces from the Museo Nazionale, including the collection of the Ludovisi noble family. In the frescoed salons you can see the *Galata Suicida,* a poignant sculptural work portraying a barbarian warrior who chooses death for himself and his wife, rather than humiliation by the enemy. Another highlight is the large Ludovisi sarcophagus, magnificently carved from marble. In a place of honor is the *Ludovisi Throne,* which shows a goddess emerging from the sea and being helped by her acolytes. For centuries this was heralded as one of the most sublime Greek sculptures, but, today, at least one authoritative art historian considers it a colossally overrated fake. Look for the framed explanations of the exhibits that detail (in English) how and exactly where Renaissance sculptors, Bernini among them, added missing pieces to the classical works. In the lavishly frescoed Loggia stand busts of the Caesars. In the wing once occupied by early-20th-century poet Gabriele d'Annunzio (who married into the Altemps family), three rooms host the museum's Egyptian collection. ⊠ *Piazza di Sant'Apollinare 46, Piazza Navona* ☎ *06/39967701* ⊕ *www.coopculture.it* ⊠ *€8, or €10 including 3 other Museo Nazionale Romano sites over 1 week (Crypta Balbi, Palazzo Massimo alle Terme, Museo delle Terme di Diocleziano); €11, or €13 (including 3 other sites) if a special exhibit is on.*

Palazzo Spada

CASTLE/PALACE | In this neighborhood of huge, austere palaces, Palazzo Spada strikes an almost frivolous note, with its pretty ornament-encrusted courtyard and its upper stories covered with stuccoes and statues. While the palazzo houses an impressive collection of Old Master paintings, it's most famous for its trompe-l'oeil garden gallery, a delightful example of the sort of architectural games rich Romans of the 17th century found irresistible. Even if you don't go into the gallery, step into the courtyard and look through the glass window of the library to the colonnaded corridor in the adjacent courtyard. See—or seem to see—a 26-foot-long gallery quadrupled in depth, a sort of optical telescope taking the Renaissance's art of perspective to another level, as it stretches out for a great distance with a large statue at the end. In fact the distance is an illusion: the corridor grows progressively narrower and the columns progressively smaller as they near the statue, which is just 2 feet tall. The Baroque period is known for special effects, and this is rightly one of the most famous. It was long thought that Borromini was responsible for this ruse; it's now known that it was designed by an Augustinian priest, Giovanni Maria da Bitonto. Upstairs is a seignorial picture gallery with the paintings shown as they would have been, piled on top of each other clear to the ceiling. Outstanding works include Brueghel's *Landscape with Windmills*, Titian's *Musician*, and Andrea del Sarto's *Visitation*. Look for the fact-sheets that have descriptive notes about the objects in each room. ⊠ *Piazza Capo di Ferro 13, Campo de' Fiori* ☎ *06/6874896* ⊕ *www.galleriaspada. beniculturali.it* ⊠ *€5* ☻ *Closed Tues.*

★ Pantheon

RELIGIOUS BUILDING | The best preserved ancient building in the city, this former Roman temple is a marvel of architectural harmony and proportion. It was entirely rebuilt by the emperor Hadrian around AD 120 on the site of an earlier Pantheon (from the Greek: *pan,* all, and *theon,* gods) erected in 27 BC by Augustus's right-hand man and son-in-law, Agrippa. The most striking thing about the Pantheon is not its size, immense though it is, nor even the phenomenal technical difficulties posed by so massive a construction; rather, it's the remarkable unity of the building. The diameter described by the dome is exactly equal to its height. It's the use of such simple mathematical balance that gives classical architecture its characteristic sense of proportion and its nobility. The opening at the apex of the dome, the *oculus,* is nearly 30 feet in diameter and was intended to symbolize the "all-seeing eye of the heavens." On a practical note, this means when it rains, it rains inside: look out for the drainage holes in the floor. Although little is known for sure about the Pantheon's origins or purpose, it's worth noting that the five levels of trapezoidal coffers (sunken panels in the ceiling) represent the course of the five then-known planets and their concentric spheres. Ruling over them is the sun, represented symbolically and literally by the 30-foot-wide eye at the top. The heavenly symmetry is further paralleled by the coffers: 28 to each row, the number of lunar cycles. In the center of each would have shone a small bronze star. Down below, the seven large niches were occupied not by saints, but, it's thought, by statues of Mars, Venus, the deified Caesar, and the other "astral deities," including the moon and sun, the "sol invictus." (Academics still argue, however, about which gods were most probably worshipped here.) One of the reasons the Pantheon is so well preserved is the result of it being consecrated as a church in AD 608. (It's still a working church today.) No building, church or not, though, escaped some degree of plundering through the turbulent centuries of Rome's history after the fall of the empire. In 655, for example, the gilded bronze covering the dome was stripped. The Pantheon is also one of the city's important burial places. Its most famous tomb is that of Raphael (between the second and third chapels on the left as you enter). Mass takes place on Sunday and on religious holidays at 10:30; it's open to the public, but you are expected to arrive before the beginning and stay until the end. General access usually resumes at about 11:30. ⊠ *Piazza della Rotonda, Piazza Navona* ☎ *06/68300230* ⊕ *www.pantheonroma.com* ⊠ *Free; audio guide €7.*

★ Piazza Navona

PLAZA/SQUARE | Always camera-ready, the beautiful Baroque plaza known as Piazza Navona has Bernini sculptures, three gorgeous fountains, a magnificently Baroque church (Sant'Agnese in Agone), and under it all the remains of a Roman athletics track. Pieces of the arena are still visible near the adjacent Piazza Sant'Apollinare, and the ancient spirit of entertainment lives on in the buskers and mimes who populate the piazza today. The piazza took on its current look during the 17th century, after Pope Innocent X of the Pamphilj family decided to make over his family palace (now the Brazilian embassy and an ultra-luxe hotel) and the rest of the piazza. Center stage is the Fontana dei Quattro Fiumi, created for Innocent by Bernini in 1651. Bernini's powerful figures of the four rivers represent the longest rivers of the four known continents at the time: the Nile (his head covered because the source was unknown); the Ganges; the Danube; and the Plata (the length of the Amazon was then unknown). Popular legend has it that the figure of the Plata—the figure closest to Sant'Agnese in Agone—raises his hand before his eyes because he can't bear to look upon the church's "inferior" facade designed by Francesco Borromini, Bernini's rival. If you want a café with one of the most beautiful, if pricey, views in Rome, grab a seat at Piazza Navona. Just be aware that all the restaurants here are heavily geared toward tourists, so while it's a beautiful place for a coffee, you can find cheaper, more authentic, and far better meals elsewhere. ⊠ *Piazza Navona.*

Portico d'Ottavia

RUINS | Looming over the Jewish Ghetto, this huge portico, with a few surviving columns, is one of the area's most picturesque set pieces, with the church of Sant'Angelo in Pescheria built right into its ruins. Named by Augustus in honor of his sister Octavia, it was originally 390 feet wide and 433 feet long, encompassed two temples, a meeting hall, and a library, and served as a kind of grandiose entrance foyer for the adjacent Teatro di Marcello. The ruins of the portico became Rome's *pescheria* (fish market) during the Middle Ages. A stone plaque on a pillar (a copy; the original is in the Musei Capitolini) states in Latin that the head of any fish surpassing the length of the plaque was to be cut off "up to the first fin" and given to the city fathers, or else the vendor was to pay a fine of 10 gold florins. The heads were used to make fish soup and were considered a great delicacy. ⊠ *Via Portico d'Ottavia 29, Jewish Ghetto.*

★ San Luigi dei Francesi

CHURCH | A pilgrimage spot for art lovers, San Luigi's Contarelli Chapel (the fifth and last chapel on the left, toward the main altar) is adorned with three stunningly dramatic works by Caravaggio (1571–1610), the Baroque master of the heightened approach to light and dark. They were commissioned for the tomb of Mattheiu Cointerel in one of Rome's French churches (San Luigi is St. Louis, patron saint of France). The inevitable coin machine will light up his *Calling of Saint Matthew, Saint Matthew and the Angel,* and *Martyrdom of Saint Matthew* (seen from left to right), and Caravaggio's mastery of light takes it from there. When painted, they caused considerable consternation among the clergy of San Luigi, who thought the artist's dramatically realistic approach was scandalously disrespectful. A first version of the altarpiece was rejected; the priests were not particularly happy with the other two, either. Time has fully vindicated Caravaggio's patron, Cardinal Francesco del Monte, who secured the commission for these works and stoutly defended them. ⊠ *Piazza di San Luigi dei Francesi, Piazza Navona* ☎ *06/688271* ⊕ *www.saintlouis-rome.net.*

★ Santa Maria sopra Minerva

CHURCH | The name of the church reveals that it was built *sopra* (over) the ruins of a temple of Minerva, the ancient goddess of wisdom. Erected in 1280 by Dominicans along severe Italian Gothic lines, it has undergone a number of more or less happy restorations to the interior. Certainly, as the city's major Gothic church, it provides a refreshing contrast to Baroque flamboyance. Have a €1 coin handy to illuminate the Cappella Carafa in the right transept, where Filippino Lippi's (1457–1504) glowing frescoes are well worth the small investment, opening up the deepest azure expanse of sky where musical angels hover around the Virgin. Under the main altar is the tomb of St. Catherine of Siena, one of Italy's patron saints. Left of the altar you'll find Michelangelo's *Risen Christ* and the tomb of the gentle artist Fra Angelico. Bernini's unusual and little-known monument to the Blessed Maria Raggi is on the fifth pier of the left-hand aisle. In front of the church, Bernini's *Elephant and Obelisk* is perhaps the city's most charming sculpture. An inscription on the base references the church's ancient patroness, reading something to the effect that it takes a strong mind to sustain solid wisdom. ⊠ *Piazza della Minerva, Piazza Navona* ☎ *06/792257* ⊕ *www.santamariasopraminerva.it.*

Sant'Andrea della Valle

CHURCH | Topped by the highest dome in Rome after St. Peter's (designed by Maderno), this huge and imposing 17th-century church is remarkably balanced in design. Fortunately, its facade, which had turned a sooty gray from pollution, has been cleaned to a near-sparkling white. Use one of the handy mirrors to examine the early-17th-century frescoes by Domenichino in the choir vault and those by Lanfranco in the dome. One of the earliest ceilings done in full Baroque style, its upward vortex was influenced by Correggio's dome in Parma, of which Lanfranco was also a citizen. (Bring a few coins to light the paintings, which can be very dim.) The three massive paintings of Saint Andrew's martyrdom are by Mattia Preti (1650–51). Richly marbled and decorated chapels flank the nave, and in such a space, Puccini set the first act of *Tosca.* ⊠ *Piazza Vidoni 6, Corso Vittorio Emanuele II, Campo de' Fiori* ☎ *06/6861339* ⊕ *www.santandrea.teatinos.org.*

★ Sant'Ignazio

CHURCH | Rome's second Jesuit church, this 17th-century landmark set on a rococo piazza harbors some of the city's most magnificent trompe l'oeils. To get the full effect of the marvelous illusionistic ceiling by priest-artist Andrea Pozzo, stand on the small yellow disk set into the floor of the nave. The heavenly vision above you, seemingly extending upward almost indefinitely, represents the *Allegory of the Missionary Work of the Jesuits* and is part of Pozzo's cycle of works in this church exalting the early history of the Jesuit Order, whose founder was the reformer Ignatius of Loyola. The saint soars heavenward, supported by a cast of thousands, creating a jaw-dropping effect that was fully intended to rival the glorious ceiling produced by Baciccia in the nearby mother church of Il Gesù. Be sure to have coins handy for the machine that switches on the lights so you can marvel at the false dome, which is actually a flat canvas—a trompe l'oeil trick Pozzo used when the architectural budget drained dry. The dazzling church hardly stops there: scattered around the nave are several awe-inspiring altars; their soaring columns, gold-on-gold decoration, and gilded statues are pure splendor. The church is often host to concerts of sacred music performed by choirs from all over the world. Look for posters by the main doors or check the website for more information. ⊠ *Via del Caravita 8A, Piazza Navona* ☎ *06/6794406* ⊕ *www.chiesasantignazio.it.*

Sant'Ivo alla Sapienza

CHURCH | The main facade of this eccentric Baroque church, probably Borromini's best, is on the stately courtyard of an austere building that once housed Rome's university. Sant'Ivo has what must surely be one of the most delightful "domes" in all of Rome—a dizzying spiral said to have been inspired by a bee's stinger. The apian symbol is a reminder that Borromini built the church on commission from the Barberini pope Urban VIII (a swarm of bees figure on the Barberini family crest), although it was completed by Alexander VII. The interior, open only for three hours on Sunday morning, is worth a look, especially if you share Borromini's taste for complex mathematical architectural idiosyncrasies. "I didn't take up architecture solely to be a copyist," he once said. Sant'Ivo is certainly the proof. ✉ Corso del Rinascimento 40, Piazza Navona ☎ 06/6864987 ⊙ Closed Aug., and Mon.–Sat.

Sinagoga

RELIGIOUS BUILDING | This synagogue has been the city's largest Jewish temple, and a Roman landmark with its aluminum dome, since its construction in 1904. The building also houses the Jewish Museum, with its precious ritual objects and other exhibits, which document the uninterrupted presence of a Jewish community in the city for nearly 22 centuries. Until the 16th century, Jews were esteemed citizens of Rome. Among them were bankers and physicians to the popes, who had themselves given permission for the construction of synagogues. But in 1555, during the Counter-Reformation, Pope Paul IV decreed the building of the walls of the Ghetto, confining the Jews to this small area and imposing a series of restrictions, some of which continued to be enforced until 1870. For security reasons, entrance is via guided visit only, and tours in English start every hour at about 10 minutes past the hour; entrance to the synagogue is through the museum located in Via Catalana (Largo 16 Ottobre 1943). ✉ Lungotevere de' Cenci 15, Jewish Ghetto ☎ 06/68400661 ⊕ www. museoebraico.roma.it ☎ €11 ⊙ Museum closed Sat. and Jewish holidays.

★ Via Giulia

STREET | Still a Renaissance-era diorama and one of Rome's most exclusive addresses, Via Giulia was the first street in Rome since ancient times to be deliberately planned. Straight as a die, it was named for Pope Julius II (of Sistine Chapel fame), who commissioned it in the early 1500s as part of a scheme to open up a grandiose approach to St. Peter's Basilica, and it is flanked with elegant churches and palaces. Although the pope's plans to change the face of the city were only partially completed, Via Giulia became an important thoroughfare in Renaissance Rome. Today, after more than four centuries, it remains the "salon of Rome," address of choice for Roman aristocrats, although controversy has arisen about a recent change—the decision to add a large parking lot along one side of the street—that meant steamrolling through ancient and medieval ruins underneath. A stroll will reveal elegant palaces and churches (one, San Eligio, on the little side street Via di Sant'Eligio, was designed by Raphael himself). The area around Via Giulia is wonderful to wander through and get the feel of daily life as carried on in a centuries-old setting. Among the buildings that merit your attention are Palazzo Sacchetti (Via Giulia 66), with an imposing stone portal (inside are some of Rome's grandest staterooms, still, after 300 years, the private quarters of the Marchesi Sacchetti), and the forbidding brick building that housed the Carceri Nuove (New Prison; Via Giulia 52), Rome's prison for more than two centuries and now the offices of Direzione Nazionale Antimafia. Near the bridge that arches over the southern end of Via Giulia is the church of Santa Maria dell'Orazione e Morte (Holy Mary of Prayer and Death), with stone skulls on its door. These are a symbol of a confraternity that was charged with burying the bodies of the unidentified dead found in the city streets. Home since 1927 to the Hungarian Academy, the Palazzo Falconieri (Via Giulia 06/6889671) was designed by Borromini—note the architect's rooftop belvedere adorned with statues of the family "falcons," best viewed from around the block along the Tiber embankment. (The Borromini-designed salons and loggia are sporadically open as part of a guided tour; call the Hungarian Academy for information.) Remnant of a master plan by Michelangelo, the arch over the street was meant to link massive Palazzo Farnese, on the east side of Via Giulia, with the building across the street and a bridge to the Villa Farnesina, directly across the river. Finally, on the right and rather green with age, dribbles that star of many a postcard, the Fontana del Mascherone. ✉ *Via Giulia, between Piazza dell'Oro and Piazza San Vincenzo Palloti, Campo de' Fiori.*

🍴 Restaurants

Armando al Pantheon

$$ | ROMAN | In the shadow of the Pantheon, this small family-run trattoria, open since 1961, delights tourists and locals alike. There's an air of authenticity to the Roman staples here, and the quality of the ingredients and the cooking mean booking ahead is a must. **Known for:** good wine list; traditional Roman cooking beautifully executed; spaghetti *cacio e pepe.* [$] *Average main: €16* ✉ *Salita dei Crescenzi 31, Piazza Navona* ☎ *06/68803034* 🌐 *www.armandoalpantheon.it* 🕒 *Closed Sun., and Dec.–Jan. 6. No dinner Sat.*

★ **Ba' Ghetto**

$$ | ITALIAN | FAMILY | This hot spot on the main promenade in the Jewish Ghetto has been going strong for years, with pleasant indoor and outdoor seating. The kitchen is kosher (many places featuring Roman Jewish fare are not) and serves meat dishes (so no dairy) from the Roman Jewish tradition as well as from elsewhere in the Mediterranean; down the street is Ba'Ghetto Milky (Via del Portico d'Ottavia 2/a), the kosher dairy version of the original. **Known for:** outside tables on the pedestrianized street; *carciofi alla giudia* (deep-fried artichokes) and other Roman Jewish specialities; casual family atmosphere. [$] *Average main: €22* ✉ *Via del Portico d'Ottavia 57, Jewish Ghetto* ☎ *06/68892868* 🌐 *www.baghetto.com* 🕒 *Dinner Fri. and lunch Sat. are strictly for those who observe Shabbat with advance payment.*

Bar del Fico

$ | ITALIAN | FAMILY | Everyone in Rome knows Bar del Fico, located right behind Piazza Navona, so if you're looking to hang out with the locals, this is the place to come for a drink or something to eat at any time of day or night. Just about every evening of the year, it's packed with people sipping cocktails in the square. **Known for:** buzzy atmosphere; outside tables in a pretty square; Italian-style brunch. [$] *Average main: €10* ✉ *Piazza de Fico 26, Piazza Navona* ☎ *06/68891373* 🌐 *www.bardelfico.com.*

Bellacarne

$$ | ROMAN | *Bellacarne* means "beautiful meat," and that's the focus of the menu here, though the double entendre is that it's also what a Jewish Italian grandmother might say while pinching her grandchild's cheek. The kosher kitchen makes its own pastrami, though the setting is definitely more fine-dining than deli. **Known for:** deep-fried artichokes; outside seating; house-made pastrami. [$] *Average main: €17* ✉ *Via Portico d'Ottavia 51, Jewish Ghetto* ☎ *06/6833104* 🌐 *www.bellacarne.it* 🕒 *No dinner Fri. No lunch Sat.*

★ **Cul de Sac**

$ | WINE BAR | This popular wine bar near Piazza Navona is among the city's oldest and offers a book-length selection of wines from Italy, France, the Americas, and elsewhere. Offering great value and pleasant service a stone's throw from Piazza Navona, it's open all afternoon, making it a great spot for a late lunch or an early dinner when most restaurants aren't open yet. **Known for:** relaxed atmosphere and outside tables; great wine list (and wine bottle–lined interior); eclectic Italian and Mediterranean fare. $ Average main: €14 Piazza di Pasquino 73, Piazza Navona 06/68801094 www. enotecaculdesacroma.it.

Ditirambo

$$ | ITALIAN | Don't let the country-kitchen ambience fool you: at this little spot off Campo de' Fiori, the constantly changing selection of offbeat takes on Italian classics makes this a step beyond the ordinary. There are several good options for vegetarians. **Known for:** good vegetarian options; hearty meat and pasta dishes; cozy and casual atmosphere. $ Average main: €16 Piazza della Cancelleria 74, Campo de' Fiori 06/6871626 www. ristoranteditirambo.it Closed Aug.

★ Emma

$$$ | ROMAN | FAMILY | With dough by Rome's renowned family of bakers, the Rosciolis, this large, sleek, modern pizzeria is smack in the middle of the city, with the freshest produce right outside the door. The wine list features many local Lazio options. **Known for:** tasty fritti (classic fried Roman pizzeria appetizers); light and airy, casual atmosphere; thin-crust Roman pizza. $ Average main: €25 Via Monte della Farina 28–29, Campo de' Fiori 06/64760475 www. emmapizzeria.com.

Enoteca Corsi

$ | ITALIAN | Very convenient for a good-value lunch in the centro storico, this trattoria is undeniably old-school—renovations were done a few years back, but you wouldn't know it—and that's all part of the charm. It's packed at lunch with a mix of civil servants from the nearby government offices, construction workers, and in-the-know tourists, when a few specials—classic pastas, a delicious octopus salad, and some secondi like roast veal with peas—are offered. **Known for:** brusque but friendly service; casual atmosphere; Roman specialities. $ Average main: €12 Via del Gesù 88, Piazza Navona 06/6790821 www. enotecacorsi.com Closed Sun., and 3 wks in Aug. No dinner Sat.

★ Etablì

$ | MEDITERRANEAN | On a narrow vicolo (alley) off lovely cobblestone Piazza del Fico, this multifunctional restaurant and lounge space is decorated according to what could be called a modern Italian farmhouse-chic aesthetic, with vaulted wood-beam ceilings, wrought-iron touches, plush leather sofas, and chandeliers. The food is Mediterranean, with touches of international flavors. **Known for:** great location by Piazza Navona; popular after-dinner spot for sipping; casually romantic boho-chic atmosphere. $ Average main: €12 Vicolo delle Vacche 9/a, Piazza Navona 06/97616694 www. etabli.it.

Filetti di Baccalà

$ | ITALIAN | The window reads "Filetti di Baccalà," but the official name of this small restaurant that specializes in one thing—deliciously battered and deep-fried fillets of salt cod—is Dar Filettaro a Santa Barbara. The location, down the street from Campo de' Fiori in a little piazza in front of the beautiful Santa Barbara church, practically begs you to eat at one of the outdoor tables, where service is brusque. **Known for:** tables outside on the pretty square; filetti di baccalà; functional "hole-in-the-wall" interior. $ Average main: €6 Largo dei Librari 88, Campo de' Fiori 06/6864018 Closed Mon., and Aug.

★ Il Convivio Troiani

$$$$ | MODERN ITALIAN | In a tiny, nondescript alley north of Piazza Navona, the three Troiani brothers—Angelo in the kitchen, and brothers Giuseppe and Massimo presiding over the dining room and wine cellar—have been quietly

redefining the experience of Italian *alta cucina* (haute cuisine) since 1990 at this well-regarded establishment. Service is attentive without being overbearing, and the wine list is exceptional. **Known for:** amazing wine cellar and a great sommelier; fine dining in elegant surroundings; inventive modern Italian cooking with exotic touches. [$] *Average main: €38* ✉ *Vicolo dei Soldati 31, Piazza Navona* ☎ *06/6869432* 🌐 *www.ilconviviotroiani.it* 🕓 *Closed Sun., and 1 wk in Aug. No lunch.*

Il Sanlorenzo

$$$$ | SEAFOOD | This gorgeous space, with its chandeliers and soaring original brickwork ceilings, houses one of the best seafood restaurants in the Eternal City. Order à la carte, or if you're hungry, the eight-course tasting menu is extremely tempting—it might include the likes of cuttlefish-ink tagliatelle with mint, artichokes, and roe, or shrimp from the island of Ponza with rosemary, bitter herbs, and porcini mushrooms—and, given the quality of the fish, a relative bargain at €90. **Known for:** elegant surroundings; top-quality fish and seafood; spaghetti *con ricci* (sea urchins). [$] *Average main: €36* ✉ *Via dei Chiavari 4/5, Campo de' Fiori* ☎ *06/6865097* 🌐 *www.ilsanlorenzo.it* 🕓 *Closed Sun., and 2 wks in Aug. No lunch Sat. and Mon.*

La Ciambella

$$ | ITALIAN | The sprawling space is styled after American restaurants, with a lively bar in front, but the structure itself is all Roman, with brick archways, high ceilings, and a skylight in one of the dining rooms that allows guests to gaze at the fantastic Roman sky. The emphasis here is on high-quality ingredients and classic Italian culinary traditions. **Known for:** great location near the Pantheon; elegant setting; sophisticated classic Italian cuisine. [$] *Average main: €17* ✉ *Via dell'Arco della Ciambella 20, Piazza Navona* ☎ *06/6832930* 🌐 *www.la-ciambella.it* 🕓 *Closed Mon.*

L'Angolo Divino

$$ | WINE BAR | There's something about this cozy wine bar that feels as if it's in a small university town instead of a bustling metropolis. Serene blue-green walls lined with wooden shelves of wines from around the Italian peninsula add to the warm atmosphere, and the kitchen stays open until the wee hours on weekends. **Known for:** late-night snacks; excellent wine selection and advice; cozy atmosphere. [$] *Average main: €13* ✉ *Via dei Balestrari 12, Campo de' Fiori* ☎ *06/6864413* 🌐 *www.angolodivino.it* 🕓 *Closed 2 wks in Aug.*

Osteria dell'Ingegno

$$ | MODERN ITALIAN | This casual, trendy place is a great spot to enjoy a glass of wine or a gourmet meal in an ancient piazza in the city center, but the modern interior—vibrant with colorful paintings by local artists—brings you back to the present day. The simple but innovative menu includes dishes like Roman artichokes with *baccalà*, beef *tagliata* (sliced grilled steak) with a red-wine reduction, and a perfectly cooked duck breast with red fruit sauce. **Known for:** outdoor seating with views of ancient ruins; a great spot both for aperitifs and/or a meal; beautiful location on a pedestrian square. [$] *Average main: €22* ✉ *Piazza di Pietra 45, Piazza Navona* ☎ *06/6780662* 🌐 *www.osteriadellingegno.com.*

Pesci Fritti

$$ | SOUTHERN ITALIAN | This cute jewel box of a restaurant sits on the seating of the ancient Theatre of Pompey just behind Campo de' Fiori (note the curve of the street). Step inside, and the whitewashed walls with touches of pale sea blue will make you feel like you've escaped to the Mediterranean for seafood favorites. **Known for:** cozy setting; fried fish and seafood choices; spaghetti with clams. [$] *Average main: €18* ✉ *Via di Grottapinta 8, Campo de' Fiori* ☎ *06/68806170* 🌐 *www.pescifritti.it* 🕓 *Closed Mon. and Aug.*

★ Pianostrada

$$ | **MODERN ITALIAN** | This gourmet restaurant has an open kitchen, where you can watch the talented women owners cook up a storm of inventive delights—this is a "kitchen *lab*," after all, where top local ingredients are whipped into delicious plates. The spaghetti with tomato sauce, smoked ricotta, parmigiano, basil, and lemon peel is one of the signature dishes, and the amped up traditional recipe is a delicious indication of how interesting the food can get. **Known for:** homey atmosphere; freshly baked focaccia with various toppings; creative burgers and salads. $ *Average main: €20* ⊠ *Via delle Zoccolette 22, Campo de' Fiori* ☎ *06/89572296.*

★ Pierluigi

$$$ | **ITALIAN** | This popular seafood restaurant is a fun spot on balmy summer evenings, with tables out on the pretty Piazza de' Ricci. As at most Italian restaurants, fresh fish is sold per hectogram (100 grams, or about 3.5 ounces), so you may want to double-check the cost after it's been weighed. **Known for:** elegant atmosphere with great service; tables on the pretty pedestrianized piazza; top-quality fish and seafood. $ *Average main: €30* ⊠ *Piazza de' Ricci 144, Campo de' Fiori* ☎ *06/6861302* ⊕ *www.pierluigi.it.*

★ Salumeria Roscioli

$$ | **WINE BAR** | The shop in front of this wine bar will beckon you in with top-quality comestibles like hand-sliced cured ham from Italy and Spain, more than 300 cheeses, and a dizzying array of wines—but venture farther inside to try an extensive selection of unusual dishes and interesting takes on the classics. There are tables in the cozy wine cellar downstairs, but try and bag a table at the back on the ground floor (reserve well ahead; Roscioli is very popular). **Known for:** best prosciutto in town; extensive wine list; arguably Rome's best spaghetti alla carbonara. $ *Average main: €22* ⊠ *Via dei Giubbonari 21, Campo de' Fiori*

☎ *06/6875287* ⊕ *www.salumeriaroscioli. com* ⊙ *Closed Sun. and 1 wk in Aug.*

☕ Coffee and Quick Bites

★ Gelateria Del Teatro

$ | **ICE CREAM** | **FAMILY** | In a window next to the entrance of this renowned gelateria, you can see the fresh fruit being used in the laboratory to create the flavors of the day, which highlight the best of Italy, from Amalfi lemons to hazelnuts from Alba. In addition to traditional flavors, they serve a few interesting combinations, like raspberry and sage or white chocolate with basil. **Known for:** charming location on a cobblestone street; seasonal, all natural ingredients; sublime gelato. $ *Average main: €3* ⊠ *Via dei Coronari 65/66, Piazza Navona* ☎ *06/45474880* ⊕ *www.gelateriadelteatro.it.*

★ Giolitti

$ | **ITALIAN** | **FAMILY** | Open since 1900, Giolitti near the Pantheon is Rome's old-school gelateria par excellence. Pay in advance at the register by the door and take your receipt to the counter, where you can choose from dozens of flavors, including chocolate, cinnamon, and pistachio. **Known for:** wide selection of flavors; excellent gelato; old-school ambiance. $ *Average main: €3* ⊠ *Via degli Uffici del Vicario 40, Piazza Navona* ☎ *06/6991243* ⊕ *www.giolitti.it.*

Pasticceria Boccione

$ | **BAKERY** | This tiny, old-school bakery is an institution in the Ghetto area and is famed for its Roman Jewish sweet specialties. Service is brusque, choices are few, what's available depends on the season, and when it's sold out, it's sold out. **Known for:** old-school bakery, so no frills and no seats; pizza ebraica ("Jewish pizza," a dense baked sweet rich in nuts and raisins); ricotta and cherry tarts. $ *Average main: €4* ⊠ *Via del Portico d'Ottavia 1, Jewish Ghetto* ☎ *06/6878637* ⊙ *Closed Sat.*

Sant'Eustachio il Caffè

$ | **CAFÉ** | Frequented by tourists and government officials from the nearby Senate alike, this café is considered by many to make Rome's best coffee. Take it at the counter Roman-style: servers are hidden behind a huge espresso machine, where they vigorously mix the sugar and coffee to protect their "secret method" for the perfectly prepared cup (if you want your caffè without sugar here, ask for it *senza zucchero*). **Known for:** '30s interior; *gran caffè* (large sugared espresso); old-school Roman coffee bar vibe. $ *Average main: €2* ✉ *Piazza Sant'Eustachio 82, Piazza Navona* ☎ *06/68802048* ⊕ *www.santeustachioilcaffe.it.*

 ## Hotels

Albergo Santa Chiara

$$$ | **HOTEL** | If you're looking for a good location and top-notch service at great rates—not to mention comfortable beds and a quiet stay—look no further than this historic hotel, run by the same family for some 200 years. **Pros:** lovely sitting area in front, overlooking the piazza; great location near the Pantheon; free Wi-Fi. **Cons:** street-side rooms can be noisy; some rooms are on the small side and need updating; Wi-Fi can be slow. $ *Rooms from: €210* ✉ *Via Santa Chiara 21, Piazza Navona* ☎ *06/6872979* ⊕ *www.albergosantachiara.com* 🛏 *96 rooms* ⦿ *Free Breakfast.*

Casa di Santa Brigida

$ | **B&B/INN** | The friendly sisters of Santa Brigida oversee simple, straightforward, and centrally located accommodations in one of Rome's loveliest convents, with a rooftop terrace overlooking Palazzo Farnese. **Pros:** free Wi-Fi; large library and sunroof; insider papal tickets. **Cons:** no TVs in the rooms (though there is a common TV room); weak air-conditioning; far from a Metro stop. $ *Rooms from: €50* ✉ *Piazza Farnese 96, entrance around the corner at Via Monserrato 54, Campo de' Fiori* ☎ *06/68892596* ⊕ *www.brigidine.org* 🛏 *20 rooms* ⦿ *Free Breakfast.*

Chapter Roma

$$$ | **HOTEL** | This hip new member of Design Hotels has an edgy, of-the-moment design that juxtaposes plush midcentury Italian furnishings with street art murals and industrial touches. **Pros:** healthy food options at the Market café; trendy design; coworking space available. **Cons:** no spa; no gym; service can be a bit spotty. $ *Rooms from: €230* ✉ *Via di Santa Maria de' Calderari 47, Jewish Ghetto* ☎ *06/89935351* ⊕ *www.chapter-roma.com* 🛏 *47* ⦿ *Free Breakfast.*

D.O.M Hotel Roma

$$$$ | **HOTEL** | In an old convent on Via Giulia, one of Rome's romantic ivy-covered streets, the D.O.M (Deo Optimo Maximo) is an ultrachic luxury hotel that resembles an aristocratic *casa nobile*. **Pros:** hip decor; complimentary Acqua di Parma toiletries; heated towel racks. **Cons:** delicious but expensive cocktails; an armed guard at the anti-terrorism headquarters opposite the hotel may be off-putting for some; standard rooms are small for a five-star hotel. $ *Rooms from: €320* ✉ *Via Giulia 131, Campo de' Fiori* ☎ *06/6832144* ⊕ *www.domhotelroma.com* 🛏 *18 rooms* ⦿ *Free Breakfast.*

Hotel de' Ricci

$$$$ | **HOTEL** | This intimate boutique hotel from the team behind Pierluigi is a top spot for wine lovers. **Pros:** perks include complimentary aperitivo and priority reservations at Pierluigi; excellent wine cellar and wine tastings; great location on a quiet street. **Cons:** the bar is only open to hotel guests; there's a charge of 50 euros per day to bring pets; there's no spa or gym. $ *Rooms from: €350* ✉ *Via della Barchetta 14, Campo de' Fiori* ☎ *06/6874775* ⊕ *www.hoteldericci.com* 🛏 *8 rooms* ⦿ *No Meals.*

Hotel Genio

$$ | **HOTEL** | Just off one of Rome's most beautiful piazzas—Piazza Navona—this pleasant hotel has a lovely rooftop terrace perfect for enjoying a cappuccino or a glass of wine while taking in the view. **Pros:** spacious, elegant bathrooms; free Wi-Fi; breakfast buffet is abundant. **Cons:** spotty Internet; rooms facing the street can be noisy; beds can be too firm for some. $ *Rooms from: €160* ⊠ *Via Giuseppe Zanardelli 28, Piazza Navona* ☎ *06/6833781* ⊕ *www.hotelgenioroma.it* ⤶ *60 rooms* ⦿*l Free Breakfast* Ⓜ *Spagna.*

Hotel Ponte Sisto

$$$ | **HOTEL** | Situated in a remodeled Renaissance palazzo with one of the prettiest patio-courtyards in Rome, this hotel is a relaxing retreat close to Trastevere and Campo de' Fiori. **Pros:** luxury bathrooms; beautiful courtyard garden; rooms with views (and some with balconies and terraces). **Cons:** carpets starting to show signs of wear; some upgraded rooms are small and not worth the price difference; street-side rooms can be a bit noisy. $ *Rooms from: €250* ⊠ *Via dei Pettinari 64, Campo de' Fiori* ☎ *06/6863100* ⊕ *www.hotelpontesisto.it* ⤶ *106 rooms* ⦿*l Free Breakfast.*

Pantheon Iconic Hotel

$$$ | **HOTEL** | A member of Marriott's Autograph Collection, this boutique hotel is a sleek retreat in the center of the action. **Pros:** Marriott Bonvoy members can use and redeem points; restaurant by one of the city's best chefs; modern design and amenities. **Cons:** no spa or gym; some rooms lack external views; design might be considered a bit cold and corporate. $ *Rooms from: €250* ⊠ *Via di Santa Chiara 4A, Piazza Navona* ☎ *06/87807070* ⊕ *www.thepantheonhotel.com* ⤶ *79 rooms* ⦿*l No Meals.*

Nightlife

★ Bar del Fico

CAFÉS | Bar del Fico looks a lot different from the days of yore when raucous outdoor chess matches accompanied cocktails at the once-bare-bones local hangout. Though the chess tables are still sitting in the shade of the historic fig tree, Bar del Fico is now a happening bar, restaurant, evening cocktail spot, and late-night hangout. ⊠ *Piazza del Fico 26, Piazza Navona* ☎ *06/68891373* ⊕ *www. bardelfico.com/en/bar.*

Etablì

WINE BARS | If you set up a wine bar in your living room, it'd feel a lot like Etablì. This is the perfect spot for meeting friends before a night out on the town. ⊠ *Vicolo delle Vacche 9, Piazza Navona* ☎ *06/97616694* ⊕ *www.etabli.it.*

Jerry Thomas Project

COCKTAIL LOUNGES | One of just a handful of hidden bars in Rome, this intimate bar looks like a Prohibition-era haunt and serves the kind of classic cocktails you find in New York speakeasies. It's seating room only, so reservations must be made in advance. Upon booking, you'll receive a password via email. ⊠ *Vicolo Cellini 30, Piazza Navona* ☎ *370/1146287* ⊕ *www. thejerrythomasproject.it.*

L'Angolo Divino

WINE BARS | Nestled on a quiet side street around the corner from the ever-vivacious Campo de' Fiori, this wood-paneled enoteca is a hidden treasure of wines. Its extensive selection lists more than 1,000 labels to go along quite nicely with its quaint menu of delicious homemade pastas and local antipasti. And because it's open every night until 1:30 am, it's the ideal place for a late-night tipple. ⊠ *Via dei Balestrari 12, Campo de' Fiori* ☎ *06/6864413* ⊕ *www.angolodivino.it.*

★ **Roof Garden Bar at**
Grand Hotel de la Minerve

COCKTAIL LOUNGES | During warm months, this lofty perch offers perhaps the most inspiring view in Rome—directly over the Pantheon's dome. The Roof Garden has an equally impressive cocktail menu. Take advantage of summer sunsets and park yourself in a front-row seat as the dome glows. Even if you're just going for a drink, it's a good idea to book a table, especially on weekends. ⊠ *Grand Hotel de la Minerve, Piazza della Minerve 69, Piazza Navona* ☎ *06/695201* ⊕ *www. minervaroofgarden.it.*

Vinoteca Novecento

WINE BARS | A lovely, tiny enoteca with a very old-fashioned vibe, Vinoteca Novecento has a seemingly unlimited selection of wines, proseccos, vini santi, and grappe, along with salami-and-cheese tasting menus. Inside is standing-room only; in good weather, sit outside on one of the oak barriques. ⊠ *Piazza delle Coppelle 47, Piazza Navona* ☎ *06/6833078.*

 Performing Arts

★ **Teatro Argentina**

THEATER | A gorgeous 18th-century theater, the Teatro Argentina evokes glamour and sophistication with its velvet upholstery, large crystal chandeliers, and beautifully dressed theatergoers, who come to see international productions of stage and dance performances. ⊠ *Largo di Torre Argentina 52, Campo de' Fiori* ☎ *06/684000314* ⊕ *www.teatrodiroma.net.*

 Shopping

CERAMICS AND
DECORATIVE ARTS

★ **IN.OR. dal 1952**

CRAFTS | For more than 50 years, IN.OR. dal 1952 has served as a trusty friend for Romans in desperate need of an exclusive wedding gift or those oh-so-perfect china place settings for a

fancy Sunday dinner. Entrance is via a secluded 15th-century courtyard and up a flight of stairs. The store specializes in work handcrafted by the silversmiths of Pampaloni and Bastianelli in Florence. ⊠ *Via della Stelletta 23, Piazza Navona* ☎ *06/6878579.*

CLOTHING

★ **L'Archivio di Monserrato**

WOMEN'S CLOTHING | This airy, spacious boutique curated by Soledad Twombly (daughter-in-law of painter Cy Twombly) showcases her original designs as well as a sophisticated mix of antique Turkish and Indian textiles, jewelry, shoes, and small homewares picked up on her travels. Tailored jackets trimmed with exotic fabrics, dresses in eclectic prints and bold colors, and smart linen suits are some of Twombly's signatures. ⊠ *Via di Monserrato 150, Campo de' Fiori* ☎ *06/6868168* ⊕ *www. soledadtwombly.com.*

Le Tartarughe

WOMEN'S CLOTHING | A familiar face on the catwalks of Rome's fashion shows, designer Susanna Liso, a Rome native, adds suggestive elements of playful experimentation to her haute couture and ready-to-wear lines, which are much loved by Rome's aristocracy and intelligentsia. With intense, enveloping designs, she mixes raw silks or cashmere and fine merino wool together to form captivating garments that combine seduction and linear form. ⊠ *Via Piè di Marmo 17, Piazza Navona* ☎ *06/6792240* ⊕ *www.letartarughe.eu.*

Vestiti Usati Cinzia

MIXED CLOTHING | Vintage-clothes hunters, costume designers, and stylists alike love browsing through the racks at Vestiti Usati Cinzia. The shop is fun and very inviting and stocked with wall-to-wall funky 1960s and '70s apparel and loads of goofy sunglasses. There's definitely no shortage of flower-power bell-bottoms and hippie shirts, embroidered tops, trippy and psychedelic boots, and other awesome accessories that will take you back to the days of peace and love. ✉ *Via del Governo Vecchio 45, Piazza Navona* ☎ *06/6832945.*

FOOD AND WINE

Moriondo e Gariglio

CANDY | Not exactly Willy Wonka (but in the same vein), Moriondo e Gariglio is a chocolate lover's paradise, churning out some of the finest chocolate delicacies in town. The shop dates back to 1850 and adheres strictly to family recipes passed on from generation to generation. Whether you favor marrons glacés or dark-chocolate truffles, you'll delight in choosing from more than 80 delicacies. ✉ *Via Piè di Marmo 21, Piazza Navona* ☎ *06/6990856.*

JEWELRY

MMM—Massimo Maria Melis

JEWELRY & WATCHES | Drawing heavily on ancient Roman and Etruscan designs, Massimo Maria Melis jewelry will carry you back in time. Working with 21-carat gold, he often incorporates antique coins in many of his exquisite bracelets and necklaces. Some of his pieces are done with an ancient technique, much-loved by the Etruscans, in which tiny gold droplets are fused together to create intricately patterned designs. ✉ *Via dell'Orso 57, Piazza Navona* ☎ *06/6869188* ⊕ *www.massimomariamelis.com.*

Quattrocolo

JEWELRY & WATCHES | This historic shop dating to 1938 showcases exquisite antique micro-mosaic jewelry painstakingly crafted in the style perfected by the masters at the Vatican mosaic studio. You'll also find 18th- and 19th-century cameos and beautiful engraved stones as well as contemporary jewelry handmade in the studio. The small works were beloved by cosmopolitan clientele of the Grand Tour age and offer modern-day shoppers a taste of yesteryear's grandeur. ✉ *Via della Scrofa 48, Piazza Navona* ☎ *06/68801367* ⊕ *www.quattrocolo.com.*

SHOES AND ACCESSORIES

★ Chez Dede

OTHER SPECIALTY STORE | Husband-and-wife duo Andrea Ferolla and Daria Reina (he's a fashion illustrator, she's a photographer) curate an edited selection of clothes, bags, vintage jewelry, books, home decor, and anything else you might need in this cult favorite lifestyle-concept shop. Their signature bags are designed to go from the plane straight to the beach, and they regularly release collectible items featuring Ferolla's whimsical illustrations. ✉ *Via di Monserrato 35, Campo de' Fiori* ☎ *06/83772934* ⊕ *www.chezdede.com.*

Ibiz

LEATHER GOODS | In business since 1972, this family team creates colorful, stylish leather handbags, belts, and sandals near Piazza Campo de' Fiori. Choose from the premade collection or order something in the color of your choice; their workshop is visible in the boutique. ✉ *Via dei Chiavari 39, Campo de' Fiori* ☎ *06/68307297* ⊕ *www.ibizroma.it.*

★ Maison Halaby

HANDBAGS | Lebanese designer and artist Gilbert Halaby was featured in fashion magazines like *Vogue* and created jewelry for Lady Gaga before giving up the rat race and opening his own shop, where the ethos is all about slow fashion. He designs boldly colored leather handbags incorporating suede, python, fringe, raffia, or jeweled handles, as well as silk scarves printed with his original watercolors, which he sells in this small boutique that feels like an extension of his home, with a velvet sofa, plenty of books and plants, and his own paintings on the walls. The shop is mainly open by appointment, but if Gilbert is there when you pass by, ring the bell and he'll invite you in for coffee or Campari. ✉ *Via di Monserrato 21, Campo de' Fiori* ☎ *06/96521585* ⊕ *www.maisonhalaby.com* ☉ *Open by appointment.*

STATIONERY

★ Cartoleria Pantheon dal 1910

STATIONERY | Instead of sending a post-card home, head to the simply sumptuous Cartoleria Pantheon dal 1910 for fine handmade paper to write that special letter. In addition to simple, stock paper and artisanal sheets of handcrafted Amalfi paper, there are hand-bound leather journals in an extraordinary array of colors and sizes. The store has two locations in the neighborhood. ⊠ *Via della Maddalena 41, Piazza Navona* ☎ *06/6795633* ⊕ *www.cartoleriapantheon.it.*

TOYS

Al Sogno

TOYS | **FAMILY** | If you're looking for quality toys that encourage imaginative play and learning, look no further than Al Sogno. With an emphasis on the artistic as well as the multisensory, the shop has a selection of toys that are both discerning and individual, making them perfect for children of all ages. Carrying an exquisite collection of fanciful puppets, collectible dolls, masks, stuffed animals, and illustrated books, this Navona jewel, around since 1945, is crammed top-to-bottom with beautiful, well-crafted playthings. If you believe that children's toys don't have to be high-tech, you will adore reliving some of your best childhood memories here. ⊠ *Piazza Navona 53, corner of Via Agonale, Piazza Navona* ☎ *06/6864198* ⊕ *www.alsogno.com.*

★ Bartolucci

TOYS | **FAMILY** | This shop opened in the '90s, but the Bartolucci family has been making whimsical, handmade curiosities out of pine, including clocks, bookends, bedside lamps, and wall hangings, since 1936. You can even buy a child-size motorbike entirely made of wood (wheels, too). Don't miss the life-size Pinocchio pedaling furiously on a wooden bike. ⊠ *Via dei Pastini 98, Piazza Navona* ☎ *06/69190894* ⊕ *www.bartolucci.com.*

Piazza di Spagna

In spirit (and in fact) this section of the city is its most grandiose. The overblown Vittoriano monument, the labyrinthine treasure-chest palaces of Rome's surviving aristocracy, even the diamond-draped denizens of Via Condotti's shops—all embody the exuberant ego of a city at the center of its own universe. Here's where you'll see ladies in furs gobbling pastries at café tables and walk through a thousand snapshots as you climb the famous Spanish Steps, admired by generations from Byron to Versace. Cultural treasures abound around here: gilded 17th-century churches, glittering palazzi, and the greatest example of portraiture in Rome, Velázquez's incomparable *Innocent X* at the Galleria Doria Pamphilj. Have your camera ready—along with a coin or two—for that most beloved of Rome's landmarks, the Trevi Fountain.

GETTING HERE AND AROUND

Piazza di Spagna is a short walk from Piazza del Popolo, the Pantheon, and the Trevi Fountain. One of Rome's handiest subway stations, Spagna, is tucked just left of the steps. Buses No. 117 (from the Colosseum) and No. 119 (from Piazza del Popolo) hum through the area; the latter tootles up Via del Babuino, famed for its shopping.

Sights

★ Ara Pacis Augustae

(*Altar of Augustan Peace*)

MONUMENT | In a city better known for its terra-cotta–colored palazzi, this pristine monument sits inside one of Rome's newer architectural landmarks: a gleaming, rectangular glass-and-travertine structure designed by American architect Richard Meier. Overlooking the Tiber on one side and the ruins of the marble-clad Mausoleo di Augusto (Mausoleum of Augustus) on the other, the result is a serene, luminous oasis right in the center of Rome. The altar itself dates back to 13 BC; it was commissioned to celebrate the Pax Romana, the era of peace ushered in by Augustus's military victories. Like all ancient Roman monuments of this kind, you have to imagine its spectacular and moving relief sculptures painted in vibrant colors, now long gone. The reliefs on the short sides portray myths associated with Rome's founding and glory; the long sides display a procession of the imperial family. It's fun to try to play "who's who"—although half of his body is missing, Augustus is identifiable as the first full figure at the procession's head on the south-side frieze—but academics still argue over exact identifications of most of the figures. This one splendid altar is the star of the small museum downstairs, which hosts rotating exhibits on Italian culture, with themes ranging from design to film. ⊠ *Lungotevere in Augusta, at the corner of Via Tomacelli, Piazza di Spagna* ☎ *06/0608* ⊕ *www.arapacis.it* ⓣ *€10.50, €17 when there's an exhibit* Ⓜ *Flaminio.*

Keats-Shelley Memorial House

HISTORIC HOME | Sent to Rome in a last-ditch attempt to treat his consumptive condition, English Romantic poet John Keats lived—and died—in this house at the foot of the Spanish Steps. At the time, this was the heart of the colorful bohemian quarter of Rome that was especially favored by English expats. He took his last breath here on February 23, 1821, and is now buried in the Non-Catholic Cemetery in Testaccio. Even before his death, Keats was celebrated for such poems as "Ode to a Nightingale" and "Endymion." In this "Casina di Keats," you can visit his final home and see his death mask, though all his furnishings were burned after his death as a sanitary measure by the local authorities. You'll also find a rather quaint collection of memorabilia of English literary figures of the period—Lord Byron, Percy Bysshe Shelley, Joseph Severn, and Leigh Hunt, as well as Keats—and

an exhaustive library of works on the Romantics. ⊠ *Piazza di Spagna 26, Piazza di Spagna* ☎ *06/6784235* ⊕ *www.keats-shelley-house.org* ⓣ *€6* ⊘ *Closed Sun.* Ⓜ *Spagna.*

Mausoleo di Augusto

TOMB | The largest circular tomb in the world, the mausoleum certainly made a statement about the glory of Augustus, Julius Caesar's successor. He was only 35 years old when he commissioned it following his victory over Marc Anthony and Cleopatra. Though the ruins we see now are brick and stone, it was originally covered in marble and travertine, with evergreen trees planted on top, a colossal statue of the emperor at the summit, and a pair of bronze pillars inscribed with his achievements at the entrance. The mausoleum's innermost sepulchral chamber housed the ashes of several members of the Augustan dynasty, but it was subsequently raided and the urns were never found. Between the 13th and 20th centuries, it lived several other lives as a garden, an amphitheater that hosted jousting tournaments, and a concert hall, which Mussolini tore down in 1936 in a bid to restore the monument to its imperial glory. His plans were interrupted by World War II, after which the mausoleum was all but abandoned until a recent restoration reopened it to the public. A new public piazza is currently being constructed around it. ⊠ *Piazza Augusto Imperatore, Piazza di Spagna* ☎ *06/0608* ⊕ *www.mausoleodiaugusto.it* ⓣ *€4* Ⓜ *Spagna.*

Monumento a Vittorio Emanuele II, or Altare della Patria (*Victor Emmanuel II Monument, or Altar of the Nation*)

MONUMENT | The huge white mass known as the "Vittoriano" is an inescapable landmark that has been likened to a huge wedding cake or an immense typewriter. Present-day Romans joke that you can only avoid looking at it if you are standing on it, but it was the source of great civic pride at the time of its construction at the turn of the 20th century. To create this elaborate marble monster and the vast piazza on which it stands, its architects blithely destroyed many ancient and medieval buildings and altered the slope of the Campidoglio (Capitoline Hill), which abuts it. Built to honor the unification of Italy and the nation's first king, Victor Emmanuel II, it also shelters the eternal flame at the tomb of Italy's Unknown Soldier, killed during World War I. You can't miss the Monumento, so enjoy neo-imperial grandiosity at its most bombastic. The underwhelming exhibit inside the building tells the history of the country's unification, but the truly enticing feature of the Vittoriano is its rooftop terrace, which offers some of the best panoramic views of Rome. The only way up is by elevator (the entrance is located several flights of stairs up on the right as you face the monument). ⊠ *Entrances on Piazza Venezia, Piazza del Campidoglio, and Via di San Pietro in Carcere, Piazza di Spagna* ☎ *06/0608* ⊕ *vittoriano.benicul- turali.it* ⛶ *€10* Ⓜ *Colosseo.*

★ **Palazzo Colonna**

HISTORIC HOME | Rome's grandest family built themselves Rome's grandest private palace, a fusion of 17th- and 18th-century buildings that has been occupied by the Colonna family for more than 20 generations. The immense palatial residence faces Piazza dei Santi Apostoli on one side and the Quirinale (Quirinal Hill) on the other (with a little bridge over Via della Pilotta linking to the gardens on the hill). The palazzo is still home to some Colonna patricians, but it also holds an exquisite art gallery, which is open to the public on Saturday mornings. The gallery is itself a setting of aristocratic grandeur; you might recognize the Sala Grande as the site where Audrey Hepburn meets the press in *Roman Holiday*. An ancient red marble column (*colonna* in Italian), which is the family's emblem, looms at one end, but the most spectacular feature is the ceiling fresco of the Battle of Lepanto painted by Giovanni Coli

and Filippo Gherardi beginning in 1675. Adding to the opulence are works by Poussin, Tintoretto, and Veronese, and a number of portraits of illustrious members of the family, such as Vittoria Colonna, Michelangelo's muse and longtime friend. There is a guided tour in English at noon that is includd in the entrance fee and can help you to navigate through the array of madonnas, saints, goddesses, popes, and cardinals to see Annibale Carracci's lonely *Beaneater*, spoon at the ready and front teeth missing. The gallery also has a café with a pleasant terrace. ⊠ *Via della Pilotta 17, Piazza di Spagna* ☎ *06/6784350* ⊕ *www.galleriacolonna.it* ⛶ *€12* ⊗ *Closed Sun.–Fri.* Ⓜ *Barberini.*

★ **Palazzo Doria Pamphilj**

HISTORIC HOME | Along with the Palazzo Colonna and the Galleria Borghese, this dazzling family palace provides the best glimpse of aristocratic Rome. The main attractions in the gilded galleries are the legendary Old Master paintings, including treasures by Velázquez and Caravaggio; the splendor of the halls themselves; and a unique suite of private family apartments. The understated beauty of the graceful facade, designed by Gabriele Valvassori in 1730, is best admired by crossing to the opposite side of the street for a good view, but it barely hints at the opulence that awaits inside. The palace passed through several hands before becoming the property of the Pamphilj family, who married into the famous seafaring Doria family of Genoa in the 18th century. The family still lives in part of the palace. The gallery contains 550 paintings, including three by Caravaggio—a young *St. John the Baptist, Mary Magdalene*, and the breathtaking *Rest on the Flight to Egypt*. Off the eye-popping **Galleria degli Specchi** (Gallery of Mirrors)—a smaller version of the one at Versailles—are the famous Velázquez *Pope Innocent X*, considered by some historians to be the greatest portrait ever painted, and the Bernini bust of the same Pamphilj pope. The delightful

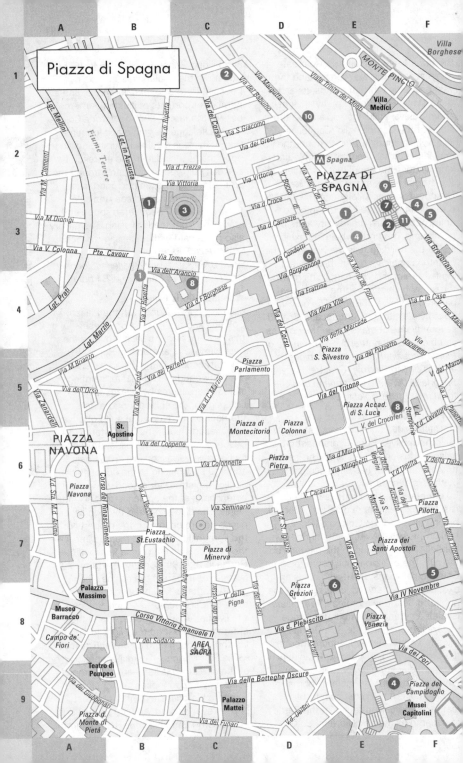

Sights ▼

1 Ara Pacis Augustae **B3**
2 Keats-Shelley Memorial House... **E3**
3 Mausoleo di Augusto **C3**
4 Monumento a Vittorio
  Emanuele II, or Altare
  della Patria **E9**
5 Palazzo Colonna **F7**
6 Palazzo Doria Pamphilj............. **E8**
7 The Spanish Steps.................. **E3**
8 Trevi Fountain **F5**

Restaurants ▼

1 Il Marchese **B4**
2 Mirabelle **G2**
3 Moma **I3**
4 Ristorante Nino **E3**
5 Settimo.............................. **G2**

Quick Bites ▼

1 Antico Caffè Greco **E3**

Hotels ▼

1 Aleph Rome Hotel **H3**
2 Babuino 181 .... **C1**
3 Baglioni Hotel Regina **H2**
4 The Hassler......................... **F3**
5 Hotel de la Ville **F3**
6 Hotel d'Inghilterra **D3**
7 Hotel Eden.......................... **G2**
8 Hotel Vilòn.......................... **C4**
9 Il Palazzetto **E2**
10 Margutta 19 .... **D2**
11 Scalinata di Spagna............... **F3**

KEY

1 *Sights*

1 *Restaurants*

1 *Quick Bites*

1 *Hotels*

audio guide is included in the ticket price and narrated by the current heir, Prince Jonathan Doria Pamphilj, who divulges an intimate family history. ⊠ *Via del Corso 305, Piazza di Spagna* ☎ *06/6797323* ⊕ *www.doriapamphilj.it* ⊗ *Closed Mon.–Thurs.* ⚲ *reservations required* ⊠ *€14* Ⓜ *Barberini.*

★ The Spanish Steps

NOTABLE BUILDING | FAMILY | The iconic Spanish Steps (often called simply *la scalinata,* or "the staircase," by Italians) and the Piazza di Spagna from which they ascend both get their names from the Spanish Embassy to the Vatican on the piazza—even though the staircase was built with French funds by an Italian in 1723. In honor of a diplomatic visit by the King of Spain, the hillside was transformed by architect Francesco de Sanctis with a spectacular piece of urban planning to link the church of Trinità dei Monti at the top with the Via Condotti below. In an allusion to the church, the staircase is divided by three landings (beautifully lined by potted azaleas mid-April–mid-May). Bookending the bottom of the steps are two beloved holdovers from the 18th century, when the area was known as the "English Ghetto": to the right, the Keats-Shelley House, and to the left, Babington's Tea Rooms—both beautifully redolent of the era of the Grand Tour. For weary sightseers who find the 135 steps too daunting, there is an elevator at Vicolo del Bottino 8, next to the Metro entrance. (Those with mobility problems should be aware that there is still a small flight of stairs after, however, and that the elevator is sporadically closed for repair.) At the bottom of the steps, Bernini's splendid "Barcaccia" (sinking ship) fountain dates to the early 17th century and still spouts drinking water from the ancient Aqua Vergine aqueduct. ⊠ *Piazza di Spagna* Ⓜ *Spagna*

★ Trevi Fountain

FOUNTAIN | Alive with rushing waters commanded by an imperious sculpture of Oceanus, the Fontana di Trevi has been all about theatrical effects from the start; it is an aquatic marvel in a city filled with them. The fountain's unique drama is largely due to its location: its vast basin is squeezed into the tight confluence of three little streets (the *tre vie,* which may give the fountain its name), with cascades emerging as if from the wall of Palazzo Poli. The dream of a fountain emerging full-force from a palace was first envisioned by Bernini and Pietro da Cortona from Pope Urban VIII's plan to rebuild an older fountain, which had earlier marked the end-point of the ancient Acqua Vergine aqueduct, created in 18 BC by Agrippa. Three popes later, under Pope Clement XIII, Nicola Salvi finally broke ground with his winning design. Unfortunately, Salvi did not live to see his masterpiece of sculpted seashells, roaring sea beasts, and diva-like mermaids completed; he caught a cold and died while working in the culverts of the aqueduct 11 years before the fountain was finally finished in 1762. Everyone knows the famous legend that if you throw a coin into the Trevi Fountain you will ensure a return trip to the Eternal City, but not everyone knows how to do it the right way. You must toss a coin with your right hand over your left shoulder, with your back to the fountain. One coin means you'll return to Rome; two, you'll return *and* fall in love; three, you'll return, find love, and marry. The fountain grosses some €600,000 a year, with every cent going to the Italian Red Cross, which is why Fendi was willing to foot the bill and fully funded the Trevi's marvelous recent restoration. ⊠ *Piazza di Trevi, Piazza di Spagna* Ⓜ *Barberini.*

🍽 Restaurants

★ Il Marchese

$$ | **ITALIAN** | This rustic-meets-glamorous bistro attracts locals for its flawless execution of Roman classics (many served photogenically in metal cooking pans) as well as original dishes. Its bar is known among amaro connoisseurs for having the largest selection in Rome, and the bitter liquors are the stars of the expertly crafted cocktail menu. **Known for:** extensive selection of amaros and great cocktails; well-executed classics; beautiful design. $ *Average main: €18* ⊠ *Via di Ripetta 162, Piazza di Spagna* ☎ *06/90218872* ⊕ *www.ilmarcheseroma. it* Ⓜ *Spagna.*

Mirabelle

$$$$ | **MODERN ITALIAN** | Old World elegance is the name of the game here—think white-jacketed waiters who attend to your every need, classic decor, and impeccable dishes, which are the most modern thing about this restaurant on the seventh floor of the Hotel Splendide Royal. Be sure to request a table on the terrace, which boasts panoramic views of leafy Villa Borghese and the center of Rome. **Known for:** top-notch food and service; romantic atmosphere; panoramic terrace. $ *Average main: €54* ⊠ *Hotel Splendide Royal, Via di Porta Pinciana 14, Piazza di Spagna* ☎ *06/42168838* ⊕ *www. robertonaldicollection.com/ristorante-mirabelle* ⌂ *business casual* Ⓜ *Spagna, Barberini.*

★ Moma

$$$ | **MODERN ITALIAN** | In front of the American embassy, a favorite of the design *trendoisie,* modern, Michelin-starred Moma attracts well-heeled businessmen at lunch but turns into a more intimate affair for dinner. The kitchen turns out hits as it creates *alta cucina* (haute cuisine) made using Italian ingredients sourced from small producers. **Known for:** affordable fine dining; creative presentation; pasta with a twist.

$ *Average main: €25* ⊠ *Via San Basilio 42/43, Piazza di Spagna* ☎ *06/42011798* ⊕ *www.ristorantemoma.it* ⌀ *Closed Sun.* Ⓜ *Barberini.*

Ristorante Nino

$$$ | **ITALIAN** | Almost more of a landmark than an eatery, Nino has been a favorite among international journalists and the rich and famous since the 1930s and does not seem to have changed at all over the decades. The interior is country rustic *alla toscana,* and the menu accordingly sticks to the Tuscan classics. **Known for:** *ribollita* (Tuscan bean soup); warm crostini spread with pâté; upscale old-school Italian vibe. $ *Average main: €26* ⊠ *Via Borgognona 11, Piazza di Spagna* ☎ *06/6786752* ⊕ *www.ristorantenino.it* ⌀ *Closed Sun. and Aug.* Ⓜ *Spagna.*

Settimo

$$$ | **ITALIAN** | Crowning the Sofitel Rome Villa Borghese hotel, this chic restaurant serves fancified takes on Rome's *cucina povera* (peasant cooking) in a chic space with graphic punches of color. The terrace offers fantastic views that stretch from Villa Borghese to the dome of St. Peter's, but the interior dining room, with its floor-to-ceiling windows and terrazzo-inspired floors, is lovely too. **Known for:** terrace with great views; amped up version of classic Roman recipes; colorful, modern design. $ *Average main: €26* ⊠ *Sofitel Rome Villa Borghese, Via Lombardia 47, Piazza di Spagna* ☎ *06/478021* ⊕ *www.settimoristorante.it* Ⓜ *Barberini.*

☕ Coffee and Quick Bites

Antico Caffè Greco

$ | **CAFÉ** | Pricey Antico Caffè Greco is a national landmark and Rome's oldest café; its red-velvet chairs, marble tables, and marble busts have seen the likes of Byron, Shelley, Keats, Goethe, and Casanova. Add to this the fact that it's in the middle of the shopping madness on the upscale Via dei Condotti, and you won't be surprised that the place is often filled with tourists. **Known for:** crystal goblets and high prices to match; perfect espresso; lavish historic design. $ *Average main: €12* ✉ *Via dei Condotti 86, Piazza di Spagna* ☎ *06/6791700* ⊕ *www.caffegreco.shop* Ⓜ *Spagna.*

Hotels

Aleph Rome Hotel

$$$$ | HOTEL | Fashionable couples tend to favor the Aleph, a former bank–turned–luxury Rome hotel, where the motto seems to be "more marble, everywhere." Now part of Hilton's Curio Collection, the hotel has ample facilities that include two pools (one in the spa and one on the roof), a cigar lounge, a cocktail bar, and two restaurants, one on the ground floor and one on the rooftop. **Pros:** terrace with pool; free access to the spa for hotel guests; award-winning design. **Cons:** rooftop views don't showcase Rome's most flattering side; rooms are too petite for the price; buffet breakfast not included. $ *Rooms from: €380* ✉ *Via San Basilio 15, Piazza di Spagna* ☎ *06/4229001* ⊕ *alephrome.com* ⤳ *88 rooms* ⦿ *No Meals* Ⓜ *Barberini.*

Babuino 181

$$$ | HOTEL | On chic Via del Babuino, known for its high-end boutiques, jewelry stores, and antiques shops, this discreet and stylish hotel is an ideal Roman pied à terre that has spacious rooms spread over two historic buildings. **Pros:** iPhone docks and other handy in-room amenities; spacious suites; luxury Frette linens. **Cons:** breakfast is nothing special; rooms can be a bit noisy; annex rooms feel removed from service staff. $ *Rooms from: €250* ✉ *Via del Babuino 181, Piazza di Spagna* ☎ *06/32295295* ⊕ *www.romeluxurysuites.com/babuino* ⤳ *24 rooms* ⦿ *Free Breakfast* Ⓜ *Flaminio, Spagna.*

Baglioni Hotel Regina

$$$$ | HOTEL | The former home of Queen Margherita of Savoy, the Baglioni Hotel Regina, which enjoys a prime spot on the Via Veneto, is still a favorite among today's international jet-setters. **Pros:** excellent on-site restaurant and bar; nice decor; luxury on-site spa. **Cons:** service is hit-or-miss; some rooms are noisy; location isn't as prestigious as it once was. $ *Rooms from: €319* ✉ *Via Veneto 72, Piazza di Spagna* ☎ *06/421111* ⊕ *www.baglionihotels.com/rome* ⤳ *114 rooms* ⦿ *No Meals* Ⓜ *Barberini.*

★ The Hassler

$$$$ | HOTEL | When it comes to million-dollar views, the best place to stay in the whole city is the Hassler, so it's no surprise many rich and famous (Tom Cruise, Jennifer Lopez, and the Beckhams among them), are willing to pay top dollar for a room at this exclusive hotel atop the Spanish Steps. **Pros:** sauna access included with each reservation; prime location and panoramic views; private rooftop with bar service upon request. **Cons:** breakfast not included (continental option is €29 plus 10% V.A.T. per person); VIP rates (10% V.A.T. not included); rooms are updated on a rolling basis, leaving some feeling dated. $ *Rooms from: €600* ✉ *Piazza Trinità dei Monti 6, Piazza di Spagna* ☎ *06/699340, 800/223–6800 in U.S.* ⊕ *www.hotelhasslerroma.com* ⤳ *87 rooms* ⦿ *No Meals* Ⓜ *Spagna.*

★ Hotel de la Ville

$$$$ | HOTEL | Occupying a prime position at the top of the Spanish Steps, the sister property to the beloved Hotel de Russie is the most glamorous new hotel in town. **Pros:** must-visit rooftop bar with panoramic views; pampering spa uses signature made-in-Italy organic products; prestigious location atop the Spanish Steps. **Cons:** some rooms are a bit small; service can be a bit slow at the bar; no pets allowed. $ *Rooms from: €594* ✉ *Via Sistina 69, Piazza di Spagna* ☎ *06/977931* ⊕ *www.roccofortehotels.com/hotels-and-resorts/hotel-de-la-ville* ⤳ *104 rooms* ⦿ *No Meals* Ⓜ *Spagna.*

Hotel d'Inghilterra

$$$ | **HOTEL** | Situated in a stately 16th-century building and founded in 1845, Hotel d'Inghilterra has a long, storied history: it has been used as a guesthouse for aristocratic travelers visiting a noble family who once lived across the cobblestone street and has been the home away from home for various monarchs and movie stars, like Elizabeth Taylor, not to mention some of the greatest writers of all time—Lord Byron, John Keats, Mark Twain, and Ernest Hemingway among them. **Pros:** excellent in-house restaurant; distinct character and opulence; turndown service (with chocolates). **Cons:** the location, despite soundproofing, is still noisy; elevator is small; some rooms badly in need of renovations and maintenance. $ *Rooms from: €280* ⊠ *Via Bocca di Leone 14, Piazza di Spagna* 🕾 *06/699811* ⊕ *www.starhotelscollezione.com/en/ our-hotels/hotel-d-inghilterra-rome* 🛏 *84 rooms* ⫶❍⫶ *Free Breakfast* Ⓜ *Spagna.*

⭐ Hotel Eden

$$$$ | **HOTEL** | Once a favorite haunt of Ingrid Bergman, Ginger Rogers, and Fellini, this superlative hotel combines dashing elegance, exquisitely lush decor, and stunning vistas of Rome with true Italian hospitality to create one of the city's top luxury lodgings. **Pros:** 24-hour room service; gorgeous rooftop terrace restaurant; tranquil spa facilities. **Cons:** gym is standard but small; breakfast not included (and very expensive, at €45); some rooms overlook an unremarkable courtyard. $ *Rooms from: €780* ⊠ *Via Ludovisi 49, Piazza di Spagna* 🕾 *06/478121* ⊕ *www.dorchestercollection.com/en/rome/hotel-eden* 🛏 *98 rooms* ⫶❍⫶ *No Meals* Ⓜ *Spagna.*

⭐ Hotel Vilòn

$$$$ | **HOTEL** | This intimate hotel in the 16th-century mansion annexed to Palazzo Borghese might be Rome's best-kept secret. **Pros:** fantastic location; gorgeous design; attentive staff. **Cons:** some rooms are a bit small; no spa or gym; not much outdoor space. $ *Rooms from: €460* ⊠ *Via dell'Arancio 69, Piazza di Spagna* 🕾 *06/878187* ⊕ *www.hotelvilon.com* 🛏 *18 rooms* ⫶❍⫶ *Free Breakfast* Ⓜ *Spagna.*

Il Palazzetto

$$$ | **B&B/INN** | Once a retreat for one of Rome's richest noble families, this 15th-century house is one of the most intimate and luxurious hotels in Rome, with gorgeous terraces and a rooftop bar where you can watch the never-ending theater of the Spanish Steps. **Pros:** guests have full access to the Hassler's services; location and view; free Wi-Fi. **Cons:** bedrooms do not access communal terraces; restaurant often rented out for crowded special events; often books up far in advance, particularly in high season. $ *Rooms from: €250* ⊠ *Vicolo del Bottino 8, Piazza di Spagna* 🕾 *06/69934560* ⊕ *www. ilpalazzettoroma.com* 🛏 *4 rooms* ⫶❍⫶ *No Meals* Ⓜ *Spagna.*

Margutta 19

$$$$ | **HOTEL** | Tucked away on a quiet, leafy street known for its art galleries, this 22-suite property is like your very own hip, New York–style loft in the center of old-world Rome, with top-drawer amenities, contemporary design, and a restaurant with a verdant terrace. **Pros:** deluxe furnishings; studio-loft feel in center of town; complete privacy. **Cons:** no elevator in the annex to reach rooms on higher floors; no spa or gym; entry-level rooms lack views. $ *Rooms from: €400* ⊠ *Via Margutta 19, Piazza di Spagna* 🕾 *06/97797979* ⊕ *www.romeluxurysuites.com/margutta* 🛏 *22 suites* ⫶❍⫶ *Free Breakfast* Ⓜ *Spagna.*

Scalinata di Spagna

$ | **B&B/INN** | Perched atop the Spanish Steps, this charming boutique hotel makes guests fall in love over and over again—so popular, in fact, it's often booked far in advance. **Pros:** friendly and helpful concierge; free Wi-Fi throughout; fresh fruit in guest rooms. **Cons:** no porter and no elevator; small rooms; hike up the hill to the hotel. $ *Rooms from: €116* ✉ *Piazza Trinità dei Monti 17, Piazza di Spagna* ☎ *06/45686150* ⊕ *www. hotelscalinata.com* ⇆ *30 rooms* ⦿ *Free Breakfast* Ⓜ *Spagna.*

Nightlife

Wine Bar at the Palazzetto
COCKTAIL LOUNGES | The prize for perfect aperitivo spot goes to the Palazzetto, with excellent drinks and appetizers, as well as a breathtaking view of Rome's domes and rooftops—all from its fifth-floor rooftop overlooking Piazza di Spagna. Reach it by climbing the Spanish Steps or getting a lift from the elevator inside the Spagna Metro station. Just keep an eye on the sky, as any chance for a rainy day will close the terrace (as do special events). ✉ *Vicolo del Bottino 8, Piazza di Spagna* ⇌ *The main entrance is a small gate at the top of the Spanish Steps* ☎ *06/69934560* ⊕ *www.ilpalazzettoroma.com* Ⓜ *Spagna.*

Shopping

ACCESSORIES
Furla
HANDBAGS | Furla very well might be the best deal in Italian leather, selling high-end quality handbags and purses at affordable prices. There are multiple locations throughout the Eternal City (including one at Fiumicino Airport), but its flagship store can be found in the heart of Piazza di Spagna. Be prepared to fight your way through crowds of passionate handbag lovers, all anxious to possess one of the delectable bags, wallets, or whimsical key chains in trendy sherbet hues or timeless bold color combos. ✉ *Piazza di Spagna 22, Piazza di Spagna* ☎ *06/6797159* ⊕ *www.furla.com* Ⓜ *Spagna.*

CLOTHING
★ Brioni
MEN'S CLOTHING | Founded in 1945, Brioni is hailed for its impeccable craftsmanship in creating made-to-measure menswear. The classic brand hires the best men's tailors in Italy, who design bespoke suits to exacting standards, measured to the millimeter and completely personalized from a selection of more than 5,000 spectacular fabrics. A single made-to-measure wool suit will take a minimum of 32 hours to create. Their prêt-à-porter line is also praised for peerless cutting and stitching. Past and present clients include Clark Gable, Barack Obama, and, of course, James Bond. ✉ *Via Condotti 21A, Piazza di Spagna* ☎ *06/6783428* ⊕ *www.brioni.com* ⊙ *Closed Sun.* Ⓜ *Spagna.*

Dolce & Gabbana
MIXED CLOTHING | Dolce and Gabbana met in 1980 when both were assistants at a Milan fashion atelier, and they opened their first store in 1982. With a modern aesthetic that screams sex appeal, the brand has always thrived on excess and is known for its bold, creative designs. The Rome store has a glass ceiling above a sparkling chandelier to allow natural light to spill in, illuminating the marble floors, antique brass accents, and (of course) the latest lines for men, women, and even children, plus an expansive accessories area. ✉ *Via Condotti 49–51, Piazza di Spagna* ☎ *06/69924999* ⊕ *www.dolcegabbana.com* Ⓜ *Spagna.*

Elena Mirò
WOMEN'S CLOTHING | Elena Mirò is a high-end brand that specializes in sophisticated, beautifully feminine clothes for curvy, European-styled women size 46 (U.S. size 12, U.K. size 14) and up. There are several locations in Rome, including one on Via Nazionale. ✉ *Via Frattina 11, Piazza di Spagna* ☎ *06/6784367* ⊕ *www. elenamiro.com* Ⓜ *Spagna.*

Fendi

MIXED CLOTHING | Fendi has been a fixture of the Roman fashion landscape since "Mamma" Fendi first opened shop with her husband in 1925. With an eye for crazy genius, she hired Karl Lagerfeld, who began working with the group at the start of his career. His furs and runway antics made him one of the most influential designers of the 20th century and brought international acclaim to Fendi along the way. The atelier, now owned by the Louis Vuitton group, continues to symbolize Italian glamour at its finest, though the difference in ownership is noticeable. It's also gotten new life in the Italian press for its "Fendi for Fountains" campaign, which included funding the restoration of Rome's Trevi Fountain, and for moving its global headquarters to a striking Mussolini-era building known as the "square Colosseum" in the city's EUR neighborhood. The flagship store in Rome can be found on the ground floor of Palazzo Fendi. The upper floors are home to the brand's seven private suites (the first ever Fendi hotel), and the rooftop hosts Zuma, a modern Japanese restaurant with an oh-so-cool bar that has sweeping views across Rome. ✉ *Largo Carlo Goldoni 420, Piazza di Spagna* ☎ *06/33450896* ⊕ *www.fendi.com* Ⓜ *Spagna.*

Giorgio Armani

MIXED CLOTHING | One of the most influential designers of Italian haute couture, Giorgio Armani creates fluid silhouettes and dazzling evening gowns with sexy peek-a-boo cutouts; his signature cuts are made with the clever-handedness and flawless technique achievable only by working with tracing paper and Italy's finest fabrics over the course of a lifetime. His menswear collection uses traditional textiles like wide-ribbed corduroy and stretch jersey in nontraditional ways while staying true to a clean, masculine aesthetic. The iconic Italian brand has an Emporio Armani shop on Via del Babuino, but the flagship store is the best place to find pieces that range from exotic runway-worthy masterpieces to more wearable collections emphasizing casual Italian elegance with just the right touch of whimsy and sexiness. ✉ *Via dei Condotti 77, Piazza di Spagna* ☎ *06/6991460* ⊕ *www.armani.com* Ⓜ *Spagna.*

Gucci

MIXED CLOTHING | Guccio Gucci opened his first leather shop selling luggage in Florence in 1921, and as the glamorous fashion label celebrates its centennial, the success of the double-G trademark is unquestionable. Tom Ford joined as creative director in 1994, helping the fashion house move into a new era that continues today, maintaining the label's trendiness while bringing in a breath of fresh air, thanks to old-school favorites like reinterpreted horsebit styles and Jackie Kennedy scarves. Now helmed by Alessandro Michele, Gucci remains a fashion must for virtually every A-list celebrity, and their designs have moved from heart-stopping sexy rock star to something classically subdued and retrospectively feminine, making the handbags and accessories more covetable than ever. ✉ *Via Condotti 6–8, Piazza di Spagna* ☎ *06/6790405* ⊕ *www.gucci.com* Ⓜ *Spagna.*

★ Laura Biagiotti

WOMEN'S CLOTHING | Until her death in 2017, Laura Biagiotti was a worldwide ambassador of Italian fashion. Considered the Queen of Cashmere, her soft-as-velvet pullovers have been worn by Sophia Loren, and her snow-white cardigans were said to be a favorite of the late pope John Paul II. Princess Diana even sported one of Biagiotti's cashmere maternity dresses. In addition to stocking the luxe clothing line, the flagship store has a bold red lounge where shoppers can indulge in sampling her line of his-and-her perfumes or sip a Campari cocktail while purchases are customized with Swarovski crystals. ✉ *Via Belsiana 57, Piazza di Spagna* ☎ *06/6791205* ⊕ *www. laurabiagiotti.it* Ⓜ *Spagna.*

★ Patrizia Pepe

WOMEN'S CLOTHING | One of Florence's best-kept secrets for up-and-coming designs, Patrizia Pepe first emerged on the scene in 1993 with an aesthetic that's both minimalist and bold, combining classic styles with low-slung jeans and jackets with oversize lapels that are bound to draw attention. Her line of shoes is hot-hot-hot for those who can walk on stilts. As a relative newcomer to the crowded Italian fashion scene, the brand's stand-alone fame is still under the radar, but take a look at this shop before the line becomes the next fast-tracked craze. ⊠ *Via Frattina 44, Piazza di Spagna* ☎ *06/6781851* ⊕ *www.patrizia-pepe.com* Ⓜ *Spagna.*

Prada

MIXED CLOTHING | Besides the devil, plenty of serious shoppers wear Prada season after season, especially those willing to sell their souls for one of their ubiquitous handbags. If you are looking for that blend of old-world luxury with a touch of fashion-forward finesse, you'll hit it big here. Mario Prada first founded the Italian luggage brand in 1913, but it has been his granddaughter, Miuccia, who updated the designs into the timeless investment pieces of today. You'll find the Rome store more service-oriented than the New York City branches—a roomy elevator delivers you to a series of thickly carpeted salons where a flock of discreet assistants will help you pick out dresses, shoes, lingerie, and fashion accessories. The men's store is located at Via dei Condotti 88/90, while the women's is down the street at 92/95. ⊠ *Via dei Condotti 88/90 and 92/95, Piazza di Spagna* ☎ *06/6790897* ⊕ *www.prada.com* Ⓜ *Spagna.*

Schostal

MIXED CLOTHING | A Piazza di Spagna fixture since 1870, the shop was once the go-to place for women looking to stock up on corsets, bonnets, stockings, and petticoats. Today, it's the place to stop for those essential basics that are increasingly difficult to find, like fine-quality shirts, underwear, and handkerchiefs made of wool and pure cashmere at affordable prices. ⊠ *Via della Fontanella di Borghese 29, Piazza di Spagna* ☎ *06/6791240* ⊕ *www.schostalroma1870.com* ☺ *Closed Sun.* Ⓜ *Spagna.*

Valentino

MIXED CLOTHING | Since taking the Valentino reins, creative director Pierpaolo Piccioli has faced numerous challenges, the most basic of which is keeping Valentino true to Valentino after the designer's retirement in 2008. He served as accessories designer under Valentino for more than a decade and understands exactly how to make the next generation of Hollywood stars swoon. Valentino has taken over most of Piazza di Spagna, where he lived for decades in a lovely palazzo next to one of the multiple boutiques showcasing his eponymous designs with a romantic edginess; think studded heels or a showstopping prêt-à-porter evening gown worthy of the Oscars. Rock stars and other music lovers can also have their Valentino guitar straps personalized when they buy one at this enormous boutique. ⊠ *Piazza di Spagna 38, Piazza di Spagna* ☎ *06/94515710* ⊕ *www.valentino.com* Ⓜ *Spagna.*

Versace

MIXED CLOTHING | Versace's Rome flagship is a gem of architecture and design, with Byzantine-inspired mosaic floors and futuristic interiors with transparent walls, not to mention, of course, fashion: here shoppers will find apparel, jewelry, watches, fragrances, cosmetics, and home furnishings in designs every bit as flamboyant as Donatella and Allegra (Gianni's niece), drawing heavily on the sexy rocker gothic underground vibe. ⊠ *Piazza di Spagna 12, Piazza di Spagna* ☎ *06/6784600* ⊕ *www.versace.com* Ⓜ *Spagna.*

DEPARTMENT STORES

★ La Rinascente

DEPARTMENT STORE | Italy's best-known department store is located in a dazzling space that has seven stories packed with the best luxury goods the world has to offer. Here, one can find oodles of cosmetics on the ground floor, as well as a phalanx of ready-to-wear designer sportswear and blockbuster handbags and accessories, and kitchen and home-ware in the basement. Even if you're not planning on buying anything, the base-ment excavations of a Roman aqueduct and the roof terrace bar with its splendid view are well worth a visit. There's also a location at Piazza Fiume. ⊠ *Via del Tritone 61, Piazza di Spagna* ☎ *06/879161* ⊕ *www.rinascente.it* Ⓜ *Barberini.*

JEWELRY

Bulgari

JEWELRY & WATCHES | Every capital city has its famous jeweler, and Bulgari is to Rome what Tiffany is to New York and Cartier to Paris. The jewelry giant has developed a reputation for meticulous craftsmanship melding noble metals with precious gems. In the middle of the 19th century, the great-grandfather of the cur-rent Bulgari brothers began working as a silver jeweler in his native Greece and is said to have moved to Rome with less than 1,000 lire in his pocket. The recent makeover of the store's temple-inspired interior pays homage to the brand's ties to both places. Today the mega-brand emphasizes colorful and playful jew-elry as the principal cornerstone of its aesthetic. Popular collections include Bul-gari-Bulgari and B.zero1. ⊠ *Via dei Con-dotti 10, Piazza di Spagna* ☎ *06/696261* ⊕ *www.bulgari.com* Ⓜ *Spagna.*

SHOES

A. Testoni

SHOES | Amedeo Testoni, the brand's founder and original designer, was born in 1905 in Bologna, the heart of Italy's shoe-making territory. In 1929, he opened his first shop and began producing shoes as artistic as the Cubist and Art Deco artwork of the period. His shoes have adorned the feet of Fred Astaire, proving that lightweight footwear can be comfortable and luxurious and still turn heads. Today the Testoni brand includes a line of enviable handbags and classically cool leather jackets—all found at this Roman boutique, exclusively dedicated to the women's collection. For gentlemen there are dreamy calfskin sneakers and matching messenger bags. ⊠ *Via Borgognona 21, Piazza di Spagna* ☎ *06/6787718* ⊕ *www.testoni.com* Ⓜ *Spagna.*

★ Braccialini

HANDBAGS | Founded in 1954 by Flor-entine stylist Carla Braccialini and her husband, Robert, Braccialini—currently managed by their sons—makes bags that are authentic works of art in bright colors and delightful shapes, such as London black cabs or mountain chalets. The ador-ably quirky tote bags have picture-post-card scenes of luxury destinations made of brightly colored appliquéd leather. Be sure to check out their eccentric Temi (Theme) creature bags; the snail-shape handbag made out of python skin makes an unforgettable fashion statement. ⊠ *Galleria Alberto Sordi 20/21, Piazza Colonna, Piazza di Spagna* ☎ *06/6784339* ⊕ *www.braccialini.it* Ⓜ *Spagna.*

Fausto Santini

SHOES | Shoe lovers with a passion for minimalist design flock to Fausto Santini to get their hands on his nerdy-chic shoes with their statement-making lines. Santini has been in business since 1970 and caters to a sophisticated, avant-gar-de clientele looking for elegant, classic shoes with a kick and a rainbow color palette. An outlet at Via Cavour 106, named for Fausto's father, Giacomo, sells last season's shoes at a big discount. ⊠ *Via Frattina 120, Piazza di Spagna* ☎ *06/6784114* ⊕ *www.faustosantini.com* Ⓜ *Spagna.*

Repubblica and the Quirinale

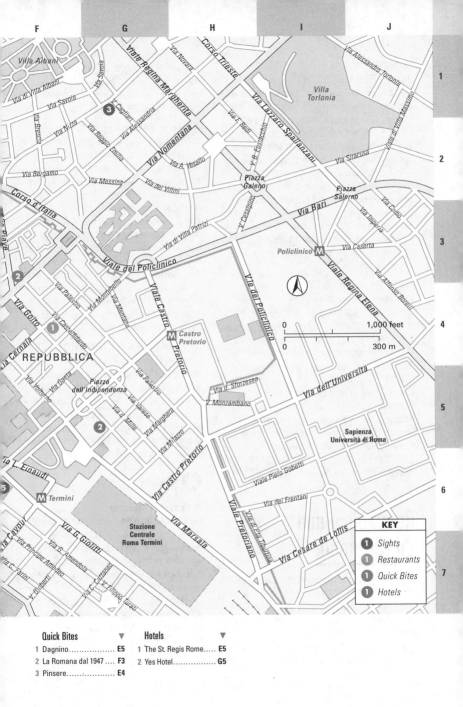

Quick Bites ▼

1 Dagnino.................. **E5**
2 La Romana dal 1947 .... **F3**
3 Pinsere................... **E4**

Hotels ▼

1 The St. Regis Rome..... **E5**
2 Yes Hotel................. **G5**

★ Tod's

SHOES | First founded in the 1920s, Tod's has grown from a small family brand into a global powerhouse so wealthy that its owner, Diego Della Valle, donated €20 million to the Colosseum restoration project. The shoe baron's trademark is his simple, classic, understated designs and butter-soft leather. Sure to please are his light and flexible slip-on Gommino driving shoes with rubber-bottomed soles for extra driving-pedal grip. There is also a location on Via dei Condotti. ⊠ *Via della Fontanella di Borghese 56a–57, Piazza di Spagna* ☎ *06/68210066* ⊕ *www.tods. com* Ⓜ *Spagna.*

HEALTH & BEAUTY

Modàfferi Barber Shop

OTHER HEALTH & BEAUTY | Run by two friendly brothers, who took over the business from their father, this barbershop is preferred by actors performing at the nearby Teatro Sistina. It was founded in the 1970s and still has charmingly retro decor. They offer haircuts, beard care, manicures, pedicures, facials, and massages and have their own line of products. For extra privacy, you can request the private room. ⊠ *Via dei Cappuccini 11, Piazza di Spagna* ☎ *06/4817077* ⊕ *www.modafferibarbershop.it* ⊘ *Closed Sun. & Mon.* Ⓜ *Barberini.*

Repubblica and the Quirinale

This sector of Rome stretches down from the 19th-century district built up around the Piazza della Repubblica—originally laid out to serve as a monumental foyer between the Termini train station and the rest of the city—and over the rest of the Quirinale. The highest of ancient Rome's famed seven hills, the Quirinale is crowned by the massive Palazzo Quirinale, home to the popes until 1870 and now Italy's presidential palace. Along the way, you can see ancient Roman sculptures, early Christian churches, and highlights from the 16th and 17th centuries, when Rome was conquered by the Baroque—and by Bernini.

Although Bernini's work feels omnipresent in much of the city center, the Renaissance-man range of his creations is particularly notable here. The artist as architect considered the church of Sant'Andrea al Quirinale one of his best; Bernini the urban designer and water worker is responsible for the muscle-bound sea god who blows his conch so provocatively in the fountain at the center of whirling Piazza Barberini. And Bernini the master gives religious passion a joltingly corporeal treatment in what is perhaps his greatest work, the *Ecstasy of St. Teresa,* in the church of Santa Maria della Vittoria.

GETTING HERE AND AROUND

Located between Termini station and the Spanish Steps, this area is about a 15-minute walk from either. Bus No. 40 will get you from Termini to the Quirinale in two stops; from the Vatican take Bus No. 64. The very central Repubblica Metro stop is on the piazza of the same name.

Sights

★ Capuchin Museum

RELIGIOUS BUILDING | Devoted to teaching visitors about the Capuchin order, this museum is mainly notable for a crypt visitable at the end of the museum circuit. Not for the easily spooked, the crypt under the church of Santa Maria della Concezione holds the bones of some 4,000 dead Capuchin monks. With bones arranged in odd decorative designs around the shriveled and decayed remains of their kinsmen, a macabre reminder of the impermanence of earthly life, the crypt is strangely touching and beautiful. As one sign proclaims: "What you are, we once were. What we are, you someday will be." Upstairs in the church, the first chapel on the right contains Guido Reni's mid-17th-century *Archangel St. Michael Trampling the Devil.* The painting caused great scandal after an astute contemporary observer remarked that the face of the devil bore a surprising resemblance to Pope Innocent X, archenemy of Reni's Barberini patrons. Compare the devil with the bust of the pope that you saw in the Palazzo Doria Pamphilj and judge for yourself. ⊠ *Via Veneto 27, Quirinale* ☎ *06/88803695* ⊕ *www.cappucciniviaveneto.it* ☒ *€8.50* Ⓜ *Barberini.*

Fontana delle Api (*Fountain of the Bees*)
FOUNTAIN | Decorated with the famous heraldic bees of the Barberini family, the upper shell and the inscription are from a fountain that Bernini designed for Pope Urban VIII; the rest was lost when the fountain was moved to make way for a new street. The inscription was the cause of a considerable uproar when the fountain was first built in 1644. It said that the fountain had been erected in the 22nd year of the pontiff's reign, although in fact the 21st anniversary of Urban's election to the papacy was still some weeks away. The last numeral was hurriedly erased, but to no avail—Urban died eight days before the beginning of his 22nd year as pope. The superstitious Romans, who had immediately recognized the inscription as a foolhardy tempting of fate, were vindicated. ⊠ *Piazza Barberini, Quirinale* Ⓜ *Barberini.*

MACRO
ART MUSEUM | Formerly known as Rome's Modern and Contemporary Art Gallery, and before that as the Peroni beer factory, this redesigned industrial space has brought new life to the gallery and museum scene of a city hitherto hailed for its "then," not its "now." The collection here covers Italian contemporary artists from the 1960s through today. The goal is to bring current art to the public in innovative spaces and, not incidentally, to give support and bring recognition to Rome's contemporary art scene, which labors in the shadow of the city's artistic heritage. After a few days—or millennia—of dusty marble, it's a breath of fresh air. ■**TIP**→ **Check the website for occasional late-night openings and events.** ⊠ *Via Nizza 138, Repubblica* ☎ *06/696271* ⊕ *www.museomacro.it* ☒ *Free* ☽ *Closed Mon.* Ⓜ *Castro Pretorio.*

★ Palazzo Barberini/Galleria Nazionale d'Arte Antica
CASTLE/PALACE | One of Rome's most splendid 17th-century buildings, the Palazzo Barberini is a landmark of the Roman Baroque style. The grand facade was designed by Carlo Maderno (aided by his nephew, Francesco Borromini), but when Maderno died, Borromini was passed over in favor of his great rival, Gian Lorenzo Bernini. Now home to the Galleria Nazionale d'Arte Antica, the palazzo holds a splendid collection that includes Raphael's *La Fornarina,* a luminous portrait of the artist's lover (a resident of Trastevere, she was reputedly a baker's daughter). Also noteworthy are Guido Reni's portrait of the doomed *Beatrice Cenci* (beheaded in Rome for patricide in 1599)—Hawthorne called it "the saddest picture ever painted" in his Rome-based novel, *The Marble Faun*—and Caravaggio's dramatic *Judith Beheading Holofernes.* The showstopper here is the palace's Gran Salone, a vast ballroom with a ceiling painted in 1630 by the third (and too-often-neglected) master of the Roman Baroque, Pietro da Cortona. It depicts the *Glorification of Urban VIII's Reign* and has the spectacular conceit of glorifying Urban VIII as the agent of Divine Providence, escorted by a "bomber squadron" (to quote art historian Sir Michael Levey) of huge Barberini bees, the heraldic symbol of the family. ⊠ *Via delle Quattro Fontane 13, Quirinale* ☎ *06/4814591* ⊕ *www.barberinicorsini. org* ☽ *Closed Mon.* ☒ *€10, includes Galleria Corsini* Ⓜ *Barberini.*

★ Palazzo Massimo alle Terme

ART MUSEUM | Come here to get a real feel for ancient Roman art—the collection rivals even the Vatican's. The Museo Nazionale Romano, with a collection ranging from striking classical Roman paintings to marble bric-a-brac, has four locations: Palazzo Altemps, Crypta Balbi, the Museo delle Terme di Diocleziano, and this, the Palazzo Massimo alle Terme. This vast structure holds the great ancient treasures of the archaeological collection and also the coin collection. Highlights include the *Dying Niobid*, the famous bronze *Boxer at Rest*, and the *Discobolus Lancellotti*. But the best part of the museum are the ancient frescoes on view on the top floor, stunningly set up to "re-create" the look of the homes they once decorated. These include stuccoes and wall paintings found in the area of the Villa Farnesina (in Trastevere) and the legendary frescoes from Empress Livia's villa at Prima Porta, delightful depictions of a garden in bloom and an orchard alive with birds. Their colors are remarkably well preserved. These delicate decorations covered the walls of cool, sunken rooms in Livia's summerhouse outside the city. ⊠ *Largo di Villa Peretti 2, Repubblica* ☎ *06/39967700* ⊕ *www.museonazionaleromano.benic-ulturali.it* ✉ *€10, or €12 for a combined ticket including access to Crypta Balbi, Museo delle Terme di Diocleziano, and Palazzo Altemps (valid for 3 days)* ⊙ *Closed Mon.* ⚊ *Reservations required* Ⓜ *Repubblica, Termini.*

Piazza del Quirinale

PLAZA/SQUARE | This strategic location atop the Quirinale has long been of great importance. It served as home of the Sabines in the 7th century BC—at that time, deadly enemies of the Romans, who lived on the Campidoglio and Palatino (all of 1 km [½ mile] away). Today, it's the foreground for the presidential residence, **Palazzo del Quirinale**, and home to the **Palazzo della Consulta,** where Italy's Constitutional Court sits. The open side

of the piazza has an impressive vista over the rooftops and domes of central Rome and St. Peter's. The **Fontana di Montecavallo,** or Fontana dei Dioscuri, comprises a huge Roman statuary group and an obelisk from the tomb of the emperor Augustus. The group of the Dioscuri trying to tame two massive marble steeds was found in the Baths of Constantine, which occupied part of the summit of the Quirinale. Unlike just about every other ancient statue in Rome, this group survived the Dark Ages intact and accordingly became one of the city's great sights, especially during the Middle Ages. Next to the figures, the ancient obelisk from the Mausoleo di Augusto (Tomb of Augustus) was put here by Pope Pius VI at the end of the 18th century. ⊠ *Piazza del Quirinale, Quirinale* Ⓜ *Barberini.*

Piazza della Repubblica

PLAZA/SQUARE | Often the first view that spells "Rome" to weary travelers walking from Termini station, this round piazza was laid out in the late 1800s and follows the line of the caldarium of the vast ancient public baths, the Terme di Diocleziano. At its center, the exuberant Fontana delle Naiadi (Fountain of the Naiads) teems with voluptuous bronze ladies happily wrestling with marine monsters. The nudes weren't there when the pope unveiled the fountain in 1888—sparing him any embarrassment—but when the figures were added in 1901, they caused a scandal. It's said that the sculptor, Mario Rutelli (grandfather of Francesco Rutelli, former mayor of Rome), modeled them on the ample figures of two musical-comedy stars of the day. The colonnades now house the luxe hotel Palazzo Naiadi and various shops and cafés. Ⓜ *Repubblica.*

San Carlo alle Quattro Fontane

CHURCH | Sometimes known as San Carlino because of its tiny size, this is one of Borromini's masterpieces. In a space no larger than the base of one of the piers of St. Peter's Basilica, he created a church that is an intricate exercise in geometric perfection, with a coffered dome that seems to float above the curves of the walls. Borromini's work is often bizarre, definitely intellectual, and intensely concerned with pure form. In San Carlo, he invented an original treatment of space that creates an effect of rippling movement, especially evident in the double-S curves of the facade. Characteristically, the interior decoration is subdued, in white stucco with no more than a few touches of gilding, so as not to distract from the form. Don't miss the cloister: a tiny, understated Baroque jewel, with a graceful portico and loggia above, echoing the lines of the church. ✉ *Via del Quirinale 23, Quirinale* ☎ *06/4883261* 🌐 *www.sancarlino.eu* [M] *Barberini.*

★ Santa Maria della Vittoria

CHURCH | Designed by Carlo Maderno, this church is best known for Bernini's sumptuous Baroque decoration of the Cappella Cornaro (Cornaro Chapel, the last on the left as you face the altar), which houses his interpretation of divine love, the *Ecstasy of St. Teresa*. Bernini's masterly fusion of sculpture, light, architecture, painting, and relief is a multimedia extravaganza, with the chapel modeled as a theater, and one of the key examples of the Roman high Baroque. The members of the Cornaro family meditate on the communal vision of the great moment of divine love before them: the swooning saint's robes appear to be on fire, quivering with life, and the white marble group seems suspended in the heavens as golden rays illuminate the scene. An angel assists at the moment of Teresa's vision as the saint abandons herself to the joys of heavenly love. Bernini represented this mystical experience in what, to modern eyes, may seem very earthly terms. Or, as the visiting French dignitary Charles de Brosses put it in the 18th century, "If this is divine love, I know all about it." ✉ *Via XX Settembre 17, Largo Santa Susanna, Repubblica* ☎ *06/42740571* [M] *Repubblica.*

★ Sant'Andrea al Quirinale

CHURCH | Designed by Bernini, this small church is one of the triumphs of the Roman Baroque period. His son wrote that Bernini considered it his best work and that he used to come here occasionally, just to sit and contemplate. Bernini's simple oval plan, a classic form in Baroque architecture, is given drama and movement by the church's decoration, which carries the story of St. Andrew's martyrdom and ascension into heaven, starting with the painting over the high altar, up past the figure of the saint above, to the angels at the base of the lantern and the dove of the Holy Spirit that awaits on high. ✉ *Via del Quirinale 30, Quirinale* ☎ *06/4819399* 🌐 *santandrea.gesuiti.it* 🕒 *Closed Mon.* [M] *Barberini.*

🍴 Restaurants

Trimani Il Winebar

$$ | WINE BAR | This wine bar is run by the Trimani family of wine merchants, whose shop next door has been in business for nearly two centuries. Hot food is served at lunch and dinner in the minimalist interior, and it is also perfect for an aperitif or an early supper (it opens for evening service at 5:30). **Known for:** 6,000 wines on sale from around the world; candlelit second floor for sipping; *torte salate* (savory tarts). [$] *Average main: €18* ✉ *Via Cernaia 37, Repubblica* ☎ *06/4469630* 🌐 *www.trimani.com* 🕒 *Closed Sun. and Aug.* [M] *Castro Pretorio.*

☕ Coffee and Quick Bites

Dagnino

$ | SICILIAN | Hidden inside a covered arcade, this Sicilian pasticceria, which opened in 1955 and proudly wears its mid-century modern design, boasts pastry cases filled with sweets like cannoli, cassata, cakes, and marzipan. Go for breakfast and try the cornetto filled with ricotta and chocolate chips—this is one of the few places in Rome where you can find it. **Known for:** Sicilian desserts; mid-century modern design; cornetti filled with ricotta and chocolate chips. $ *Average main: €3* ✉ *Via Vittorio Emanuele Orlando 75, Repubblica* ☎ *06/4818660* ⊕ *www.pasticceriadagnino.com* Ⓜ *Repubblica.*

La Romana dal 1947
$ | **ICE CREAM** | In summertime, the line at this gelateria stretches out the door and around the corner. Though it's a franchise that originated in Rimini, La Romana is loved by Romans for its rich, creamy gelato made with organic milk, fresh fruit, nuts, and chocolate. **Known for:** modern decor; big portions; reasonably priced. $ *Average main: €3* ✉ *Via Venti Settembre 60, Repubblica* ☎ *06/42020828* ⊕ *www.gelateriaromana.com* Ⓜ *Repubblica.*

Pinsere
$ | **PIZZA** | **FAMILY** | In Rome, you'll usually find either pizza *tonda* or pizza *al taglio,* but there's also pizza *pinsa*: it's an oval-shape individual pie, and a little thicker than the classic Roman pizza. Pinsere is mostly a take-out shop, with people eating on the street for their lunch break, so it's the perfect quick meal. **Known for:** mortadella and pistachio pizzas; budget-friendly options; seasonal toppings. $ *Average main: €6* ✉ *Via Flavia 98, Repubblica* ☎ *06/42020924* ⊕ *www.facebook.com/Pinsere* ⊘ *Closed weekends and Aug.* Ⓜ *Castro Pretorio.*

Hotels

The St. Regis Rome
$$$$ | **HOTEL** | Originally opened by César Ritz in 1894, this grand dame is looking fabulous thanks to a $40 million renovation completed in 2018. **Pros:** fresh off a complete renovation; the library lounge serves a lovely afternoon tea; every room comes with butler service. **Cons:** the restaurant feels more like a lounge than a proper restaurant; breakfast is not included; no pets allowed. $ *Rooms*

from: €650 ✉ *Via Vittorio E. Orlando 3, Repubblica* ☎ *06/47091* ⊕ *www.stregisrome.com* ⇥ *161 rooms* ⦿ *No Meals* Ⓜ *Repubblica.*

Yes Hotel
$ | **HOTEL** | This chic hotel may fool you into thinking the digs are expensive, but the contemporary coolness of Yes Hotel, located around the corner from Termini station, actually comes at a bargain. **Pros:** a great value without the budget feel; around the corner from Termini station; discount if you pay in cash. **Cons:** not near many top sights; small rooms; neighborhood can be noisy at night. $ *Rooms from: €80* ✉ *Via Magenta 15, Repubblica* ☎ *06/44363836* ⊕ *www.yeshotelrome.com* ⇥ *42 rooms* ⦿ *Free Breakfast* Ⓜ *Termini, Castro Pretorio.*

 Performing Arts

★ Teatro dell'Opera
OPERA | Long considered a far younger sibling of La Scala in Milan and La Fenice in Venice, the company commands an audience during its mid-November–May season. In the hot summer months, they move to the Terme di Caracalla for its outdoor opera series. As can be expected, the oft-preferred performance is *Aida,* for its spectacle, which once included real elephants. The company has lately taken a new direction, using projections atop the ancient ruins to create cutting-edge sets. ✉ *Piazza Beniamino Gigli 1, Repubblica* ☎ *06/481601, 06/4817003 tickets* ⊕ *www.operaroma.it* Ⓜ *Repubblica.*

Villa Borghese and Around

Touring Rome's artistic masterpieces while staying clear of its hustle and bustle can be, quite literally, a walk in the park. Some of the city's finest sights are tucked away in or next to green lawns and pedestrian piazzas, offering a breath of fresh air for weary sightseers, especially in the Villa Borghese park. One of Rome's largest, this park can alleviate gallery gout by offering an oasis in which to cool off under the ilex, oak, and umbrella pine trees. If you feel like a picnic, have an *alimentari* (food shop) make you some panini before you go; food carts within the park are overpriced.

GETTING HERE AND AROUND

The Metro stop for Piazza del Popolo is Flaminio on Line A. The Villa Giulia, the Galleria Nazionale d'Arte Moderna e Contemporanea, and the Bioparco in Villa Borghese are accessible from Via Flaminia, 1 km (½ mile) from Piazza del Popolo. Tram No. 19 and Bus No. 3 stop at each. Bus No. 160 and No. 628 connect Piazza del Popolo to Piazza Venezia. Bus No. 116 goes into Villa Borghese.

 # Sights

★ Galleria Borghese

ART MUSEUM | It's a real toss-up as to which is more magnificent: the museum built for Cardinal Scipione Borghese in 1612 or the art that lies within it. The luxury-loving cardinal had the museum custom built as a showcase for his fabulous collection of both antiquities and more "modern" works, including those he commissioned from the masters Caravaggio and Bernini. Today, it's a monument to Roman interior decoration at its most extravagant. One of the most famous works in the collection is Canova's neoclassical sculpture *Pauline Borghese as Venus Victorious*. The next three rooms hold three key early Baroque sculptures: Bernini's *David, Apollo and Daphne*, and *The Rape of Persephone*. All were done when the artist was in his twenties, and all illustrate Bernini's extraordinary skill. *Apollo and Daphne* shows the moment when, to aid her escape from the pursuing Apollo, Daphne is turned into a laurel tree. Leaves and twigs sprout from her fingertips as she stretches agonizingly away from Apollo.

In *The Rape of Persephone*, Pluto has just plucked Persephone (or Proserpina) from her flower-picking, or perhaps he's returning to Hades with his prize. (Don't miss the realistic way his grip causes dimples in Persephone's flesh.) This is the stuff that makes the Baroque exciting—and moving. Other Berninis on view in the collection include a large, unfinished figure called *Verità*, or Truth. Room 8 contains six paintings by Caravaggio, the hotheaded genius who died at age 37. All of his paintings, even the charming *Boy with a Basket of Fruit*, seethe with an undercurrent of darkness. The disquieting *Sick Bacchus* is a self-portrait of the artist who, like the god, had a fondness for wine. *David and Goliath*, painted in the last year of Caravaggio's life—while he was on the run, murder charges hanging over his head—includes his self-portrait in the head of Goliath. Upstairs, the Pinacoteca (Picture Gallery) boasts paintings by Raphael (including his moving *Deposition*), Pinturicchio, Perugino, Bellini, and Rubens. Probably the gallery's most famous painting is Titian's allegorical *Sacred and Profane Love*, a mysterious and yet-unsolved image with two female figures, one nude, one clothed. ■ **TIP→ Admission to the Galleria is by reservation only. Visitors are admitted in two-hour shifts 9–5. Prime-time slots can sell out days in advance, so reserve directly through the Borghese's website.** ✉ *Piazzale Scipione Borghese 5, off Via Pinciana, Villa Borghese* ☎ *06/32810 reservations, 06/8413979 info* ⊕ *www.galleriaborghese.it* 🎫 *€15, including €2 reservation fee; increased fee during temporary exhibitions* 𝇇 *Closed Mon.* ⚲ *Reservations required.*

MAXXI—Museo Nazionale delle Arti del XXI Secolo (*National Museum of 21st-Century Arts*)

ART MUSEUM | Designed by the late Iraqi-British starchitect Zaha Hadid, this modern building plays with lots of natural light, curving and angular lines, and big open spaces, all meant to question the

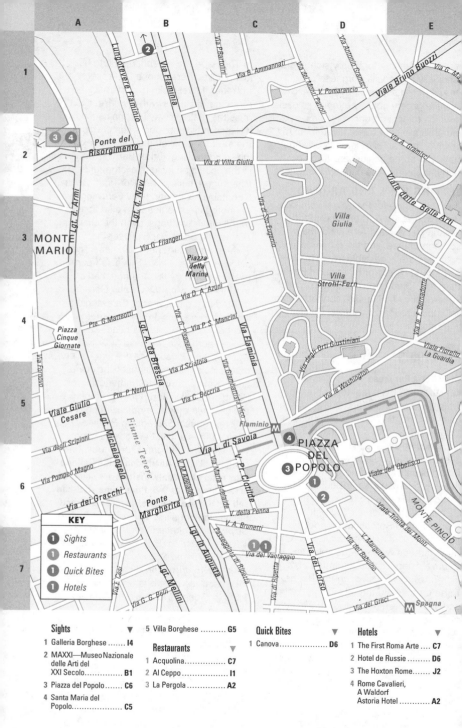

Sights ▼

1 Galleria Borghese **I4**

2 MAXXI—Museo Nazionale delle Arti del XXI Secolo.............. **B1**

3 Piazza del Popolo....... **C6**

4 Santa Maria del Popolo................... **C5**

5 Villa Borghese **G5**

Restaurants ▼

1 Acquolina................. **C7**

2 Al Ceppo **I1**

3 La Pergola **A2**

Quick Bites ▼

1 Canova.................... **D6**

Hotels ▼

1 The First Roma Arte **C7**

2 Hotel de Russie **D6**

3 The Hoxton Rome....... **J2**

4 Rome Cavalieri, A Waldorf Astoria Hotel **A2**

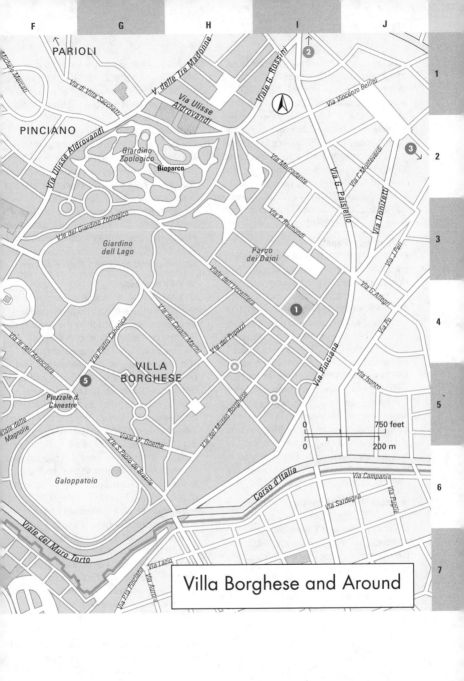

Villa Borghese and Around

division between "within" and "without" (think glass ceilings and steel staircases that twist through the air). The MAXXI hosts temporary exhibitions of art, architecture, film, and more. The permanent collection, exhibited on a rotating basis, boasts more than 350 works from modern and contemporary artists, including Andy Warhol, Francesco Clemente, and Gerhard Richter. ✉ *Via Guido Reni 4/A, Flaminio* ☎ *06/3201954* ⊕ *www.maxxi.art* ✉ *€12* ⊘ *Closed Mon.* Ⓜ *Flaminio, then Tram No. 2 to Apollodoro.*

★ Piazza del Popolo

PLAZA/SQUARE | With its obelisk and twin churches, this immense square is a famed Rome landmark. It marks what was for centuries the northern entrance to the city, where all roads from the north converge and where visitors, many of them pilgrims, would get their first impression of the Eternal City. The desire to make this entrance to Rome something special had been a pet project of popes and their architects for more than three centuries. The piazza, crowded with fashionable carriages and carnival revelers in the past, is a pedestrian zone today. At election time, it's the scene of huge political rallies, and on New Year's Eve, Rome stages a mammoth alfresco party here. ✉ *Piazza del Popolo* Ⓜ *Flaminio*

★ Santa Maria del Popolo

CHURCH | Standing inconspicuously in a corner of the vast Piazza del Popolo, this church often goes unnoticed, but the treasures inside make it a must for art lovers. Bramante enlarged the apse, which was rebuilt in the 15th century on the site of a much older place of worship. Inside, in the first chapel on the right, you'll see some frescoes by Pinturicchio from the mid-15th century; the adjacent Cybo Chapel is a 17th-century exercise in decorative marble. Raphael designed the famous Chigi Chapel, the second on the left, with vault mosaics—showing God the Father in benediction—as well as statues of Jonah and Elijah. More than

a century later, Bernini added the oval medallions on the tombs and the statues of Daniel and Habakkuk. Finally, the Cerasi Chapel, to the left of the high altar, holds two Caravaggios: *The Crucifixion of St. Peter* and *The Conversion of St. Paul.* Exuding drama and realism, both are key early Baroque works that show how "modern" 17th-century art can appear. Compare their style with the much more restrained and classically "pure" *Assumption of the Virgin* by Annibale Carracci, which hangs over the altar of the chapel. ✉ *Piazza del Popolo 12, near Porta Pinciana, Piazza del Popolo* ☎ *3923612243* ⊕ *www.smariadel-popolo.com/it* ⊘ *Closed Sun.* Ⓜ *Flaminio.*

★ Villa Borghese

CITY PARK | **FAMILY** | Rome's Central Park, the Villa Borghese was originally laid out as a recreational garden in the early 17th century by Cardinal Scipione Borghese. The word "villa" was used to mean suburban estate, of the type developed by the ancient Romans and adopted by Renaissance nobles. Today's gardens cover a much smaller area—by 1630, the perimeter wall was almost 5 km (3 miles) long. At the end of the 18th century, Scottish painter Jacob More remodeled the gardens into the English style popular at the time. In addition to the gloriously restored Galleria Borghese, the highlights of the park are Piazza di Siena, a graceful amphitheater, and the botanical garden on Via Canonica, where there is a pretty little lake as well as the neoclassical faux–Temple of Aesculapius, the Biopark zoo, Rome's own replica of London's Globe Theatre, and the Villa Giulia museum. The Carlo Bilotti Museum (www.museo-carlobilotti.it) is particularly attractive for Giorgio de Chirico fans, and there is more modern art in the nearby Galleria Nazionale d'Arte Moderna e Contemporanea. The 63-seat children's movie theater, Cinema dei Piccoli, shows films for adults in the evening. There's also Casa del Cinema, where film buffs can screen films or sit at the sleek, cherry-red, indoor-outdoor caffè (you can find a schedule of events at www.casadelcinema.it). ✉ *Main entrances at Porta Pinciana, the Pincio, Piazzale Flaminio (Piazza del Popolo), Viale delle Belle Arti, and Via Mercadante, Villa Borghese* [M] *Flaminio.*

🍴 Restaurants

Acquolina

$$$$ | **MODERN ITALIAN** | This Michelin-starred restaurant turns out delicious and high-quality seafood dishes that incorporate top-of-the-line ingredients like truffles and caviar. Tortelli are served with butter, anchovies, and black truffle, and all the dishes are artfully presented. **Known for:** sophisticated desserts; elaborate tasting menus; linguine with clams. [$] *Average main: €40* ✉ *The First Roma Arte, Via del Vantaggio 14, Piazza del Popolo* ☎ *06/3201590* 🌐 *www.acquolinaristorante.it* 🕒 *Closed Sun. and 10 days in Aug. No lunch* [M] *Flaminio.*

Al Ceppo

$$$ | **ITALIAN** | The well-heeled, the business-minded, and those of refined palates frequent this outpost of tranquility. The owners hail from Le Marche, the region northeast of Rome that encompasses inland mountains and the Adriatic coastline, and these ladies dote on their customers as you'd wish a sophisticated Italian mamma would. **Known for:** authentic Le Marche cuisine; excellent wine list; grilled meat and fish. [$] *Average main: €30* ✉ *Via Panama 2, Villa Borghese* ☎ *06/8419696* 🌐 *www.ristorantealceppo.it* 🕒 *Closed 3 wks in Aug.*

★ La Pergola

$$$$ | **MODERN ITALIAN** | Dinner here is a truly spectacular and romantic event, with incomparable views across the city matched by a stellar dining experience that includes top-notch service as well as sublimely inventive fare. The difficulty comes in choosing from among Michelin-starred chef Heinz Beck's alta cucina specialties. **Known for:** weekend reservations that book up three months in advance; fagotelli La Pergola stuffed with pecorino, eggs, and cream with guanciale and zucchini; award-winning wine list. [$] *Average main: €65* ✉ *Rome Cavalieri, A Waldorf Astoria Resort, Via Alberto Cadlolo 101, Monte Mario* ☎ *06/35092152* 🌐 *www.romecavalieri.com/lapergola.php* 🕒 *Closed Sun. and Mon., 3 wks in Aug., and Jan. No lunch* 👔 *Jacket and tie.*

☕ Coffee and Quick Bites

Canova

$$ | **ITALIAN** | Esteemed director Federico Fellini, who lived around the corner on Via Margutta, used to come here all the time and even had an office in the back. His drawings and black-and-white stills from his films remain on display in the hallway that leads to the interior dining room, but the best place to sit for people-watching with a coffee, light lunch, or aperitivo is on the terrace out front. **Known for:** Fellini's old hangout; great people-watching on Piazza del Popolo; sandwiches and other light fare. [$] *Average main: €15* ✉ *Piazza del Popolo 16, Piazza del Popolo* ☎ *06/3612231* 🌐 *www.canovapiazzadelpopolo.it* [M] *Flaminio.*

🛏 Hotels

The First Roma Arte

$$$$ | **HOTEL** | Set in a 19th-century neoclassical palace, this cozy boutique hotel was remodeled to feature high-tech, elegant guest rooms while keeping the core structure, including unique windows and tall ceilings, intact. **Pros:** more than 200 works of art on display from Galleria Mucciaccia; fitness room with Technogym equipment; incredible staff that is eager to please. **Cons:** many rates don't include breakfast; some rooms can be a bit dark; not a lot of in-room storage for luggage. [$] *Rooms from: €450* ✉ *Via del Vantaggio 14, Piazza del Popolo* ☎ *06/45617070* 🌐 *www.thefirsthotel.com/arte* 🔑 *29 rooms* 🍽 *No Meals* [M] *Flaminio.*

★ **Hotel de Russie**

$$$$ | **HOTEL** | Occupying a 19th-century hotel that once hosted royalty, Picasso, and Cocteau, the Hotel de Russie is now the first choice in Rome for government bigwigs and Hollywood high rollers seeking ultimate luxury in a secluded retreat. **Pros:** excellent Stravinskij cocktail bar also has tables in the garden; big potential for celebrity sightings; well-equipped gym and world-class spa with hydropool Jacuzzi, steam room, and sauna. **Cons:** expensive; faster Internet comes at a fee; breakfast not included. $ *Rooms from: €700 ⊠ Via del Babuino 9, Piazza del Popolo ☎ 06/328881 ⊕ www.roccofortehotels. com/hotels-and-resorts/hotel-de-russie ⤳ 120 rooms ◉ No Meals Ⓜ Flaminio.*

The Hoxton Rome

$$ | **HOTEL** | British brand The Hoxton's first foray into Italy is a design lover's dream filled with 1970s-inspired bespoke furniture, art tomes, and plants that transform the large lobby into intimate seating nooks perfect for socializing and co-working. **Pros:** great food and drinks; stylish design; friendly staff. **Cons:** rooms have little storage space for clothes; location far from tourist sites, with no metro nearby; no gym or spa. $ *Rooms from: €189 ⊠ Largo Benedetto Marcello 220, Parioli ☎ 06/94502700 ⊕ www.thehoxton.com/rome ⤳ 192 rooms ◉ No Meals.*

Rome Cavalieri, A Waldorf Astoria Hotel

$$$$ | **RESORT** | A hilltop oasis far from the noise of the centro storico, the Rome Cavalieri comes with magnificent views, three outdoor pools, one indoor pool, and a palatial spa perched atop the Monte Mario amid 15 acres of lush Mediterranean parkland. **Pros:** impressive on-site restaurant; famed art collection, including a Tiepolo triptych from 1725; complimentary shuttle to city center. **Cons:** outside the city center; you definitely pay for the luxury of staying here—everything is expensive; not all rooms have great views. $ *Rooms from:* €370 ⊠ *Via Alberto Cadlolo 101, Monte Mario ☎ 06/35091 ⊕ www.romecavalieri. com ⤳ 370 rooms ◉ No Meals.*

 Nightlife

★ **Stravinskij Bar at the Hotel de Russie**

COCKTAIL LOUNGES | The Stravinskij Bar, in the Hotel de Russie's gorgeous garden, is the best place to catch a glimpse of la dolce vita. Celebrities, blue bloods, and VIPs hang out in the private courtyard garden where mixed drinks and cocktails are well above par. There are also healthy smoothies and bites if you need to refuel. ⊠ *Hotel de Russie, Via del Babuino 9, Piazza del Popolo ☎ 06/328881 ⊕ www. roccofortehotels.com/hotels-and-resorts/ hotel-de-russie/restaurant-and-bar/stravinskij-bar* Ⓜ *Flaminio.*

⚞ Performing Arts

★ **Auditorium Parco della Musica**

CONCERTS | Architect Renzo Piano conceived and constructed the Auditorium Parco della Musica, a futuristic complex made up of three enormous, pod-shaped concert halls, which have hosted some of the world's greatest music acts. The Sala Santa Cecilia is a massive hall for grand orchestra and choral concerts; the Sala Sinopoli is more intimately scaled for smaller troupes; and the Sala Petrassi was designed for alternative events. All three are arrayed around the Cavea (amphitheater), a vast outdoor Greco-Roman-style theater. The Auditorium also hosts seasonal festivals, including the Rome Film Fest, a Christmas market, and a gardening festival in May. ⊠ *Viale Pietro de Coubertin 30, Flaminio ☎ 06/80241281 ⊕ www.auditorium.com* Ⓜ *Flaminio, then Tram No. 2 to Ankara/Tiziano.*

Teatro Olimpico

THEATER | Part of Rome's theater circuit, the 1930s-era Teatro Olimpico is one of the main venues for cabaret, contemporary dance companies, visiting international ballet companies, and touring Broadway hows. ⊠ *Piazza Gentile da Fabriano 17, Flaminio* ☎ *06/32659916* ⊕ *www.tea-roolimpico.it* Ⓜ *Flaminio, then Tram 2.*

Shopping

★ Il Marmoraro

ANTIQUES & COLLECTIBLES | This tiny shop is a holdout of Via Margutta's days as a street full of artists and artisans. Sandro Fiorentino's father opened the shop in 1969 (he carved plaques like the one that marks Federico Fellini's house up the street) and Sandro still engraves the marble by hand. The shop is packed full of plaques, many with clever phrases, which make a great souvenir. Sandro will also engrave a message of your choice upon request. ⊠ *Via Margutta 53B, Piazza del Popolo* ☎ *06/3207660* ⊗ *Closed Sun.* Ⓜ *Spagna.*

★ Saddlers Union

HANDBAGS | Saddlers Union first launched in 1957 and quickly gained a cult following among those who valued Italian artistry and a traditional aesthetic. If you're searching for a sinfully fabulous handbag in a graceful, classic shape or that "I have arrived" attorney's briefcase, these preppy creations will always hit the mark. Prices are a bit steep, but the quality is definitely worth it. ⊠ *Via Paolo Frisi 50, Parioli* ☎ *06/32120237* ⊕ *www.saddlersunion.com.*

Trastevere

Across the Tiber from the Jewish Ghetto is Trastevere (literally "across the Tiber"), long cherished as Rome's Greenwich Village and now subject to rampant gentrification. In spite of this, Trastevere remains about the most tightly knit community in the city, the Trasteverini proudly proclaiming their descent from the ancient Romans. Ancient bridges—the Ponte Fabricio and the Ponte Cestio—link Trastevere and the Ghetto to Isola Tiberina (Tiber Island), a diminutive sandbar and one of Rome's most picturesque sights.

GETTING HERE AND AROUND

From the Vatican or Spanish Steps, expect a 30- to 40-minute walk to reach Trastevere. From Termini station, take Bus No. 40 Express or No. 64 to Largo di Torre Argentina, where you can switch to Tram No. 8 to get to Trastevere. If you don't feel like climbing the steep Gianicolo, take Bus No. 115 from Largo dei Fiorentini, then enjoy the walk down to the northern reaches of Trastevere or explore the leafy residential area of Monteverde Vecchio on the other side of the hill.

Sights

Isola Tiberina (*Tiber Island*)

ISLAND | It's easy to overlook this tiny island in the Tiber, but you shouldn't. In terms of history and sheer loveliness, charming Isola Tiberina—shaped like a boat about to set sail—gets high marks. Cross onto the island via Ponte Fabricio, Rome's oldest remaining bridge, constructed in 62 BC; on the north side of the island crumbles the romantic ruin of the Ponte Rotto (Broken Bridge), which dates back to 179 BC. Descend the steps to the lovely river embankment to see a Roman relief of the intertwined-snakes symbol of Aesculapius, the great god of healing. In imperial times, Romans sheathed the entire island with marble to make it look like Aesculapius's ship, replete with a towering obelisk as a mast. Amazingly, a fragment of the ancient sculpted ship's prow still exists. You can marvel at it on the downstream end of the embankment. Today, medicine still reigns here. The island is home to the hospital of Fatebenefratelli (literally, "Do good, brothers"). Nearby is San Bartolomeo, built at the end of the 10th century by the Holy Roman Emperor Otto III and restored in the 18th century. ⊠ *Trastevere* ⚓ *Isola Tiberina can be accessed by Ponte Fabricio or Ponte Cestio.*

Palazzo Corsini

GARDEN | A brooding example of Baroque style, the palace (once home to Queen Christina of Sweden) is across the road

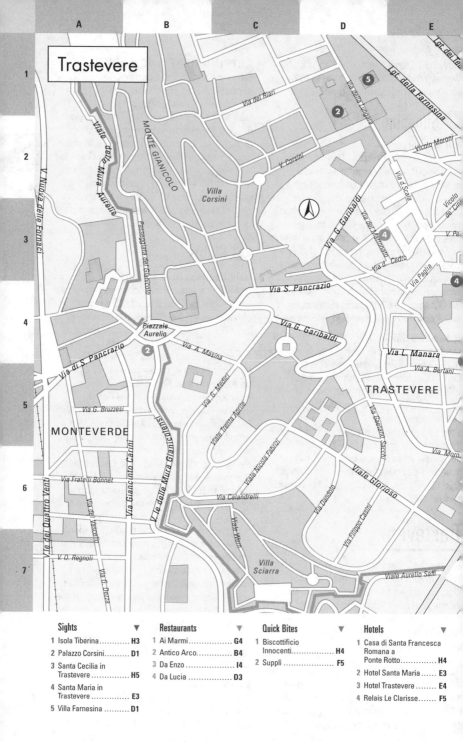

Trastevere

Sights ▼
1 Isola Tiberina............ **H3**
2 Palazzo Corsini.......... **D1**
3 Santa Cecilia in
   Trastevere **H5**
4 Santa Maria in
   Trastevere **E3**
5 Villa Farnesina **D1**

Restaurants ▼
1 Ai Marmi................. **G4**
2 Antico Arco.............. **B4**
3 Da Enzo **I4**
4 Da Lucia **D3**

Quick Bites ▼
1 Biscottificio
   Innocenti................ **H4**
2 Supplì **F5**

Hotels ▼
1 Casa di Santa Francesca
   Romana a
   Ponte Rotto.............. **H4**
2 Hotel Santa Maria **E3**
3 Hotel Trastevere **E4**
4 Relais Le Clarisse....... **F5**

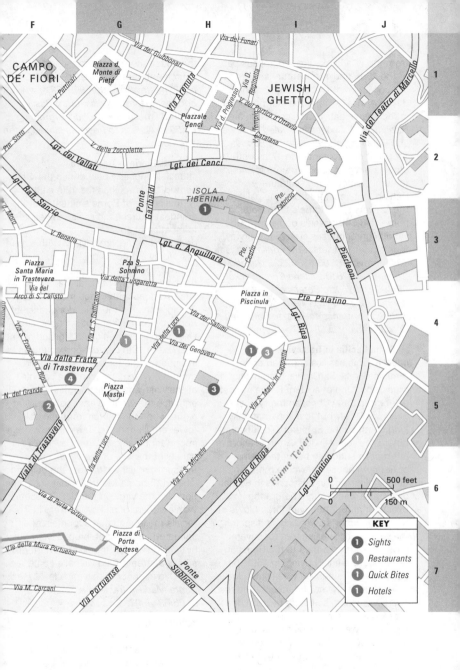

from the Villa Farnesina and houses part of the 16th- and 17th-century sections of the collection of the Galleria Nazionale d'Arte Antica. Among the star paintings in this manageably sized collection are Rubens's *St. Sebastian Healed by Angels* and Caravaggio's *St. John the Baptist.* Stop in if only to climb the 17th-century stone staircase, itself a drama of architectural shadows and sculptural voids. Behind, but separate from, the palazzo is the University of Rome's Orto Botanico, home to 3,500 species of plants, with various greenhouses around a stairway/fountain with 11 jets. ⊠ *Via della Lungara 10, Trastevere* ☎ *06/68802323 Galleria Corsini, 06/32810 Galleria Corsini tickets, 06/49917107 Orto Botanico* ⊕ *www.barberinicorsini.org* ✆ *Galleria Corsini €12, including entrance to Palazzo Barberini; Orto Botanico* ✆ *€8* ⊙ *Closed Tues.*

★ Santa Cecilia in Trastevere

CHURCH | This basilica commemorates the aristocratic St. Cecilia, patron saint of musicians. One of ancient Rome's most celebrated Early Christian martyrs, she was most likely put to a supernaturally long death by the Emperor Diocletian just before the year AD 300. After an abortive attempt to suffocate her in the baths of her own house (a favorite means of quietly disposing of aristocrats in Roman days), she was brought before the executioner. But not even three blows of the executioner's sword could dispatch the young girl. She lingered for several days, converting others to the Christian cause, before finally dying. In 1595, her body was exhumed—it was said to look as fresh as if she still breathed—and the heart-wrenching sculpture by eyewitness Stefano Maderno that lies below the main altar was, the sculptor insisted, exactly how she looked. Time your visit to enter the cloistered convent to see what remains of Pietro Cavallini's *Last Judgment,* dating to 1293. It's the only major fresco in existence known to have been painted by Cavallini, a contemporary of Giotto. To visit the frescoes, ring the bell of the convent to the left of the church entrance. ⊠ *Piazza di Santa Cecilia 22, Trastevere* ☎ *06/5899289* ⊕ *www.benedettinesantacecilia.it/htm/Basilica.html* ✆ *Frescoes €2.50, underground €2.50* ⊙ *Access to frescoes closed in the afternoon.*

★ Santa Maria in Trastevere

CHURCH | Originally built during the 4th century and rebuilt in the 12th century, this is one of Rome's oldest and grandest churches. It is also the earliest foundation of any Roman church to be dedicated to the Virgin Mary. With a nave framed by a processional of two rows of gigantic columns (22 in total) taken from the ancient Baths of Caracalla, and an apse studded with gilded mosaics, the interior conjures the splendor of ancient Rome better than any other in the city. Overhead is Domenichino's gilded ceiling (1617). The 18th-century portico draws attention to the facade's 800-year-old mosaics, which represent the parable of the Wise and Foolish Virgins. They enhance the whole piazza, especially at night, when the church front and bell tower are illuminated. The church's most important mosaics, Pietro Cavallini's six panels of the *Life of the Virgin,* cover the semicircular apse. Note the building labeled "Taberna Meritoria" just under the figure of the Virgin in the Nativity scene, with a stream of oil flowing from it; it recalls the legend that a fountain of oil appeared on this spot, prophesying the birth of Christ. Off the piazza's northern side is a street called Via delle Fonte dell'Olio in honor of this miracle. ⊠ *Piazza Santa Maria in Trastevere, Trastevere* ☎ *06/5814802.*

★ Villa Farnesina

CASTLE/PALACE | Money was no object to the extravagant Agostino Chigi, a banker from Siena who financed many papal projects. His munificence is evident in this elegant villa, built for him about 1511. He was especially proud of the decorative frescoes in the airy loggias, some painted by Raphael himself, notably a luminous *Triumph of Galatea*. Agostino entertained the popes and princes of 16th-century Rome, impressing his guests at riverside suppers by having his servants clear the table by casting the precious silver and gold dinnerware into the Tiber (indeed, nets were unfurled a foot or two beneath the water's surface to retrieve the valuable ware). In the magnificent Loggia of Psyche on the ground floor, Giulio Romano and others worked from Raphael's designs. Raphael's lovely *Galatea* is in the adjacent room. On the floor above you can see the trompe-l'oeil effects in the aptly named Hall of Perspectives by Peruzzi. Agostino Chigi's bedroom, next door, was frescoed by Il Sodoma with the *Wedding of Alexander and Roxanne*, which is considered to be the artist's best work. The palace also houses the Gabinetto Nazionale delle Stampe, a treasure trove of old prints and drawings. ⊠ *Via della Lungara 230, Trastevere* 🕾 *06/68027268 info, 06/68027397 tour reservations* ⊕ *www.villafarnesina.it* 🎫 *€10* ⊗ *Closed Sun.*

 **Restaurants**

Ai Marmi

$ | **PIZZA** | **FAMILY** | This place is about as lively as it gets—indeed, it's packed pretty much every night, with diners munching on crisp pizzas that come out of the wood-burning ovens at top speed. It's best not to go during peak dining hours, so go early or late if you don't want to wait. **Known for:** open until midnight for a late-night bite; excellent wood-oven pizzas; fried starters, such as *supplì* (breaded fried rice balls). **$** *Average main: €12* ⊠ *Viale Trastevere 53, Trastevere* 🕾 *06/5800919* ⊗ *Closed Wed. and 3 wks in Aug. Lunch only on Sun.*

★ Antico Arco

$$$ | **MODERN ITALIAN** | Founded by three friends with a passion for wine and fine food, Antico Arco attracts foodies from Rome and beyond with its refined culinary inventiveness. The location on top of the Janiculum Hill makes for a charming setting, and inside, the dining rooms are plush, modern spaces, with whitewashed brick walls, dark floors, and black velvet chairs. **Known for:** open noon until midnight daily; changing seasonal menu; molten chocolate soufflé cake. **$** *Average main: €29* ⊠ *Piazzale Aurelio 7, Trastevere* 🕾 *06/5815274* ⊕ *www.anticoarco.it* ⊗ *Closed Tues.*

★ Da Enzo

$$ | **ROMAN** | In the quieter part of Trastevere, the family-run Da Enzo is everything you would imagine a classic Roman trattoria to be. There are just a few tables, but diners from around the world line up to eat here—a testament to the quality of the food. **Known for:** small space with long waits; *cacio e pepe*, carbonara, and other Roman classics; boisterous, authentic atmosphere. **$** *Average main: €14* ⊠ *Via dei Vascellari 29, Trastevere* 🕾 *06/5812260* ⊕ *www.daenzoal29.com* ⊗ *Closed Sun. and 2 wks in Aug.*

Da Lucia

$$ | **ROMAN** | There's no shortage of old-school trattorias in Trastevere, but Da Lucia has a strong following among them. Both locals and expats enjoy the brusque but "authentic" service and the hearty Roman fare; snag a table outside in warm weather for the true Roman experience of cobblestone-terrace dining. **Known for:** beef rolls *(involtini)*; *bombolotti* (a tubular pasta) *all'amatriciana*; spaghetti *cacio e pepe*. **$** *Average main: €14* ⊠ *Vicolo del Mattonato 2, Trastevere* 🕾 *06/5803601* ⊗ *Closed Mon.–Wed. and Aug.*

☕ Coffee and Quick Bites

Biscottificio Innocenti

$ | **ITALIAN** | **FAMILY** | The scent of cookies wafts out into the street as you approach this family-run bakery, where a small team of bakers makes sweet treats the old-school way in an oven bought in the

1960s. There are dozens of varieties of baked goods, mostly sweet but some savory. **Known for:** dozens of varieties of baked goods; brutti ma buoni cookies; old-school family-run bakery. $ *Average main: €3* ✉ *Via della Luce 21, Trastevere* ☎ *06/5803926* ◷ *Closed 2 wks in Aug.*

Supplì

$ | **ROMAN** | Trastevere's best *supplì* have been served at this hole-in-the-wall take-out spot since 1979. At lunchtime, the line spills out onto the street with locals who've come for the namesake treats, as well as fried baccalà fillets and stuffed zucchini flowers. **Known for:** pistachio and salmon pasta; old-fashioned baked pizza with zucchini and straciatella cheese; gnocchi on Thursday (the traditional day for it in Rome). $ *Average main: €5* ✉ *Via di San Francesco a Ripa 137, Trastevere* ☎ *06/5897110* ⊕ *www.suppliroma.it* ◷ *Closed Sun. and 2 wks in Aug.*

Hotels

Casa di Santa Francesca Romana a Ponte Rotto

$ | **HOTEL** | In the heart of Trastevere but tucked away from the hustle and bustle of the medieval quarter, this cheap, clean, comfortable hotel in a former monastery is centered on a lovely green courtyard. **Pros:** excellent restaurants nearby; away from rowdy tourist side of Trastevere; rates can't be beat. **Cons:** spotty Wi-Fi; few amenities besides TV room and reading room; a bit far from Metro, but there are tram and bus stops nearby. $ *Rooms from: €98* ✉ *Via dei Vascellari 61, Trastevere* ☎ *06/5812125* ⊕ *www.sfromana.it* ⇱ *37 rooms* ◉ *Free Breakfast.*

Hotel Santa Maria

$ | **HOTEL** | A Trastevere treasure with a pedigree going back four centuries, this ivy-covered, mansard-roof, rosy-brick-red, erstwhile Renaissance-era convent—just steps away from the glorious Santa Maria in Trastevere church and a few blocks from the Tiber—has sweet and simple

guest rooms: a mix of brick walls, "cotto" tile floors, oak furniture, and matching bedspreads and curtains. **Pros:** a quaint and pretty oasis in a central location; lovely rooftop terrace; free bicycles to use during your stay. **Cons:** some rooms can be noisy; not the best value for money; tricky to find. $ *Rooms from: €120* ✉ *Vicolo del Piede 2, Trastevere* ☎ *06/5894626* ⊕ *www.hotelsantamariatrastevere.it* ⇱ *20 rooms* ◉ *Free Breakfast.*

Hotel Trastevere

$$ | **HOTEL** | This hotel captures the villagelike charm of the Trastevere district and offers basic, clean, comfortable rooms. **Pros:** friendly staff; convenient to tram and bus; good rates for location. **Cons:** few amenities; rooms are a little worn on the edges; standard rooms are quite small. $ *Rooms from: €130* ✉ *Via Luciano Manara 24/a, Trastevere* ☎ *06/5814713* ⊕ *www.hoteltrastevere. net* ⇱ *14 rooms* ◉ *Free Breakfast.*

Relais Le Clarisse

$ | **B&B/INN** | Set within the former cloister grounds of the Santa Chiara order, with beautiful gardens, Le Clarisse makes you feel like a personal guest at a friend's villa, thanks to the comfortable size of the guest rooms and personalized service. **Pros:** complimentary high-speed Wi-Fi; spacious rooms with comfy beds; high-tech showers/tubs with good water pressure. **Cons:** check when booking as you may be put in neighboring building; this part of Trastevere can be noisy at night; no restaurant or bar. $ *Rooms from: €70* ✉ *Via Cardinale Merry del Val 20, Trastevere* ☎ *06/58334437* ⊕ *www. leclarissetrastevere.com* ⇱ *17 rooms* ◉ *Free Breakfast.*

Nightlife

★ Freni e Frizioni

CAFÉS | This hipster hangout has a cute artist vibe, and is great for an afternoon coffee, tea, or aperitivo, or for late-night socializing. Though the vibe is laid-back, the bartenders take their cocktails seriously—and have the awards to prove it. In warmer weather, the crowd overflows into the large terrazzo overlooking the Tiber and the side streets of Trastevere. ⊠ *Via del Politeama 4, Trastevere* ☎ *06/45497499* ⊕ *www.freniefrizioni.com.*

Shopping

BOOKSTORES

Almost Corner Bookshop

BOOKS | Bursting at the seams, with not an ounce of space left on its shelves, this tiny little bookshop is a favorite meeting point for English speakers in Trastevere. Irish owner Dermot O'Connell goes out of his way to find what you're looking for, and if he doesn't have it in stock he'll make a special order for you. The shop carries everything from popular best sellers to translated Italian classics, as well as lots of good books about Rome. ⊠ *Via del Moro 45, Trastevere* ☎ *06/5836942.*

FLEA MARKETS

Porta Portese

MARKET | One of the biggest flea markets in Italy, Porta Portese welcomes visitors in droves every Sunday from 7 am to 2 pm. Treasure seekers and bargain hunters love scrounging around tents for new and used clothing, antique furniture, used books, accessories, and other odds 'n' ends. Bring your haggling skills, and cash (preferably small bills—it'll work in your favor when driving a bargain); many stallholders don't accept credit cards, and the nearest ATM is a hike. ⊠ *Via Portuense and adjacent streets between Porta Portese and Via Ettore Rolli, Trastevere.*

SHOES

Joseph Debach

SHOES | With his shoe boutique in Rome that is open only in the evenings (or by appointment), Joseph Debach has made eccentric creations that are more art than footwear. Entirely handmade from wood, metal, and leather in his small and chaotic studio, his abacus wedge is worthy of a museum. The sometimes outrageous styles earn a "wow" and are occasionally finished with hand-painted strings, odd bits of comic books, newspapers, and other unexpected baubles. ⊠ *Piazza de' Renzi 21, Trastevere* ☎ *3460255265* ⊕ *www.josephdebach.it.*

Aventino and Testaccio

The **Aventino** district is somewhat rarefied, where some houses still have their own bell towers and private gardens are called "parks," without exaggeration. Like the emperors of old on the Palatine, the fortunate residents here look out over the Circus Maximus and the river, winding its way far below. **Testaccio** is perhaps the world's only district built on broken pots: the hill of the same name was born from discarded pottery used to store oil, wine, and other goods loaded from nearby Ripa, when Rome had a port and the Tiber was once a mighty river to an empire. It's quiet during the day, but on Saturday buzzes with the loud music from rows of discos and clubs.

Sights

★ Centrale Montemartini

ART MUSEUM | A decommissioned power plant (Rome's first electricity plant) was reopened as a permanent exhibition space in 2005 and today houses the overflow of ancient art from the Musei Capitolini collection. After strolling Rome's medieval lanes, the Centrale Montemartini's early-20th-century style can feel positively modern. A 15-minute walk from the heart of Testaccio in one direction will lead you past walls covered in street art to the urban district of Ostiense. Head southwest and saunter under the train tracks to admire buildings bedecked with four-story-high murals until you reach the Centrale Montemartini. With Roman sculptures and mosaics

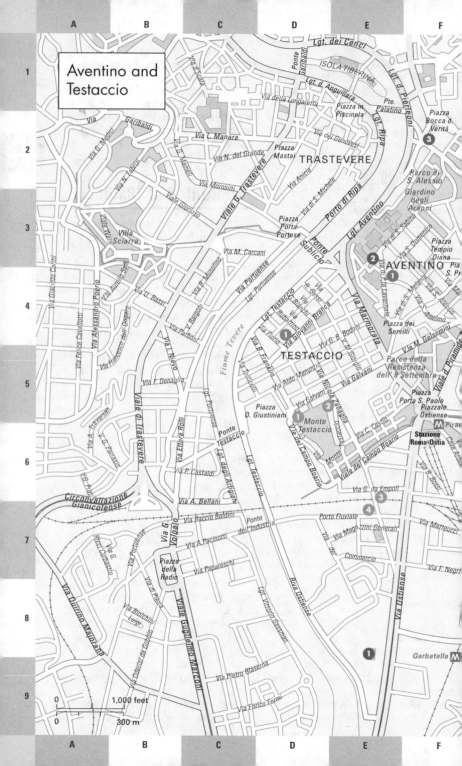

Aventino and Testaccio

A | **B** | **C** | **D** | **E** | **F**

Lgt. dei Cenci

ISOLA TIBERINA

Ponte Garibaldi

Via di Scala

Lgt. d. Anguillara

Lgt. d. Pierleoni

Via della Lungaretta

Piazza in Piscinula

Pte. Palatino

Piazza Bocca d. Verità

Via G. Medici

Via Garibaldi

Via L. Manara

Via dei Genovesi

Lgt. Ripa

Via E. Manali

Via N. del Grande

Piazza Mastai

Via della Ripa

TRASTEVERE

Parco di S. Alessio

Via N. Tabrini

Via Morosini

Via Amicia

Via di S. Michele

Porto di Ripa

Giardino degli Acanci

Villa Sciarra

Viale G. Trastevere

Viale Glorioso

Piazza Porta Portese

Ponte Sublicio

Lgt. Aventino

Via di S. Sabina

Via di S. Domenico

Piazza Tempio Diana

AVENTINO

Via Giacomo Carini

Via Aurelio Saffi

Via Alessandro Poerio

Via U. Bassi

Via M. Carcani

Via Portuense

Lgt. Portuense

Via Marmorata

Via di S. Prisca

Via di S. Melania

Via S. Anselmo

Piazza dei Servilli

Via Felice Cavallotti

Via Francesco dell'Ongaro

Via F. Nievo

Via B. Musolino

Via I. Bargoni

Via Portuense

Lgt. Testaccio

Via Ginori

Via R. Gessi

Via A. Rubattino

Via Florio

Via Giovanni Branca

Via G.B. Bodoni

Via M. Gelsomini

TESTACCIO

Parco della Resistenza dell'8 Settembre

Via F. Denaglia

Via B. Franklin

Via Aldo Manunzio

Via Nicola Zabaglia

Via Galvani

Piazza Porta S. Paolo

Piazzale Ostiense

Via A. traversari

Viale di Trastevere

Via V. G. Paradisi

Via Ettore Rolli

Piazza O. Giustiniani

Via Galvani

Monte Testaccio

Via C. Cestio

Stazione Roma-Ostia

Via G. Pascoli

Ponte Testaccio

Lgt. dell'Arignan

Monte

Viale del Campo Boario

Via U. Piramide

Via P. Castaldi

Circonvallazione Gianicolense

Via A. Bellani

Via G. da Empoli

Via B. Blasi

Via G. Volpato

Via Baccio Baldini

Ponte dell'Industria

Porto Fluviale

Via Magazzini Generali

Via Matteucci

Via G. Ricci Curbastro

Via A. Pacinotti

Via Pa-

Via Pa-

Commercio

Via F. Negri

Via Portuense

Piazza della Radio

Via Papareschi

Riva Ostiense

Via di Pietra

Viale Guglielmo Marconi

Lgt. Ostiense

Via Quirino Majorana

Via Brovchini Luigi

Via Cristoforo da Gubbio

Via Pietro Blaserna

Via Vittorio Gassman

Via Ustiense

Garbatella

Via Enrico Fermi

0 — 1,000 feet

0 — 300 m

Fiume Tevere

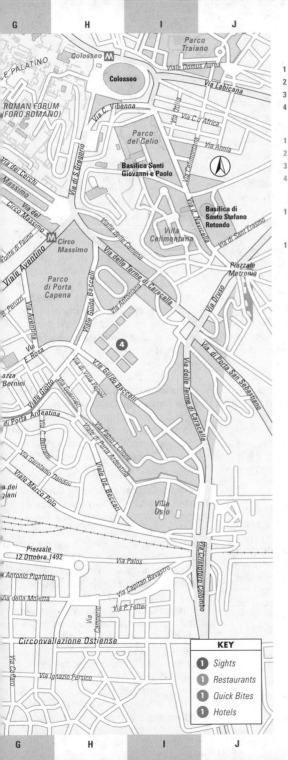

Sights ▼

1 Centrale Montemartini.............**E8**
2 Piazza dei Cavalieri di Malta......**E3**
3 Santa Maria in Cosmedin..........**F2**
4 Terme di Caracalla................**H4**

Restaurants ▼

1 Checchino dal 1887...............**D5**
2 Flavio al Velavevodetto **D5**
3 Marigold **E6**
4 Porto Fluviale....................**E7**

Quick Bites ▼

1 Trapizzino........................**D4**

Hotels ▼

1 Hotel San Anselmo................**E4**

set against industrial machinery and pipes, nowhere else in Rome is the contrast between old and new more apparent or enjoyable. A pleasure, too, is the fact that you're likely to be one of the few visitors here, making it the perfect stop for those feeling claustrophobic from Rome's crowds. Unusually, the collection is organized by the area in which the ancient pieces were found. Highlights include the former boiler room filled with ancient marble statues that once decorated Rome's private villas, such as the beautiful *Esquiline Venus*, as well as a large mosaic of a hunting scene. ✉ *Via Ostiense 106, Testaccio* ☎ *06/0608* ⊕ *www.centralemontemartini.org* ⚑ *€10* ⊗ *Closed Mon.* Ⓜ *Garbatella.*

★ **Piazza dei Cavalieri di Malta**

PLAZA/SQUARE | Peek through the keyhole of the Priorato di Malta, the walled compound of the Knights of Malta, and you'll get a surprising eyeful: a picture-perfect view of the dome of St. Peter's Basilica, far across the city. The top of the church is flawlessly framed by trimmed hedges that lie beyond a nondescript, locked green door. The square and the priory within the walls are the work of Giovanni Battista Piranesi, an 18th-century engraver who is more famous for etching Roman views than for orchestrating them, but he fancied himself a bit of an architect and did not disappoint. As for the Order of the Knights of Malta, it is the world's oldest and most exclusive order of chivalry, founded in the Holy Land during the Crusades. Though nominally ministering to the sick in those early days—a role that has since become the order's raison d'être—the knights amassed huge tracts of land in the Middle East. From 1530 they were based on the Mediterranean island of Malta, but in 1798 Napoléon expelled them, and, in 1834, they established themselves in Rome. Tours are sometimes available if you would like to go inside; call for more information. ✉ *Via Santa Sabina and Via Porta Lavernale,* *Aventino* ☎ *06/5779193 tour reservations* Ⓜ *Circo Massimo; Tram No. 3.*

★ **Santa Maria in Cosmedin**

CHURCH | FAMILY | Although this is one of Rome's oldest churches, with a haunting interior, it plays second fiddle to the renowned artifact installed out in the portico. The **Bocca della Verità** (Mouth of Truth) is in reality nothing more than an ancient drain cover, unearthed during the Middle Ages. Legend has it, however, that the teeth will clamp down on a liar's hand if they dare to tell a fib while holding their fingers up to the fearsome mouth. Hordes of tourists line up to take the test every day (kids especially get a kick out of it), but there is never a wait to enter the church itself, which was built in the 6th century. Head inside to stand before the flower-crowned skull of St. Valentine, who is celebrated every February 14th, but go ahead and pass on the trip down to the tiny, empty crypt. Heavily restored at the end of the 19th century, the church stands across from the **Piazza della Bocca della Verità,** originally the location of the Forum Boarium, ancient Rome's cattle market, and later the site of public executions. ✉ *Piazza della Bocca della Verità 18, Aventino* ☎ *06/6787759* ⊕ *www.cosmedin.org* Ⓜ *Circo Massimo.*

Terme di Caracalla (*Baths of Caracalla*)

RUINS | FAMILY | The Terme di Caracalla are some of Rome's most massive—yet least visited—ruins. Begun in AD 206 by the emperor Septimius Severus and completed by his son, Caracalla, the 28-acre complex could accommodate 1,600 bathers at a time. Along with an Olympic-size swimming pool and baths, the complex also had two gyms, a library, and gardens. The impressive baths depended on slave labor, particularly the unseen stokers who toiled in subterranean rooms to keep the fires roaring in order to heat the water. Rather than a simple dip in a tub, Romans turned "bathing" into one of the most lavish leisure activities imaginable. A bath began in the sudatoria, a series of small rooms resembling saunas, which then led to the caldarium, a circular room that was humid rather than simply hot. Here a strigil, or scraper, was used to get the dirt off the skin. Next stop: the warm(-ish) tepidarium, which helped start the cool-down process. Finally, it ended with a splash around the frigidarium, a chilly swimming pool. Today, the complex is a shell of its former self. Some black-and-white mosaic fragments remain, but most of the opulent mosaics, frescoes, and sculptures have found their way into Rome's museums. However, the towering walls and sheer size of the ruins give one of the best glimpses into ancient Rome's ambitions. If you're here in summer, don't miss the chance to catch an open-air opera or ballet in the baths, put on by the **Teatro dell'Opera di Roma**. ✉ *Viale delle Terme di Caracalla 52, Aventino* ☎ *06/39967702* 🌐 *www.coopculture.it* 🎫 *€8 (includes Villa dei Quintili and Tomba di Cecilia Metella)* [M] *Circo Massimo.*

🍴 Restaurants

Checchino dal 1887

$$ | **ROMAN** | Literally carved into the side of a hill made up of ancient shards of amphorae, Checchino is an example of a classic, upscale, family-run Roman establishment, with one of the best wine cellars in the region. One of the first restaurants to open near Testaccio's (now long closed) slaughterhouse, they still serve classic offal dishes (though the white-jacketed waiters can also suggest other options). **Known for:** *coda alla vaccinara* (Roman-style oxtail); old-school Roman cooking; old-school Roman waiters. [$] *Average main: €23* ✉ *Via di Monte Testaccio 30, Testaccio* ☎ *06/5743816* 🌐 *www.checchino-dal-1887.com* 🕒 *Closed Mon., Aug., and 1 wk at Christmas* [M] *Piramide.*

★ **Flavio al Velavevodetto**

$$ | **ROMAN** | It's everything you're looking for in a true Roman eating experience: authentic, in a historic setting, and filled with Italians eating good food at good prices. In this very *romani di Roma* (Rome of the Romans) neighborhood, surrounded by discos and bars sharing Monte Testaccio, you can enjoy a meal of classic local dishes, from vegetable antipasto to cacio e pepe (said to be the best version in the city) and lamb chops. **Known for:** *polpette di bollito* (fried breaded meatballs); authentic Roman atmosphere and food; outdoor covered terrace in summer. [$] *Average main: €16* ✉ *Via di Monte Testaccio 97, Testaccio* ☎ *06/5744194* 🌐 *www.ristorantevelavevodetto.it* [M] *Piramide.*

Marigold

$ | **SCANDINAVIAN** | Run by a husband-and-wife team (she's Danish, he's Italian), this hip restaurant blends the best of both their cultures with a Scandinavian-meets-Italian design and menu. It draws a young, international crowd who come for the sourdough, cinnamon buns, and veggie-forward dishes. **Known for:** minimalist design; Danish breads and baked goods; weekend brunch. [$] *Average main: €13* ✉ *Via Giovanni da Empoli 37, Testaccio* ☎ *06/87725679* 🌐 *www.marigoldroma.com* 🕒 *Closed Mon., Dinner Fri. and Sat. only* [M] *Ostiense.*

Porto Fluviale

$ | **ITALIAN** | This massive structure takes up the better part of a block on a street that's gone from gritty clubland to popular nightspot, thanks largely to Porto Fluviale. The place pulls double duty as a bar, café, pizzeria, lunch buffet, and lively evening restaurant. **Known for:** *cicchetti* (Venetian-style tapas); good cocktails; pizza from wood-burning oven. [$] *Average main: €13* ✉ *Via del Porto Fluviale 22, Testaccio* ☎ *06/5743199* 🌐 *www.portofluviale.com* [M] *Piramide.*

☕ Coffee and Quick Bites

Trapizzino

$ | **ROMAN** | **FAMILY** | Stefano Callegari is one of Rome's most famous pizza makers, but at Trapizzino he's doing something a bit different. The name of the restaurant is derived from the Italian words for sandwich (*tramezzino*) and pizza, and the result is something like an upscale pizza pocket, stuffed on the spot with local specialties like chicken alla cacciatore, or trippa, or roast pumpkin, pecorino, and almonds. **Known for:** Italian craft beer; casual setting, with seating available next door; eggplant parmigiana and meatball sandwiches. [$] *Average main: €4* ✉ *Via Giovanni Branca 88, Testaccio* ☎ *06/43419624* 🌐 *www.trapizzino.it* ⏲ *Closed 1 wk in Aug.* [M] *Piramide.*

Hotels

Hotel San Anselmo

$ | **HOTEL** | This refurbished 19th-century villa is a romantic retreat from the city, set in a *molto* charming garden atop the Aventine Hill. **Pros:** historic building with artful interior; garden where you can enjoy breakfast; free Wi-Fi. **Cons:** no full restaurant; limited public transportation; some rooms are quite small. [$] *Rooms from: €80* ✉ *Piazza San Anselmo 2, Aventino* ☎ *06/570057* 🌐 *www.aventinohotels.com* 🛏 *34 rooms* 🍴 *Free Breakfast* [M] *Circo Massimo.*

Esquilino and Via Appia Antica

Esquilino, covering Rome's most sprawling hill—the Esquiline—lies at the edge of the tourist maps, near the Termini station. Today, culturally diverse inhabitants of different nationalities live and work in the area. It's not the cobblestone-street atmosphere that most think of when they think of Rome. Far south lies catacomb country—the haunts of the fabled underground graves of Rome's earliest Christians, arrayed to either side of the Queen of Roads, the Via Appia Antica (Appian Way). Strewn with classical ruins and dotted with grazing sheep, the road stirs images of chariots and legionnaires returning from imperial conquests. It was completed in 312 BC by Appius Claudius, who laid it out to connect Rome with settlements in the south, in the direction of Naples. Though time and vandals have taken their toll on the ancient relics along the road, the catacombs remain to cast their spirit-warm spell. Today, the dark, gloomy catacombs contrast strongly with the Appia Antica's fresh air, verdant meadows, and evocative classical ruins.

GETTING HERE AND AROUND

The Esquilino Hill can be reached via the Vittorio Emanuele subway station, one stop from Termini station. Bus No. 150F runs from Piazza del Popolo to Esquilino.

The initial stretch of the Via Appia Antica is not pedestrian-friendly—there is fast, heavy traffic and no sidewalk all the way from Porta San Sebastiano to the Catacombe di San Callisto. To reach the catacombs, take Bus No. 218 from San Giovanni in Laterano. Alternatively, take Metro Line A to Colli Albani and then Bus No. 660 to the Tomba di Cecilia Metella.

Sights

Catacombe di San Callisto

(*Catacombs of St. Calixtus*)

CEMETERY | Burial place of several very early popes, this is Rome's oldest and best-preserved underground cemetery. One of the (English-speaking) friars who act as custodians of the catacomb will guide you through its crypts and galleries, some adorned with Early Christian frescoes. Watch out for wrong turns: this catacomb is five stories deep! **TIP→ The large parking area means this is favored by large groups; it can get busy.** ✉ *Via Appia Antica 110, Via Appia Antica* ☎ *06/5130151* 🌐 *www.catacombe.roma.it* 🎟 *€8* ⏲ *Closed Wed. and mid-Jan.–Feb.*

★ **Catacombe di San Sebastiano**

(*Catacombs of St. Sebastian*)

CEMETERY | The 4th-century church was named after the saint who was buried in the catacomb, which burrows underground on four different levels. This was the only Early Christian cemetery

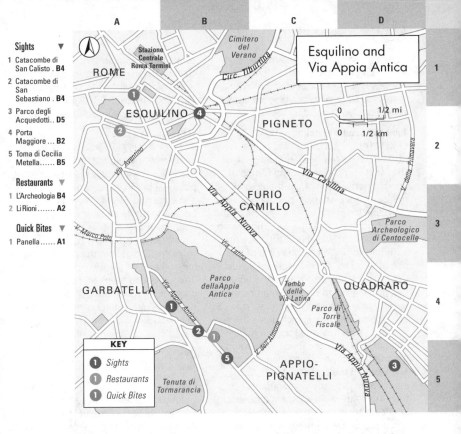

to remain accessible during the Middle Ages, and it was from here that the term *catacomb* is derived—it's in a spot where the road dips into a hollow, known to the Romans as *catacumba* (Greek for "near the hollow"). ⊠ *Via Appia Antica 136, Via Appia Antica* ☏ *06/7850350* ⊕ *www. catacombe.org* ⊡ *€8* ⊘ *Closed Sun.*

Parco degli Acquedotti

CITY PARK | **FAMILY** | This massive park was named for the six remaining aqueducts that formed part of the famously elaborate system that carried water to ancient Rome. It's technically part of the Parco dell'Appia Antica and you can indeed walk on a piece of an ancient Roman road that once went all the way to Benevento, a city near Naples. The park has some serious film cred: it was featured in the opening scene of *La Dolce Vita* and in a rather memorable scene depicting some avant-garde

performance art in *La Grande Bellezza*. On weekends, it's a popular place for locals to picnic, exercise, and bring their kids or dogs. ⊠ *Via Lemonia 221, Via Appia Antica* ⊕ *www.parcodegliacquedotti.it* Ⓜ *Giulio Agricola, Subaugusta.*

Porta Maggiore (*Great Gate*)

RUINS | The massive 1st-century-AD arch was built as part of the original Aqua Claudia and then incorporated into the walls hurriedly erected in the late 3rd century as Rome's fortunes began to decline; the great arch of the aqueduct subsequently became a *porta* (city gate). It gives an idea of the grand scale of ancient Roman public works. On the Piazzale Labicano side, to the east, is the curious **Baker's Tomb,** erected in the 1st century BC by a prosperous baker (predating both the aqueduct and the city walls); it's shaped like an oven to signal the deceased's trade. The site is now in the middle of a public transport node, and is close to Rome's first tram depot (going back to 1889). ✉ *Piazza di Porta Maggiore, Esquilino* [M] *Tram No. 3, 5, 14, or 19.*

Tomba di Cecilia Metella

CEMETERY | For centuries, sightseers have flocked to this famous landmark, one of the most complete surviving tombs of ancient Rome. One of the many round mausoleums that once lined the Appian Way, this tomb is a smaller version of the Mausoleum of Augustus, but impressive nonetheless. It was the burial place of a Roman noblewoman: the wife of the son of Crassus, who was one of Julius Caesar's rivals and known as the richest man in the Roman Empire (infamously entering the English language as "crass"). The original decoration includes a frieze of bulls' skulls near the top. The travertine stone walls were made higher and the medieval-style crenellations were added when the tomb was transformed into a fortress by the Caetani family in the 14th century. An adjacent chamber houses a small museum of the area's geological phases. Entrance to this site also includes access to the splendid Villa dei Quintili, but you can get a super view without going in. ✉ *Via Appia Antica 161, Via Appia Antica* ☎ *06/7886254* 🌐 *www.parcoarcheologicoappiaantica.it* 🎫 *€10, includes all the sites in the Parco dell'Appia Antica (Villa dei Quintili, Antiquarium di Lucrezia Romana, Complesso di Capo di Bove, Tombe della Via Latina, and the Villa dei Setti Bassi)* 🕒 *Closed Mon.*

🍴 Restaurants

L'Archeologia

$$ | **ITALIAN** | In this farmhouse just beyond the catacombs, founded around 1890, you can dine indoors beside the fireplace in cool weather or in the garden under age-old vines in summer. Specialties include *mezze maniche all'amatriciana*, lamb with smoked potatoes and artichokes, and fresh seafood. **Known for:** romantic setting; ancient wine cellar La Cantina; hand-painted frescoes. [$] *Average main: €24* ✉ *Via Appia Antica 139, Via Appia Antica* ☎ *06/7880494* 🌐 *www.larcheologia.it* 🕒 *Closed Tues.*

Li Rioni

$ | **PIZZA** | **FAMILY** | This busy pizzeria conveniently close to the Colosseum has been serving real-deal Roman-style pizza—super thin and cooked to a crisp—since the mid-1980s. The magic might be due to the fact that they let their pizza dough rise 24–48 hours before baking to guarantee an extra-light pizza, said to be more easily digested than others. **Known for:** homemade tiramisu; olive *ascolane* (fried, breaded olives stuffed with sausage); pizza margherita. [$] *Average main: €12* ✉ *Via dei Santi Quattro 24, Esquilino* ☎ *06/70450605* 🌐 *www.lirioni.it* 🕒 *Closed 2 wks in Aug. No lunch* [M] *Colosseo.*

☕ Coffee and Quick Bites

Panella

$ | **BAKERY** | Opened in 1929, this nearly century-old spot is one of Rome's best bakeries and sells both sweet and savory baked goods, including over 70 types of bread. Line up for the pizza al taglio at lunchtime or sit down at one of the outdoor tables for a cappuccino and cornetto or an aperitivo replete with mini sandwiches made on homemade buns. **Known for:** over 70 types of bread; crostata, tartlettes, and other sweet treats; one of Rome's best bakeries. [$] *Average main: €5* ✉ *Via Merulana 54, Esquilino* ☎ *06/4872435* 🌐 *www.panellaroma.com* 🕒 *Closed Sun.* [M] *Vittorio Emanuele.*

Chapter 4

4

VENICE

Updated by
Liz Humphreys

 Sights
★★★★★

 Restaurants
★★★★☆

 Hotels
★★★★★

 Shopping
★★★☆☆

 Nightlife
★★☆☆☆

WELCOME TO VENICE

TOP REASONS TO GO

★ **Cruising the Grand Canal:** The beauty of its palaces, enhanced by the play of light on the water, make a trip down Venice's "Main Street" unforgettable.

★ **Basilica di San Marco:** Don't miss the gorgeous mosaics inside—they're worth standing in line for.

★ **Santa Maria Gloriosa dei Frari:** Its austere, cavernous interior houses Titian's *Assumption*—one of the world's most beautiful altarpieces—plus several other spectacular art treasures.

★ **Gallerie dell'Accademia:** Legendary masterpieces of Venetian painting will overwhelm you in this fabled museum.

★ **Sipping wine and snacking at a bacaro:** For a sample of tasty local snacks and excellent Veneto wines in a uniquely Venetian setting, head for one of the city's many wine bars.

1 **San Marco.** The neighborhood at the center of Venice is filled with fashion boutiques, art galleries, and grand hotels.

2 **Dorsoduro.** This graceful residential area is home to renowned art galleries; the Campo Santa Margherita is a lively student hangout.

3 **San Polo and Santa Croce.** These bustling *sestieri* (districts) have all sorts of shops, several major churches, and the Rialto fish and produce markets.

4 **Cannaregio.** This sestiere has some of the sunniest open-air canalside walks in town; the Jewish Ghetto has a fascinating history.

5 **Castello.** With its gardens, park, and narrow, winding walkways, it's the sestiere least influenced by Venice's tourist culture.

6 **San Giorgio Maggiore and the Giudecca.** San Giorgio is graced with its magnificent namesake church, and the Giudecca has wonderful views of Venice.

7 **Islands of the Lagoon.** Each island in Venice's northern lagoon has its own allure.

EATING AND DRINKING WELL IN VENICE

The catchword in Venetian restaurants is "fish." How do you learn about the catch of the day? A visit to the Rialto's *pescheria* (fish market) is more instructive than any book, and when you're dining at a well-regarded restaurant, ask for a recommendation.

Traditionally, fish is served with a bit of salt, maybe some chopped parsley, and a drizzle of olive oil—no lemon; lemon masks the flavor. Ask for an entire wild-caught fish; it's much more expensive than its farmed cousin, but certainly worth it. Antipasto may be pro-sciutto *di San Daniele* (from the Veneto region) or *sarde in saor* (fresh panfried sardines marinated with onions, raisins, and pine nuts). Risotto, cooked with shellfish or veggies, is a great first course. Pasta? Enjoy it with seafood: this is *not* the place to order spaghetti with tomato sauce. Other pillars of regional cooking include *pasta e fagioli* (thick bean soup with pasta); polenta, often with *fegato alla veneziana* (liver with onion); and that dessert invented in the Veneto, tiramisu.

GOING BACARO

You can sample regional wines and scrumptious *cicheti* (small snacks) in *bacari* (wine bars), a great Venetian tradition. Crostini and *polpette* (meat, fish, or vegetable croquettes) are popular cicheti, as are small sandwiches, seafood salads, *baccalà mantecato* (creamy, whipped salt cod), and toothpick-speared items like roasted peppers, marinated artichokes, and mozzarella balls.

SEAFOOD

Granseola (crab), *moeche* (tiny, locally caught soft-shell crabs), sweet *canoce* (mantis shrimp), *capelunghe* (razor clams), calamari, and *seppie* or *seppioline* (cuttlefish) are all prominently featured, as well as *rombo* (turbot), *branzino* (sea bass), *San Pietro* (John Dory), *sogliola* (sole), *orate* (gilthead bream), and *triglia* (mullet). Trademark dishes include sarde in saor, *frittura mista* (tempura-like fried fish and vegetables), and *baccalà mantecato*.

RISOTTO, PASTA, POLENTA

As a first course, Venetians favor the creamy rice dish risotto *all'onda* ("undulating," as opposed to firm), prepared with vegetables or shellfish. When pasta is served, it's generally accompanied by seafood sauces, too: *pasticcio di pesce* is lasagna-type pasta baked with fish, and *bigoli* is a strictly local whole-wheat pasta shaped like thick spaghetti, usually served *in salsa* (an anchovy-onion sauce with a dash of cinnamon), or with *nero di seppia* (cuttlefish-ink sauce). *Pasta e fagioli* is another classic first course, and polenta is a staple—served creamy or fried in wedges, generally as an accompaniment to stews or *seppie in nero* (cuttlefish in black ink).

VEGETABLES

The larger islands of the lagoon are known for their legendary vegetables, such as the Sant'Erasmo *castraure*, sinfully expensive but heavenly tiny white artichokes that appear for a few days in spring. Spring treats include the fat white asparagus from neighboring Bassano or Verona, and artichoke bottoms (*fondi*), usually sautéed with olive oil, parsley, and garlic. From December to March the prized local radicchio *di Treviso* is grilled and frequently served with a bit of melted Taleggio cheese from Lombardy. Fall brings small wild mushrooms called *chiodini* and *zucca di Mantova,* a yellow squash with a gray-green rind used in soups, puddings, and ravioli stuffing.

SWEETS

Tiramisu lovers will have ample opportunity to sample this creamy delight made from ladyfingers soaked in espresso and rum or brandy and covered with mascarpone cream and cinnamon. Gelato, *sgroppino* (prosecco, vodka, and lemon sorbet), and *semifreddo* (soft homemade ice cream) are other sweets frequently seen on Venetian menus, as are almond cakes and dry cookies served with dessert wine. Try *focaccia veneziana,* a sweet raised cake made in the late fall and winter.

Venice is often called La Serenissima, or "the most serene," a reference to the majesty, wisdom, and power of this city that was for centuries a leader in trade between Europe and Asia and a major center of European culture. Built on water by people who saw the sea as defender and ally, and who constantly invested in its splendor with magnificent architectural projects, Venice is a city unlike any other.

No matter how often you've seen it in photos and films, the real thing is more dreamlike than you could ever imagine. Its most notable landmarks, the Basilica di San Marco and the Palazzo Ducale, are exotic mixes of Byzantine, Romanesque, Gothic, and Renaissance styles, reflecting Venice's ties with the rest of Italy and with Constantinople to the east. Shimmering sunlight and silvery mist soften every perspective here; it's easy to understand how the city became renowned in the Renaissance for its artists' use of color. It's full of secrets, inexpressibly romantic, and frequently given over to pure, sensuous enjoyment.

You'll see Venetians going about their daily affairs in vaporetti, in the *campi* (squares), and along the *calli* (narrow streets). Despite their many challenges (including more frequent flooding and overcrowding), they are proud of their city and its history and are still quite helpful to those who show proper respect for Venice and its way of life.

Planning

Making the Most of Your Time

The hordes of tourists here are legendary, especially in spring and fall but during other seasons too—there's really no "off-season" in Venice. Unfortunately, tales of impassable tourist-packed streets and endless queues to get into the Basilica di San Marco are not exaggerated. A little bit of planning, however, will help you avoid the worst of the crowds.

Most tourists do little more than take the vaporetto down the Grand Canal to Piazza San Marco, see the piazza and the basilica, and walk up to the Rialto and back to the station. You'll want to visit these areas, too, but do so in the early morning, before most tourists have finished their breakfast cappuccinos.

Because many tourists are other Italians who come for a weekend outing, you can further decrease your competition for Venice's pleasures by choosing to visit the city on weekdays.

Away from San Marco and the Rialto, the streets and quays of Venice's beautiful medieval and Renaissance residential districts receive only a moderate amount of traffic. Besides the Grand Canal and the Piazza San Marco, and perhaps Torcello, the other historically and artistically important sites are seldom overcrowded. Even on weekends you probably won't have to queue up for the Gallerie dell'Accademia.

Getting Oriented

Venice proper is quite compact, and you should be able to walk across it in a couple of hours, even counting a few minutes for getting lost. Vaporetti will save wear and tear on tired feet, but won't always save you much time.

Venice is divided into six sestieri: Cannaregio, Castello, Dorsoduro, San Polo, and Santa Croce. More sedate outer islands float around them—San Giorgio Maggiore and the Giudecca just to the south; beyond them the Lido, the barrier island; and to the north, Murano, Burano, and Torcello.

Getting Here and Around

AIR
Aeroporto Marco Polo. ☎ 041/2609260 ⊕ www.veniceairport.it.
LAND TRANSFERS
ATVO. ☎ 0421/594672 ⊕ www.atvo.it.
WATER TRANSFERS
From Marco Polo terminal, it's a mostly covered seven-minute walk to the dock where boats depart for Venice's historic center. The ride is in a closed boat so you won't get much of a view; plus, it's more expensive and generally slower than the bus to Piazzale Roma (unless your hotel is near a boat station).

Alilaguna. ☎ 041/2401701 ⊕ www. alilaguna.it.
CAR
Venice is at the end of the SR11, just off the east–west A4 autostrada. There are no cars in Venice; if possible, return your rental when you arrive.

A warning: don't be waylaid by illegal touts, often wearing fake uniforms, who try to flag you down and offer to arrange parking and hotels. Use one of the established garages and consider reserving a space in advance. The **Autorimessa Comunale** (041/2727307, avm.avmspa.it) costs €26–€29 for 24 hours (slight discounts if you book online). The **Garage San Marco** (041/5232213, www.garagesanmarco. it) costs €35 for 24 hours, with slight discounts for prepaid online reservations. On its own island, **Tronchetto** (041/5207555, www.tronchettoparking. it) charges €21 for 24 hours. Watch for signs coming over the bridge—you turn right just before Piazzale Roma. Many hotels and the casino have guest discounts with San Marco or Tronchetto garages. Another alternative is to park in Mestre, on the mainland, and take a train (10 minutes, €1) or bus into Venice. The garage across from the station and the Bus No. 2 stop costs €8 per day.

PUBLIC TRANSPORTATION
WATER BUSES
ACTV. ☎ 041/041 041 ⊕ www.actv.it.
WATER TAXIS
A *motoscafo* isn't cheap: you'll spend about €70 for a short trip in town, €90 to the Lido, and €100 or more per hour to visit the outer islands. It is strongly suggested to book through the **Consorzio Motoscafi Venezia** (041/5222303, www. motoscafivenezia.com) to avoid an argument with your driver over prices. A water taxi can carry up to 10 passengers, with an additional charge of €10 per person for more than 5 people, so if you're

traveling in a group, it may not be that much more expensive than a vaporetto.

TRAIN

Venice has rail connections with many major cities in Italy and Europe. Note that Venice's train station is **Venezia Santa Lucia,** not to be confused with Venezia Mestre, which is the mainland stop prior to arriving in the historic center. Some trains don't continue beyond the Mestre station; in such cases you can catch the next Venice-bound train. Get a ticket on the Trenitalia app or a paper ticket from the kiosk on the platform and validate it (in the yellow time-stamp machine) to avoid a fine.

Restaurants

Dining options in Venice range from ultra-high-end establishments, where jackets are required, to very casual eateries. Once staunchly traditional, many restaurants have revamped their dining rooms and their menus, creating dishes that blend classic elements with ingredients and methods less common to the region. Mid- and upper-range restaurants often offer innovative options as well as mainstays like sarde in saor and *fegato alla veneziana.*

Unfortunately, Venice also has its share of overpriced, mediocre eateries. Restaurants catering to tourists have little motivation to maintain quality since most diners are one-time patrons. You are better off at a restaurant frequented by locals, who are interested in the food, not the views. Avoid places with cajoling waiters outside, as well as those that don't display their prices or have showy tourist menus translated into a dozen languages. For the same €15–€20 you'd spend at such places, you could do better at a *bacaro* making a meal of *cicheti.*

Restaurant listings have been shortened. For full information, visit Fodors.com.

WHAT IT COSTS in Euros

$	$$	$$$	$$$$
AT DINNER			
under €15	€15–€24	€25–€35	over €35

Hotels

Venetian magic lingers when you retire for the night, whether you're staying in a grand hotel or budget *locanda* (inn). Hotels usually occupy very old buildings, often without elevators or lounge areas. It's not at all unusual for each room to be different, even on the same floor: windows overlooking charming canals and bleak alleyways are both common. Venice is one of the most popular destinations on Earth—so book your lodging as far in advance as possible.

In terms of location, the area in and around San Marco is the most crowded and expensive. Still convenient but more tranquil areas include Dorsoduro, Santa Croce, and Cannaregio (though the area around the train station can be hectic), or even Castello in the area beyond the Pietà church. Also take into consideration the proximity of a vaporetto stop, especially if you have heavy baggage. Regardless of where you stay, it's essential that you have detailed directions to your hotel: note not only its street address but also its sestiere as well as a nearby landmark or two. Even if you arrive by water taxi, you may still have a bit of a walk.

Hotel reviews have been shortened. For full information, visit Fodors.com.

WHAT IT COSTS in Euros

$	$$	$$$	$$$$
LODGING FOR TWO			
under €125	€125–€200	€201–€300	over €300

Nightlife

Nightlife offerings in Venice are, even by rather sedate standards, fairly tame. Most bars must close by midnight, especially those that offer outdoor seating. Piazza San Marco is a popular meeting place in nice weather, when the cafés stay open relatively late and all seem to compete to offer the best live music. The younger crowd, Venetians and visitors alike, tend to gravitate toward the area around the Ponte di Rialto, with Campi San Bartolomeo and San Luca on one side and Campo Rialto Nuovo on the other. Especially popular with university students and young people from the mainland are the bars around Campo Santa Margherita. Visit 2night.it/venezia for nightlife listings and reviews.

Performing Arts

Visit www.agendavenezia.org for a preview of musical, artistic, and sporting events. *Venezia News* (*VENews*), available at newsstands, has similar information but also includes in-depth articles about noteworthy events. The tourist office publishes a handy, free quarterly *Calendar* in Italian and English, listing daily events and current museum and venue hours. *Venezia da Vivere* (www.veneziadavivere. com) is a seasonal guide listing cool cultural happenings and places. And don't ignore the posters you see plastered on the walls as you walk—often they contain the most up-to-date information you can find.

■ TIP→ **For more information on festivals in Venice, see On the Calendar in Travel Smart.**

CARNEVALE

Although Carnevale has traditionally been associated with the time leading up to the Roman Catholic period of Lent, it originally started out as a principally secular annual period of partying and feasting to celebrate Venice's victory over Ulrich II, Patriarch of Aquileia, in 1162. To commemorate the annual tribute Ulrich was forced to pay, a bull and 12 pigs were slaughtered in Piazza San Marco each year on the day before Lent. Since then, the city has marked the days preceding *Quaresima* (Lent) with abundant feasting and wild celebrations. The word *carnevale* is derived from the words *carne* (meat) and *levare* (to remove), as eating meat was restricted during Lent. The use of masks for Carnevale was first mentioned in 1268, and its direct association with Lent was not made until the end of the 13th century.

Venice earned its international reputation as the "city of Carnevale" in the 18th century, when partying would begin several months before Lent and the city seemed to be one continuous masquerade. During this time, income from tourists became a major source of funds in La Serenissima's coffers. With the Republic's fall in 1797, Carnevale was prohibited by the French and the Austrians. From Italian reunification in 1866 until the fall of Fascism in the 1940s, the event was alternately allowed or banned, depending on the government's stance.

It was revived for good in the 1970s, when residents began taking to the calli and campi in their own impromptu celebrations. It didn't take long for the tourist industry to embrace Carnevale as a means to stimulate business in low season. And their faith is well placed: each year over the 10- to 12-day Carnevale period (ending on the Tuesday before Ash Wednesday), more than a half-million people attend concerts, theater and street performances, masquerade balls, historical processions, fashion shows, and contests. Since 2008 Carnevale has been organized by **Venezia Marketing & Eventi** (www.carnevale.venezia. it). *A Guest in Venice* is also a complete guide to public and private Carnevale festivities. Stop by the **tourist office** (*041/2424* www.veneziaunica.it) or the Venice Pavilion for information, but be aware they can be mobbed. If you're not planning on joining in the revelry, you'd be wise to choose another time to visit Venice. Crowds throng the streets (which become one-way, with police directing foot traffic), bridges are designated "no-stopping" zones to avoid gridlock, and prices skyrocket.

Shopping

Alluring shops abound in Venice. You'll find countless vendors of such trademark wares as glass, lace, and high-end textiles. The authenticity of some goods can be suspect, but they're often pleasing to the eye, regardless of origin. You will also find interesting craft and art studios with high-quality, one-of-a-kind articles. Antiques, especially antique Venetian glass, are almost invariably cheaper outside of Venice, because Venetians are ready to pay high prices for their own heritage.

The San Marco area is full of shops and couture boutiques, such as Armani, Missoni, Valentino, Fendi, and Versace. Leading from Piazza San Marco, you'll find some of Venice's busiest shopping streets—Le Mercerie, the Frezzeria, Calle dei Fabbri, and Calle Larga XXII Marzo. Other good shopping areas surround Calle del Teatro and Campi San Salvador, Manin, San Fantin, and San Bartolomeo. You can find somewhat less expensive, more varied, and more imaginative shops between the Ponte di Rialto and San Polo and in Santa Croce, and art galleries in Dorsoduro from the Salute to the Accademia. Regular store hours are usually 9 to 12:30 and 3:30 or 4 to 7:30; some stores close Saturday afternoon or Monday morning.

Passes and Discounts

Avoid lines and hassle with the online **Venezia Unica City Pass** (www.veneziaunica.it). This all-in-one pass can be used for public transportation and entry to

museums, churches, and other attractions; you only pay for the services you wish to add. You'll receive an email with the pass, which you can show for entry at sights, though you'll still need to physically collect your transportation pass at an ACTV automatic ticket machine or ticket point located around the city.

Fifteen of Venice's most significant churches covered by the Venezia Unica City Pass are part of the **Chorus Foundation** umbrella group (*041/2750462, www.chorusvenezia.org*), which coordinates their administration, hours, and admission fees. Churches in this group are open to visitors all day except Sunday morning. Single church entry costs €3; you have a year to visit all 15 with the €12 Chorus Pass, which you can get at any participating church or online.

The Museum Pass (€35) from **Musei Civici** (*041/2405211, www.visitmuve.it/en/tickets*) includes single entry to 12 Venice city museums for six months.

Tours

Venice has a variety of tours with expert guides; just be sure to choose a guide that's authorized if you book a private tour. Some excursions also include a boat tour as a portion of a longer walking tour.

PRIVATE TOURS
A Guide in Venice
GUIDED TOURS | This popular company offers a wide variety of innovative, entertaining, and informative themed tours—including master artisan, art, and architecture tours—for groups of up to eight people. Individual tours are also available and generally last two to three hours. The guide fee is €75 per hour, which does not include admissions or transportation fees. Small group tours running May–October are also available at €62.50 per person. ☎ *0347/7876846 Sabrina Scaglianti ⊕ www.aguideinvenice.com.*

Continued on page 158

CRUISING THE GRAND CANAL

THE BEST INTRODUCTION TO VENICE IS A TRIP DOWN MAIN STREET

Venice's Grand Canal is one of the world's great thoroughfares. It winds its way from Piazzale Roma to Piazza San Marco, passing 200 palazzi built from the 13th to the 18th centuries by Venice's richest and most powerful families. There's a theatrical quality to a boat ride on the canal: it's as if each pink- or gold-tinted facade is trying to steal your attention from its rival across the way.

In medieval and Renaissance cities, wars and sieges required defense to be an element of design; but in rich, impregnable Venice, you could safely show off what you had. But more than being simply an item of conspicuous consumption, a Venetian's palazzo was an embodiment of his person—not only his wealth, but also his erudition and taste.

The easiest and cheapest way to see the Grand Canal is to take the Line 1 vaporetto (water bus) from Piazalle Roma to San Marco. The ride takes about 35 minutes. Invest in a day ticket and you can spend the better part of a day hopping on and off at the vaporetto's many stops, visiting the sights along the banks. Keep your eyes open for the highlights listed here; some have fuller descriptions later in this chapter.

FROM PIAZZALE ROMA TO RIALTO

Palazzo Labia
Tiepolo's masterpiece, the cycle of Antony and Cleopatra, graces the grand ballroom in this palazzo. The Labia family, infamous for their ostentation, commissioned the frescos to celebrate a marriage and had Tiepolo use the face of the family matriarch, Maria Labia, for that of Cleopatra. Luckily, Maria Labia was known not only for her money, but also for her intelligence and her beauty.

Santa Maria di Nazareth

Ponte di Scalzi

R. DI BIASI

Stazione Ferrovia Santa Lucia

FERROVIA

SANTA CROCE

Ponte di Calatrava

After you pass the Ferrovia, the baroque church immediately to your left is the Baroque **Santa Maria di Nazareth**, called the Chiesa degli Scalzi (Church of the Barefoot).

After passing beneath the Ponte di Scalzi, ahead to the left, where the Canale di Cannaregio meets the Grand Canal, you'll spy **Palazzo Labia**, an elaborate 18th-century palace built for the social-climbing Labia family.

Known for their ostentation even in this city where modesty was seldom a virtue, the Labias chose a location that required three facades instead of the usual one.

A bit farther down, across the canal, is the 13th-century **Fondaco dei Turchi**, an elegant residence that served as a combination commercial center and ghetto for the Turkish community. Try not to see the side towers and the crenellations; they were

added during a 19th-century restoration.

Beyond it is the obelisk-topped **Ca' Belloni-Battagia**, designed for the Belloni family by star architect Longhena. Look for the family crest he added prominently on the facade.

On the opposite bank is architect Mauro Codussi's magnificent **Palazzo Vendramin-Calergi**, designed just before 1500. Codussi ingeniously married the fortress-like Renaissance style of the Florentine Alberti's Palazzo Rucellai to the lacy delicacy of the Venetian Gothic, creating the prototype of the Venetian Renaissance palazzo. The palazzo is now Venice's casino.

Palazzo Vendramin-Calergi
Venice's first Renaissance palazzo. Immediately recognized as a masterpiece, it was so highly regarded that later, when its subsequent owners, the Calergi, were convicted of murder and their palace was to be torn down as punishment, the main building was spared.

Church of San Marcuola

HETTO

S. MARCUOLA

Ca' Belloni-Battagia

S. STAE

Fondaco dei Turchi

Depositi del Megio

San Stae Church

SAN POLO

Ca' Corner della Regina

Ca' Pesaro

CA' D'ORO

Ca' d'Oro
Inspired by stories of Nero's Domus Aurea (Golden House) in Rome, the first owner had parts of the façade gilded with 20,000 sheets of gold leaf. The gold has long worn away, but the Ca' D'Oro is still Venice's most beautiful Gothic palazzo.

Ca' da Mosto
Venice's oldest surviving palazzo gives you an idea of Marco Polo's Venice. More than any other Byzantine palazzo in town, it maintains its original 13th-century appearance.

Rialto Mercato

Pescheria
Stop by in the morning to see the incredible variety of fish for sale. Produce stalls fill the adjacent fondamenta. Butchers and cheesemongers occupy the surrounding shops.

Fondaco dei Tedeschi

Ca' dei Camerlenghi

RIALTO

SAN MARCO

The whimsically Baroque church of **San Stae** on the right bank is distinguished by a host of marble saints on its facade.

Farther along the bank is one of Longhena's Baroque masterpieces, **Ca' Pesaro**. It is now the Museum of Modern Art.

Next up on the left is **Ca' d'Oro** (1421-1438), the canal's most spendid example of Venetian Gothic domestic design. Across from this palazzo is the loggia of the neo-Gothic **pescheria**, Venice's fish market.

Slightly farther down, on the bank opposite from the vegetable market, is the early 13th-century **Ca' da Mosto**, the oldest building on the Grand Canal. The upper two floors are later additions, but the ground floor and piano nobile give you a good idea of a rich merchant's house during the time of Marco Polo.

As you approach the Rialto Bridge, to the left, just before the bridge, is the

Fondaco dei Tedeschi. German merchants kept warehouses, offices, and residences here; its facade was originally frescoed by Titian and Giorgione.

FROM RIALTO TO THE PONTE DELL' ACCADEMIA

SAN POLO

Ponte di Rialto

RIAL

Ca' Foscari
The canal's most imposing Gothic masterpiece, Ca' Foscari was built to blot out the memory of a traitor to the Republic.

Palazzo Barzizza

Ca' Loredan

S. SILVESTRO

Ca' Farsetti

Palazzo Pisani Moretta

Ca' Grimani

TOMA

S. ANGELO

Ca' Garzoni

Ca' Balbi

Palazzo Grassi

Ca' Rezzonico

REZZONICO

SAN MARCO

ACCADEMIA

Gallerie dell'Accademia

DORSODURO

The shop-lined **Ponte di Rialto** was built in stone after former wooden bridges had burned or collapsed. As you pass under the bridge, on your left stands star architect Sansovino's Palazzo Dolfin Manin. The white stone–clad Renaissance palace was built at huge expense and over the objections of its conservative neighbors.

A bit farther down stand **Ca' Loredan** and **Ca' Farsetti**, 13th-century Byzantine palaces that today make up Venice's city hall.

Along the same side is the **Ca' Grimani**, by the Veronese architect Sanmichele. Legend has it that the palazzo's oversized windows were demanded by the young Grimani's fiancée, who insisted that he build her a palazzo on the Canale Grande with windows larger than the portal of her own house.

At the Sant'Angelo landing, the vaporetto passes close to Codussi's **Ca' Corner-Spinelli**. Back on the right bank, in a lovely salmon color, is the graceful **Palazzo Pisani Moretta**, built in the mid-15th century and typical of the Venetian Gothic palazzo of the generation after the Ca' D'Oro.

A bit farther down the right bank, crowned by obelisks, is **Ca' Balbi**. Niccolò Balbi built this elegant palazzo in order to upstage his former landlord, who had insulted him in public.

Farther down the right bank, where the Canale makes a sharp turn, is the imposing **Ca' Foscari**. Doge Francesco Foscari tore down an earlier palazzo on this spot and built this splendid palazzo to erase memory of the traitorous former owner. It is now the seat of the University of Venice.

Continuing down the right bank you'll find Longhena's **Ca' Rezzonico**, a magnificent baroque palace. Opposite stands the Grand Canal's youngest palace, Giorgio Massari's **Palazzo Grassi**, commissioned in 1749. It houses part of the François Pinot contemporary art collection.

Near the canal's fourth bridge, is the former church and monastery complex that houses the world-renowned **Gallerie dell'Accademia**, the world's largest and most distinguished collection of Venetian art.

ARCHITECTURAL STYLES ALONG THE GRAND CANAL

BYZANTINE: 13th century
Distinguishing characteristics: high, rounded arches, relief panels, multicolored marble.
Examples: Fondaco dei Turchi, Ca' Loredan, Ca' Farsetti, Ca' da Mosto

GOTHIC: 14th and 15th centuries
Distinguishing characteristics: pointed arches, high ceilings, and many windows.
Examples: Ca' d'Oro, Ca' Foscari, Palazzo Pisani Moretta, Ca' Barbaro (and, off the canal, Palazzo Ducale)

RENAISSANCE: 16th century
Distinguishing characteristics: classically influenced emphasis on harmony and motifs taken from classical antiquity.

Examples: Palazzo Vendramin-Calergi, Ca' Grimani, Ca' Corner-Spinelli, Ca' dei Camerlenghi, Ca' Balbi, Palazzo Corner della Ca' Granda, Palazzo Dolfin Manin, and, off the canal, Libreria, Sansoviniana on Piazza San Marco

BAROQUE: 17th century
Distinguishing characteristics: Renaissance order wedded with a more dynamic style, achieved through curving lines and complex decoration.

Examples: churches of Santa Maria di Nazareth, San Stae, and Santa Maris della Salute; Ca' Belloni Battaglia, Ca' Pesaro, Ca' Rezzonico

FROM THE PONTE DELL'ACCADEMIA TO SAN ZACCARIA

Ca' Barbaro
John Singer Sargent, Henry James, and Cole Porter are among the guests who have stayed at Ca' Barbaro. It was a center for elegant British and American society during the turn of the 20th century.

Santa Maria Della Salute
Baldessare Longhena was only 26 when he designed this church, which was to become one of Venice's major landmark. Its rotunda form and dynamic Baroque decoration predate iconic Baroque churches in other Italian cities.

Ponte dell' Accademia

SAN MARCO

Ca' Pisani-Gritti

Palazzo Corner della Ca' Granda

ACCADEMIA

Casetta Rossa

S. M. DEL GIGLIO

DORSODURO

SALUTE

Ca' Barbarigo

Palazzo Salviati

S. Maria della Salute

Palazzo Venier dei Leoni
Eccentric art dealer Peggy Guggenheim's personal collection of modern art is here. At the Grand Canal entrance to the palazzo stands Marino Marini's sexually explicit equestrian sculpture, the Angel of the Citadel. Numerous entertaining stories have been spun around the statue and Ms. Guggenheim's overtly libertine ways.

Ca' Dario
Graceful and elegant Ca' Dario is reputed to carry a curse. Almost all its owners since the 15th century have met violent deaths or committed suicide. It was, nevertheless, a center for elegant French society at the turn of the 20th century.

Down from the Accademia bridge, on the left bank next door to the fake Gothic Ca' Franchetti, is the beautiful **Ca' Barbaro**, designed by Giovanni Bon, who was also at work about that time on the Ca' D'Oro.

Farther along on the left bank Sansovino's first work in Venice, the **Palazzo Corner della Ca' Granda**, begun in 1533, still shows the influence of his Roman Renaissance contemporaries, Bramante and Giulio Romano. It faces the uncompleted **Palazzo Venier dei Leoni**, which holds the Peggy Guggenheim Collection, a good

cross-section of the visual arts from 1940 to 1960.

Ca' Dario a bit farther down, was originally a Gothic palazzo, but in 1487 it was given an early Renaissance multi-colored marble facade.

At this point on the canal the cupola of **Santa Maria della Salute** dominates the scene. The commission for the design of the church to celebrate the Virgin's

rescuing Venice from the disastrous plague of 1630, was given to the 26-year-old Longhena. The young architect stressed the new and inventive aspects of his design, likening the rotunda shape to a crown for the Virgin.

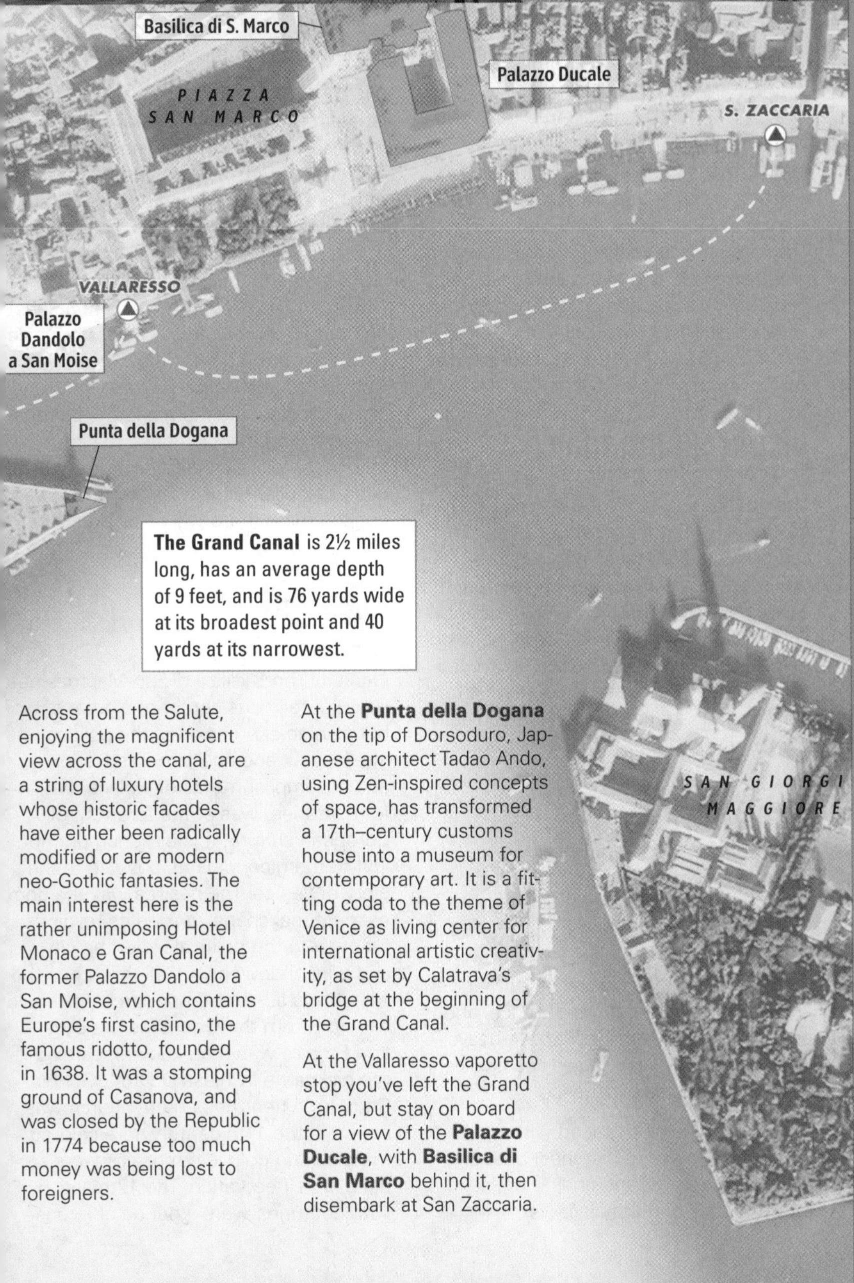

Basilica di S. Marco

Palazzo Ducale

PIAZZA SAN MARCO

S. ZACCARIA

VALLARESSO

Palazzo Dandolo a San Moise

Punta della Dogana

SAN GIORGIO MAGGIORE

The Grand Canal is 2½ miles long, has an average depth of 9 feet, and is 76 yards wide at its broadest point and 40 yards at its narrowest.

Across from the Salute, enjoying the magnificent view across the canal, are a string of luxury hotels whose historic facades have either been radically modified or are modern neo-Gothic fantasies. The main interest here is the rather unimposing Hotel Monaco e Gran Canal, the former Palazzo Dandolo a San Moise, which contains Europe's first casino, the famous ridotto, founded in 1638. It was a stomping ground of Casanova, and was closed by the Republic in 1774 because too much money was being lost to foreigners.

At the **Punta della Dogana** on the tip of Dorsoduro, Japanese architect Tadao Ando, using Zen-inspired concepts of space, has transformed a 17th–century customs house into a museum for contemporary art. It is a fitting coda to the theme of Venice as living center for international artistic creativity, as set by Calatrava's bridge at the beginning of the Grand Canal.

At the Vallaresso vaporetto stop you've left the Grand Canal, but stay on board for a view of the **Palazzo Ducale**, with **Basilica di San Marco** behind it, then disembark at San Zaccaria.

See Venice

GUIDED TOURS | Luisella Romeo is a delightful guide capable of bringing to life even the most convoluted aspects of Venice's art and history. She can customize tours depending on guests' areas of interest, including Murano and glass art, music in Venice, and photography tours. ☎ *0349/0848303* ⊕ *www.seevenice.it.*

Walks Inside Venice

GUIDED TOURS | For a host of particularly creative group and private tours—from history to art to gastronomy—check out Walks Inside Venice. The maximum group size is 6, and tour guides include people with advanced university degrees and published authors. ☎ *041/5241706, 041/2750687* ⊕ *www.walksinsidevenice. com.*

Visitor Information

The multilingual staff of the **Venice tourism office** (041/2424, www.veneziaunica.it) can provide directions and up-to-the-minute information. Branches can be found at Marco Polo Airport; the Venezia Santa Lucia train station; Garage Comunale, on Piazzale Roma; and at Piazza San Marco near Museo Correr at the southwest corner. The train station branch is open daily 7–9; other branches have similar hours.

San Marco

Extending from Piazza San Marco (St. Mark's Square) to the Ponte di Rialto, this sestiere is the historical and commercial heart of Venice. Restaurants in its eponymous square—the only one in Venice given full stature as a "piazza" and, hence, often referred to simply as "the Piazza"—heave with tourists, but enjoying an aperitivo here is an unforgettable experience.

This sestiere is also graced with some of Venice's loveliest churches, best-endowed museums, and finest hotels (often with Grand Canal views). In addition, it's the city's main shopping district. Some of the famous Venetian glass producers from Murano have boutiques in San Marco, as do many Italian designers. Its mazes of streets are also lined with shops that sell elegantly wrought jewelry among other items.

TIMING

You can easily spend several days seeing the historical and artistic monuments in and around Piazza San Marco alone, but at a bare minimum, plan on at least an hour for the basilica and its wonderful mosaics. Add on another half hour if you want to see its Pala d'Oro, Galleria, and Museo di San Marco. You'll want at least an hour to appreciate the Palazzo Ducale. Leave another hour for the Museo Correr, through which you also enter the archaeological museum and the Libreria Sansoviniana. If you choose to simply take in the piazza itself from a café table at an establishment with an orchestra, keep in mind there will be an additional charge for the music.

 Sights

★ **Basilica di San Marco**

CHURCH | The Basilica di San Marco is not only the religious center of a great city, but also an expression of the political, intellectual, and economic aspiration and accomplishments of a place that, for centuries, was at the forefront of European culture. It is a monument not just to the glory of God, but also to the glory of Venice. The basilica was the doges' personal chapel, linking its religious function to the political life of the city, and was endowed with all the riches the Republic's admirals and merchants could carry off from the Orient (as the Byzantine Empire was then known), earning it the nickname "Chiesa D'Oro," (Golden Church). When the present church was begun in the 11th century, rare colored marbles and gold leaf mosaics were used in its decoration. The 12th and 13th centuries were a period of intense military expansion, and by the early 13th century, the facades began to bear testimony to Venice's conquests, including gilt-bronze ancient Roman horses taken from Constantinople in 1204. The low lighting, the single massive Byzantine chandelier, the giant iconostasis (altar screen), the matroneum (women's gallery) high above the naves—even the Greek-cross ground plan—give San Marco an exotic aspect quite unlike that of most Western Christian churches. The effect is remarkable. Here the pomp and mystery of Oriental magnificence are wedded to Christian belief, creating an intensely awesome impression. The glory of the basilica is, of course, its medieval mosaic work; about 30% of the mosaics survive in something close to their original form. The earliest date from the late 12th century, but the great majority date from the 13th century. The taking of Constantinople in 1204 was a deciding moment for the mosaic decoration of the basilica. Large amounts of mosaic material were brought in, and a Venetian school of mosaic decoration began to develop. Moreover, a 4th- or 5th-century treasure—the Cotton Genesis, the earliest illustrated Bible—was brought from Constantinople and supplied the designs for the exquisite mosaics of the Creation and the stories of Abraham, Joseph, and Moses that adorn the narthex (entrance hall). They are among the most beautiful and best preserved in all the basilica. In the Sanctuary, the main altar is built over the tomb of St. Mark, its green marble canopy lifted high on 6th-century carved alabaster columns—again, pillaged art. The Pala d'Oro, a dazzling gilt-silver, gem-encrusted screen containing 255 enameled panels, was commissioned in 976 in Constantinople by the Venetian doge Pietro I Orseolo and enlarged over the subsequent four centuries. Remember that this is a sacred place: guards may deny admission to people in shorts, sleeveless dresses, and tank tops. ✉ *Piazza San Marco, San Marco 328, San Marco* ☎ *041/2708311* ⊕ *www.basilicasanmarco.it* ✉ *Basilica €3, treasury €3, sanctuary and Pala d'Oro €5, museum €7* Ⓜ *Vallaresso/San Zaccaria.*

Campanile

VIEWPOINT | Construction of Venice's famous brick bell tower (325 feet tall, plus the angel) began in the 9th century; it took on its present form in 1514. During the 15th century, the tower was used as a place of punishment: immoral clerics were suspended in wooden cages from the tower, some forced to subsist on bread and water for as long as a year; others were left to starve. In 1902, the tower unexpectedly collapsed, taking with it Jacopo Sansovino's marble loggia (1537–49) at its base. The largest original bell, called the Marangona, survived. The crushed loggia was promptly reconstructed, and the new tower, rebuilt to the old plan, reopened in 1912. Today, on a clear day the stunning view includes the Lido, the lagoon, and the mainland as far as the Alps, but strangely enough, none of the myriad canals that snake through the city. ✉ *Piazza San Marco* ☎ *041/2708311* ⊕ *www.basilicasanmarco.it* ✉ *€10* Ⓜ *Vaporetto: Vallaresso, San Zaccaria.*

★ Museo Correr

HISTORY MUSEUM | This museum of Venetian art and history contains an important sculpture collection by Antonio Canova and important paintings by Giovanni Bellini, Vittore Carpaccio (Carpaccio's famous painting of the Venetian courtesans is here), and other major local painters. There are nine sumptuously decorated Imperial Rooms, where the Empress of Austria once stayed, and several rooms convey the city's proud naval history through highly descriptive paintings and numerous maritime objects, including ships' cannons and some surprisingly large iron mast-top navigation lights. The museum also houses curiosities like the absurdly high-soled shoes worn by 16th-century Venetian ladies (who walked with the aid of a servant) and has

4

Venice SAN MARCO

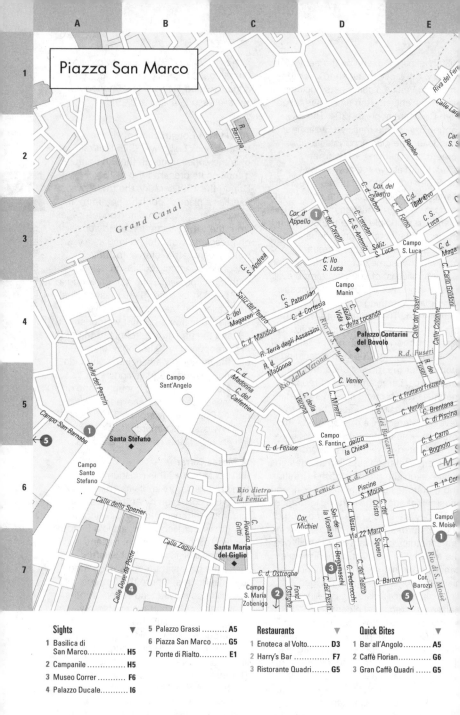

Piazza San Marco

Sights ▼

1 Basilica di
   San Marco **H5**
2 Campanile **H5**
3 Museo Correr **F6**
4 Palazzo Ducale **I6**
5 Palazzo Grassi **A5**
6 Piazza San Marco **G5**
7 Ponte di Rialto **E1**

Restaurants ▼

1 Enoteca al Volto **D3**
2 Harry's Bar **F7**
3 Ristorante Quadri **G5**

Quick Bites ▼

1 Bar all'Angolo **A5**
2 Caffè Florian **G6**
3 Gran Caffè Quadri **G5**

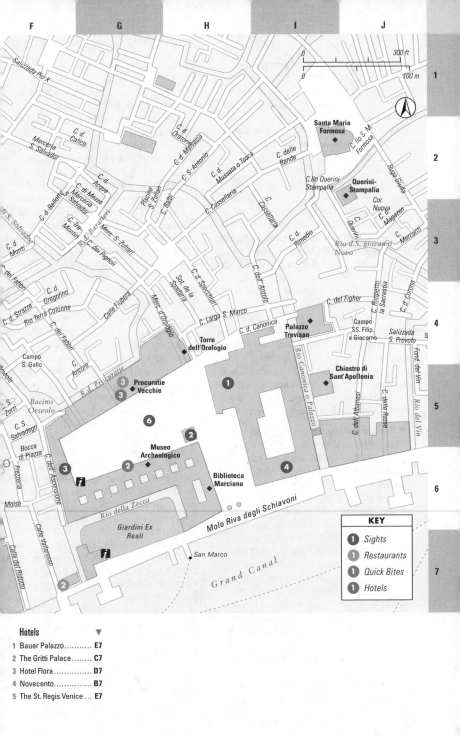

Hotels ▼

a significant collection of antique gems. It's also the main repository of Venetian drawings and prints, which, unfortunately, can be seen only by special arrangement, or during special exhibitions. The Correr exhibition rooms lead directly into the **Museo Archeologico**, which houses the Grimani collection—an important 16th- and 17th-century collection of Greek and Roman art, still impressive even after the transfer of many objects to Paris and Vienna during the Napoleonic and Austrian occupations—and the Stanza del Sansovino, the only part of the **Biblioteca Nazionale Marciana** open to visitors. ☒ *Piazza San Marco, Ala Napoleonica, opposite basilica, Piazza San Marco* ☏ *041/2405211* ⊕ *correr.visitmuve.it* ☞ *The tour is currently limited to the first floor only, including the Procuratie Nuove and Imperial Apartments.* 🎟 *Museums of San Marco Pass €25, includes Museo Correr, Museo Archeologico, Biblioteca Nazionale Marciana, and Palazzo Ducale. Museum Pass €36, includes all four museums plus eight civic museums* Ⓜ *Vaporetto: Vallaresso, San Zaccaria.*

★ **Palazzo Ducale** (*Doge's Palace*)
HISTORY MUSEUM | Rising grandly above the Piazzetta San Marco, this Gothic fantasia of pink-and-white marble is a majestic expression of Venetian prosperity and power. Although the site was the doges' residence from the 10th century, the building began to take its present form around 1340; what you see now is essentially a product of the first half of the 15th century. It served not only as a residence, but also as the central administrative center of the Venetian Republic. Unlike other medieval seats of authority, the Palazzo Ducale is free of any military defenses—a sign of the Republic's self-confidence. The position of the loggias below instead of above the retaining wall, and the use of pink marble to emphasize the decorative function of that wall, gave the palazzo a light and airy aspect, one that could impress visitors—and even intimidate them,

through opulence and grace rather than fortresslike bulk. You'll find yourself in an immense courtyard that holds some of the first evidence of Renaissance architecture in Venice, such as Antonio Rizzo's Scala dei Giganti (Stairway of the Giants), erected between 1483 and 1491, directly ahead, guarded by Sansovino's huge statues of Mars and Neptune, added in 1567. Though ordinary mortals must use the central interior staircase, its upper flight is the lavishly gilded Scala d'Oro (Golden Staircase), also designed by Sansovino, in 1555. The palace's sumptuous chambers have walls and ceilings covered with works by Venice's greatest artists. Visit the Anticollegio, a waiting room outside the Collegio's chamber, where you can see the *Rape of Europa* by Veronese and Tintoretto's *Bacchus, Ariadne,* and *Venus.* The ceiling of the Sala del Senato (Senate Chamber), featuring *The Triumph of Venice* by Tintoretto, is magnificent, but it's dwarfed by his masterpiece, *Paradise,* in the Sala del Maggiore Consiglio (Great Council Hall). A vast work commissioned for a vast hall, this dark, dynamic piece is the world's largest oil painting (23 feet by 75 feet). The room's carved gilt ceiling is breathtaking, especially with Veronese's majestic *Apotheosis of Venice* filling one of the center panels. A narrow canal separates the palace's east side from the cramped cell blocks of the Prigioni Nuove (New Prisons). High above the water arches the enclosed marble Ponte dei Sospiri (Bridge of Sighs), which earned its name in the 19th century, from Lord Byron's *Childe Harold's Pilgrimage.* Reserve your spot for the palazzo's popular Secret Itineraries tour well in advance. You'll visit the doge's private apartments, through hidden passageways to the interrogation (torture) chambers, and into the rooftop *piombi* (lead) prison, named for its lead roofing. Venetian-born writer and libertine Giacomo Casanova (1725–98), along with an accomplice, managed to escape from the piombi in 1756; they were the only men ever to do so.

Let's Get Lost

Getting around Venice presents some unusual problems: the city's layout has few straight lines; house numbering seems nonsensical; and the six sestieri of San Marco, Cannaregio, Castello, Dorsoduro, Santa Croce, and San Polo all duplicate each other's street names. What's more, addresses in Venice are given by sestiere rather than street, making them of limited help in getting around. Venetians commonly give directions by pinpointing a major landmark, such as a church, and telling you where to go from there.

The numerous vaporetto lines can be bewildering, too, and often the only option for getting where you want to go is to walk. Yellow signs, posted on many busy corners, point toward the major landmarks—San Marco, Rialto, Accademia, and so forth—but don't count on finding such markers once you're deep into residential neighborhoods. Even buying a good map at a newsstand—the kind showing all street names and vaporetto routes—won't necessarily keep you from getting lost. To make matters worse, map apps on smart phones, for some reason, give frequently erroneous results for Venice.

Fortunately, as long as you maintain your patience, getting lost in Venice can be a pleasure. For one thing, being lost is a sign that you've escaped the tourist throngs. And although you might not find the Titian masterpiece you'd set out to see, you could wind up coming across an ageless *bacaro* (a traditional wine bar) or a quirky shop that turns out to be the highlight of your afternoon. Opportunities for such serendipity abound. Keep in mind that the city is self-contained: sooner or later, perhaps with the help of a patient native, you can rest assured you'll regain your bearings.

4

Venice SAN MARCO

✉ *Piazzetta San Marco, Piazza San Marco* ☎ *041/42730892 tickets, 848/082000 outside Italy* ⊕ *palazzoducale.visitmuve. it* 🎟 *Museums of San Marco Pass €25, includes Palazzo Ducale, Museo Correr, Museo Archeologico, and Biblioteca Nazionale Marciana. Museum Pass €36, includes all four museums plus eight civic museums. Secret Itineraries tour €29* Ⓜ *Vaporetto: San Zaccaria, Vallaresso.*

Palazzo Grassi

ART MUSEUM | Built between 1748 and 1772 by Giorgio Massari for a Bolognese family, this palace is one of the last of the great noble residences on the Grand Canal. Once owned by auto magnate Gianni Agnelli, it was bought by French businessman François Pinault in 2005 to showcase his highly esteemed collection of modern and contemporary art (which has now grown so large that Pinault rented the Punta della Dogana, at the entryway to the Grand Canal, for his newest acquisitions). Pinault brought in Japanese architect Tadao Ando to remodel the Grassi's interior. Check online for a schedule of temporary art exhibitions. ✉ *Campo San Samuele 3231, San Marco* ☎ *041/2001057* ⊕ *www.palazzograssi.it* 🎟 *€15* Ⓜ *Vaporetto: Sant'Angelo (Line 1).*

★ Piazza San Marco

PLAZA/SQUARE | FAMILY | One of the world's most beautiful squares, Piazza San Marco (St. Mark's Square) is the spiritual and artistic heart of Venice, a vast open space bordered by an orderly procession of arcades marching toward the fairy-tale cupolas and marble lacework of the Basilica di San Marco. From midmorning on, it is generally packed with tourists. (If Venetians have business in the piazza, they try to conduct it in the early morning, before the crowds swell.) At night the piazza can be magical, especially in winter, when mists swirl around the lampposts and the campanile. Facing the basilica, on your left, the long, arcaded building is the Procuratie Vecchie, renovated to its present form in 1514 as offices and residences for the powerful procurators, or magistrates. On your right is the Procuratie Nuove, built half a century later in a more imposing, classical style. It was originally planned by Venice's great Renaissance architect Jacopo Sansovino (1486–1570), to carry on the look of his Libreria Sansoviniana (Sansovinian Library), but he died before construction on the Nuove had begun. Vincenzo Scamozzi (circa 1552–1616), a pupil of Andrea Palladio (1508–80), completed the design and construction. Still later, the Procuratie Nuove was modified by architect Baldassare Longhena (1598–1682), one of Venice's Baroque masters. When Napoléon (1769–1821) entered Venice with his troops in 1797, he expressed his admiration for the piazza and promptly gave orders to alter it. His architects demolished a church with a Sansovino facade in order to build the Ala Napoleonica (Napoleonic Wing), or Fabbrica Nuova (New Building), which linked the two 16th-century procuratie and effectively enclosed the piazza. Piazzetta San Marco is the "little square" leading from Piazza San Marco to the waters of Bacino San Marco (St. Mark's Basin); its *molo* (landing) once served as the grand entrance to the Republic. Two imposing columns tower above the waterfront. One is topped by the winged lion, a traditional emblem of St. Mark that became the symbol of Venice itself; the other supports St. Theodore, the city's

first patron, along with his dragon. (A third column fell off its barge and ended up in the bacino before it could be placed alongside the others.) Although the columns are a glorious vision today, the Republic traditionally executed convicts here—and some superstitious Venetians still avoid walking between them. ⊠ *San Marco* Ⓜ *Vaporetto: Calle Valaresso, Giardinetti, or San Zaccaria*

★ **Ponte di Rialto** (*Rialto Bridge*)
BRIDGE | FAMILY | The competition to design a stone bridge across the Grand Canal attracted the best architects of the late 16th century, including Michelangelo, Palladio, and Sansovino, but the job went to the less famous (if appropriately named) Antonio da Ponte (1512–95). His pragmatic design, completed in 1591, featured shop space and was high enough for galleys to pass beneath. Putting practicality and economy over aesthetic considerations—unlike the classical plans proposed by his more famous contemporaries—da Ponte's bridge essentially followed the design of its wooden predecessor. But it kept decoration and cost to a minimum at a time when the Republic's coffers were low, due to continual wars against the Turks and competition brought about by the Spanish and Portuguese opening of oceanic trade routes. Along the railing you'll enjoy one of the city's most famous views: the Grand Canal vibrant with boat traffic. ⊠ *San Marco* Ⓜ *Vaporetto: Rialto.*

🍴 Restaurants

Enoteca al Volto
$$ | VENETIAN | A short walk from the Ponte di Rialto, this bar has been around since 1936, and the satisfying cicheti and primi have a lot to do with its staying power. Grab one of the tables out front, or take refuge in two small, dark rooms with a ceiling plastered with wine labels

hat provide a classic backdrop for simple fare, including a delicious risotto that is served daily from noon, plus a solid wine list of both Italian and foreign vintages. **Known for:** fantastic main courses, including risotto and pasta with seafood; great local and international wine selection; tasty and inexpensive cicheti. $ *Average main: €17* ⊠ *Calle Cavalli, San Marco 4081, San Marco* ☎ *041/5228945* ⊕ *enotecaalvolto.com* Ⓜ *Vaporetto: Rialto.*

★ Harry's Bar

$$$$ | **VENETIAN** | For those who can afford t, lunch or dinner at Harry's Bar is as much a part of a visit to Venice as a walk across the Piazza San Marco or a vaporetto ride down the Grand Canal. Inside, the suave, subdued beige-on-white decor is unchanged from the 1930s, and the classic Venetian fare is carefully and excellently prepared. **Known for:** signature crepes flambées and famous Cipriani chocolate cake; being the birthplace of the Bellini cocktail; see-and-be-seen atmosphere. $ *Average main: €58* ⊠ *Calle Vallaresso, San Marco 1323, San Marco* ☎ *041/5285777* ⊕ *www.cipriani. com* 🍴 *Jacket required* Ⓜ *Vaporetto: San Marco (Calle Vallaresso).*

★ Ristorante Quadri

$$$$ | **VENETIAN** | Although the lavish interior has been updated by designer Philippe Starck, this restaurant above the famed café of the same name is still steeped in Venetian ambience and history (it was where Turkish coffee was introduced to the city in the 1700s). When the Alajmo family (of the celebrated Le Calandre near Padua) took over, they put their accomplished sous-chef from Padua in charge of the kitchen, resulting in the addition of dishes—best sampled with a tasting menu—that are complex and sophisticated, with a wonderful wine list to match. **Known for:** revitalized designer decor; seasonal tasting menus; sophisticated and modern Italian cuisine. $ *Average main: €60* ⊠ *Piazza San Marco 121, San Marco* ☎ *041/5222105* ⊕ *alajmo.it*

⊗ *Closed Mon. and Tues. No lunch Wed.– Fri.* Ⓜ *Vaporetto: San Marco.*

☕ Coffee and Quick Bites

Bar all'Angolo

$ | **CAFÉ** | This corner of Campo Santo Stefano is a pleasant place to sit and watch the Venetian world go by. The café staff are in constant motion, so you'll receive your coffee, spritz, panino, or *tramezzino* (sandwich on untoasted white bread, usually with a mayonnaise-based filling) in short order; consume it at your leisure at one of the outdoor tables, at the bar, or at the tables in the back. **Known for:** good people-watching; simple yet satisfying fare, like tramezzini and panini; tasty homemade desserts, including tiramisu and cakes. $ *Average main: €10* ⊠ *Campo Santo Stefano, San Marco 3464, just in front of Santo Stefano church, San Marco* ☎ *041/5220710* ⊗ *Closed Sun. and Jan.* Ⓜ *Vaporetto: Sant'Angelo.*

★ Caffè Florian

$$ | **CAFÉ** | Florian is not only Italy's first café (1720), but also one of its most beautiful, with glittering, neo-Baroque decor and 19th-century wall panels depicting Venetian heroes. The coffee, drinks, and snacks are good, but most people—including Venetians from time to time—come for the atmosphere and history: this was the only café to serve women during the 18th century (hence Casanova's patronage); it was frequented by artistic notables like Wagner, Goethe, Goldoni, Lord Byron, Marcel Proust, and Charles Dickens; and it was the birthplace of the international art exhibition that became the Venice Biennale. **Known for:** hot chocolate, coffee, and quick nibbles; prime location on St. Mark's Square; beautiful, historic interior. $ *Average main: €16* ⊠ *Piazza San Marco, San Marco 56, San Marco* ☎ *041/5205641* ⊕ *www.caffeflorian.com* ⊗ *Closed early Jan.* Ⓜ *Vaporetto: San Marco.*

★ Gran Caffè Quadri

$$ | **CAFÉ** | Come for breakfast, a pre-dinner aperitivo, or anything in between at this always lively historic coffee-house—opened in 1775 and taken over by the famous culinary Alajmo family in 2011—in the center of the action on Piazza San Marco. Choose from a wide selection of pastries at breakfast (though the cappuccino and brioche combo is always a classic), pizzas at lunch, and *tramezzini* all day long, including one with lobster. **Known for:** prime people-watching; extensive (though pricey) aperitivo; celebrity owners. $ *Average main: €17* ⊠ *Piazza San Marco, San Marco 121, San Marco* ☏ *041/5222105* ⊕ *www.alajmo.it* Ⓜ *Vaporetto: San Marco.*

 Hotels

Bauer Palazzo

$$$$ | **HOTEL** | This palazzo with an ornate 1930s neo-Gothic facade facing the Grand Canal has large (by Venetian standards), lavishly decorated guest rooms with high ceilings, tufted walls of Bevilacqua and Rubelli fabrics, Murano glass, marble bathrooms, damask drapes, and reproduction antique furniture. **Pros:** pampering service; Venice's highest rooftop terrace; high-end luxury. **Cons:** decor could be a bit dark and old-fashioned for some; furnishings are, as is the facade, an imitation; no spa on-site. $ *Rooms from: €406* ⊠ *Campo San Moisè, San Marco 1413/D, San Marco* ☏ *041/5207022* ⊕ *www.bauervenezia. com* ⍥ *No Meals* ⤳ *191 rooms* Ⓜ *Vaporetto: Vallaresso.*

★ The Gritti Palace

$$$$ | **HOTEL** | With handblown chandeliers, sumptuous textiles, and sweeping canal views, this grande dame (whose history dates from 1525, when it was built as the residence of the prominent Gritti family) represents aristocratic Venetian living at its best. **Pros:** classic Venetian experience; truly historical property; Grand Canal location. **Cons:** food served at the hotel gets mixed reviews; major

splurge; few spa amenities. $ *Rooms from: €1000* ⊠ *Campo Santa Maria del Giglio, San Marco 2467, San Marco* ☏ *041/794611* ⊕ *www.thegrittipalace. com* ⤳ *82 rooms* ⍥ *No Meals* Ⓜ *Vaporetto: Santa Maria del Giglio.*

Hotel Flora

$$ | **HOTEL** | The elegant and refined facade announces a charming, and reasonably priced, place to stay; the hospitable staff, the tastefully decorated rooms, and the lovely garden, where guests can breakfast or drink, do not disappoint. **Pros:** central location; excellent breakfast; peaceful hidden garden. **Cons:** old-fashioned lobby doesn't invite hanging out; no water views; some rooms can be on the small side. $ *Rooms from: €160* ⊠ *Calle Bergamaschi, San Marco 2283/A, just off Calle Larga XXII Marzo, San Marco* ☏ *041/5205844* ⊕ *www.hotelflora.it* ⤳ *40 rooms* ⍥ *Free Breakfast* Ⓜ *Vaporetto: San Marco (Vallaresso).*

★ Novecento

$$ | **HOTEL** | A stylish yet intimate retreat tucked away on a quiet calle midway between Piazza San Marco and the Accademia Bridge offers exquisite rooms tastefully decorated with original furnishings and tapestries from the Mediterranean and Far East. **Pros:** complimentary afternoon tea; unique design sensibility; intimate, romantic atmosphere. **Cons:** most rooms only have showers, not tubs; some rooms can be noisy; no elevator. $ *Rooms from: €170* ⊠ *Calle del Dose, San Marco 2683/84, off Campo San Maurizio, San Marco* ☏ *041/2413765* ⊕ *www. novecento.biz* ⤳ *9 rooms* ⍥ *Free Breakfast* Ⓜ *Vaporetto: Santa Maria del Giglio.*

★ The St. Regis Venice

$$$$ | **HOTEL** | Whimsical design details evoking the Venetian landscape abound in this elegant, contemporary hotel (the former Westin Europa & Regina) constructed from five historic palazzi with phenomenal views onto the Grand Canal. **Pros:** terraces with unbeatable views; St. Regis butler service for all guests;

vonderful central location. **Cons:** few spa amenities (no pool or saunas); standard ooms on the small side; sleek modern style not for fans of Venetian opulence. *$ Rooms from: €627 ✉ San Marco 2159, San Marco ☎ 041/2400001 🌐 www.marriott.com/hotels/travel/vcexr-the-st-regis-venice 🍽 Free Breakfast 🛏 169 rooms* Ⓜ *Vaporetto: Vallaresso.*

Nightlife

B Bar Lounge

BARS | This gold mosaic-lined bar in the Bauer Venezia hosts live jazz bands Wednesday to Sunday nights, plus a ate-night DJ on Friday and Saturday. *✉ Bauer Palazzo, Campo San Moisè, San Marco 1459, San Marco ☎ 041/5207022 🌐 www.bbarvenezia.com* Ⓜ *Vaporetto: Vallaresso.*

Bacaro Jazz

BARS | This Venetian-style dive bar has strong cocktails, a jazz soundtrack, and hundreds of bras hanging from the ceiling. The lively daily happy hour is a great time to visit. *✉ San Marco 5546, San Marco ☎ 041/5285249 🌐 bacarojazz.it* Ⓜ *Vaporetto: Rialto.*

★ Bar Longhi

BARS | The Gritti Palace is home to one of the most exclusive watering holes in town (though thankfully open to the public), lined with 18th-century paintings and Murano chandeliers. You can also enjoy your cocktail on the patio with prime views onto the Grand Canal. *✉ The Gritti Palace, Campo Santa Maria del Giglio, San Marco 2467, San Marco ☎ 041/794611 🌐 www.thegrittipalace.com* Ⓜ *Vaporetto: Giglio.*

Shopping

Arnoldo/Battois

WOMEN'S CLOTHING | Venetian designers Silvano Arnoldo and Massimiliano Battois create beautifully crafted handbags, accessories, and women's clothing in rich colors using luxurious materials. There's a second store in San Marco at Calle dei Fuseri. *✉ Campo San Maurizio, San Marco 2671, San Marco ☎ 0348/4123797 🌐 www.arnoldoebattois.com* Ⓜ *Vaporetto: Giglio.*

★ Atelier Segalin di Daniela Ghezzo

SHOES | This artist turned master shoemaker produces one-of-a-kind creations from exotic leathers. Though the shoes start at €650 and usually take at least six weeks to finish, you'll truly feel like you're wearing a masterpiece. *✉ Calle dei Fuseri, San Marco 4365, San Marco ☎ 041/5222115 🌐 www.danielaghezzo.it* Ⓜ *Vaporetto: Rialto.*

★ Bevilacqua

FABRICS | This renowned studio has kept the weaving tradition alive in Venice since 1875, using 18th-century hand looms for its most precious creations. Its repertoire of 3,500 different patterns and designs yields a ready-to-sell selection of hundreds of brocades, Gobelins, damasks, velvets, taffetas, and satins. You'll also find tapestry, cushions, and braiding. Fabrics made by this prestigious firm have been used to decorate the Vatican, the Royal Palace of Stockholm, and the White House. There is another location behind the San Marco Basilica. If you're interested in seeing the actual 18th-century looms in action making the most precious fabrics, request an appointment at the Luigi Bevilacqua production center in Santa Croce. *✉ Campo di Santa Maria del Giglio, San Marco 2520, San Marco ☎ 041/2410662 main retail outlet, 041/5287581 retail outlet behind Basilica, 041/721566 Santa Croce production center 🌐 www.bevilacquatessuti.com* Ⓜ *Vaporetto: Giglio.*

★ Dittura Massimo

SHOES | Run by a second-generation shoemaker, this shop is one of the only places left in the city still producing Venice's iconic *friulane* slippers, invented in the 19th century and handstitched from velvet and rubber. The shoes are still worn by gondoliers today. ⊠ *Calle Fiubera, San Marco 943, San Marco* ☏ *041/5231163* ⊕ *ditturamassimo.it* Ⓜ *Vaporetto: San Marco.*

Fondaco dei Tedeschi

HATS & GLOVES | This 15th-century Renaissance commercial center served as Venice's main post office for many years, but was remodeled and returned to its historical roots as a luxury department store. Here you can find a large assortment of high-end jewelry, clothing, and other luxury items, plus fabulous views from the rooftop terrace; book online for a free 15-minute visit. ⊠ *Calle Fondaco dei Tedeschi, near San Marco end of Ponte di Rialto, San Marco* ☏ *041/3142000* ⊕ *www.dfs.com/en/venice/stores/t-fondaco-dei-tedeschi-by-dfs* Ⓜ *Vaporetto: Rialto.*

Giuliana Longo

SOUVENIRS | A hat shop that's been around since 1901 offers an assortment of Venetian and gondolier straw hats, Panama hats from Ecuador, caps and berets, and some select scarves of silk and fine wool; there's even a special corner dedicated to accessories for antique cars. ⊠ *Calle del Lovo, San Marco 4813, San Marco* ☏ *041/5226454* ⊕ *www.giulianalongo.com* Ⓜ *Vaporetto: San Marco.*

★ Jesurum

FABRICS | A great deal of so-called Burano Venetian lace is now machine-made in China—and there really is a difference. Unless you have some experience, you're best off going to a trusted place. Jesurum has been the major producer of handmade Venetian lace since 1870. Its lace is, of course, all modern production, but if you want an antique piece, the people at Jesurum can point you in the right direction. ⊠ *Calle Veste, San Marco 2024, San Marco* ☏ *041/5238969*

⊕ *www.jesurum.it* Ⓜ *Vaporetto: San Marco (Vallaresso).*

★ Venini

GLASSWARE | When connoisseurs of Venetian glass think of the firms who have restored Venice to its place as the epicenter of artistic glass production, Venini is, without any major discussion, the firm that immediately comes to mind. Since the beginning of the 20th century, Venini has found craftsmen and designers that have made their trademark synonymous with the highest quality both in traditional and in creative glass design. A piece of Venini glass, even one of modest price and proportions, will be considered not only a charming decorative object, but also a work of art that will maintain its value for years to come. While Venini's more exciting and innovative pieces may cost thousands of dollars, the Venini showrooms in the Piazza San Marco and on Fondamenta Vetrai in Murano also have small, more conventional designs for prices as low as €100. ⊠ *Piazzetta Leoncini, San Marco 314, San Marco* ☏ *041/5224045 San Marco, 041/2737211 Murano* ⊕ *www.venini.com* Ⓜ *Vaporetto: San Marco (San Zaccaria).*

Dorsoduro

The sestiere Dorsoduro (named for its "hard back" solid clay foundation) is across the Grand Canal to the south of San Marco. It is a place of meandering canals, the city's finest art museums, monumental churches, and *scuole* (Renaissance civic institutions) filled with works by Titian, Veronese, and Tiepolo, and a promenade called the Zattere, where on sunny days you'll swear half the city is out for *passeggiata* (a stroll). The eastern tip of the peninsula, the

Venetian Art Glass

The glass of Murano is Venice's number-one product, and you'll be confronted by mind-boggling displays of traditional and contemporary glassware—much of it kitsch and not made in Venice. Traditional Venetian glass is hot blown glass, not lead crystal; it comes in myriad forms that range from the classic ornate goblets and chandeliers, to beads, vases, sculpture, and more. Beware of paying "Venetian" prices for glass made elsewhere. A piece claiming to be made in Murano may guarantee its origin, but not its value or quality; the prestigious Venetian glassmakers—like Venini, Seguso, Salviati, and others—sign their pieces, but never use a "made in Murano" label. To make a smart purchase, take your time and be selective. You can learn a great deal without sales pressure at the Museo del Vetro (museovetro.visitmuve.it) on Murano; unfortunately, you'll likely find the least attractive glass where public demonstrations are offered. Although prices in Venice and on Murano are comparable, shops in Venice with wares from various glassworks may charge slightly less.

■TIP→ A "free" taxi to Murano always comes with sales pressure. Take the vaporetto included in your transit pass, and, if you prefer, a private guide who specializes in the subject but has no affinity to any specific furnace.

Punta della Dogana, is capped by the dome of Santa Maria della Salute and was once the city's customs point; the old customs house is now a museum of contemporary art.

Dorsoduro is home to the Gallerie dell'Accademia, with an unparalleled collection of Venetian painting, and the gloriously restored Ca' Rezzonico, which houses the Museo del Settecento Veneziano. Another of its landmark sites, the Peggy Guggenheim Collection, has a fine selection of 20th-century art. Add to this some wonderful restaurants, charming places to stay, and inviting bars for an early-evening spritz, and you've got a sestiere well worth exploring,

TIMING

You can easily spend a full day in the neighborhood. Devote at least a half hour to admiring the Titians in the imposing and monumental Santa Maria della Salute, and another half hour for the wonderful Veroneses in the peaceful, serene church of San Sebastiano. The Gallerie dell'Accademia demands a few hours, but if time is short an audio guide can help you cover the highlights in about an hour. Ca' Rezzonico deserves at least an hour, as does the Peggy Guggenheim Collection.

◉ Sights

★ Ca' Rezzonico

HISTORY MUSEUM | Designed by Baldassare Longhena in the 17th century, this gigantic palace was completed nearly 100 years later by Giorgio Massari and became the last home of English poet Robert Browning (1812–89). Stand on the bridge by the Grand Canal entrance to spot the plaque with Browning's poetic excerpt, "Open my heart and you will see graved inside of it, Italy…" on the left side of the palace. The spectacular centerpiece is the eye-popping Grand

Venice's Scuola Days

An institution you'll inevitably encounter from Venice's glory days is the *scuola*. These weren't schools, as the word today translates, but important fraternal institutions. The smaller ones (*scuole piccole*) were established by different social groups—enclaves of foreigners, tradesmen, followers of a particular saint, and parishioners. The *scuole grandi*, however, were open to all citizens and included people of different occupations and ethnicities. They formed a more democratic power base than the Venetian governmental Grand Council, which was limited to nobles.

For the most part secular, despite their devotional activities, the scuole concentrated on charitable work, either helping their own membership or assisting the city's neediest citizens. The tradesmen's and servants' scuole formed social-security nets for elderly and disabled members. Wealthier scuole assisted orphans or provided dowries so poor girls could marry. By 1500 there were more than 200 minor scuole in Venice, but only six scuole grandi, some of which contributed substantially to the arts. The Republic encouraged their existence—the scuole kept strict records of the names and professions of contributors to the brotherhood, which helped when it came time to collect taxes.

Ballroom, which has hosted some of the grandest parties in the city's history, from its 18th-century heyday to the 1969 Bal Fantastica (a Save Venice charity event that attracted every notable of the day, from Elizabeth Taylor to Aristotle Onassis). Today the upper floors of the Ca' Rezzonico are home to the especially delightful **Museo del Settecento** (Museum of Venice in the 1700s). Its main floor successfully retains the appearance of a magnificent Venetian palazzo, decorated with period furniture and tapestries in gilded salons, as well as Gianbattista Tiepolo ceiling frescoes and oil paintings. Upper floors contain a fine collection of paintings by 18th-century Venetian artists, including the famous Pulcinella frescoes by Tiepolo's son, Giandomenico, moved here from the Villa di Zianigo. There's even a restored apothecary, complete with powders and potions. ⊠ *Fondamenta Rezzonico, Dorsoduro 3136, Dorsoduro* ☎ *041/2410100* ⊕ *carezzonico. visitmuve.it* ⊠ *€10 (free with Museum Pass)* ⊘ *Closed Tues.* Ⓜ *Vaporetto: Ca' Rezzonico.*

Campo Santa Margherita
PLAZA/SQUARE | Lined with cafés and restaurants generally filled with students from the nearby university, Campo Santa Margherita also has produce vendors and benches where you can sit and take in the bustling local life of the campo. Also close to the Ca' Rezzonico and the Scuola Grande dei Carmini, and only a 10-minute walk from the Gallerie dell'Accademia, the square is the center of Dorsoduro social life. It takes its name from the church to one side, closed since the early 19th century and now used as an auditorium. On weekend evenings it sometimes attracts hordes of high school students from the mainland. ⊠ *Campo Santa Margherita, Dorsoduro* Ⓜ *Vaporetto: San Basilio.*

★ Gallerie dell'Accademia
ART MUSEUM | The greatest collection of Venetian paintings in the world

hangs in these galleries founded by Napoléon back in 1807 on the site of a religious complex he had suppressed. The galleries were carefully and subtly restructured between 1945 and 1959 by the renowned architect Carlo Scarpa. Jacopo Bellini is considered the father of the Venetian Renaissance, and in Room 2 you can compare his *Madonna and Child with Saints* with such later works as *Madonna of the Orange Tree* by Cima da Conegliano (circa 1459–1517) and *Ten Thousand Martyrs of Mt. Ararat* by Vittore Carpaccio (circa 1455–1525). Jacopo's more accomplished son Giovanni (circa 1430–1516) attracts your eye not only with his subject matter but also with his rich color. Rooms 4 and 5 have a good selection of his madonnas. Room 5 contains *The Tempest* by Giorgione (1477–1510), a revolutionary work that has intrigued viewers and critics for centuries. It is unified not only by physical design elements, as was usual, but more importantly by a mysterious, somewhat threatening atmosphere. In Room 10, *Feast in the House of Levi*, commissioned as a Last Supper, got Veronese summoned to the Inquisition over its depiction of dogs, jesters, and other extraneous figures. The artist responded with the famous retort, *"Noi pittori ci prendiamo le stesse libertà dei poeti e dei pazzi"* (We painters permit ourselves the same liberties as poets and madmen). He resolved the problem by simply changing the title, so that the painting represented a different, less solemn biblical feast. Don't miss the views of 15th- and 16th-century Venice by Carpaccio and Gentile Bellini, Giovanni's brother—you'll see how little the city has changed. Booking tickets in advance isn't essential but helps during busy seasons and costs only an additional €1.50. A free map notes art and artists, and the bookshop sells a more informative English-language booklet. In the main galleries a €4 audio guide saves reading but adds little to each room's excellent annotation.

✉ *Dorsoduro 1050, Campo della Carità just off Accademia Bridge, Dorsoduro* ☎ *041/5222247, 041/5200345 reservations* ⊕ *www.gallerieaccademia.it/en* 💶 *€12, subject to increases for special exhibitions* Ⓜ *Vaporetto: Accademia.*

Gesuati (*Church of Santa Maria del Rosario*)

CHURCH | When the Dominicans took over the church of Santa Maria della Visitazione from the suppressed order of Gesuati laymen in 1668, Giorgio Massari, the last of the great Venetian Baroque architects, was commissioned to build this structure between 1726 and 1735. It has an important Gianbattista Tiepolo (1696–1770) illusionistic ceiling and several other of his works, plus those of his contemporaries, Giambattista Piazzetta (1683–1754) and Sebastiano Ricci (1659–1734). ✉ *Zattere, Dorsoduro* ☎ *041/2750462* ⊕ *www.chorusvenezia. org* ⊗ *Closed Sun.* 💶 *€3 (free with Chorus Pass)* Ⓜ *Vaporetto: Zattere.*

Peggy Guggenheim Collection

ART MUSEUM | FAMILY | Housed in the incomplete but nevertheless charming Palazzo Venier dei Leoni, this choice selection of 20th-century painting and sculpture represents the taste and extraordinary style of the late heiress Peggy Guggenheim. Through wealth, social connections, and a sharp eye for artistic trends, Guggenheim (1898–1979) became an important art dealer and collector from the 1930s through the 1950s, and her personal collection here includes works by Picasso, Kandinsky, Pollock, Motherwell, and Ernst (her onetime husband). The museum serves beverages, snacks, and light meals in its refreshingly shady and artistically sophisticated garden. ✉ *Fondamenta Venier dei Leoni, Dorsoduro 701, Dorsoduro* ☎ *041/2405411* ⊕ *www.guggenheim-venice.it* 💶 *€15* ⊗ *Closed Tues.* ☞ *Timed tickets must be purchased online in advance. Weekend tickets*

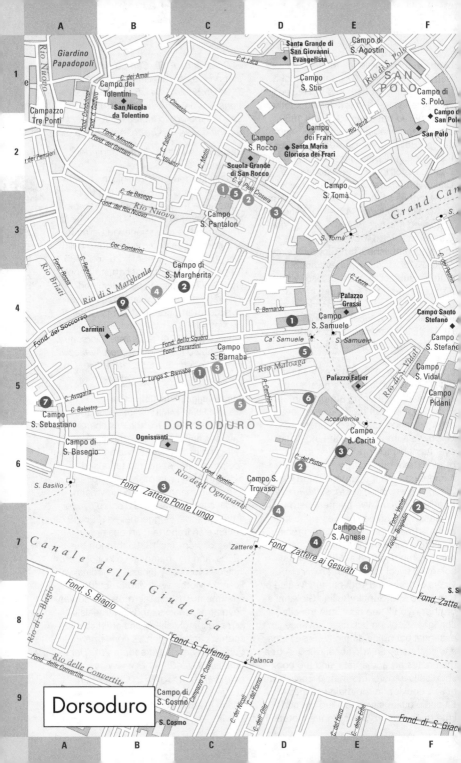

Sights ▼

1 Ca' Rezzonico D4
2 Campo Santa Margherita.........C4
3 Gallerie dell'Accademia E6
4 Gesuati............................. D7
5 Peggy Guggenheim Collection... G6
6 Punta della Dogana I6
7 San Sebastiano A5
8 Santa Maria della Salute H6
9 Scuola Grande dei Carmini.......B4

Restaurants ▼

1 Estro Vino e Cucina................C2
2 Impronta Cafe.....................C3
3 La Bitta..............................C5
4 Osteria alla Bifora B4
5 Osteria Enoteca ai Artisti C5

Quick Bites ▼

1 Caffè Ai Artisti C5
2 Cantinone già Schiavi.............D6
3 Imagina Café D3
4 Osteria al Squero D7
5 Pasticceria Tonolo.................C3

Hotels ▼

1 Ca' Maria Adele.....................H7
2 Hotel American–Dinesen..........F7
3 Il Palazzo Experimental B6
4 La Calcina E7
5 Palazzo Stern......................D5
6 Pensione Accademia
  Villa Maravege....................D5

KEY

- **1** Sights
- **1** Restaurants
- **1** Quick Bites
- **1** Hotels

must be booked at least one day ahead
Ⓜ *Vaporetto: Accademia.*

★ Punta della Dogana

ART MUSEUM | Funded by the billionaire who owns a major share in Christie's Auction House, the François Pinault Foundation had Japanese architect Tadao Ando redesign this fabled customs house—sitting at the *punta,* or very head, of the Grand Canal—now home to a changing roster of works from Pinault's renowned collection of contemporary art. The streaming light, polished surfaces, and clean lines of Ando's design contrast beautifully with the massive columns, sturdy beams, and brick of the original Dogana. Even if you aren't into contemporary art, a visit is worthwhile just to see Ando's amazing architectural transformation. Be sure to walk down to the punta for a magnificent view of the Venetian basin. Check online for a schedule of temporary exhibitions. ✉ *Punta della Dogana, Dorsoduro* ☎ *041/2001057* ⊕ *www.palazzograssi.it* ⊘ *Closed Tues.* ◩ *€15; €20 with Palazzo Grassi* Ⓜ *Vaporetto: Salute.*

★ San Sebastiano

CHURCH | Paolo Veronese (1528–88), though still in his twenties, was already the official painter of the Republic when he began the oil panels and frescoes at San Sebastiano, his parish church, in 1555. For decades he continued to embellish the church with very beautiful illusionistic scenes. The cycles of panels in San Sebastiano are considered to be his supreme accomplishment. Veronese is buried beneath his bust near the organ. The church itself, remodeled by Scarpagnino and finished in 1548, offers a rare opportunity to see a monument in Venice where both the architecture and the pictorial decoration all date from the same period. Be sure to check out the portal of the ex-convent, now part of the University of Venice, to the left of the church; it was designed in 1976–78 by Carlo Scarpa, one of the most important

Italian architects of the 20th century. ✉ *Campo San Sebastiano, Dorsoduro* ☎ *041/2750462* ⊕ *www.chorusvene-zia.org* ◩ *€3 (free with Chorus Pass)* ⊘ *Closed Sun.* Ⓜ *Vaporetto: San Basilio.*

★ Santa Maria della Salute

CHURCH | The most iconic landmark of the Grand Canal, La Salute (as this church is commonly called) is most unforgettably viewed from the Riva degli Schiavoni at sunset, or from the Accademia Bridge by moonlight. En route to becoming Venice's most important Baroque architect, 32-year-old Baldassare Longhena won a competition in 1631 to design a shrine honoring the Virgin Mary for saving Venice from a plague that in the space of two years (1629–30) killed 47,000 residents, or one-third of the city's population. It was not completed, however, until 1687—five years after Longhena's death. Outside, this ornate white Istrian stone octagon is topped by a colossal cupola with snail-like ornamental buttresses—in truth, piers encircled by finely carved "ropes," an allusion to the sail-making industry of the city (or so say today's art historians). Inside, a white-and-gray color scheme is complemented by a polychrome marble floor and the six chapels. The Byzantine icon above the main altar has been venerated as the Madonna della Salute (Madonna of Health) since 1670, when Francesco Morosini brought it here from Crete. Above it is a sculpture showing Venice on her knees before the Madonna as she drives the wretched plague from the city. Do not leave the church without visiting the **Sacrestia Maggiore,** which contains a dozen works by Titian, including his *San Marco Enthroned with Saints* altarpiece. You'll also see Tintoretto's *Wedding at Cana.* For the Festa della Salute, held November 21, a votive bridge is constructed across the Grand Canal, and Venetians make a pilgrimage here to light candles in prayer for another year's health. ✉ *Punta della Dogana, Dorsoduro* ☎ *041/2743928*

🌐 *basilicasalutevenezia.it* 🎫 *Church free, sacristy €4* [M] *Vaporetto: Salute.*

Scuola Grande dei Carmini

HISTORIC SIGHT | When the order of Santa Maria del Carmelo commissioned Baldassare Longhena to finish the work on the Scuola Grande dei Carmini in the 1670s, their brotherhood of 75,000 members was the largest in Venice and one of the wealthiest. Little expense was spared in the stuccoed ceilings and carved ebony paneling, and the artwork is remarkable. The paintings by Gianbattista Tiepolo that adorn the Baroque ceiling of the **Sala Capitolare** (Chapter House) are particularly alluring. In what many consider his best work, the artist's nine canvases vividly transform some rather conventional religious themes into dynamic displays of color and movement. ✉ *Campo dei Carmini, Dorsoduro 2617, Dorsoduro* ☎ *041/5289420* 🌐 *www.scuolagrande-carmini.it* 🕒 *Closed Mon.–Wed.* 🎫 *€7* [M] *Vaporetto: Ca' Rezzonico.*

🍴 Restaurants

★ Estro Vino e Cucina

$$$ | MODERN ITALIAN | Wine lovers shouldn't miss this cozy and compact eatery run by the Spezzamonte brothers, which offers a fantastic selection of natural wines along with modern takes on classic Venetian dishes, such as scampi in saor and local grilled amberjack. If you can't choose, let the helpful servers suggest the perfect vino from their list of more than 700 bottles to pair with your à la carte dishes or tasting menu. **Known for:** vibrant atmosphere; extensive natural wine list; ambitious local cuisine. [$] *Average main: €28* ✉ *Calle San Pantalon, Dorsoduro 3778, Dorsoduro* ☎ *041/4764914* 🌐 *www.estrovenezia.com* 🕒 *Closed Tues. No lunch Wed.* [M] *Vaporetto: San Tomà.*

Impronta Cafe

$$ | VENETIAN | This sleek café is a favorite lunchtime haunt for professors from the nearby university and local businesspeople, when you can easily have a beautifully prepared primo or secondo, plus a glass of wine, for a reasonable price; there's also a good selection of sandwiches and salads. Unlike most local eateries, this spot is open from breakfast through late dinner, and you can dine well and economically in the evening on classic pasta, seafood, and meat dishes. **Known for:** all-day dining; contemporary decor; well-prepared classic Venetian dishes. [$] *Average main: €20* ✉ *Intersection of Calle Crosera and Calle San Pantalon, Dorsoduro 3815, Dorsoduro* ☎ *041/2750386* 🌐 *www.improntacafe-venice.com* 🕒 *Closed Sun. and 2 wks in Aug.* [M] *Vaporetto: San Tomà.*

★ La Bitta

$$ | NORTHERN ITALIAN | For a break from all the fish and seafood options in Venice, this is your place; the meat- and veggie-focused menu (inspired by the cuisine of the Venetian terra firma) presents a new temptation at every course, and market availability keeps the dishes changing almost every day. The homemade desserts are all luscious (it's been said that La Bitta serves the best *panna cotta* in town), and you can trust the owner's selections from her excellent wine and grappa lists. **Known for:** friendly and efficient service; meat dishes (no seafood); seasonally inspired menus. [$] *Average main: €18* ✉ *Calle Lunga San Barnaba, Dorsoduro 2753/A, Dorsoduro* ☎ *041/5230531* 🕒 *Closed Sun. No lunch* [M] *Vaporetto: Ca' Rezzonico.*

★ Osteria alla Bifora

$$ | VENETIAN | A beautiful and atmospheric bacaro, Alla Bifora has such ample, satisfying fare that most Venetians consider it a full-fledged restaurant. Offerings include overflowing trays of cold, sliced meats and cheeses; various preparations of baccalà; and Venetian classics, such as polpette, sarde in saor, and marinated anchovies. **Known for:** warm and friendly owners; *seppie in nero con polenta* (cuttlefish in ink with polenta); good selection of regional wines by the glass. $ *Average main: €18* ⊠ *Campo Santa Margherita, Dorsoduro 2930, Dorsoduro* ☏ *041/5236119* ⊘ *Closed Jan. and Aug.* Ⓜ *Vaporetto: Ca' Rezzonico.*

★ Osteria Enoteca ai Artisti

$$$ | VENETIAN | Pop into this canalside restaurant at lunch for a satisfying primo or come for dinner to sample fine and fresh offerings; the candle-lighted tables that line the *fondamenta* suggest romance, and the service is friendly and welcoming. The posted menu—with choices like tagliatelle with porcini mushrooms and tiger prawns, or a filleted John Dory with tomatoes and pine nuts—changes daily (spot the date at the top) and seasonally. **Known for:** truly helpful service; delicious pasta and seafood offerings; superlative tiramisu. $ *Average main: €25* ⊠ *Fondamenta della Toletta, Dorsoduro 1169a, Dorsoduro* ☏ *041/5238944* ⊕ *www.enotecaartisti. com* ⊘ *Closed Sun. and Mon.*

☕ Coffee and Quick Bites

Caffè Ai Artisti

$ | CAFÉ | Caffè Ai Artisti gives locals, students, and travelers alike good reason to pause and refuel. The location is central, pleasant, and sunny—perfect for people-watching and taking a break before the next destination—and the hours are long. **Known for:** chilling with the locals; relaxing with a coffee; evening Aperol spritz or wine. $ *Average main: €8* ⊠ *Dorsoduro 2771, Dorsoduro* ☏ *393/9680135* Ⓜ *Vaporetto: Ca' Rezzonico.*

★ Cantine del Vino già Schiavi

$ | WINE BAR | A mainstay for anyone living or working in the area, this beautiful, family-run, 19th-century bacaro across from the *squero* (gondola boatyard) of San Trovaso has original furnishings and one of the city's best wine cellars, and the walls are covered floor-to-ceiling with bottles for purchase. The cicheti

here are some of the most inventive—and freshest—in Venice (feel free to compliment the Signora, who makes them up to twice a day); everything's eaten standing up, as there's no seating. **Known for:** boisterous local atmosphere; excellent quality cicheti; plenty of wine choices. $ *Average main: €8* ⊠ *Fondamenta Nani, Dorsoduro 992, Dorsoduro* ☏ *041/5230034* ⊕ *www.cantinaschiavi. com* ⊘ *Closed Sun. and 3 wks in Aug.* Ⓜ *Vaporetto: Zattere, Accademia.*

Imagina Cafè

$ | ITALIAN | This friendly café and art gallery, located between Campo Santa Margherita and Campo San Barnaba, is a great place to stop for a spritz, or even for a light lunch or dinner. The highlights are the freshly made salads, but their panini and tramezzini are also among the best in the area. **Known for:** pleasant outdoor seating; tasty sandwiches and salads; good wines and cocktails. $ *Average main: €10* ⊠ *Rio Terà Canal, Dorsoduro 3126, Dorsoduro* ☏ *041/2410625* ⊕ *www.imaginacafe.it/english.html* Ⓜ *Vaporetto: Ca' Rezonnico.*

Osteria al Squero

$$ | ITALIAN | It wasn't long after this lovely little wine bar (not, as its name implies, a restaurant) appeared across from the Squero San Trovaso that it became a neighborhood—and citywide—favorite. The Venetian owner has created a personal vision of what a good bar should offer: a variety of sumptuous cicheti, panini, and cheeses to be accompanied by just the right regional wines (ask for his recommendation). **Known for:** tasty cicheti; good veggie options; pretty canal views. $ *Average main: €20* ⊠ *Fondamenta Nani, Dorsoduro 943/944, Dorsoduro* ☏ *335/6007513* ⊕ *osteriaalsquero. wordpress.com* ⊘ *Closed Sun.* Ⓜ *Vaporetto: Accademia, Zattere.*

Pasticceria Tonolo

$ | BAKERY | Venice's premier confectionery has been in operation since 1886. During Carnevale it's still one of the best places in town for *frittelle,* or fried doughnuts (traditional raisin, or cream-filled), and at Christmas and Easter, this is where Venetians order their *focaccia veneziana,* the traditional raised cake—well in advance. **Known for:** can't-miss doughnuts; arguably the best pastries in Venice; excellent coffee. [$] *Average main: €5* ✉ *Calle San Pantalon, Dorsoduro 3764, Dorsoduro* ☎ *041/5237209* 🌐 *pasticceria-tonolo-venezia.business.site* ⏲ *Closed Sun. afternoon and Mon.* [M] *Vaporetto: San Tomà.*

Hotels

★ Ca' Maria Adele

$$$$ | **HOTEL** | One of the city's most intimate and elegant getaways blends terrazzo floors, dramatic Murano chandeliers, and antique-style furnishings with contemporary touches, particularly in the African-wood reception area and breakfast room. **Pros:** quiet and romantic; tranquil yet convenient spot near Santa Maria della Salute; imaginative decor. **Cons:** no restaurant (just breakfast room); bathrooms on the small side; no elevator and lots of stairs. [$] *Rooms from: €462* ✉ *Campo Santa Maria della Salute, Dorsoduro 111, Dorsoduro* ☎ *041/5203078* 🌐 *www.camariaadele.it* ⏲ *Closed 3 wks in Jan.* 🛏 *14 rooms* 🍴 *Free Breakfast* [M] *Vaporetto: Salute.*

Hotel American–Dinesen

$$ | **HOTEL** | If you're in Venice to see art, you can't beat the location of this hotel, where all the spacious rooms have brocade fabrics and Venetian-style lacquered furniture. **Pros:** on a bright, quiet, exceptionally picturesque canal; some rooms have canal-view terraces; wonderfully located near Gallerie dell'Accademia, Peggy Guggenheim Collection, and Punta della Dogana. **Cons:** bathrooms can feel cramped; style could be too understated for those expecting Venetian opulence; canal-view rooms are more expensive. [$] *Rooms from: €171* ✉ *San Vio, Dorsoduro 628, Dorsoduro* ☎ *041/5204733* 🌐 *www.hotelamerican.it* 🛏 *34 rooms* 🍴 *No Meals* [M] *Vaporetto: Accademia, Salute, and Zattere.*

Il Palazzo Experimental

$$$ | **HOTEL** | Of-the-moment Parisian designer Dorothée Meilichzon composed the striped pastel color palette at this hip boutique hotel— the first Experimental Group property in Italy—hidden inside a Renaissance palazzo across from the Giudecca Canal. **Pros:** quiet location away from the Venice crowds; trendy cocktail bar on-site; fun, whimsical decor. **Cons:** no gym; little storage space in bathrooms; not all rooms have water views. [$] *Rooms from: €270* ✉ *Fondamenta Zattere Al Ponte Lungo, Dorsoduro 1411, Dorsoduro* ☎ *041/0980200* 🌐 *www.palazzoexperimental.com* 🛏 *32 rooms* 🍴 *No Meals* [M] *Vaporetto: Zattere, San Basilio.*

La Calcina

$$ | **HOTEL** | Many notables (including Victorian-era art critic John Ruskin) have stayed at this hotel, which has an enviable location along the sunny Zattere, as well as comfy rooms and apartments with parquet floors, original 19th-century furniture, and firm beds. **Pros:** well-regarded restaurant with terrace over the Giudecca Canal; panoramic views from some rooms; quiet, peaceful atmosphere. **Cons:** no elevator; not for travelers who prefer ultramodern surroundings; most rooms on the small side. [$] *Rooms from: €130* ✉ *Zattere, Dorsoduro 780, Dorsoduro* ☎ *041/5206466* 🌐 *www.lacalcina.com* 🛏 *25 rooms* 🍴 *Free Breakfast* [M] *Vaporetto: Zattere.*

★ Palazzo Stern

$$ | **HOTEL** | This opulently refurbished neo-Gothic palazzo features marble-column arches, terrazzo floors, frescoed ceilings, mosaics, and a majestic carved

staircase, and some rooms have tufted walls and parquet flooring, but the gracious terrace that overlooks the Grand Canal is almost reason alone to stay here. **Pros:** modern renovation retains historic ambience; lovely views from many rooms; excellent hotel service. **Cons:** standard rooms don't have views; no restaurant, gym, or spa; Grand Canal–facing rooms can be a bit noisy. [$] *Rooms from: €192* ✉ *Calle del Traghetto, Dorsoduro 2792, Dorsoduro* ☎ *041/2770869* 🌐 *www.palazzostern.com* 🍴 *Free Breakfast* 🛏 *24 rooms* [M] *Vaporetto: Ca' Rezzonico.*

Pensione Accademia Villa Maravege

$$ | **HOTEL** | Behind iron gates in one of the most densely packed parts of the city, you'll find yourself in front of a large and elegant garden and Gothic-style villa where accommodations are charmingly decorated with Venetian-style antique reproductions and fine tapestry. **Pros:** a unique villa in the heart of Venice; complimentary drinks and snacks at the bar; two gardens where guests can breakfast, drink, and relax. **Cons:** no guest rooms have Grand Canal views; bathrooms can be on the small side; no restaurant. [$] *Rooms from: €128* ✉ *Fondamenta Bollani, Dorsoduro 1058, Dorsoduro* ☎ *041/5210188* 🌐 *www.pensioneaccademia.it* 🛏 *27 rooms* 🍴 *Free Breakfast* [M] *Vaporetto: Accademia.*

Nightlife

Al Chioschetto

BARS | Although this popular place consists only of a kiosk set up to serve some outdoor tables, it is located on the Zattere, and thus provides panoramic views. It's a handy meet-up for locals and a stop-off for tourists in nice weather for a spritz, a panino, or a sunny read as the Venetian world eases by. But go for the view and the sunshine; the food and drink, while acceptable, are not exceptional. ✉ *Near Ponte Lungo, Dorsoduro 1406/A, Dorsoduro* ☎ *348/3968466* [M] *Vaporetto: Zattere.*

★ **Il Caffè** (*Bar Rosso*)

BARS | Commonly called "Bar Rosso" for its bright-red exterior, Il Caffè has far more tables outside than inside. A favorite with students and faculty from the nearby university, it's a good place to enjoy a spritz—the preferred Venetian aperitif of white wine, Campari or Aperol, soda water, an olive, and a slice of orange. It has excellent tramezzini (among the best in town) and panini, and a hip, helpful staff. It's been recently frequented by high-school students from the mainland on weekend nights, so it can be more enjoyable around lunchtime or in the early evening. ✉ *Campo Santa Margherita, Dorsoduro 2963, Dorsoduro* ☎ *041/5287998* [M] *Vaporetto: Ca' Rezzonico.*

Orange

BARS | Modern, hip, and complemented by an internal garden, this welcoming bar anchors the south end of Campo Santa Margherita, the liveliest campo in Venice. You can have *piadine* sandwiches, salads, and drinks while watching soccer games on a massive screen inside, or sit at the tables in the campo. Despite being close to the university, Orange is frequented primarily by young working people from the mainland and tourists. ✉ *Campo Santa Margherita, Dorsoduro 3054/A, Dorsoduro* ☎ *041/5234740* [M] *Vaporetto: Ca' Rezzonico.*

Venice Jazz Club

LIVE MUSIC | Owner Federico and his band play live jazz, in styles including classic, modern, Latin jazz, and bossa nova, at this intimate venue. Concerts usually start at 9 pm every night except Thursday and Sunday, and dinner is available beforehand for an extra charge. ✉ *Ponte dei Pugni, Dorsoduro 3102, Dorsoduro* ☎ *041/5232056* 🌐 *venicejazzclub.weebly.com* [M] *Vaporetto: Ca' Rezzonico.*

🛍 Shopping

Il Grifone

HANDBAGS | Of Venice's few remaining artisan leather shops, Il Grifone is the standout with respect to quality, tradition, and the guarantee of an exquisite product. For more than 30 years, Antonio Peressin has been making bags, purses, belts, and smaller leather items that have a wide following because of his precision and attention to detail. His goods remain reasonably and accessibly priced. ✉ *Fondamenta del Gaffaro, Dorsoduro 3516, Dorsoduro* ☎ *041/5229452* ⊕ *www.ilgrifonevenezia.it* Ⓜ *Vaporetto: Piazzale Roma.*

Marina and Susanna Sent

JEWELRY & WATCHES | The beautiful and elegant glass jewelry of Marina and Susanna Sent has been featured in *Vogue*. Look also for vases and other exceptional design pieces. Other locations are on the Fondamenta Serenella on Murano and in the Sottoportico de Rialto in San Polo. ✉ *Campo San Vio, Dorsoduro 669, Dorsoduro* ☎ *041/5208136 for Dorsoduro, 041/5210016 for San Polo, 041/5274665 for Murano* ⊕ *www.marinaesusannasent.com* Ⓜ *Vaporetto: Accademia, Zattere, Giglio, Murano Serenella.*

San Polo and Santa Croce

The two smallest of Venice's six sestieri, San Polo and Santa Croce, were named after their main churches, although the Chiesa di Santa Croce was demolished in 1810. The city's most famous bridge, the Ponte di Rialto, unites San Marco (east) with San Polo (west). The Rialto takes its name from Rivoaltus, the high ground on which it was built. You'll find some of Venice's most lauded restaurants here, and shops abound in the area surrounding the Ponte di Rialto. On the San Marco side you'll find fashion, on the San Polo side, food.

TIMING

To do the area justice requires at least half a day. If you want to take part in the food shopping, come early to beat the crowds. Campo San Giacomo dell'Orio, west of the main thoroughfare that takes you from the Ponte di Rialto to Santa Maria Gloriosa dei Frari, is a peaceful place for a drink and a rest. The museums of Ca' Pesaro are a time commitment—you'll want at least two hours to see them both.

👁 Sights

Ca' Pesaro

ART MUSEUM | Baldassare Longhena's grand Baroque palace, begun in 1676, is the beautifully restored home of two impressive collections. The Galleria Internazionale d'Arte Moderna has works by 19th- and 20th-century artists, such as Klimt, Kandinsky, Matisse, and Miró. It also has a collection of representative works from the Venice Biennale that amounts to a panorama of 20th-century art. The pride of the Museo Orientale is its collection of Japanese art—and especially armor and weapons—of the Edo period (1603–1868). It also has a small but striking collection of Chinese and Indonesian porcelains and musical instruments. ✉ *Santa Croce 2076, Santa Croce* ☎ *041/721127 Galleria, 041/5241173 Museo Orientale* ⊕ *capesaro.visitmuve.it* 🎟 *€10, includes both museums (free with Museum Pass)* 🕐 *Closed Mon.* Ⓜ *Vaporetto: San Stae.*

Campo San Polo

PLAZA/SQUARE | Only Piazza San Marco is larger than this square, and the echo of children's voices bouncing off the surrounding palaces makes the space seem even bigger. Campo San Polo once hosted bull races, fairs, military parades, and packed markets, and now comes especially alive on summer nights, when

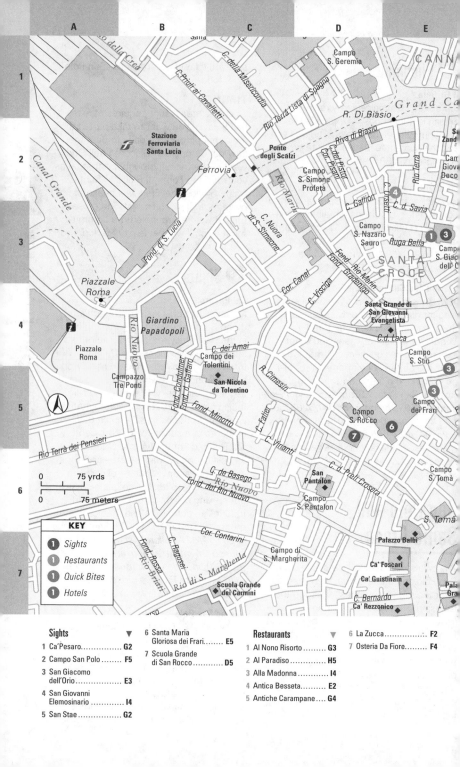

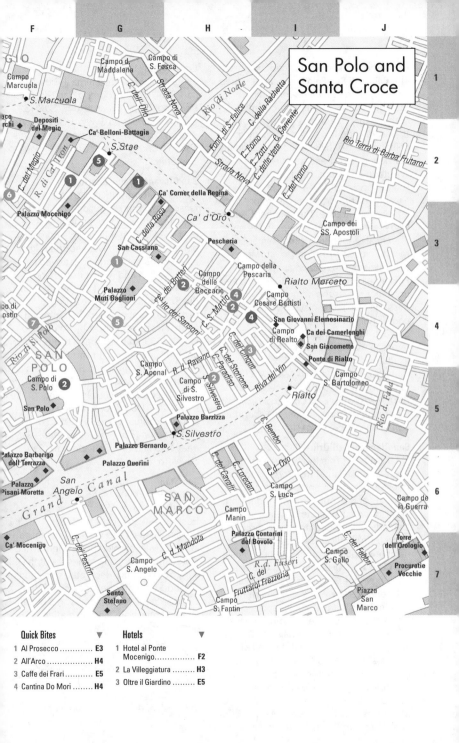

San Polo and Santa Croce

Quick Bites ▼

1 Al Prosecco **E3**
2 All'Arco **H4**
3 Caffe dei Frari **E5**
4 Cantina Do Mori **H4**

Hotels ▼

1 Hotel al Ponte
Mocenigo **F2**
2 La Villeggiatura **H3**
3 Oltre il Giardino **E5**

it's home to the city's outdoor cinema. The **Chiesa di San Polo** has been restored so many times that little remains of the original 9th-century church, and the 19th-century alterations were so costly that, sadly, the friars sold off many great paintings to pay bills. Although Gianbattista Tiepolo is represented here, his work is outdone by 16 paintings by his son Giandomenico (1727–1804), including the *Stations of the Cross* in the oratory to the left of the entrance. The younger Tiepolo also created a series of expressive and theatrical renderings of the saints. Look for altarpieces by Tintoretto and Veronese that managed to escape auction. San Polo's bell tower (begun 1362) remained unchanged over the centuries—don't miss the two lions, playing with a disembodied human head and a serpent, that guard it. Tradition has it that the head refers to that of Marino Faliero, the doge executed for treason in 1355. ⊠ *Campo San Polo, San Polo* ☎ *041/2750462 Chorus Foundation* ⊕ *www.chorusvenezia. org* ⊗ *Closed Sun.* ⌨ *Chiesa di San Polo €3 (free with Chorus Pass)* Ⓜ *Vaporetto: San Silvestro, San Tomà.*

San Giacomo dell'Orio

PLAZA/SQUARE | This lovely square was named after a laurel tree (*orio*), and today trees lend it shade and character. Add benches and a fountain (with a drinking bowl for dogs), and the pleasant, oddly shaped campo becomes a welcoming place for friendly conversation and neighborhood kids at play. Legend has it the **Chiesa di San Giacomo dell'Orio** was founded in the 9th century on an island still populated by wolves. The current church dates from 1225; its short, unmatched Byzantine columns survived renovation during the Renaissance, and the church never lost the feel of an ancient temple sheltering beneath its 14th-century ship's-keel roof. In the sanctuary, large marble crosses are surrounded by a group of small medieval Madonnas. The altarpiece is *Madonna with Child and Saints* (1546) by Lorenzo

Lotto (1480–1556), and the sacristies contain 12 works by Palma il Giovane (circa 1544–1628). ⊠ *Campo San Giacomo dell'Orio, Santa Croce* ☎ *041/2750462 Chorus Foundation* ⊕ *www.chorusvenezia.org* ⌨ *Church €3 (free with Chorus Pass)* ⊗ *Church closed Sun.* Ⓜ *Vaporetto: San Stae.*

San Giovanni Elemosinario

CHURCH | Storefronts make up the facade, and market guilds—poulterers, messengers, and fodder merchants—built the altars at this church intimately bound to the Rialto Market. The original church was completely destroyed by a fire in 1514 and rebuilt in 1531 by Scarpagnino, who had also worked on the Scuola di San Rocco. During a more recent restoration, workers stumbled upon a frescoed cupola by Pordenone (1484–1539) that had been painted over centuries earlier. Don't miss Titian's *St. John the Almsgiver* and Pordenone's *Sts. Catherine, Sebastian, and Roch.* ⊠ *Rialto Ruga Vecchia San Giovanni, Santa Croce* ☎ *041/2750462 Chorus Foundation* ⊕ *www.chorusvenezia.org* ⌨ *€3 (free with Chorus Pass)* ⊗ *Closed Mon.–Sat. after 1:15 and Sun.* Ⓜ *Vaporetto: San Silvestro, Rialto.*

San Stae

CHURCH | The church of San Stae—the Venetian name for Sant'Eustachio (St. Eustace)—was reconstructed in 1687 by Giovanni Grassi and given a new facade in 1707 by Domenico Rossi. Renowned Venetian painters and sculptors of the early 18th century decorated this church around 1717 with the legacy left by Doge Alvise II Mocenigo, who's buried in the center aisle. San Stae affords a good opportunity to see the early works of Gianbattista Tiepolo, Sebastiano Ricci, and Piazzetta, as well as those of the previous generation of Venetian painters, with whom they had studied. ⊠ *Campo San Stae, Santa Croce* ☎ *041/2750462 Chorus Foundation*

⊕ *www.chorusvenezia.org* ⊘ *Closed Sun.* 📧 *€3 (free with Chorus Pass)* Ⓜ *Vaporetto: San Stae.*

★ Santa Maria Gloriosa dei Frari

CHURCH | Completed in 1442, this immense Gothic church of russet-color brick, known locally as "I Frari," is famous worldwide for its array of spectacular Venetian paintings. Visit the sacristy first, to see Giovanni Bellini's 1488 triptych *Madonna and Child with Saints* in all its mellow luminosity, painted for precisely this spot. The Corner Chapel on the other side of the chancel is graced by Bartolomeo Vivarini's (1415–84) 1474 altarpiece *St. Mark Enthroned and Saints John the Baptist, Jerome, Peter, and Nicholas,* which is much more conservative, displaying an attention to detail generally associated with late medieval painting. In the first south chapel of the chorus, there is a fine sculpture of St. John the Baptist by Donatello, dated 1438 (perhaps created before the artist came to Venice), which conveys a psychological intensity rare for early Renaissance sculpture. You can see the rapid development of Venetian Renaissance painting by contrasting Bellini with the heroic energy of Titian's *Assumption,* over the main altar, painted only 30 years later. Unveiled in 1518, it was the artist's first public commission and, after causing a bit of controversy, did much to establish his reputation. Upon viewing this painting at the far end of the nave, you'll first think it has been specially spotlit: up close, however, you'll discover this impression is due to the painter's unrivaled use of light and color. Titian's beautiful *Madonna di Ca' Pesaro* is in the left aisle. The painting took seven years to complete (finished in 1526), and in it Titian disregarded the conventions of his time by moving the Virgin out of center and making the saints active participants. The composition, built on diagonals, anticipates structural principals of Baroque painting in the following century. The Frari also holds a Sansovino sculpture of St. John

the Baptist and Longhena's impressive Baroque tomb designed for Doge Giovanni Pesaro. ✉ *Campo dei Frari, San Polo* ☎ *041/2728618, 041/2750462 Chorus Foundation* ⊕ *www.basilicadeifrari.it* 📧 *€3 (free with Chorus Pass)* Ⓜ *Vaporetto: San Tomà.*

★ Scuola Grande di San Rocco

HISTORY MUSEUM | This elegant example of Venetian Renaissance architecture was built between 1517 and 1560 for the essentially secular charitable confraternity bearing the saint's name. The Venetian "scuole" were organizations that sometimes had loose religious affiliations, through which the artisan class could exercise some influence upon civic life. Although San Rocco is bold and dramatic outside, its contents are even more stunning—a series of more than 60 paintings by Tintoretto. In 1564, Tintoretto edged out competition for a commission to decorate a ceiling by submitting not a sketch, but a finished work, which he moreover offered free of charge. *Moses Striking Water from the Rock, The Brazen Serpent,* and *The Fall of Manna* represent three afflictions—thirst, disease, and hunger—that San Rocco, and later his brotherhood, sought to relieve. ✉ *Campo San Rocco, San Polo 3052, San Polo* ☎ *041/5234864* ⊕ *www.scuolagrandesanrocco.it* 📧 *€10* Ⓜ *Vaporetto: San Tomà.*

🍴 Restaurants

Al Nono Risorto

$$ | **VENETIAN** | **FAMILY** | Although in the Santa Croce neighborhood, this friendly trattoria popular with the locals is really only a short walk from the Rialto Market. The pizza—not a Venetian specialty, generally speaking—is pretty good here, but the star attractions are the generous appetizers and excellent shellfish pastas, and in good weather you can enjoy your meal in the pergola-covered courtyard (do reserve if you want to snag a table there). **Known for:** pretty outdoor garden seating; traditional starters and pastas; quite tasty pizzas. [$] *Average main: €19* ✉ *Ramo Quinto Gallion O del Pezzetto 2338, Santa Croce* ☎ *041/5241169* 🌐 *alnonorisortovenezia.com* 🕒 *Closed Wed. and Jan.* [M] *Vaporetto: Rialto Mercato.*

★ Al Paradiso

$$$ | MODERN ITALIAN | In a small dining room made warm and cozy by its pleasing and unpretentious decor, proprietor Giordano makes all diners feel like honored guests. Unlike many elegant restaurants, Al Paradiso serves generous portions, and many of the delicious antipasti and primi are quite satisfying; you may want to follow the traditional Italian way of ordering and wait until you've finished your antipasto or your primo before you order your secondo. **Known for:** central location near the Ponte di Rialto; large appetizer and pasta portions; tasty meat and fish mains. [$] *Average main: €26* ✉ *Calle del Scaleter 767, San Polo* ☎ *041/5234910* 🌐 *fantecchiathos.wixsite.com/ristorantealparadiso* 🕒 *Closed 3 wks Jan.–Feb.* [M] *Vaporetto: San Silvestro.*

Alla Madonna

$ | VENETIAN | "The Madonna" used to be world-famous as "the" classic Venetian trattoria, but in recent decades has settled into middle age. Owned and operated by the Rado family since 1954, this Venetian institution looks like one, with wood beams, stained-glass windows, and a panoply of paintings on white walls; folks still head here to savor the classic Venetian repertoire, with a strong focus on seafood. **Known for:** old-time atmosphere; traditional Venetian cuisine; freshly prepared seafood. [$] *Average main: €14* ✉ *Calle della Madonna, San Polo 594, San Polo* ☎ *041/5223824* 🌐 *www.ristoranteallamadonna.com* 🕒 *Closed Wed. and Jan.* [M] *Vaporetto: San Silvestro.*

Antica Besseta

$$ | VENETIAN | Tucked away in a quiet corner of Santa Croce, with a few tables under an ivy shelter, the Antica Besseta dates from the 19th century, and it retains some of its old feel. The menu focuses on vegetables and fish, according to what's at the market, with some pasta and meat dishes, too. **Known for:** charming old-fashioned feel; classic Italian pastas, like spaghetti con vongole (with clams); simple menu of fish and meat choices. [$] *Average main: €22* ✉ *Salizzada de Ca' Zusto, Santa Croce 1395, Santa Croce* ☎ *041/721687* 🌐 *www.anticabesseta.it* [M] *Vaporetto: Riva di Biasio.*

★ Antiche Carampane

$$$ | SEAFOOD | Judging by its rather modest and unremarkable appearance, you wouldn't guess that Piera Bortoluzzi Librai's trattoria is among the finest fish restaurants in the city both because of the quality of the ingredients and because of the chef's creative magic. You can choose from a selection of classic dishes with a modern and creative touch. **Known for:** popular with visitors and locals (so book ahead); superlative fish and seafood; modernized Venetian dishes. [$] *Average main: €25* ✉ *Rio Terà delle Carampane, San Polo 1911, San Polo* ☎ *041/5240165* 🌐 *www.antichecarampane.com* 🕒 *Closed Sun. and Mon., 10 days in Jan., and 3 wks July–Aug.* [M] *Vaporetto: San Silvestro.*

La Zucca

$$ | NORTHERN ITALIAN | Simple place settings, wood lattice walls, and a mélange of languages make La Zucca (The Pumpkin) feel much like a typical, somewhat sophisticated vegetarian restaurant that you could find in any European city. What makes La Zucca special is the use of fresh, local ingredients—many of which, like the particularly sweet zucca itself, aren't normally found outside northern Italy—and simply great cooking. **Known for:** flan di zucca, a luscious pumpkin pudding topped with aged ricotta cheese; seasonal vegetarian-focused dishes; home-style Italian cooking. [$] *Average main: €21* ✉ *Calle del Tintor, at Ponte del Megio, Santa Croce 1762, Santa*

Croce ☎ 041/5241570 🌐 www.lazucca.it ⏲ Closed Sun. [M] Vaporetto: San Stae.

★ Osteria Da Fiore

$$$$ | **VENETIAN** | The understated atmosphere, simple decor, and quiet elegance featured alongside Da Fiore's modern take on traditional Venetian cuisine certainly merit its international reputation. With such beautifully prepared cuisine, you would expect the kitchen to be run by a chef with a household name; however, the kitchen is headed by owner Maurizio Martin's wife, Mara, who learned to cook from her grandmother. **Known for:** reservations required in advance; sophisticated traditional Venetian dishes; delicious tasting menus. [$] *Average main: €40* ✉ *Calle del Scaleter, San Polo 2002, San Polo* ☎ *041/721308* 🌐 *www.dafiore.net* ⏲ *Closed 3 wks in Jan.* [M] *Vaporetto San Tomà.*

Coffee and Quick Bites

Al Prosecco

$$ | **WINE BAR** | Locals drop into this friendly bacaro to explore wines from this region and elsewhere in Italy. They accompany a carefully chosen selection of meats, cheeses, and other food from small, artisanal producers, used in tasty panini like the *porchetta romane verdure* (roasted pork with greens) and in elegant cold platters. **Known for:** outdoor seating on the lively campo; great selection of biodynamic wines, including prosecco; lovely meat and cheese platters. [$] *Average main: €20* ✉ *Campo San Giacomo da l'Orio 1503, Santa Croce* ☎ *041/5240222* 🌐 *www.alprosecco.com* ⏲ *Closed Sun.* [M] *Vaporetto: San Stae.*

All'Arco

$ | **WINE BAR** | Just because it's noon and you only have enough time between sights for a sandwich doesn't mean that it can't be a satisfying, even awe-inspiring, one. There's no menu at All'Arco, but a scan of what's behind the glass counter is all you need; order what entices you, or have Roberto or Matteo (father and son) suggest a cicheto or panino. **Known for:** friendly and helpful service; top-notch cicheti; platters of meats and cheeses. [$] *Average main: €8* ✉ *Calle Arco, San Polo 436, San Polo* ☎ *041/5205666* ⏲ *Closed Sun, 2 wks in Feb., and Aug. No dinner* [M] *Vaporetto: San Silvestro.*

Caffè dei Frari

$ | **CAFÉ** | Just over the bridge in front of the Frari church is this old-fashioned place where you'll find an assortment of sandwiches and snacks, but it is the atmosphere, and not the food, that is the main attraction. Established in 1870, it's one of the last Venetian tearooms with its original decor, and while prices are a bit higher than in cafés in nearby Campo Santa Margherita, the vibe and the friendly "retro" atmosphere make the added cost worthwhile. **Known for:** quality *cicheti* (finger food); lovely historic setting; well-made cocktails. [$] *Average main: €8* ✉ *Fondamenta dei Frari, San Polo 2564, San Polo* ☎ *347/8293158* ⏲ *Closed Sun and Mon. No dinner* [M] *Vaporetto: San Tomà.*

Cantina Do Mori

$ | **WINE BAR** | This is the original bacaro, in business continually since 1462; cramped but warm and cozy under hanging antique copper pots, it has served generations of workers from the Rialto Market. In addition to young local whites and reds, the well-stocked cellar offers reserve labels, many available by the glass; between sips you can choose to munch the myriad cicheti on offer, or a few tiny well-stuffed tramezzini, appropriately called *francobolli* (postage stamps). **Known for:** delicious baccalà mantecato, with or without garlic and parsley; good choice of wines by the glass; fine selection of cicheti and sandwiches. [$] *Average main: €8* ✉ *Calle dei Do Mori, San Polo 429, San Polo* ☎ *041/5225401*

Closed Sun. Ⓜ *Vaporetto: Rialto Mercato.*

Hotels

★ Hotel al Ponte Mocenigo

$ | HOTEL | At this hotel—once home to the Santa Croce branch of the Mocenigo family, which counts a few doges in its lineage—a columned courtyard welcomes you, and guest room decor nods to the building's history, with canopied beds, striped damask fabrics, lustrous terrazzo flooring, and gilt-accented furnishings. **Pros:** enchanting courtyard (the perfect spot for an aperitivo); fantastic value; friendly and helpful staff. **Cons:** standard rooms are small; beds are on the hard side; rooms in the annex can be noisy. Ⓢ *Rooms from: €110* ✉ *Fondamento de Rimpeto a Ca' Mocenigo, Santa Croce 2063, Santa Croce* ☎ *041/5244797* ⊕ *www.alpontemocenigo.com* ⊸ *11 rooms* ⦿ *Free Breakfast* Ⓜ *Vaporetto: San Stae.*

La Villeggiatura

$ | HOTEL | If eclectic Venetian charm is what you seek, this luminous residence near the Rialto has it: each of the individually decorated guest rooms has its own theater-themed wall painting by a local artist. **Pros:** relaxed atmosphere and friendly, personalized service; well located near markets, artistic monuments, and restaurants; meticulously maintained. **Cons:** no restaurant (though breakfast is served); no view to speak of, despite the climb; no elevator and lots of stairs. Ⓢ *Rooms from: €104* ✉ *Calle dei Botteri, San Polo 1569, San Polo* ☎ *041/5244673* ⊕ *www.lavilleggiatura.it* ⊸ *6 rooms* ⦿ *Free Breakfast* Ⓜ *Vaporetto: Rialto Mercato.*

★ Oltre il Giardino

$$$ | HOTEL | Behind a brick wall, just over the bridge from the Frari church, this palazzo is hard to find but well worth the effort: a sheltered location, large garden, and individually decorated guest rooms make it feel like a country house. **Pros:** friendly owners happy to share their Venice tips; peaceful, gracious, and convenient setting; glorious walled garden. **Cons:** rooms book up quickly; a beautiful, but not particularly Venetian, ambience; no in-house restaurant (though breakfast served). Ⓢ *Rooms from: €218* ✉ *Fondamenta Contarini, San Polo 2542, San Polo* ☎ *041/2750015* ⊕ *www.oltreil-giardino-venezia.com* *Closed Jan.* ⊸ *6 rooms* ⦿ *Free Breakfast* Ⓜ *Vaporetto: San Tomà.*

Nightlife

★ Il Mercante

COCKTAIL LOUNGES | When the clock strikes 6 pm, historic Caffè dei Frari transforms into this lively craft cocktail bar. Relax on a velvet sofa while enjoying your inventive drink, which is sure to have an intricate story behind it. There's also a good selection of small bites on offer. ✉ *Fondamenta dei Frari, San Polo 2564, San Polo* ☎ *041/4767305* ⊕ *www.ilmercantevenezia.com* Ⓜ *Vaporetto: San Tomà.*

Naranzaria

BARS | At the friendliest of the several bar-restaurants that line the Erbaria, near the Rialto Market, enjoy a cocktail outside, along the Canal Grande, or at a cozy table inside the renovated 16th-century warehouse. Although the food is acceptable, the ambience is really the main attraction. After the kitchen closes at 10:30, light snacks are served until midnight, and there is live music (usually jazz, Latin, or rock) occasionally on Sunday evening. ✉ *L'Erbaria, San Polo 130, along Grand Canal, San Polo* ☎ *041/7241035* ⊕ *www.naranzaria.it* Ⓜ *Vaporetto: Rialto Mercato.*

Shopping

Gilberto Penzo

ANTIQUES & COLLECTIBLES | FAMILY | Find amazingly detailed handmade wooden models of all types of Venetian ships and boats, as well as affordable kits for kids to create their own boats at home. ⊠ *Calle Seconda dei Saoneri, San Polo 2681, San Polo* ☎ *041/5246139* ⊕ *www. veniceboats.com* Ⓜ *Vaporetto: San Tomà.*

★ **Il Tabarro San Marco di Monica Daniele**

OTHER SPECIALTY STORE | This petite shop is the best place in town to find traditional Venetian wool capes, known as *tabarro*, and classic hats, such as the Ezra Pound (curved hat with a brim), the *tricorno* (three-cornered hat), and the *cilindro* (top hat). ⊠ *Calle del Scaleter, San Polo 2235, San Polo* ☎ *041/5246242* ⊕ *www. monicadaniele.com* Ⓜ *Vaporetto: San Stae, San Silvestro.*

Laberintho

JEWELRY & WATCHES | A tiny bottega near Campo San Polo is run by a team of young goldsmiths and jewelry designers specializing in inlaid stones. The work on display in their shop is exceptional, and they also create customized pieces. ⊠ *Calle del Scaleter, San Polo 2236, San Polo* ☎ *041/710017* ⊕ *www.laberintho.com* Ⓜ *Vaporetto: San Stae, San Silvestro.*

Cannaregio

Seen from above, this part of town seems like a wide field plowed by several long, straight canals linked by perpendicular streets—not typical of Venice, where the shape of the islands usually defines the shape of the canals. Cannaregio's main thoroughfare, the Strada Nova (New Street, as it was converted from a canal in 1871), is the longest street in Venice; it runs parallel to the Grand Canal. Today the Strada Nova serves as a pedestrian walkway from the train station almost to the Rialto. Cannaregio, first settled in the 14th century, is one of the more "modern" of Venice's neighborhoods, with *fondamente* (walkways) along the major canals north of the Strada Nova, making it ideal for canalside strolls with views of spectacular Gothic and Baroque facades. There are also some fine eateries and pretty palazzo hotels—all of them away from the San Marco crowds.

TIMING

Although it's more residential and less sight-rich than other Venice neighborhoods, you'll still need several hours here to explore the Ca' d'Oro palace and Madonna dell'Orto and Santa Maria dei Miracoli churches, and to wander the Jewish Ghetto. Cannaregio is a great place to spend a morning before taking the vaporetto to Murano and Burano, which departs from the Fondamente Nove stop.

Sights

★ **Ca' d'Oro**

HISTORY MUSEUM | One of the classic postcard sights of Venice, this exquisite Venetian Gothic palace was once literally a "Golden House," when its marble tracery and ornaments were embellished with gold. It was created by Giovanni and Bartolomeo Bon between 1428 and 1430 for the patrician Marino Contarini, who had read about the Roman emperor Nero's golden house in Rome, the Domus Aurea, and wished to imitate it as a present to his wife. Her family owned the land and the Byzantine *fondaco* (palace-trading house) previously standing on it; you can still see the round Byzantine arches incorporated into the Gothic building's entry porch. The last proprietor, Baron Giorgio Franchetti, left Ca' d'Oro to the city after having it carefully restored and furnished with antiquities, sculptures, and paintings that today make up the Galleria Franchetti. Besides Andrea Mantegna's *St. Sebastian* and other Venetian works, the Galleria Franchetti contains the type of fresco that

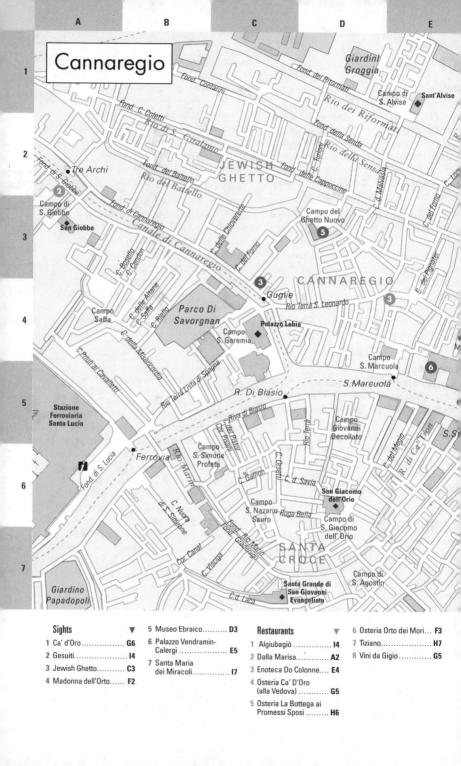

Cannaregio

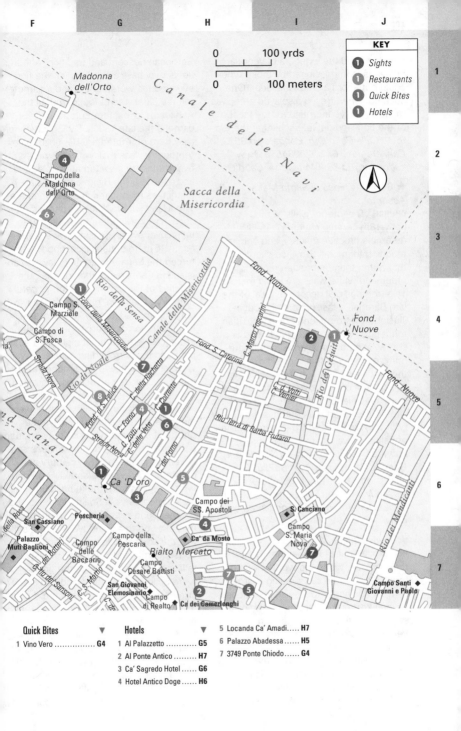

KEY

1 Sights
1 Restaurants
1 Quick Bites
1 Hotels

Madonna dell'Orto

Canale delle Navi

4 Campo della Madonna dell'Orto

6

Sacca della Misericordia

0   100 yrds

0   100 meters

Rio della Sensa

Fond. della Misericordia

Canale della Misericordia

Fond. Nuove

1 Campo S. Marziale

Fond. S. Caterina

C. Mocol Foscarini

Campo di S. Fosca

Rio di Noale

7 C. della Rachetta

C. Larga

C. Larga

2 Fond. Nuove

1 Fond. Nuove

Strada Nova

Fond. di S. Felice

8

C. Pesaro

4 C. Zotti

C. delle Vere

1

6

Rio Terra d' Barba Frutarol

C.V. Volti Venier

Rio dei Gesuiti

Fond. Nuove

C. del forno

5

Strada Nova

1 Ca 'D'oro

3

Campo dei SS. Apostoli

4

S. Canciano

della Rosa

San Cassiano

Pescheria

Campo della Pescaria

Campo S. Maria Nova

7

Palazzo Muti Baglioni

Campo delle Beccarie

Rialto Mercato

Ca' da Mosto

C.lo Rio dei Boteri

Campo Cesare Battisti

Rio dei Mendicanti

C.S. Mattio

San Giovanni Elemosinario

Campo di Rialto

2

Ca dei Camerlenghi

7

5

Campo Santi Giovanni e Paolo

Quick Bites ▼
1 Vino Vero **G4**

Hotels ▼
1 Al Palazzetto **G5**
2 Al Ponte Antico **H7**
3 Ca' Sagredo Hotel **G6**
4 Hotel Antico Doge **H6**

5 Locanda Ca' Amadi..... **H7**
6 Palazzo Abadessa **H5**
7 3749 Ponte Chiodo...... **G4**

once adorned the exteriors of Venetian buildings (commissioned by those who could not afford a marble facade). One such detached fresco displayed here was made by the young Titian for the facade of the Fondaco dei Tedeschi near the Rialto. ✉ *Calle Ca' d'Oro, Cannaregio 3933, Cannaregio* ☎ *041/5200345* ⊕ *www. cadoro.org* 🎫 *€6* Ⓜ *Vaporetto: Ca' d'Oro.*

★ **Gesuiti** (*Chiesa di Santa Maria Assunta*)

CHURCH | The interior walls of this early-18th-century church (1715–30) resemble brocade drapery, and only touching them will convince skeptics that rather than embroidered cloth, the green-and-white walls are inlaid marble. This trompe-l'oeil decor is typical of the late Baroque's fascination with optical illusion. Toward the end of his life, Titian tended to paint scenes of suffering and sorrow in a nocturnal ambience. A dramatic example of this is on display above the first altar to the left: Titian's daring *Martyrdom of St. Lawrence* (1578), taken from an earlier church that stood on this site. To the left of the church is the Oratory of the Crociferi, which features some of Palma Giovane's best work, painted between 1583 and 1591. ✉ *Campo dei Gesuiti, Cannaregio* ☎ *041/5286579* 🎫 *Gesuiti €1; oratory €3* 🕐 *Oratory closed Mon.–Wed., Jan.–mid-Feb., and Sept.–Oct.* Ⓜ *Vaporetto: Fondamente Nove.*

★ **Jewish Ghetto**

HISTORIC DISTRICT | The neighborhood that gave the world the word *ghetto* is today a quiet area surrounding a large campo. It is home to Jewish institutions, several kosher restaurants, a rabbinical school, and five synagogues. Present-day Venetian Jews live all over the city, and the contemporary Jewish life of the ghetto, with the exception of the Jewish Museum and the synagogues, is an enterprise conducted almost exclusively by American Hasidic Jews of eastern European descent and tradition. Although Jews may have arrived earlier, the first synagogues weren't built and a cemetery (on the Lido) wasn't founded until the Ashkenazi, or eastern European Jews, came in the late 1300s. Dwindling coffers may have prompted the Republic to sell temporary visas to Jews, who were over the centuries alternately tolerated and expelled. The Rialto commercial district, as mentioned in Shakespeare's *The Merchant of Venice,* depended on Jewish moneylenders for trade and to help cover ever-increasing war expenses. In 1516, relentless local opposition forced the Senate to confine Jews to an island in Cannaregio, then on the outer reaches of the city, named for its *geto* (foundry). The term "ghetto" also may come from the Hebrew "ghet," meaning separation or divorce. Gates at the entrance were locked at night, and boats patrolled the surrounding canals. Jews were allowed only to lend money at low interest, operate pawnshops controlled by the government, trade in textiles, or practice medicine. Jewish doctors were highly respected and could leave the ghetto at any hour when on duty. Though ostracized, Jews were nonetheless safe in Venice, and in the 16th century, the community grew considerably—primarily with refugees from the Inquisition, which persecuted Jews in Spain, Portugal, and southern and central Italy. The ghetto was allowed to expand twice, but it still had the city's densest population and consequently ended up with the city's tallest buildings. Although the gates were pulled down after Napoléon's 1797 arrival, the ghetto was reinstated during the Austrian occupation. The Jews realized full freedom only in 1866 with the founding of the Italian state. Many Jews fled Italy as a result of Mussolini's 1938 racial laws, so that on the eve of World War II, there were about 1,500 Jews left in the ghetto. Jews continued to flee, and the remaining 247 were deported by he Nazis; only eight returned. The area has Europe's highest density of Renaissance-era synagogues, and visiting them is interesting not only culturally, but also aesthetically. Though each is marked by the tastes of its individual builders, Venetian influence is evident throughout. Women's galleries resemble those of theaters from the same era, and some synagogues were decorated by artists who were simultaneously active in local churches; Longhena, the architect of Santa Maria della Salute, renovated the Spanish synagogue in 1635. ⊠ *Campo del Ghetto Nuovo, Cannaregio.*

★ Madonna dell'Orto

CHURCH | Though built toward the middle of the 14th century, this church takes its character from its beautiful late-Gothic facade, added between 1460 and 1464; it's one of the most beautiful Gothic churches in Venice. Tintoretto lived nearby, and this, his parish church, contains some of his most powerful work. Lining the chancel are two huge (45 feet by 20 feet) canvases, *Adoration of the Golden Calf* and *Last Judgment.* In glowing contrast to this awesome spectacle is Tintoretto's *Presentation of the Virgin at the Temple* and the simple chapel where he and his children, Marietta and Domenico, are buried. Paintings by Domenico, Cima da Conegliano, Palma il Giovane, Palma Il Vecchio, and Titian also hang in the church. A chapel displays a photographic reproduction of a precious *Madonna with Child* by Giovanni Bellini. The original was stolen one night in 1993. Don't miss the beautifully austere, late-Gothic cloister (1460), which you enter through the small door to the right of the church; it is frequently used for exhibitions but may be open at other times as well. ⊠ *Campo della Madonna dell'Orto, Cannaregio* ☎ *041/795991* ⛴ *€3* Ⓜ *Vaporetto: Orto.*

Museo Ebraico (*Jewish Museum*)

SYNAGOGUE | The small but well-arranged museum highlights centuries of Venetian Jewish culture with splendid silver Hanukkah lamps and Torahs, and beautifully decorated wedding contracts handwritten in Hebrew. Tours of the ghetto and its five synagogues in Italian and English leave from the museum hourly (on the half hour). ⊠ *Campo del Ghetto Nuovo, Cannaregio 2902/B, Cannaregio* ☎ *041/715359* ⊕ *www.museoebraico. it* ⛴ *€10* 🕐 *Closed Sat.* Ⓜ *Vaporetto: San Marcuola, Guglie.*

Palazzo Vendramin-Calergi

CASINO | Hallowed as the site of Richard Wagner's death and today Venice's most glamorous casino, this magnificent edifice found its fame centuries earlier: Venetian star architect Mauro Codussi (1440–1504) essentially invented Venetian Renaissance architecture with this design. Built for the Loredan family around 1500, Codussi's palace married the fortresslike design of the Florentine Alberti's Palazzo Rucellai with the lightness and delicacy of Venetian Gothic. Note how Codussi beautifully exploits the flickering light of Venetian waterways to play across the building's facade and to pour in through the generous windows. Venice has always prized the beauty of this palace. In 1652 its owners were convicted of a rather gruesome murder, and the punishment would have involved, as was customary, the demolition of their palace. The murderers were banned from the Republic, but the palace, in view of its beauty and historical importance, was spared. Only a newly added wing was torn down. ⊠ *Cannaregio 2040, Cannaregio* ☎ *041/5297111* ⊕ *www.casinovenezia.it* ⛴ *Casino €5–€10; free for visitors staying at a Venice hotel* Ⓜ *Vaporetto: San Marcuola.*

★ Santa Maria dei Miracoli

CHURCH | Tiny yet harmoniously proportioned, this Renaissance gem, built between 1481 and 1489, is sheathed in marble and decorated inside with exquisite marble reliefs. Architect Pietro Lombardo (circa 1435–1515) miraculously compressed the building to fit its lot, then created the illusion of greater size by varying the color of the exterior, adding extra pilasters on the building's canal side and offsetting the arcade windows to make the arches appear deeper. The church was built to house *I Miracoli,* an image of the Virgin Mary by Niccolò di Pietro (1394–1440) that is said to have performed miracles—look for it on the high altar. ✉ *Campo Santa Maria Nova, Cannaregio* ☎ *041/2750462 Chorus Foundation* ⊕ *www.chorusvenezia.org* ⊠ *€3 (free with Chorus Pass)* ☉ *Closed Sun.* Ⓜ *Vaporetto: Rialto.*

# Restaurants

Algiubagiò

$$$ | ITALIAN | Algiubagiò has a dual personality: at lunch it serves big salads (a better bet than the pizza) and other light fare; at dinner, you'll find heartier primi like their classic guinea fowl ravioli followed by secondi like Angus fillets with rosemary. The young, friendly staff also serve ice cream, drinks, and sandwiches all day. **Known for:** lovely waterfront seating with views of the Dolomites; airy respite for lunch or a snack; romantic spot for dinner. Ⓢ *Average main: €30* ✉ *Fondamente Nove, Cannaregio 5039, Cannaregio* ☎ *041/5236084* ⊕ *www.algiubagio.net* Ⓜ *Vaporetto: Fondamente Nove.*

★ Dalla Marisa

$$ | ITALIAN | This is the most famous workingman's restaurant in Venice; if you can get a table for lunch, you'll eat, without any choice, what Marisa prepares for her blue-collar clientele—generally, enormous portions of excellent pasta, followed by a hearty roast meat course (frequently game, more infrequently fish) for an unbelievably inexpensive fixed price. Dinner is a bit more expensive, and you may have some choice, but not much; for the authentic "Marisa experience," go for lunch. **Known for:** very reasonable prices; authentic, well-prepared Venetian food; limited menu choices. Ⓢ *Average main: €15* ✉ *Fondamenta di San Giobbe 652b,*

Cannaregio ☎ *041/720211* ☉ *Closed 1 wk in Aug. No dinner Sun.–Mon. and Wed.*

Enoteca Do Colonne

$ | WINE BAR | Venetians from this working-class neighborhood frequent this friendly bacaro, not just for a glass of very drinkable wine, but also because of its excellent selection of traditional Venetian cicheti for lunch. There's a large assortment of sandwiches and panini, as well as luscious tidbits like grilled vegetables, breaded and fried sardines and shrimp, and a superb version of baccalà mantecato, along with Venetian working-class specialties, such as *museto* (a sausage made from pigs' snouts served warm with polenta) and *nervetti* (veal tendons with lemon and parsley). **Known for:** the best *musetto* (sausage with polenta) in town; a cozy place for locals to hang out; classic cicheti and sandwiches. Ⓢ *Average main: €8* ✉ *Rio Terà Cristo, Cannaregio 1814, Cannaregio* ☎ *041/5240453* ⊕ *www.docolonne.it* Ⓜ *Vaporetto: San Marcuola.*

Osteria Ca' d'Oro (alla Vedova)

$ | VENETIAN | "The best polpette in town," you'll hear fans of the venerable Vedova say, and that explains why it's an obligatory stop on any *giro d'ombra* (bacaro tour); the polpette are always hot and crunchy—and also gluten-free, as they're made with polenta. Ca' d'Oro is a full-fledged trattoria as well, but make sure to reserve ahead: it's no secret to those seeking traditional Venetian fare at reasonable prices, locals and travelers alike. **Known for:** house wine served in tiny traditional glasses; famous polpette (meatballs); classic Venetian cuisine. Ⓢ *Average main: €12* ✉ *Calle del Pistor, Cannaregio 3912, off Strada Nova, Cannaregio* ☎ *041/5285324* ☉ *Closed Aug. No lunch Sun.* Ⓜ *Vaporetto: Ca' d'Oro.*

Osteria La Bottega ai Promessi Sposi

$$ | VENETIAN | Join locals at the *banco* (counter) premeal for an *ombra* (small glass of wine) and cicheti like polpette or violet eggplant rounds, or reserve a table for a full meal in the dining room or the intimate courtyard. A varied, seasonal menu includes local standards like calf's liver or grilled *canestrelli* (tiny Venetian scallops), along with creative variations on classic Venetian fare, such as home-made ravioli stuffed with radicchio di Treviso or orecchiette with a scrumptious minced-duck sauce. **Known for:** friendly, helpful service; creative cicheti and wine; regularly changing menu with both traditional and modern choices. $ *Average main: €18* ✉ *Calle de l'Oca, just off Campo Santi Apostoli, Cannaregio 4367, Cannaregio* ☎ *041/2412747* ⊘ *No lunch Mon.* Ⓜ *Vaporetto: Ca' d'Oro.*

Osteria Orto dei Mori
$$$ | **ITALIAN** | This small, popular neighborhood osteria—located canalside, just under the nose of the campo's famous corner statue—specializes in creative versions of classic Italian (but not necessarily Venetian) dishes; don't skip dessert, as their tiramisu wins raves. When the weather's nice, dining outside in the square can be a truly memorable experience. **Known for:** buzzing atmosphere with locals and tourists alike; traditional Italian dishes with modern accents; choice local wine selection. $ *Average main: €26* ✉ *Campo dei Mori, Fondamenta dei Mori, Cannaregio 3386, Cannaregio* ☎ *041/5243677* ⊕ *www. osteriaortodeimori.com* ⊘ *Closed Tues. and Wed.* Ⓜ *Vaporetto: Orto, Ca' d'Oro, San Marcuola.*

Tiziano
$ | **ITALIAN** | A fine variety of excellent tramezzini lines the display cases at this *tavola calda* (roughly the Italian equivalent of a cafeteria) on the main thoroughfare from the Rialto to Santi Apostoli; inexpensive salad plates and daily pasta specials are also served. This is a great place for a light meal or snack before a performance at the nearby Teatro Malibran. **Known for:** efficient (if occasionally grumpy) service; quick meals or snacks, especially tramezzini; modest prices. $ *Average*

main: €8 ✉ *Salizada San Giovanni Crisostomo, Cannaregio 5747, Cannaregio* ☎ *041/5235544* Ⓜ *Vaporetto: Rialto.*

★ Vini da Gigio
$$ | **VENETIAN** | A brother-sister team run this refined trattoria, where you're made to feel as if you've been personally invited to lunch or dinner. Indulge, perhaps, in rigatoni with duck sauce or arugula-stuffed ravioli, seafood risotto made to order, or sesame-encrusted tuna. Just note, though, that it's the meat dishes that steal the show: the steak with red-pepper sauce and the *tagliata di agnello* (sautéed lamb fillet with a light, crusty coating) are both superb, and you'll never enjoy a better *fegato alla veneziana* (Venetian-style liver with onions). **Known for:** superb meat dishes like *fegato alla veneziana* (Venetian-style liver with onions); helpful and professional service; one of the city's best wine cellars. $ *Average main: €24* ✉ *Fondamenta San Felice, Cannaregio 3628/A, Cannaregio* ☎ *041/5285140* ⊕ *www.vinidagigio.com* ⊘ *Closed Mon. and Tues. and 2 wks in Aug.* Ⓜ *Vaporetto: Ca' d'Oro.*

☕ Coffee and Quick Bites

★ Vino Vero
$ | **WINE BAR** | Swing by this pint-sized wine bar for cicheti and crostini that's just a bit different and fresher than what you'll find elsewhere, along with a fine selection of natural wines. Though there's not much space inside, try to snag one of the coveted seats by the canal. **Known for:** pretty canalside seating; large selection of both Italian and international natural wines; delectable small bites. $ *Average main: €10* ✉ *Fondamenta de la Misericordia, Cannaregio 2497, Cannaregio* ☎ *041/2750044* ⊕ *vinovero. wine* ⊘ *No lunch Mon.* Ⓜ *Vaporetto: Madonna dell'Orto, Ca' d'Oro.*

Hotels

Al Palazzetto

$$ | **B&B/INN** | **FAMILY** | Understated Venetian decor, original exposed-beam ceilings and terrazzo flooring, and large rooms suitable for families or small groups are hallmarks of this intimate, family-owned guesthouse. **Pros:** good value for money; authentic 18th-century palace; clean and quiet. **Cons:** not many amenities; old-fashioned decor; a bit rough around the edges. Ⓢ *Rooms from: €149* ✉ *Calle delle Vele, Cannaregio 4057, Cannaregio* ☏ *041/2750897* ⊕ *www.guesthouse.it* ⟿ *5 rooms* ⦿❙ *Free Breakfast* Ⓜ *Vaporetto: Ca' d'Oro.*

★ Al Ponte Antico

$$$$ | **HOTEL** | This hospitable 16th-century palace inn has lined its Gothic windows with tiny white lights, creating an inviting glow that's emblematic of the luxurious, distinctively Venetian warmth inside. **Pros:** upper-level terrace overlooks Grand Canal; superior service; family run. **Cons:** books up quickly; beds a little hard for some; in one of the busiest areas of the city (although not particularly noisy). Ⓢ *Rooms from: €330* ✉ *Calle dell'Aseo, Cannaregio 5768, Cannaregio* ☏ *041/2411944* ⊕ *www.alponteantico. com* ⟿ *9 rooms* ⦿❙ *Free Breakfast* Ⓜ *Vaporetto: Rialto.*

★ Ca' Sagredo Hotel

$$$ | **HOTEL** | This expansive palace has been the Sagredo family residence since the mid-1600s and has the decor to prove it: a massive staircase has Longhi wall panels soaring above it; large common areas are adorned with original art by Tiepolo, Longhi, and Ricci; and a traditional Venetian style dominates guest rooms, many of which have canal views and some of which have original art and architectural elements. **Pros:** rooftop terrace and indoor bar; excellent location; some of the city's best preserved interiors. **Cons:** heat in rooms controlled by front desk; more opulent than intimate; no coffee- or tea-making facilities in rooms. Ⓢ *Rooms from: €280* ✉ *Campo Santa Sofia, Cannaregio 4198/99, Cannaregio* ☏ *041/2413111* ⊕ *www.casagredohotel.com* ⟿ *42 rooms* ⦿❙ *No Meals* Ⓜ *Vaporetto: Ca' d'Oro.*

Hotel Antico Doge

$$ | **HOTEL** | Once the home of Marino Faliero, a 14th-century doge who was executed for treason, this palazzo has been attentively "modernized" in elegant 18th-century Venetian style: all rooms are adorned with brocades, damask-tufted walls, gilt mirrors, and parquet floors—even the breakfast room has a stuccoed ceiling and Murano chandelier. **Pros:** some rooms have whirlpool tubs; convenient to the Rialto and beyond; romantic, atmospheric decor. **Cons:** no elevator; no outdoor garden or terrace; area outside hotel can get very busy. Ⓢ *Rooms from: €200* ✉ *Campo Santi Apostoli, Cannaregio 5643, Cannaregio* ☏ *041/2411570* ⊕ *www.anticodoge.com* ⟿ *20 rooms* ⦿❙ *Free Breakfast* Ⓜ *Vaporetto: Ca' d'Oro, Rialto.*

Locanda Ca' Amadi

$$ | **HOTEL** | A historic 13th-century palazzo near the Rialto Market is a welcome retreat on a tranquil *corte,* and individually decorated rooms have tufted walls and views of a lively canal or a quiet courtyard. **Pros:** handy for sightseeing; classic Venetian style; some canal-view rooms. **Cons:** no restaurant (simple continental breakfast served, though); rooms vary a lot in size and quality; reception staff not always helpful or available. Ⓢ *Rooms from: €138* ✉ *Corte Amadi, Cannaregio 5815, Cannaregio* ☏ *041/5285210* ⊕ *www.caamadi.it* ⟿ *6 rooms* ⦿❙ *Free Breakfast* Ⓜ *Vaporetto: Rialto.*

★ Palazzo Abadessa

$$ | **HOTEL** | At this late-16th-century palazzo, you can experience gracious

hospitality, a luxurious atmosphere, a lush private garden, and unusually spacious guest rooms well appointed with antique-style furniture, frescoed or stuccoed ceilings, and silk fabrics. **Pros:** superb guest service; enormous walled garden, a rare and delightful treat in crowded Venice; unique and richly decorated guest rooms. **Cons:** no restaurant (buffet breakfast served); some bathrooms are small and plain; Wi-Fi can be iffy. $ *Rooms from: €170* ✉ *Calle Priuli, Cannaregio 4011, off Strada Nova, Cannaregio* ☎ *041/2413784* ⊕ *www.abadessa.com* ⊗ *Closed last 2 wks in Jan.* ➦ *15 rooms* ⊙ *Free Breakfast* Ⓜ *Vaporetto: Ca' d'Oro.*

3749 Ponte Chiodo

$ | **B&B/INN** | Spending time at this charming guesthouse near the Ca' d'Oro vaporetto stop is like staying with a friend: service is warm and helpful, with lots of suggestions for dining and sightseeing. **Pros:** highly attentive service; pretty private garden; relaxed atmosphere. **Cons:** not for those looking for large-hotel amenities (no spa or gym); no restaurant, though breakfast is served in the garden; some bathrooms are smallish. $ *Rooms from: €98* ✉ *Calle Racheta, Cannaregio 3749, Cannaregio* ☎ *041/2413935* ⊕ *www.pontechiodo.it* ➦ *6 rooms* ⊙ *Free Breakfast* Ⓜ *Vaporetto: Ca' d'Oro.*

🍸 Nightlife

El Sbarlefo

WINE BARS | The odd name is Venetian for "smirk," although you'll be hard-pressed to find one at this cheery, familiar bacaro with a wine selection as ample as the cicheti on offer. The spread of delectables ranges from classic polpette of meat and tuna to tomino cheese rounds to speck and robiola rolls, and the selection of wines is equally intriguing. There's often live jazz and blues on Friday and Saturday nights. El Sbarlefo has a second location in Dorsoduro, in the calle just behind the

church of San Pantalon. ✉ *Salizada del Pistor, off Campo Santi Apostoli, Cannaregio 4556/C, Cannaregio* ☎ *041/5246650* ⊕ *www.elsbarlefo.it* Ⓜ *Vaporetto: Ca' d'Oro.*

Time Social Bar

COCKTAIL LOUNGES | The seasonal cocktails at this charming mixology bar, many of which use fruit and homemade bitters, win rave reviews from visitors and locals alike. There are also small nibbles on offer if hunger strikes. ✉ *Rio Terà Farsetti, Cannaregio 1414, Cannaregio* ☎ *0338/3636951* Ⓜ *Vaporetto: San Marcuola Casino.*

Un Mondo di Vino

WINE BARS | Recharge with some wine or a cicheto or two—meat, fish, and vegetarian choices are on offer—at this cozy, friendly spot near the Miracoli church. Numerous wines are available by the glass, and the helpful servers are often happy to crack open a bottle for sampling if there's something you fancy. ✉ *Salizzada San Cancian, Cannaregio* ☎ *041/5211093* ⊕ *www.bacarounmondodivino.it* Ⓜ *Vaporetto: Rialto, Ca' d'Oro.*

Shopping

★ Gianni Basso Stampatore

STATIONERY | This traditional printer creates handmade business cards, stationery, and invitations using vintage letterpress machinery. You can choose from the selection on offer, or have your own custom designed and shipped to you at home. ✉ *Calle del Fumo, Cannaregio 5306, Cannaregio* ☎ *041/5234681* Ⓜ *Vaporetto: Fondamente Nove.*

Vittorio Constantini

ANTIQUES & COLLECTIBLES | **FAMILY** | This glass artist's workshop features unusual, intricate pieces inspired by nature—birds, butterflies, beetles, and other insects—appreciated by adults and children alike. ✉ *Calle del Fumo, Cannaregio 5311, Cannaregio* ☎ *041/5222265* ⊕ *www.*

vittoriocostantini.com *Vaporetto: Fondamente Nove.*

Castello

Castello, Venice's largest sestiere, includes all of the land from east of Piazza San Marco to the city's easternmost tip. Its name probably comes from a fortress that once stood on one of the eastern islands. Not every well-off Venetian family could find a spot or afford to build a palazzo on the Grand Canal. Many who couldn't instead settled in western Castello, taking advantage of its proximity to the Rialto and San Marco, and built the noble palazzi that today distinguish this area from the fisher's enclave in the more easterly streets of the sestiere. During the days of the Republic, eastern Castello was the primary neighborhood for workers in the shipbuilding Arsenale located in its midst and now home to the Venice Biennale. Foodies flock here for some of the city's most creative modern Italian cuisine.

TIMING

Unless you're here during the Biennale—in which case, you'll be spending at least a full day or two at the Arsenale—you can check out the neighborhood's three gorgeous churches (San Francesco della Vigna, Santi Giovanni e Paolo, and San Zaccaria), as well as the lovely rooms in the Scuola di San Giorgio degli Schiavoni (if it's open, which it isn't always), in half a day.

◉ Sights

Arsenale

MILITARY SIGHT | Visible from the street, the Porta Magna (1460), an impressive Renaissance gateway designed by Antonio Gambello, was the first classical structure to be built in Venice. It is guarded by four lions—war booty of Francesco Morosini, who took the Peloponnese from the Turks in 1687. The 10-foot-tall lion on the left stood sentinel more

than 2,000 years ago near Athens, and experts say its mysterious inscription is runic "graffiti" left by Viking mercenaries hired to suppress 11th-century revolts in Piraeus. If you look at the winged lion above the doorway, you'll notice that the Gospel at his paws is open but lacks the customary *Pax* inscription; praying for peace perhaps seemed inappropriate above a factory that manufactured weapons. The interior is not regularly open to the public, since it belongs to the Italian Navy, but it opens for the Biennale di Arte and for Venice's festival of traditional boats, Mare Maggio, held every May. If you're here at those times, don't miss the chance to look inside; you can enter from the back via a northern-side walkway leading from the Ospedale vaporetto stop. The Arsenale is said to have been founded in 1104 on twin islands. The immense facility that evolved—it was the largest industrial complex in Europe built prior to the Industrial Revolution—was given the old Venetian dialect name *arzanà,* borrowed from the Arabic *darsina'a,* meaning "workshop." At the height of its activity, in the early 16th century, it employed as many as 16,000 *arsenalotti,* workers who were among the most respected shipbuilders in the world. The Arsenale developed a type of pre–Industrial Revolution assembly line, which allowed it to build ships with astounding speed and efficiency. (This innovation existed even in Dante's time, and he immortalized these toiling workers armed with boiling tar in his *Inferno,* canto 21.) The Arsenale's efficiency was confirmed time and again—whether building 100 ships in 60 days to battle the Turks in Cyprus (1597) or completing one perfectly armed warship, start to finish, while King Henry III of France attended a banquet. ⊠ *Campo de la Tana 2169, Castello* Ⓜ *Vaporetto: Arsenale.*

★ San Francesco della Vigna

CHURCH | Although this church contains some interesting and beautiful paintings and sculptures, it's the architecture that makes it worth the hike through a lively, middle-class residential neighborhood. The Franciscan church was enlarged and rebuilt by Jacopo Sansovino in 1534, giving it the first Renaissance interior in Venice; its proportions are said to reflect the mystic significance of the numbers three and seven dictated by Renaissance neo-Platonic numerology. The soaring but harmonious facade was added in 1562 by Palladio. The church represents a unique combination of the work of the two great stars of 16th-century Veneto architecture. As you enter, a late Giovanni Bellini *Madonna with Saints* is down some steps to the left, inside the Cappella Santa. In the Giustinian chapel to the left is Veronese's first work in Venice, an altarpiece depicting the Virgin and child with saints. In another, larger chapel on the left are bas-reliefs by Pietro and his son Tullio Lombardo. Be sure to ask to see the attached cloisters, which are usually open to visitors and quite lovely. ⊠ *Campo di San Francesco della Vigna, Castello* ☎ *041/5206102* ⊠ *Free* ⊘ *Closed weekends* Ⓜ *Vaporetto: Celestia.*

★ San Zaccaria

CHURCH | More a museum than a church, San Zaccaria has a striking Renaissance facade, with central and upper portions representing some of Mauro Codussi's best work. The lower portion of the facade and the interior were designed by Antonio Gambello. The original structure of the church was 14th-century Gothic, with its facade completed in 1515, some years after Codussi's death in 1504, and it retains the proportions of the rest of the essentially Gothic structure. Inside is one of the great treasures of Venice, Giovanni Bellini's celebrated altarpiece, *La Sacra Conversazione,* easily recognizable in the left nave. Completed in 1505, when the artist was 75, it shows Bellini's ability to incorporate the aesthetics of the High Renaissance into his work. It bears a closer resemblance to the contemporary works of Leonardo (it dates from approximately the same time

as the *Mona Lisa*) than it does to much of Bellini's early work. The Cappella di San Tarasio displays frescoes by Tuscan Renaissance artists Andrea del Castagno (1423–57) and Francesco da Faenza (circa 1400–51). Castagno's frescoes (1442) are considered the earliest examples of Renaissance painting in Venice. The three outstanding Gothic polyptychs attributed to Antonio Vivarini earned it the nickname "Golden Chapel." ⊠ *Campo San Zaccaria, 4693 Castello, Castello* ☎ *041/5221257* ⊠ *Church free, chapels and crypt €1.50* ⊘ *Closed Sun. morning* Ⓜ *Vaporetto: San Zaccaria.*

★ Santi Giovanni e Paolo

CHURCH | A venerated jewel, this gorgeous church looms over one of the most picturesque squares in Venice: the Campo Giovanni e Paolo, centered on the magnificent 15th-century equestrian statue of Bartolomeo Colleoni by the Florentine Andrea del Verrocchio. Also note the beautiful facade of the Scuola Grande di San Marco (now the municipal hospital), begun by Pietro Lombardo and completed after the turn of the 16th century by Mauro Codussi. The massive Italian Gothic church itself is of the Dominican order and was consecrated in 1430. Bartolomeo Bon's portal, combining Gothic and classical elements, was added between 1458 and 1462, using columns salvaged from Torcello. The 15th-century stained-glass window near the side entrance is breathtaking for its brilliant colors and beautiful figures; it was made in Murano from drawings by Bartolomeo Vivarini and Girolamo Mocetto (circa 1458–1531). The second official church of the Republic after San Marco, San Zanipolo is the Venetian equivalent of London's Westminster Abbey, with a great number of important people, including 25 doges, buried here. Artistic highlights include an early (1465) polyptych by Giovanni Bellini (right aisle, second altar) where the influence of Mantegna is still very evident, Alvise Vivarini's *Christ Carrying the Cross*

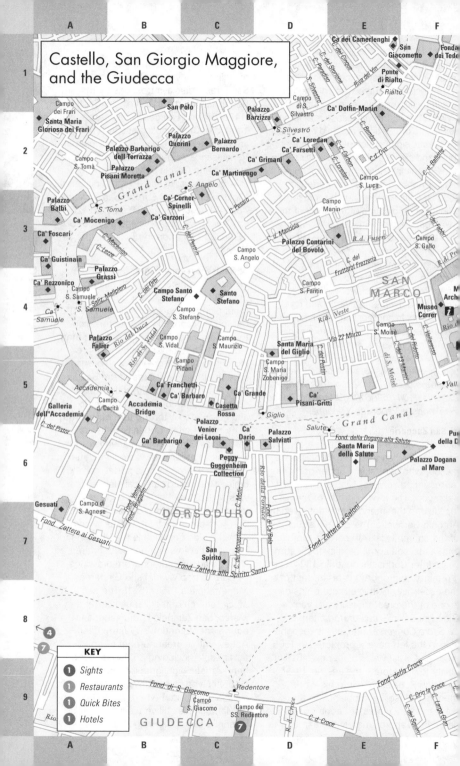

Castello, San Giorgio Maggiore, and the Giudecca

Campo
dei Frari
Santa Maria
Gloriosa dei Frari
San Polo
Palazzo
Barzizza
Ca dei Camerlenghi
San
Giacometto
Fonda
dei Tede
Ponte
di Rialto
Rialto
Campo
di S.
Silvestro
Ca' Dolfin-Manin
S. Silvestro
Palazzo
Barbarigo
dell'Terrazza
Palazzo
Querini
Palazzo
Bernardo
Ca' Loredan
Ca' Farsetti
Campo
S. Tomà
Palazzo
Pisani Moretta
Ca' Grimani
Campo
S. Luca
Grand Canal
Ca' Martinengo
S. Angelo
Palazzo
Balbi
Ca' Corner-
Spinelli
Campo
Manin
Ca' Mocenigo
Ca' Garzoni
Ca' Foscari
Palazzo Contarini
del Bovolo
R.d. Fusen
Campo
S. Gallo
Ca' Guistinain
Palazzo
Grassi
Campo
S. Angelo
C. del
Fruttarol Frezzeria
SAN
MARCO
Ca' Rezzonico
Campo
S. Samuele
S. Samuele
Campo Santo
Stefano
Santo
Stefano
Ca'
Samuele
Campo
S. Fantin
Museo
Correr
Palazzo
Falier
Campo
S. Vidal
Campo
S. Stefano
Campo
S. Maurizio
R.d. Veste
Campo
S. Moise
Via 22 Marzo
Santa Maria
del Giglio
Campo
Pidani
Campo
S. Maria
Zobenigo
Accademia
Ca' Franchetti
Ca' Barbaro
Ca' Grande
Ca'
Pisani-Gritti
Galleria
dell''Accademia
Campo
d. Carità
Accademia
Bridge
Casetta
Rossa
Giglio
Salute
Grand Canal
C. del Pistor
Palazzo
Venier
dei Leoni
Ca'
Dario
Palazzo
Salviati
Fond. della Dogana alla Salute
Pu
della D
Ca' Barbarigo
Peggy
Guggenheim
Collection
Santa Maria
della Salute
Palazzo Dogana
al Mare
Gesuati
Campo di
S. Agnese
DORSODURO
Fond. Zattere ai Gesuati
Fond. Zattere ai Saloni
San
Spirito
Fond. Zattere allo Spirito Santo

Fond. di S. Giacomo
Redentore
Fond. della Croce

KEY
1 Sights
1 Restaurants
1 Quick Bites
1 Hotels

Campo
S. Giacomo
Campo del
SS. Redentore
GIUDECCA

Sights ▼

1 Arsenale	J4
2 Fondazione Giorgio Cini	I7
3 San Francesco della Vigna	J1
4 San Giorgio Maggiore	I6
5 San Zaccaria	I3
6 Santi Giovanni e Paolo	H1
7 Santissimo Redentore	C9
8 Scuola di San Giorgio degli Schiavoni	J2

Restaurants ▼

1 Al Covo	J4
2 Alle Testiere	H2
3 Cip's Club	H8
4 Corte Sconta	J3
5 CoVino	J3
6 Il Ridotto	H3
7 La Palanca	A8
8 Local	J2
9 Osteria di Santa Marina	G1

Quick Bites ▼

1 Aciugheta	H3
2 El Rèfolo	J4
3 Wine Bar 5000	I2

Hotels ▼

1 Belmond Hotel Cipriani	H8
2 Ca' dei Dogi	H3
3 Ca' di Dio	J4
4 Hilton Molino Stucky Venice	A8
5 Hotel Danieli	H4
6 Hotel La Residenza	J3
7 Metropole	J4
8 Ruzzini Palace Hotel	H1

(sacristy), and Lorenzo Lotto's *Charity of St. Antonino* (right transept). Don't miss the Cappella del Rosario (Rosary Chapel), off the left transept, built in the 16th century to commemorate the 1571 victory of Lepanto in western Greece, when Venice led a combined European fleet to defeat the Turkish Navy. The chapel was devastated by a fire in 1867 and restored in the early years of the 20th century with works from other churches, among them the sumptuous Veronese ceiling paintings. However quick your visit, don't miss the Pietro Mocenigo tomb to the right of the main entrance, by Pietro Lombardo and his sons. Note also Tullio Lombardo's tomb of Andrea Vendramin, the original home of Tullio's *Adam*, which has recently been restored in New York City's Metropolitan Museum of Art. ⊠ *Campo dei Santi Giovanni e Paolo, Castello* ☎ *041/5235913* ⊕ *www.santigiovanniepaolo.it* ✉ *€3.50* 𝕊 *Closed weekends* Ⓜ *Vaporetto: Fondamente Nove, Rialto.*

★ **Scuola di San Giorgio degli Schiavoni**

HISTORIC HOME | Founded in 1451 by the Dalmatian community, this small *scuola,* or confraternity, was, and still is, a social and cultural center for migrants from what is now Croatia. It contains one of Italy's most beautiful rooms, harmoniously decorated between 1502 and 1507 by Vittore Carpaccio. Although Carpaccio generally painted legendary and religious figures against backgrounds of contemporary Venetian architecture, here is perhaps one of the first instances of "Orientalism" in Western painting. Note the turbans and exotic dress of those being baptized and converted, and even the imagined, arid Middle Eastern or North African landscape in the background of several of the paintings. In this scuola for immigrants, Carpaccio focuses on "foreign" saints especially venerated in Dalmatia: Sts. George, Tryphone, and Jerome. He combined keen empirical observation with fantasy, a sense of warm color, and late medieval realism.

(Look for the priests fleeing St. Jerome's lion, or the body parts in the dragon's lair.) ■ TIP→ **Opening hours are quite flexible. Since this is a must-see site, check in advance so you won't be disappointed.** ⊠ *Calle dei Furlani, Castello 3259/A, Castello* ☎ *041/5228828* ⊕ *www.scuoladalmatavenezia.com* ✉ *€5* 𝕊 *Closed Tues. and Wed.* Ⓜ *Vaporetto: Arsenale, San Zaccaria.*

🍴 Restaurants

Al Covo

$$$ | VENETIAN | For years, Diane and Cesare Binelli's Al Covo has set the standard of excellence for traditional, refined Venetian cuisine; the Binellis are dedicated to providing their guests with the freshest, highest-quality fish from the Adriatic, and vegetables, when at all possible, from the islands of the Venetian lagoon and the fields of the adjacent Veneto region. Although their cuisine could be correctly termed "classic Venetian," it always offers surprises, like the juicy crispness of their legendary fritto misto—reliant upon a nonconventional secret ingredient in the batter—or the heady aroma of their fresh anchovies marinated in wild fennel, an herb somewhat foreign to Veneto. **Known for:** Diane's chocolate cake for dessert; sophisticated Venetian flavors; top-notch local ingredients. 𝕊 *Average main: €29* ⊠ *Campiello Pescaria, Castello 3968, Castello* ☎ *041/5223812* ⊕ *www.ristorantealcovo.com* 𝕊 *Closed Wed.–Thurs., 3 wks. in Jan., and 10 days in Aug.* Ⓜ *Vaporetto: Arsenale.*

★ Alle Testiere

$$$ | VENETIAN | The name is a reference to the old headboards that adorn the walls of this tiny, informal restaurant, but the food (not the decor) is undoubtedly the focus. Local foodies consider this one of the most refined eateries in the city thanks to chef Bruno Cavagni's gently creative take on classic Venetian fish dishes; the chef's artistry seldom draws

attention to itself, but simply reveals new dimensions to familiar fare, creating dishes that stand out for their lightness and balance. **Known for:** wonderful wine selection; daily changing fish offerings, based on what's fresh at the market; excellent pasta with seafood. $ *Average main: €29* ✉ *Castello 5801, Castello* ☎ *041/5227220* ⊕ *www.osterialletestiere.it* ⊗ *Closed Sun. and Mon., 3 wks in Jan.–Feb., and 4 wks in July–Aug.*

★ Corte Sconta

$$$ | **SEAFOOD** | The heaping seafood antipasti alone is reason enough to visit this classic seafood-focused eatery close to the Biennale—think tuna and swordfish carpaccio, spider crab, clams, crab paté, and a variety of fish. But you'll also want to stay for the excellent mains, particularly soft-shell crab, mixed grilled fish, and spaghetti vongole, plus the lovely courtyard setting. **Known for:** service with a sense of humor; charming atmosphere with outdoor seating; some of the best seafood in town. $ *Average main: €25* ✉ *Calle del Pestrin, Castello 3886, Castello* ☎ *041/5227024* ⊕ *www. cortescontavenezia.com* ⊗ *Closed Sun. and Mon.* Ⓜ *Vaporetto: Arsenale.*

★ CoVino

$$ | **MODERN ITALIAN** | You'll feel like a part of the action in this miniscule natural wine–focused eatery, where the seasonal, organic dishes are prepared right in front of you in the open kitchen. The wine list includes more than 100 labels available by the bottle, or ask for their expert advice on pairing terroir-driven wines with your Slow Food meal. **Known for:** friendly atmosphere; focus on local ingredients; fixed-price menus (2–3 courses for lunch and 3 courses for dinner). $ *Average main: €22* ✉ *Calle del Pestrin, Castello 3829, Castello* ☎ *041/2412705* ⊕ *www. covinovenezia.com* ⊗ *Closed Tues. and Wed.* Ⓜ *Vaporetto: Arsenale.*

★ Il Ridotto

$$$$ | **MODERN ITALIAN** | Longtime restaurateur Gianni Bonaccorsi (proprietor of the popular Aciugheta nearby) has established an eatery where he can pamper a limited number of lucky patrons with his imaginative cuisine and impeccable taste in wine. *Ridotto* means "small, private place," which this very much is, evoking an atmosphere of secrecy and intimacy; the innovative menus tend toward lighter but wonderfully tasty versions of classic dishes. Ask them to recommend a wine from the excellent cantina. **Known for:** extensive wine recommendations; some of the most creative cuisine in Venice; excellent five-, seven-, or nine-course tasting menus. $ *Average main: €40* ✉ *Campo SS. Filippo e Giacomo, Castello 4509, Castello* ☎ *041/5208280* ⊕ *www. ilridotto.com* ⊗ *Closed Tues. and Wed.* Ⓜ *Vaporetto: San Zaccaria.*

★ Local

$$$$ | **VENETIAN** | In a simple yet charming setting with beamed ceilings and terrazzo floors, a sister and brother team oversee their "New Venetian Cuisine," where local ingredients are used to prepare reinvented traditional dishes, often with Japanese influences. Menus are tasting-menu only, ranging from three to 12 courses (with a less expensive three-course option at weekday lunch), and wine pairings from their extensive list are a recommended treat. **Known for:** highly attentive staff; ingredients from Italian producers; risotto with *gò* (goby fish), nori seaweed, and *katsuobushi* (dried smoked tuna). $ *Average main: €95* ✉ *Salizzada dei Greci, Castello 3303, Castello* ☎ *041/2411128* ⊕ *www.ristorantelocal.com* ⊗ *Closed Tues. and Wed.* Ⓜ *Vaporetto: San Zaccaria.*

★ Osteria di Santa Marina

$$$ | **VENETIAN** | The candlelit tables on this romantic campo are inviting enough, but it's the intimate restaurant's imaginative kitchen that's likely to win you over; you can order consistently excellent pasta, fish, or meat dishes à la carte or opt for one of the rewarding tasting menus. The wine list is ample and well thought out, and service is gracious, warm, and professional. **Known for:** charming and romantic setting; innovative and artfully presented modern Venetian food; wonderful wine pairings. $ *Average main: €28* ⊠ *Campo Santa Marina, Castello 5911, Castello* ☎ *041/5285239* ⊕ *www. osteriadisantamarina.com* ⊘ *Closed Sun. and 2 wks in Aug. No lunch Mon.* Ⓜ *Vaporetto: Rialto.*

 Coffee and Quick Bites

Aciugheta

$$ | WINE BAR | Almost an institution, the "Tiny Anchovy" (as the name translates) doubles as a pizzeria-trattoria, but the real reason for coming is the bar's tasty cicheti, like the eponymous anchovy minipizzas, the *arancioni* rice balls, and the polpette. Wines by the glass change daily, but there is always a good selection of local wines on hand, as well as some Tuscan and Piedmontese choices thrown in for good measure. **Known for:** good selection of Italian wines by the glass; *pizzetta con l'acciuga* (minipizza with anchovy); mix of traditional and more modern cicheti. $ *Average main: €15* ⊠ *Campo SS. Filippo e Giacomo, Castello 4357, Castello* ☎ *041/5224292* ⊕ *www. aciugheta.com* ⊘ *Closed Mon.* Ⓜ *Vaporetto: San Zaccaria.*

El Rèfolo

$$ | WINE BAR | At this contemporary cantina and hip hangout in a very Venetian neighborhood, the owner pairs enthusiastically chosen wines and artisanal beers with select meat, savory cheese, and seasonal vegetable combos. With outside-only seating (not particularly comfortable), it's more appropriate for an aperitivo and a light meal. **Known for:** boisterous atmosphere outside in nice weather; good selection of wine and beer; filling meat and cheese plates. $ *Average main: €15* ⊠ *Via Garibaldi,*

Castello 1580, Castello ☎ *344/1636759* ⊕ *www.elrefolo.it* ⊘ *Closed Mon.* Ⓜ *Vaporetto: Arsenale.*

Wine Bar 5000

$ | WINE BAR | Nibble on a selection of cicheti or a cheese or meat plate at this cozy wine bar on Campo San Severo, near the Basilica dei Frari. You can either dine inside the brick-walled, Murano glass-chandeliered space, or watch the gondolas sail by at a table outdoors next to the quiet adjacent Severno canal. **Known for:** small but well-prepared choice of cicheti; lovely outdoor seating area; large wine list, including biodynamic options. $ *Average main: €10* ⊠ *Campo San Severo, Castello 5000, Castello* ☎ *041/5201557* ⊕ *www.lunasentada.it/ winebar5000* ⊘ *Closed Tues. and Wed.* Ⓜ *Vaporetto: San Zaccaria.*

Hotels

★ Ca' dei Dogi

$ | HOTEL | A quiet courtyard secluded from the San Marco melee offers an island of calm in six guest rooms and two apartments (some with private terraces overlooking the Doge's Palace, one with a Jacuzzi), which are individually decorated with contemporary furnishings and accessories. **Pros:** traditional Italian restaurant on-site; amazing location close to Doge's Palace and Piazza San Marco; balconies with wonderful views. **Cons:** no elevator and lots of stairs; rooms are on the small side; bathrooms can feel cramped. $ *Rooms from: €116* ⊠ *Corte Santa Scolastica, Castello 4242, Castello* ☎ *041/2413751* ⊕ *www.cadeidogi. it* ⊘ *Closed 3 wks. in Dec.* ➥ *6 rooms* ⊙¶ *Free Breakfast* Ⓜ *Vaporetto: San Zaccaria.*

Ca' di Dio

$$$$ | HOTEL | Housed in a palace dating from 1272, with interiors updated by of-the-moment architect Patricia

Urquiola, this deluxe hotel offers rooms with views of San Giorgio Maggiore Island, two restaurants, and two internal courtyards, all within striking distance of the Venice Biennale grounds. **Pros:** convenient to the Biennale; most guest rooms are suites; on-site gym and spa. **Cons:** not for fans of traditional design; quite expensive; a walk from traditional Venetian sights. $ *Rooms from: €500* ⊠ *Riva Ca' di Dio, Castello 5866, Castello* ⊕ *vretreats.com/en/ca-di-dio* ¶Ol *Free Breakfast* Ⓜ *Vaporetto: Arsenale.*

★ Hotel Danieli

$$$$ | HOTEL | One of the city's most famous lodgings—built in the 14th century and run as a hotel since 1822—lives up to its reputation: the chance to explore the wonderful, highly detailed lobby is itself a reason to book an overnight stay, plus the views along the lagoon are fantastic, the rooms gorgeous, and the food fabulous. **Pros:** historical and inviting lobby; tasty cocktails at Bar Dandolo; amazing rooftop views. **Cons:** service can be indifferent; some rooms feel dated; lots of American tourists. $ *Rooms from: €500* ⊠ *Riva degli Schiavoni, Castello 4196, Castello* ☎ *041/5226480* ⊕ *www.marriott.com/hotels/travel/vcelc-ho-tel-danieli-a-luxury-collection-hotel-venice* ¶ *210 rooms* ¶Ol *No Meals* Ⓜ *Vaporetto: San Zaccaria.*

Hotel La Residenza

$ | HOTEL | Set in a quiet campo, this renovated 15th-century Gothic-Byzantine palazzo has simple but spacious rooms and lovely public spaces filled with chandeliers, 18th-century paintings, and period reproduction furnishings. **Pros:** affordable rates; lavish salon and breakfast room; quiet residential area, steps from Riva degli Schiavoni and 10 minutes from Piazza San Marco. **Cons:** basic guest rooms; no elevator; sparse breakfast. $ *Rooms from: €80* ⊠ *Campo Bandiera e Moro (or Bragora), Castello 3608, Castello* ☎ *041/5285315* ⊕ *www.*

venicelaresidenza.com ¶ *15 rooms* ¶Ol *No Meals* Ⓜ *Vaporetto: Arsenale.*

★ Metropole

$$$ | HOTEL | Atmosphere prevails in this labyrinth of opulent, intimate spaces featuring classic Venetian decor combined with exotic Eastern influences: the owner—a lifelong collector of unusual objects—has filled the common areas and sumptuously appointed guest rooms with an assortment of antiques and curiosities. **Pros:** great restaurant and bar; hotel harkens back to the gracious Venice of a bygone era; suites have private roof terraces with water views. **Cons:** rooms with views are considerably more expensive; one of the most densely touristed locations in the city; quirky, eccentric collections on display not for everyone. $ *Rooms from: €216* ⊠ *Riva degli Schiavoni, Castello 4149, Castello* ☎ *041/5205044* ⊕ *www.hotelmetropole.com* ¶ *67 rooms* ¶Ol *Free Breakfast* Ⓜ *Vaporetto: San Zaccaria.*

Ruzzini Palace Hotel

$$ | HOTEL | Renaissance- and Baroque-style common areas are soaring spaces with Venetian terrazzo flooring, frescoed and exposed beam ceilings, and Murano chandeliers; guest rooms tastefully mix historical style with contemporary furnishings and appointments. **Pros:** great buffet breakfast (not included in all rates); a luminous, aristocratic ambience; located on a lively Venetian campo not frequented by tourists. **Cons:** relatively far from a vaporetto stop; plain bathrooms; no restaurant on-site. $ *Rooms from: €192* ⊠ *Campo Santa Maria Formosa, Castello 5866, Castello* ☎ *041/2410447* ⊕ *www.ruzzinipalace.com* ¶ *28 rooms* ¶Ol *No Meals* Ⓜ *Vaporetto: San Zaccaria, Rialto.*

Nightlife

Bar Dandolo

COCKTAIL LOUNGES | Even if you're not staying at Hotel Danieli, it's worth a stop to marvel at its bar's over-the-top decor inside a 14th-century palace. Though pricey, it's a highly atmospheric place to sample their signature Vesper martini (gin, vodka, martini dry, and Angostura bitters), or another cocktail of your choice, usually accompanied by live piano music. ⊠ Hotel Danieli, Riva degli Schiavoni, Castello 4196, Castello ☎ 041/5226480 ⊕ www.marriott.com Ⓜ Vaporetto: San Zaccaria.

Zanzibar

CAFÉS | This kiosk bar is very popular on warm summer evenings with Venetians-in-the-know and tourists. Although there's food, it's mostly limited to conventional Venetian sandwiches and commercial ice cream. The most interesting thing about the place is its location with a view of the church of Santa Maria Formosa, which makes it a pleasant place for a drink and a good place for people-watching. ⊠ Campo Santa Maria Formosa, Castello 5840, Castello ☎ 345/9423998 Ⓜ Vaporetto: San Zaccaria.

Shopping

★ Banco Lotto No. 10

WOMEN'S CLOTHING | All of the one-of-a-kind clothes and bags on sale at this vintage-inspired boutique were designed and created by residents of the women's prison on Giudecca Island. ⊠ Salizada Sant'Antonin, Castello 3478/A, Castello ☎ 041/5221439 Ⓜ Vaporetto: San Zaccaria.

★ Papier Mache–Laboratorio di Artigianato Artistico

OTHER SPECIALTY STORE | FAMILY | If you're looking for an authentic Venetian mask, this is the place to come. Owner Stefano and his talented team of artists create exquisite handmade masks that can be custom ordered if you don't see what you want, as well as shipped worldwide. ⊠ Calle Lunga Santa Maria Formosa, Castello 5174/B, Castello ☎ 041/5229995 ⊕ www.papiermache.it Ⓜ Vaporetto: Ospedale.

San Giorgio Maggiore and the Giudecca

Beckoning travelers across St. Mark's Basin is the island of San Giorgio Maggiore, separated by a small channel from the Giudecca. A tall brick campanile on that distant bank nicely complements the Campanile of San Marco. Beneath it looms the stately dome of one of Venice's greatest churches, San Giorgio Maggiore, the creation of Andrea Palladio. To the west, on the Giudecca, is Palladio's other masterpiece, the church of the Santissimo Redentore.

You can reach San Giorgio Maggiore via Vaporetto Line 2 from San Zaccaria. The next three stops on the line take you to the Giudecca. The island's past may be shrouded in mystery, but despite recent gentrification by artists and well-to-do bohemians, it's still down-to-earth and one of the city's few remaining primarily working-class neighborhoods. Interestingly, you find that most Venetians don't even consider the Giudecchini Venetians at all.

Did You Know?

The nobility in Venice used to be extremely competitive about their gondolas, decorating them in flamboyant colors and over-the-top ornaments. A law in the 16th century put an end to that. Today, all gondolas in Venice must be painted boring black, though they are allowed three flourishes: a curly tail, a pair of seahorses, and a multi-pronged prow.

TIMING

A half day should be plenty of time to visit the area. Allow about a half hour to see each of the churches and an hour or two to look around the Giudecca.

Sights

★ Fondazione Giorgio Cini
(*Cini Foundation*)

OTHER MUSEUM | Adjacent to San Giorgio Maggiore is a complex that now houses the Cini Foundation; it contains a very beautiful cloister designed by Palladio in 1560, his refectory, and a library designed by Longhena, as well as 10 "Vatican Chapels" created for the 2018 Architecture Biennale by renowned architects, including Norman Foster, now on permanent display. Guided tours are given from 11 am to 2:30 pm daily (except Wednesday) from November through mid-March and from 10 am to 6 pm daily from mid-March through October; reservations are required. ⊠ *Isola di San Giorgio Maggiore, San Giorgio Maggiore* ☎ *041/2710237* ⊕ *www.cini.it* 🔂 *Reservations required* 🖃 *€14 for guided tour of either the Foundation buildings or the Vatican Chapels; €18 for guided tour of both the Foundation buildings and the Vatican Chapels* ⊗ *Closed Wed. Nov.–mid-Mar.* Ⓜ *Vaporetto: San Giorgio.*

★ San Giorgio Maggiore

CHURCH | There's been a church on this island since the 8th century, with the addition of a Benedictine monastery in the 10th. Today's refreshingly airy and simply decorated church of brick and white marble was begun in 1566 by Palladio and displays his architectural hallmarks of mathematical harmony and classical influence. *The Last Supper* and the *Gathering of Manna*, two of Tintoretto's later works, line the chancel. To the right of the entrance hangs *The Adoration of the Shepherds* by Jacopo Bassano (1517–92); affection for his home in the foothills, Bassano del Grappa, is evident in the bucolic subjects and terra-firma colors he chooses. If they have time, monks are happy to show Carpaccio's *St. George and the Dragon,* which hangs in a private room. The campanile dates from 1791, the previous structures having collapsed twice. ⊠ *Isola di San Giorgio Maggiore, San Giorgio Maggiore* ☎ *041/5227827 San Giorgio Maggiore* ⊕ *www.abbaziasangiorgio.it* 🖃 *Church free, campanile €6* Ⓜ *Vaporetto: San Giorgio.*

Santissimo Redentore

CHURCH | After a plague in 1576 claimed some 50,000 people—nearly one-third of the city's population (including Titian)—Andrea Palladio was asked to design a commemorative church. The Giudecca's Capuchin friars offered land and their services, provided the building's design was in keeping with the simplicity of their hermitage. Consecrated in 1592, after Palladio's death, the Redentore (considered Palladio's supreme achievement in ecclesiastical design) is dominated by a dome and a pair of slim, almost minaretlike bell towers. Its deceptively simple, stately facade leads to a bright, airy interior. There aren't any paintings or sculptures of note, but the harmony and elegance of the interior makes a visit worthwhile. For hundreds of years, on the third weekend in July, it was tradition for the doge to make a pilgrimage here and give thanks to the Redeemer for ending the 16th-century plague. The event has become the Festa del Redentore, a favorite Venetian festival featuring boats, fireworks, and outdoor feasting. It's the one time of the year when you can walk to the Giudecca—across a temporary pontoon bridge connecting Redentore with the Zattere. ⊠ *Fondamenta San Giacomo, Giudecca* ☎ *041/5231415, 041/2750462 Chorus Foundation* ⊕ *www.chorusvenezia. org* 🖃 *€3 (free with Chorus Pass)* ⊗ *Closed Sun.* Ⓜ *Vaporetto: Redentore.*

Restaurants

Cip's Club

$$$$ | VENETIAN | Though it's all about the views at the Belmond Cipriani's indoor/outdoor restaurant—on the water's edge, looking out at the Venice skyline—the well-prepared renditions of Venetian classics and extensive wine list certainly don't play second fiddle. Taking the complimentary 10-minute boat ride to and from San Marco also adds to the thoroughly romantic feel. **Known for:** relaxing lunch destination; sophisticated service; sublime Venice vistas. $ *Average main: €48* ⊠ *Belmond Hotel Cipriani, Giudecca 10, Giudecca* ☎ *041/240801* ⊕ *www.belmond.com/hotels/europe/italy/venice/belmond-hotel-cipriani/dining* Ⓜ *Vaporetto: Zitelle.*

La Palanca

$$ | ITALIAN | It's all about the views at this classic wine bar–restaurant, where tables perched on the water's edge are often filled with both locals and visitors, particularly at lunchtime. The homemade pasta and fish dishes are highly recommended, and although they don't really serve dinner, a filling selection of cicheti is offered in the evening. **Known for:** superlative views; sea bass ravioli; good wine list. $ *Average main: €15* ⊠ *Isola della Giudecca 448, Giudecca* ☎ *041/5287719* ⊘ *Closed Sun.* Ⓜ *Vaporetto: Palanca.*

Ⓗ Hotels

★ Belmond Hotel Cipriani

$$$$ | HOTEL | With amazing service, wonderful rooms, fab restaurants, and a large pool and spa—all just a five-minute boat ride from Piazza San Marco (the hotel water shuttle leaves every 15 minutes, 24 hours a day)—the Cipriani is Venetian luxe at its best. **Pros:** old-world charm; Michelin-starred restaurant; Olympic-size saltwater pool. **Cons:** amazingly expensive; some rooms not quite up to par; gym not open 24 hours. $ *Rooms from: €1406* ⊠ *Giudecca 10, Giudecca* ☎ *041/240801* ⊕ *www.belmond.com/hotels/europe/italy/venice/belmond-hotel-cipriani* ⊘ *Closed mid-Nov.–late Mar.* ⇥ *96 rooms* ⦿ *Free Breakfast* Ⓜ *Vaporetto: Zitelle.*

Hilton Molino Stucky Venice

$$ | HOTEL | FAMILY | Wooden beams and iron columns are some of the original details still visible in this redbrick — former flour mill turned hotel— which also features sublime views across the lagoon to Venice, particularly from the lively rooftop bar. **Pros:** extremely helpful staff; ample breakfast buffet; convenient boat shuttle to Venice proper. **Cons:** can hear noise from other rooms; hotel itself a bit confusing to navigate; food offerings on the pricey side. $ *Rooms from: €192* ⊠ *Giudecca 810, Giudecca* ☎ *041/2723311* ⊕ *www3.hilton.com/en/hotels/italy/hilton-molino-stucky-venice-VCEHIHI/index.html* ⦿ *No Meals* ⇥ *379 rooms* Ⓜ *Vaporetto: Palanca.*

Nightlife

★ Skyline Rooftop Bar

COCKTAIL LOUNGES | For arguably the best views of Venice anywhere, visit this buzzy eighth-floor hotel cocktail bar. There are regular DJ and live music events during the summer months. ⊠ *Hilton Molino Stucky Venice, Giudecca 810, Giudecca* ☎ *041/2723316* ⊕ *www.skylinebarvenice.it* Ⓜ *Vaporetto: Palanca.*

Ⓢ Shopping

★ Fortuny Showroom and Factory

FABRICS | While you can't visit the factory where exquisite Fortuny fabrics have been produced since 1921, the showroom is open to the public on weekdays year-round, and fabric is available for purchase. ⊠ *Fondamenta San Biagio, Giudecca 805, Giudecca* ☎ *0393/8257651 showroom* ⊕ *fortuny.com/venice* Ⓜ *Vaporetto: Palanca.*

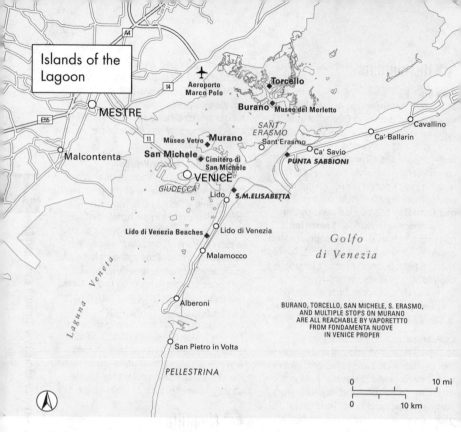

BURANO, TORCELLO, SAN MICHELE, S. ERASMO,
AND MULTIPLE STOPS ON MURANO
ARE ALL REACHABLE BY VAPORETTTO
FROM FONDAMENTA NUOVE
IN VENICE PROPER

Islands of the Lagoon

The perfect vacation from your Venetian vacation is an escape to Murano, Burano, and sleepy Torcello, the islands of the northern lagoon, or to the Lido, Venice's barrier island that forms the southern border of the Venetian Lagoon. Torcello is legendary for its beauty and breathing room, and makes a wonderful destination for a picnic (be sure to pack a lunch). Burano, which has a long history of lace production, is an island of fishing traditions and houses painted in a riot of colors—blue, yellow, pink, ocher, and dark red. Murano is renowned for its glass, and you can tour a glass factory here, but be warned that you will be pressured to buy. San Michele, a vaporetto stop on the way to Murano, is the cemetery island of Venice, the resting place of many international artists who have chosen to spend eternity in this beautiful city. Finally, the Lido, which protects Venice from the waters of the Adriatic, forms the beach of Venice, and is home to a series of elegant bathing establishments.

TIMING

Hitting all the sights on all the islands takes a busy, full day. If you limit yourself to Murano and San Michele, you can easily explore for an ample half day; the same goes for Burano and Torcello. In summer the express Vaporetto Line 7 will take you to Murano from San Zaccaria (the Jolanda landing) in 25 minutes; Line 3 will take you from Piazzale Roma to Murano via the Canale di Cannaregio in 21 minutes; otherwise, local Line 4.1 makes a 45-minute trip from San Zaccaria every 20 minutes, circling the east end of Venice, stopping at Fondamente Nove and San Michele island cemetery on the way. To see glassblowing, get off at Colonna; the Museo stop will put you near the Museo del Vetro.

Line 12 goes from Fondamente Nove direct to Murano and Burano every 30 minutes (from there, Torcello is a 5-minute ferry ride on Line 9); the full trip takes 45 minutes each way. To get to Burano and Torcello from Murano, pick up Line 12 at the Faro stop (Murano's lighthouse). Line 1 runs from San Marco to the Lido in about 15 minutes.

Sights

Cimitero di San Michele (San Michele Cemetery)
CEMETERY | It's no surprise that serenity prevails on San Michele in Venice's northern lagoon. The city's island cemetery is surrounded by ocher brick walls and laced with cypress-lined pathways amid plots filled with thousands of graves; there's also a modern extension completed by British architect David Chipperfield in 2017. Among those who have made this distinctive island their final resting place are such international arts and sciences luminaries as Igor Stravinsky, Sergei Diaghilev, Ezra Pound, and the Austrian mathematician Christian Doppler (of the Doppler effect). You're welcome to explore the grounds if you dress respectfully and adhere to a solemn code of conduct. Photography and picnicking are not permitted. ⊠ *Isola di San Michele, San Michele* ☎ *041/7292841* ⛴ *Free* Ⓜ *Vaporetto: San Michele.*

Lido di Venezia Beaches
BEACH | **FAMILY** | Venice's legendary beachfront, the Lido, still retains elements of Belle Époque grandeur. Most hotels here have access to charming beach clubs with cabanas, striped umbrellas, and chaise longues—all of which are often available for nonguests to use for a fee. On either end of the long barrier island, the public beaches offer a more rustic but still delightful setting for nature lovers to dig their toes in the sand. **Amenities:** food and drink; lifeguards; showers; toilets. **Best for:** swimming; walking. ⊠ *Lido di Venezia, Lido* Ⓜ *Vaporetto: Lido.*

Museo del Merletto (Lace Museum)
OTHER MUSEUM | **FAMILY** | Home to the Burano Lace School from 1872 to 1970, the palace of Podestà of Torcello now houses a museum dedicated to the craft for which this island is known. Detailed explanations of the manufacturing process and Burano's distinctive history as a lace-making capital provide insight into displays that showcase everything from black Venetian Carnival capes to fingerless, elbow-length "mitten gloves" fashionable in 17th-century France. Portraits of Venice's aristocracy as well as embroidered silk and brocade gowns with lace embellishments provide greater societal context on the historical use of lace in European fashion. You can also watch interesting lace-making demonstrations. ⊠ *Piazza Galuppi 187, Burano* ☎ *041/730034* ⊕ *museomerletto.visitmuve.it/en* ⊗ *Closed Mon.* ⛴ *€5* Ⓜ *Vaporetto: Burano.*

★ Museo Vetro (Glass Museum)
ART MUSEUM | **FAMILY** | This compact yet informative museum displays glass items dating from the 3rd century AD to today. You'll learn all about techniques introduced through the ages (many of which are still in use), including 15th-century gold-leaf decoration, 16th-century filigree work that incorporated thin bands of white or colored glass into the crystal, and the 18th-century origins of Murano's iconic chandeliers. A visit here will help you to understand the provenance of the glass you'll see for sale—and may be tempted to buy—in shops around the island. ⊠ *Fondamenta Marco Giustinian 8, Murano* ☎ *041/739586* ⊕ *museovetro.visitmuve.it/en/home* ⛴ *€10* Ⓜ *Vaporetto: Museo Murano.*

🍴 Restaurants

Acquastanca

$$ | VENETIAN | Grab a seat among locals at this charming, intimate eatery—the perfect place to pop in for a lunchtime primo or to embark on a romantic evening. The name, referring to the tranquillity of the lagoon at the turn of the tide, reflects this restaurant's approach to food and service, and you'll find such tempting seafood-based dishes as gnocchi with scallops and zucchini and curried scampi with black *venere* rice.
Known for: relaxing atmosphere; light and fresh traditional food; focus on seafood dishes. [$] *Average main: €20* ✉ *Fondamenta Manin 48, Murano* ☎ *041/3195125* ⊕ *www.acquastanca.it* ☉ *Closed Sun. No dinner Tues.–Thurs. and Sat.* Ⓜ *Vaporetto: Murano Colonna, Murano Faro.*

Al Gatto Nero da Ruggero

$$ | SEAFOOD | Around since 1965, Al Gatto Nero da Ruggero offers the best fish on Burano. No matter what you order, though, you'll savor the pride the owner and his family have in their lagoon, their island, and the quality of their cucina (maybe even more so when enjoying it on the picturesque fondamenta).
Known for: the freshest fish and seafood around; tagliolini with spider crab; risotto Burano-style, using local ghiozzi fish. [$] *Average main: €22* ✉ *Fondamenta della Giudecca 88, Burano* ☎ *041/730120* ⊕ *www.gattonero.com* ☉ *Closed Mon., 1 wk in July, and 3 wks in Nov. No dinner Sun.* Ⓜ *Vaporetto: Burano.*

Busa alla Torre da Lele

$$ | VENETIAN | If you're shopping for glass on Murano and want to sample some first-rate home cooking for lunch, you can't do better than stopping in this unpretentious trattoria in the island's central square. Friendly waiters will bring you ample portions of pasta, with freshly made seafood-based sauces, and a substantial variety of carefully grilled or baked fish. **Known for:** outdoor dining on a square; tasty local fish and seafood; reliable lunch stop in Murano. [$] *Average main: €20* ✉ *Campo Santo Stefano 3, Murano* ☎ *041/739662* ☉ *No dinner* Ⓜ *Vaporetto: Murano Colonna.*

Locanda Cipriani Restaurant

$$$ | VENETIAN | A nearly legendary restaurant—Hemingway came here often to eat, drink, and brood under the green veranda—established by a nephew of Giuseppe Cipriani (the founder of Harry's Bar), this inn profits from its idyllic location on the island of Torcello. The food is not exceptional, especially considering the high prices, but dining here is more about getting lost in Venetian magic.
Known for: a peaceful lunch choice when you want to get away from Venice; wonderful historic atmosphere; traditional Venetian cuisine, with a focus on seafood. [$] *Average main: €34* ✉ *Piazza Santa Fosca 29, Torcello* ☎ *041/730150* ⊕ *www.locandacipriani.com* ☉ *Closed Tues. and Jan.–early Feb. No dinner Sun.–Mon. and Wed.–Thurs.* Ⓜ *Vaporetto: Torcello.*

★ Venissa

$$$$ | MODERN ITALIAN | Stroll across the bridge from Burano to the islet of Mazzorbo to see some of the Venetian islands' only working vineyards, amid which sits this charming restaurant where seasonal dishes incorporate vegetables, herbs, and flowers from its own gardens and fish fresh from the lagoon. To accompany your meal, pick out a local wine like the Venissa Vino Bianco, made with the island's native Dorona grape.
Known for: perfect wine pairings; creative, sometimes avant-garde dishes; relaxed setting with tables overlooking the vines. [$] *Average main: €53* ✉ *Fondamenta Santa Caterina 3, Burano* ☎ *041/5272281* ⊕ *www.venissa.it/en/restaurant* ☉ *Closed Tues. and Nov.–Mar.* Ⓜ *Vaporetto: Mazzorbo.*

Hotels

Hotel Excelsior Venice Lido Resort
$$$$ | **HOTEL** | **FAMILY** | Built in 1908, this grand hotel with Moorish decor has old-fashioned charm and loads of amenities—from a private beach with white cabanas and a seasonal bar and restaurant to a swimming pool, gym, and tennis courts (though, oddly, no spa). **Pros:** convenient water shuttle every 30 mins to and from Venice proper; friendly, welcoming staff; lovely beachfront location. **Cons:** can get very busy in summer and around the Venice Film Festival; could do with a refresh; restaurant on the expensive side. [$] *Rooms from: €515* ✉ *Lungomare Marconi 41, Lido* ☎ *041/5260201* 🌐 *www.hotelexcelsiorvenezia.com* 🛏 *196* 🍴 *No Meals* [M] *Vaporetto: Lido.*

Hyatt Centric Murano Venice
$$ | **HOTEL** | Befitting its location on Murano, this well-situated hotel is in a former glass-making factory and has vitreous works of art throughout; it also has spacious, contemporary guest rooms with dark-wood floors, brown-and-cream color schemes, and good-size bathrooms with rain showers. **Pros:** vaporetto stop right outside the hotel, free airport transfers; easy walk to restaurants and shops; excellent breakfast buffet. **Cons:** most rooms have no views; gym is basic; extra charge for using wellness center. [$] *Rooms from: €190* ✉ *Riva Longa 49, Murano* ☎ *041/2731234* 🌐 *www.hyatt.com* 🛏 *119 rooms* 🍴 *No Meals* [M] *Vaporetto: Museo Murano.*

JW Marriott Venice Resort & Spa
$$$$ | **RESORT** | Once you get a taste of the resort's lush gardens, fabulous spa, and fantastic pools—all set on an exclusive island called Isole Delle Rose, a 20-minute boat ride from Venice—you may find yourself quickly settling in to *la dolce vita* (the sweet life). **Pros:** loads of amenties not found at hotels in Venice proper; relaxed vibe far from the Venice crowds; spacious rooms. **Cons:** not much Venetian style in rooms; getting to and from Venice can feel like a hassle; extra charge for spa. [$] *Rooms from: €450* ✉ *Isola delle Rose, Laguna di San Marco, Venezia Succursale 12, Venice* ☎ *041/8521300* 🌐 *www.jwvenice.com* 🕓 *Closed mid-Nov.–Feb.* 🛏 *266 rooms* 🍴 *No Meals.*

Shopping

Davide Penso
JEWELRY & WATCHES | This Venice-born, Murano-based artist makes gorgeous glass necklaces, earrings, and bracelets using the lampwork technique, where he shapes colored glass rods over a flame. ✉ *Fondamenta Riva Longa 48, Murano* ☎ *041/5274634* 🌐 *www.davidepenso.com* [M] *Vaporetto: Museo Murano.*

★ **Emilia Burano**
FABRICS | This is not your grandmother's lace—these fourth-generation lace makers have updated their designs to produce exquisite bed linens, lampshades, sleepwear, and other items with lace trims and insets. There's also a small museum of antique lace and wedding garments from the 16th and 17th centuries. ✉ *Piazza Galuppi 205, Burano* ☎ *041/735245* 🌐 *www.emiliaburano.it* [M] *Vaporetto: Burano.*

★ **Mama Salvadore Murano**
GLASSWARE | To see more of glassmaking's artistic side, visit this gallery/shop that highlights works from international contemporary glass artists, including renowned 11th-generation Venice glassworker Davide Salvadore. ✉ *Fondamenta dei Vetrai 113, Corte del Fabbro 120, Murano* ☎ *0331/6224359* 🌐 *www.mamamurano.com* [M] *Vaporetto: Murano.*

★ Salviati

GLASSWARE | One of the oldest and most prestigious Italian glassmakers (founded in 1859), Salviati partners with renowned international designers, including Tom Dixon, to create beautiful contemporary pieces. ✉ *Fondamenta Radi 16, Murano* ☎ *041/5274085* ⊕ *www.salviati.com* Ⓜ *Vaporetto: Murano Museo, Murano Navagero.*

★ Simone Cenedese

GLASSWARE | This talented second-generation glass master produces intricately designed and often whimsical glass chandeliers and sculptures. ✉ *Calle Bertolini, 6, Murano* ☎ *041/5274455* ⊕ *www.simonecenedese.it* Ⓜ *Vaporetto: Murano Faro, Murano Colonna.*

NORTHERN ITALY

Updated by
Nick Bruno, Patricia Rucidlo,
and Liz Shemaria

⊙ Sights	🍴 Restaurants	🛏 Hotels	🛍 Shopping	☂ Nightlife
★★★★★	★★★★★	★★★★★	★★★★☆	★★★☆☆

WELCOME TO NORTHERN ITALY

TOP REASONS TO GO

★ **Giotto's frescoes in the Cappella degli Scrovegni:** In this Padua chapel, Giotto's expressive and innovative frescoes foreshadowed the Renaissance.

★ **Leonardo's *Last Supper*:** Behold one of the world's most famous works of art for yourself house within Santa Maria delle Grazie in Milan.

★ **Hiking in the Cinque Terre:** Hike the famous Cinque Terre trails past gravity-defying vineyards, colorful, rock-perched villages, and the deep blue Mediterranean Sea.

★ **The signature food of Emilia-Romagna:** This region's food—prosciutto crudo, Parmigiano-Reggiano, balsamic vinegar, and above all, pasta—makes the trip to Italy worthwhile.

★ **Breathtaking mosaics:** The intricate tiles in Ravenna's Mausoleo di Galla Placidia, in brilliantly well-preserved colors, depict vivid portraits and pastoral scenes.

Northern Italy holds some of the country's most memorable towns, cities, and regions. The Veneto region, just west of Venice, holds the beautiful, artistically rich cities of Padua, Vincenza, and Verona. Farther west, Milan is a major transportation hub and may be your point of entry into the country. South of Milan, you'll find the gorgeous beaches of the Italian Riviera, with the colorful villages of the Cinque Terre being a highlight. Between Florence and Venice, the region of Emilia-Romagna holds prosperous, highly cultured cities, where the locals have mastered the art of living—and especially eating—well.

1 Padua. A city of both high-rises and history, Padua is most noted for Giotto's frescoes in the Cappella degli Scrovegni.

2 Vicenza. This elegant art city bears the signature of the great 16th-century architect Andrea Palladio.

3 Verona. One of the best preserved and most beautiful cities in Italy.

4 Milan. The country's center of finance and commerce is constantly looking to the future. Home of the Italian stock exchange, it's also one of the world's fashion capitals and has cultural and artistic treasures that rival those of Florence and Rome.

5 Riomaggiore. The first of the Cinque Terre villages has a small harbor and coastal views.

6 Manarola. Terraced vineyards, olive trees, and pastel houses fill the town.

7 Corniglia. Climb (365 steps) to the most remote Cinque Terre town.

8 Vernazza. Enjoy lively piazzas and a postcard-worthy port view.

9 Monterosso al Mare. Come here for festivals, beaches, clear water, and plentiful hotels.

10 Bologna. Emilia's principal cultural and intellectual center is famed for its arcaded sidewalks, medieval towers, and sublime restaurants.

11 Ferrara. This prosperous, tidy town north of Bologna has a rich medieval past and distinctive cuisine.

12 Ravenna. The main attractions of this well-preserved Romagna city are its mosaics—glittering treasures left from Byzantine rule.

EATING AND DRINKING WELL IN THE VENETO AND FRIULI–VENEZIA GIULIA

With the decisive seasonal changes of the Venetian Arc, it's little wonder that many restaurants shun printed menus. Elements from field and forest define much of the region's cuisine, including white asparagus, herbs, chestnuts, radicchio, and wild mushrooms.

Restaurants of the Venetian Arc tend to cling to tradition, not only in the food they serve, but also when they serve it. From 2:30 in the afternoon until about 7:30 in the evening most places are closed (though you can pick up a snack at a bar during these hours), and on Sunday afternoon restaurants are packed with Italian families and friends indulging in the weekly ritual of lunching out.

Meals are still sacred for most Italians, so don't be surprised if you get disapproving looks as you gobble down a sandwich or a slice of pizza while seated on the church steps or a park bench. (In many places it's actually illegal to do so.)

THE BEST IN BEANS

Pasta e fagioli (a thick bean soup with pasta, served slightly warm or at room temperature) is made all over Italy. Folks in the Veneto, though, take special pride in their version, made from particularly fine beans grown around the village of Lamon, near Belluno. *Il fagiolo di Lamon* derives from the *Borlotto di Vigevano* bean and was first introduced by a monk in the 1500s via the Spanish court's colonial links to Mexico and Guatemela.

FISH

The catch of the day is always a good bet, whether it's sweet and succulent Adriatic shellfish, sea bream, bass, or John Dory, or freshwater fish from Lake Garda, near Verona. A staple in the Veneto is *baccalà*: this is dried salt cod, which, alongside *stoccafisso*, air-dried cod, was introduced to Italy during the Renaissance by northern European traders. Dried cod is soaked in water or milk and then prepared in a different way in each city. In Vicenza, baccalà *alla vicentina* confusingly uses stoccafisso, which is cooked with onions, milk, and cheese, and is generally served with polenta.

MEAT

In the Veneto, traditional dishes feature offal as much as the prime cuts. Beef (including veal), pork, rabbit, horse, and donkey meat are standard, while goose, duck, and guinea fowl are common poultry options. In Friuli–Venezia Giulia, menus show the influence of Austria-Hungary: you may find deer and hare on the menu, as well as Eastern European–style goulash. One unusual treat served throughout the Veneto is *nervetti*—cubes of gelatin from a calf's knee prepared with onions, parsley, olive oil, and lemon.

PASTA, RISOTTO, POLENTA

For *primi* (first courses), the Veneto dines on *bigoli* (thick whole-wheat pasta), generally served with an anchovy-onion sauce delicately flavored with cinnamon, or creamy risotto flavored with vegetables or shellfish. Polenta is everywhere, whether it's a stiff porridge topped with Gorgonzola, or a stew, or a patty grilled and served alongside meat or fish.

RADICCHIO DI TREVISO

In fall and winter be sure to try the radicchio di Treviso, a red endive grown near that town but popular all over the region. Cultivation is very labor-intensive, so it can be expensive. It's best in a veal or chicken stew, in a risotto, or just grilled or baked with a drizzle of olive oil and perhaps a little Taleggio cheese from neighboring Lombardy.

WINE

The Veneto produces more D.O.C. (Denominazione di Origine Controllata) wines than any other region in Italy. Amarone, the region's crowning achievement, is a robust, full-bodied red. The best of the whites are Soave, prosecco, and *pinot bianco* (pinot blanc). In Friuli–Venezia Giulia, local wines include *friulano*, a dry, lively white made from the sauvignon vert grape, and *picolit*, a dessert wine.

EATING AND DRINKING WELL IN EMILIA-ROMAGNA

Italians rarely agree about anything, but many concede that some of the country's finest foods originated in Emilia-Romagna. Tortellini, fettuccine, Parmesan cheese, prosciutto crudo, and balsamic vinegar are just a few of the Italian delicacies born here.

One of the beauties of Emilia-Romagna is that its exceptional food can be had without breaking the bank. Many trattorias serve up classic dishes, mastered over the centuries, at reasonable prices. Cutting-edge restaurants and wine bars are often more expensive; their inventive menus are full of *fantasia*—reinterpretations of the classics. For the budget-conscious, Bologna, a university town, has great places for cheap eats.

Between meals, you can sustain yourself with the region's famous sandwich, the *piadina*. It's made with pitalike thin bread, usually filled with prosciutto or mortadella, cheese, and vegetables, then put under the grill and served hot, with the cheese oozing at the sides. These addictive sandwiches can be savored at sit-down places or ordered to go.

THE REAL RAGÙ

Emilia-Romagna's signature dish is *tagliatelle al ragù* (flat noodles with meat sauce), known as "spaghetti Bolognese" most everywhere else. This *primo* (first course) is on every menu, and no two versions are the same. The sauce starts in a sauté pan with finely diced carrots, onions, and celery. Purists add nothing but minced beef, but some use *guanciale* (pork cheek), sausage, veal, or chicken. Regular ministrations of broth are added, and sometimes wine, milk, or cream.

PORK PRODUCTS

It's not just mortadella and cured pork products like prosciutto crudo and *culatello* that Emilia-Romagnans go crazy for—they're wild about the whole hog. You'll frequently find cotechino and zampone, both *secondi* (second courses), on menus. *Cotechino* is a savory, thick, fresh sausage served with lentils on New Year's Eve (the combination is said to augur well for the new year) and with mashed potatoes year-round. *Zampone,* a stuffed pig's foot, is redolent of garlic and deliciously fatty.

BOLLITO MISTO

The name means "mixed boil," and they do it exceptionally well in this part of Italy. According to Emilia-Romagnans, *bollito misto* was invented here, although other Italians—especially those from Milan and Piedmont—might dispute this claim. Chicken, beef, tongue, and zampone are tossed into a stockpot and boiled; they're then removed from the broth and served with a fragrant *salsa verde* (green sauce), made with parsley and spiced with anchovies, garlic, and capers. This simple yet rich dish is usually served with mashed potatoes on the side, and savvy diners will mix some of the piquant salsa verde into the potatoes as well.

STUFFED PASTA

Among the many Emilian variations on stuffed pasta, *tortellini* are the smallest. Tortelli and *cappellacci* are larger pasta "pillows," about the size of a brussels sprout, but with the same basic form as tortellini. They're often filled with pumpkin or spinach and cheese. Tortelloni are, in theory, even bigger, although their size varies. Stuffed pastas are generally served simply, with melted butter, sage, and Parmigiano-Reggiano cheese or, in the case of tortellini, in brodo (in beef, chicken, or capon broth or some combination thereof), which brings out the subtle richness of the filling.

WINES

Emilia-Romagna's wines accompany the region's fine food rather than vying with it for accolades. The best-known is *Lambrusco,* a sparkling red produced on the Po Plain that has some admirers and many detractors. It's praised for its tartness and condemned for the same; it does, however, pair brilliantly with the local fare. The region's best wines include Sangiovese di Romagna (somewhat similar to Chianti), from the Romagnan hills, and barbera from the Colli Piacentini and Apennine foothills. Castelluccio, Bonzara, Zerbina, Leone Conti, and Tre Monti are among the region's top producers.

The prosperous north has Italy's most diverse landscape. Venice is a rare jewel of a city, while Milan and Turin are centers of commerce and style. Along the country's northern border, the mountain peaks of the Dolomites and the Valle d'Aosta attract skiers in winter and hikers in summer, while the Lake District and the coastline of the Italian Riviera are classic summertime playgrounds.

Food here is exceptional, from the French-influenced cuisine of Piedmont to Italian classics prepared with unrivaled skill in Emilia-Romagna.

MAJOR REGIONS

The **Veneto**, for centuries influenced by the city of Venice on the marshy Adriatic coast, is a prosperous region dotted by fortified cities with captivating history and undulating vineyards. Padua's alluring architecture, art, and canal network may reflect the Venetian influence as the closest terra firma dominion, but its ancient, pioneering university—famed for its humanist alumni—creates a beguiling buzz of cycling students, food markets, and commerce. With the cooling Dolomite Alpine waters of the Adige River snaking through its medieval, Roman, and Venetian heart, Verona combines splendor with intimacy. Perfectly formed and wealthy Vicenza is where the peerless Palladio put his harmonious architectural plans into bricks, mortar, and gleaming marble. To the west lies **Milan**, the country's economic engine. South, on the Gulf of Genoa, are five isolated seaside villages known collectively as the **Cinque Terre**. Gourmets the world over claim that **Emilia-Romagna's** greatest contribution to humankind has been gastronomic, but Bologna's palaces, Ferrara's medieval alley, and the Byzantine beauty of mosaic-rich Ravenna are all breathtaking.

Planning

When to Go

The ideal times to visit are late spring and early summer (May and June) and in early fall (September and October). Summers tend to be hot and humid—though if you're an opera buff, it's worth tolerating the heat in order to see a performance at the Arena di Verona (where the season runs from July through September).

Winter is a good time to avoid travel to these regions; although the dense fog can be beautiful, it makes for bad driving conditions, and wet, bone-chilling cold isn't unusual November through March. That being said, you'll get some of the best ates and some of the smallest crowds if you do decide to visit during this time.

Making the Most of Your Time

Lined up in a row west of Venice are Padua, Vicenza, and Verona—three prosperous small cities that are each worth at least a day on a northern Italy itinerary. Verona has the most charm and the widest selection of hotels and restaurants, so it's probably the best choice for a base in the area, even though it also draws the most tourists. The hills north of Venice make for good drives, with appealing villages set amid a visitor-friendly wine country.

Italy's commercial hub isn't usually at the top of the list for visiting tourists, but Milan is the nation's most modern city, with its own sophisticated appeal: its fashionable shops rival those of New York and Paris, its soccer teams are Italy's answer to the Yankees and the Mets, its opera performances set the standard for the world, and its art treasures are well worth the visit.

The Italian Riviera and Cinque Terre is extremely seasonal. From April to October, the area's bustling with shops, cafés, clubs, and restaurants that stay open late. In high season (Easter and June–August), it can be very crowded and lively. Yet, the rest of the year, the majority of resorts close down, and you'll be hard-pressed to find accommodations or restaurants open.

Plan on spending at least two days in Bologna, the region's cultural and historical capital. Also plan on visiting Ferrara, a misty, mysterious medieval city. If you have time, go to Ravenna for its memorable Byzantine mosaics and Modena for its harmonious architecture and famous balsamic vinegar.

Getting Here and Around

Aeroporto Malpensa, 50 km (31 miles) northwest of Milan, is the major northern Italian hub for intercontinental flights and also sees substantial European and domestic traffic. Venice's **Aeroporto Marco Polo** also serves international destinations. There are regional airports in Turin, Genoa, Bologna, Verona, Trieste, Treviso, Bolzano, and Parma, and Milan has a secondary airport, Linate. You can reach all of these on connecting flights from within Italy and from other European cities. You can also get around northern Italy by train using the Italian national rail system, **Ferrovie dello Stato** (199303060 *toll-free within Italy*). Shuttle buses run three times an hour (less often after 10 pm) between Malpensa and Milan's main train station, Stazione Centrale; the trip takes about 75 minutes, depending on traffic. The Malpensa Express Train, which leaves twice an hour, takes 40 minutes and delivers you to Cadorna metro station in central Milan.

The cities in these regions are connected by well-maintained highways and an efficient railway system. A car provides added freedom, but city driving and parking can be a challenge.

Restaurants

You'll find lots of traditional northern Italian restaurants in this region, and can pretty much count on menus divided into pasta, fish, and meat options. As in the rest of Italy, it's common for dishes to feature seasonal and local ingredients. Although the Veneto is not considered one of Italy's major cuisine areas, the region offers many opportunities for exciting gastronomic adventures. The fish offerings are among the most varied and freshest in Italy, and possibly Europe, and the vegetables from the islands in the Venetian lagoon are considered a national treasure. Take a break from pasta and try the area's wonderful, creamy risottos and hearty polenta. Meal prices in Milan tend to be higher than in the rest of the region (and quite high for European cities in general), though this is also where you'll see examples of the latest food trends and more adventurous choices on the menus. While fine dining can be found in Cinque Terre, you are more likely to enjoy a casual atmosphere, often with an amazing sea view. Expect both the decor and dishes to be simple but flavorful.

In Emilia-Romagna, dining options range from mom-and-pop-style informal trattorias to three-star Michelin restaurants. Food here is not for the faint of heart (or those on diets): it is rich, creamy, and cheesy. Local wines pair remarkably well with this sumptuous fare. You may want to rethink Lambrusco, as it marries well with just about everything on the menu.

Hotels

Rates tend to be higher in Padua and Verona; in Verona especially, seasonal rates vary widely and soar during trade fairs and the opera season. There are fewer good lodging choices in Vicenza, perhaps because more overnighters are drawn to the better restaurant scenes in Verona and Padua. *Agriturismo* (farm stay) information is available at tourist offices and sometimes on their websites. High-season in Milan depends on what fairs and exhibitions are being staged. Prices in almost all hotels can go up dramatically during the Furniture Fair in early April. Fashion, travel, and tech fairs also draw big crowds throughout the year, raising prices. In contrast to other cities in Italy, however, you can often find discounts on weekends. In Cinque Terre, lodging tends to be pricey in high season, particularly June to August; reservations for this region should also be made far in advance as places book up very quickly. Emilia-Romagna has a reputation

for demonstrating a level of efficiency uncommon in most of Italy. Even the smallest hotels are usually well run, with high standards of quality and service. Bologna is very much a businessperson' city, and many hotels here cater to the business traveler, but there are smaller, more intimate hotels as well. It's smart to book in advance—the region hosts many fairs and conventions that can fill up hotels even during low season.

Hotel reviews have been shortened. For full information, visit Fodors.com.

WHAT IT COSTS in Euros			
$	$$	$$$	$$$$
RESTAURANTS			
under €15	€15–€24	€25–€35	over €35
HOTELS			
under €125	€125–€200	€201–€300	over €300

Padua

A romantic warren of arcaded streets, Padua is a major cultural center in northern Italy. It has first-rate artistic monuments and, along with Bologna, is one of the few cities in the country where you can catch a glimpse of student life.

Its university, founded in 1222 and Italy's second oldest, attracted such cultural icons as Dante (1265–1321), Petrarch (1304–74), and Galileo (1564–1642), thus earning the city the sobriquet *"la Dotta"* (the Learned). Padua's Basilica di Sant'Antonio, begun around 1238, attracts droves of pilgrims, especially on his feast day, June 13. Three great artists—Giotto (1266–1337), Donatello (circa 1386–1466), and Mantegna (1431–1506)—left significant works in Padua. Giotto's Capela degli Scrovegni here is one of the best-known and most meticulously preserved works of art the country. Today, a bicycle-happy student body—some 60,000 strong—influences every aspect of local culture; don't be surprised if you spot a *laurea* (graduation) ceremony marked by laurel leaves, mocking lullabies, and X-rated caricatures.

GETTING HERE AND AROUND

Many people visit Padua from Venice: the train trip between the cities is short, and regular bus service originates from Venice's Piazzale Roma. By car from Milan or Venice, Padua is on the Autostrada Torino–Trieste (A4/E70). Take the San Carlo exit and follow Via Guido Reni to Via Tiziano Aspetti into town. From the south, take the Autostrada Bologna–Padova (A13). Regular bus service connects Venice's Marco Polo airport with downtown Padua.

Padua is a walker's city—parking is difficult, and cars are prohibited in much of the city center. If you arrive by car, leave your vehicle at your hotel or in one of the parking lots on the outskirts. Unlimited bus service is included with the PadovaCard (€18 or €24, valid for 48 or 72 hours), which allows entry to all the city's principal sights (€1 extra for a Capella degli Scrovegni reservation). It's available at tourist information offices and at some museums.

VISITOR INFORMATION

CONTACTS PadovaCard. ☎ *049/2010020 for Cappella degli Scrovegni reservations* ⊕ *www.cappelladegliscrovegni.it.* **Padua Tourism Office.** ✉ *Padova Railway Station, Piazzale Stazione, Padua* ☎ *049/5207415* ⊕ *www.turismopadova.it.*

Sights

Abano Terme

TOWN | A very popular hot-springs spa town about 12 km (7 miles) southwest of Padua, Abano Terme lies at the foot of the Euganean Hills among hand-tilled vineyards. If a bit of pampering sounds better than traipsing through yet another church or castle, indulge yourself with a soak, a massage, stone therapy, a skin peel, or a series of mud treatments, which are especially recommended for joint aches. A good-value day pass (€35) is available at the central and well-equipped Hotel Antiche Terme Ariston Molino Buja (*www.aristonmolino.it*). For a longer stay check out the latest offers on the Abano spa hotel hub website (*www.abano.it*). The nearest railway stop on the Bologna–Padua line is Terme Euganee–Montegrotto. Alternatively, you can board a train on the Milan–Venice line, disembark at Padua, and board an Abano-bound bus in front of the train station. The trip takes about half an hour. ✉ *Abano Terme* ⊕ *Take the Padua West exit off A4, or the Terme Euganee exit off A13* ⊕ *www.abano.it; www.aristonmolino.it.*

★ Basilica di Sant'Antonio

(*Basilica del Santo*)

CHURCH | Thousands of faithful make the pilgrimage here each year to pray at the tomb of St. Anthony, while others come to admire works by the 15th-century Florentine master Donatello. His equestrian statue (1453) of the condottiere Erasmo da Narni, known as Gattamelata, in front of the church is one of the great masterpieces of Italian Renaissance sculpture. It was inspired by the ancient statue of Marcus Aurelius in Rome's Campidoglio. Donatello also sculpted the series of bronze reliefs in the imposing interior illustrating the miracles of St. Anthony, as well as the bronze statues of the Madonna and saints on the high altar. The huge church, which combines elements of Byzantine, Romanesque, and Gothic styles, was probably begun around 1238, seven years after the death of the Portuguese-born saint. It underwent structural modifications into the mid-15th century. Masses are held in the basilica almost constantly, which makes it difficult to see these artworks. More accessible is the restored Cappella del Santo (housing the tomb of the saint), dating from the 16th century. Its walls are covered with impressive

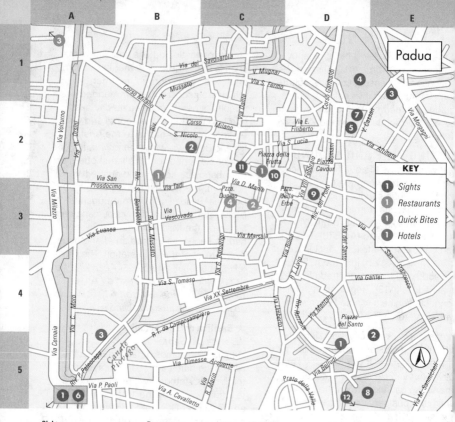

Padua

KEY

- ① Sights
- ① Restaurants
- ① Quick Bites
- ① Hotels

The Venetian Arc, Past and Present

Long before Venetians made their presence felt on the mainland in the 15th century, Ezzelino III da Romano (1194–1259) laid claim to Verona, Padua, and the surrounding lands and towns. He was the first of a series of brutal and aggressive rulers who dominated the cities of the region until the rise of Venetian rule.

After Ezzelino was ousted, powerful families, such as Padua's Carrara and Verona's Della Scala (Scaligeri), vied throughout the 14th century to dominate these territories. With the rise of Venetian rule came a time of relative peace, when noble families from the lagoon and the mainland commissioned Palladio and other accomplished architects to design their palazzi and villas. This rich classical legacy, superimposed upon medieval castles and fortifications, is central to the identities of present-day Padua, Vicenza, and Verona.

The region remained under Venetian control until the Napoleonic invasion and the fall of the Venetian Republic in 1797. The Council of Vienna ceded it, along with Lombardy, to Austria in 1815. The region revolted against Austrian rule and joined the Italian Republic in 1866.

Friuli–Venezia Giulia's complicated history is reflected in its architecture, language, and cuisine. It's been marched through, fought over, hymned by patriots, and romanticized by writers who include James Joyce, Rainer Maria Rilke, Ernest Hemingway, Pier Paolo Pasolini, Italo Svevo, and Jan Morris. The region has seen Fascists and Communists, Romans, Hapsburgs, and Huns. It survived by forging sheltering alliances—Udine beneath the wings of San Marco (1420), Trieste choosing Duke Leopold of Austria (1382) over Venetian domination.

Some of World War I's fiercest fighting took place in Friuli–Venezia Giulia, where memorials and cemeteries commemorate the hundreds of thousands who died before the arrival of Italian troops in 1918 finally liberated Trieste from Austrian rule. Trieste, along with the whole of Venezia Giulia, was annexed to Italy in 1920. During World War II, Germany occupied the area and placed Trieste in an administrative zone along with parts of Slovenia. The only Nazi extermination camp on Italian soil, the Risiera di San Sabba, was in a suburb of Trieste. After the war, during a period of Cold War dispute, Trieste was governed by an Allied military administration; it was officially re-annexed to Italy in 1954, when Italy ceded the Istrian peninsula to the south to Yugoslavia. These arrangements were not finally ratified by Italy and Yugoslavia until 1975.

reliefs by important Renaissance sculptors. The Museo Antoniano part of the basilica complex contains a Mantegna fresco and works by Tiepolo, Carpaccio, and Piazzetta. ⊠ *Piazza del Santo, Padua* ☎ *049/8225652* ⊕ *www.basilicadelsanto. it* ⊠ *Basilica free, museum complex €7* ⊗ *Museum complex closed Mon.*

Burchiello Excursion, Brenta Canal

BODY OF WATER | During the 16th century the Brenta was transformed into a mainland version of Venice's Grand Canal with the building of nearly 50 waterside villas. Back then, boating parties viewed them in *burchielli*—beautiful boats. Today the Burchiello excursion boat makes full- and half-day tours along the Brenta in season, departing from Padua and Venice; tickets can also be bought at travel agencies. You visit three houses, including the Villas Pisani and Foscari, with a lunch-time break in Oriago (€23 or €30 extra). Note that most houses are on the left side coming from Venice, or the right from Padua. ⊠ *Via Porciglia 34, Padua* ☎ *049/8760233* ⊕ *www.ilburchiello.it* ⊠ *€70 for half day, €99 for full day; lunch extra* ⊗ *Closed Mon. and Nov.–Feb.*

★ Cappella degli Scrovegni
(*The Arena Chapel*)
CHURCH | The spatial depth, emotional intensity, and naturalism of the frescoes illustrating the lives of Mary and Jesus in this world-famous chapel broke new ground in Western art. Enrico Scrovegni commissioned these frescoes to atone for the sins of his deceased father, Reginaldo, the usurer condemned to the Seventh Circle of the Inferno in Dante's *Divine Comedy*. Giotto and his assistants worked on the frescoes from 1303 to 1305, arranging them in tiers to be read from left to right. Opposite the altar is a *Last Judgment*, most likely designed and painted by Giotto's assistants.
■ **TIP→ Mandatory timed-entry reservations (nonrefundable) should be made in advance at the ticket office, online, or by phone. Payments online or by phone by credit card must be made one day in advance. Reservations are necessary even if you have a PadovaCard.** To preserve the artwork, doors are opened only every 15 minutes. A maximum of 25 visitors must spend 15 minutes in an acclimatization room before making a 15-minute chapel visit (20 minutes in certain months). Tickets should be picked up at least one hour before your reservation. It's sometimes possible to buy admission on the spot. A good place to get some background before visiting the chapel is the multimedia room. ⊠ *Piazza Eremitani 8, Padua* ☎ *049/2010020 reservations* ⊕ *www.cappelladegliscrovegni.it* ⊠ *€14, includes Musei Civici and Palazzo Zuckermann.*

Chiesa degli Eremitani
CHURCH | This 13th-century church houses substantial fragments of Andrea Mantegna's frescoes (1448–50), which were damaged by Allied bombing in World War II. Despite their fragmentary condition, Mantegna's still beautiful and historically important depictions of the martyrdom of St. James and St. Christopher show the young artist's mastery of extremely complex problems of perspective. ⊠ *Piazza Eremitani, Padua* ☎ *049/8756410.*

Montegrotto Terme
TOWN | At this spa town about 13 km (8 miles) southwest of Padua, you can luxuriate in thermal mineral pools. Montegrotto Terme has several hotels whose treatments vary from simple massage and thermal and mud baths to hydrokinetic therapy. Scuba enthusiasts head here for the world's deepest indoor pool, Y-40 Deep Joy. The nearest railway stop, on the Bologna–Padua line, is Terme Euganee–Montegrotto. Taxis are available outside the station. ⊠ *Montegrotto Terme* ⊹ *Terme Euganee exit off A13* ⊕ *www.visitabanomontegrotto.com.*

★ Musei Civici degli Eremitani
(*Civic Museum*)
OTHER MUSEUM | Usually visited along with the neighboring Cappella degli Scrovegni, this former monastery houses a rich array of exhibits and has wonderful cloister gardens with a mix of ancient architectural fragments and modern sculpture. The Pinacoteca displays works of medieval and modern masters, including some by Tintoretto, Veronese, and Tiepolo. Standouts are the Giotto Crucifix, which once hung in the Cappella degli Scrovegni, and the *Portrait of a Young Senator*, by Giovanni Bellini (1430–1516). Among the archaeological finds is an intriguing Egyptian section, while the *Gabinetto Fotografico* is an important collection of photographs. Set aside at least 60–90 minutes to appreciate the scope of this fabulous museum complex. ⊠ *Piazza Eremitani 8, Padua* ☎ *049/8204551*

€10, €14 with Scrovegni Chapel and Palazzo Zuckermann; free with PadovaCard ⊘ Closed Mon.

Orto Botanico (*Botanical Garden*)

GARDEN | The Venetian Republic ordered the creation of Padua's botanical garden in 1545 to supply the university with medicinal plants, and it retains its original layout. You can stroll the arboretum—still part of the university—and wander through hothouses and beds of plants that were introduced to Italy in this late-Renaissance garden. A St. Peter's palm, planted in 1585, inspired Goethe to write his 1790 essay, "The Metamorphosis of Plants." ⊠ *Via Orto Botanico 15, Padua* ☎ *049/8273939* ⊕ *www.ortobotanicopd.it* €10 (€5 with PadovaCard) ⊘ Closed Mon. May–Mar.

Palazzo del Bo

COLLEGE | The University of Padua, founded in 1222, centers around this predominantly 16th-century palazzo with an 18th-century facade. It's named after the Osteria del Bo (*bo* means "ox"), an inn that once stood on the site. It's worth a visit to see the perfectly proportioned anatomy theater (1594), the beautiful Old Courtyard, and a hall with a lectern used by Galileo. You can enter only as part of a guided tour; most guides speak English, but it is worth checking ahead by phone. ⊠ *Via 8 Febbraio, Padua* ☎ *049/8275111 university switchboard, 049/8273939* ⊕ *www.unipd.it* €7 ⊘ Closed Sat. and Sun.

Palazzo della Ragione

CASTLE/PALACE | Also known as Il Salone, the spectacular arcaded reception hall in Padua's original law courts is as notable for its grandeur—it's 85 feet high—as for its colorful setting, surrounded by shops, cafés, and open-air fruit and vegetable markets. Nicolò Miretto and Stefano da Ferrara, working from 1425 to 1440, painted the frescoes after Giotto's plan, which was destroyed by a fire in 1420. The stunning space hosts art shows, and an enormous wooden horse, crafted for

a public tournament in 1466, commands pride of place. It is patterned after the famous equestrian statue by Donatello in front of the Basilica di Sant'Antonio, and may, in fact, have been designed by Donatello himself in the last year of his life. ⊠ *Piazza della Ragione, Padua* ☎ *049/8205006* ⊘ Closed Sat. and Sun. €7 (free with PadovaCard).

Piazza dei Signori

PLAZA/SQUARE | Some fine examples of 15th- and 16th-century buildings line this square. On the west side, the **Palazzo del Capitanio** (facade constructed 1598–1605) has an impressive **Torre dell'Orologio,** with an astronomical clock dating from 1344 and a portal made by Falconetto in 1532 in the form of a Roman triumphal arch. The 12th-century **Battistero del Duomo** (Cathedral Baptistry), with frescoes by Giusto de' Menabuoi (1374–78), is a few steps away. ⊠ *Piazza dei Signori, Padua* ☎ *049/656914* Battistero €4 (free with PadovaCard).

Villa Pisani

CASTLE/PALACE | FAMILY | Extensive grounds with rare trees, ornamental fountains, and garden follies surround this extraordinary palace in Stra, 13 km (8 miles) southeast of Padua. Built in 1721 for the Venetian doge Alvise Pisani, it recalls Versailles more than a Veneto villa. This was one of the last and grandest of many stately residences constructed along the Brenta River from the 16th to 18th century by wealthy Venetians for their villeggiatura escape from midsummer humidity. Gianbattista Tiepolo's (1696–1770) spectacular fresco on the ballroom ceiling, *The Apotheosis of the Pisani Family* (1761), alone is worth the visit. For a relaxing afternoon, explore the gorgeous park and maze. To get here from Padua, take the SITA bus, or from Venice or Padua, take ACTV Bus No. 53E. The villa is a five-minute walk from the bus stop in Stra. ■TIP➔ **Mussolini invited Hitler here for their first meeting, but they stayed only one night**

because of the mosquitoes, which remain. If visiting on a late afternoon in summer, carry bug repellent. ✉ *Via Doge Pisani 7, Stra* ☎ *049/502074* 🌐 *www.villapisani.beniculturali.it* 🎫 *€7.50, €4.50 park only* 🕒 *Closed Mon.*

🍴 Restaurants

Enoteca dei Tadi

$$ | ITALIAN | In this cozy and atmospheric cross between a wine bar and a restaurant you can put together a fabulous, inexpensive dinner from various classic dishes from all over Italy. Portions are small, but prices are reasonable—just follow the local custom and order a selection, perhaps starting with fresh *burrata* (mozzarella's creamier cousin) with tomatoes, or a selection of prosciutti or salami. **Known for:** bountiful wine and grappa list; several kinds of lasagna; intimate and rustic setting. [$] *Average main: €21* ✉ *Via dei Tadi 16, Padua* ☎ *049/8364099, 388/4083434 mobile* 🌐 *www.enotecadeitadi.it* 🕒 *Closed Mon., 2 wks in Jan., and 2 wks late June–July. No lunch.*

L'Anfora

$$ | WINE BAR | This mix between a traditional *bacaro* (wine bar) and an osteria is a local institution, opened in 1922. Stand at the bar with a cross section of Padovano society, from construction workers to professors, and peruse the reasonably priced menu of simple *casalinga* (home-cooked dishes), plus salads and a selection of cheeses. **Known for:** very busy at lunchtime; no-nonsense traditional Veneto food; atmospheric art-filled osteria with wood interior. [$] *Average main: €19* ✉ *Via Soncin 13, Padua* ☎ *049/656629* 🕒 *Closed Sun. (except in Dec.), 1 wk in Jan., and 1 wk in Aug.*

Le Calandre

$$$$ | MODERN ITALIAN | Traditional Veneto recipes are given a highly sophisticated and creative treatment here, and the whole theatrical tasting-menu experience and gorgeous table settings can seem by turns revelatory or overblown at this high-profile place. Owner-chef Massimiliano Alajmo's creative, miniscule-portion dishes, passion for design (bespoke lighting, carved wooden tables, and quirky plates), and first-class wine list make this an option for a pricey celebratory meal. **Known for:** reservations essential; theatrical, sensory dining experience; playful (or to some pretentious) touches. [$] *Average main: €175* ✉ *Via Liguria 1, Sarmeola* ✥ *7 km (4 miles) west of Padua* ☎ *049/630303* 🌐 *www.calandre.com* 🕒 *Closed Sun., Mon., and Jan. 1–22. No lunch Tues.*

Osteria Dal Capo

$$ | VENETIAN | Located in the heart of what used to be Padua's Jewish ghetto, this friendly trattoria serves almost exclusively traditional Veneto dishes, and it does so with refinement and care. Everything from the well-crafted dishes to the unfussy ship's dining cabin–like decor and elegant plates reflect decades of Padovano hospitality. **Known for:** limited tables mean reservations essential; liver and onions with grilled polenta; intimate and understated dining at decent prices. [$] *Average main: €21* ✉ *Via degli Obizzi 2, Padua*

Cocktail Hour on Padua's Piazzas 🍴

A great Padua tradition is the outdoor consumption of *aperitivi*—a *spritz* (a mix of Aperol or Campari, soda water, and wine), prosecco, or wine—in the Piazza delle Erbe and Piazza delle Frutta. Several bars there provide drinks in plastic cups so you can take them outside and mingle among the crowds. The ritual begins at 6 or so, and may be accompanied with tasty cocktail stick–pierced appetizers known to the Padovani as *spunciotti*. Bars generally close shortly after midnight.

🖾 049/663105 ⊕ www.osteriadalcapo.it
🕓 Closed Sun. No lunch Mon.

Coffee and Quick Bites

Bar Romeo

$ | **NORTHERN ITALIAN** | Deep in the atmospheric Sotto Salone market, this busy bar does a fab selection of filled *tramezzini* (triangular sandwiches), panini, and other snacks. It's a great place to hear the local dialect and mingle with the market workers and shoppers any time of day; grab a breakfast caffè and brioche, a cheeky glass of Falanghina, or a bit later—after 11 am perhaps—an apertivo with snacks. **Known for:** superb selection of wine by the glass; good value sandwiches; friendly staff and Padovano vibe. $ *Average main: €5* 🖾 *26 Sotto Salone, Padua* 🖾 *340/556 0611.*

🛏 Hotels

Al Fagiano

$ | **HOTEL** | The refreshingly funky surroundings in this self-styled art hotel include sponge-painted walls, brush-painted chandeliers, and views of the spires and cupolas of the Basilica di Sant'Antonio. **Pros:** convenient location; relaxed, quirky, homey atmosphere; great for art lovers or those after a unique atmosphere. **Cons:** some find the way-out-there (some risqué) art a bit much; not all rooms have views; lots of stairs. $ *Rooms from: €90* 🖾 *Via Locatelli 45, Padua* 🖾 *049/8750073* ⊕ *www.alfagiano.com* 🛏 *40 rooms* ⦿ *No Meals.*

Albergo Verdi

$ | **HOTEL** | One of the best-situated hotels in the city provides understated modern rooms and public areas that tend toward the minimalist without being severe, while the intimate breakfast room with stylish Eames Eiffel chairs and adjoining terrace is a tranquil place to start the day. **Pros:** excellent location close to the Piazza dei Signori; 24-hour bar service; attentive staff. **Cons:** steep stairs and

small elevator; few views; student noise in piazza-facing rooms. $ *Rooms from: €100* 🖾 *Via Dondi dell'Orologio 7, Padua* 🖾 *049/8364163* ⊕ *www.albergoverdipadova.it* 🛏 *14 rooms* ⦿ *Free Breakfast.*

Methis Hotel & Spa

$$ | **HOTEL** | Four floors of sleekly designed guest rooms reflect the elements at this modern spa hotel: there are gentle earth tones and fiery red in the Classic rooms; watery, cool blues in Superior rooms; and airy white in the top-floor suites. **Pros:** gym, sauna, Turkish bath, and spa treatments; superb canal walks nearby; better views of canal across road from front rooms. **Cons:** public spaces lack some character; 15-minute walk from major sights and restaurants; some maintenance issues. $ *Rooms from: €130* 🖾 *Riviera Paleocapa 70, Padua* 🖾 *049/8725555* ⊕ *www.methishotel.com* 🛏 *59 rooms* ⦿ *Free Breakfast.*

Nightlife

★ Caffè Pedrocchi

CAFÉS | No visit to Padua is complete without taking time to sit in this historic café and iconic Padovano venue, patronized by luminaries like the French novelist Stendhal in 1831. Nearly 200 years later, it remains central to the city's social life. The café was built in the Egyptian Revival style, and it's now famed for its innovative aperitivi and signature mint coffee. The accomplished, innovative restaurant serves breakfast, lunch, and dinner. The grand salons and terrace provide a backdrop for the occasional jazz, swing, and cover bands. 🖾 *Piazzetta Pedrocchi, Padua* 🖾 *049/8781231* ⊕ *www.caffepedrocchi.it.*

Shopping

★ Mercato Sotto il Salone

FOOD | Under the Salone there's an impressive food market where shops sell choice salami and cured meats, local cheeses, wines, coffee, and tea. With the adjacent Piazza delle Erbe fruit and vegetable market, you can pick up all the makings of a fine picnic. On weekends and public holidays, the piazza is often filled with fabulous street food, as well as wine and beer stalls. ⊠ *Piazza della Ragione, Padua* ⊕ *mercatosottoilsalone. it.*

Zotti Antiquariato

ANTIQUES & COLLECTIBLES | Owned by antiques dealer Pietro Maria Zotti—who has worked for more than 40 years in the trade—this always-changing shop has fascinating finds from Venetian artworks to stylish midcentury furniture, plus lots of smaller, more affordable items including books, prints, jewelry, militaria, and coins. ⊠ *Selciato San Nicolò 5, Padua* ☎ *338/2930830* ⊕ *www.zottiantiquariato.it.*

Vicenza

A visit to Vicenza is a must for any student or fan of architecture. This elegant, prosperous city bears the distinctive signature of the architect Andrea Palladio (1508–80), whose name has been given to the Palladian style of architecture.

Palladio emphasized the principles of order and harmony using the classical style of architecture established by Renaissance architects such as Brunelleschi, Alberti, and Sansovino. He used these principles and classical motifs not only for public buildings but also for private dwellings. His elegant villas and palaces were influential in propagating classical architecture in Europe, especially in Britain, and later in America—most notably at Thomas Jefferson's Monticello.

In the mid-16th century Palladio was commissioned to rebuild much of Vicenza, which had been greatly damaged during wars waged against Venice by the League of Cambrai (1505), an alliance of the papacy, France, the Holy Roman Empire, and several neighboring city-states. He made his name with the renovation of Palazzo della Ragione, begun

in 1549 in the heart of Vicenza, and then embarked on a series of noble buildings, all of which adhere to the same principles of classicism and harmony.

GETTING HERE AND AROUND
Vicenza is midway between Padua and Verona, and several trains leave from both cities every hour. By car, take the Autostrada Brescia–Padova/Torino–Trieste (A4/E70) to SP247 North directly into Vicenza.

CONTACT Vicenza Tourism Office. ⊠ *Piazza Giacomo Matteotti 12, Vicenza* ☎ *0444/320854* ⊕ *www.vicenzae.org.*

 Sights

Palazzo Barbaran da Porto (Palladio Museum)

CASTLE/PALACE | Palladio executed this beautiful city palace for the Vicentine noble Montano Barbarano between 1570 and 1575. The noble patron, however, did not make things easy for Palladio; the architect had to incorporate at least two preexisting medieval houses, with irregularly shaped rooms, into his classical, harmonious plan. It also had to support the great hall of the *piano mobile* (moving floor) above the fragile walls of the original medieval structure. The wonder of it is that this palazzo is one of Palladio's most harmonious constructions; the viewer has little indication that this is actually a transformation of a medieval structure. The palazzo also contains a museum dedicated to Palladio and is the seat of a center for Palladian studies. ⊠ *Contrà Porti 11, Vicenza* ☎ *0444/323014* ⊕ *www.palladiomuseum. org* ⌨ *€8; €20 Vicenza Card, includes Palazzo Chiericati and Teatro Olimpico, plus others* ⊘ *Closed Mon.*

Palazzo Chiericati

CASTLE/PALACE | This imposing Palladian palazzo (1550) would be worthy of a visit even if it didn't house Vicenza's **Museo Civico.** Because of the ample space surrounding the building, Palladio combined

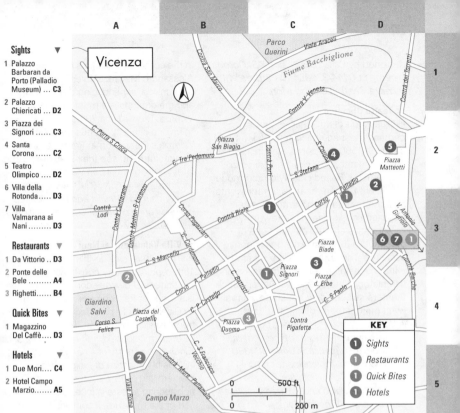

elements of an urban palazzo with those he used in his country villas. The museum's important Venetian holdings include significant paintings by Cima, Tiepolo, Piazzetta, and Tintoretto, but its main attraction is an extensive collection of rarely found works by painters from the Vicenza area, among them Jacopo Bassano (1515–92) and the eccentric and innovative Francesco Maffei (1605–60), whose work foreshadowed important currents of Venetian painting of subsequent generations. ✉ *Piazza Matteotti, Vicenza* ☎ *0444/222811* ⊕ *www.musei-civicivicenza.it* 🎫 *€7; €20 Vicenza Card, includes Palazzo Barbaran da Porto and Teatro Olimpico, plus others.*

Piazza dei Signori

PLAZA/SQUARE | At the heart of Vicenza, this square contains the **Palazzo della Ragione** (1549), the project with which

Palladio made his name by successfully modernizing a medieval building, grafting a graceful two-story exterior loggia onto the existing Gothic structure. Commonly known as Palladio's basilica, the palazzo served as a courthouse and public meeting hall (the original Roman meaning of the term *basilica*) and is now open only when it houses exhibits. The main point of interest, though, the loggia, is visible from the piazza. Take a look also at the **Loggia del Capitaniato,** opposite, which Palladio designed but never completed. ✉ *Vicenza.*

Santa Corona

CHURCH | An exceptionally fine *Baptism of Christ* (1502), a work of Giovanni Bellini's maturity, hangs over the altar on the left, just in front of the transept of this church. Santa Corona also houses the elegantly simple Valmarana chapel, designed by Palladio. ✉ *Contrà S. Corona, Vicenza* ☎ *0444/320854* ✉ *€3 (free with Vicenza Card)* ⊘ *Closed Mon.*

★ Teatro Olimpico

PERFORMANCE VENUE | Palladio's last, perhaps most spectacular work was begun in 1580 and completed in 1585, after his death, by Vincenzo Scamozzi (1552–1616). Based closely on the model of ancient Roman theaters, it represents an important development in theater and stage design and is noteworthy for its acoustics and the cunning use of perspective in Scamozzi's permanent backdrop. The anterooms are frescoed with images of important figures in Venetian history. One of the few Renaissance theaters still standing, it can be visited (with guided tours) during the day and is used for concerts, operas, and other performances. ✉ *Ticket office, Piazza Matteotti 12, Vicenza* ☎ *0444/964380* ⊕ *www.teatrolimpicovicenza.it* ✉ *€11; €20 Vicenza Card, includes Palazzo Barbaran da Porto and Palazzo Chiericati, plus others* ⊘ *Closed Mon.*

★ Villa della Rotonda

(*Villa Almerico Capra*)

HISTORIC HOME | Commissioned in 1556 as a suburban residence for Paolo Almerico, this beautiful Palladian villa is the purest expression of Palladio's architectural theory and aesthetic. More a villa-temple than a residence, it contradicts the rational utilitarianism of Renaissance architecture and demonstrates the priority Palladio gave to the architectural symbolism of celestial harmony over practical considerations. A visit to view the interior can be difficult to schedule—the villa remains privately owned, and visiting hours are limited and constantly change—but this is a worthwhile stop, if only to see how Palladio's harmonious arrangement of smallish interconnected rooms around a central domed space paid little attention to the practicalities of living. The interior decoration, mainly later Baroque stuccowork, contains some allegorical frescoes in the cupola by Palladio's contemporary, Alessandro Maganza. Even without a peek inside, experiencing the exterior and the grounds is a must for any visit to Vicenza. The villa is a 20-minute walk from town or a cab (€10) or bus ride (#8) from Vicenza's Piazza Roma. Private tours are by appointment; see their website for the latest visiting details. ✉ *Via della Rotonda, Vicenza* ☎ *0444/321793* ⊕ *www.villa-larotonda.it* ✉ *€10 villa and grounds, €5 grounds only* ⊘ *Interior closed weekdays early Apr.–early Dec.*

★ Villa Valmarana ai Nani

HISTORIC HOME | Inside this 17th- to 18th-century country house, named for the statues of dwarfs adorning the garden, is a series of frescoes executed in 1757 by Gianbattista Tiepolo depicting scenes from classical mythology, *The Iliad*, Tasso's *Jerusalem Delivered*, and Ariosto's *Orlando furioso* (*The Frenzy of Orlando*). They include his *Sacrifice of Iphigenia*, a major masterpiece of 18th-century painting. The neighboring *foresteria* (guesthouse) is also part of the museum; it contains frescoes showing 18th-century life at its most charming, and scenes of chinoiserie popular in the 18th century, by Tiepolo's son Giandomenico (1727–1804). The garden dwarfs are probably taken from designs by Giandomenico. You can reach the villa on foot by following the same path that leads to Palladio's Villa della Rotonda. ✉ *Via dei Nani 2/8, Vicenza* ☎ *0444/321803* ⊕ *www.villavalmarana.com* ✉ *€11.*

🍽 Restaurants

Da Vittorio

$ | PIZZA | FAMILY | You'll find little in the way of atmosphere or style at this tiny, casual place, but Vicentini flock here for what may be the best pizza north of Naples. There's an incredible array of toppings, from the traditional to the exotic (think mango), but the pizzas taste so authentic you may feel transported to the Bay of Naples. **Known for:** tightly packed tables create a warm atmosphere;

uthentic wood-fired Neapolitan pizza convenient to Palladio villas; cheery naive artworks. [$] *Average main: €12* ✉ *Borgo Berga 52, Vicenza* ☎ *0444/525059* 🕓 *Closed Tues., No lunch Sat. and Sun.*

Ponte delle Bele
$$ | **NORTHERN ITALIAN** | Many of Vicenza's wealthier residents spend at least part of the summer in the Alps to escape the heat, and the dishes of this popular and friendly trattoria reflect the hearty Alpine influences on local cuisine. The house specialty, *stinco di maiale al forno* (roast pork shank), is wonderfully fragrant, with herbs and aromatic vegetables. **Known for:** mountain cheeses and cold cuts; hearty Vicentina classics including baccalà served with polenta; unfussy, relaxed atmosphere and kitschy Alpine decor. [$] *Average main: €15* ✉ *Contrà Ponte delle Bele 5, Vicenza* ☎ *0444/320647* 🌐 *www.pontedellebele.it* 🕓 *Closed Sun. and 2 wks in Aug.*

Righetti
$ | **ITALIAN** | Vicentini of all generations gravitate to this popular cafeteria for classic dishes that don't put a dent in your wallet. Expect hearty helpings of fare such as *orzo e fagioli* (barley and bean soup) and baccalà *alla vicentina* (stockfish Vicenza style). **Known for:** entertaining local atmosphere; classic dishes; very popular, especially for lunch. [$] *Average main: €12* ✉ *Piazza Duomo 3, Vicenza* ☎ *0444/543135* 🕓 *Closed weekends and 1 wk in Jan. and Aug.*

Coffee and Quick Bites

Magazzino Del Caffè
$ | **NORTHERN ITALIAN** | Il Magazzino is a great spot to grab a snack any time of day, as this well-run, modern place covers all the bases from caffè and brioche breakfast fixes, to brunch panini and plates of pasta or risotto with a glass of wine later. Check out their fab selection of brioche pastries with novel fruit and nutty fillings, as well as heaped salads. **Known for:** tempting biscuits and gelato; aperitivi with stuzzichini snacks; friendly, youthful staff. [$] *Average main: €8* ✉ *Corso Palladio 152, Vicenza* ☎ *335/573 9054.*

Hotels

★ **Due Mori**
$ | **HOTEL** | The public areas and guest rooms at one of the oldest (1883) hotels in the city, just off the Piazza dei Signori, are filled with turn-of-the-20th-century antiques, and regulars favor the place because the high ceilings in the main building make it feel light and airy. **Pros:** free Wi-Fi; comfortable, tastefully furnished rooms in central location; rate same year-round. **Cons:** no help with luggage; no AC, although ceiling fans minimize the need for it; no TVs in rooms. [$] *Rooms from: €100* ✉ *Contrà Do Rode 24, Vicenza* ☎ *0444/321886* 🌐 *www.hotelduemori.com* 🕓 *Closed 2 wks in early Aug. and 2 wks in late Dec.* 🛏 *30 rooms* 🍴 *No Meals.*

Hotel Campo Marzio
$$ | **HOTEL** | Rooms at this comfortable full-service hotel—a five-minute walk from the train station and right in front of the city walls—are ample in size, with a mix of contemporary and traditional accents. **Pros:** set back from the street, so it's quiet and bright; free Wi-Fi in rooms; free bike hire. **Cons:** breakfast room a tad uninspiring; no in-room tea- or coffee-making facilities; businesslike exterior. [$] *Rooms from: €125* ✉ *Viale Roma 21, Vicenza* ☎ *0444/5457000* 🌐 *www.hotelcampomarzio.com* 🛏 *36 rooms* 🍴 *Free Breakfast.*

Verona

On the banks of the fast-flowing River Adige and 60 km (37 miles) west of Vicenza, enchanting Verona has timeless monuments, a picturesque town center, fascinating museums, and a romantic reputation as the setting of Shakespeare's *Romeo and*

Palladio's Architecture

Wealthy 16th-century patrons commissioned Andrea Palladio to design villas that would reflect their sense of cultivation and status. Using a classical vocabulary of columns, arches, and domes, he gave them a series of masterpieces in the towns and hills of the Veneto that exemplify the neo-Platonic ideals of harmony and proportion. Palladio's creations are the perfect expression of how a learned 16th-century man saw himself and his world, and as you stroll through them today, their serene beauty is as powerful as ever. Listen closely and you might even hear that celestial harmony, the music of the spheres, that so moved Palladio and his patrons.

Town and Country
Although the *villa*, or country residence, was still a relatively new phenomenon in the 16th century, it quickly became all the rage once the great lords of Venice turned their eyes from the sea toward the fertile plains of the Veneto. They were forced to do this once their trade routes had faltered when Ottoman Turks conquered Constantinople in 1456 and Columbus opened a path for Spain to the riches of America in 1492. In no time, canals were built, farms were laid out, and the fashion for villeggiatura became a favored lifestyle. As a means of escaping an overheated Rome, villas had been the original brainchild of the ancient emperors, and it was no accident that the Venetian lords wished to emulate this palatial style of country residence. Palladio's method of evaluating the standards, and standbys, of ancient Roman life through the eye of the Italian Renaissance, combined with his innate sense of proportion and symmetry, became the lasting foundation of his art. In turn, Palladio threw out the mélange of styles prevalent in Venetian architecture—Byzantine, Gothic, and Renaissance—for the pure, noble lines found in the buildings of the Caesars.

Andrea Palladio (1508–80)
"Face dark, eyes fiery. Dress rich. His appearance that of a genius." So was Palladio described by his wealthy mentor, Count Trissino. Trissino encouraged the young student to trade in his birth name, Andrea di Pietro della Gondola, for the elegant Palladio. He did, and it proved a wise move indeed. Born in Padua in 1508, Andrea moved to nearby Vicenza in 1524 and was quickly taken up by the city's power elite. He experienced a profound revelation on his first trip, in 1541, to Rome, where he sensed the harmony of the ancient ruins and saw the elements of classicism that were working their way into contemporary architecture. This experience led to his spectacular conversion of Vicenza's Palazzo della Ragione into a Roman basilica, recalling the great meeting halls of antiquity. In years to come, after relocating to Venice, he created some memorable churches, such as San Giorgio Maggiore (1564). Despite these varied projects, Palladio's unassailable position as one of the world's greatest architects is tied to the countryside villas, which he spread across the Veneto plains like a firmament of stars. Nothing else in the Veneto illuminates more clearly the idyllic beauty of the region than these elegant residences, their stonework now nicely mellowed and suntanned after five centuries.

Vicenza

To see Palladio's pageant of palaces, head for Vicenza. His Palazzo della Ragione marks the city's heart, the Piazza dei Signori. This building rocketed young Palladio from an unknown to an architectural star. Across the way is his redbrick Loggia del Capitaniato. One block past the loggia is Vicenza's main street, appropriately named Corso Andrea Palladio. Just off this street is the Contrà Porti, where you'll find the Palazzo Barbaran da Porto (1570) at No. 11, with its fabulously rich facade erupting with Ionic and Corinthian pillars. Today, this is the Centro Internazionale di Studi di Architettura Andrea Palladio (www.palladiomuseum.org), a study center that mounts impressive temporary exhibitions. A few steps away, on the Contrà San Gaetano Thiene, is the Palazzo Thiene (1542–58), designed by Giulio Romano and completed by Palladio. Doubling back to Contrà Porti 21, you find the Palazzo Iseppo da Porto (1544), the first palazzo where you can see the neoclassical effects of young Palladio's trip to Rome. Following the Contrà Riale, you come to Corso Fogazzaro 16 and the Palazzo Valmarana Braga (1565). Its gigantic pilasters were a first for domestic architecture. Returning to the Corso Palladio, head left to the opposite end of the Corso, about five blocks, to the Piazza Matteotti and Palazzo Chiericati (1550). This was practically a suburban area in the 16th century, and for the palazzo Palladio combined elements of urban and rural design. The pedestal raising the building and the steps leading to the entrance— unknown in urban palaces—were to protect from floods and to keep cows from wandering in the front door. Across the Corso Palladio is Palladio's last and one of his most spectacular works, the Teatro Olimpico (1580). By careful study of ancient ruins and architectural texts, he reconstructed a Roman theater with archaeological precision. Palladio died before it was completed, but he left clear plans for the project. Although it's on the outskirts of town, the Villa Almerico Capra, better known as La Rotonda or Villa della Rotonda (1566), is an indispensable part of any visit to Vicenza. It's the iconic Palladian building, the purest expression of his aesthetic.

Palladio Country

At the Villa Barbaro (1554) near the town of Maser in the province of Treviso, 48 km (30 miles) northeast of Vicenza, you can see the results of a onetime collaboration between two of the greatest artists of their age. Palladio was the architect, and Paolo Veronese decorated the interior with an amazing cycle of trompe-l'oeil frescoes—walls dissolve into landscapes, and illusions of courtiers and servants enter rooms and smile down from balustrades. Legend has it a feud developed between Palladio and Veronese, with Palladio feeling the illusionistic frescoes detracted from his architecture; but there is practically nothing to support the idea of such a rift. It's also noteworthy that Palladio for the first time connected the two lateral granaries to the main villa. This was a working farm, and Palladio thus created an architectural unity by connecting the working parts of the estate to the living quarters with graceful arcades, bringing together the Renaissance dichotomy of the active and the contemplative.

Juliet. Verona grew to power and prosperity within the Roman Empire as a result of its key commercial and military position in northern Italy. With its Roman arena, theater, and city gates, it has the most significant monuments of Roman antiquity north of the Eternal City itself. After the fall of the empire, the city continued to flourish under the guidance of barbarian kings, such as Theodoric, Alboin, Pepin, and Berengar I. It reached its cultural and artistic peak in the 13th and 14th centuries under the Della Scala (Scaligeri) dynasty. (Look for the *scala*, or ladder, emblem all over town.) In 1404 Verona traded its independence for security and placed itself under the control of Venice. (The other recurring architectural motif is the lion of St. Mark, a symbol of Venetian rule.)

With its well-heeled yet lively Veneto atmosphere and proximity to Lake Garda, Verona attracts many tourists, especially Germans and Austrians. Tourism peaks during summer's renowned season of open-air opera in the arena and during spring's Vinitaly, one of the world's most important wine and spirits expos.

If you're going to visit more than one or two sights, it's worth purchasing a VeronaCard, available at museums, churches, and tobacconists for €20 (for 24 hours) or €25 (48 hours). It buys single admission to most of the city's significant museums and churches, and allows you to ride for free on city buses. If you're mostly interested in churches, a €6 cumulative ticket is sold at Verona's major houses of worship and gains you entry to the Duomo, San Fermo Maggiore, San Zeno Maggiore, and Sant'Anastasia (all covered by the VeronaCard as well). Verona's churches enforce a dress code: no shorts, short skirts, or sleeveless shirts.

GETTING HERE AND AROUND

Verona is midway between Venice and Milan. Its small Aeroporto Valerio Catullo accommodates domestic and European flights, though many travelers fly into Venice or Milan and drive or take the train to Verona. Several trains per hour depart from points along the Milan–Venice line. By car, from the east or west, take the Autostrada Trieste–Torino (A4/E70) to the SS12 and follow it north into town. From the north or south, take the Autostrada del Brennero (A22/E45) to the SR11 East (initially called the Strada Bresciana) directly into town.

VISITOR INFORMATION

CONTACTS Verona Tourism Office (IAT Verona). ⊠ *Via degli Alpini 9, Verona* 🕾 *045/8068680* ⊕ *www.veronatouristoffice.it/en.* **VeronaCard.** ⊕ *www.turismoverona.eu.*

Sights

Arche Scaligere

TOMB | On a little square off the Piazza dei Signori are the fantastically sculpted Gothic tombs of the Della Scala family, who ruled Verona during the late Middle Ages. The 19th-century English traveler and critic John Ruskin described the tombs as graceful places where people who have fallen asleep live. The tomb of Cangrande I (1291–1329) hangs over the portal of the adjacent church and is the work of the Maestro di Sant'Anastasia. The tomb of Mastino II, begun in 1345, has an elaborate baldachin, originally painted and gilded, and is surrounded by an iron grillwork fence and topped by an equestrian statue. The latest and most elaborate tomb is that of Cansignorio (1375), the work principally of Bonino da Campione. The major tombs are all visible from the street. ⊠ *Via Arche Scaligere, Verona.*

★ Arco dei Gavi

RUINS | This stunning structure is simpler and less imposing, but also more graceful, than the triumphal arches in Rome. Built in the 1st century AD by the architect Lucius Vitruvius Cerdo to celebrate the accomplishments of the patrician Gavia family, it was highly esteemed by several Renaissance architects, including Palladio. ⊠ *Corso Cavour, Verona.*

Arena di Verona

RUINS | FAMILY | Only Rome's Colosseum and Capua's arena would dwarf this amphitheater, built for gymnastic competitions, choreographed sacrificial rites, and games involving hunts, fights, battles, and wild animals. Although four arches are all that remain of the arena's outer arcade, the main structure is complete and dates from AD 30. In summer, you can join up to 16,000 (3,000 during COVID-19 restrictions) for spectacular opera productions and pop or rock concerts (extra costs for these events). ■TIP→ **The opera's the main thing here: when there is no opera performance, you can still enter the interior, but the arena is less impressive inside than the Colosseum or other Roman amphitheaters.** ⊠ *Piazza Bra 5, Verona* 🕾 *045/8003204* ⊕ *www.arena.it* 🖾 *€10 (free with VeronaCard); €11 includes entrance to nearby Museo Lapidario Maffeiano* 🕘 *Closed Mon. Oct.–May.*

★ Castelvecchio

CASTLE/PALACE | This crenellated, russet brick building with massive walls, towers, turrets, and a vast courtyard was built for Cangrande II della Scala in 1354 and presides over a street lined with attractive old buildings and palaces of the nobility. Only by going inside the **Museo di Castelvecchio** can you really appreciate this massive castle complex with its vaulted halls. You also get a look at a significant collection of Venetian and Veneto art, medieval weapons, and jewelry. The interior of the castle was restored and redesigned as a museum between 1958 and 1975 by Carlo Scarpa, one of Italy's most accomplished architects. Behind the castle is the Ponte Scaligero (1355), which spans the River Adige. ⊠ *Corso Castelvecchio 2, Verona* 🕾 *045/8062611* ⊕ *museodicastelvecchio.comune.verona. it* 🖾 *€4.50 (free with VeronaCard).*

Duomo

CHURCH | The present church was begun in the 12th century in the Romanesque style; its later additions are mostly Gothic. On pilasters guarding the main entrance are 12th-century carvings thought to represent Oliver and Roland, two of Charlemagne's knights and heroes of several medieval epic poems. Inside, Titian's *Assumption* (1532) graces the first chapel on the left. ⊠ *Via Duomo, Verona* 🕾 *045/592813* ⊕ *www.chieseverona.it* 🖾 *€3 (free with Church Cumulative Ticket or VeronaCard).*

★ Funicular of Castel San Pietro

VIEWPOINT | Opened in 2017, this funicular ride ascends 500 feet from near Teatro Romano up to a panoramic terrace in just 90 seconds, affording fabulous Veronese views. For the adventurous, there's scope for long walks around the parkland paths and quiet lanes crisscrossing the elevated city walls. ⊠ *Via Fontanelle S. Stefano, Verona* 🕾 *342/8966695* ⊕ *www. funicolarediverona.it* 🖾 *€2.50 round-trip, €1.50 one way.*

Loggia del Consiglio

GOVERNMENT BUILDING | This graceful structure on the north flank of the Piazza dei Signori was finished in 1492 and built to house city council meetings. Although the city was already under Venetian rule, Verona still had a certain degree of autonomy, which was expressed by the splendor of the loggia. Very strangely for a Renaissance building of this quality, its architect remains unknown, but it's the finest surviving example of late-15th-century architecture in Verona. The building is not open to the public, but the exterior is worth a visit. ⊠ *Piazza dei Signori, Verona.*

Museo Archeologico and Teatro Romano

HISTORY MUSEUM | The archaeological holdings of this museum in a 15th-century former monastery consist largely of the donated collections of Veronese citizens proud of their city's classical past. You'll find few blockbusters here, but there are some noteworthy pieces (especially among the bronzes), and it is interesting to see what cultured Veronese collected between the 17th and 19th century. The

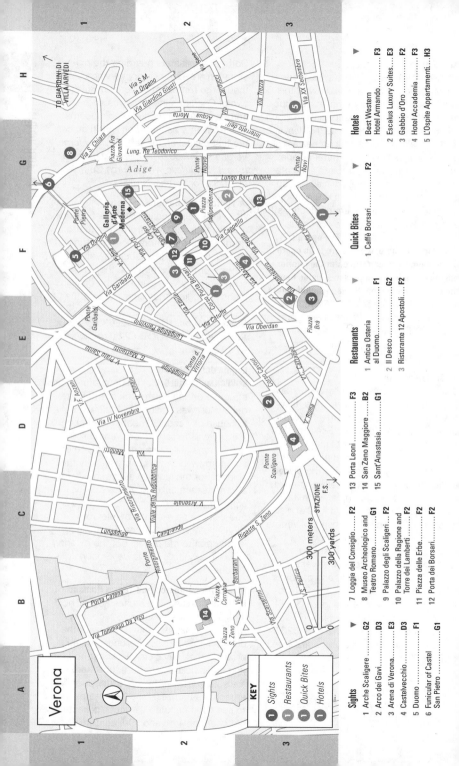

Verona

KEY
- Sights
- Restaurants
- Quick Bites
- Hotels

Sights
1 Arche Scaligere **G2**
2 Arco dei Gavi............. **D3**
3 Arena di Verona.......... **E3**
4 Castelvecchio............. **D3**
5 Duomo...................... **F1**
6 Funicular of Castel
  San Pietro **G1**
7 Loggia del Consiglio...... **F2**
8 Museo Archeologico and
  Teatro Romano............ **G1**
9 Palazzo degli Scaligeri... **F2**
10 Palazzo della Ragione and
   Torre dei Lamberti **F2**
11 Piazza delle Erbe.......... **F2**
12 Porta dei Borsari.......... **F2**
13 Porta Leoni **F3**
14 San Zeno Maggiore **B2**
15 Sant'Anastasia............ **G1**

Restaurants
1 Antica Osteria
  al Duomo.................... **F1**
2 Il Desco..................... **G2**
3 Ristorante 12 Apostoli.... **F2**

Quick Bites
1 Caffè Borsari.............. **F2**

Hotels
1 Best Western
  Hotel Armando............. **F3**
2 Escalus Luxury Suites.... **E3**
3 Gabbio d'Oro.............. **F2**
4 Hotel Accademia.......... **F3**
5 L'Ospite Appartamenti.... **H3**

TO GIARDINI DI
VILLA ARVEDI

Adige

Piazza Brà

STAZIONE
F.S.

0   300 meters
0   300 yards

museum complex includes the Teatro Romano, Verona's 1st-century-AD theater, which is open to visitors. ✉ *Rigaste del Redentore 2, Verona* ☎ *045/8000360* ⊕ *museoarcheologico.comune.verona.it* ✉ *€4.50 (free with VeronaCard).*

Palazzo degli Scaligeri
(*Palazzo di Cangrande*)
CASTLE/PALACE | The Della Scala family ruled Verona from this stronghold built (over Roman ruins) at the end of the 13th century and then inhabited by Cangrande I. At that time Verona controlled the mainland Veneto from Treviso and Lombardy to Mantua and Brescia, hence the building's alternative name as a seat of Domini di Terraferma (Venetian administration): Palazzo del Podestà. The portal facing the Piazza dei Signori was added in 1533 by the accomplished Renaissance architect Michele Sanmicheli. You have to admire the palazzo from the outside, as it's not open to the public. ✉ *Piazza dei Signori, Verona.*

★ Palazzo della Ragione and Torre dei Lamberti
VIEWPOINT | An elegant 15th-century pink marble staircase leads up from the *mercato vecchio* (old market) courtyard to the magistrates' chambers in this 12th-century palace, built at the intersection of the main streets of the ancient Roman city. The interior now houses exhibitions of art from the **Galleria d'Arte Moderna Achille Forti.** You can get the highest view in town from atop the attached 270-foot-high Romanesque Torre dei Lamberti. About 50 years after a lightning strike in 1403 knocked its top off, it was rebuilt and extended to its current height. ✉ *Piazza dei Signori, Verona* ☎ *045/9273027* ⊕ *torredeilamberti.it* ✉ *Gallery and tower €8 (free with VeronaCard); tower €5 on Mon.* ☽ *Gallery closed Mon.*

Piazza delle Erbe
PLAZA/SQUARE | Frescoed buildings surround this medieval square, where a busy Roman forum once stood; during the week it's still bustling, as vendors sell produce and trinkets, much as they have been doing for generations. Eyes are drawn to the often sun-sparkling Madonna Verona fountain (1368) and its Roman statue (the body is from AD 380, with medieval additions). ✉ *Verona.*

★ Porta dei Borsari
RUINS | As its elegant decoration suggests, this is the main entrance to ancient Verona—dating, in its present state, from the 1st century AD. It's at the beginning of the narrow, pedestrianized Corso Porta Borsari, now a smart shopping street leading to Piazza delle Erbe. ✉ *Corso Porta Borsari, Verona.*

Porta Leoni
RUINS | The oldest of Verona's elegant and graceful Roman portals, the Porta Leoni (on Via Leoni, just a short walk from Piazza delle Erbe) dates from the 1st century BC, but its original earth-and-brick structure was sheathed in local marble during the early imperial era. It has become the focus of a campaign against violence—there are often flowers and messages by the monument—in memory of the murder of a young Veronese here in 2009. ✉ *Via Leoni, Verona.*

★ San Zeno Maggiore
CHURCH | One of Italy's finest Romanesque churches is filled with treasures, including a rose window by the 13th-century sculptor Brioloto that represents a wheel of fortune, with six of the spokes formed by statues depicting the rising and falling fortunes of mankind. The 12th-century porch is the work of Maestro Niccolò; it's flanked by marble reliefs by Niccolò and Maestro Guglielmo depicting scenes from the Old and New Testaments and from the legend of Theodoric. The bronze doors date from the 11th and 12th centuries; some were probably imported from Saxony, and some are from Veronese workshops. They combine allegorical representations with scenes from the lives of saints. Inside, look for the 12th-century statue of San Zeno to the left of the main altar.

In modern times it has been dubbed the "Laughing San Zeno" because of a misinterpretation of its conventional Romanesque grin. A famous *Madonna and Saints* triptych by Andrea Mantegna (1431–1506) hangs over the main altar, and a peaceful cloister (1120–38) lies to the left of the nave. The detached bell tower was finished in 1173. ✉ *Piazza San Zeno, Verona* ☎ *045/592813* 🌐 *www.chieseverona.it* 🎫 *€3 (free with Church Cumulative Ticket or VeronaCard).*

Sant'Anastasia

CHURCH | Verona's largest church, begun in 1290 but only consecrated in 1471, is a fine example of Gothic brickwork and has a grand doorway with elaborately carved biblical scenes. The main reason for visiting this church, however, is *St. George and the Princess* (dated 1434, but perhaps earlier) by Pisanello (1377–1455). It's above the Pellegrini Chapel off the main altar. As you come in, look also for the *gobbi* (hunchbacks) supporting the holy-water basins. ✉ *Piazza Sant'Anastasia, Verona* ☎ *045/592813* 🌐 *www.chieseverona.it* 🎫 *€3 (free with Church Cumulative Ticket or VeronaCard).*

🍴 Restaurants

★ Antica Osteria al Duomo

$$ | NORTHERN ITALIAN | This side-street eatery, lined with old wood paneling and decked out with musical instruments, serves traditional Veronese classics, like *bigoli* (thick whole-wheat spaghetti) with donkey ragù and *pastissada con polenta* (horsemeat stew with polenta). Don't be deterred by the unconventional meats—they're tender and delicious, and this is probably the best place in town to sample them. **Known for:** popular and busy; blackboard menu, bar, and wooden interiors; occasional live music. [$] *Average main: €19* ✉ *Via Duomo 7/A, Verona* ☎ *045/8004505* 🕒 *Closed Sun. except in Dec. and during wine fair.*

★ Il Desco

$$$$ | MODERN ITALIAN | Opened in 1981 by Elia Rizzo, the nationally renowned fine-dining Desco cuisine is now crafted by talented son Matteo. True to Italian and Rizzo culinary traditions, he preserves natural flavors through careful ingredient selection, adding daring combinations inspired by stints in kitchens around the world. **Known for:** pricey tasting menus; inventive, colorful plates of food; elegant, arty surroundings fit for a modern opera. [$] *Average main: €50* ✉ *Via Dietro San Sebastiano 7, Verona* ☎ *045/595358* 🌐 *www.ristoranteildesco.it* 🕒 *Closed Sun. and Mon. (open for dinner Mon. in July, Aug., and Dec.).*

Ristorante 12 Apostoli

$$$$ | NORTHERN ITALIAN | Run by the Gioco family for over a century, 12 Apostoli offers a fine-dining experience amid gorgeous frescoes and dramatically lit place settings. Near Piazza delle Erbe, this historic palazzo setting stands on the foundations of a Roman temple: you can view architectural fragments and a model in the wine cellar. **Known for:** innovative tasting menus; elegant, atmospheric rooms and cantina; slow and sumptuous dining. [$] *Average main: €40* ✉ *Vicolo Corticella San Marco 3, Verona* ☎ *045/596999* 🌐 *www.12apostoli.com* 🕒 *Closed Sun. and Mon. No lunch weekdays.*

☕ Coffee and Quick Bites

★ Caffè Borsari

$ | NORTHERN ITALIAN | This bustling caffè-bar is famed for its excellent creamy coffee and freshly made brioche—pre-Covid it was cheek-by-jowl *al banco* (at the bar), but for now the Veronese patrons must spill outside. The narrow space on the charming Corso Borsari cobbles is packed with coffee- and tea-making pots and cups, as are its walls with colorful gifts and oddities according to the time of year. **Known for:** fab staff may decorate your *schiuma* (froth); indulgent hot chocolate; selection of coffee, tea, candies, and chocolates to take away. Ⓢ *Average main: €4* ✉ *Corso Portoni Borsari 15, Verona* ☎ *045/8031313.*

 Hotels

Best Western Hotel Armando

\$\$ | **HOTEL** | In a residential area a few minutes' walk from the Arena, this contemporary Best Western hotel offers respite from the busy city as well as easier parking. **Pros:** free Wi-Fi; good breakfast; large rooms for Italy. **Cons:** simple room decor; no parking valet; noise from neighboring restaurant. Ⓢ *Rooms from: €167* ✉ *Via Dietro Pallone 1, Verona* ☎ *045/8000206* ⊕ *www.hotelarmando.it* �)️ *Closed 2 wks late Dec.–early Jan.* ⇘ *28 rooms* ⑩ *Free Breakfast.*

Escalus Luxury Suites

\$\$\$ | **HOTEL** | **FAMILY** | Near the Arena and Verona's marble-paved main shopping street, Via Mazzini, these suites and mini-apartments offer contemporary minimalist style in muted colors; the larger ones have handy kitchenettes, and all have swank bathrooms. **Pros:** large showers; chic location near sights and shopping; family-friendly Glamour Deluxe Suite with balcony. **Cons:** constant passeggiata hum from Via Mazzini; checkout is before 11 am; minimalist decor not to everyone's taste. Ⓢ *Rooms from: €250* ✉ *Vicolo Tre Marchetti 12, Verona* ☎ *045/8036754* ⊕ *www.escalusverona.com* ⇘ *6 suites* ⑩ *Free Breakfast.*

Gabbia d'Oro

\$\$\$\$ | **HOTEL** | Occupying a historic building off Piazza delle Erbe in the ancient heart of Verona, this hotel is a romantic fantasia of ornamentation, rich fabrics, and period-style furniture. **Pros:** great breakfast; central location; romantic atmosphere. **Cons:** some guests may find the decor overly ornate, even stuffy; some very small rooms, especially considering the price; small bathrooms. Ⓢ *Rooms from: €350* ✉ *Corso Porta Borsari 4/a, Verona*

☎ *045/8003060* ⊕ *www.hotelgabbiadoro. it* ⑩ *Free Breakfast* ⇘ *27 rooms.*

Hotel Accademia

\$\$\$ | **HOTEL** | The Palladian facade of columns and arches here hint at the well-proportioned interior layout: expect an elegant contemporary take on art deco in public spaces and immaculate if impersonal traditional-style decor in guest rooms. **Pros:** rooftop solarium; central location; good fitness room. **Cons:** rates increase greatly during summer opera season and trade fairs; expensive parking; service can be patchy. Ⓢ *Rooms from: €292* ✉ *Via Scala 12, Verona* ☎ *045/596222* ⊕ *www.accademiavr.it* ⇘ *96 rooms* ⑩ *Free Breakfast.*

L'Ospite Appartamenti

\$ | **HOTEL** | Friendly and energetic Federica has transformed this three-story property, owned by her family (of De Rossi pasticceria fame), into some of the most stylish contemporary apartments—and one of the best values—in Verona, complete with kitchenettes. **Pros:** immaculately clean; great location in the Veronetta near the university and the Adige River; helpful host offers tips and some cooking courses. **Cons:** on a busy road; narrow pavement outside; books up early. Ⓢ *Rooms from: €105* ✉ *Via Venti Settembre 3, Verona* ☎ *045/8036994, 329/4262524 (mobile)* ⊕ *www.lospite.com* �)️ *Closed early Jan.* ⇘ *6 apartments* ⑩ *No Meals.*

Milan

Rome may be bigger and wield political power, but Milan and the affluent north are what really make the country go. Leonardo da Vinci's *The Last Supper* and other great works of art are here, as well as a spectacular Gothic Duomo, the finest of its kind. Milan even reigns supreme where it really counts (in the minds of many Italians), routinely trouncing the rest of the nation with its two premier soccer teams.

And yet, Milan hasn't won the battle for hearts and minds when it comes to tourism. Most visitors prefer Tuscany's hills and Venice's canals to Milan's hectic efficiency and wealthy indifference, and it's no surprise that in a country of medieval hilltop villages and skilled artisans, a city of grand boulevards and global corporations leaves visitors asking the real Italy to please stand up. They're right, of course: Milan is more European than Italian, a new buckle on an old boot, and although its old city can stand cobblestone to cobblestone against the best of them, seekers of Roman ruins and fairy-tale towns may pass. But Milan's secrets reveal themselves slowly to those who look. A side street conceals a garden complete with flamingos (Giardini Invernizzi, on Via dei Cappuccini, just off Corso Venezia; closed to the public, but you can still catch a glimpse), and a renowned 20th-century-art collection hides modestly behind an unspectacular facade a block from Corso Buenos Aires (the Casa-Museo Boschi di Stefano). Visitors tempted by world-class shopping will appreciate Milan's European sophistication while discovering unexpected facets of a country they may have only thought they knew.

Virtually every invader in European history—Gaul, Roman, Goth, Lombard, and Frank—as well as a long series of rulers from France, Spain, and Austria, took a turn at ruling the city. After being completely sacked by the Goths in AD 539 and by the Holy Roman Empire under Frederick Barbarossa in 1157, Milan became one of the first independent city-states of the Renaissance. Its heyday of self-rule proved comparatively brief. From 1277 until 1500 it was ruled first by the Visconti and then the Sforza dynasties. These families were known, justly or not, for a peculiarly aristocratic mixture of refinement, classical learning, and cruelty; much of the surviving grandeur of Gothic and Renaissance art and architecture is their doing. Be on the lookout

in your wanderings for the Visconti family emblem—a viper, its jaws straining wide, devouring a child.

GETTING HERE AND AROUND

The city center is compact and walkable; trolleys and trams make it even more accessible, and the efficient Metropolitana (subway) and buses provide access to locations farther afield. Driving in Milan is difficult and parking a real pain, so a car is a liability. In addition, drivers within the second ring of streets (the *bastioni*) must pay a daily congestion charge on weekdays between 7:30 am and 7:30 pm (until 6 pm on Thursday). You can pay the charge at news vendors, tobacconists, Banca Intesa Sanpaolo ATMs, or online at *areac.atm-mi.it/Areac/iweb/Acquisto. aspx*; parking meters and parking garages in the area also include it in the cost. There is also a public bike sharing system called BikeMi.

BIKE CONTACT BikeMi. ☎ *02/48607607* ⊕ *www.bikemi.com.*

PUBLIC TRANSPORTATION

A standard public transit ticket within the central zones of Milan costs €2 and is valid for a 90-minute trip on a subway, bus, or tram. An all-inclusive subway, bus, and tram pass costs €7 for 24 hours or €12 for 48 hours. Another option is a Carnet (€18), good for 10 tram, bus, or subway rides. Individual tickets and passes can be purchased from news vendors, tobacconists, at ticket machines at all subway stops, at ticket offices at the Duomo and other subway stops, and on your phone via the ATM Milano app. You can also pay for the subway using a contactless card at the turnstile.

Once you have your ticket, either stamp it or insert it into the slots in station turnstiles or on poles inside trolleys and buses. (Electronic tickets won't function if they become bent or demagnetized. If you have a problem, contact a station manager, who can usually issue a new ticket.) Trains run from 6 am to 12:30 am.

PUBLIC TRANSPORTATION CONTACTS

ATM. (*Azienda Trasporti Milanesi*) ☎ *02/48607607* ⊕ *www.atm.it/en.* **Radiobus.** ☎ *02/48034803* ⊕ *www.atm.it/en.*

Taxi fares in Milan are higher than in American cities; a short ride can run about €15 during rush hour or fashion week. You can get a taxi at a stand with an orange "Taxi" sign, or by calling one of the taxi companies. Most also have apps you can download to order taxis from your phone; some let you text or use WhatsApp to hail a cab. Dispatchers may speak some English; they'll ask for the phone number you're calling from, and they'll tell you the number of your taxi and how long it'll take to arrive. If you're in a restaurant or bar, ask the staff to call a cab for you.

TAXI CONTACTS 026969. ☎ *02/6969* ⊕ *www.026969.it.* **Autoradiotaxi.** ☎ *02/8585* ⊕ *www.028585.it.* **Radio Taxi Freccia.** ☎ *02/4000* ⊕ *www.024000.it.* **Taxiblu.** ☎ *02/4040* ⊕ *www.taxiblu.it.*

TOURS
CONTACT City Sightseeing Milano. ☎ *02/867131* ⊕ *www.city-sightseeing.it/en/milan.*

VISITOR INFORMATION
CONTACT Milan Tourism Office. ✉ *Piazza del Duomo 14, next to Palazzo Reale, Duomo* ☎ *02/88455555* ⊕ *www.yesmilano.it.*

Duomo

Milan's main streets radiate out from the massive Duomo, a late-Gothic cathedral begun in 1386. Heading north is the handsome Galleria Vittorio Emanuele II, an enclosed shopping arcade that opens at one end to the world-famous opera house known as La Scala. Via Manzoni leads northeast from La Scala to the Quadrilatero della Moda, or fashion district. Heading northeast from the Duomo is the pedestrian-only street Corso Vittorio Emanuele II. Northwest of the Duomo is Via Dante, at the to, is the imposing outline of the C. Sforzesco.

 Sights

★ Duomo

CHURCH | There is no denying that for sheer size and complexity, the Duomo is unrivaled in Italy. It is the second-largest church in the country—the largest being St. Peter's in Rome—and the fourth largest in the world. This intricate Gothic structure has been fascinating and exasperating visitors and conquerors alike since it was begun by Gian Galeazzo Visconti III (1351–1402), first duke of Milan, in 1386. Consecrated in the 15th or 16th century, it was not completed until just before the coronation of Napoléon as king of Italy in 1809. The building is adorned with 135 marble spires and 2,245 marble statues. The oldest part is the apse. Its three colossal bays of curved and counter-curved tracery—especially the bay adorning the exterior of the stained-glass windows—should not be missed. At the end of the southern transept down the right aisle lies the tomb of Gian Giacomo Medici. The tomb owes some of its design to Michelangelo but was executed by Leone Leoni (1509–90) and is generally considered his masterpiece; it dates from the 1560s. Directly ahead is the Duomo's most famous sculpture, the gruesome but anatomically instructive figure of San Bartolomeo (St. Bartholomew), who was flayed alive. As you enter the apse to admire those splendid windows, glance at the sacristy doors to the right and left of the altar. The lunette on the right dates from 1393 and was decorated by Hans von Fernach. The one on the left also dates from the 14th century and is ascribed jointly to Giacomo da Campione and Giovannino de' Grassi. The roof is worth a look: walk out the left (north) transept to the stairs and elevator. As you stand among the forest of marble

virtually every
...ice, including
...with precious
...quarries near
...nti's team
...rpose and
...als. Exhib-
...mo shed light
...ral's history and include
...ne of the treasures removed from
the exterior for preservation purposes,
while the early Christian Baptistry of St.
John can be seen in the archaeological
area underneath the cathedral. ⊠ *Piazza del Duomo, Duomo* 🕾 *02/361691*
⊕ *www.duomomilano.it* 🎫 *Cathedral €5;
museum €5; cathedral, museum, and
archaeological area €10; stairs to roof
€15; elevator €20* Ⓜ *Duomo.*

Battistero Paleocristiano/Baptistry of San Giovanni alle Fonti

CHURCH | More specifically known as the
Baptistry of San Giovanni alle Fonti, this
4th-century baptistry is one of two that
lie beneath the Duomo. Although opinion
remains divided, it is widely believed to
be where Ambrose, Milan's first bishop
and patron saint, baptized Augustine.
Tickets also include a visit to the Duomo
and its museum. ⊠ *Piazza del Duomo,
Duomo* 🕾 *02/72022656* ⊕ *www.duom-
omilano.it* 🎫 *€10, including admission
to Duomo and museum; €20, including
Duomo, museum, and roof* Ⓜ *Duomo.*

★ Galleria Vittorio Emanuele II

STORE/MALL | This spectacular
late-19th-century Belle Époque tunnel is
essentially one of the planet's earliest
and most select shopping malls, with
upscale tenants that include Gucci,
Prada, and Versace. This is the city's
heart, midway between the Duomo and
La Scala. It teems with life, which makes
for great people-watching from the tables
that spill out from bars and restaurants,
where you can enjoy an overpriced
coffee. Books, clothing, food, hats, and
jewelry are all for sale. Known as Milan's
"parlor," the Galleria is often viewed as a

barometer of the city's well-being. The
historic, if somewhat overpriced and
inconsistent, Savini Restaurant hosts the
beautiful and powerful of the city, just
across from McDonald's. Even in poor
weather the great glass dome above
the octagonal center is a splendid sight.
The paintings at the base of the dome
represent Europe, Asia, Africa, and the
Americas. Those at the entrance arch
are devoted to science, industry, art, and
agriculture. And the floor mosaics are
a vastly underrated source of pleasure,
even if they are not to be taken too seriously. Be sure to follow tradition and spin
your heels once or twice on the more
"delicate" parts of the bull beneath your
feet in the northern apse; the Milanese
believe it brings good luck. ⊠ *Piazza del
Duomo, Duomo* Ⓜ *Duomo.*

Milano Osservatorio—Fondazione Prada

OTHER MUSEUM | This contemporary
photography exhibition space, developed
in partnership with Fondazione Prada,
is spread over two floors in the Galleria
Vittorio Emanuele II. Exhibitions, which
rotate several times a year, explore
the cultural and social implications of
photography. The space itself, bombed
after World War II and then fully restored,
is worth visiting just for the unique view
of the Galleria dome through the large
windows. You can reach the gallery via
the elevator next to the Prada store. A
ticket for the Osservatorio includes entry
to the main Fondazione Prada museum
(good for seven days). ⊠ *Galleria Vittorio
Emanuele II, Piazza del Duomo, Duomo*
🕾 *02/56662611* ⊕ *www.fondazioneprada.
org/visit/milano-osservatorio* 🎫 *€10; €15,
including Fondazione Prada* ☉ *Closed
Tues.* Ⓜ *Duomo.*

Museo del Novecento

ART MUSEUM | Ascend a Guggenheim-es-
que spiral walkway to reach the modern
works at this petite yet dense collection
of Italian contemporary art, adjacent
to the Duomo. The museum highlights
20th-century Italian artists, including a

strong showing of Futurists, like Boccioni and Severini, and sculptures from Marini, along with a smattering of works by other European artists, including Picasso, Braque, and Matisse. ✉ *Via Marconi 1, Duomo* ☎ *02/88444061* ⊕ *www.muse-odelnovecento.org* 🎫 *€10 (free every 1st and 3rd Tues. of month after 2 and 1st Sun. of month)* ⊙ *Closed Mon. morning* Ⓜ *Duomo.*

★ Palazzo Reale

ART MUSEUM | Elaborately decorated with painted ceilings and grand staircases, this former royal palace close to the Duomo is almost worth a visit in itself; however, it also functions as one of Milan's major art galleries, with a focus on modern artists. Recent exhibitions have highlighted works by Picasso, Chagall, Warhol, Pollock, and Kandinsky. Check the website before you visit to see what's on; purchase tickets online in advance to save time in the queues, which are often long and chaotic. ✉ *Piazza del Duomo 12, Duomo* ☎ *02/884 45 181* ⊕ *www.palazzorealemilano.it* 🎫 *Varies by exhibition* ⊙ *Closed Mon. morning* Ⓜ *Duomo.*

Pinacoteca Ambrosiana

ART MUSEUM | Cardinal Federico Borromeo, one of Milan's native saints, founded this picture gallery in 1618 with the addition of his personal art collection to a bequest of books to Italy's first public library. The core works of the collection include such treasures as Caravaggio's *Basket of Fruit,* Raphael's monumental preparatory drawing (known as a "cartoon") for *The School of Athens,* which hangs in the Vatican, and Leonardo da Vinci's *Portrait of a Musician.* The highlight for many is Leonardo's *Codex Atlanticus,* which features thousands of his sketches and drawings. In addition to works by Lombard artists are paintings by Botticelli, Luini, Titian, and Jan Brueghel. A wealth of charmingly idiosyncratic items on display include 18th-century scientific instruments and gloves worn by Napoléon at Waterloo. Access to

the library, the Biblioteca [...] is limited to researchers [...] entrance tickets. ✉ *Piazza [...] mo* ☎ *02/806921* ⊕ *www [...] en* 🎫 *€15* ⊙ *Closed Mon. [...]*

Santa Maria Presso San Satiro

CHURCH | Just a few steps from the Duomo, this architectural gem was first built in 876 and later perfected by Bramante (1444–1514), demonstrating his command of proportion and perspective—hallmarks of Renaissance architecture. Bramante tricks the eye with a famous optical illusion that makes a small interior seem extraordinarily spacious and airy, while accommodating a beloved 13th-century fresco. ✉ *Via Torino 17–19, Duomo* ☎ *02/874683* Ⓜ *Duomo; Tram No. 2, 3, 4, 12, 14, 19, 20, 24, or 27.*

🍴 Restaurants

Giacomo Arengario

$$$ | **ITALIAN** | Join businesspeople, ladies who lunch, and in-the-know travelers at this elegant restaurant atop the Museo del Novecento and with a glorious Duomo view (be sure to request a window table, though, or risk being relegated to a viewless back room). To complement the vistas, choose from a selection of well-prepared seafood, pasta, and meat courses for lunch and dinner; the servers are happy to recommend pairings from the extensive wine list. **Known for:** wine pairings; amazing Duomo views from tables by the windows; contemporary Milanese dishes. 🟥 *Average main: €30* ✉ *Via Marconi 1, Duomo* ☎ *02/72093814* ⊕ *giacomoarengario.com* Ⓜ *Duomo.*

La Vecchia Latteria

$$ | **VEGETARIAN** | In its two small dining rooms, this family-owned lunch spot serves an impressive amount of vegetarian cuisine. Nestled on a small street just steps away from the Duomo, it offers an array of freshly prepared seasonal selections from a daily-changing menu; try the *misto forno* (mixed plate), which

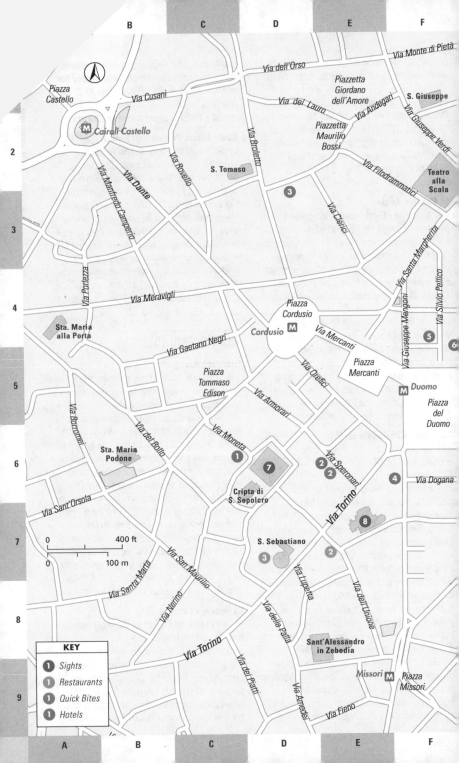

Duomo

offers a taste of several different small dishes. **Known for:** retro '50s atmosphere; Italian-focused vegetarian cuisine; daily-changing tasting menu. $ *Average main: €15* ⊠ *6 Via dell'Unione, Duomo* ☎ *02/874401* ☽ *Closed Sun. No dinner* Ⓜ *Duomo or Missori.*

Piz

$ | **PIZZA** | **FAMILY** | Fun, lively, and full of locals, this casual and inexpensive pizzeria on a side street near the Duomo has just three kinds of thin-crust pizza on the menu—luckily, all are excellent. Choose from margherita, bianca (white, with no tomato), and marinara (with no mozzarella); although you'll inevitably need to wait, you'll likely get a free glass of prosecco and a slice of pizza with cheese while you do. **Known for:** bustling vibe; seasonal changing bianca pizza; free before- and after-dinner drinks. $ *Average main: €9* ⊠ *Via Torino 34, Duomo* ☎ *02/86453482* Ⓜ *Duomo; Tram No. 2, 3, or 14.*

🍴 Coffee and Quick Bites

Camparino in Galleria

$$$ | **CAFÉ** | One thing has remained constant in the Galleria: the Camparino, whose inlaid counter, mosaics, and wrought-iron fixtures have been welcoming tired shoppers since 1867. It's been given a fresh twist by star chef Davide Oldani with a menu of Pan'cot—roasted bread topped with veggies, fish, or meat, to be enjoyed with a Campari aperitif—served in pretty Bar di Passo downstairs, while a more extensive range of Campari cocktails paired with food for aperitivo or dinner is available in elegant Sala Spiritello upstairs. **Known for:** contemporary versions of Campari cocktails; prime people-watching; high-end aperitivo. $ *Average main: €30* ⊠ *Galleria Vittorio Emanuele, Piazza del Duomo 21, Duomo* ☎ *02/86464435* ⊕ *www.camparino.it* Ⓜ *Duomo.*

Piccolo Peck

$$ | **SANDWICHES** | The café at this foodie paradise near the Duomo features Italian specialty foods such as excellent cheeses, charcuterie, vegetables in olive oil, seafood, and sandwiches. It also reinterprets classic dishes like Russian salad and paté, which can be washed down with a fine selection of wines by the glass or a bottle from its cellar of global labels. **Known for:** casual atmosphere; wide bakery selection, including classic brioche; delicious Italian treats from the famed Peck deli. $ *Average main: €20* ⊠ *Via Spadari 9, Duomo* ☎ *02/8023161* ⊕ *www.peck.it/en/restaurants/piccolo-peck* Ⓜ *Tram No. 2, 12, 14, 16, or 19.*

Rinascente Food & Restaurants

$ | **ECLECTIC** | The seventh floor of this famous Italian department store is a gourmet food market surrounded by several small restaurants that can be a good option for lunch, an aperitivo overlooking the Duomo, or dinner after a long day of shopping. There are several places to eat, including the popular mozzarella bar Obica, God Save the Food for juices and healthy bowls, De Santis for "slow food" sandwiches, and the sophisticated Maio restaurant. **Known for:** inexpensive meals and snacks; terrace overlooking the Duomo; culinary gifts to take home. $ *Average main: €10* ⊠ *Piazza Duomo, Duomo* ☎ *02/8852454* ⊕ *www.rinascente.it* Ⓜ *Duomo.*

🛏 Hotels

Hotel Gran Duca di York

$$ | **HOTEL** | The spare but classically elegant and efficient rooms at this hotel are arranged around a courtyard—four have private terraces—and offer good value for pricey Milan. **Pros:** good breakfast; central location; friendly staff. **Cons:** many rooms on the small side; limited amenities (no restaurant or gym); showers can be tiny. $ *Rooms from: €191* ⊠ *Via Moneta 1, Duomo* ☎ *02/874863* ⊕ *www.ducadiyork.com* ⇆ *33 rooms* ⑩ *Free Breakfast*

Ⓜ *Cordusio or Duomo; Tram No. 2, 12, 14, 16, or 27.*

Hotel Spadari al Duomo

$$$ | HOTEL | That this chic city-center inn is owned by an architect's family comes through in details like the custom-designed furniture and paintings by young Milanese artists in the stylish guest rooms. **Pros:** good breakfast; attentive staff; central location. **Cons:** no restaurant; street noise can be a problem; some rooms on the small side. Ⓢ *Rooms from: €260* ✉ *Via Spadari 11, Duomo* ☎ *02/72002371* ⊕ *www.spadarihotel.com* ⦿ *Free Breakfast* ⤳ *40 rooms* Ⓜ *Duomo; Tram No. 2, 3, 12, 14, 16, 24, or 27.*

Hotel Star

$ | HOTEL | The price is extremely reasonable, the staff are helpful, and the rooms are well equipped and comfortable, some with touches like whirlpool tubs and balconies. **Pros:** breakfast is included; centrally located near key attractions; reasonably priced. **Cons:** street noise can be an issue; quirky animal prints in some rooms not for everyone; some bathrooms are extremely small. Ⓢ *Rooms from: €115* ✉ *Via dei Bossi 5, Duomo* ☎ *02/801501* ⊕ *www.hotelstar.it* ⤳ *30 rooms* ⦿ *Free Breakfast.*

Maison Milano | UNA Esperienze

$$$ | HOTEL | Inside this faithfully restored palazzo dating from the early 1900s, spaciousness is accentuated with soft white interiors, muted fabrics and marble, and contemporary lines. **Pros:** the warmth of a residence and the luxury of a design hotel; friendly staff; lovely bathrooms. **Cons:** no restaurant or bar; not much of a lobby; breakfast not included. Ⓢ *Rooms from: €239* ✉ *Via Mazzini 4, Duomo* ☎ *02/726891* ⊕ *www.gruppouna.it/esperienze/maison-milano* ⦿ *No Meals* ⤳ *27 rooms* Ⓜ *Duomo; Tram No. 2, 3, 12, 14, 16, 24, or 27.*

★ Park Hyatt Milan

$$$$ | HOTEL | Extensive use of warm travertine stone and modern art creates a sophisticated yet inviting backdrop at the Park Hyatt, where spacious, opulent guest rooms have walk-in closets and bathrooms with double sinks, glass-enclosed rain showers, and separate soaking tubs. **Pros:** excellent restaurant; central location; contemporary decor and amenities. **Cons:** very expensive; not particularly intimate; some rooms showing a little wear. Ⓢ *Rooms from: €1,400* ✉ *Via Tommaso Grossi 1, Duomo* ☎ *02/88211234* ⊕ *milan.park.hyatt.com* ⤳ *106 rooms* ⦿ *No Meals* Ⓜ *Duomo; Tram No. 1.*

★ Room Mate Giulia

$$$ | HOTEL | For hip, affordable, design-focused lodging with a friendly feel and prime location right next to the Galleria and around the corner from the Duomo, you can't do much better than the city's first outpost from Spanish hotel chain Room Mate. **Pros:** relatively affordable rates for Milan; fresh, appealing design; amazing location. **Cons:** gym on the small side; breakfast room a bit cramped; busy location means some noise in rooms. Ⓢ *Rooms from: €249* ✉ *Via Silvio Pellico 4, Duomo* ☎ *02/80888900* ⊕ *www.room-matehotels.com/en* ⤳ *85 rooms* ⦿ *No Meals* Ⓜ *Duomo; Tram No. 1.*

Ⓨ Nightlife

Bar STRAF

BARS | This architecturally stimulating but dimly lit place has such artistic features as recycled fiberglass panels and vintage 1970s furnishings. The music is an eclectic mix of chill-out tunes during the daytime, with more upbeat and vibrant tracks pepping it up at night. Located on a quiet side street near the Duomo, STRAF draws a young and lively, if tourist-heavy, crowd. ✉ *Via San Raffaele 3, Duomo* ☎ *02/805081* ⊕ *www.straf.it/bar* Ⓜ *Duomo.*

 Performing Arts

Conservatorio

MUSIC | The two halls belonging to the Conservatorio host some of the leading names in classical music. Series are organized by several organizations, including the venerable chamber music society the **Società del Quartetto**. ⊠ *Via del Conservatorio 12, Duomo* ☎ *02/762110, 02/795393 Società del Quartetto* ⊕ *www. consmilano.it* Ⓜ *San Babila; Tram No. 9, 12, 23, or 27; Bus No. 60 or 73.*

★ Teatro alla Scala

OPERA | You need know nothing of opera to sense that La Scala is closer to a cathedral than a concert hall. Hearing opera sung in this magical setting is an unparalleled experience: it is, after all, where Verdi established his reputation and where Maria Callas sang her way into opera lore. It stands as a symbol—both for the performer who dreams of singing here and for the opera buff—and its notoriously demanding audiences are apt to jeer performers who do not measure up. If you are lucky enough to be here during opera season, do whatever is necessary to attend. Tickets go on sale two months before the first performance and are usually sold out the same day. The opening gala is December 7, the feast day of Milan patron St. Ambrose, and performances run all year, except for the end of July and August, and major holidays. For tickets, visit the Box Office at Largo Ghiringhelli 1, Piazza della Scala, every day from 12 to 6 pm and two hours before the beginning of each performance, for same-day shows. Tickets are also available online. Tickets purchased online can be presented at the entrance with your smartphone or tablet. Although you might not get seats for the more popular operas with big-name stars, it is worth trying; ballets are easier. There are also 140 reduced-visibility balcony tickets available for each performance on a first-come, first-served basis; for evening operas and ballets, registration for the list begins at 1 pm, and ticket recipients (with a maximum of two tickets per person) are announced at 5:30 pm. At the Museo Teatrale alla Scala you can admire an extensive collection of librettos, paintings of the famous names of Italian opera, posters, costumes, antique instruments, and design sketches for the theater. It is also possible to take a look at the theater itself. Special exhibitions reflect current productions. ⊠ *Piazza della Scala, Largo Ghiringhelli 1, Duomo* ☎ *02/72003744 theater, 02/88797473 museum* ⊕ *www. teatroallascala.org* ⊠ *Museum €9.75* Ⓜ *Duomo or Cordusio; Tram No. 1.*

Shopping

Borsalino

HATS & GLOVES | The kingpin of milliners, Borsalino has managed to stay trendy since it opened in 1857. ⊠ *Galleria Vittorio Emanuele II 92, Duomo* ☎ *02/89015436* ⊕ *www.borsalino.com* Ⓜ *Duomo; Tram No. 1.*

Gucci

MIXED CLOTHING | This Florence-born brand attracts lots of fashion-forward tourists in hot pursuit of its monogrammed bags, shoes, and accessories. ⊠ *Galleria Vittorio Emanuele II, Duomo* ☎ *02/8597991* ⊕ *www.gucci.com* Ⓜ *Duomo; Tram No. 1.*

La Rinascente

DEPARTMENT STORE | The flagship location of this always bustling and very central department store—adjacent to both the Duomo and the Galleria Vittorio Emanuele II—carries a wide range of Italian and international brands (both high-end and casual) for men, women, and children. There's also a fine selection of beauty and home products. ⊠ *Piazza Duomo, Duomo* ☎ *02/9138 7388* ⊕ *www.rinascente.it* Ⓜ *Duomo; Tram No. 1, 2, 12, 14, 16, or 27.*

Trussardi

JEWELRY & WATCHES | This family-run label offers sleek, fashion-forward accessories, leather goods, and clothes at its flagship store. ⊠ *Piazza della Scala 5, Duomo*

☎ *02/80688242* ⊕ *www.trussardi.com*
Ⓜ *Duomo; Tram No. 1.*

Castello

This 15th-century castle is home to crypts, battlements, tunnels, and an interesting array of museums.

◉ Sights

Castello Sforzesco

HISTORIC SIGHT | Wandering the grounds of this tranquil castle and park near the center of Milan is a great respite from the often-hectic city, and the interesting museums inside are an added bonus. The castle's crypts and battlements, including a tunnel that emerges well into the Parco Sempione behind, can be visited with privately reserved guides from Ad Artem or Opera d'Arte. For the serious student of Renaissance military engineering, the Castello must be something of a travesty, so often has it been remodeled or rebuilt since it was begun in 1450 by the condottiere, or mercenary, who founded the city's second dynastic family: Francesco Sforza, fourth duke of Milan. Although today "mercenary" has a pejorative ring, during the Renaissance, all Italy's great soldier-heroes were professionals hired by the cities and principalities they served. Of them—and there were thousands—Francesco Sforza (1401–66) is considered one of the greatest, most honest, and most organized. It is said he could remember the names not only of all his men but of their horses as well. His rule signaled the enlightened age of the Renaissance but preceded the next foreign rule by a scant 50 years. Since the turn of the 20th century, the Castello has been the depository of several city-owned collections of Egyptian and other antiquities, musical instruments, arms and armor, decorative arts and textiles, prints and photographs, paintings, and sculpture. Highlights include the Sala delle Asse, a frescoed room attributed

to Leonardo da Vinci (1452–1519), and Michelangelo's unfinished *Rondanini Pietà*, believed to be his last work—an astounding achievement for a man nearly 90, and a moving coda to his life—which is housed in the Museo Pietà Rondanini. The *pinacoteca* (picture gallery) features 230 paintings from medieval times to the 18th century, including works by Antonello da Messina, Canaletto, Andrea Mantegna, and Bernardo Bellotto. The Museo dei Mobili e delle Sculture Lignee (Furniture Museum), which illustrates the development of Italian furniture design from the Middle Ages to the present, includes a delightful collection of Renaissance treasure chests of exotic woods with tiny drawers and miniature architectural details. A single ticket purchased in the office in an inner courtyard admits visitors to these separate installations, which are dispersed around the castle's two immense courtyards. ✉ *Piazza Castello, Castello* ☎ *02/88463700* ⊕ *www. milanocastello.it* ✍ *Castle free, museums €10 (free every 1st and 3rd Tues. of month after 2, and €5 1st Sun. of month)* ☉ *Museums closed Mon.* Ⓜ *Cadorna, Lanza, or Cairoli; Tram No. 1, 2, 4, 12, 14, or 19; Bus No. 18, 37, 50, 58, 61, or 94.*

⊙ Performing Arts

Teatro Dal Verme

CONCERTS | Frequent classical, rock, and jazz concerts by international artists are staged here from October to May. ✉ *Via San Giovanni sul Muro 2, Castello* ☎ *02/87905* ⊕ *www.dalverme.org* Ⓜ *Cairoli; Tram No. 1 or 4.*

Sempione

Just beyond the Sforzesco Castle grounds is a large park that holds an aquarium, the Triennale museum, and the Torre Branca.

Sights

Acquario Civico di Milano
(*Civic Aquarium of Milan*)
AQUARIUM | FAMILY | The third oldest aquarium in Europe, opened in 1906, is known as much for its art nouveau architecture as for its small but interesting collection of marine life. You'll find 36 pools that house more than 100 species of fish, including an emphasis on Italian freshwater fish and their habitat, and one tank of species from the Red Sea. ⊠ *Viale Gerolamo Gadio 2, Sempione* ☎ *02/88465750* ⊕ *www.acquariocivicomilano.eu* ⊒ *€5; free every 1st and 3rd Tues. of month after 2 and 1st Sun. of month* ⊙ *Closed Mon.* Ⓜ *Lanza; Tram No. 2, 4, 12, or 14; Bus No. 57.*

Parco Sempione
CITY PARK | FAMILY | Originally the gardens and parade grounds of the Castello Sforzesco, this open space was reorganized during the Napoleonic era, when the arena on its northeast side was constructed, and then turned into a park during the building boom at the end of the 19th century. It is still the lungs of the city's fashionable western neighborhoods, and the **Aquarium** still attracts Milan's schoolchildren. The park became a bit of a design showcase in 1933 with the construction of the Triennale. ⊠ *Sempione* ⊒ *Free* Ⓜ *Cairoli, Lanza or Cadorna; Tram No. 1, 2, 4, 12, 14, 19, or 27; Bus No. 43, 57, 61, 70, or 94*

Torre Branca
VIEWPOINT | It is worth visiting Parco Sempione just to see the Torre Branca. Designed by the architect Gio Ponti (1891–1979), who was behind so many of the projects that made Milan the design capital that it is, this steel tower rises 330 feet over the Triennale. Take the elevator to get a nice view of the city, then have a drink at the glitzy Just Cavalli Restaurant and Club at its base. ⊠ *Parco Sempione, Sempione* ☎ *02/3314120* ⊕ *museobranca.it/torre-branca-2/* ⊒ *€6*

⊙ *Closed Sun. and Mon.; closed Mon., Tues., Thurs., and Fri. mid-Sept.–mid-May* Ⓜ *Cadorna; Tram No. 1; Bus No. 61.*

Triennale Design Museum
ART MUSEUM | In addition to honoring Italy's design talent, the Triennale also offers a regular series of exhibitions on design from around the world. A spectacular bridge entrance leads to a permanent collection, an exhibition space, and a stylish café and rooftop restaurant with expansive views. The Triennale also manages the fascinating museum-studio of designer Achille Castiglioni, in nearby Piazza Castello (hour-long guided tours Tuesday–Friday at 10, 11, and noon; €15. Call or email in advance to book: *02/8053606, info@achillecastiglioni.it*. ⊠ *Via Alemagna 6, Sempione* ☎ *02/72434244* ⊕ *www. triennale.org* ⊒ *€12* ⊙ *Closed Mon.* Ⓜ *Cadorna; Bus No. 61.*

Brera

To the north of the Duomo lie the winding streets of this elegant neighborhood, once the city's bohemian quarter.

Sights

★ Pinacoteca di Brera (*Brera Gallery*)
ART MUSEUM | The collection here is star-studded even by Italian standards. The museum has nearly 40 rooms, arranged in chronological order—so pace yourself. One highlight is the somber, moving *Cristo Morto* (*Dead Christ*) by Mantegna, which dominates Room VI with its sparse palette of umber and its foreshortened perspective. Mantegna's shocking, almost surgical precision tells of an all-too-human agony. It's one of Renaissance painting's most quietly wondrous achievements, finding an unsuspected middle ground between the excesses of conventional gore and beauty in representing the Passion's saddest moment. Room XXIV offers two additional highlights of the gallery: Raphael's (1483–1520) *Sposalizio*

della Vergine (*Marriage of the Virgin*), with its mathematical composition and precise, alternating colors, portrays the betrothal of Mary and Joseph. *La Vergine con il Bambino e Santi* (*Madonna with Child and Saints*), by Piero della Francesca (1420–92), is an altarpiece commissioned by Federico da Montefeltro (shown kneeling, in full armor, before the Virgin); it was intended for a church to house the duke's tomb. Room XXXVIII houses one of the most romantic paintings in Italian history: *Il Bacio,* by Francesco Hayez (1791–1882), depicts a couple from the Middle Ages engaged in a passionate kiss. The painting was meant to portray the patriotic spirit of Italy's Unification and freedom from the Austro-Hungarian Empire. ✉ *Via Brera 28, Brera* ☎ *02/722631* 🌐 *www.pinacotecabrera.org* 🎟 *€15* 🕒 *Closed Mon.* [M] *Montenapoleone or Lanza; Tram No. 1, 4, 12, 14, or 27; Bus No. 61.*

🍴 Restaurants

★ Cittamani

$$ | **MODERN INDIAN** | Celebrity chef Ritu Dalmia runs well-regarded Italian restaurants in India, so it's no surprise that her first restaurant in Italy offers a mash-up of modern Indian food with Italian and international ingredients; even the decor, with shelves of pottery and terrazzo floors, is a cultural combo. Look for unexpected flavors and a mix of small plates, more substantial mains, and utterly delicious fusion desserts. **Known for:** sleek contemporary setting; Indian food quite different from the norm; nontraditional naans. [$] *Average main: €21* ✉ *Piazza Mirabello 5, Brera* ☎ *02/38240935* 🌐 *www.cittamani.com* 🕒 *Closed Mon.* [M] *Moscova or Turati; Bus No. 43 or 94.*

Fioraio Bianchi Caffè

$$$ | **MODERN ITALIAN** | A French-style bistro in the heart of Milan, Fioraio Bianchi Caffè was opened more than 40 years ago by Raimondo Bianchi, a great lover of flowers; in fact, eating at this restaurant is a bit like dining in a Parisian boutique with floral decor. Despite the French atmosphere, the dishes have Italian flair and ensure a classy, inventive meal. **Known for:** great spot for morning coffee and pastries; charming, flower-filled, shabby-chic setting; creative Italian-style bistro food. [$] *Average main: €28* ✉ *Via Montebello 7, Brera* ☎ *02/29014390* 🌐 *www.fioraiobianchicaffe.it* 🕒 *Closed 3 wks in Aug.* [M] *Turati.*

☕ Coffee and Quick Bites

N'Ombra de Vin

$ | **WINE BAR** | This enoteca serves wine by the glass and, in addition to the plates of *salumi* (Italian cold cuts) and cheese nibbles, has light food and not-so-light desserts. It's a great place for people-watching on Via San Marco, while indoors offers a more dimly lit, romantic setting; check out the impressive vaulted basement, where bottled wines and spirits are sold. **Known for:** Italian and French wines; solid tapas dishes; atmospheric setting in an old Augustinian refectory. [$] *Average main: €14* ✉ *Via S. Marco 2, Brera* ☎ *02/6599650* 🌐 *www.nombradevin.it* [M] *Lanza, Turati, or Montenapoleone; Tram No. 1, 2, 4, 12, or 14.*

🛏 Hotels

Bulgari Hotel Milano

$$$$ | **HOTEL** | Housed in an 18th-century palazzo on a quiet street a short stroll from the shops of Brera and Montenapoleone, the Bulgari offers up chic yet restrained rooms, an enormous garden, and a celebrity-chef-helmed restaurant. **Pros:** excellent spa, with heated pool, sauna, and Jacuzzi; convenient location for sightseeing; trendy and fashionable guests. **Cons:** extremely expensive; service not quite up to par; rooms are a bit bland. [$] *Rooms from: €750* ✉ *Via Privata Fratelli Gabba 7b, Brera* ☎ *02/8058051* 🌐 *www.bulgarihotels.com/en_US/milan* 🔑 *61 rooms* 🍽 *No Meals* [M] *Montenapoleone.*

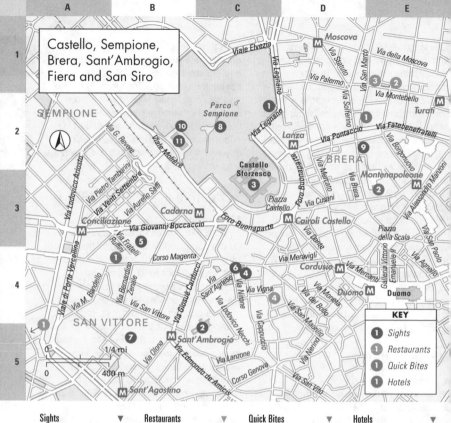

Castello, Sempione, Brera, Sant'Ambrogio, Fiera and San Siro

KEY
- **1** Sights
- **1** Restaurants
- **1** Quick Bites
- **1** Hotels

Sights ▼

1 Acquario Civico
di Milano **C2**

2 Basilica di
Sant'Ambrogio **C5**

3 Castello Sforzesco **C3**

4 Chiesa di
San Maurizio al
Monastero Maggiore ... **C4**

5 The Last Supper/
Il Cenacolo/Santa Maria
delle Grazie **B3**

6 Museo Civico
Archeologico **C4**

7 Museo Nazionale della
Scienza e Tecnologia
Leonardo da Vinci **B5**

8 Parco Sempione **C2**

9 Pinacoteca di Brera **D2**

10 Torre Branca **B2**

11 Triennale
Design Museum **B2**

Restaurants ▼

1 Al Rifugio Pugliese **A4**

2 Cittamani **E1**

3 Fioraio Bianchi Caffè **E1**

4 Taverna Moriggi **C4**

Quick Bites ▼

1 N'Ombra de Vin **E2**

Hotels ▼

1 Antica Locanda
Leonardo **B4**

2 Bulgari Hotel Milano **E3**

Nightlife

Bar at Bulgari Hotel Milano

BARS | Having drinks or a light lunch at the Bulgari Hotel bar lets you step off the asphalt and into one of the city's most impressive private urban gardens—even indoors you seem to be outside, separated from the elements by a spectacular wall of glass. The Bar is a great place to run into international hotel guests and jet-setting Milanese, and the staff mix up a wide range of traditional and novel drinks—including the Bulgari Cocktail with gin, Aperol, and orange, pineapple, and lime juices. ⊠ *Via Privata Fratelli Gabba 7/b, Brera* ☏ *02/8058051* ⊕ *www.bulgarihotels.com/en_US/milan/bar-and-restaurant/il-bar* Ⓜ *Montenapoleone; Tram No. 1.*

Shopping

Mercato di Via S. Marco

MARKET | The Monday- and Thursday-morning markets here cater to the wealthy residents of the central Brera neighborhood. In addition to food stands where you can get cheese, roast chicken, and dried beans and fruits, there are several clothing and shoe stalls that are important stops for some of Milan's most elegant women. ⊠ *Via San Marco, near Via Castelfidardo, Brera* Ⓜ *Lanza; Tram No. 2, 4, 12, or 14.*

Sant'Ambrogio

If the part of the city to the north of the Duomo is dominated by shopping, Sant'Ambrogio and other parts to the south are known for art. The most famous piece is *Il Cenacolo*—known in English as *The Last Supper*. If you have time for nothing else, make sure you see this masterpiece, which is housed in the refectory of Santa Maria delle Grazie. Reservations are required to see it, and you should make yours at least three weeks before you depart for Italy, so you can plan the rest of your time in Milan.

Sights

Basilica di Sant'Ambrogio

(*Basilica of St. Ambrose*)

CHURCH | Milan's bishop, St. Ambrose (one of the original Doctors of the Catholic Church), consecrated this church in AD 387. St. Ambroeus, as he is known in Milanese dialect, is the city's patron saint, and his remains—dressed in elegant religious robes, a miter, and gloves—can be viewed inside a glass case in the crypt below the altar. Until the construction of the more imposing Duomo, this was Milan's most important church. Much restored and reworked over the centuries (the gold-and-gem-encrusted altar dates from the 9th century), Sant'Ambrogio still preserves its Romanesque characteristics, including 5th-century mosaics. The church is often closed for weddings on Saturday. ⊠ *Piazza Sant'Ambrogio 15, Sant'Ambrogio* ☏ *02/86450895* ⊕ *www.basilicasantambrogio.it* Ⓜ *Sant'Ambrogio; Bus No. 50, 58, or 94.*

Chiesa di San Maurizio al Monastero Maggiore

CHURCH | Next to the Museo Civico Archeologico, you'll find this little gem of a church, constructed starting in 1503 and decorated almost completely with magnificent 16th-century frescoes. The modest exterior belies the treasures inside, including a concealed back room once used by nuns that includes a fascinating fresco of Noah loading the ark with animals, including two unicorns. ⊠ *Corso Magenta 15, Sant'Ambrogio* ☏ *02/88445208* Ⓜ *Cadorna or Cairoli; Tram No. 16 or 27; Bus No. 50, 58, or 94.*

★ The Last Supper/Il Cenacolo/ Santa Maria delle Grazie

CHURCH | Leonardo da Vinci's *The Last Supper,* housed in this church and former Dominican monastery, has had an almost unbelievable history of bad luck and neglect. Its near destruction in an American bombing raid in August 1943 was only the latest chapter in a series of misadventures, including—if one 19th-century source is to be believed—being whitewashed over by monks. Well-meant but disastrous attempts at restoration have done little to rectify the problem of the work's placement: it was executed on a wall unusually vulnerable to climatic dampness. Yet Leonardo chose to work slowly and patiently in oil pigments, which demand dry plaster, instead of proceeding hastily on wet plaster according to the conventional fresco technique. After years of restorers patiently shifting from one square centimeter to another, Leonardo's masterpiece is finally free of centuries of retouching, grime, and dust. Astonishing clarity and luminosity have been regained. Despite Leonardo's carefully preserved preparatory sketches, in which the apostles are clearly labeled by name, there still remains some small debate about a few identities in the final arrangement. There can be no mistaking Judas, however—small and dark, his hand calmly reaching forward to the bread, isolated from the terrible confusion that has taken the hearts of the others. Art historian Frederick Hartt offers an elegantly terse explanation for why the composition works: it combines "dramatic confusion" with "mathematical order." Certainly, the amazingly skillful and unobtrusive repetition of threes—in the windows, in the grouping of the figures, and in their placement—adds a mystical aspect to what at first seems simply the perfect observation of spontaneous human gesture. Reservations are required to view the work. Viewings are in 15-minute timed-entry slots, and visitors must arrive 20 minutes before their assigned time in order not to lose their place. Reservations can be made online. Reserve at least three weeks ahead if you want a Saturday slot, two weeks for a weekday slot. Some city bus tours include a visit in their regular circuit, which may be a good option. The painting was executed in what was the order's refectory, which is now referred to

as the Cenacolo Vinciano. Take a moment to visit Santa Maria delle Grazie itself. It's a handsome, completely restored church with a fine dome and a cloister, both of which Bramante added around the time Leonardo was commissioned to paint *The Last Supper.* ✉ *Piazza Santa Maria delle Grazie 2, off Corso Magenta, Sant'Ambrogio* ☎ *02/92800360 reservations, 02/4676111 church* ⊕ *www.cenacolovinciano.net* ⊙ *Closed Mon.* ⊠ *Last Supper €15 (free 1st Sun. of month)* Ⓜ *Cadorna or Conciliazione; Tram No. 18.*

Museo Civico Archeologico

(*Municipal Archaeological Museum*)
HISTORY MUSEUM | Appropriately situated in the heart of Roman Milan, this museum housed in a former monastery displays everyday utensils, jewelry, silver plate, and several fine examples of mosaic pavement from Mediolanum, the ancient Roman name for Milan. The museum opens into a garden that is flanked by the square tower of the Roman circus and the polygonal Ansperto tower, adorned with frescoes dating to the end of the 13th and 14th centuries that portray St. Francis and other saints receiving the stigmata. ✉ *Corso Magenta 15, Sant'Ambrogio* ☎ *02/88445208* ⊕ *www.museoarcheologicomilano.it* ⊠ *€5 (free every 1st and 3rd Tues. of month after 2)* ⊙ *Closed Mon.* Ⓜ *Cadorna or Cairoli; Tram No. 16 or 27; Bus No. 50, 58, or 94.*

Museo Nazionale della Scienza e Tecnologia Leonardo da Vinci (*National Museum of Science and Technology*)

SCIENCE MUSEUM | FAMILY | This converted cloister is best known for the collection of models based on Leonardo da Vinci's sketches. One of the most visited rooms features interactive, moving models of the famous *vita aerea* (aerial screw) and *ala battente* (beating wing), thought to be forerunners of the modern helicopter and airplane, respectively. The museum also houses a varied collection of industrial artifacts, including trains, and several reconstructed workshops, including a watchmaker's, a lute maker's, and an antique pharmacy. Reserve tickets for the celebrated Italian-built submarine, the S-506 *Enrico Toti,* online or by phone to avoid disappointment. Displays also illustrate papermaking and metal founding, which were fundamental to Milan's—and the world's—economic growth. There's a bookshop and a bar. ■ **TIP→ Avoid this museum on weekends. It's a popular spot for families, and there are long lines on those days.** ⊠ *Via San Vittore 21, Sant'Ambrogio* ☎ *02/02485551* ⊕ *www. museoscienza.org* ✉ *€10, €18 including tour of submarine (€20 when reserved in advance)* ⊘ *Closed Mon.* Ⓜ *Sant'Ambrogio; Bus No. 50, 58, or 94.*

🍴 Restaurants

Taverna Moriggi

$$ | **MILANESE** | This wood-paneled traditional Milanese taverna near the stock exchange, within a house from the 14th century, is the perfect spot to enjoy a mix of both traditional and more innovative fare. Pasta, risotto, and more robust secondi like tenderloin with a Barolo wine reduction are available at both lunch and dinner; a reservation is a good idea. **Known for:** historical setting; well-prepared risotto and cotoletta alla Milanese; fantastic wine selection. ⓢ *Average main: €21* ⊠ *Via Morigi 8, Sant'Ambrogio* ☎ *02/36755232* ⊕ *www.tavernamoriggi. com* ⊘ *Closed Mon. No lunch Tues.* Ⓜ *Cairoli or Cordusio; Tram 1, 2, 4, 12, 14, 16, or 27.*

🛏 Hotels

Antica Locanda Leonardo

$ | **HOTEL** | A feeling of relaxation prevails in this 19th-century building, and the neighborhood—the church that houses *The Last Supper* is a block away—is one of Milan's most desired and historic. **Pros:** friendly, helpful staff; very quiet and homey; breakfast is ample. **Cons:** old-fashioned decor; more like a

bed-and-breakfast than a hotel; breakfast is an extra fee. ⓢ *Rooms from: €118* ⊠ *Corso Magenta 78, Sant'Ambrogio* ☎ *02/48014197* ⊕ *www.anticalocandaleonardo.com* ⊘ *Closed 1st wk in Jan. and 3 wks in Aug.* ➟ *16 rooms* ⦿ *No Meals* Ⓜ *Conciliazione, Sant'Ambrogio, or Cadorna; Tram No. 1, 16, 19, or 27.*

Fiera and San Siro

Fiera is a quiet suburb northwest of the city center. Neighboring San Siro is home to Stadio Meazza (commonly known as San Siro Stadium), where AC and Inter Milan play their home matches.

🍴 Restaurants

Al Rifugio Pugliese

$$ | **SOUTHERN ITALIAN** | Outside the center of town, this is a fun place to sample specialties from the Puglia region of southern Italy. These include homemade orecchiette and other pastas served with a variety of sauces; dishes are piled high, so share or come with a big appetite. **Known for:** lively atmosphere; more than 10 different salads; burrata dishes. ⓢ *Average main: €20* ⊠ *Via Costanza 2, Fiera* ☎ *02/48000917* Ⓜ *Wagner; Tram No. 14, 16, or 19.*

🏃 Activities

San Siro Stadium (Stadio Meazza)

SOCCER | AC Milan and Inter Milan, two of the oldest and most successful teams in Europe, vie for the heart of soccer-mad Lombardy. For residents, the city is *Milano* but the teams are *Milan,* a vestige of their common founding as the Milan Cricket and Football Club in 1899. When an Italian-led faction broke off in 1908, the new club was dubbed F. C. Internazionale (or "Inter") to distinguish it from the bastion of English exclusivity that would become AC Milan (or simply "Milan"). Since then, the picture has become more clouded: although Milan used to pride itself as the true team of the city and of its working class, and Inter more persuasively claimed pan-Italian support, the divide among the fan base is not so clear-cut. AC Milan and Inter Milan share the use of San Siro Stadium (Stadio Meazza) during their August–May season. With more than 60,000 of the 80,000 seats appropriated by season-ticket holders and another couple of thousand allocated to visiting fans, tickets to Sunday games can be difficult to come by. You can purchase advance AC Milan tickets online at the club's website (*www.acmilan.com*), at the Casa Milan ticket office at Via Aldo Rossi 8, at Banca Popolare di Milano branches, or at VivaTicket sales points. They're also sold at the stadium booth on match days. For true fans, the AC Milan headquarters, called Casa Milan, includes a museum with interactive exhibits, a store selling team merchandise, and a restaurant. Inter tickets are available on the club's website (*www.inter.it*). If you're a soccer fan but can't get in to see a game, consider taking one of the stadium tours (*www.sansirostadium.com/en/museum-tour/tour*). ✉ *Piazzale Angelo Moratti, San Siro* ☎ *02/48798201* 🌐 *www.sansirostadium.com* [M] *San Siro Stadio; Tram No. 16; Bus No. 49.*

Quadrilatero

Via Manzoni, which lies northeast of La Scala, leads to Milan's Quadrilatero della Moda, or fashion district.

👁 Sights

Museo Bagatti Valsecchi

HISTORIC HOME | Glimpse the lives of 19th-century Milanese aristocrats in a visit to this lovely historic house museum, once the home of two brothers, Barons Fausto and Giuseppe Bagatti. Family members inhabited the house until 1974; it opened to the public as a museum in 1984. The house is decorated with the brothers' fascinating collection of 15th- and 16th-century Renaissance art, furnishings, and objects, including armor, musical instruments, and textiles. The detailed audio guide included with admission provides a thorough insight into the history of the artworks and intriguing stories of the family itself. ✉ *Via Gesu 5, Quadrilatero* ☎ *02/76006132* 🌐 *museobagattivalsecchi.org* 🕒 *Closed Mon.* 🎫 *€10* [M] *Montenapoleone; Tram No. 1.*

Museo Poldi-Pezzoli

ART MUSEUM | This exceptional museum, opened in 1881, was once a private residence and collection, and contains not only pedigreed paintings but also porcelain, textiles, and a cabinet with scenes from Dante's life. The gem is undoubtedly *Portrait of a Lady*, by Piero del Pollaiolo (1431–98), one of the city's most prized treasures and the source of the museum's logo. The collection also includes masterpieces by Botticelli (1445–1510), Andrea Mantegna (1431–1506), Giovanni Bellini (1430–1516), and Fra Filippo Lippi (1406–69). ✉ *Via Manzoni 12, Quadrilatero* ☎ *02/794889* 🌐 *www.museopoldipezzoli.it* 🎫 *€10* 🕒 *Closed Tues.* [M] *Montenapoleone or Duomo; Tram No. 1.*

🍴 Restaurants

Don Carlos

$$$$ | **ITALIAN** | One of the few restaurants open after La Scala lets out, Don Carlos, in the Grand Hotel et de Milan, is nothing like its indecisive operatic namesake (whose betrothed was stolen by his father). Flavors are bold, presentation is precise and full of flair, service is attentive, and the walls are blanketed with sketches of the theater. **Known for:** veal Milanese; late-night hours; homemade pasta. [$] *Average main: €39* ✉ *Via Manzoni 29, Quadrilatero* ☎ *02/72314640* 🕒 *No lunch* [M] *Montenapoleone; Tram No. 1 or 2.*

Seta

$$$ | MODERN ITALIAN | Modern Italian cuisine made using interesting ingredients is the draw at this restaurant with sophisticated brown-and-green decor in Milan's Mandarin Oriental Hotel. The best way to experience the intricate dishes is through the seven-course tasting menu; or a less expensive option, opt for the three-course "carte blanche" lunch menu. **Known for:** top-notch service; wonderful Italo-centric wine list; ultra-creative dishes. $ *Average main: €120* ⊠ *Via Andegari 9, Quadrilatero* ☎ *02/87318897* ⊕ *www.mandarinoriental.com/milan/la-scala/fine-dining/restaurants/italian-cuisine/seta* ⊗ *Closed Sun.,1st wk of Jan., and three wks in Aug.* Ⓜ *Montenapoleone; Tram No. 1.*

☕ Coffee and Quick Bites

Chic & Go Milano

$ | MODERN ITALIAN | Step into these stylish and trendy surroundings for a quick sandwich as exquisite as the fashions in the nearby shops. Though the lobster panini will run you a pretty penny, other top-notch items—like crab, salmon, prosciutto, Angus tartare, and mozzarella di bufala—are not a bad deal. **Known for:** convenient location near shopping; gourmet sandwiches; regional meats. $ *Average main: €8* ⊠ *Via Montenapoleone 25, Quadrilatero* ☎ *02/782648* ⊕ *www.chic-and-go.com* Ⓜ *Montenapoleone; Tram No. 1.*

🛏 Hotels

★ Armani Hotel Milano

$$$ | HOTEL | Located in Milan's fashion district, this minimalist boutique hotel looks like it has been plucked from the pages of a sleek shelter magazine, and it should: it was designed by fashion icon Giorgio Armani to evoke the same sculptural, streamlined aesthetic—and tailored comfort—as his signature clothing. **Pros:** great location near major

shopping streets; complimentary (except for alcohol) minibar; lovely spa area and 24-hour gym. **Cons:** some noise issues from neighboring rooms; breakfast (only included in some rates) not up to par; a few signs of wear and tear. $ *Rooms from: €760* ⊠ *Via Manzoni 31, Quadrilatero* ☎ *02/88838888* ⊕ *www.armanihotelmilano.com* ⇌ *95 rooms* ⦿ *No Meals* Ⓜ *Montenapoleone.*

Four Seasons Hotel Milano

$$$$ | HOTEL | Built in the 15th century as a convent, with a colonnaded cloister, this sophisticated retreat in the heart of Milan's upscale shopping district certainly exudes a feeling that is anything but urban. **Pros:** quiet, elegant setting that feels removed from noisy central Milan; friendly and helpful staff; large rooms. **Cons:** decor is a bit old-fashioned; breakfast isn't included in the rate; expensive. $ *Rooms from: €810* ⊠ *Via Gesù 6–8, Quadrilatero* ☎ *02/77088* ⊕ *www.fourseasons.com/milan* ⇌ *118 rooms* ⦿ *No Meals* Ⓜ *Montenapoleone; Tram No. 1.*

Grand Hotel et de Milan

$$$$ | HOTEL | Only blocks from La Scala, you'll find everything you would expect from a traditionally elegant European hotel, where tapestries and persimmon velvet enliven a 19th-century look without sacrificing dignity and luxury. **Pros:** traditional and elegant; staff go above and beyond to meet guest needs; great location off Milan's main shopping streets. **Cons:** gilt decor may not suit those who like more modern design; no spa; some small rooms. $ *Rooms from: €466* ⊠ *Via Manzoni 29, Quadrilatero* ☎ *02/723141* ⊕ *www.grandhoteletdemilan.it* ⇌ *72 rooms and 23 suites* ⦿ *Free Breakfast* Ⓜ *Montenapoleone.*

Hotel Senato

$$$ | HOTEL | The central courtyard of this boutique hotel near Milan's fashion district is covered in a layer of water, a cheeky nod to the Naviglio Grande canal that once ran in front of the 19th-century palace, which now has a sleek, minimalist

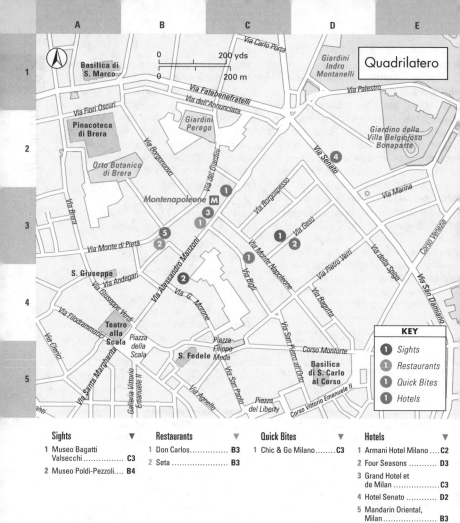

Sights ▼

1 Museo Bagatti
  Valsecchi **C3**
2 Museo Poldi-Pezzoli.... **B4**

Restaurants ▼

1 Don Carlos **B3**
2 Seta **B3**

Quick Bites ▼

1 Chic & Go Milano **C3**

Hotels ▼

1 Armani Hotel Milano **C2**
2 Four Seasons **D3**
3 Grand Hotel et
  de Milan **C3**
4 Hotel Senato **D2**
5 Mandarin Oriental,
  Milan **B3**

design and artsy touches like brass ginkgo biloba–leaf lamps, serpentine mosaic floor patterns, and flowers and music selected by "curators." Relatively simple white-on-white guest rooms have black and gray accents, high ceilings, oak parquet floors, and white Carrara marble bathrooms; try for a room with a private terrace overlooking the peaceful courtyard. **Pros:** convenient location; lovely breakfast buffet with local products; cool designer touches. **Cons:** some rooms on the small side; basic gym facilities; noise can be an issue. ⓢ *Rooms from: €286* ⊠ *Via Senato 22, Quadrilatero* ☏ *02/781236* ⊕ *www. senatohotelmilano.it* ⟿ *43 rooms* ⦿ *Free Breakfast* Ⓜ *Turati or Palestro; Tram No. 1; Bus No. 61 or 94.*

★ **Mandarin Oriental, Milan**

$$$$ | HOTEL | FAMILY | A sense of refined luxury pervades the guest rooms and public spaces of this sophisticated hotel, located just off the main Via Montenapoleone shopping street; from the elegant bedrooms with super-comfortable beds and oversize bathrooms with underfloor heating to the highly rated restaurant and one of the largest spas in Milan (9,700 square feet), you'll be taken care of here. **Pros:** tranquil spa and 24-hour fitness center; wonderful and attentive service; top restaurant on-site. **Cons:** can be difficult to find; very expensive; only some rooms have views. ⓢ *Rooms from: €700* ⊠ *Via Andegari 9, Quadrilatero* ☏ *02/87318888* ⊕ *www.mandarinoriental.com* ⟿ *104 rooms* ⦿ *No Meals* Ⓜ *Montenapoleone; Tram No. 1.*

ⓨ Nightlife

Armani/Bamboo Bar

BARS | The Bamboo Bar at the Armani Hotel Milano has kept Milan abuzz since its opening in 2011. With high ceilings, louvered windows, and expansive views of the city's rooftops, this modern architectural marvel is a great spot to enjoy a relaxing cup of tea or a pre-dinner aperitivo. ⊠ *Via Manzoni 31, Quadrilatero* ☏ *02/88838888* ⊕ *www.armanihotelmilano.com* Ⓜ *Montenapoleone; Tram No. 1.*

Shopping

Armani Megastore

OTHER SPECIALTY STORE | Armani Junior, Emporio Armani, Armani Fiori (flowers), Armani Dolci (chocolate), and Armani Libri (books) are all under this monumental store's roof. ⊠ *Via Manzoni 31, Quadrilatero* ☏ *02/62312600* ⊕ *www.armani. com* Ⓜ *Montenapoleone; Tram No. 1.*

★ DMAG Outlet

JEWELRY & WATCHES | This store has some of the best prices in the area for luxury items, such as Prada, Gucci, Lanvin, and Cavalli. DMAG has two other locations, at Via Forcella 13 and Via Bigli 4. ⊠ *Via Manzoni 44, Quadrilatero* ☏ *02/36514365* ⊕ *www.dmag.eu* Ⓜ *Montenapoleone; Tram No. 1.*

★ Dolce & Gabbana

JEWELRY & WATCHES | This fabulous duo has created an empire based on sultry designs for men and women. The gorgeous three-story flagship store features clothing for both, plus accessories. ⊠ *Via della Spiga 2, Quadrilatero* ☏ *02/795747* ⊕ *www.dolcegabbana.it* Ⓜ *San Babila; Tram No. 61 or 94.*

Dondup

MIXED CLOTHING | Started in 1999, Dondup is a Milanese brand that has captured the essence of casual chic. But it's no longer just a brand for denim lovers: its flagship store houses menswear, women's wear, accessories, and shoe collections. ⊠ *Via della Spiga 50, Quadrilatero* ☏ *02/20242232* ⊕ *www.dondup.com* Ⓜ *Montenapoleone; Tram No. 1.*

Giorgio Armani

MIXED CLOTHING | Find Armani's apparel and accessories for both men and women in the brand's newest boutique. ⊠ *Via Sant'Andrea 9, Quadrilatero* ☏ *02/76003234* ⊕ *www.armani.com* Ⓜ *San Babilo.*

Missoni

MIXED CLOTHING | Famous for their kaleido-scope-pattern knits, this family-run brand sells whimsical designs for men and women. ✉ *Via Sant'Andrea 2, Quadrilatero* ☎ *02/76003555* ⊕ *www.missoni.com* Ⓜ *Montenapoleone or San Babila; Tram No. 1.*

Miu Miu

MIXED CLOTHING | Prada's more upbeat, youthful brand has a wide offering of boldly printed women's fashions and accessories. ✉ *Via Sant'Andrea 21, Quadrilatero* ☎ *02/76001799* ⊕ *www. miumiu.com* Ⓜ *Montenapoleone, San Babila, or Palestro; Tram No. 1.*

Moschino

MIXED CLOTHING | Known for its bold prints, colors, and appliqués, Moschino is a brand for daring fashionistas. ✉ *Via Sant'Andrea 25, Quadrilatero* ☎ *02/76022639* ⊕ *www.moschino. com* Ⓜ *Montenapoleone, San Babila, or Palestro; Tram No. 1.*

Prada

MIXED CLOTHING | Founded in Milan, Prada has several locations throughout the city. Its stores on Via Montenapoleone show-case its women's (Via Montenapoleone 8) and men's fashions (Via Montenapole-one 6). ✉ *Via Montenapoleone 8, Quad-rilatero* ☎ *02/7771771* ⊕ *www.prada. com* Ⓜ *Montenapoleone, San Babila, or Palestro; Tram No. 1.*

Roberto Cavalli

MIXED CLOTHING | Famous for his wild-an-imal prints, Roberto Cavalli creates sexy designs for men and women. ✉ *Via Montenapoleone 6/A, Quadrilatero* ☎ *02/7630771* ⊕ *www.robertocavalli.com* Ⓜ *San Babila.*

Salvatore Ferragamo Donna

WOMEN'S CLOTHING | This Florence-based brand is a leader in leather goods and accessories, and carries designs for women in this store. ✉ *Via Montenapo-leone 3, Quadrilatero* ☎ *02/76000054* ⊕ *www.ferragamo.com* Ⓜ *San Babila.*

Salvatore Ferragamo Uomo

MEN'S CLOTHING | Ferragamo's men's accessories, leather goods, and ties are a staple for Milan's male fashion set. ✉ *Via Montenapoleone 20/4, Quadrilater* ☎ *02/76006660* ⊕ *www.ferragamo.com* Ⓜ *Montenapoleone; Tram No. 1.*

Tod's

MIXED CLOTHING | This leather-goods leader sells luxury handbags as well as a variety of shoes for men and women. It also offers complete lines of men's and women's clothing. ✉ *Via Montenapo-leone 13, Quadrilatero* ☎ *02/76002423* ⊕ *www.tods.com* Ⓜ *Montenapoleone, San Babila, or Palestro; Tram No. 1.*

Valentino

MIXED CLOTHING | Even after the departure of its founding father, Valentino Gara-vani, this fashion brand still flourishes. ✉ *Via Montenapoleone 20, Quadrilatero* ☎ *02/76006182* ⊕ *www.valentino.com* Ⓜ *Montenapoleone; Tram No. 1.*

Versace

MIXED CLOTHING | Run by flamboyant Donatella Versace and known for its rock-and-roll styling, the first store of this fashion house opened on Via della Spiga in 1978, not far from its current location in the Quadrilatero della Moda shopping district. ✉ *Via Monte Napole-one, 11, Quadrilatero* ☎ *02/7600 8528* ⊕ *www.versace.com* Ⓜ *San Babila or Montenapoleone.*

Porta Garibaldi

This stylish, upscale, and buzzing district is home to the emblematic 10 Corso Como concept store and the colorful and lively Piazza Gae Aulenti, which is a study in Milan's modern architecture, includ-ing the 757-foot UniCredit Tower. New construction, stylish restaurants, and urban parks provide a modern break from historical sight-seeing.

Sights

Piazza Gae Aulenti

PLAZA/SQUARE | Welcome to the modern era. The piazza named for the famed Italian female architect is a stroll into the future of architectural design. Here you'll find Italy's tallest skyscraper (the 757-foot mirrored and spired Unicredit Tower), BM Studios (a curved and wood-slatted innovation lab), a Tesla dealership, and an LED tree surrounded by reflective pools. Nearby are Bosco Verticale—two apartment buildings covered in more than 900 hanging trees—part of Stefano Boeri's "Vertical Forest" project, which launched in 2014 to improve air quality in cities (the studio has since created similar structures in more than 20 locations across the globe). Stroll through a botanical garden, Biblioteca degli Alberi (library of trees), and join locals picnicking when the weather cooperates. ⊠ *Piazza Gae Aulenti, Garibaldi* Ⓜ *Garibaldi.*

ADI Design Museum Compasso d'Oro

OTHER MUSEUM | More than 350 of the most renowned Italian industrial design objects from the last 65 years are showcased in this former Enel electricity plant (with two original transformers still visible in one gallery), which opened as a museum in 2021. The items in the permanent collection were selected during biennial judging for Compasso d'Oro (golden compass) awards from 1954 until today. Some of the exhibits are grouped by category, like cars (1960 Abarth-Fiat Monza Zagato, 1959 Fiat 500, and 2014 Ferrari F12berlinetta) and coffee makers Alessi's 9090 from 1979 and Napoletana from 1981). There's even a 1960 Flying Dutchman boat from Alpa. There are also playful groupings by color, such as 1970's orange winners (Soriana sofa from Cassina and Elvi's 390 automatic processing unit). One of the galleries is dedicated to "grandfathers of design," such as Giulio Castelli, founder of Milan-based furniture maker Kartell, and Camillo Olivetti and his eponymous information technology company, which started out making typewriters (its Lettera 22, which won in 1954, is also on display). Peruse a design library in the bookstore and sip coffee or wine in the cafe, taking a seat in more than a dozen chairs from various Italian designers. ⊠ *Piazza Compasso d'Oro, 1, Garibaldi* ☎ *02/36693790* ⊕ *www. adidesignmuseum.org* ≊ *€12* ⊘ *Closed Mon.* ☞ *Tickets may be purchased online, or at the museum with a credit card or mobile wallet (no cash accepted).* Ⓜ *Garibaldi.*

Restaurants

★ Ceresio 7 Pools & Restaurant

$$$$ | CONTEMPORARY | Book well in advance for one of Milan's most fashionable eateries, where the tables are lacquered red and modern artwork crowds the walls—exactly what you'd expect from the twin brothers, Dean and Dan Caten, behind the fashion label Dsquared2. The food cred matches the scene—with fresh, creative, sophisticated pastas and other dishes. **Known for:** swimming pools and terrace views; place for seeing and being seen; luxe ingredients like lobster, king crab, and truffles. Ⓢ *Average main: €36* ⊠ *Via Ceresio 7, Garibaldi* ☎ *02/31039221* ⊕ *www.ceresio7.com* Ⓜ *Garibaldi; Tram No. 2, 4, 12, or 14; Bus No. 37 or 190.*

Ratanà

$$ | NORTHERN ITALIAN | Chef Cesare Battisti infuses the Milanese dishes of his childhood with a contemporary twist at this lively restaurant. Its two patios face a park with skyline views, and its dining room is decorated with vintage items (like an Olivetti typewriter and Scandalli accordion). **Known for:** more than 500 wines; meat- and fish-focused menu with contemporary and traditional dishes; setting in a former historical house. Ⓢ *Average main: €24* ⊠ *Via Gaetano de Castillia 28, Garibaldi* ☎ *02/87128855* ⊕ *www.ratana.it* ⊘ *2 wks in Aug. and 2 wks in Dec.* Ⓜ *Gioia.*

Coffee and Quick Bites

Zàini

$ | BAKERY | The Zàini family opened its chocolate factory here in 1913, on a side street off Corso Como. Today, its black-and-white marble-tile–floored and chandelier-lit cafe, is found just past flagship stores for Dsquared2 and Moschino. **Known for:** elegant breakfast or aperitivo spot; decadent hot chocolate; artfully wrapped chocolate gifts. $ Average main: €10 ☒ Via Carlo de Cristoforis, 5, Garibaldi ☏ 02/694914449 ⊕ www.zainispa.com Ⓜ Garibaldi.

Hotels

Hotel Viu Milan

$$$ | HOTEL | A short walk from trendy Corso Como and the historic Cimitero Monumentale, this sleek business-focused hotel features vertical gardens outside and contemporary Italian-designed furnishings within—but its true pièce de résistance is an inviting rooftop pool with panoramic views. **Pros:** stylish modern decor; spacious bathrooms; high-quality food. **Cons:** hotel has a signature scent, which may bother perfume-averse guests; rooftop terrace sometimes not useable due to events; out-of-the-way location for central Milan. $ Rooms from: €240 ☒ Via Aristotile Fioravanti 6, Garibaldi ☏ 02/80010910 ⊕ www.hotelviumilan.com ⇆ 124 rooms Ⓘ No Meals Ⓜ Monumentale; Tram No. 10, 12, or 14.

Ⓨ Nightlife

Blue Note

LIVE MUSIC | The first European branch of the famous New York nightclub features regular performances by some of the most famous names in jazz, as well as blues and rock concerts. Dinner is also available. ☒ Via Borsieri 37, Garibaldi ☏ 02/69016888 ⊕ www.bluenotemilano.com Ⓜ Isola; Tram No. 7, 31, or 33.

Dry Milano

BARS | A hot spot for both classic and creative cocktails, this trendy industrial space packed with hip locals has a pizza joint in the back if you get hungry. There's a second location at Viale Vittorio Veneto 28. ☒ Via Solferino 33, Garibaldi ☏ 02/63793414 ⊕ www.drymilano.it Ⓜ Moscova, Turati, or Repubblica; Tram No. 1, 9, or 33; Bus No. 37.

Shopping

★ 10 Corso Como

OTHER SPECIALTY STORE | A shrine to Milan's creative fashion sense, the concept store 10 Corso Como was founded by the former fashion editor and publisher Carla Sozzani. The clothing and design establishment also includes a restaurant-café, gallery, bookstore, and small hotel. There's also a second store at Via Tazzoli 3. ☒ Corso Como 10, Corso Como ☏ 02/290113581 ⊕ www.10corsocomo.com Ⓜ Porta Garibaldi.

Repubblica

Some of the city's best restaurants and hotels can be found around the Piazza della Repubblica.

Coffee and Quick Bites

★ Pavè

$ | BAKERY | Your main problem at Pavè will be deciding what to order among rows of cakes, tarts, classic Italian brioches (with sweet fillings like cream and jam), and other pastries. When everything is this drool-worthy, your best strategy is to come with friends and share your favorites. **Known for:** sandwiches and crostini on housemade bread; vegan pastries; chocolate and fruit-filled tarts. $ Average main:€10 ☒ Via Felice Casati 27, Repubblica ☏ 02/37905491 ⊕ www.pavemilano.com ⊙ No dinner Ⓜ Repubblica.

Hotels

Hotel Principe di Savoia Milano

$$$ | **HOTEL** | Milan's grande dame has all the exquisite trappings of a traditional luxury hotel: lavish mirrors, drapes, and carpets; limousine services; and some of the city's largest guest rooms, outfitted with eclectic fin-de-siècle furnishings. **Pros:** substantial health club–spa; shuttle to Duomo and shopping district; close to Central Station. **Cons:** located in a not-very-central or attractive neighborhood; breakfast and other meals overly expensive; showing a bit of wear and tear. $ *Rooms from: €400* ⊠ *Piazza della Repubblica 17, Repubblica* ☎ *02/62301* ⊕ *www.dorchestercollection.com/en/milan/hotel-principe-di-savoia* ⇨ *301 rooms* ⦿I *No Meals* Ⓜ *Repubblica; Tram No. 1, 9, or 33.*

ME Milan Il Duca

$$$$ | **HOTEL** | The first Italian outpost of the Spanish hotel brand ME by Meliá has a lively party atmosphere, with rousing music playing in the lobby, a design-conscious vibe, and a happening rooftop bar with panoramic city views. **Pros:** great rooftop bar; young, vibrant atmosphere; spacious rooms. **Cons:** no spa; may feel overdesigned to some; can be noisy. $ *Rooms from: €328* ⊠ *Piazza della Repubblica 13, Repubblica* ☎ *02/35403218* ⊕ *www.melia.com/en/hotels/italy/milan/me-milan-il-duca/index.htm* ⇨ *132 rooms* ⦿I *No Meals* Ⓜ *Repubblica; Tram No. 1, 5, 9, 10, or 33.*

Westin Palace

$$$$ | **HOTEL** | Don't be fooled by the functional 1950s-era exterior of one of Milan's premier business addresses: inside, rooms have a contemporary look with soothing gray walls and brown marble bathrooms. **Pros:** full-service hotel with extensive amenities; good-size gym open 24/7; renovated rooms in both modern and more traditional styles. **Cons:** Wi-Fi can be spotty in some rooms; not in the most central or attractive location; lacking in local character. $ *Rooms from: €313* ⊠ *Piazza della Repubblica 20, Repubblica* ☎ *02/63361* ⊕ *www.marriott.com/hotels/travel/milwi-the-westin-palace-milan* ⇨ *231 rooms* ⦿I *Free Breakfast* Ⓜ *Repubblica; Tram No. 1, 5, 9, or 33.*

Nightlife

Radio Rooftop Bar

COCKTAIL LOUNGES | Some of Milan's most beautiful people congregate for an Aperol spritz and a selection of international tapas on this terrace with panoramic views of the city. Located at the top of the ME Milan Il Duca, the bar has heat lamps to keep visitors here even in cooler weather. You can also enjoy lunch Monday through Friday. ⊠ *Piazza della Repubblica 13, Repubblica* ☎ *02/84220109* ⊕ *www.radiorooftop.com/milan* Ⓜ *Repubblica; Tram No. 1, 5, 9, 10, or 33.*

Shopping

Antonioli

MIXED CLOTHING | Antonioli raises the bar for Milan's top trendsetters. Uniting the most cutting-edge looks of each season, it is among the fashion-forward concept stores in the city. Aside from Italian brands like Valentino, it also stocks a competitive international array of designers, like Ann Demeulemeester, Rick Owens, Givenchy, Jil Sander, Maison Margiela, and Vetements. ⊠ *Via Pasquale Paoli 1, Centro Direzionale* ☎ *02/36561860* ⊕ *www.antonioli.eu* Ⓜ *Porta Genova; Tram No. 2; Bus No. 47 or 74.*

Cinque Giornate

Located just east of the city center, Cinque Giornate marks the location of the Five Days revolt against Austrian rule in Milan.

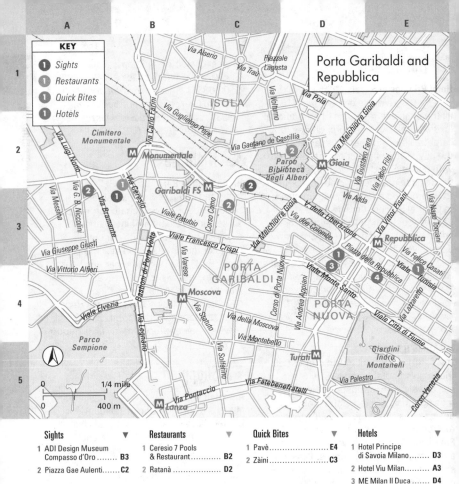

Porta Garibaldi and Repubblica

KEY
- **1** Sights
- **1** Restaurants
- **1** Quick Bites
- **1** Hotels

Sights ▼	Restaurants ▼	Quick Bites ▼	Hotels ▼
1 ADI Design Museum Compasso d'Oro **B3**	1 Ceresio 7 Pools & Restaurant **B2**	1 Pavè **E4**	1 Hotel Principe di Savoia Milano **D3**
2 Piazza Gae Aulenti **C2**	2 Ratanà **D2**	2 Zàini **C3**	2 Hotel Viu Milan **A3**
			3 ME Milan Il Duca **D4**
			4 Westin Palace **E4**

Restaurants

a Giacomo

$$ | **ITALIAN** | The fashion and publishing rowds, as well as international bankers nd businesspeople, favor this Tuscan-Ligurian restaurant. The emphasis is n fish, and with its tile floor and bank f fresh seafood, the place has a refined eighborhood-bistro style. **Known for:** xtensive wines, cocktails, and after-diner drinks; sophisticated dining; specialty *nocchetti alla Giacomo* (with seafood nd tomato). $ *Average main: €32* ⊠ *Via ? Sottocorno 6, entrance in Via Cellini, Cinque Giornate* ☎ *02/76023313* ⊕ *www. giacomoristorante.com* Ⓜ *Tram No. 9, 12, 23, or 27; Bus No. 60 or 73.*

Palestro

Nestled just below the Giardini Pubblici ndro Montanelli park, Palestro is filled vith galleries, museums, and historical andmarks.

Sights

GAM: Galleria d'Arte Moderna/Villa Reale

HISTORIC HOME | One of the city's most beautiful buildings is an outstanding example of neoclassical architecture, built between 1790 and 1796 as a residence for a member of the Belgiojoso family. After it was donated to Napoléon, who lived here briefly with Empress Josephine, it became known as the Villa Reale. Its residential origins are evident in its elegant proportions and private back garden. The museum provides a unique glimpse of the splendors hiding behind Milan's discreet and often stern facades. The collection consists of works donated by prominent Milanese art collectors. It emphasizes 18th- and 19th-century Italian works, but also has a smattering of 20th-century Italian pieces as well as some international works by Van Gogh and Picasso, among others. The museum

also presents regularly scheduled rotating exhibitions. ⊠ *Via Palestro 16, Palestro* ☎ *02/88445947* ⊕ *www.gam-milano.com* ⚏ *€5 (Free every 1st and 3rd Tues. of month after 2)* ☉ *Closed Mon.* Ⓜ *Palestro or Turati; Tram No. 1 or 2; Bus No. 94 or 61.*

Villa Necchi Campiglio

NOTABLE BUILDING | In 1932, architect Piero Portaluppi designed this sprawling estate in an art deco style, with inspiration coming from the decadent cruise ships of the 1920s. Once owned by the Necchi Campiglio industrial family, the tasteful and elegant home—which sits on Via Mozart, one of Milan's most exclusive streets—is a reminder of the refined, modern culture of the nouveaux riches who accrued financial power in Milan during that era. There is also a cafe on the grounds that is open 10 am–6 pm. ■**TIP**→ **Tours of the estate last about one hour; English-speaking tours are offered Wed.–Sat. between 10:30 am and 2:15 pm.** ⊠ *Via Mozart 14, Palestro* ☎ *02/76340121* ⊕ *www.fondoambiente.it/villa-necchi-campiglio-eng* ⚏ *€14 or €20 for guided visits; garden-only €4.* ☉ *Closed Mon. and Tues.* Ⓜ *Palestro, San Babila, or Montenapoleone; Bus No. 54, 61, or 94.*

Porta Venezia

This district is home to parks and gardens, museums, galleries, and one end of the famed Corso Buenos Aires shopping street.

Sights

Giardini Pubblici Indro Montanelli (*Public Gardens Indro Montanelli*)

GARDEN | **FAMILY** | Giuseppe Piermarini, architect of La Scala, laid out these gardens across Via Palestro from the Villa Reale in 1770. Designed as public pleasure gardens, today they are still popular with families who live in the city center. Generations of Milanese have taken pony rides and gone on the miniature train and merry-go-round. The park also contains a small planetarium and the **Museo Civico di Storia Naturale** (Municipal Natural History Museum). ✉ *Corso Venezia 55, Porta Venezia* ☎ *02/88463337* ⊕ *www. assodidatticamuseale.it* ☞ *Gardens free, museum €5 (free every 1st and 3rd Tues. of month after 2 and 1st Sun. of month)* ⊙ *Museum closed Mon.* Ⓜ *Palestro; Tram No. 9, 29, or 30.*

🍴 Restaurants

Joia
$$$$ | **VEGETARIAN** | At this hushed, haute-cuisine vegetarian haven near Piazza della Repubblica, delicious dishes—all without eggs and many without flour—are served in a minimalist beige room that puts the focus solely on the artistry of the food. Vegetarians, who often get short shrift in Italy, will marvel at the variety of culinary offerings made from many organic and biodynamic ingredients. **Known for:** well-thought-out wine selection; imaginative presentations; ever-changing menu. $ *Average main: €40* ✉ *Via Panfilo Castaldi 18, Porta Venezia* ☎ *02/29522124* ⊕ *joia.it* ⊙ *Closed 2 wks in Aug. and Dec. 24–Jan.6* Ⓜ *Repubblica or Porta Venezia; Tram No. 1, 5, 9, or 33.*

LùBar
$$ | **SICILIAN** | Dining at LùBar, which was started by three children of Milan fashion designer Luisa Beccaria and which is tucked into the side of the Galleria d'Arte Moderna, feels like eating inside a greenhouse—only with fashionable people among the trees and plants. The cozy, chic environs lend themselves perfectly to nibbling on small plates of modern Sicilian food—for lunch, an afternoon snack, or a light dinner—all served on Caltagirone ceramics straight from Sicily. **Known for:** Sicilian street food like arancini and polpette (meatballs); LùBar Spritz made with Amara, a Sicilian blood orange amaro; charming, relaxed atmosphere.

$ *Average main: €16* ✉ *Via Palestro 16, Porta Venezia* ☎ *02/83527769* ⊕ *www. lubar.it* Ⓜ *Palestro or Turati; Tram No. 1 or 2; Bus No. 94 or 61.*

Buenos Aires

This street in northeastern Milan is one of the busiest in the city and has over 350 stores and outlets to choose from.

⊙ Sights

Casa-Museo Boschi di Stefano (*Boschi di Stefano House and Museum*)
HISTORIC HOME | To most people, Italian art means Renaissance art, but the 20th century in Italy was also a time of artistic achievement. An apartment on the second floor of a stunning art deco building designed by Milan architect Portaluppi houses this collection, which was donated to the city of Milan in 2003 and is a tribute to the enlightened private collectors who replaced popes and nobles as Italian patrons. The walls are lined with the works of postwar greats, such as Fontana, de Chirico, and Morandi. Along with the art, the museum holds distinctive postwar furniture and stunning Murano glass chandeliers. ✉ *Via Jan 15, Buenos Aires* ☎ *02/88463614* ⊕ *www.fondazione-boschidistefano.it* ☞ *Free* ⊙ *Closed Mon.* Ⓜ *Lima; Tram No. 33; Bus No. 60.*

☕ Coffee and Quick Bites

★ Marghe
$ | **NEOPOLITAN** | At Marghe, crafting Neopolitan-style pizza is art—as the line of people outside the restaurant each night suggests. Put your name down (they don't accept reservations), or better, arrive right before they open at 7:30 pm to grab a table in the rustic and lively dining room with exposed concrete walls, floral tiled floors, and pendant lights, where pizzas are delivered quickly and piping hot. **Known for:** pizza made from Type 1 flour and dough

at rises for 48 hours; ingredients from aples and the Amalfi Coast; local atmos-here. $ *Average main: €10* ✉ *Via Plinio , Buenos Aires* ☎ *02/54118711* ⊕ *www. arghepizza.com* Ⓜ *Lima.*

oreto

ocated in the northeastern part of the ty, Piazzale Loreto has a rather grim ecent history: In August 1944, the estapo in Milan publicly executed 15 alian resistance fighters here. Less han a year later, Benito Mussolini and number of other high-ranking fascists, vere captured and shot, with their bod-s displayed here. There are no placards r signs to mark this history, and the quare itself has since been widened to ccomodate more traffic.

🍴 Restaurants

a Abele

| **ITALIAN** | The superb risotto dishes at his neighborhood trattoria change with he season; you'll find at least three on he menu—meat, fish, and vegetari-n—and it's tempting to try them all. he setting is relaxed and the service is nformal. **Known for:** reasonable prices; neat-focused main courses like tripe; :ozy neighborhood favorite. $ *Average nain: €13* ✉ *Via Temperanza 5, Loreto* ☎ *02/2613855* ⊕ *www.trattoriadaabele.it* ⏱ *Closed Mon. No dinner weekdays and Sun.* Ⓜ *Pasteur.*

Bicocca

his university and business district plays nost to musicals and concerts as well as rt installations.

👁 Sights

Pirelli HangarBicocca

ARTS CENTER | Anselm Kiefer's *The Seven Heavenly Palaces*—seven cement towers extending 43–52 feet high, along with five of Kiefer's large-scale paintings—is the must-see permanent installation at this impressive gallery in a former train factory. There are also temporary exhibitions of contemporary art through-out the year; check the website for the latest showings. ✉ *Via Chiese 2, Bicocca* ☎ *02/66111573* ⊕ *www.hangarbicocca. org* ⏱ *Free* ⏱ *Closed Sat.–Tues.* Ⓜ *Via Chiese; Bus No. 87 or 51.*

Porta Romana

Home to some of Milan's wealthiest res-idents, Porta Romana is a hip and vibrant neighborhood.

👁 Sights

★ Fondazione Prada

ART MUSEUM | New structures of metal and glass and revamped buildings once part of a distillery from the 1910s now contain this museum's roughly 205,000 square feet. The modern art showcased here is not for the faint of heart. Perma-nent pieces, such as *Haunted House,* featuring works by Louise Bourgeois and Robert Gober, are avant-garde and chal-lenging, and temporary exhibitions high-light cutting-edge Italian and international artists. Don't hesitate to ask one of the helpful, knowledgeable staffers for guid-ance navigating the expansive grounds, which can be confusing. And don't miss the Wes Anderson–designed café, Luce Bar, for a drink or snack, or the Restau-rant Torre for an aperitivo or a full meal with panoramic views from on high. The Fondazione is a hike from the city center; expect a 10-minute walk from the metro station to the galleries. ✉ *Largo Isarco 2, Porta Romana* ☎ *02/56662611* ⊕ *www. fondazioneprada.org* ⏱ *€15 for full visit*

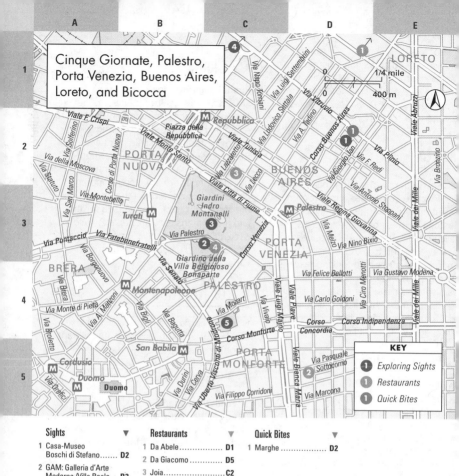

Cinque Giornate, Palestro, Porta Venezia, Buenos Aires, Loreto, and Bicocca

KEY
- 1 *Exploring Sights*
- 1 *Restaurants*
- 1 *Quick Bites*

Sights ▼

1 Casa-Museo Boschi di Stefano **D2**

2 GAM: Galleria d'Arte Moderna./Villa Reale .. **B3**

3 Giardini Pubblici Indro Montanelli **C3**

4 Pirelli HangarBicocca **C1**

5 Villa Necchi Campiglio **C4**

Restaurants ▼

1 Da Abele **D1**

2 Da Giacomo **D5**

3 Joia **C2**

4 LùBar **C3**

Quick Bites ▼

1 Marghe **D2**

admission, which includes a ticket to Milano Osservatorio; €8-10 for temporary exhibitions or permanent projects only. ☉ *Closed Tues.* Ⓜ *Lodi TIBB; Tram No. 24; Bus No. 65.*

Restaurants

U Barba
$ | **NORTHERN ITALIAN** | Simple, fresh, authentic Ligurian (in that region's dialect the name means "the uncle") specialties will take you back to lazy summer days on the Italian Riviera—even during Milan's gray winters. Such coastal classics as *trofie al pesto* (an egg-free pasta served with pesto) and *bagnun di acciughe* (anchovy soup), coupled with a basket of warm focaccia, or a side of *farinata* (a chickpea pancake) reign supreme in this Milan favorite. **Known for:** focaccia and farinata; fresh pasta, also available to take home; charming setting with vintage furniture. $ *Average main: €14* ⊠ *Via Pier Candido Decembrio 33, Porta Romana* ☎ *02/45487032* ⊕ *www. ubarba.it* ☉ *Closed Mon. No lunch Tues.– Fri.* Ⓜ *Lodi TIBB; Tram No. 16; Bus No. 90.*

Ticinese

This boho district is also home to the Basilica di San Lorenzo Maggiore and the Basilica di Sant'Eustorgio.

Sights

MUDEC (Museo delle Culture)
ART MUSEUM | Home to a permanent collection of ethnographic displays as well as temporary exhibitions of big-name artists such as Basquiat and Miró, MUDEC is in the vibrant and developing Zona Tortona area of the city. British architect David Chipperfield designed the soaring space in a former factory. The permanent collection includes art, objects, and documents from Africa, Asia, and the Americas. Book in advance

Formula 1 Racing

Italian Grand Prix. Italy's Formula 1 fans are passionate and huge numbers converge in early September for the Italian Grand Prix, held 15 km (9 miles) northeast of Milan in Monza. The racetrack was built in 1922 within the **Parco di Monza.** Check the website for dates, as well as for special category races, like classic cars and motorcycles. Visitors are allowed to zoom around the track on certain days—guided by a professional driver, of course. ⊠ *Monza Eni Circuit, Via Vedano 5, Parco di Monza, Monza* ⊕ *www. monzanet.it.*

for the most popular temporary exhibits. There's also a highly rated restaurant, Enrico Bartolini Mudec, as well as a more casual bistro. ⊠ *Via Tortona 56, Ticinese* ☎ *02/54917* ⊕ *www.mudec.it* ⊠ *Permanent collection free, special exhibitions €10–€17* ☉ *Closed Mon. until 2:30 pm* Ⓜ *Sant'Agostino or Porta Genova; Tram No. 2 or 14; Bus No. 68 or 90/91.*

San Lorenzo Maggiore alle Colonne
CHURCH | Sixteen ancient Roman columns line the front of this sanctuary; 4th-century Paleo-Christian mosaics survive in the Cappella di Sant'Aquilino (Chapel of St. Aquilinus). ⊠ *Corso di Porta Ticinese 35, Ticinese* ☎ *02/89404129* ⊕ *www. sanlorenzomaggiore.com* ⊠ *Mosaics €2* Ⓜ *Missori.*

Restaurants

★ [bu:r] di Eugenio Boer
$$$$ | **MODERN ITALIAN** | Named after the phonetic spelling of the Dutch-Italian chef's last name, this innovative, high-concept restaurant, whose quiet dining rooms are done up in gray and gold, offers a choice of interesting tasting

menus and à la carte options. Boer's contemporary Italian food is beautifully presented and full of complex flavors, and the well-matched wines lean toward the natural. **Known for:** helpful and well-informed service; personalized cuisine; traditional dishes with an ultramodern spin. [$] *Average main: €65* ✉ *Via Mercalli ang. Via SF D'Assisi, Ticinese* ☎ *02/62065383* 🌐 *www.restaurantboer.com* 🕓 *Closed Sun. No lunch.* [M] *Crocetta; Tram No. 15; Bus No. 94.*

Hotels

★ The Yard

$$$ | **HOTEL** | The decor in this eclectic, extremely hip hotel at the foot of the lively Corso di Porta Ticinese and by the Navigli canals features sports memorabilia from golf, horseback riding, boxing, and others. **Pros:** very friendly staff; contemporary flair; interesting location near many restaurants and bars. **Cons:** about a half-hour hike from the Duomo and central attractions; lacking some of the amenities of large hotels; bar noise can be heard in some rooms. [$] *Rooms from: €229* ✉ *Piazza XXIV Maggio 8, Porta Ticinese* ☎ *02/89415901* 🌐 *www.theyardmilano.com* 🛏 *32 rooms* 🍴 *Free Breakfast* [M] *Tram No. 3 or 9.*

Navigli

One of the oldest neighborhoods in the city, Navigli is a quiet, artistic hub by day and a lively hot spot by night.

Sights

★ Navigli District

HISTORIC DISTRICT | In medieval times, a network of *navigli,* or canals, crisscrossed the city. Almost all have been covered over, but two—Naviglio Grande and Naviglio Pavese—are still navigable. The area's chock-full of boutiques, art galleries, cafés, bars, and restaurants, and at night the Navigli serves up a scene about as close as you will get to southern Italian–style street life in Milan. On weekend nights, it is difficult to walk among the youthful crowds thronging the narrow streets along the canals. Check out the antiques fair on the last Sunday of the month from 9 to 6. **TIP→ During the summer months, be sure to put on some mosquito repellent.** ✉ *South of Corso Porta Ticinese, Navigli* [M] *Porta Genova; Tram No. 2, 3, 9, 14, 15, 29, or 30.*

"Let's Go to the Columns"

Andiamo al Le Colonne, in Milanese youthspeak, is the cue to meet up at the sober Roman columns in front of the Basilica San Lorenzo Maggiore. Attracted to the Corso di Porta Ticinese by its bars and shops, hipsters spill out on the street to chat and drink. Neighbors may complain about the noise and confusion, but students and nighthawks find it indispensable for socializing at all hours. It's a street—no closing time.

Nightlife

Rita

BARS | Though it's a bit difficult to find, on a side street in the popular aperitivo haunt of Navigli, the expertly mixed cocktails, well-prepared snacks, and excellent playlist make this classic worth the hunt. It also serves burgers, sandwiches, and more substantial plates for dinner. ✉ *Via Angelo Fumagalli 1, Navigli* ☎ *02/837 2865* [M] *Porta Genova; Tram No. 2.*

★ Ugo Bar

BARS | Flanked by a long bar and tables lit by candles, and featuring floral wallpaper and eclectic framed paintings of animals, this bar has a moody living-room vibe.

It's a charming place for a drink, if you can squeeze past the crowds. There is also a handful of outdoor tables for prime people-watching. ⊠ *Via Corsico 12, Navigli* ☎ *02/39811557* ⊕ *www.ugobar.it* Ⓜ *Porta Genova; Tram No. 9 or 10.*

Performing Arts

Auditorium di Milano Fondazione Cariplo
CONCERTS | This modern hall, known for its excellent acoustics, is home to the **Orchestra Sinfonica di Milano Giuseppe Verdi (Symphonic Orchestra)** and **Coro Sinfonico di Milano Giuseppe Verdi (Symphonic Choir)**. The season, which runs from September to June, includes many top international performers and rotating guest conductors. ⊠ *Largo Gustav Mahler, at Corso San Gottardo, Navigli* ☎ *02/83389401* ⊕ *www.laverdi.org* Ⓜ *Tram No. 3 or 15; Bus No. 59 or 91.*

Tortona

Tortona's former factories, warehouses, and workshops are now a creative hub packed with shops, studios, and the MUDEC, a museum with modern and contemporary art and special exhibitions.

Sights

★ Armani/Silos
OTHER MUSEUM | About 600 pieces, from about 1980 to the present, by famed Milanese fashion designer Giorgio Armani are displayed on four floors of this airy 48,000-square-foot museum, housed in a 1950s building that was formerly a Nestlé cereal storage facility. The collection is divided by theme: Ethnicities; Androgynous, including many of Armani's famous suits; and Stars, with clothes worn to the Oscars and other celebrity-studded events. A digital archive lets you explore Armani's full body of work, and a café lets you stop for a restorative espresso. Temporary exhibitions explore photography, architecture, and other themes

related to design. ⊠ *Via Bergognone 40, Ticinese* ☎ *02/91630010* ⊕ *www.armanisilos.com* 💳 *€12* ⏱ *Closed Mon. and Tues.* Ⓜ *Sant'Agostino or Porta Genova; Tram No. 2 or 14; Bus No. 68 or 90/91.*

Hotels

Hotel Magna Pars Suites Milano
$$$$ | HOTEL | Next to the trendy Navigli canals area, this ultrastylish all-suites boutique hotel in a former perfume factory has Italian-designed furnishings; paintings by local Brera Academy artists; and sleek, white accommodations—each with its own signature scent (such as fruity, woodsy, or floral) and all overlooking one of two tranquil courtyards. **Pros:** wonderful food at the attached restaurant; modern, design-y feel; attentive service. **Cons:** a bit of a trek to central attractions; spa on the small side; perfumed rooms not for everyone. 💲 *Rooms from: €327* ⊠ *Via Forcella 6, Tortona* ☎ *02/8338371* ⊕ *www.magnapars-suitesmilano.it* 🛏 *60 suites* ⑪ *No Meals* Ⓜ *Porta Genova; Tram No. 2, 9, or 19.*

Riomaggiore

17 km (11 miles) southwest of La Spezia, 101 km (60 miles) southeast of Genoa.

At the eastern end of the Cinque Terre, Riomaggiore is built into a river gorge (hence the name, which means "major river") and is easily accessible from La Spezia by train or car. The landscape is terraced and steep—be prepared for many stairs!—and leads to a small harbor, protected by large slabs of alabaster and marble that serve as tanning beds for sunbathers. The harbor is also the site of several outdoor cafés with fine views. According to legend, the settlement of Riomaggiore dates as far back as the 8th century, when Greek religious refugees came here to escape persecution by the Byzantine emperor.

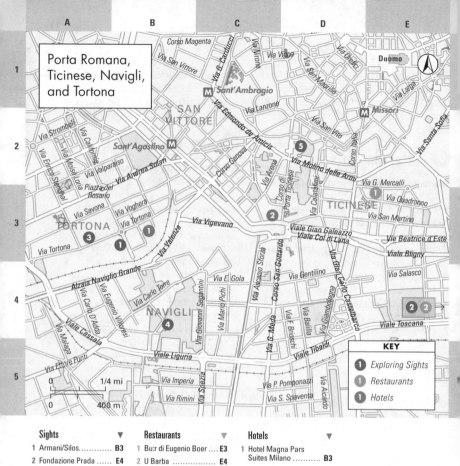

Porta Romana,
Ticinese, Navigli,
and Tortona

Duomo

Corso Magenta
Via San Vittore
Via G. Carducci
Via Nirone
Via Vigna
Via Orefici
Via San Maurilio
Via Larga
M Sant'Ambrogio
Via Edmondo de Amicis
Via Lanzone
Via San Vito
M Missori
SAN VITTORE
Via Stromboli
Via California
Via Moisè Loria
Sont'Agostino M
Via Valparaiso
Corso Genova
Via Arena
Corso di Porta Ticinese
Via Molino delle Armi
Via G. Mercalli
TICINESE
Via Quadronno
Via Enrico Stendhal
Via Andrea Solari
Piazza del Rosario
Via Savona
Via Voghera
Via Calatafimi
Via San Martino
TORTONA
Via Tortona
Via Vigevano
Viale Gian Galeazzo
Vle Beatrice d'Este
Via Tortona
Viale Col di Lana
Viale Bligny
Alzaia Naviglio Grande
Via Valenza
Via E. Gola
Via Ascanio Sforza
Via Gentilino
Via Salasco
Via Carlo Torre
Via Eugenio Villoresi
Via Carlo D'Adda
Via Giovanni Segantini
Via Mario Pichi
Corso San-Gottardo
Via F. Brioschi
Via Barilla
Via Gian Carlo Castelbarco
Viale Toscana
NAVIGLI
Viale Cassala
Via Malaga
Viale Liguria
Via G. Meda
Viale Tibaldi
Via Ettore Ponti
Via Imperia
Via Spezia
Via P. Pomponazzi
Via Alcaldo
Via Rimini
Via S. Spaventa

0   1/4 mi
0   400 m

KEY	
1	Exploring Sights
1	Restaurants
1	Hotels

Sights	▼	Restaurants	▼	Hotels	▼
1 Armani/Silos............. **B3**		1 Bu:r di Eugenio Boer **E3**		1 Hotel Magna Pars	
2 Fondazione Prada **E4**		2 U Barba **E4**		Suites Milano **B3**	
3 MUDEC				2 The Yard **C3**	
(Museo delle Culture).. **A3**					
4 Navigli District **B4**					
5 San Lorenzo Maggiore					
alle Colonne **D2**					

Accessing Cinque Terre Trails

When to Go

The ideal times to visit the Cinque Terre are September and May, when the weather is mild and the summer tourist season isn't in full swing (June through August can be unbearably hot and crowded).

Getting Here and Around

There is now a local train between La Spezia and Levanto that stops at each of the Cinque Terre villages, and runs approximately every 30 minutes throughout the day. Tickets for each leg of the journey (€1.90–€2.20) are available at all five train stations. In Corniglia, the only one of the Cinque Terre that isn't at sea level, a shuttle service (€1.50) is provided for those who don't wish to climb (or descend) the 300-plus steps that link the train station with the clifftop town.

Along the Cinque Terre coast two ferry lines operate. From June to September, Golfo Paradiso runs from Genoa and Camogli to Monterosso al Mare and Vernazza (a one-day ticket costs €38). The smaller but more frequent Golfo dei Poeti stops at each village from Lerici (east of Riomaggiore) to Monterosso, with the exception of Corniglia, four times a day (a one-day ticket costs €35).

Admission

Entrance tickets for using the trails are available at ticket booths located at the start of each section of Trail No. 2, and at information offices in the Levanto, Monterosso, Vernazza, Corniglia, Manarola, Riomaggiore, and La Spezia train stations. A one-day pass costs €7.50, which includes a trail map and an information leaflet; a two-day pass is €14.50.

The Cinque Terre Card combines park entrance fees with unlimited daily use of the regional train between La Spezia, the five villages, and Levanto just north of Monterosso, and costs €16 for a one-day pass and €29 for a two-day pass.

For More Information

www.cinqueterre.com; www.lecinque-terre.org; www.parconazionale5terre.it; www.rebuildmonterosso.com; www.savevernazza.com; www.littleparadiso.com (blog).

The village is divided into two parts. If you arrive by train, you will have to pass through a tunnel that flanks the train tracks to reach the historic side of town. To avoid the crowds and get a great view of the Cinque Terre coast, walk straight uphill as soon as you exit the station. This winding road takes you over the hill to the 14th-century **church of St. John the Baptist,** toward the medieval town center and the Genovese-style tower houses that dot the village. Follow Via Roma (the Old Town's main street) downhill, pass under the train tracks, and you'll arrive in the charming fishermen's port.

Lined with traditional fishing boats and small trattorias, this is a lovely spot for a romantic lunch or dinner. Unfortunately, Riomaggiore doesn't have as much old-world charm as its sister villages; its easy accessibility has brought traffic and more construction here than elsewhere in the Cinque Terre.

GETTING HERE AND AROUND

The enormous parking problems presented by these cliff-dwelling villages have been mitigated somewhat by a large, covered parking structure at La Spezia Centrale station, which costs €2.30 per hour in summer. It's clean and secure (you cannot enter without a ticket code to open the door), and it's open 24/7. This is a good backup solution for those with cars, although others may choose to take a day trip from Pisa or Lucca and rely on bus and train services. Arrive early, as it can fill up by mid-morning, especially in high season.

Sights

Riomaggiore

TOWN | This village at the eastern end of the Cinque Terre is built into a river gorge (hence the name, which means "river major"). It has a tiny harbor protected by large slabs of alabaster and marble, which serve as tanning beds for sunbathers, as well as being the site of several outdoor cafés with fine views. According to legend, the settlement of Riomaggiore dates as far back as the 8th century, when Greek religious refugees came here to escape persecution by the Byzantine emperor. ✉ *Stazione Ferroviaria, Riomaggiore* ☎ *0187/762187* 🌐 *www.turismoinliguria.it.*

Restaurants

Dau Cila

$$ | **LIGURIAN** | There's wonderful seaside dining on Riomaggiore harbor, with a menu of local Ligurian dishes and an extensive wine list. **■ TIP→ On bad-weather days, take advantage of the lovely dining room with vaulted ceilings, built into the rock. Known for:** local flavors; sea views; extensive wine list. [$] *Average main: €22* ✉ *Via San Giacomo 65, Riomaggiore* ☎ *0187/760032* 🕓 *Closed Tues.*

Manarola

16 km (10 miles) southwest of La Spezia, 117 km (73 miles) southeast of Genoa.

The enchanting pastel houses of Manarola spill down a steep hill overlooking a spectacular turquoise swimming cove and a bustling harbor. The whole town is built on black rock. Above the town, ancient terraces still protect abundant vineyards and olive trees. This village is the center of wine and olive oil production in the region, and its streets are lined with shops selling local products.

Surrounded by steep terraced vineyards, Manarola's one road tumbles from the **Chiesa di San Lorenzo** (14th century) high above the village, down to the rocky port. Since the Cinque Terre wine cooperative is located in **Groppo,** a hamlet overlooking the village (reachable by foot or by the green Park bus; ask at Park offices for schedules), the vineyards are accessible. If you'd like to snap a shot of the most famous view of the town, you can walk from the port area to the cemetery above. Along the way you'll pass the town's playground, uncrowded bathrooms, and a tap with clean drinking water.

Sights

Manarola

TOWN | Enchanting pastel houses spill down a steep hill overlooking a spectacular turquoise swimming cove and a bustling harbor. The whole town is built on black rock. Above the town, ancient terraces still protect abundant vineyards and olive trees. This village is the center of the wine and olive oil production of the region, and its streets are lined with shops selling local products. 🌐 *www.turismoinliguria.it, www.parconazionale5terre.it.*

Hotels

★ **La Torretta**

$$$ | **HOTEL** | One of the Cinque Terre's few "boutique" hotels is in a 17th-century tower that sits high on the hill above the rainbow-hue village of Manarola, with truly lovely views of the terraced vineyards, colorful village homes, and the Mediterranean sea; inside, decor is chic, sleek, and antiques-bedecked. **Pros:** no-smoking policy; stellar staff; free luggage transfer. **Cons:** steep walk up to the hotel; books

Hiking the Cinque Terre

Though often described as relaxing and easy, the Cinque Terre also have several hiking options if you wish to exert yourself a little. Many people do not realize just how demanding parts of these trails can be—it's best to come prepared. We recommend bringing a Cinque Terre Card and cash (smaller shops, eateries, and the park entrances do not accept credit cards).

When all trails are completely open, a hike through the entire region takes about four to five hours; add time for exploring each village and taking a lunch break—it's an all-day, if not two-day, trek. We recommend an early start, especially in summer when midday temperatures can rise to 90°F. Note that only Sentiero Azzurro (Trail No. 2) requires the Cinque Terre Card. The other 20-plus trails in the area are free. All trails are well marked with a red-and-white sign. Trails from village to village get progressively steeper from south (Riomaggiore) to north (Monterosso). If you're a day-tripper with a car, use the underground lot at La Spezia Centrale train station (€2.30 per hour in summer) and take the train to Riomaggiore (6–8 minutes).

Our Favorites

Other trails to consider include **Monterosso to Santuario Madonna di Soviore**, a fairly strenuous but rewarding 1½ hours up to a lovely 8th-century sanctuary. There is also a restaurant and a priceless view. **Riomaggiore to Montenero and Portovenere** is one hour up to the sanctuary and another three hours to Portovenere, passing through some gorgeous, less-traveled terrain. **Manarola to Volastra to Corniglia** runs high above the main trail and through vineyards and lesser-known villages. **Monterosso to Levanto** is a good 2½-hour hike, passing over Punta Mesco with glorious views of the Cinque Terre to the south, Corsica to the west, and the Alps to the north.

Each town has something that passes for a beach (usually with lots of pebbles or slabs of terraced rock), but there is only one option for both sand and decent swimming—in Monterosso, just across from the train station. It's equipped with chairs, umbrellas, and snack bars.

Precautions

If you're hitting the trails, carry water with you, wear sturdy shoes (hiking boots are best), and have a hat and sunscreen handy. Note that the lesser-used trails aren't as well maintained as Trail No. 2. If you're undertaking the full Trail No. 1 hike, bring something to snack on as well as your water bottle. Note that currently the Via dell'Amore and the portion of Trail No. 2 between Manarola and Corniglia are closed indefinitely due to landslides.

■ TIP→ **Check weather reports, especially in late fall and winter; thunderstorms can make shelterless trails slippery and dangerous. Rain in October and November can cause landslides and close trails altogether.**

up quickly; strict no-refund policy. [$] *Rooms from: €250* ✉ *Vico Volto 20, Cinque Terre, Manarola* ☎ *0187/920327* 🌐 *www.torrettas.com* 🕓 *Closed Dec.–Feb.* 🛏 *15 rooms* 🍴 *Free Breakfast.*

Corniglia

27 km (17 miles) northwest of La Spezia, 100 km (60 miles) southeast of Genoa.

The buildings, narrow lanes, and stairways of Corniglia are strung together amid vineyards high on the cliffs. On a clear day, views of the entire coastal strip are excellent, from Elba in the south to the Italian Alps in the north. The high perch and lack of harbor make this farming community the most remote and therefore least crowded of the Cinque Terre. In fact, the 365 steps that lead up from the train station to the town center dissuade many tourists from making the hike to the village. You can also take the green Park bus, but they run infrequently and are usually packed with tired hikers.

Corniglia is built along one road edged with small shops, bars, gelaterias, and restaurants. Midway along Via Fieschi is the **Largo Taragio,** the main square and heart of the village. Shaded by leafy trees and umbrellas, this is a lovely spot for a mid-hike gelato break. Here you'll find the 14th-century **Chiesa di San Pietro.** The church's rose window of marble imported from Carrara is impressive, particularly considering the work required to get it here!

Sights

Corniglia

TOWN | Stone buildings, narrow lanes, and stairways are strung together amid vineyards high on the cliffs; on a clear day views of the entire coastal strip are excellent. The high perch and lack of harbor make this farming community the most remote of the Cinque Terre. ✉ *Corniglia* ☎ *0187/762600* 🌐 *www.parconazionale5terre.it.*

San Pietro

CHURCH | On a pretty pastel square sits the 14th-century church of San Pietro. The rose window of marble imported from Carrara is impressive, particularly considering the work required to get it here. ✉ *Main Sq., Corniglia.*

Vernazza

27 km (17 miles) west of La Spezia, 96 km (59 miles) southeast of Genoa.

With its narrow streets and small squares, Vernazza is arguably the most charming of the Cinque Terre towns, and usually the most crowded. Historically, it was the most important of them and—since Vernazza was the only one fortunate enough to have a natural port—the wealthiest, as evinced by the elaborate arcades, loggias, and marble work lining Via Roma and Piazza Marconi.

The village's pink slate-roof houses and colorful squares contrast with the remains of the medieval fort and castle, including two towers, in the Old Town. The Romans first inhabited this rocky spit of land in the 1st century. Today, Vernazza has a fairly lively social scene. **Piazza Marconi** looks out across Vernazza's small sandy beach to the sea, toward Monterosso. The numerous restaurants and bars crowd their tables and umbrellas on the outskirts of the piazza, creating a patchwork of sights and sounds that form one of the most unique and beautiful places in the world.

Sights

Vernazza

TOWN | With narrow streets and small squares, the village that many consider to be the most charming of the five towns has the best access to the

Continued on page 282

HIKING THE CINQUE TERRE

FIVE REMOTE VILLAGES MAKE ONE MUST-SEE DESTINATION

"Charming" and "breathtaking" are adjectives that get a workout when you're traveling in Italy, but it's rare that both apply to a single location. The Cinque Terre is such a place, and this combination of characteristics goes a long way toward explaining its tremendous appeal.

The area is made up of five tiny villages (Cinque Terre literally means "Five Lands") clinging to the cliffs along a gorgeous stretch of the Ligurian coast. The terrain is so steep that for centuries footpaths were the only way to get from place to place. It just so happens that these paths provide beautiful views of the rocky coast tumbling into the sea, as well as access to secluded beaches and grottoes.

Backpackers "discovered" the Cinque Terre in the 1970s, and its popularity has been growing ever since. Despite summer crowds, much of the original appeal is intact. Each town has maintained its own distinct charm, and views from the trails in between are as breathtaking as ever.

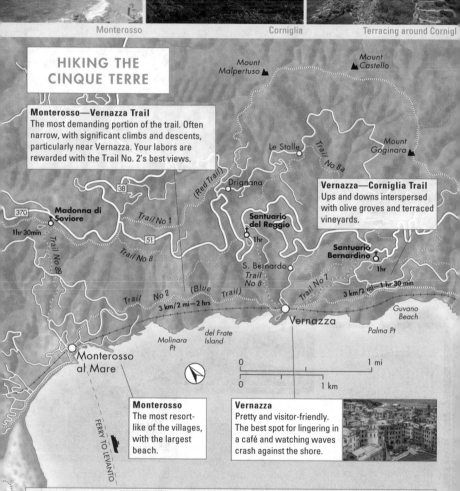

Monterosso · Corniglia · Terracing around Cornigl[i]

HIKING THE CINQUE TERRE

Monterosso—Vernazza Trail
The most demanding portion of the trail. Often narrow, with significant climbs and descents, particularly near Vernazza. Your labors are rewarded with the Trail No. 2's best views.

Vernazza—Corniglia Trail
Ups and downs interspersed with olive groves and terraced vineyards.

Mount Malpertuso ▲

Mount Castello ▲

Mount Gaginara ▲

Le Stalle

Trail No 8a

(Red Trail)

Drignana

38

370

Madonna di Soviore

1hr 30min

Trail No 89

Trail No 1

51

Trail No 8

Santuario del Reggio

1hr

S. Bernardo

Trail No 8

Santuario Bernardino ♦

1hr

Trail No 7

3 km/2 mi—1 hr 30 min

Trail No 2 (Blue Trail)

3 km/2 mi—2 hrs

Guvano Beach

Molinara Pt

del Frate Island

Vernazza

Palma Pt

0 — 1 mi

0 — 1 km

Monterosso al Mare

FERRY TO LEVANTO

Monterosso
The most resort-like of the villages, with the largest beach.

Vernazza
Pretty and visitor-friendly. The best spot for lingering in a café and watching waves crash against the shore.

THE CLASSIC HIKE

Hiking is the most popular way to experience the Cinque Terre, and Trail No. 2, the Sentiero Azzurro (Blue Trail), is the most traveled path. To cover the entire trail is a full day: it's approximately 13 km (8 miles) in length, takes you to all five villages, and requires about five hours, not including stops, to complete. The best approach is to start at the eastern-most town of Riomaggiore and warm up your legs on the easiest segment of the trail. As you work your way west, the hike gets progressively more demanding. Between Corniglia and Manarola take the ferry (which provides its own beautiful views) or the inland train running between the towns instead.

Manarola

Along Lovers' Lane

Via dell'Amore

**rniglia—
anarola Trail**
is section of the trail
currently closed.

Manarola—Riomaggiore Trail
Known as the Via dell'Amore (Lovers'
Lane). A wide, paved, flat path with
fine views.

KEY

....	*Major footpaths*
- - - - - - - -	*Sanctuary footpaths*
- - - - - - - -	*Connecting footpaths*
↗ 45min	*Hiking times*
♀	*Sanctuaries*

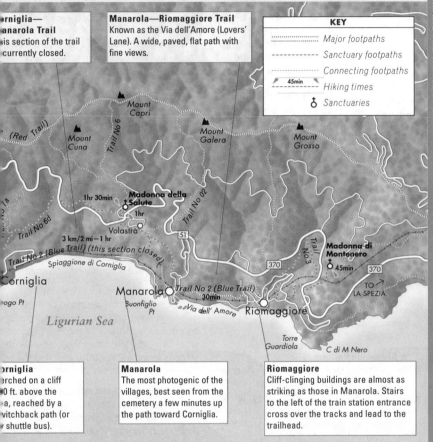

(Red Trail)

Mount
Capri

Mount
Cuna

Trail No 6

Mount
Galera

Mount
Grosso

1hr 30min

**Madonna della
Salute**
♀

Trail No 02

Trail No 6d

1hr

Volastra

3 km/2 mi—1 hr

Trail No 2 (Blue Trail) (this section closed)

Spiaggione di Corniglia

51

370

**Madonna di
Montenero**
♀ 45min

Trail
No 3

370

TO →
LA SPEZIA

Corniglia

ogo Pt

Ligurian Sea

Manarola

Buonfiglio
Pt

Trail No 2 (Blue Trail)

30min

Via dell' Amore

Riomaggiore

Torre
Guardiola

C di M Nero

orniglia
erched on a cliff
0 ft. above the
a, reached by a
vitchback path (or
v shuttle bus).

Manarola
The most photogenic of the
villages, best seen from the
cemetery a few minutes up
the path toward Corniglia.

Riomaggiore
Cliff-clinging buildings are almost as
striking as those in Manarola. Stairs
to the left of the train station entrance
cross over the tracks and lead to the
trailhead.

BEYOND TRAIL NO.2

Trail No. 2 is just one of a network of
trails crisscrossing the hills. If you're
a dedicated hiker, spend a few nights
and try some of the other routes.
Trail No. 1, the Sentiero Rosso (Red
Trail), climbs from Portovenere (east of
Riomaggiore) and returns to the sea at
Levanto (west of Monterosso al Mare).
To hike its length takes from 9 to 12
hours; the ridge-top trail provides spectacular views from high above the villages, each of which can be reached via
a steep path. Other shorter trails go from
the villages up into the hills, some leading to religious sanctuaries. Trail No. 9,
for example, starts from the old section
of Monterosso and ends at the Madonna
di Soviore Sanctuary.

sea—a geographic reality that made the village wealthier than its neighbors, as evidenced by the elaborate arcades, loggias, and marble work. The village's pink, slate-roof houses and colorful squares contrast with the remains of the medieval fort and castle, including two towers, in the old town. The Romans first inhabited this rocky spit of land in the 1st century. Today Vernazza has a fairly lively social scene. It's a great place to refuel with a hearty seafood lunch or linger in a café between links of the seaside hike. ⊠ *Vernazza* ⊕ *www.turismoinliguria. it,www.parconazionale5terre.it.*

 Restaurants

Gambero Rosso

$$ | **LIGURIAN** | Relax on Vernazza's main square at this fine trattoria looking out onto the church of Santa Maria d'An-tiochi. Enjoy such delectable dishes as shrimp salad, vegetable torte, and squid-ink risotto. **Known for:** pesto dishes; piazza view; fresh seafood. $ *Average main: €22* ⊠ *Piazza Marconi 7, Vernazza* ☎ *0187/812265* ⊕ *www.ristorantegam-berorosso.net* ⊗ *Closed Thurs. and Nov.–Mar.*

★ Ristorante Belforte

$$ | **LIGURIAN** | High above the sea in one of Vernazza's remaining medieval stone towers is this unique spot serving deli-cious Cinque Terre cuisine such as branzi-no *sotto sale* (cooked under salt), stuffed mussels, and *insalata di polpo* (octopus salad). The setting is magnificent, so try for an outdoor table. **Known for:** lively atmosphere; incredible views; octopus salad. $ *Average main: €20* ⊠ *Via Guido-ni 42, Vernazza* ☎ *0187/812222* ⊕ *www. ristorantebelforte.it* ⊗ *Closed Tues. and Nov.–Easter.*

Hotels

La Malà

$$$ | **B&B/INN** | A cut above other lodging options in the Cinque Terre, these small guest rooms are equipped with flat-screen TVs, AC, marble showers, and comfortable bedding and have views of the sea or the port, which can also be enjoyed at their most bewitching from a shared terrace literally suspended over the Mediterranean. **Pros:** helpful, attentive staff; views; clean, fresh-feeling rooms. **Cons:** child-friendly (either a pro or a con); books up quickly; some stairs are involved. $ *Rooms from: €250* ⊠ *Giovan-ni Battista 29, Vernazza* ☎ *334/2875718* ⊕ *www.lamala.it* ⊗ *Closed Jan. 8–Mar. 1* ⟿ *4 rooms* ❙◯❙ *Free Breakfast.*

Monterosso al Mare

32 km (20 miles) northwest of La Spezia, 89 km (55 miles) southeast of Genoa.

It's the combined draw of beautiful beaches, rugged cliffs, crystal-clear tur-quoise waters, and plentiful small hotels and restaurants that has made Monteros-so al Mare the largest of the Cinque Terre villages (population 1,800) and also the busiest in midsummer.

And Monterosso has festivals enough to match its size. They start with the Lemon Feast on the Saturday before Ascension Sunday. Then, on the second Sunday after Pentecost, comes the Flower Festival of Corpus Christi: during the afternoon, the streets and alleyways of the historic center are decorated with thousands of colorful flower petals, set in beautiful designs, over which an evening procession passes. Finally, the Salted Anchovy and Olive Oil Festival takes place each year during the second weekend of September.

Sights

Heading west from the train station, you pass through a tunnel and exit into the centro storico (historic center) of the village. Nestled into the wide valley that leads to the sea, Monterosso is built above numerous streams, which have been covered to make up the major streets of the village. Via Buranco, the oldest street in Monterosso, leads to the most characteristic piazza of the village, Piazza Matteotti. Locals pass through here daily to shop at the supermarket and butcher. This piazza also contains the oldest and most typical wineshop in the village, Enoteca da Eliseo—stop here between 6 pm and midnight to share tables with fellow tourists and locals over a bottle of Cinque Terre wine. There's also the **Chiesa di San Francesco**, built in the 12th century and an excellent example of the Ligurian Gothic style. Its distinctive black stripes and marble rose window make it one of the most photographed sites in the Cinque Terre.

Fegina, the newer side of the village (and site of the train station), has relatively modern homes ranging from the Liberty style (art nouveau) to the early 1970s. At the far eastern end of town, you'll run into a private sailing club sheltered by a vast rock carved with an impressive statue of Neptune. From here, you can reach the challenging trail to Levanto (a great 2½-hour hike). This trail has the added bonus of a five-minute detour to the **ruins of a 14th-century monastery**. The expansive view from this vantage point allowed the monks who were housed here to easily scan the waters for enemy ships that might invade the villages and alert residents to coming danger. Have your camera ready for this Cinerama-like vista.

Although it has the most nightlife in the Cinque Terre (thanks to its numerous wine bars and pubs), Monterosso is also the most family-friendly. With its expanse of free and equipped beaches, extensive pedestrian areas, large children's play park, and summer activities, Monterosso is a top spot for kids.

The **local outdoor market** is held on Thursday and attracts crowds of tourists and villagers from along the coast to shop for everything from pots, pans, and underwear to fruits, vegetables, and fish. Often a few stands sell local art and crafts, as well as olive oil and wine.

Restaurants

Enoteca Internazionale

$ | **WINE BAR** | Located on the main street, this bar offers a large selection of wines, both local and from farther afield, plus delicious light fare; its umbrella-covered patio is a welcoming spot to recuperate after a day of hiking. Susanna, the owner, is a certified sommelier who's always forthcoming with helpful suggestions on pairing local wines with their tasty bruschettas. **Known for:** helpful staff; extensive wine list; patio dining. [$] *Average main: €13* ✉ *Via Roma 62, Monterosso al Mare* ☎ *0187/817278* 🌐 *www.enotecainternazionale.com* ⏲ *Closed Jan.–Feb.*

★ **Miky**

$$$ | **SEAFOOD** | This is arguably the best restaurant in Monterosso, specializing in tasty, fresh seafood dishes like grilled calamari and monkfish ravioli. The *catalana* (poached lobster and shrimp with sliced raw fennel and carrot) is a winner. **Known for:** fine dining; sunny seaside setting; fresh seafood. [$] *Average main: €33* ✉ *Via Fegina 104, Monterosso al Mare* ☎ *0187/817608* 🌐 *www.ristorantemiky.it* ⏲ *Closed mid-Nov.–mid-Mar.*

Hotels

Bellambra B&B

$ | **B&B/INN** | Modern rooms with charm and comfort in the heart of the old town make this a terrific base for exploring the Cinque Terre. **Pros:** an apartment can sleep up to 6 people; location; spacious rooms and bathrooms. **Cons:** books up quickly; no elevator with steep, narrow stairs; can be a bit noisy. [$] *Rooms from: €120* ✉ *Via Roma 64, Monterosso al Mare* ☎ *39/3920121912* 🌐 *www.bellambra5terre.com* 🛏 *4 rooms* 🍴 *No Meals.*

Il Giardino Incantato
$$ | **B&B/INN** | With wood-beam ceilings and stone walls, the stylishly restored and updated rooms in this 16th-century house in the historic center of Monterosso ooze comfort and old-world charm. **Pros:** gorgeous garden; excellent hosts; spacious rooms. **Cons:** some rooms are small; books up quickly; no views. [$] *Rooms from: €180* ✉ *Via Mazzini 18, Monterosso al Mare* ☎ *0187/818315* 🌐 *www.ilgiardinoincantato.net* 🍴 *Free Breakfast* ⏲ *Closed Nov.–Easter* 🛏 *4 rooms.*

Porto Roca
$$$$ | **HOTEL** | Far from the madding crowds, one of Cinque Terre's only high-end hotels is perched on the famous terraced cliffs right over the main beach, with large balconies to savor panoramic views of the magnificent sea. **Pros:** unobstructed sea views; pool; tranquil location. **Cons:** somewhat removed from town; back-facing rooms can be a bit dark; some of the rooms could use a revamp. [$] *Rooms from: €380* ✉ *Via Corone 1, Monterosso al Mare* ☎ *0187/817502* 🌐 *www.portoroca.it* 🛏 *43 rooms* 🍴 *Free Breakfast* ⏲ *Closed Nov.–Easter.*

Bologna

Bologna, a city rich with cultural jewels, has long been one of the best-kept secrets in northern Italy. Tourists in the know bask in the shadow of its leaning medieval towers and devour the city's wonderful food.

The charm of the centro storico, with its red-arcaded passageways and sidewalks, can be attributed to wise city counselors who, at the beginning of the 13th century, decreed that roads couldn't be built without *portici* (porticoes). Were these counselors to return to town eight centuries later, they'd marvel at how little has changed.

Bologna, with a population of about 388,000, has a university-town vibe—and it feels young and lively in a way that many other Italian cities don't. It also feels full of Italians in a way that many other towns, thronged with tourists, don't. Bolognesi come out at aperitivo time, and you might be struck by the fact that it's not just youngsters who are out for the passeggiata or a glass of wine with *affettati misti*.

From as early as the Middle Ages the town was known as "Bologna the Fat" for the agricultural prosperity that resulted in a well-fed population. In the 21st century Bolognese food remains, arguably, the best in Italy. With its sublime cuisine, lively spirit, and largely undiscovered art, Bologna is a memorable destination.

GETTING HERE AND AROUND

Frequent train service from Florence to Bologna makes getting here easy. The Italo and Frecciarossa and Frecciargento (high-speed trains) run several times an hour and take just under 40 minutes. Otherwise, you're left with the *regionale* (regional) trains, which putter along and get you to Bologna in around 1¾ hours. The historic center is an interesting and relatively effortless walk from the station—though it takes about 20 minutes.

If you're driving from Florence, take the A1, exiting onto the A14, and then get on the RA1 to Exit 7–Bologna Centrale. The trip takes about an hour. From Milan, take the A1, exiting to the A14 as you near the city; from there, take the A13 and exit at Bologna; then follow the RA1 to Exit 7–Bologna Centrale. The trip takes just under three hours.

VISITOR INFORMATION

CONTACTS Bologna Tourism Offices.
✉ *Aeroporto di Bologna, Bologna*
☎ *051/6472201* ⊕ *www.bolognawel-come.com.*

 Sights

Basilica di San Petronio

CHURCH | Construction on this vast cathedral began in 1390; and the work, as you can see, still isn't finished more than 600 years later. The wings of the transept are missing and the facade is only partially decorated, lacking most of the marble that was intended to adorn it. The main doorway was carved in 1425 by the great Sienese master Jacopo della Quercia. Above the center of the door is a Madonna and Child flanked by saints Ambrose and Petronius, the city's patrons. Michelangelo, Giulio Romano, and Andrea Palladio (among others), submitted designs for the facade, which were all eventually rejected. The Bolognesi had planned an even bigger church—you can see the columns erected to support the larger version outside the east end—but had to tone down construction when the university seat was established next door in 1561. The **Museo di San Petronio** contains models showing how it was originally supposed to look. The most important art in the church is in the fourth chapel on the left: these frescoes by Giovanni di Modena date to 1410–15. ✉ *Piazza Maggiore* ☎ *051/231415* ⊕ *www.basilicadisanpetronio.org* ⊠ *Free* ⊘ *Museo di San Petronio closed Mon.*

Fontana del Nettuno

FOUNTAIN | Sculptor Giambologna's elaborate 1563–66 Baroque fountain and monument to Neptune occupying Piazza Nettuno has been aptly nicknamed "Il Gigante" (The Giant). Its exuberantly sensual mermaids and undraped god of the sea drew fire when it was constructed—but not enough, apparently, to dissuade the populace from using the fountain as a public washing stall for centuries. ✉ *Piazza del Nettuno, Piazza Maggiore.*

Le Due Torri

NOTABLE BUILDING | Two landmark medieval towers, mentioned by Dante in *The Inferno,* stand side by side in the compact Piazza di Porta Ravegnana. Once, every family of importance had a tower as a symbol of prestige and power (and as a potential fortress). Now only 24 remain out of nearly 100 that once presided over the city. Torre Garisenda (late 11th century), which tilts 10 feet off perpendicular, was shortened to 157 feet in the 1300s and is now closed to visitors. Torre degli Asinelli (1119) is 318 feet tall and leans 7½ feet. If you're up to a serious physical challenge—and not claustrophobic—you may want to climb its 498 narrow, wooden steps to get the view over Bologna. ✉ *Piazza di Porta Ravegnana, East of Piazza Maggiore* ⊕ *www.duetorribologna.com* ⊠ *€5.*

MAMbo

ART MUSEUM | The museum—the name stands for Museo d'Arte Moderna di Bologna, or Bologna's Museum of Modern Art—houses a permanent collection of modern art (defined as post–World War II until five minutes ago) and stages a revolving series of temporary exhibitions by cutting-edge artists. All of this is set within a remarkable space: you might have a hard time telling that the sleek minimalist structure was built in 1915 as the Forno del Pane, a large bakery that made bread for city residents. A bookshop and a restaurant complete the complex, the latter offering Sunday brunch and delicious aperitivi. ✉ *Via Don Minzoni 14, Bologna* ☎ *051/6496611* ⊕ *www.mambo-bologna.org* ⊠ *€6* ⊘ *Closed Mon.*

Museo Internazionale e Biblioteca della Musica di Bologna

OTHER MUSEUM | The music museum in the spectacular Palazzo Aldini-Sanguinetti, with its 17th- and 18th-century frescoes, offers among its exhibits a 1606 harpsichord and a collection of beautiful music manuscripts dating from the

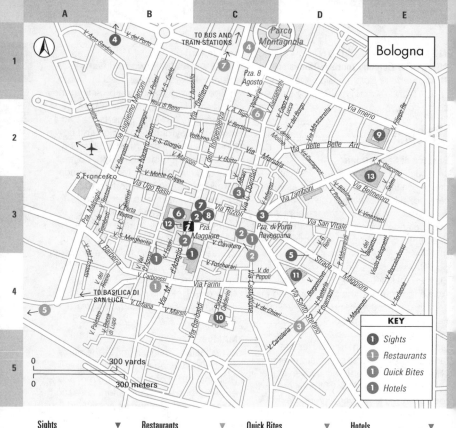

Bologna

KEY

- ❶ Sights
- ❶ Restaurants
- ❶ Quick Bites
- ❶ Hotels

Sights ▼	Restaurants ▼	Quick Bites ▼	Hotels ▼
1 Basilica di San Petronio **B3**	1 Da Cesari **B4**	1 Sfoglia Rina.............. **C3**	1 Art Hotel Novecento ... **B3**
2 Fontana del Nettuno..... **C3**	2 Da Gianni a la Vecia Bulagna................... **C3**	2 Tamburini **C3**	2 Art Hotel Orologio **B3**
3 Le Due Torri............... **C3**	3 Drogheria della Rosa... **D4**		3 Hotel Corona D'Oro...... **C3**
4 MAMbo.................. **B1**	4 Ristorante I Portici....... **C1**		
5 Museo Internazionale e Biblioteca della Musica di Bologna **D4**	5 RIstorante Marconi..... **A4**		
6 Palazzo Comunale...... **B3**	6 Trattoria del Rosso....... **C2**		
7 Palazzo del Podestà..... **C3**	7 Trattoria di Via Serra **C1**		
8 Palazzo Re Enzo.......... **C3**			
9 Pinacoteca Nazionale... **E2**			
10 San Domenico **C4**			
11 Santo Stefano........... **D4**			
12 Torre dell'Orologio (Clock Tower)............. **B3**			
13 Università di Bologna ... **E2**			

500s. ✉ *Strada Maggiore 34, University area* 🕾 *051/2757711* ⊕ *www.museibologna.it* 🕙 *Closed Mon.* 🎟 *€5.*

Palazzo Comunale

GOVERNMENT BUILDING | When Bologna was an independent city-state, this huge palace dating from the 13th to 15th century was the seat of government—a function it still serves today in a building that is a mélange of styles. Over the door is a statue of Bologna-born Pope Gregory XIII (reigned 1572–85), most famous for reorganizing the calendar. There are good views from the upper stories. The first-floor Sala Rossa (Red Room) and the Sala del Consiglio Comunale (City Council Hall) are open with advance request and during some exhibitions. Within the palazzo are two museums. The Collezioni Comunali d'Arte exhibits medieval paintings as well as some Renaissance works by Luca Signorelli (circa 1445–1523) and Tintoretto 1518–94). Underground caves and the foundations of the old cathedral can be visited by appointment; contact the tourist office. The old stock exchange, part of the Palazzo Comunale, which you enter from Piazza Nettuno, has been turned into a library. Dubbed the Sala Borsa, it has an impressive interior courtyard. ✉ *Piazza Maggiore 6, Piazza Maggiore* 🕾 *051/2193998 Collezioni Comunali d'Arte, 051/2194400 Sala Borsa* ⊕ *www.museibologna.it* 🎟 *Collezioni Comunali d'Arte €6; Sala Borsa free* 🕙 *Collezioni Comunali d'Arte closed Mon.; Sala Borsa closed Sun.*

Palazzo del Podestà

NOTABLE BUILDING | This classic Renaissance palace facing the Basilica di San Petronio was erected from 1484–94, and attached to it is the soaring Torre dell'Arengo. The bells in the tower have rung whenever the city has celebrated, mourned, or called its citizens to arms. It's not open to the public. ✉ *Piazza Maggiore 1, Piazza Maggiore.*

Palazzo Re Enzo

CASTLE/PALACE | Built in 1244, this palace became home to King Enzo of Sardinia, who was imprisoned here in 1249 after he was captured during the fierce battle of Fossalta. He died here 23 years later. The palace has other macabre associations as well: common criminals received last rites in the tiny courtyard chapel before being executed in Piazza Maggiore. The courtyard is worth a peek, but the palace merely houses government offices as well as special events. ✉ *Piazza del Nettuno 1/c, Piazza Maggiore* 🕾 *051/6583121.*

Pinacoteca Nazionale

ART GALLERY | Bologna's principal art gallery contains many works by the immortals of Italian painting; its prize possession is the *Ecstasy of St. Cecilia* by Raphael (1483–1520). There's also a beautiful polyptych by Giotto (1267–1337), as well as *Madonna with Child and Saints Margaret, Jerome, and Petronius* (altarpiece of St. Margaret) by Parmigianino (1503–40); note the rapt eye contact between St. Margaret and the Christ child. ✉ *Via delle Belle Arti 56, University area* 🕾 *051/4209411* ⊕ *www.pinacotecabologna.beniculturali.it* 🕙 *Closed Mon.* 🎟 *€6.*

San Domenico

CHURCH | The tomb of St. Dominic, who died here in 1221, is called the **Arca di San Domenico,** and is found in this church in the sixth chapel on the right. Many artists participated in its decoration, notably Niccolò di Bari, who was so proud of his 15th-century contribution that he changed his name to Niccolò dell'Arca to recall this famous work. The young Michelangelo (1475–1564) carved the angel on the right and the image of San Petronio. In the right transept of the church is a tablet marking the last resting place of hapless King Enzo, the Sardinian ruler imprisoned in the Palazzo Re Enzo. The attached museum contains religious relics. ✉ *Piazza San Domenico 13, off Via Garibaldi, South of Piazza Maggiore* 🕾 *051/6400411* ⊕ *www.sandomenicobologna.it.*

★ Santo Stefano

CHURCH | This splendid and unusual basilica contains between four and seven connected churches (authorities differ). A 4th-century temple dedicated to Isis originally occupied this site, but much of what you see was erected between the 10th and 12th centuries. The oldest existing building is **Santi Vitale e Agricola,** parts of which date from the 5th century. The exquisite beehive-shape San Sepolcro contains a Nativity scene much loved by Bologna's children, who come at Christmastime to pay their respects to the Christ child. Just outside the church, which probably dates from the 5th century (with later alterations), is the **Cortile di Pilato** (Pilate's Courtyard), named for the basin in the center. Despite the fact that the basin was probably crafted around the 8th century, legend has it that Pontius Pilate washed his hands in it after condemning Christ. Also in the building are a museum displaying various medieval religious works and its shop, which sells honey, shampoos, and jams made by the monks. ✉ *Piazza Santo Stefano, Via Santo Stefano 24, University area* ☎ *320/9065699* 🌐 *www.santostefanobologna.it* 🕒 *Closed during services.*

Università di Bologna

COLLEGE | Take a stroll through the streets of the university area: a jumble of buildings, some dating as far back as the 15th century and most to the 17th and 18th. The neighborhood, as befits a college town, is full of bookshops, coffee bars, and inexpensive restaurants. Though not particularly distinguished, they're characteristic of student life in the city. Try eating at the *mensa universitaria* (cafeteria) if you want to strike up a conversation with local students (most speak English). Political slogans and sentiments are scrawled on walls all around the university and tend to be ferociously leftist, sometimes juvenile, and often entertaining. Among the university museums, the most interesting is the **Museo di Palazzo Poggi,** which displays scientific instruments plus paleontological, botanical, and university-related artifacts. ✉ *Via Zamboni 33, University area* ☎ *051/2099610 museum* 🌐 *www.museopalazzopoggi.unibo.it* 🕒 *Closed Mon.* 🎟 *€5 museum.*

Torre dell'Orologio (Clock Tower)

CLOCK | For a spectacular view of Piazza Maggiore and the Bolognesi hills from two terraces as well as a look at how Bologna's oldest clock keeps the city punctual, climb the Torre dell'Orologio, or d'Arccursio tower. Opened to the public in 2021, it was built in 1249 as University of Bologna law professor Accursio da Bagnolo's monumental timepiece for his home in the piazza. The clock mechanism you'll see dates from 1773, as found on the horologist's inscription "Rinaldo Gandofli Accademic Clementi Fece 1773," among the clock's movement, gears, and swinging pendulum. An audio guide for your mobile phone, accessible via a QR code, shares the story of the tower and the clock's history. ✉ *Piazza Maggiore, 6, Bologna* ☎ *051/658 3111* 🌐 *www.bolognawelcome.com* 🎟 *€8* 🕒 *Closed Mon.* ✍ *Reservations required.*

🍴 Restaurants

★ Da Cesari

$$ | **EMILIAN** | Host Paolino Cesari has been presiding over his eatery since 1962, and he and his staff go out of their way to make you feel at home. The food's terrific, and if you love pork products, try anything on the menu with *mora romagnola:* Paolino has direct contact with the people who raise this breed that nearly became extinct (he calls it "my pig"). **Known for:** traditional setting; pork dishes like flavorful salame; wine list with lots of local bottles. [$] *Average main: €18* ✉ *Via de' Carbonesi 8, South of Piazza Maggiore* ☎ *051/237710* 🌐 *www.da-cesari.it* 🕒 *Closed Sun., Aug., and 1 wk in Jan.*

★ Da Gianni a la Vecia Bulagna

$$ | EMILIAN | At the bottom of an alley off Piazza Maggiore, this unassuming place—known to locals as simply "Da Gianni"—is all about food. The usual starters are on hand—including a tasty *tortellini in brodo*—in addition to daily specials; *bollito misto* (mixed boiled meat) is a fine option here, and the *cotechino con puré di patate* (pork sausage with mashed potatoes) is elevated to sublimity by the accompanying salsa verde. **Known for:** busy local spot; tortellini in brodo; efficient and friendly service. $ *Average main: €16* ⊠ *Via Clavature 18, Piazza Maggiore* ☎ *051/229434* ⊕ *www.trattoria-gianni.it* ⊘ *Closed Mon. and 1 wk early Jan. No dinner Sun.*

Drogheria della Rosa

$$ | EMILIAN | Chef Emanuele Addone, who presides over his intimate little restaurant set in an ex-pharmacy, hits the food markets every day and buys what looks good, ensuring seasonality. He sauces his tortelli stuffed with *squacquerone* and *stracchino* (two creamy, fresh cow's-milk cheeses) with artichokes, zucchini flowers, or mushrooms, depending on the time of year. **Known for:** no written menu; idiosyncratic surroundings; seasonal filled tortelli. $ *Average main: €18* ⊠ *Via Cartoleria 10, University area* ☎ *051/222529* ⊕ *www.drogheriadellarosa.it* ⊘ *Closed Sun.*

Ristorante I Portici

$$$$ | EMILIAN | The frescoed ceiling, parquet flooring, and live classical music are clues that this sophisticated restaurant (part of the hotel of the same name) occupies a former theater and *café-chantant*, or musical venue, from the late 19th century. It's the perfect setting for an evening of fine dining featuring mainly Emilian dishes with modern touches—and even the odd southern influence picked up by the award-winning chef Emanuele Petrosino from his years working in Naples. **Known for:** sophisticated culinary offerings; refined and attentive service; sumptuous surroundings in a former theater. $ *Average main: €43* ⊠ *Via dell'Indipendenza 69, North of Piazza Maggiore* ☎ *051/42185* ⊕ *www.iporticihotel.com* ⊘ *Closed Sun. and Mon. No lunch.*

Ristorante Marconi

$$$ | EMILIAN | Siblings Aurora and Massimo Mazzucchelli have succeeded in enticing a steady stream of Bolognesi to their celebrated eatery 15 km (9 miles) south of the city to sample their startlingly modern gourmet creations. Ingredients are fresh, rich, and well balanced in dishes featuring pigeon breast and eel, while flavorsome desserts include a sorbet of the day. **Known for:** discreet but attentive service; sober style; intriguing and unusual dishes in tasting menus. $ *Average main: €30* ⊠ *Via Porrettana 291, Sasso Marconi* ☎ *051/846216* ⊕ *www.ristorantemarconi.it* ⊘ *Closed Mon. and 10 days in Aug. No dinner Sun.*

Trattoria del Rosso

$ | EMILIAN | Here, in the mirrored interior, a mostly young crowd chows down on classic regional fare at affordable prices. Nimble staff bearing multiple plates sashay neatly between the closely spaced tables delivering such standards as tortellini in brodo and *Cotoletta alla Bolognese* (veal with Parmigiano-Reggiano and prosciutto). **Known for:** fun atmosphere; student haunt with great-value regional food; affordable wine list. $ *Average main: €10* ⊠ *Via Augusto Righi 30/A, University area* ☎ *051/236730* ⊘ *Closed Mon. No dinner Sun.*

Trattoria di Via Serra

$$ | EMILIAN | At this simple trattoria off the main tourist circuit, much care has been taken with the decor: the rooms, overseen by host Flavio, are small and intimate, and the wooden walls painted a creamy whitish gray. Chef Tommaso gives equal care to the menu and deftly turns out Bolognese classics, as well as dishes with a modern twist—among the antipasti, his *tosone fresco avvolto nella* *pancetta* incorporates Parmigiano-Reggiano, unsmoked bacon, and greens. **Known for:** convivial atmosphere; all locally sourced ingredients; modern riffs on classic dishes. [$] *Average main: €18* ✉ *Via Serra 9B, Bologna* ☎ *051/6312330* 🌐 *www.trattoriadiviaserra.it* ⏲ *Closed Mon.*

Coffee and Quick Bites

Sfoglia Rina

$ | **ITALIAN** | **FAMILY** | The *pastaio* (pasta-maker) tradition in this bright honeycomb tiled pasta shop and restaurant—which often has a line around the block—started nearly 60 years ago in a town about six miles southwest of Bologna. There, Rina De Franceschi rolled *sfoglia* (dough) following family recipes. **Known for:** affordable and wide-ranging menu; fresh pasta in many varieties; weekly vegetarian-friendly specials. [$] *Average main: €10* ✉ *Via Castiglione, 5/b, Bologna* ☎ *051/9911710* 🌐 *www.sfogliarina.it.*

Tamburini

$$ | **WINE BAR** | Two small rooms inside plus kegs and bar stools outside make up this lively, packed little spot. The overwhelming plate of *affettati misti* is crammed with top-quality local cured meats and succulent cheeses, and the adjacent salumeria offers many wonderful items to take away. **Known for:** lively atmosphere with a vast wine selection; cheese and cured meat plates; abundant portions. [$] *Average main: €15* ✉ *Via Caprarie 1, Piazza Maggiore* ☎ *051/234726* 🌐 *www.tamburini.com.*

Hotels

★ **Art Hotel Novecento**

$$ | **HOTEL** | This swank place, with decor inspired by European design of the 1930s, is in a little piazza just minutes from Piazza Maggiore. **Pros:** spacious single rooms ideal for solo travelers; sumptuous buffet breakfast; friendly, capable concierge service. **Cons:** cheapest doubles are small; the piazza outside can get noisy; expensive parking. [$] *Rooms from: €139* ✉ *Piazza Galileo 4/3, Piazza Maggiore* ☎ *051/7457311* 🌐 *www.art-hotel-novecento.com* 🍴 *Free Breakfast* 🛏 *24 rooms.*

★ **Art Hotel Orologio**

$$ | **HOTEL** | **FAMILY** | The location of this stylish and welcoming family-run hotel can't be beat: it's right around the corner from Piazza Maggiore on a quiet piazza. **Pros:** central location; welcomes all animals; family-friendly rooms. **Cons:** needs some updating; pet-friendly environment may not appeal to allergy sufferers; limited facilities. [$] *Rooms from: €185* ✉ *Via IV Novembre 10, Piazza Maggiore* ☎ *051/7457411* 🌐 *www.art-hotel-orologio.com* 🛏 *32 rooms* 🍴 *Free Breakfast.*

Hotel Corona D'Oro

$$$ | **HOTEL** | Elegance and historic charm are the keynotes of this central lodging, converted from a medieval palazzo and just a short stroll from Piazza Maggiore and all the main attractions. **Pros:** spacious and silent rooms; historic character; helpful, friendly staff. **Cons:** some rooms are small; no restaurant; steps on some floors are not ideal for anyone with mobility issues. [$] *Rooms from: €208* ✉ *Via Oberdan 12, Bologna* ☎ *051/7457611* 🌐 *www.hco.it* 🛏 *40 rooms* 🍴 *Free Breakfast.*

Nightlife

BARS

Bar Calice

BARS | A year-round indoor-outdoor operation (with heat lamps), this bar is extremely popular with thirtysomethings, sometimes pushing baby carriages. Its large menu includes raw oysters. There's also a dining room upstairs. ✉ *Via Clavature 13, at Via Marchesana, Piazza Maggiore* ☎ *051/236523.*

e Stanze

BARS | At Le Stanze you can sip an aperitivo or a late-night drink amid a young and noisy clientele. The decor includes 17th-century frescoes in what was once the private chapel of the Palazzo Bentivoglio. The adjoining restaurant offers a small selection of Bologna favorites. ☒ *Via del Borgo di San Pietro 1, University area* ☎ *051/228767* ⊕ *www.lestanzecafe.it.*

★ Nu Lounge Bar

BARS | This high-energy tiki bar draws a cocktail-loving crowd that enjoys fun drinks such as "Hellvis," made with lime, agave syrup, rum, grenadine, ginger, and Angostura. ☒ *Via de' Musei 6, off Buca San Petronio, Piazza Maggiore* ☎ *051/222532* ⊕ *www.nuloungebar.com.*

Osteria del Sole

WINE BARS | Although "osteria" in an establishment's name suggests that food will be served, such is not the case here. This place is all about drinking wine; the entrance door has warnings such as "He who doesn't drink will please stay outside" and "Dogs who don't drink are forbidden to come in." It's been around since 1465, and locals pack in, bearing food from outside to accompany the wine. ☒ *Vicolo Ranocchi 1/d, Piazza Maggiore* ☎ *347/9680171* ⊕ *www.osteriadelsole.it.*

CAFÉS

★ Zanarini

CAFÉS | Chic Bolognesi congregate at this bar that serves coffee in the morning and swank aperitivi in the evening. Tasty sandwiches and pastries are also available. ☒ *Piazza Galvani 1, Piazza Maggiore* ☎ *051/2750041.*

MUSIC VENUES

Cantina Bentivoglio

LIVE MUSIC | With live music including jazz staged nearly every evening, Cantina Bentivoglio is one of Bologna's most renowned nightspots. You can enjoy light and more substantial meals here as well. ☒ *Via Masarella 4/B, University area* ☎ *051/265416* ⊕ *www.cantinabentivoglio.it.*

Osteria Buca delle Campane

LIVE MUSIC | In a 13th-century building, this underground tavern has good, inexpensive food, and the after-dinner scene is popular with locals, including students, who come to listen to the live music on weekends and some other nights. The kitchen stays open until long past midnight. Reservations are strongly advised. ☒ *Via Benedetto XIV 4, University area* ☎ *051/220918* ⊕ *www.bucadellecampane.it.*

Performing Arts

MUSIC AND OPERA

Teatro Comunale

MUSIC | This 18th-century theater presents concerts by Italian and international orchestras throughout the year, but the highly acclaimed opera performances from January to July and October to December are the main attraction. Reserve seats for those performances well in advance. ☒ *Largo Respighi 1, University area* ☎ *051/529019* ⊕ *www.tcbo.it.*

Shopping

CLOTHING

Castel Guelfo The Style Outlets

OUTLET | If you don't feel like paying Galleria Cavour prices, this mall is about 20 minutes outside Bologna. It includes more than 50 stores, among them such top brands as Swarovski. ☒ *Via del Commercio 4/2, Loc. Poggio Piccolo, Castel Guelfo* ⊹ *Take the A14 toward Imola, Castel San Pietro Terme exit; 299 m (980 feet) after tollbooth, turn right onto Via San Carlo* ☎ *0542/670765* ⊕ *www.thestyleoutlets.it.*

Galleria Cavour

MALL | One of the most upscale malls in Italy, the Galleria houses many of the fashion giants, including Armani, Gucci, Saint Laurent, and Tod's. ☒ *Via Luigi Carlo Farini, South of Piazza Maggiore* ⊕ *www.galleriacavour.it.*

WINE AND FOOD

Eataly

FOOD | At this lively shop—the original location in the now international Italian cuisine empire—with an attached bookstore, you can grab a bite to eat or have a glass of wine while stocking up on high-quality olive oil, vinegar, cured meats, and artisanal pasta. On the top floor, you can have a full-fledged trattoria meal. There's a second entrance on Via Pescherie Vecchie. ✉ *Via degli Orefici 19, Piazza Maggiore* ☎ *051/0952820* ⊕ *www.eataly.net.*

Enoteca Italiana

WINE/SPIRITS | Consistently recognized as one of the best wine stores in the country, Enoteca Italiana lives up to its reputation—as it says, "every good bottle has a good story"—with shelves lined with excellent selections from all over Italy at reasonable prices. In addition, the delicious plates of cured meats served with wines by the glass, make a great light lunch. ✉ *Via Marsala 2/b, North of Piazza Maggiore* ☎ *051/235989* ⊕ *www. enotecaitaliana.it.*

La Baita Vecchia Malga

FOOD | Fresh tagliolini, tortellini, and other Bolognese pasta delicacies are sold here, along with sublime food to eat at small tables here or take away. The cheese counter is laden with superlative local specimens. ✉ *Via Pescherie Vecchie 3/a, Piazza Maggiore* ☎ *051/223940* ⊕ *www. vecchiamalganegozi.com.*

Majani

CANDY | Classy Majani has been producing chocolate since 1796. Its staying power may be attributed to high-quality confections that are as pretty to look at as they are to eat. ✉ *Via de' Carbonesi 5, Piazza Maggiore* ☎ *051/234302* ⊕ *www.majani.it.*

Mercato delle Erbe

FOOD | This food market and food hall that opened in 1910 bustles year-round. ✉ *Via Ugo Bassi 23, Piazza Maggiore* ☎ *335/4112427* ⊕ *www.mercatodelleerbe.it.*

Mercato di Mezzo

FOOD | This former fruit and vegetable market has morphed into a food hall. Various stalls offer a wide range of Italian and Romagnolo cuisine from pasta to fis to pizza and cured meats and cheeses. Order from whatever place strikes your fancy, and sit anywhere there's room. There's a second entrance on Via Pesche rie Vecchie. ✉ *Via Clavature 12, Piazza Maggiore* ☎ *051/228782.*

Paolo Atti & Figli

FOOD | This place has been producing some of Bologna's finest pastas, cakes, and other delicacies since 1868. There's a second branch at Via Drapperie 6. ✉ *Via Caprarie 7, Piazza Maggiore* ☎ *051/220425* ⊕ *www.paoloatti.com.*

★ Roccati

CANDY | Sculptural works of chocolate, as well as basic bonbons and simpler sweets, have been crafted here since 1909. ✉ *Via Clavature 17/a, Piazza Maggiore* ☎ *051/261964* ⊕ *www.roccaticioccolato.com.*

Ferrara

47 km (29 miles) northeast of Bologna, 74 km (46 miles) northwest of Ravenna.

When the legendary Ferrarese filmmaker Michelangelo Antonioni called his beloved hometown "a city that you can see only partly, while the rest disappears to be imagined," perhaps he was referring to the low-lying mist that rolls in off the Adriatic each winter and shrouds Ferrara's winding knot of medieval alleyways, turreted palaces, and ancient wine bars—once frequented by the likes of Copernicus—in a ghostly fog. But perhaps Antonioni was also suggesting that Ferrara's striking beauty often conceals a dark and tortured past.

Today you're likely to be charmed by Ferrara's prosperous air and meticulous cleanliness, its excellent restaurants and chic bars (for coffee and any other liquid refreshment), and its lively wine-bar scene. You'll find aficionados gathering outside any of the wine bars near the Duomo even on the foggiest of weeknights. Although Ferrara is a UNESCO World Heritage Site, the city draws amazingly few tourists—which only adds to its appeal.

GETTING HERE AND AROUND

Train service is frequent from Bologna (usually three trains per hour) and takes either a half hour or 50 minutes, depending on which train type you take. It's around 35 minutes from Florence to Bologna, and then about a half hour from Bologna to Ferrara. The walk from the station is easy (about 20 minutes) and not particularly interesting. You can also take Bus No. 1, No. 6, No. 9, or No. 11 from the station to the center; buy your ticket at the newsagent inside and remember to stamp your ticket upon boarding the bus.

If you're driving from Bologna, take the RA1 out of town, then the A13 in the direction of Padua, exiting at Ferrara Nord. Follow the SP19 directly into the center of town. The trip should take about 45 minutes.

VISITOR INFORMATION

CONTACT Ferrara Tourism Office. ⊠ *Castello Estense, Piazza Castello, Ferrara* 🕾 *0532/209370* ⊕ *www.ferrarainfo.com.*

Sights

Casa Romei

CASTLE/PALACE | Built by the wealthy banker Giovanni Romei (1402–83), this vast structure with a graceful courtyard ranks among Ferrara's loveliest Renaissance palaces. Mid-15th-century frescoes adorn rooms on the ground floor; the piano nobile contains detached frescoes from local churches as well as lesser-known Renaissance sculptures. The Sala delle Sibille has a very large 15th-century fireplace and beautiful coffered wood

ceilings. ⊠ *Via Savonarola 30, Ferrara* 🕾 *0532/234130* ⊕ *www.ferraraterraeacqua.it* 🎟 *€3 (free 1st Sun. of the month Oct.–Mar.).*

★ Castello Estense

CASTLE/PALACE | The former seat of Este power, this massive castle dominates the center of town, a suitable symbol for the ruling family: cold and menacing on the outside, lavishly decorated within. The public rooms are grand, but deep in the bowels of the castle are dungeons where enemies of the state were held in wretched conditions. The prisons of Don Giulio, Ugo, and Parisina have some fascinating features, like 15th-century graffiti. Lovers Ugo and Parisina (stepmother and stepson) were beheaded in 1425 because Ugo's father, Niccolò III, didn't like the fact that his son was cavorting with his stepmother. The castle was established as a fortress in 1385, but work on its luxurious ducal quarters continued into the 16th century. Representative of Este grandeur are the Sala dei Giochi, painted with athletic scenes, and the Sala dell'Aurora, decorated to show the times of the day. The terraces of the castle and the hanging garden have fine views of the town and countryside. You can traverse the castle's drawbridge and wander through many of its arcaded passages whenever the castle gates are open. ⊠ *Piazza Castello, Ferrara* 🕾 *0532/419180* ⊕ *www.castelloestense. it* 🎟 *€12.*

Duomo

CHURCH | The magnificent Gothic cathedral, a few steps from the Castello Estense, has a three-tier facade of slender arches and beautiful sculptures over the central door. Work began in 1135 and took more than 100 years to complete. The interior was completely remodeled in the 17th century. At this writing, the facade is scaffolded and the interior closed as part of a major restoration. ⊠ *Piazza della Cattedrale, Ferrara* 🕾 *0532/207449* ⊕ *www. cattedralediferrara.it.*

Museo della Cattedrale

ART MUSEUM | Some of the original decorations of the town's main church, the former church, and the cloister of San Romano reside in the Museo della Cattedrale, across the piazza from the Duomo. Inside you'll find 22 codices commissioned between 1477 and 1535; early-13th-century sculptures by the Maestro dei Mesi; a mammoth oil on canvas by Cosmè Tura from 1469; and an exquisite Jacopo della Quercia, the *Madonna della Melagrana*. Although this last work dates from 1403 to 1408, the playful expression on the Christ child seems very 21st century. ⊠ *Via San Romano 1, Ferrara* ☎ *0532/761299* ⊕ *www.artecultura.fe.it* ⊠ *€6* ⊙ *Closed Mon.*

Museo Nazionale dell'Ebraismo Italiano e della Shoah (*Museum of Italian Judaism and the Shoah*)

OTHER MUSEUM | The collection of ornate religious objects and multimedia installations at this museum (commonly known as MEIS) bears witness to the long history of the city's Jewish community. This history had its high points—1492, for example, when Ercole I invited the Jews to come over from Spain—and its lows, notably 1627, when Jews were enclosed within the ghetto, where they were forced to live until the advent of a united Italy in 1860. The triangular warren of narrow cobbled streets that made up the ghetto originally extended as far as Corso Giovecca (originally Corso Giudecca, or Ghetto Street). When it was enclosed, the neighborhood was restricted to the area between Via Scienze, Via Contrari, and Via di San Romano. The museum is located about a 15-minute walk from the former Jewish ghetto. Guided tours may be booked in advance by emailing or calling the museum. ⊠ *Via Piangipane 81, Ferrara* ☎ *0532/769137* ⊕ *www. meisweb.it* ⊠ *€10* ⊙ *Closed Mon.*

Palazzina di Marfisa d'Este

CASTLE/PALACE | On the busy Corso Giovecca, this grandiose 16th-century palace belonged to a great patron of the arts. It has painted ceilings, fine 16th-century furniture, and a garden containing a grotto and an outdoor theater. ⊠ *Corso Giovecca 170, Ferrara* ☎ *0532/244949* ⊕ *www. artecultura.fe.it* ⊙ *Closed Mon.* ⊠ *€4.*

Palazzo dei Diamanti

(*Palace of Diamonds*)

ART MUSEUM | Named for the 8,500 small pink-and-white marble pyramids (or "diamonds") that stud its facade, this building was designed to be viewed in perspective—both faces at once—from diagonally across the street. Work began in the 1490s and finished around 1504. Inside the palazzo is the Pinacoteca Nazionale and Modern and Contemporary Art Gallery, which host temporary exhibits. ⊠ *Corso Ercole I d'Este 21, Ferrara* ☎ *0532/244949* ⊕ *www.palazzodiamanti. it* ⊠ *€6* ⊙ *Closed Mon.*

★ Palazzo Schifanoia

HISTORIC SIGHT | The oldest, most characteristic area of Ferrara is south of the Duomo, stretching between the Corso Giovecca and the city's ramparts. Here various members of the Este family built pleasure palaces, the best known of which is the Palazzo Schifanoia (*schifanoia* means "carefree" or, literally, "fleeing boredom"). Begun in the late 14th century, the palace was remodeled between 1464 and 1469. Inside is Museo Schifanoia, with its lavish interior—particularly the Salone dei Mesi, which contains an extravagant series of frescoes showing the months of the year and their mythological attributes. ⊠ *Via Scandiana 23, Ferrara* ☎ *0532/244949* ⊕ *www.artecultura.fe.it* ⊠ *€10* ⊙ *Closed Mon.*

Via delle Volte

STREET | One of the best-preserved medieval streets in Europe, the Via delle Volte clearly evokes Ferrara's past. The series of ancient *volte* (arches) along the narrow cobblestone alley once joined the merchants' houses on the south side of the street to their warehouses on the north side. The street ran parallel to the banks of the Po River, which was home to Ferrara's busy port. ✉ *Ferrara.*

Restaurants

★ Enoteca al Brindisi

$ | WINE BAR | Ferrara is a city of wine bars, beginning with this one (allegedly Europe's oldest), which opened in 1435—Copernicus drank here while a student in the late 1400s, and the place still has an undergraduate aura. The twentysomething staff pours well-chosen wines by the glass, and they serve *cappellacci di zucca* (pasta stuffed with squash) with two different sauces (ragù or butter and sage). **Known for:** full of locals, students, and visitors; set menus at great prices; marvelous salads. $ *Average main: €12* ✉ *Via Adelardi 11, Ferrara* ☎ *0532/473744* ⊕ *www.albrindisi.net* ⊘ *Closed Mon. and 1 wk late Jan.*

Il Mandolino

$$ | EMILIAN | At this idiosyncratic trattoria on the historic Via delle Volte try tearing your attention away from the countless paintings, photographs, and musical instruments that cover the walls, and instead focusing on the excellent fare on offer. Typical dishes include the classic cappellacci di zucca (pasta stuffed with squash in a meat sauce), and the lasagna may be one of the best you'll ever have. **Known for:** friendly staff; fascinating decor; local home cooking like excellent lasagna. $ *Average main: €15* ✉ *Via delle Volte 52, Ferrara* ☎ *0532/760080* ⊕ *www. ristoranteilmandolino.it* ⊘ *Closed Tues. No dinner Sun. and Mon.*

Il Sorpasso

$$ | EMILIAN | Named after a 1962 cult movie, *Il Sorpasso* (*The Easy Life*) serves terrific, honestly priced food in an unassuming space: white walls lined with movie posters, and white floors. No matter—the fine cooking and the sourcing of local ingredients whenever possible help this trattoria surpass many others. **Known for:** vegan and vegetarian options; excellent pastas and desserts; using local ingredients whenever possible. $ *Average main: €15* ✉ *Via Saraceno 118, Ferrara* ☎ *0532/790289* ⊕ *www. trattoriailsorpasso.it* ⊘ *Closed Tues. No dinner Mon.*

L'Oca Giuliva

$$ | EMILIAN | Food, service, and ambience harmonize blissfully at this casual but elegant restaurant inside a 12th-century building. The chef shows a deft hand with area specialties and shines with the fish dishes. **Known for:** tasting menus; creative antipasti and seafood dishes; cappellacci di zucca (pumpkin-stuffed pasta). $ *Average main: €20* ✉ *Via Boccacanale di Santo Stefano 38/40, Ferrara* ☎ *0532/207628* ⊕ *www.ristorantelocagiuliva.it* ⊘ *Closed Tues.*

Molto Più Che Centrale

$ | EMILIAN | A winning combination of traditional and innovative dishes is the big draw at this stylish restaurant spread over two floors. With red and white walls adorned with splashy modern art, and elegant wooden tables and chairs, the ambience is colorful and contemporary without being garish. **Known for:** attentive waitstaff; local dishes with modern flourishes; upbeat, contemporary setting. $ *Average main: €14* ✉ *Via Boccaleone 8, Ferrara* ☎ *0532/1880070* ⊘ *Closed Thurs.*

★ Quel Fantastico Giovedì

$$ | EMILIAN | Locals and other cognoscenti frequent this sleek eatery just minutes away from Piazza del Duomo, where chef Gabriele Romagnoli uses prime local ingredients to create gustatory sensations on a menu that changes daily. Fish and seafood figure prominently among his dishes, such as with a *gratinato* (similar to a French au gratin) with seafood. **Known for:** excellent service; seasonal menu; notable fish and seafood dishes. $ *Average main: €15* ✉ *Via Castelnuovo 9, Ferrara* ☎ *0532/760570* ⊕ *www. quelfantasticogiovedi.it* ⊘ *Closed Wed. No lunch Thurs.*

Hotels

Hotel Annunziata

$ | **HOTEL** | Brightly colored fittings enliven the white-walled, hardwood-floor guest rooms—think minimalism with a splash—at this hotel on a quiet little piazza near the forbiddingly majestic Castello Estense. **Pros:** perfect location (you can't get much more central); terrific buffet breakfast; stellar staff. **Cons:** annex 500 feet from main building; some rooms have uninspiring views; few facilities and limited public spaces. [$] *Rooms from: €74* ✉ *Piazza Repubblica 5, Ferrara* ☎ *0532/201111* 🌐 *www.annunziata.it* 🛏 *27 rooms* 🍴 *Free Breakfast.*

★ **Locanda Borgonuovo**

$ | **B&B/INN** | In the early 18th century this lodging began life as a convent (later suppressed by Napoléon), but now it's a delightful city-center bed-and-breakfast, popular with performers at the city's Teatro Comunale. **Pros:** knowledgeable local advice; bicycles can be borrowed for free; phenomenal breakfast featuring local foods and terrific cakes made in-house. **Cons:** must reserve far in advance as this place books quickly; steep stairs to reception area and rooms; decor may be a bit over-fussy for some. [$] *Rooms from: €100* ✉ *Via Cairoli 29, Ferrara* ☎ *0532/211100* 🌐 *www.borgonuovo.com* 🛏 *5 rooms* 🍴 *Free Breakfast.*

Maxxim Hotel

$ | **HOTEL** | **FAMILY** | Though given a stylish modern makeover, the courtyards, vaulted brick lobby, and breakfast room of this 15th-century palazzo retain much of their lordly Renaissance flair. **Pros:** tasteful modern makeover; beyond-helpful staff; good choice for families. **Cons:** occasional noise from neighboring rooms; split-level loft rooms impractical for some; some bathrooms are on the small side. [$] *Rooms from: €64* ✉ *Via Ripagrande 21, Ferrara* ☎ *0532/1770700* 🌐 *www.maxxim.it* 🛏 *40 rooms* 🍴 *Free Breakfast.*

Ravenna

80 km (50 miles) northwest of San Marino, 93 km (58 miles) southeast of Ferrara.

A small, quiet, and well-heeled city, Ravenna has brick palaces, cobblestone streets, magnificent monuments, and spectacular Byzantine mosaics. The high point in its civic history occurred in the 5th century, when Pope Honorious moved his court here from Rome. Gothic kings Odoacer and Theodoric ruled the city until it was conquered by the Byzantines in AD 540. Ravenna later fell under the sway of Venice, and then, inevitably, the Papal States.

Because Ravenna spent much of its past looking east, its greatest art treasures show that Byzantine influence. Churches and tombs with the most unassuming exteriors contain within them walls covered with sumptuous mosaics. These beautifully preserved Byzantine mosaics put great emphasis on nature, which you can see in the delicate rendering of sky, earth, and animals. Outside Ravenna, the town of Classe hides even more mosaic gems.

GETTING HERE AND AROUND

By car from Bologna, take the SP253 to the RA1, and then follow signs for the A14/E45 in the direction of Ancona. From here, follow signs for Ravenna, taking the A14dir Ancona–Milano–Ravenna exit. Follow signs for the SS16/E55 to the center of Ravenna. From Ferrara the drive is more convoluted, but also more interesting. Take the SS16 to the RA8 in the direction of Porto Garibaldi, taking the Roma/Ravenna exit. Follow the SS309/E55 to the SS309dir/E55, taking the SS253 Bologna/Ancona exit. Follow the SS16/E55 into the center of Ravenna.

By train, there are one or two services hourly from Bologna, taking 70 minutes.

VISITOR INFORMATION

CONTACT Ravenna Tourism Office. ✉ *Piazza San Francesco 7, Ravenna* 🕿 *0544/35755* ⊕ *www.turismo.ra.it.*

Sights

★ Basilica di San Vitale

CHURCH | The octagonal church of San Vitale was built in AD 547, after the Byzantines conquered the city, and its interior shows a strong Byzantine influence. The area behind the altar contains the most famous works, depicting Emperor Justinian and his retinue on one wall, and his wife, Empress Theodora, with her retinue, on the opposite one. Notice how the mosaics seamlessly wrap around the columns and curved arches on the upper sides of the altar area. ■ TIP→ **School groups can sometimes swamp the site from March through mid-June.** ✉ *Via San Vitale, off Via Salara, Ravenna* 🕿 *0544/541688 for info, 800/303999 for info (toll-free)* ⊕ *www.ravennamosaici.it* 🎫 *€10.50 combination ticket, includes 4–5 diocesan monuments.*

★ Battistero Neoniano

CHURCH | Next door to Ravenna's 18th-century cathedral, the baptistery has one of the town's most important mosaics. It dates from the beginning of the 5th century AD, with work continuing through the century. In keeping with the building's role, the great mosaic in the dome shows the baptism of Christ, and beneath are the Apostles. The lowest register of mosaics contains Christian symbols, the Throne of God, and the Cross. Note the naked figure kneeling next to Christ—he is the personification of the River Jordan. ✉ *Piazza Duomo, Ravenna* 🕿 *0544/541688 for info, 800/303999 for info (toll-free)* ⊕ *www.ravennamosaici.it* 🎫 *€10.50 combination ticket, includes 4–5 diocesan monuments.*

Classis Ravenna–Museo della Città e del Territorio

OTHER MUSEUM | FAMILY | In Classe, a short distance outside Ravenna, this museum dazzlingly illustrates the history of Ravenna and its environs from the pre-Roman era to the Lombard conquest in AD 751. The museum occupies a refurbished sugar refinery, and with the help of multimedia presentations and panels in Italian and English, it chronicles the Roman, Ostrogoth, and Byzantine periods. Displays include bronze statuettes, stone sculptures, glassware, and mosaic fragments. A separate room summarizes the building's more recent history. It's an easy walk from Sant'Apollinare in Classe. ■ TIP→ **To get here from Ravenna, take Bus No. 4 from the station or the local train to Classe, or use the cycle path from the city center.** ✉ *Via Classense 29, off SS71, Classe* 🕿 *0544/473717* ⊕ *www.classisravenna.it* 🎫 *€5 (€12 including Sant'Apollinare in Classe)* 🕔 *Closed Mon. Nov.–late Dec. and 10 days Jan.*

Domus dei Tappeti di Pietra

(*House of the Stone Carpets*)
RUINS | This archaeological site with lovely mosaics was uncovered in 1993 during digging for an underground parking garage near the 18th-century church of Santa Eufemia. Ten feet below ground level lie the remains of a Byzantine palace dating from the 5th and 6th centuries AD. Its beautiful and well-preserved network of floor mosaics displays elaborately designed patterns, creating the effect of luxurious carpets. ✉ *Via Barbiani 16, enter through Sant'Eufemia church, Ravenna* 🕿 *0544/32512* ⊕ *www.domusdeitappetidipietra.it* 🎫 *€4.*

★ Mausoleo di Galla Placidia

CHURCH | The little tomb and the great church stand side by side, but the tomb predates the Basilica di San Vitale by at least 100 years: these two adjacent sights are decorated with the best-known, most elaborate mosaics in Ravenna. Galla Placidia was the sister

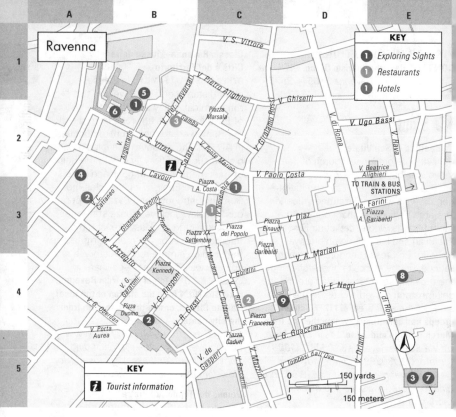

Ravenna

of the Roman emperor Honorius, who moved the imperial capital to Ravenna in AD 402. This mid-5th century mausoleum is her memorial. The simple redbrick exterior only serves to enhance by contrast the richness of the interior mosaics, in deep midnight blue and glittering gold. The tiny central dome is decorated with symbols of Christ, the evangelists, and striking gold stars. Eight of the Apostles are represented in groups of two on the four inner walls of the dome; the other four appear singly on the walls of the two transepts. There are three sarcophagi in the tomb, none of which are believed to actually contain the remains of Galla Placidia. ■TIP→ **Visit early or late in the day to avoid the school groups that can sometimes swamp the Mausoleo from March through mid-June.** ✉ *Via San Vitale, 17, off Via Salara, Ravenna* ☎ *0544/541688 for info, 800/303999 for info (toll-free)* ⊕ *www.ravennamosaici.it* ⊠ *€10.50 combination ticket, includes 4–5 diocesan monuments (€2 supplement for mausoleum).*

Museo Nazionale di Ravenna (*National Museum of Ravenna*)

OTHER MUSEUM | Next to the Church of San Vitale and housed in a former Benedictine monastery, the museum contains artifacts from ancient Rome, Byzantine fabrics and carvings, and pieces of early Christian art. The collection is well displayed and artfully lighted. In the first cloister are marvelous Roman tomb slabs from excavations nearby; upstairs, you can see a reconstructed 18th-century pharmacy. ✉ *Via San Vitale 17, Ravenna* ☎ *0544/213902* ⊕ *www.ravennantica.it/en/ravenna-national-museum-museo-nazionale-di-ravenna* ⊠ *€6* ⊗ *Closed Mon.*

Sant'Apollinare in Classe

CHURCH | This church about 5 km (3 miles) southeast of Ravenna is landlocked now, but when it was built, it stood in the center of the busy shipping port known to the ancient Romans as Classis. The arch above and the area around the high altar are rich with mosaics. Those

on the arch, older than the ones behind it, are considered superior. They show Christ in Judgment and the 12 lambs of Christianity leaving the cities of Jerusalem and Bethlehem. In the apse is the figure of Sant'Apollinare himself, a bishop of Ravenna, and above him is a magnificent Transfiguration against blazing green grass, animals in odd perspective, and flowers. ✉ *Via Romea Sud 224, off SS71, Classe* ☎ *0544/527308* ⊠ *€5 or €9 including Classis Ravenna museum* ⊗ *Closed Mon.*

★ Sant'Apollinare Nuovo

CHURCH | The mosaics displayed in this church date from the early 6th century, making them slightly older than those in San Vitale. Since the left side of the church was reserved for women, it's only fitting that the mosaics on that wall depict 22 virgins offering crowns to the Virgin Mary. On the right wall, 26 men carry the crowns of martyrdom; they approach Christ, surrounded by angels. ✉ *Via Roma 53, at Via Guaccimanni, Ravenna* ☎ *800/303999 for info (toll-free), 0544/541688 for info* ⊕ *www.ravennamosaici.it* ⊠ *€10.50 combination ticket, includes 4–5 diocesan monuments.*

Tomba di Dante

TOMB | Exiled from his native Florence, the author of *The Divine Comedy* died here in 1321, and Dante's tomb is in a small neoclassical building next door to the large church of St. Francis. The Florentines have been trying to reclaim their famous son for hundreds of years, but the Ravennans refuse to give him up, arguing that since Florence did not welcome Dante in life, it does not deserve him in death. Perhaps as penance, every September the Florentine government sends olive oil that's used to fuel the light hanging in the chapel's center. ✉ *Via Dante Alighieri 9, Ravenna* ☎ *0544/215676* ⊠ *Free.*

🍴 Restaurants

Bella Venezia

$$ | **ITALIAN** | Pastel walls, crisp white tablecloths, and warm light provide the backdrop for some seriously good Romagnolo dishes. The menu offers local specialties, but also gives a major nod to Venice—Ravenna's conqueror of long ago. **Known for:** family-owned and operated; truffle dishes, depending on the season; outdoor dining. [$] *Average main: €15* ✉ *Via IV Novembre 16, Ravenna* ☎ *0544/212746* 🌐 *www.ristorantebellavenezia.it* 🕙 *Closed Sun. No lunch Sat.*

Ca' de Vèn

$$ | **ITALIAN** | These buildings, joined by a glass-ceilinged courtyard, date from the 15th century, so the setting itself is reason enough to come; that the food is so good makes a visit here all the more satisfying. At lunchtime Ca' de Vèn teems with locals tucking in to *piadine* (a typical Romagnolo flatbread) stuffed or topped with various ingredients, and the grilled dishes—including *tagliata di pollo* (sliced chicken breast tossed with arugula and set atop exquisitely roasted potatoes)—are among the highlights. **Known for:** majestic, high-ceilinged lively setting; grilled meats; weekly menu of Romagnolo specialties. [$] *Average main: €16* ✉ *Via Corrado Ricci 24, Ravenna* ☎ *0544/30163* 🌐 *www.cadeven.it* 🕙 *Closed Mon.*

Osteria del Tempo Perso

$$ | **ITALIAN** | A couple of jazz-, rock-, and food-loving friends joined forces to open this smart little restaurant in the center. The interior's warm terra-cotta-sponged walls give off an orange glow, and wine bottles line the walls, interspersed with photographs of musical greats—but the food is what counts. **Known for:** fine wine list; housemade pastas; terrific seafood dishes. [$] *Average main: €20* ✉ *Via Gamba 12, Ravenna* ☎ *0544/215393* 🌐 *www.osteriadeltempoperso.it* 🕙 *No lunch weekdays.*

🛏 Hotels

Albergo Cappello

$$ | **HOTEL** | Originally opened in the late 19th century and restored a century later, this small, charming place exhibits a Venetian influence, with Murano chandeliers hanging from the high coffered wood ceilings in common rooms. **Pros:** wine bar and good restaurant; good location in historic area and near sights; accommodating staff. **Cons:** occasional street noise in some rooms; only seven rooms; parking sometimes hard to find. [$] *Rooms from: €134* ✉ *Via IV Novembre 41, Ravenna* ☎ *0544/219813* 🌐 *www.albergocappello.it* 🛏 *7 rooms* 🍴 *Free Breakfast.*

Hotel Sant'Andrea

$ | **B&B/INN** | **FAMILY** | For a quiet and welcoming lodging on a residential street a stone's throw from the Basilica di San Vitale, look no further—it even has a delightful garden. **Pros:** cheery and helpful staff; quiet neighborhood; good-size guest rooms and family suites, some with terraces. **Cons:** reception closes at 9 pm; can get a little noisy; few facilities. [$] *Rooms from: €93* ✉ *Via Carlo Cattaneo 33, Ravenna* ☎ *0544/215564* 🌐 *www.santandreahotel.com* 🛏 *12 rooms* 🍴 *Free Breakfast.*

🎫 Performing Arts

Teatro di Tradizione Dante Alighieri

ARTS CENTERS | Operas and dance productions are staged here from November to April. If your Italian is up to it, you could also attend any of the theatrical productions. ✉ *Via Mariani 2, Ravenna* ☎ *0544/249244* 🌐 *www.teatroalighieri.org.*

Chapter 6

FLORENCE

Updated by
Patricia Rucidlo

👁 Sights	🍴 Restaurants	🛏 Hotels	🛍 Shopping	🍸 Nightlife
★★★★★	★★★★★	★★★★★	★★★★★	★★★★☆

WELCOME TO FLORENCE

TOP REASONS TO GO

★ **Galleria degli Uffizi:**
Italian Renaissance art doesn't get much better than this vast collection bequeathed in 1737 by the last Medici, Anna Maria Luisa.

★ **Brunelleschi's Dome:**
His work of engineering genius is the city's undisputed centerpiece.

★ **Michelangelo's *David*:**
One look, up close, and you'll know why this is one of the world's most famous sculptures.

★ **The view from Piazzale Michelangelo:** From this perch the city is laid out before you. The colors at sunset heighten the experience.

★ **Piazza Santa Croce:**
After you've had your fill of Renaissance masterpieces, idle here and watch the world go by.

1 Around the Duomo.
You're in the heart of Florence here. Among the numerous highlights are the city's greatest museum (the Uffizi) and arguably its most impressive square (Piazza della Signoria).

2 San Lorenzo. The complex of the basilica of San Lorenzo, the Palazzo Medici-Riccardi, and the Galleria dell'Accademia bears the imprints of the Medici and of Michelangelo, culminating in the latter's masterful statue of *David*. Just to the north, the former convent of San Marco is an oasis of artistic treasures decorated with ethereal frescoes.

3 Santa Maria Novella.
This part of town includes the train station, 16th-century palaces, and the city's swankest shopping street, Via Tornabuoni.

4 Santa Croce. The district centers on its namesake basilica, which is filled with the tombs of Renaissance (and other) luminaries. The area is also known for its leather shops.

5 The Oltrarno. Across the Arno you encounter the massive Palazzo Pitti and the narrow streets of the Santo Spirito neighborhood.

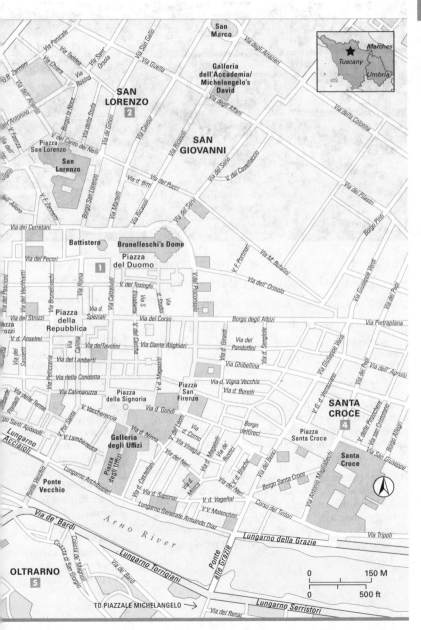

Marches

Tuscany

Umbria

San Marco

Galleria dell'Accademia/ Michelangelo's David

SAN LORENZO
2

SAN GIOVANNI

Piazza San Lorenzo

San Lorenzo

Via Pancale
Via Taddea
Via Sant' Orsola
Via San Gallo
Via Guelfa
Via degli Arrazieri
Via della Colonna

Via Chiara
Via Rosina
Borgo la Noce
Via della Stufa
Via Cavour
Via de' Ginori
Via Ricasoli
Via degli Affani

G.B. Zannoni
Via dell'Ariento
Via Faenza
V. dell'Antonino
V. del Canto dei Nelli

Borgo San Lorenzo
Via Martelli
Via Ricasoli
Via d: Bitti
Via del Pucci
Via del Servi
V. del Castellaccio
Via dei Pilastri

V.F Zannetti
Via de' Cerretani

Battistero
Brunelleschi's Dome

Piazza del Duomo
1

Via del Pecori
Via Roma
Via Calzaiuoli
V. del Tosinghi

Piazza della Repubblica
Via d. Speziali
Via S. Elisabetta
Via del Studio
V. del Proconsolo

Via del Corso
Borgo degli Albizi
Via Pietraplana

Via del Strozzi
Via de'Tavolini
Via Dante Alighieri
Via del Pandolfini
Via d. Sangiote
Via Giuseppe Verdi

V. del Anselmi
Via della Condotta
Via Ghibellina
Via dell'Agnolo

Via Calimaruzza
Piazza della Signoria
Piazza San Firenze
Via d. Vigna Vecchia
Via d. Burelli

SANTA CROCE
4

Piazza Santa Croce

Santa Croce

Galleria degli Uffizi

Ponte Vecchio

Lungarno Acciaioli

Lungarno Archibusieri

Arno River

OLTRARNO
5

TO PIAZZALE MICHELANGELO →

0   150 M
0   500 ft

EATING AND DRINKING WELL IN FLORENCE

In Florence, simply prepared meats, grilled or roasted, are the culinary stars, usually paired with seasonal vegetables like artichokes or porcini. *Bistecca* is popular here, but there's plenty more that tastes great on the grill, too.

Traditionalists go for their gustatory pleasures in *trattorie* and *osterie*, places where decor is unimportant and place mats are mere paper. Culinary innovation comes slowly in this town, though some cutting-edge restaurants have been appearing.

By American standards, Florentines eat late: 1:30 or 2 pm is typical for lunch and 9 pm for dinner is considered early. Consuming a *primo*, *secondo*, and *dolce* is largely a thing of the past. For lunch, many Florentines simply grab a panino and a glass of wine at a bar. Those opting for a simple trattoria lunch often order a plate of pasta and dessert.

STALE AND STELLAR

Stale bread is the basis for three classic Florentine primi: *pappa al pomodoro*, *ribollita*, and *panzanella*. Pappa is made with either fresh or canned tomatoes and that stale bread. Ribollita is a vegetable soup with *cavolo nero* (Tuscan kale) and cannellini beans, thickened with bread. Panzanella is reconstituted Tuscan bread combined with tomatoes, cucumber, and basil. They all are enhanced with a generous application of fragrant Tuscan olive oil.

A CLASSIC ANTIPASTO: CROSTINI DI FEGATINI

This beloved dish consists of a chicken-liver spread, served warm or at room temperature, on toasted, garlic-rubbed bread. It can be served smooth, like a pâté, or in a chunkier, more rustic version. It's made by sautéing chicken livers with finely diced carrot and onion, enlivened with the addition of wine, broth, or Marsala reductions, and mashed anchovies and capers.

A CLASSIC SECONDO: BISTECCA FIORENTINA

The town's culinary pride and joy is a thick slab of beef, resembling a T-bone steak, from large white oxen called Chianina. The meat's slapped on the grill and served rare, sometimes with a pinch of salt.

It's always seared on both sides, and just barely cooked inside.

A CLASSIC CONTORNO: CANNELLINI BEANS

Simply boiled, they provide the perfect accompaniment to bistecca. The small white beans are best when they go straight from the garden into the pot. They should be anointed with a generous dose of Tuscan olive oil; the combination is oddly felicitous, and it goes a long way toward explaining why Tuscans are referred to as *mangiafagioli* (bean eaters) by other Italians.

A CLASSIC DOLCE: BISCOTTI DI PRATO

These are sometimes the only dessert on offer. *Biscotti* means twice-cooked (or, in this case, twice-baked). They are hard almond cookies that soften considerably when dipped languidly into *vin santo* ("holy wine"), a sweet dessert wine, or into a simple *caffè*.

A CLASSIC WINE: CHIANTI CLASSICO

This blend from the region just south of Florence relies mainly on the local, hardy *sangiovese* grape; it's aged for at least one year before hitting the market. (*Riserve*—reserve—is aged at least an additional six months.)

Chianti is usually the libation of choice for Florentines. Traditionalists opt for the younger, fruitier (and usually less expensive) versions often served in straw flasks. You can sample Chianti Classico all over town, and buy it in local supermarkets.

Its magical combination of beauty and history has drawn people to Florence for centuries, and then it draws them back again. It offers myriad moments of personal illumination before its palazzi, its churches, and its art museums, as well as in interaction with the people you meet there.

Florence has captivated visitors for ages now, probably ever since the powerful Medici family first staged jousts and later lavish pageants to celebrate their weddings. Its mostly sober beauty continued to attract people from all over Europe intent on taking in the achievements of the past on their Grand Tour of Europe. Sometimes this heady combination of art and beauty has proven overwhelming, as it did for French author and diplomat Stendhal in 1817, whose visit to the church of Santa Croce occasioned palpitations and a fainting spell. Today, however, visitors are more often overwhelmed by the press of their own numbers intent on taking it all in before moving on to the next stop on their tightly scheduled tours. Florence has always been visitor-friendly—the historical center of the city can be crossed on foot in less than half an hour, and the picturesque surrounding hills are a short bus ride away. But the flood of tourists has made the natives more reticent. A visitor is more likely to bump into or to exchange views with other visitors than with native Florentines, all busy catering to tourists' needs. Few Florentines, these days, can afford to live in the center where they work. Even the university has pulled out to a suburb. By day, the city is overrun with bus-loads of processing day-trippers; come evening by droves of U.S. study-abroad students intent on immersion in the native *aperitivo* culture. Where have all the Italians gone, you wonder? Fear not, they still come out on Sundays to walk in family groups along the major shopping streets, school groups still pack museums, and they still hold parades in Renaissance costume to mark various historical or religious occasions. *Caffè* culture still thrives. All this will be revealed to the attentive visitor who sees past the crowds and takes the time to look around the corner onto a quieter street, piazza, or neighborhood.

When the sun sets over the Arno and, as Mark Twain described it, "overwhelms Florence with tides of color that make all the sharp lines dim and faint and turn the solid city to a city of dreams," it's hard not to fall under the city's spell.

Planning

Making the Most of Your Time

With some planning, you can see Florence's most famous sights in a couple of days. Start off at the city's most awe-inspiring architectural wonder, the **Duomo,** climbing to the top of the dome if you have the stamina (and are not claustrophobic: it gets a little tight going up and coming back down). On the same piazza, check out Ghiberti's bronze doors at the **Battistero.** (They're actually high-quality copies; the Museo dell'Opera del Duomo has the originals.) Set aside the afternoon for the **Galleria degli Uffizi,** making sure to reserve tickets in advance.

On Day 2, visit Michelangelo's *David* in the **Galleria dell'Accademia**—reserve tickets here, too. Linger in **Piazza della Signoria,** Florence's central square, where a copy of *David* stands in the spot the original occupied for centuries, then head east a couple of blocks to **Santa Croce,** the city's most artistically rich church. Double back and walk across Florence's landmark bridge, the **Ponte Vecchio.**

Do all that, and you'll have seen some great art, but you've just scratched the surface. If you have more time, put the **Bargello,** the **Museo di San Marco,** and the **Cappelle Medicee** at the top of your list. When you're ready for an art break, stroll through the **Boboli Gardens** or explore Florence's lively shopping scene, from the food stalls of the **Mercato Centrale** to the chic boutiques of the **Via Tornabuoni.**

HOURS

Florence's sights keep tricky hours. Some are closed Wednesday, some Monday, some every other Monday. Quite a few shut their doors each day (or on most days) by 2 in the afternoon. Things get even more confusing on weekends. Make it a general rule to check the hours closely for any place you're planning to visit; if it's someplace you have your heart set on seeing, it's worthwhile to call to confirm.

Here's a selection of major sights that might not be open when you'd expect *(consult the Sight listings within this chapter for the full details).* And be aware that, as always, hours can and do change. Also note that on the first Sunday of the month, all state museums are free. That means that the Accademia and the Uffizi, among others, do not accept reservations. Unless you are a glutton for punishment (i.e., large crowds), these museums are best avoided on that day.

The **Accademia** and the **Uffizi** are both closed Monday.

The **Battistero** is open Monday through Saturday 8:15–10:15 and 11:15–8; Sunday 8:30–2.

The **Bargello** closes at 1:50 pm, and is closed entirely on alternating Sundays and Mondays. However, it's often open much later during high season and when there's a special exhibition on.

The **Cappelle Medicee** are closed alternating Sundays and Mondays (those Sundays and Mondays when the Bargello is open).

The **Duomo** closes at 4:30 on Thursday, as opposed to 5 other weekdays, 4:45 Saturday, and Sunday it's open only 1:30–4:45. The dome of the Duomo is closed Sunday.

Museo di San Marco closes at 1:50 weekdays but stays open until 4:45 weekends—except for alternating Sundays and Mondays, when it's closed entirely.

Palazzo Medici-Riccardi is closed Wednesday.

RESERVATIONS

At most times of day you'll see a line of people snaking around the Uffizi. They're waiting to buy tickets, and you don't want to be one of them. Instead, call ahead for a reservation (055/294883; reservationists speak English). You'll be given a reservation number and a time of admission—the sooner you call, the more time-slots you'll have to choose from. Go to the museum's reservation door 10 minutes before the appointed hour, give the clerk your number, pick up your ticket, and go inside. (Know that often in high season, there's at least a half-hour wait to pick up the tickets and often an even longer wait to get into the museum.) You'll pay €4 for this privilege, but it's money well spent. You can also book tickets online through the website (www. uffizi.it/en/the-uffizi); the booking process takes some patience, but it works.

Use the same reservation service to book tickets for the Galleria dell'Accademia, where lines rival those of the Uffizi. (Reservations can also be made for the Palazzo Pitti, the Bargello, and several other sights, but they usually aren't needed—although, lately, in summer, lines can be long at Palazzo Pitti.) An alternative strategy is to check with your hotel—many will handle reservations.

Getting Here and Around

AIR

To get into the city center from the airport by car, take the autostrada A11. A SITA bus will take you directly from the airport to the center of town. Buy the tickets within the train station.

AIR CONTACTS Aeroporto A. Vespucci. ⊠ *10 km (6 miles) northwest of Florence, Florence* ☏ *055/30615* ⊕ *www.aeroporto. firenze.it.* **Aeroporto Galileo Galilei.** ⊠ *12 km (7 miles) south of Pisa and 80 km (50 miles) west of Florence, Florence* ☏ *050/849300* ⊕ *www.pisa-airport.com.*

BIKE AND MOPED

Brave souls (cycling in Florence is difficult at best) may rent bicycles at easy-to-spot locations at Fortezza da Basso, the Stazione Centrale di Santa Maria Novella, and Piazza Pitti. Otherwise, try **Alinari** (Via San Zanobi 40/r, San Marco; 055/280500). You'll be up against hordes of tourists and those pesky *motorini* (mopeds). (For a safer ride, try Le Cascine, a former Medici hunting ground turned into a large public park with paved pathways.) The historic center can be circumnavigated via bike paths lining the *viali,* the ring road surrounding the area. If you want to go native and rent a noisy Vespa (Italian for "wasp") or other make of motorcycle or *motorino,* you can do so at **Massimo** (Via Campo d'Arrigo 102/B, 055/573689).

BUS

Florence's flat, compact city center is made for walking, but when your feet get weary you can use the efficient bus system, which includes small electric buses making the rounds in the center. Buses also climb to Piazzale Michelangelo and San Miniato south of the Arno.

Maps and timetables for local bus service are available for a small fee at the ATAF (Azienda Trasporti Area Fiorentina), or for free at visitor information offices. Tickets must be bought in advance from tobacco shops, newsstands, automatic ticket machines near main stops, or ATAF booths. The ticket must be canceled in the small validation machine immediately upon boarding.

You have several ticket options, all valid for one or more rides on all lines. A €1.50 ticket is good for ninety minutes from the time it is first canceled. Another option is to buy a booklet of 10 tickets, each good for 70 minutes, for €14.

Long-distance buses provide inexpensive service between Florence and other cities in Italy and Europe. **Bus Italia** (Via

Santa Caterina da Siena 17/r, 055/47821)
s the major line.

CAR

Florence is connected to the north and
south of Italy by the Autostrada del
Sole (A1). It takes about 1½ hours of
driving on scenic roads to get to Bologna
(although heavy truck traffic over the
Apennines often makes for slower
going), about 3 hours to Rome, and 3–3½
hours to Milan. The Tyrrhenian Coast is an
hour west on the A11.

An automobile in Florence is a major
liability. If your itinerary includes parts
of Italy where you'll want a car (such as
Tuscany), pick the vehicle up on your way
out of town.

TAXI

Taxis usually wait at stands throughout
the city (in front of the train station and
in Piazza della Repubblica, for example),
or you can call for one (055/4390 or
055/4242). The meter starts at €3.30
from any taxi stand; if you call Radio
Dispatch (that means that a taxi comes
to pick you up wherever it is you are), it
starts at €5.50. Extra charges apply at
night, on Sunday, for radio dispatch, and
for luggage. Single women traveling after
9 pm seeking taxis are entitled to a 10%
discount on the fare; you must, however,
request it.

TRAIN

Florence is on the principal Italian train
route between most European capitals
and Rome, and within Italy it is served
frequently from Milan, Venice, and Rome
by Intercity (IC) and nonstop Eurostar
trains. Avoid trains that stop only at the
Campo di Marte or Rifredi station, which
are not convenient to the city center.

TRAIN CONTACTS Italo. ⊠ *Florence*
☎ *892020* ⊕ *www.italotreno.it.* **Stazione
Centrale di Santa Maria Novella.** ⊠ *Florence*
☎ *892021* ⊕ *www.trenitalia.com.*

Restaurants

Florence's popularity with tourists means
that, unfortunately, there's a higher
percentage of mediocre restaurants here
than you'll find in most Italian towns (Venice,
perhaps, might win that prize). Some
restaurant owners cut corners and let
standards slip, knowing that a customer
today is unlikely to return tomorrow,
regardless of the quality of the meal. So,
if you're looking to eat well, it pays to do
some research, starting with the recommendations
here. Dining hours start at
around 1 for lunch and 8 for dinner. Many
of Florence's restaurants are small, so
reservations are a must. You can sample
such specialties as creamy *fegatini* (a
chicken-liver spread) and *ribollita* (minestrone
thickened with bread and beans
and swirled with extra-virgin olive oil) in
a bustling, convivial trattoria, where you
share long wooden tables set with paper
place mats, or in an upscale *ristorante*
with linen tablecloths and napkins.

*Restaurants reviews have been shortened.
For full information, visit Fodors.com.*

WHAT IT COSTS in Euros			
$	$$	$$$	$$$$
AT DINNER			
under €15	€15–€24	€25–€35	over €35

Hotels

Florence is equipped with hotels for
all budgets; for instance, you can find
both budget and luxury hotels in the
centro storico (historic center) and
along the Arno. Florence has so many
famous landmarks that it's not hard to
find lodging with a panoramic view. The
equivalent of the genteel *pensioni* of
yesteryear can still be found, though they
are now officially classified as "hotels."
Generally small and intimate, they often

have a quaint appeal that usually doesn't preclude modern plumbing. Florence's importance not only as a tourist city but also as a convention center and the site of the Pitti fashion collections guarantees a variety of accommodations.

The high demand also means that, except in winter, reservations are a must. If you find yourself in Florence with no reservations, go to **Consorzio ITA** (Stazione Centrale, Santa Maria Novella, 055/282893). You must go there in person to make a booking.

Hotel reviews have been shortened. For full information, visit Fodors.com.

WHAT IT COSTS in Euros			
$	$$	$$$	$$$$
FOR TWO PEOPLE			
under €125	€125– €200	€201– €300	over €300

Shopping

Window-shopping in Florence is like visiting an enormous contemporary-art gallery. Many of today's greatest Italian artists are fashion designers, and most keep shops in Florence. Discerning shoppers may find bargains in the street markets.

■ TIP→ **Do not buy any knockoff goods from any of the hawkers plying their fake Prada (or any other high-end designer) on the streets. It's illegal, and fines are astronomical if the police happen to catch you. (You pay the fine, not the vendor.)**

Shops are generally open 9–1 and 3:30–7:30, and are closed Sunday and Monday mornings most of the year. Summer (June to September) hours are usually 9–1 and 4–8, and some shops close Saturday afternoon instead of Monday morning. When looking for addresses, you'll see two color-coded numbering systems on each street. The red numbers are commercial addresses and are indicated, for example, as "31/r." The blue or black numbers are residential addresses. Most shops take major credit cards and ship purchases, but because of possible delays it's wise to take your purchases with you.

Visitor Information

The Florence tourist office, known as the APT (Azienda di Promozione Turistica; 055/290832), has branches next to the Palazzo Medici-Riccardi, across the street from Stazione di Santa Maria Novella (the main train station), and at the Bigallo, in Piazza del Duomo. The offices are generally open from 9 in the morning until 7 in the evening. The multilingual staff will give you directions and the latest on happenings in the city. It's particularly worth a stop if you're interested in finding out about performing-arts events. The APT website (feelflorence.it) provides information in both Italian and English.

Around the Duomo

The heart of Florence, stretching from the Piazza del Duomo south to the Arno, is as dense with artistic treasures as any place in the world. Its churches, medieval towers, Renaissance palaces, and world-class museums and galleries contain some of the most outstanding achievements of Western art.

Much of the centro storico is closed to automobile traffic, but you still must dodge mopeds, cyclists, and masses of fellow tourists as you walk the narrow streets, especially in the area bounded by the Duomo, Piazza della Signoria, Galleria degli Uffizi, and the Ponte Vecchio. Via dei Calzaiuoli, between Piazza del Duomo and Piazza della Signoria, is the city's favorite *passeggiata* (constitutional).

Sights

Bargello

ART MUSEUM | This building started out as the headquarters for the Capitano del Popolo (Captain of the People) during the Middle Ages, and was later a prison. Today it houses the Museo Nazionale, home to what is probably the finest collection of Renaissance sculpture in Italy. Masterpieces by Michelangelo (1475–1564), Donatello (circa 1386–1466), and Benvenuto Cellini (1500–71) are remarkable; the works are distributed among an eclectic collection of arms, ceramics, and miniature bronzes, among other things. In 1401 Filippo Brunelleschi (1377–1446) and Lorenzo Ghiberti (circa 1378–1455) competed to earn the most prestigious commission of the day: the decoration of the north doors of the Baptistery in Piazza del Duomo. For the contest, each designed a bronze bas-relief panel depicting the sacrifice of Isaac; the panels are displayed together in the room devoted to the sculpture of Donatello, on the upper floor. According to Ghiberti, the judges chose him, though Brunelleschi maintained that they were both hired for the commission. See whom you believe after visiting. ⊠ Via del Proconsolo 4, Bargello ☎ 055/294883 ⊕ www.museodelbargello.it ⊗ Closed 1st, 3rd, 5th Mon. of month; closed 2nd and 4th Sun. of month ⊠ €8.

Battistero (*Baptistery*)

RELIGIOUS BUILDING | The octagonal Baptistery is one of the supreme monuments of the Italian Romanesque style and one of Florence's oldest structures. Local legend has it that it was once a Roman temple dedicated to Mars (it wasn't), and modern excavations suggest that its foundations date from the 1st century AD. The round Romanesque arches on the exterior date from the 11th century, and the interior dome mosaics from the beginning of the mid-13th century are justly renowned, but—glittering beauties though they are—they could never outshine the building's famed bronze Renaissance doors decorated with panels crafted by Lorenzo Ghiberti. These doors—or at least copies of them—on which Ghiberti worked most of his adult life (1403–52), are on the north and east sides of the Baptistery. The Gothic panels on the south door were designed by Andrea Pisano (circa 1290–1348) in 1330. Ghiberti's original doors were removed to protect them from the effects of pollution and acid rain and have been beautifully restored. Ghiberti's north doors depict scenes from the life of Christ; his later east doors (dating 1425–52), facing the Duomo facade, render scenes from the Old Testament. Both merit close examination, for they are very different in style and illustrate the artistic changes that marked the beginning of the Renaissance. Look at the far right panel of the middle row on the earlier (1403–24) north doors (*Jesus Calming the Waters*). Ghiberti here captured the chaos of a storm at sea with great skill and economy, but the artistic conventions he used are basically pre-Renaissance: Jesus is the most important figure, so he is the largest; the disciples are next in size, being next in importance; the ship on which they founder looks like a mere toy. The exquisitely rendered panels on the east doors are larger, more expansive, more sweeping—and more convincing. The middle panel on the left-hand door tells the story of Jacob and Esau, and the various episodes of the story—the selling of the birthright, Isaac ordering Esau to go hunting, the blessing of Jacob, and so forth—have been merged into a single beautifully realized street scene. Ghiberti's use of perspective suggests depth: the background architecture looks far more credible than on the north-door panels, the figures in the foreground are grouped realistically, and the naturalism and grace of the poses (look at Esau's left leg and the dog next to him) have nothing to do with the sacred message being conveyed. Although the religious

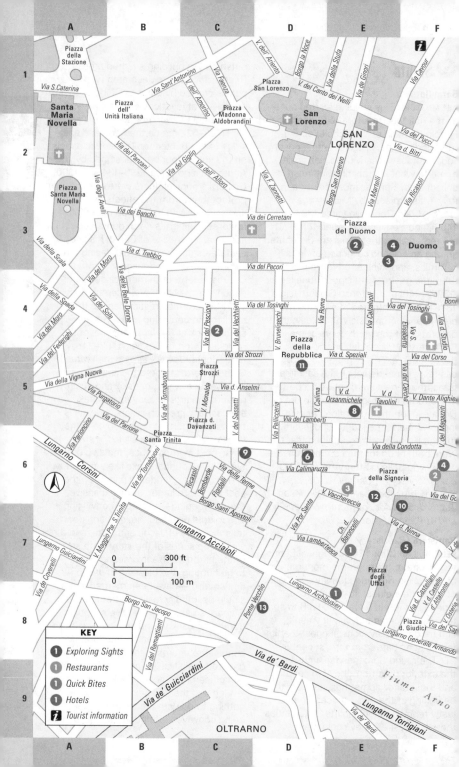

Around the Duomo

Sights ▼

1	Bargello	**G6**
2	Battistero	**E3**
3	Campanile	**E3**
4	Duomo	**E3**
5	Galleria Degli Uffizi	**F7**
6	Mercato Nuovo	**D6**
7	Museo dell'Opera del Duomo	**G3**
8	Orsanmichele	**E5**
9	Palazzo Davanzati	**C6**
10	Palazzo Vecchio	**F7**
11	Piazza della Repubblica	**D5**
12	Piazza della Signoria	**E6**
13	Ponte Vecchio	**D8**

Restaurants ▼

1	Coquinarius	**F4**
2	Gucci Osteria	**F6**
3	Rivoire	**E6**

Quick Bites ▼

1	'ino	**E7**

Hotels ▼

1	Hotel degli Orafi	**E8**
2	Hotel Helvetia and Bristol	**C4**
3	Hotel Renaissance	**F6**
4	In Piazza della Signoria	**F6**

content remains, the figures and their place in the natural world are given new prominence, and are portrayed with a realism not seen in art since the fall of the Roman Empire nearly a thousand years before. As a footnote to Ghiberti's panels, one small detail of the east doors is worth a special look. To the lower left of the Jacob and Esau panel, Ghiberti placed a tiny self-portrait bust. From either side, the portrait is extremely appealing—Ghiberti looks like everyone's favorite uncle—but the bust is carefully placed so that you can make direct eye contact with the tiny head from a single spot. When that contact is made, the impression of intelligent life—of *modern* intelligent life—is astonishing. It's no wonder that these doors received one of the most famous compliments in the history of art from an artist known to be notoriously stingy with praise: Michelangelo declared them so beautiful that they could serve as the Gates of Paradise. ✉ *Piazza del Duomo, Duomo* ☎ *055/2302885* ⊕ *www.operaduomo. firenze.it* ✍ *€10.*

Campanile

NOTABLE BUILDING | The Gothic bell tower designed by Giotto (circa 1266–1337) is a soaring structure of multicolor marble originally decorated with sculptures by Donatello and reliefs by Giotto, Andrea Pisano, and others (which are now in the Museo dell'Opera del Duomo). A climb of 414 steps rewards you with a close-up of Brunelleschi's cupola on the Duomo next door and a sweeping view of the city. ✉ *Piazza del Duomo, Duomo* ☎ *055/2302885* ⊕ *www.operaduomo. firenze.it* ✍ *€15.*

★ Duomo (*Cattedrale di Santa Maria del Fiore*)

CHURCH | In 1296 Arnolfo di Cambio (circa 1245–circa 1310) was commissioned to build "the loftiest, most sumptuous edifice human invention could devise" in the Romanesque style on the site of the old church of Santa Reparata. The immense Duomo was consecrated in 1436, but work continued over the centuries. The imposing facade dates only from the 19th century; its neo-Gothic style somewhat complements Giotto's genuine Gothic 14th-century campanile. The real glory of the Duomo, however, is Filippo Brunelleschi's dome, presiding over the cathedral with a dignity and grace that few domes to this day can match. Brunelleschi's **cupola** was an ingenious engineering feat. The space to be enclosed by the dome was so large and so high above the ground that traditional methods of dome construction—wooden centering and scaffolding—were of no use whatsoever. So Brunelleschi developed entirely new building methods, which he implemented with equipment of his own design (including a novel scaffolding method). Beginning work in 1420, he built not one dome but two, one inside the other, and connected them with ribbing that stretched across the intervening empty space, thereby considerably lessening the crushing weight of the structure. He also employed a new method of bricklaying, based on an ancient herringbone pattern, interlocking each course of bricks with the course below in a way that made the growing structure self-supporting. The result was one of the great engineering breakthroughs of all time: most of Europe's later domes, including that of St. Peter's in Rome, were built employing Brunelleschi's methods, and today the Duomo has come to symbolize Florence in the same way that the Eiffel Tower symbolizes Paris. The Florentines are justly proud of it, and to this day the Florentine phrase for "homesick" is *nostalgia del cupolone* (homesick for the dome). The interior is a fine example of Florentine Gothic. Much of the cathedral's best-known art has been moved to the nearby Museo dell'Opera del Duomo. Notable among the works that remain, however, are two massive equestrian frescoes honoring

Florence Through the Ages

Guelph vs. Ghibelline. Although Florence can lay claim to a modest importance in the ancient world, it didn't come into its own until the Middle Ages. In the early 1200s the city, like most of the rest of Italy, was rent by civic unrest. Two factions, the Guelphs and the Ghibellines, competed for power. The Guelphs supported the papacy, and the Ghibellines supported the Holy Roman Empire. Bloody battles—most notably one at Montaperti in 1260—tore Florence and other Italian cities apart. By the end of the 13th century the Guelphs ruled securely, and the Ghibellines had been vanquished. This didn't end civic strife, however: the Guelphs split into the Whites and the Blacks for reasons still debated by historians. Dante, author of *The Divine Comedy*, was banished from Florence in 1301 because he was a White.

The Guilded Age. Local merchants had organized themselves into guilds by some time beginning in the 12th century. In 1250, they proclaimed themselves the *primo popolo* (literally, "first people"), making a landmark attempt at elective, republican rule. Though the episode lasted only 10 years, it constituted a breakthrough in Western history. Such a daring stance by the merchant class was a by-product of Florence's emergence as an economic powerhouse. Florentines were papal bankers; they instituted the system of international letters of credit; the gold florin became the international standard of currency. With this economic strength came a building boom. Sculptors such as Ghiberti and Donatello decorated the new churches; painters such as Giotto and Masaccio frescoed their walls.

Mighty Medici. Though ostensibly a republic, Florence was blessed (or cursed) with one very powerful family, the Medici, who came to prominence in 1434 and were initially the de facto rulers and then the absolute rulers of Florence for several hundred years. It was under patriarch Cosimo il Vecchio (1389–1464) that the Medici's position in Florence was securely established. Florence's golden age occurred during the reign of his grandson Lorenzo de' Medici (1449–92). Lorenzo was not only an astute politician but also a highly educated man and a great patron of the arts. Called "Il Magnifico" (the Magnificent), he gathered around him poets, artists, philosophers, architects, and musicians.

Lorenzo's son Piero (1471–1503) proved inept at handling the city's affairs. He was run out of town in 1494, and Florence briefly enjoyed its status as a republic while dominated by the Dominican friar Girolamo Savonarola (1452–98). After a decade of internal unrest, the republic fell and the Medici returned to power, but Florence never regained its former prestige. By the 1530s most of the major artistic talent had left the city—Michelangelo, for one, had settled in Rome. The now-ineffectual Medici, eventually attaining the title of grand dukes, remained nominally in power until the line died out in 1737, after which time Florence passed from the Austrians to the French and back again until the unification of Italy (1865–70), when it briefly became the capital under King Vittorio Emanuele II.

famous soldiers: Niccolò da Tolentino, painted in 1456 by Andrea del Castagno (circa 1419–57), and Sir John Hawkwood, painted 20 years earlier by Paolo Uccello (1397–1475); both are on the left nave. A 1995 restoration repaired the dome and cleaned the vastly crowded fresco of the Last Judgment, executed by Giorgio Vasari (1511–74) and Zuccaro, on its interior. Originally Brunelleschi wanted mosaics to cover the interior of the great ribbed cupola, but by the time the Florentines got around to commissioning the decoration, 150 years later, tastes had changed. Too bad: it's a fairly dreadful Last Judgment and hardly worth the effort of craning your neck to see it. You can explore the upper and lower reaches of the cathedral. The remains of a Roman wall and an 11th-century cemetery have been excavated beneath the nave; the way down is near the first pier on the right. The **climb to the top of the dome** (463 steps) is not for the faint of heart, but the view is superb. ⊠ *Piazza del Duomo, Florence* ☎ *055/2302885* ⊕ *www.operaduomo.firenze.it* ⊘ *Closed Sun. morning.*

★ Galleria degli Uffizi

ART MUSEUM | The venerable Uffizi Gallery occupies two floors of the U-shape Palazzo degli Uffizi, designed by Giorgio Vasari (1511–74) in 1560 to hold the *uffici* (administrative offices) of the Medici Grand Duke Cosimo I (1519–74). Among the highlights are Paolo Uccello's *Battle of San Romano*, its brutal chaos of lances one of the finest visual metaphors for warfare ever captured in paint (it returned from a glorious restoration in 2012); the *Madonna and Child with Two Angels*, by Fra Filippo Lippi (1406–69), in which the impudent eye contact established by the angel would have been unthinkable prior to the Renaissance; *The Birth of Venus* and *Primavera*, by Sandro Botticelli (1445–1510), the goddess of the former seeming to float on air and the fairy-tale charm of the latter exhibiting the painter's idiosyncratic genius at its zenith; the portraits of the Renaissance

duke Federico da Montefeltro and his wife Battista Sforza, by Piero della Francesca (circa 1420–92); *Madonna of the Goldfinch*, by Raphael (1483–1520), distinguished by the brilliant blues that decorate the sky, as well as the eye contact between mother and child, both clearly anticipating the painful future; Michelangelo's *Doni Tondo*; the *Venus of Urbino*, by Titian (circa 1488/90–1576); and the splendid *Bacchus*, by Caravaggio (circa 1571/72–1610). In the last two works, the approaches to myth and sexuality are diametrically opposed (to put it mildly). Late in the afternoon is the least crowded time to visit. For a €4 fee, advance tickets can be reserved by phone, online, or, once in Florence, at the Uffizi reservation booth (Consorzio ITA, Piazza Pitti, 055/294883), at least one day in advance of your visit. Keep the confirmation number and take it with you to the door at the museum marked "Reservations." In the past, you were ushered in almost immediately. But overbooking (especially in high season) has led to long lines and long waits even with a reservation. Taking photographs in the Uffizi has been legal since 2014, and has contributed to making what ought to be a sublime museum-going experience more of a day at the zoo. ⊠ *Piazzale degli Uffizi 6, Piazza della Signoria* ☎ *055/294883* ⊕ *www.uffizi.firenze.it; www.polomuseale.firenze.it for reservations* ▦ *From €20* ⊘ *Closed Mon.*

Mercato Nuovo (*New Market*)

MARKET | **FAMILY** | The open-air loggia, built in 1551, teems with souvenir stands, but the real attraction is a copy of Pietro Tacca's bronze *Porcellino* (which translates as "little pig" despite the fact the animal is, in fact, a wild boar). The *Porcellino* is Florence's equivalent of the Trevi Fountain: put a coin in his mouth, and if it falls through the grate below (according to one interpretation), it means you'll return to Florence someday. What you're seeing is a copy of a copy: Tacca's original version, in the Museo Bardini, is actually a copy of an ancient Greek work. ✉ *Via Por Santa Maria at Via Porta Rossa, Piazza della Repubblica* ⏲ *Closed Sun.*

★ **Museo dell'Opera del Duomo** (*Cathedral Museum*)

ART MUSEUM | A seven-year restoration of this museum and its glorious reopening in October 2015 have given Florence one of its most modern, up-to-date museums. Exhibition space has doubled in size, and the old facade of the cathedral, torn down in the 1580s, has been re-created with a 1:1 relationship to the real thing. Both sets of Ghiberti's doors adorn the same room. Michelangelo's *Pietà* finally has the space it deserves, as does Donatello's *Mary Magdalene.* ✉ *Piazza del Duomo 9, Duomo* ☎ *055/2302885* ⊕ *www.operaduomo.firenze.it* 🎟 *€5* ⏲ *Closed Tues.–Fri.*

Orsanmichele

PUBLIC ART | This multipurpose structure began as an 8th-century oratory and then in 1290 was turned into an open-air loggia for selling grain. Destroyed by fire in 1304, it was rebuilt as a loggia-market. Between 1367 and 1380 the arcades were closed and two stories were added above; finally, at century's end it was turned into a church. Inside is a beautifully detailed 14th-century Gothic tabernacle by Andrea Orcagna (1308–68). The exterior niches contain sculptures (all copies) dating from the early 1400s to the early 1600s by Donatello and Verrocchio (1435–88), among others, which were paid for by the guilds. Although it is a copy, Verrocchio's *Doubting Thomas* (circa 1470) is particularly deserving of attention. Here you see Christ, like the building's other figures, entirely framed within the niche, and St. Thomas standing on its bottom ledge, with his right foot outside the niche frame. This one detail, the positioning of a single foot, brings the whole composition to life. It's possible to see the original sculptures at the **Museo di Orsanmichele**, which is open

Monday only. ✉ *Via dei Calzaiuoli, Piazza della Repubblica* ☎ *055/284944* ⊕ *www. polomuseale.firenze.it* ⏲ *Closed Tues.– Sun.* 🎟 *Free.*

Palazzo Davanzati

CASTLE/PALACE | The prestigious Davizzi family owned this 14th-century palace in one of Florence's swankiest medieval neighborhoods (it was sold to the Davanzati in the 15th century). The place is a delight, as you can wander through the surprisingly light-filled courtyard, and climb the steep stairs to the piano nobile (there's also an elevator), where the family did most of its living. The beautiful *Sala dei Pappagalli* (Parrot Room) is adorned with trompe-l'oeil tapestries and gaily painted birds. ✉ *Piazza Davanzati 13, Piazza della Repubblica* ☎ *055/0649460* ⊕ *www.polomuseale.firenze.it* 🎟 *€6* ⏲ *Closed Tues. and 1st, 3rd, 5th Sun. of month.*

Palazzo Vecchio (*Old Palace*)

CASTLE/PALACE | **FAMILY** | Florence's forbidding, fortress-like city hall was begun in 1299, presumably designed by Arnolfo di Cambio, and its massive bulk and towering campanile dominate Piazza della Signoria. It was built as a meeting place for the guildsmen governing the city at the time; today it is still City Hall. The interior courtyard is a good deal less severe, having been remodeled by Michelozzo (1396–1472) in 1453; a copy of Verrocchio's bronze *puttino* (cherub), topping the central fountain, softens the space. (The original is upstairs.) The main attraction is on the second floor: two adjoining rooms that supply one of the most startling contrasts in Florence. The first is the opulently vast **Sala dei Cinquecento** (Room of the Five Hundred), named for the 500-member Great Council, the people's assembly established after the death of Lorenzo the Magnificent, that met here. Giorgio Vasari and others decorated the room, around 1563–65, with gargantuan frescoes

Continued on page 323

THE DUOMO
FLORENCE'S BIGGEST MASTERPIECE

For all its monumental art and architecture, Florence has one undisputed centerpiece: the Cathedral of Santa Maria del Fiore, better known as the Duomo. Its cupola dominates the skyline, presiding over the city's rooftops like a red hen over her brood. Little wonder that when Florentines feel homesick, they say they have "nostalgia del cupolone."

The Duomo's construction began in 1296, following the design of Arnolfo da Cambio, Florence's greatest architect of the time. By modern standards, construction was slow and haphazard—it continued through the 14th and into the 15th century, with some dozen architects having a hand in the project.

In 1366 Neri di Fioravante created a model for the hugely ambitious cupola: it was to be the largest dome in the world, surpassing Rome's Pantheon. But when the time finally came to build the dome in 1418, no one was sure how—or even if—it could be done. Florence was faced with a 143-ft hole in the roof of its cathedral, and one of the greatest challenges in the history of architecture.

Fortunately, local genius Filippo Brunelleschi was just the man for the job. Brunelleschi won the 1418 competition to design the dome, and for the next 18 years he oversaw its construc-

tion. The enormity of his achievement can hardly be overstated. Working on such a large scale (the dome weighs 37,000 tons and uses 4 million bricks) required him to invent hoists and cranes that were engineering marvels. A "dome within a dome" design and a novel herringbone bricklaying pattern were just two of the innovations used to establish structural integrity. Perhaps most remarkably, he executed the construction without a supporting wooden framework, which had previously been thought indispensable.

Brunelleschi designed the lantern atop the dome, but he died soon after its first stone was laid in 1446; it wouldn't be completed until 1461. Another 400 years passed before the Duomo received its façade, a 19th-century neo-Gothic creation.

DUOMO TIMELINE

1296 Work begins, following design by Arnolfo di Cambio.

1302 Arnolfo dies; work continues, with sporadic interruptions.

1331 Management of construction taken over by the Wool Merchants guild.

1334 Giotto appointed project overseer, designs campanile.

1337 Giotto dies; Andrea Pisano takes leadership role.

1348 The Black Plague; all work ceases.

1366 Vaulting on nave completed; Neri di Fioravante makes model for dome.

1417 Drum for dome completed.

1418 Competition is held to design the dome.

1420 Brunelleschi begins work on the dome.

1436 Dome completed.

1446 Construction of lantern begins; Brunelleschi dies.

1461 Antonio Manetti, a student of Brunelleschi, completes lantern.

1469 Gilt copper ball and cross added by Verrocchio.

1587 Original façade is torn down by Medici court.

1871 Emilio de Fabris wins competition to design new facade.

1887 Facade completed.

WHAT TO LOOK FOR INSIDE THE DUOMO

The interior of the Duomo is a fine example of Florentine Gothic with a beautiful marble floor, but the space feels strangely barren—a result of its great size and the fact that some of the best art has been moved to the nearby Museo dell'Opera del Duomo.

Notable among the works that remain are two towering equestrian frescoes of famous mercenaries: Niccolò da Tolentino (1456), by Andrea del Castagno, and Sir John Hawkwood (1436), by Paolo Uccello. There's also fine terra-cotta work by Luca della Robbia. Ghiberti, Brunelleschi's great rival, is responsible for much of the stained glass, as well as a reliquary urn with gorgeous reliefs. A vast fresco of the Last Judgment, painted by Vasari and Zuccari, covers the dome's interior. Brunelleschi had wanted mosaics to go there; it's a pity he didn't get his wish.

In the crypt beneath the cathedral, you can explore excavations of a Roman wall and mosaic fragments from the late sixth century; entry is near the first pier on the right. On the way down you pass Brunelleschi's modest tomb.

1. Entrance; stained glass by Ghiberti

2. Fresco of Niccolò da Tolentino by Andrea del Castagno

3. Fresco of John Hawkwood by Paolo Uccello

4. Dante and the Divine Comedy by Domenico di Michelino

5. Lunette: Ascension by Luca della Robbia

6. Above altar: two angels by Luca della Robbia. Below the altar: reliquary of St. Zenobius by Ghiberti.

7. Lunette: Resurrection by Luca della Robbia

8. Entrance to dome

9. Bust of Brunelleschi by Buggiano

10. Stairs to crypt

11. Campanile

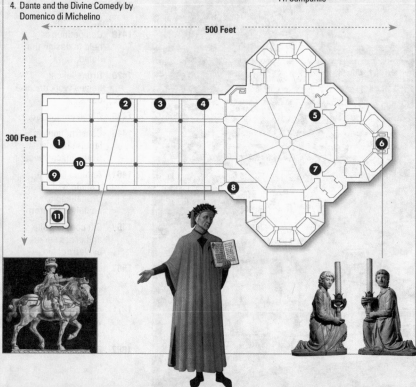

500 Feet

300 Feet

MAKING THE CLIMB

Climbing the 463 steps to the top of the dome is not for the faint of heart—or for the claustrophobic—but those who do it will be awarded a smashing view of Florence ❶. Keep in mind that the way up is also the way down, which means that while you're huffing and puffing in the ascent, people very close to you in a narrow staircase are making their way down ❷.

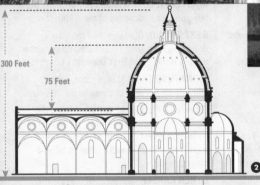

300 Feet

75 Feet

❷

DUOMO BASICS

- Even first thing in the morning during high season (May through September), a line is likely to have formed to climb the dome. Expect an hour wait.

- For an alternative to the dome, consider climbing the less trafficked campanile, which gives you a view from on high of the dome itself.

- Dress code essentials: covered shoulders, no short shorts, and hats off upon entering.

THE CRYPT

The crypt is worth a visit: computer modeling allows visitors to see its ancient Roman fabric and subsequent rebuilding. A transparent plastic model shows exactly what the earlier church looked like.

BRUNELLESCHI vs. GHIBERTI
The Rivalry of Two Renaissance Geniuses

In Renaissance Florence, painters, sculptors, and architects competed for major commissions, with the winner earning the right to undertake a project that might occupy him (and keep him paid) for a decade or more. Stakes were high, and the resulting rivalries fierce—none more so than that between Filippo Brunelleschi and Lorenzo Ghiberti.

The two first clashed in 1401, for the commission to create the bronze doors of the Baptistery. When Ghiberti won, Brunelleschi took it hard, fleeing to Rome, where he would remain for 15 years. Their rematch came in 1418, over the design of the Duomo's cupola, with Brunelleschi triumphant. For the remainder of their lives, the two would miss no opportunity to belittle each other's work.

FILIPPO BRUNELLESCHI (1377–1446)

MASTERPIECE: The dome of Santa Maria del Fiore.

BEST FRIENDS: Donatello, whom he stayed with in Rome after losing the Baptistery doors competition; the Medici family, who rescued him from bankruptcy.

SIGNATURE TRAITS: Paranoid, secretive, bad tempered, practical joker, inept businessman.

SAVVIEST POLITICAL MOVE: Feigned sickness and left for Rome after his dome plans were publicly criticized by Ghiberti, who was second-in-command. The project proved too much for Ghiberti to manage on his own, and Brunelleschi returned triumphant.

MOST EMBARRASSING MOMENT: In 1434 he was imprisoned for two weeks for failure to pay a small guild fee. The humiliation might have been orchestrated by Ghiberti.

OTHER CAREER: Shipbuilder. He built a huge vessel, *Il Badalone*, to transport marble for the dome up the Arno. It sank on its first voyage.

INSPIRED: The dome of St. Peter's in Rome.

LORENZO GHIBERTI (1378–1455)

MASTERPIECE: The Gates of Paradise, the ten-paneled east doors of the Baptistery.

BEST FRIEND: Giovanni da Prato, an underling who wrote diatribes attacking the dome's design and Brunelleschi's character.

SIGNATURE TRAITS: Instigator, egoist, know-it-all, shrewd businessman.

SAVVIEST POLITICAL MOVE: During the Baptistery doors competition, he had an open studio and welcomed opinions on his work, while Brunelleschi labored behind closed doors.

OTHER CAREER: Collector of classical artifacts, historian.

INSPIRED: *The Gates of Hell* by Auguste Rodin.

The Gates of Paradise detail

celebrating Florentine history; depictions of battles with nearby cities predominate. Continuing the martial theme, the room also contains Michelangelo's *Victory*, intended for the never-completed tomb of Pope Julius II (1443–1513), plus other sculptures of decidedly lesser quality. In comparison, the little **Studiolo**, just off the Sala dei Cinquecento's entrance, was a private room meant for the duke and those whom he invited in. Here's where the melancholy Francesco I (1541–87), son of Cosimo I, stored his priceless treasures and conducted scientific experiments. Designed by Vasari, it was decorated by him, Giambologna, and many others. Spectacular 360-degree views may be had from the battlements (only 77 steps) and from the tower (223 more). ⊠ *Piazza della Signoria, Piazza della Signoria* ☎ *055/2768325* ⊕ *museicivicifiorentini.comune.fi.it* ⊠ *From €12.50.*

Piazza della Repubblica

PLAZA/SQUARE | The square marks the site of the ancient forum that was the core of the original Roman settlement. While the street plan around the piazza still reflects the carefully plotted Roman military encampment, the Mercato Vecchio (Old Market), which had been here since the Middle Ages, was demolished and the current piazza was constructed between 1885 and 1895 as a neoclassical showpiece. The piazza is lined with outdoor cafés, affording an excellent opportunity for people-watching. ⊠ *Florence.*

Piazza della Signoria

PLAZA/SQUARE | Here, in 1497 and in 1498, the famous "bonfire of the vanities" took place, when the fanatical Dominican friar Savonarola induced his followers to hurl their worldly goods into the flames; it was also here, a year later, that he was hanged as a heretic and, ironically, burned. A plaque in the piazza pavement marks the spot of his execution. Cellini's famous bronze *Perseus* holding the severed head of Medusa is among the most important sculptures in the Loggia dei Lanzi. Other works include *The Rape of the Sabine Women* and *Hercules and the Centaur*, both late-16th-century works by Giambologna (1529–1608). In the square, the Neptune Fountain, created between 1550 and 1575 by Bartolomeo Ammannati, dominates. The Florentines call it il Biancone, which may be translated as "the big white man" or "the big white lump." Giambologna's equestrian statue, to the left of the fountain, portrays Grand Duke Cosimo I. Occupying the steps of the Palazzo Vecchio is a copy of Michelangelo's *David*, as well as Baccio Bandinelli's *Hercules*. ⊠ *Florence.*

Ponte Vecchio (*Old Bridge*)

BRIDGE | This charmingly simple bridge was built in 1345 to replace an earlier bridge swept away by a flood. Its shops first housed butchers, then grocers, blacksmiths, and other merchants. But in 1593, the Medici grand duke Ferdinand I (1549–1609), whose private corridor linking the Medici palace (Palazzo Pitti) with the Medici offices (the Uffizi) crossed the bridge atop the shops, decided that all this plebeian commerce under his feet was unseemly. So he threw out the butchers and blacksmiths and installed 41 goldsmiths and eight jewelers. The bridge has been devoted solely to these two trades ever since. The Corridoio Vasariano (Piazzale degli Uffizi 6, Piazza della Signoria, 055/294883), the private Medici elevated passageway, was built by Vasari in 1565. Though the ostensible reason for its construction was one of security, it was more likely designed so that the Medici family wouldn't have to walk amid the commoners. Take a moment to study the Ponte Santa Trinita, the next bridge downriver, from either the bridge or the corridor. It was designed by Bartolomeo Ammannati in 1567 (probably from sketches by Michelangelo), blown up by the retreating Germans during World War II, and painstakingly reconstructed after the war. The view from the Ponte Santa Trinita is beautiful, which might explain why so many young lovers seem to hang out there. ✉ *Florence.*

🍴 Restaurants

Coquinarius

$$ | **ITALIAN** | This rustically elegant space, which has served many purposes over the past 600 years, offers some of the tastiest food in town at great prices. It's the perfect place to come if you aren't sure what you're hungry for, as they offer a little bit of everything: salad lovers will have a hard time choosing from among the lengthy list (the Scozzese, with poached chicken, avocado, and bacon, is a winner); those with a yen for pasta will face agonizing choices (the ravioli with pecorino and pears is particularly good). **Known for:** service can be inconsistent; marvelous salads; reasonably priced wine list. [$] *Average main: €18* ✉ *Via delle Oche 15/r, Duomo* ☎ *055/2302153* 🌐 *www.coquinarius.it* ⏲ *No lunch Mon.–Fri.*

★ **Gucci Osteria**

$$$ | **FUSION** | Chef/artist/visionary Massimo Bottura has joined forces with creative folk at Gucci to make a marvelous menu that is both classic and innovative. Though he's trained with Ducasse and Adrià, he says his major influence was his grandmother's cooking. **Known for:** outdoor seating in one of Florence's most beautiful squares; tortellini in crema di Parmigiano Reggiano; an ever-changing creative menu. [$] *Average main: €35* ✉ *Piazza della Signoria 10, Piazza della Signoria* ☎ *055/75927038* 🌐 *www.gucci.com.*

★ **Rivoire**

$$ | **ITALIAN** | One of the best spots in Florence for people-watching offers stellar service, light snacks, and terrific aperitivi. It's been around since the 1860s, and has been famous for its hot and cold chocolate (with or without cream) for more than a century. **Known for:** the view on the piazza; hot chocolate; friendly bartenders. [$] *Average main: €15* ✉ *Via Vacchereccia 4/r, Piazza della Signoria* ☎ *055/214412* 🌐 *www.rivoire.it* ⏲ *Closed Mon.*

☕ Coffee and Quick Bites

★ **'ino**

$ | **ITALIAN** | Serving arguably the best panini in town, proprietor Alessandro Frassica sources only the very best ingredients. Located right behind the Uffizi, 'ino is a perfect place to grab a tasty sandwich and glass of wine before forging on to the next museum. **Known for:** sourcing the best ingredients; bread; interesting ingredient combinations. [$] *Average main: €8* ✉ *Via dei Georgofili 3/r–7/r, Piazza della Signoria* ☎ *055/214154* 🌐 *www.inofirenze.com* ⏲ *Closed Mon.*

🛏 Hotels

Hotel degli Orafi

$$$$ | **HOTEL** | A key scene in *A Room with a View* was shot in this pensione, which is today a luxury hotel adorned with chintz and marble. **Pros:** stellar Arno views; quiet location during the evenings rooftop bar. **Cons:** some street noise in river-facing rooms; on the path of many tour groups during the day; somewhat pricey. [$] *Rooms from: €389* ✉ *Lungarno Archibusieri 4, Piazza della Signoria* ☎ *055/26622* 🌐 *www.hoteldegliorafi.it* 🛏 *50 rooms* 🍴 *Free Breakfast.*

Hotel Helvetia and Bristol

$$$$ | **HOTEL** | From the cozy yet sophisticated lobby with its stone columns to the guest rooms decorated with prints, you might feel as if you're a guest in a sophisticated manor house. **Pros:** central location; old-world charm; excellent restaurant. **Cons:** books up quickly; breakfast is not always included in the price of a room; rooms facing the street get some noise. [$] *Rooms from: €684* ✉ *Via dei Pescioni 2, Piazza della Repubblica* ☎ *055/26651* 🌐 *www.starhotelscollezione.com* 🛏 *82 rooms* 🍴 *No Meals.*

Hotel Renaissance

$ | HOTEL | Nestled in an old building just a stone's throw from the main civic square (Piazza Signoria), this charming little boutique hotel offers peace in quiet elegance. **Pros:** the location; the staff; the sumptuous breakfast. **Cons:** some street noise in some rooms; steps up to the elevator; books up quickly. **$** *Rooms from: €180* ⊠ *Via della Condotta 4, Piazza della Signoria* ☎ *055/213996* ⊕ *www. hotelrenaissancefirenze.com* ➪ *9 rooms* ⊙*| Free Breakfast.*

★ **In Piazza della Signoria**

$$$ | B&B/INN | In this home that is part of a 15th-century palazzo, a cozy feeling permeates the charming rooms, all of which are uniquely decorated and loving-ly furnished; some have damask curtains, others fanciful frescoes in the bathroom. **Pros:** some rooms easily accommodate three; marvelous staff; tasty breakfast with a view of Piazza della Signoria. **Cons:** some of the rooms have steps up into showers and bathtubs; short flight of stairs to reach elevator; books up quickly during high season. **$** *Rooms from: €300* ⊠ *Via dei Magazzini 2, Piazza della Signoria* ☎ *055/2399546* ⊕ *www.inpiazza-dellasignoria.com* ➪ *13 rooms* ⊙*| Free Breakfast.*

Nightlife

Hard Rock Cafe

LIVE MUSIC | Hard Rock packs in young Florentines and travelers eager to sample the music hall chain's take on classic American grub. ⊠ *Via De' Brunelleschi 1 Piazza della Repubblica, Piazza della Repubblica* ☎ *055/277841* ⊕ *www. hardrock.com.*

Yab

DANCE CLUBS | Yab never seems to go out of style, though it increasingly becomes the haunt of Florentine high school and university students intent on dancing and doing vodka shots. ⊠ *Via Sassetti 5/r,* *Piazza della Repubblica* ☎ *055/215160* ⊕ *www.yab.it.*

Performing Arts

Orchestra da Camera Fiorentina

MUSIC | This orchestra performs various concerts of classical music throughout the year at Orsanmichele, the grain mar-ket–turned–church. ⊠ *Via Monferrato 2, Piazza della Signoria* ☎ *783374* ⊕ *www. orchestrafiorentina.it.*

Shopping

★ **Bernardo**

MEN'S CLOTHING | Come here for men's trousers, cashmere sweaters, and shirts with details like mother-of-pearl buttons. ⊠ *Via Porta Rossa 87/r, Piazza della Repubblica* ☎ *055/283333* ⊕ *www. bernardofirenze.it.*

Cabó

MIXED CLOTHING | Missoni knitwear is the main draw at Cabó. ⊠ *Via Porta Rossa 77–79/r, Piazza della Repubblica* ☎ *055/215774.*

Carlo Piccini

JEWELRY & WATCHES | Still in operation after four generations, this Florentine institution sells antique jewelry and makes pieces to order; you can also get old jewelry reset here. ⊠ *Ponte Vecchio 31/r, Piazza della Signoria* ☎ *055/292030.*

Diesel

MIXED CLOTHING | Trendy Diesel started in Vicenza; its gear is on the "must have" list of many Italian teens. ⊠ *Via degli Speziali 16/r, Piazza della Signoria* ☎ *055/2399963* ⊕ *www.diesel.com.*

Mandragora Art Store

SOUVENIRS | This is one of the first attempts in Florence to cash in on the museum-store craze. In store are reproductions of valued works of art and jewelry. ⊠ *Piazza del Duomo 50/r, Duomo* ☎ *055/2654384* ⊕ *www.mandragora.it.*

Mercato dei Fiori (flower market)

MARKET | Every Thursday morning from September through June the covered loggia in Piazza della Repubblica hosts a Mercato dei Fiori; it's awash in a lively riot of plants, flowers, and difficult-to-find herbs. ⊠ *Piazza della Repubblica.*

Mercato del Porcellino

MARKET | **FAMILY** | If you're looking for cheery, inexpensive trinkets to take home, roam through the stalls under the loggia of the Mercato del Porcellino. ⊠ *Via Por Santa Maria at Via Porta Rossa, Piazza della Repubblica.*

Oro Due

JEWELRY & WATCHES | Gold jewelry and other beauteous objects are priced according to the level of craftsmanship and the price of gold bullion that day. ⊠ *Via Lambertesca 12/r, Piazza della Signoria* ☎ *055/292143* ⊗ *Closed Sun.*

Patrizia Pepe

WOMEN'S CLOTHING | The Florentine designer has clothes for mostly really thin young people, especially for women with a tiny streak of rebelliousness. Sizes run extremely small. ⊠ *Via Strozzi 13/r, Duomo* ☎ *055/2302518* ⊕ *www.patrizia-pepe.com.*

★ Pegna

FOOD | Looking for some cheddar cheese to pile in your panino? Pegna has been selling both Italian and non-Italian food since 1860. ⊠ *Via dello Studio 8, Duomo* ☎ *055/282701* ⊕ *www.pegna.it.*

★ Penko

JEWELRY & WATCHES | Renaissance goldsmiths provide the inspiration for this dazzling jewelry with a contemporary feel. ⊠ *Via dell'Oca 20–22/r, Duomo* ☎ *055/2052577* ⊕ *www.paolopenko.com.*

Spazio A

WOMEN'S CLOTHING | For cutting-edge fashion, these fun and funky window displays merit a stop. The shop carries such well-known designers as Alberta Ferretti and Moschino, as well as lesser-known Italian, English, and French designers. ⊠ *Via Porta Rossa 109–115/r, Piazza della Repubblica* ☎ *055/6582109.*

San Lorenzo

A sculptor, painter, architect, and poet, Florentine native son Michelangelo was a consummate genius, and some of his finest creations remain in his hometown The Biblioteca Medicea Laurenziana is perhaps his most fanciful work of architecture. A key to understanding Michelangelo's genius can be found in the magnificent Cappelle Medicee, where both his sculptural and architectural prowess can be clearly seen. Planned frescoes were never completed, sadly, for they would have shown in one space the artistic triple threat that he certainly was. The towering yet graceful *David*, perhaps his most famous work, resides in the Galleria dell'Accademia.

After visiting San Lorenzo, resist the temptation to explore the market that surrounds the church: the market is open until 7 pm, while the churches and museums you may want to visit are not. Come back to the market later, after other sites have closed. Note that the Museo di San Marco closes at 1:50 on weekdays.

Sights

Biblioteca Medicea Laurenziana
(Laurentian Library)

LIBRARY | Michelangelo the architect was every bit as original as Michelangelo the sculptor. Unlike Brunelleschi (the architect of the Spedale degli Innocenti), however, he wasn't obsessed with proportion and perfect geometry. He was interested in experimentation and invention and in the expression of a personal vision that was at times highly idiosyncratic. It was never more idiosyncratic than in the Laurentian Library, begun in 1524 and finished in 1568 by Bartolomeo Ammannati.

s famous **vestibolo,** a strangely shaped anteroom, has had scholars scratching their heads for centuries. In a space more than two stories high, why did Michelangelo limit his use of columns and pilasters to the upper two-thirds of the wall? Why didn't he rest them on strong pedestals instead of on huge, decorative curlicue scrolls, which rob them of all visual support? Why did he recess them into the wall, which makes them look weaker still? The architectural elements here do not stand firm and strong and tall as inside San Lorenzo next door; instead, they seem to be pressed into the wall as if into putty, giving the room a soft, rubbery look that is one of the strangest effects ever achieved by 16th-century architecture. It's almost as if Michelangelo intentionally flouted the conventions of the High Renaissance to see what kind of bizarre, mannered effect might result. His innovations were tremendously influential, and produced a period of architectural experimentation. As his contemporary Giorgio Vasari put it, "Artisans have been infinitely and perpetually indebted to him because he broke the bonds and chains of a way of working that had become habitual by common usage." The anteroom's staircase (best viewed straight on), which emerges from the library with the visual force of an unstoppable lava flow, has been exempted from the criticism, however. In its highly sculptural conception and execution, it is quite simply one of the most original and fluid staircases in the world. ⊠ Piazza San Lorenzo 9, entrance to left of San Lorenzo, San Lorenzo ⊕ www. bmlonline.it 🎫 Special exhibitions €3 ⊘ Closed weekends.

Cappelle Medicee (Medici Chapels) **CHURCH** | This magnificent complex includes the **Cappella dei Principi,** the Medici chapel and mausoleum that was begun in 1605 and kept marble workers busy for several hundred years, and the **Sagrestia Nuova** (New Sacristy), designed by Michelangelo and so called

to distinguish it from Brunelleschi's Sagrestia Vecchia (Old Sacristy) in San Lorenzo. Michelangelo received the commission for the New Sacristy in 1520 from Cardinal Giulio de' Medici (1478–1534), who later became Pope Clement VII. The cardinal wanted a new burial chapel for his cousins Giuliano, Duke of Nemours (1478–1534), and Lorenzo, Duke of Urbino (1492–1519), and he also wanted to honor his father, also named Giuliano, and his uncle, Lorenzo il Magnifico. The result was a tour de force of architecture and sculpture. Architecturally, Michelangelo was as original and inventive here as ever, but it is, quite properly, the powerfully sculpted tombs that dominate the room. The scheme is allegorical: on the tomb on the right are figures representing Day and Night, and on the tomb to the left are figures representing Dawn and Dusk; above them are idealized sculptures of the two men, usually interpreted to represent the active life and the contemplative life. But the allegorical meanings are secondary; what is most important is the intense presence of the sculptural figures and the force with which they hit the viewer. ⊠ Piazza di Madonna degli Aldobrandini, San Lorenzo 🕾 055/294883 reservations ⊕ www.cappellemedicee.it 🎫 €9 ⊘ Closed 1st, 3rd, and 5th Mon., and 2nd and 4th Sun. of month.

Galleria dell'Accademia (Accademia Gallery)
ART MUSEUM | FAMILY | The collection of Florentine paintings, dating from the 13th to 18th century, is largely unremarkable, but the sculptures by Michelangelo are worth the price of admission. The unfinished Slaves, fighting their way out of their marble prisons, were meant for the tomb of Michelangelo's overly demanding patron Pope Julius II (1443–1513). But the focal point is the original David, moved here from Piazza della Signoria in 1873. David was commissioned in 1501 by the Opera del Duomo (Cathedral Works Committee), which gave the

26-year-old sculptor a leftover block of marble that had been ruined 40 years earlier by two other sculptors. Michelangelo's success with the block was so dramatic that the city showered him with honors, and the Opera del Duomo voted to build him a house and a studio in which to live and work. Today *David* is beset not by Goliath but by tourists, and seeing the statue at all—much less really studying it—can be a trial. Save yourself a long wait in line by reserving tickets in advance. A plexiglass barrier surrounds the sculpture, following a 1991 attack on it by a self-proclaimed hammer-wielding art anarchist who, luckily, inflicted only a few minor nicks on the toes. The statue is not quite what it seems. It is so poised and graceful and alert—so miraculously alive—that it is often considered the definitive sculptural embodiment of High Renaissance perfection. But its true place in the history of art is a bit more complicated. As Michelangelo well knew, the Renaissance painting and sculpture that preceded his work were deeply concerned with ideal form. Perfection of proportion was the ever-sought Holy Grail; during the Renaissance, ideal proportion was equated with ideal beauty, and ideal beauty was equated with spiritual perfection. But *David*, despite its supremely calm and dignified pose, departs from these ideals. Michelangelo didn't give the statue perfect proportions. The head is slightly too large for the body, the arms are too large for the torso, and the hands are dramatically large for the arms. The work was originally commissioned to adorn the exterior of the Duomo and was intended to be seen from a distance and on high. Michelangelo knew exactly what he was doing, calculating that the perspective of the viewer would be such that, in order for the statue to appear proportioned, the upper body, head, and arms would have to be bigger, as they are farther away from the viewer. But he also did it to express and embody, as powerfully as possible in a single figure,

an entire biblical story. David's hands *are* big, but so was Goliath, and these are the hands that slew him. Music lovers might want to check out the Museo degli Instrumenti Musicali contained within the Accademia; its Stradivarius is the main attraction. ⊠ *Via Ricasoli 60, San Marco* ☎ *055/294883 reservations, 055/2388609 gallery* ⊕ *www.polomuseale.firenze.it* ⌫ *€12; reservation fee €4* ⊘ *Closed Mon.*

★ **Mercato Centrale**

MARKET | FAMILY | Some of the food at this huge, two-story market hall is remarkably exotic. The ground floor contains meat and cheese stalls, as well as some very good bars that have panini. In 2014, a second-floor food hall opened, eerily reminiscent of food halls everywhere. The quality of the food served, however, more than makes up for this. The downstairs market is closed on Sundays: the upstairs food hall is always open. ⊠ *Piazza del Mercato Centrale, San Lorenzo* ☎ *2399798,* ⊕ *www.mercatocentrale.it.*

Museo di Casa Martelli

HISTORIC HOME | The wealthy Martelli family, long associated with the all-powerful Medici, lived, from the 16th century, in this palace on a quiet street near the basilica of San Lorenzo. The last Martelli died in 1986, and in October 2009 the *casa-museo* (house-museum) opened to the public. It's the only nonreconstructed example of such a house in all of Florence, and for that reason alone it's worth a visit. The family collected art, and while most of the stuff is B-list, a few gems by Beccafumi, Salvatore Rosa, and Piero di Cosimo adorn the walls. Reservations are essential, and you will be shown the glories of this place by well-informed, English-speaking guides. ⊠ *Via Zanetti 8, San Lorenzo* ☎ *055/294883* ⊕ *www.polomuseale.firenze.it* ⊘ *Closed Mon.–Wed., Fri., and 1st, 3rd, and 5th Sun. of month.*

Museo di San Marco

ART MUSEUM | A Dominican convent adjacent to the church of San Marco now

Florence's Trial by Fire

One of the most striking figures of Renaissance Florence was Girolamo Savonarola, a Dominican friar who, for a moment, captured the spiritual conscience of the city. In 1491 he became prior of the convent of San Marco, where he adopted a life of austerity and delivered sermons condemning Florence's excesses and the immorality of his fellow clergy. Following the death of Lorenzo de' Medici in 1492, Savonarola was instrumental in the re-formation of the republic of Florence, ruled by a representative council with Christ enthroned as monarch. In one of his most memorable acts he urged Florentines to toss worldly possessions—from sumptuous dresses to Botticelli paintings—onto a "bonfire of the vanities" in Piazza della Signoria. Savonarola's antagonism toward church hierarchy led to his undoing: he was excommunicated in 1497, and the following year was hanged and burned on charges of heresy. Today, at the Museo di San Marco, you can visit Savonarola's cell.

houses this museum, which contains many stunning works by Fra Angelico (circa 1400–55), the Dominican friar famous for his piety as well as for his painting. When the friars' cells were restructured between 1439 and 1444, he decorated many of them with frescoes meant to spur religious contemplation. His unostentatious and direct paintings exalt the simple beauties of the contemplative life. Fra Angelico's works are everywhere, from the friars' cells to the superb panel paintings on view in the museum. Don't miss the famous *Annunciation,* on the upper floor, and the works in the gallery off the cloister as you enter. Here you can see his beautiful *Last Judgment;* as usual, the tortures of the damned are far more inventive and interesting than the pleasures of the redeemed. ⊠ *Piazza San Marco 1, San Lorenzo* ☎ *055/294883* ⊕ *www.polomuseale.firenze.it* ⊠ *€8* ⊗ *Closed 1st, 3rd, and 5th Sun., and 2nd and 4th Mon. of month.*

Palazzo Medici-Riccardi

CASTLE/PALACE | The main attraction of this palace, begun in 1444 by Michelozzo for Cosimo de' Medici, is the interior chapel, the so-called **Cappella dei Magi** on the piano nobile. Painted on its walls is Benozzo Gozzoli's famous *Procession of the Magi,* finished in 1460 and celebrating both the birth of Christ and the greatness of the Medici family. Gozzoli wasn't a revolutionary painter, and today is considered by some not quite first-rate because of his technique, which was old-fashioned even for his day. Gozzoli's gift, however, was for entrancing the eye, not challenging the mind, and on those terms his success here is beyond question. Entering the chapel is like walking into the middle of a magnificently illustrated children's storybook, and this beauty makes it one of the most enjoyable rooms in the city. ⊠ *Via Cavour 1, San Lorenzo* ☎ *055/2768224* ⊕ *www.palazzomediciriccardi.it* ⊗ *Closed Wed.* ⊠ *€7.*

San Lorenzo

CHURCH | Filippo Brunelleschi designed this basilica, as well as that of Santo Spirito in the Oltrarno, in the 15th century. He never lived to see either finished. The two interiors are similar in design and effect. San Lorenzo, however, has a grid of dark, inlaid marble lines on the floor, which considerably heightens the dramatic effect. The grid makes the rigorous geometry of the interior immediately

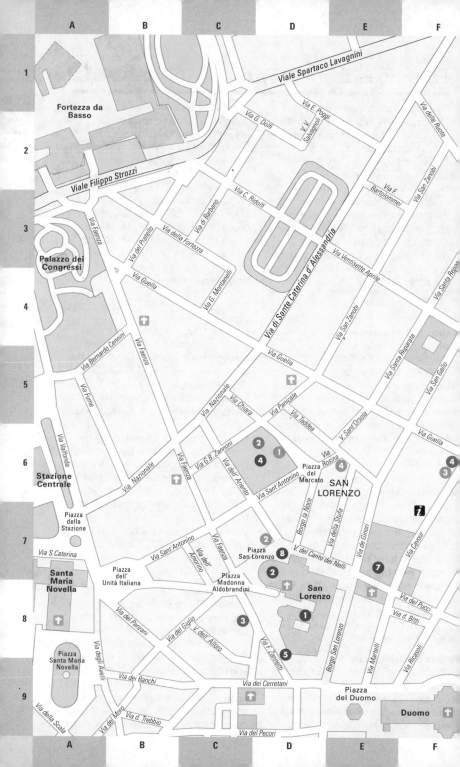

San Lorenzo

Sights ▼

1 Biblioteca Medicea
   Laurenziana **D8**
2 Cappelle Medicee **D7**
3 Galleria dell'Accademia **H5**
4 Mercato Centrale **D6**
5 Museo di Casa Martelli **D8**
6 Museo di San Marco **H4**
7 Palazzo Medici-Riccardi **E7**
8 San Lorenzo **D7**
9 Santissima Annunziata **I6**
10 Spedale degli Innocenti **I6**

Restaurants ▼

1 da Nerbone **D6**
2 da Sergio **D7**
3 Il Desco **F6**
4 Mario **E6**

Quick Bites ▼

1 Alfio e Beppe **G5**
2 Baroni **C6**

Hotels ▼

1 Antica Dimora Johanna I **G1**
2 Antica Dimora Johlea **H2**
3 Firenze Number Nine **C8**
4 Il Guelfo Bianco **F6**

KEY

1 *Exploring Sights*
1 *Restaurants*
1 *Quick Bites*
1 *Hotels*
🛈 *Tourist information*

visible, and is an illuminating lesson on the laws of perspective. If you stand in the middle of the nave at the church entrance, on the line that stretches to the high altar, every element in the church—the grid, the nave columns, the side aisles, the coffered nave ceiling—seems to march inexorably toward a hypothetical vanishing point beyond the high altar, exactly as in a single-point-perspective painting. Brunelleschi's **Sagrestia Vecchia** (Old Sacristy) has stucco decorations by Donatello; it's at the end of the left transept. ⊠ *Piazza San Lorenzo, San Lorenzo* 🎫 *€7* ☉ *Closed Sun.*

Santissima Annunziata

CHURCH | Dating from the mid-13th century, this church was restructured in 1447 by Michelozzo, who gave it an uncommon (and lovely) entrance cloister with frescoes by Andrea del Sarto (1486–1530), Pontormo (1494–1556), and Rosso Fiorentino (1494–1540). The interior is a rarity for Florence: an overwhelming example of Baroque. But it's not really a fair example, because it's merely 17th-century Baroque decoration applied willy-nilly to an earlier structure—exactly the sort of violent remodeling exercise that has given Baroque a bad name. The **Cappella dell'Annunziata,** immediately inside the entrance to the left, illustrates the point. The lower half, with its stately Corinthian columns and carved frieze bearing the Medici arms, was commissioned by Piero de' Medici in 1447; the upper half, with its erupting curves and impish sculpted cherubs, was added 200 years later. Fifteenth-century-fresco enthusiasts should also note the very fine *Holy Trinity with St. Jerome* in the second chapel on the left. Done by Andrea del Castagno (circa 1421–57), it shows a wiry and emaciated St. Jerome with Paula and Eustochium, two of his closest followers. This church, unlike many others in Florence, is highly active: please do not enter if Mass is in progress. ⊠ *Piazza di Santissima Annunziata, San Lorenzo.*

Spedale degli Innocenti

ART MUSEUM | **FAMILY** | The building built by Brunelleschi in 1419 to serve as an orphanage takes the historical prize as the very first Renaissance building. Brunelleschi designed its portico with his usual rigor, constructing it from the two shapes he considered mathematically (and therefore philosophically and aesthetically) perfect: the square and the circle. Below the level of the arches, the portico encloses a row of perfect cubes; above the level of the arches, the portico encloses a row of intersecting hemispheres. The entire geometric scheme is articulated with Corinthian columns, capitals, and arches borrowed directly from antiquity. At the time he designed the portico, Brunelleschi was also designing the interior of San Lorenzo, using the same basic ideas. But because the portico was finished before San Lorenzo, the Spedale degli Innocenti can claim the honor of ushering in Renaissance architecture. The 10 ceramic medallions depicting swaddled infants that decorate the portico are by Andrea della Robbia (1435–1525/28), done in about 1487. Within the Spedale degli Innocenti is a small museum, or Pinacoteca (*€7; Mon.–Fri. 9–1*). Most of the objects are minor works by major artists, but well worth a look is Domenico Ghirlandaio's (1449–94) *Adorazione dei Magi* (*Adoration of the Magi*), executed in 1488. His use of color and his eye for flora and fauna, shows that art from north of the Alps made a great impression on him. ⊠ *Piazza di Santissima Annunziata 12, San Lorenzo* ☎ *055/20371* ⊕ *www.istitutodeglinnocenti.it* 🎫 *€10.*

🍴 Restaurants

★ da Nerbone

$ | **TUSCAN** | This *tavola calda* (cafeteria) in the middle of the covered Mercato Centrale has been serving up food to Florentines who like their tripe since 1872. Tasty primi and secondi are available every day, but cognoscenti come for the *panino con il lampredotto* (tripe sandwich). **Known for:** favorite dishes sell out; tripe sandwich; frequented by locals (and everyone else). $ *Average main: €10 ⊠ Mercato San Lorenzo, Florence ♥ Closed Sun. No dinner.*

★ da Sergio

$ | TUSCAN | Run by the Gozzi family for just over a hundred years, the food here is delicious, affordable, and just across the way from the basilica of San Lorenzo. The menu is short, and changes daily. **Known for:** lunch only; ever-changing menu; local favorite. $ *Average main: €10 ⊠ Piazza San Lorenzo 8/r, San Lorenzo ☎ 281941 ♥ Closed Sun. No dinner Mon.–Thurs.*

Il Desco

$ | TUSCAN | The Bargiacchi family, also proprietors of the lovely hotel Guelfo Bianco just next door, source much of what is on the frequently changing menu from their organic farm in the Tuscan countryside. The menu plays to all tastes—Tuscan classics such as *peposo* (a hearty, black pepper–filled beef stew) can be found, as well as vegetarian dishes. **Known for:** clever wine list; just a few tables; fine vegetarian and vegan dishes. $ *Average main: €14 ⊠ Via Cavour 55/r, San Lorenzo ☎ 055/288330 ⊕ www. ildescofirenze.it.*

★ Mario

$ | TUSCAN | Florentines flock to this narrow family-run trattoria near San Lorenzo to feast on Tuscan favorites served at simple tables under a wooden ceiling dating from 1536. A distinct cafeteria feel and genuine Florentine hospitality prevail: you'll be seated wherever there's room, which often means with strangers. **Known for:** festive atmosphere; grilled meats; roasted potatoes. $ *Average main: €13 ⊠ Via Rosina 2/r, corner of Piazza del Mercato Centrale, San Lorenzo ☎ 055/218550 ⊕ www.trattoriamario.com ♥ Closed Sun. and Aug. No dinner.*

☕ Coffee and Quick Bites

Alfio e Beppe

$ | ITALIAN | Watch chickens roast over high flames as you decide which of the other delightful things you're going to eat with it. The beauty of this place is that it's open on Sunday when most places are not. **Known for:** roasted dishes; grilled vegetables; open Sunday. $ *Average main: €9 ⊠ Via Cavour 118–120/r, San Marco ☎ 055/214108 ♥ Closed Sat.*

★ Baroni

$ | INTERNATIONAL | The cheese collection at Baroni may be the most comprehensive in Florence. They also have high-quality truffle products, vinegars, and other delicacies. **Known for:** products packed for shipping; expansive cheese selection; top-notch foodstuffs. $ *Average main: €10 ⊠ Mercato Central, enter at Via Signa, San Lorenzo ☎ 055/289576 ⊕ www.baronialimentari.it.*

Hotels

Antica Dimora Johanna I

$ | B&B/INN | Savvy travelers and those on a budget should look no further, as this *residenza* is a tremendous value for quality and location, and though it's very much in the centro storico, the place is rather homey. **Pros:** many great, inexpensive restaurants nearby; morning tea and coffee served in your room; in a quiet neighborhood. **Cons:** no credit cards; staff go home at 7 pm; might be too removed for some. $ *Rooms from: €110 ⊠ Via Bonifacio Lupi 14, San Marco ☎ 055/481896 ⊕ www.antichedimorefiorentine.it ⤳ 10 rooms ⦿ Free Breakfast.*

★ Antica Dimora Johlea

$ | B&B/INN | Lively color runs rampant on the top floor of this 19th-century palazzo, with a charming flower-filled rooftop terrace where you can sip a glass of wine while taking in a view of Brunelleschi's cupola. **Pros:** honor bar; great staff; cheerful rooms. **Cons:** narrow staircase to get to roof terrace; staff goes home at 7:30; steps to breakfast room. Ⓢ *Rooms from: €119* ✉ *Via San Gallo 80, San Marco* ☎ *055/4633292* ⊕ *www.antichedimorefiorentine.it* ⊸ *6 rooms* ⦿ *Free Breakfast.*

Firenze Number Nine

$$$ | **HOTEL** | Those wanting an elegant hotel with a walk-in gym in the historic center have found their match: swank reception rooms, vividly decorated, have comfortable couches to sink into, and works by contemporary artists adorn the walls. **Pros:** sumptuous breakfast; location; walk-in gym and spa. **Cons:** might be too trendy for some; some street noise; books up quickly. Ⓢ *Rooms from: €300* ✉ *del Conti 9, San Lorenzo* ☎ *055/293777* ⊕ *www.firenzenumber-nine.com* ⊸ *45 rooms* ⦿ *Free Breakfast.*

Il Guelfo Bianco

$$ | **HOTEL** | The 15th-century building has all modern conveniences, but Renaissance charm still shines in the high-ceiling rooms. **Pros:** sumptuous breakfast; great staff; restaurant Il Desco is on-site. **Cons:** might be too removed for some; rooms facing the street can be noisy; not all rooms are well lit. Ⓢ *Rooms from: €140* ✉ *Via Cavour 29, San Marco* ☎ *055/288330* ⊕ *www.ilguelfobianco.it* ⦿ *Free Breakfast* ⊸ *40 rooms.*

Nightlife

Kitsch

BARS | Choose from indoor or outdoor seating and take advantage of the great list of wines by the glass. At aperitivo time €12 will buy you a truly tasty cocktail and give you access to the tremendous buffet; it's so good, you won't need dinner afterward—in fact, they called it "Apericena." That means, roughly, drink and dinner. ✉ *Via San Gallo 22/r, San Marco* ☎ *055/3841358* ⊕ *www.kitschfirenze.com.*

Shopping

Mercato Centrale

MARKET | **FAMILY** | This huge indoor food market offers a staggering selection of all things edible. Downstairs is full of vendors hawking their wares—meat, fish, fruit, vegetables; upstairs (daily 8 am–midnight) is full of food stalls serving up the best of what Italy has to offer. ✉ *Piazza del Mercato Centrale, San Lorenzo* ☎ *2399798* ⊕ *www.mercato-centrale.it* ⊘ *Downstairs closed Sun. and after 2 pm Mon.–Sat.*

Mercato di San Lorenzo

MARKET | **FAMILY** | The clothing and leather-goods stalls of the Mercato di San Lorenzo in the streets next to the church of San Lorenzo have bargains for shoppers on a budget. ✉ *Florence.*

Santa Maria Novella

Piazza Santa Maria Novella is a gorgeous, pedestrian-only square, with grass (laced with roses) and plenty of places to sit and rest your feet. The streets in and around the piazza have their share of architectural treasures, including some of Florence's most tasteful palaces. Between Santa Maria Novella and the Arno is Via Tornabuoni, Florence's swankiest shopping street.

Sights

Museo Novecento

ART MUSEUM | It began life as a 13th-century Franciscan hostel offering shelter to tired pilgrims. It later became a convalescent home, and in the late 18th century it was a school for poor girls. Now the former Ospedale di San Paolo houses a museum devoted to Italian art of the 20th century. Admittedly, most of these artists are not exactly household names, but the museum is so beautifully well done that it's worth a visit. The second floor contains works by artists from the second half of the century; start on the third floor, and go directly to the collection of Alberto della Ragione, a naval engineer who was determined to be on the cutting edge of art collecting. ⊠ *Piazza Santa Maria Novella 10, Santa Maria Novella* ☎ *055/286132* ⊕ *www. museonovecento.it* ☜ *€9.50* ☯ *Closed Thurs.*

Museo Salvatore Ferragamo

ART MUSEUM | Almost like a shrine to footwear, the shoes in this dramatically displayed collection were designed by Salvatore Ferragamo (1898–1960) beginning in the early 20th century. Born in southern Italy, Ferragamo jump-started his career in Hollywood by creating shoes for the likes of Mary Pickford and Rudolph Valentino. He then returned to Florence and set up shop in the 13th-century Palazzo Spini Ferroni. The collection includes about 16,000 shoes, and those on exhibition are frequently rotated. Special exhibitions are also mounted here and are well worth visiting—past shows have been devoted to Audrey Hepburn, Greta Garbo, and Marilyn Monroe. ⊠ *Via dei Tornabuoni 2, Santa Maria Novella* ☎ *055/3562846* ⊕ *www.ferragamo.com* ☜ *€8.*

Museo Stibbert

ART MUSEUM | Frederick Stibbert (1838–1906), born in Florence to an Italian mother and an English father, liked to collect things. Over a lifetime of doing so, he amassed some 50,000 objects. This museum, which was also his home, displays many of them. He had a fascination with medieval armor and also collected costumes, particularly Uzbek costumes, which are exhibited in a room called the Moresque Hall. These are mingled with an extensive collection of swords, guns, and other devices whose sole function was to kill people. The paintings, most of which date from the 15th century, are largely second-rate. The house itself is an interesting amalgam of neo-Gothic, Renaissance, and English eccentric. To get here, take Bus No. 4 (across the street from the station at Santa Maria Novella) and get off at the stop marked "Fabbroni 4," then follow signs to the museum. ⊠ *Via Federico Stibbert 26, Florence* ☎ *055/486049* ⊕ *www.museostibbert.it* ☜ *€6* ☯ *Closed Thurs.*

Palazzo Strozzi

HISTORIC HOME | The Strozzi family built this imposing palazzo in an attempt to outshine the nearby Palazzo Medici. Based on a model by Giuliano da Sangallo (circa 1452–1516) dating from around 1489 and executed between 1489 and 1504 under il Cronaca (1457–1508) and Benedetto da Maiaino (1442–97), it was inspired by Michelozzo's earlier Palazzo Medici-Riccardi. The palazzo's exterior is simple, severe, and massive: it's a testament to the wealth of a patrician, 15th-century Florentine family. The interior courtyard, entered from the rear of the palazzo, is another matter altogether. It is here that the classical vocabulary—columns, capitals, pilasters, arches, and cornices—is given uninhibited and powerful expression. The palazzo frequently hosts blockbuster art shows. ⊠ *Via Tornabuoni, Piazza della Repubblica* ☎ *055/2645155* ⊕ *www.palazzostrozzi.org* ☜ *Free.*

Santa Maria Novella

CHURCH | The facade of this church looks distinctly clumsy by later Renaissance standards, and with good reason: it is an architectural hybrid. The lower half was completed mostly in the 14th century; its pointed-arch niches and decorative marble patterns reflect the Gothic style of the day. About 100 years later (around 1456), architect Leon Battista Alberti was called in to complete the job. The marble decoration of his upper story clearly defers to the already existing work below, but the architectural motifs he added evince an entirely different style. The central doorway, the four ground-floor half-columns with Corinthian capitals, the triangular pediment atop the second story, the inscribed frieze

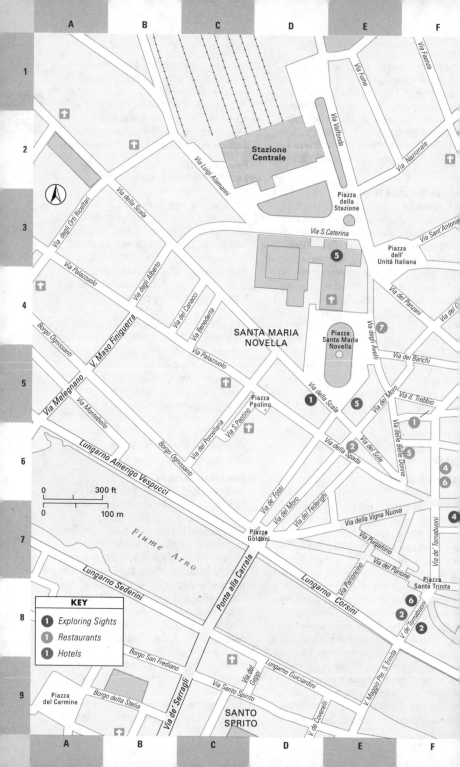

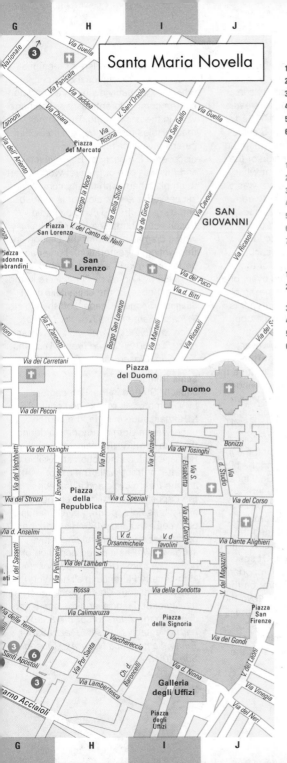

Santa Maria Novella

Sights ▼

1	Museo Novecento	**D5**
2	Museo Salvatore Ferragamo	**F8**
3	Museo Stibbert	**G1**
4	Palazzo Strozzi	**F7**
5	Santa Maria Novella	**E4**
6	Santa Trinita	**F8**

Restaurants ▼

1	Cantinetta Antinori	**F5**
2	La Spada	**E6**
3	Mangiafoco	**G8**
4	Obicà	**F6**
5	Osteria delle Belle Donne	**F6**
6	Procacci	**F6**
7	Vincanto	**E4**

Hotels ▼

1	Alessandra	**G9**
2	Antica Torre di Via Tornabuoni	**F8**
3	Gallery Hotel Art	**G9**
4	Nuova Italia	**F2**
5	The Place Firenze	**E5**
6	Torre Guelfa	**G8**

immediately below the pediment—these are borrowings from antiquity, and they reflect the new Renaissance style in architecture, born some 35 years earlier at the Spedale degli Innocenti. Alberti's most important addition—the S-curve scrolls (called volutes) surmounting the decorative circles on either side of the upper story—had no precedent whatsoever in antiquity. The problem was to soften the abrupt transition between wide ground floor and narrow upper story. Alberti's solution turned out to be definitive. Once you start to look for them, you will find scrolls such as these (or sculptural variations of them) on churches all over Italy, and every one of them derives from Alberti's example here. The architecture of the interior is, like that of the Duomo, a dignified but somber example of Florentine Gothic. Exploration is essential, however, because the church's store of art treasures is remarkable. Highlights include the 14th-century stained-glass rose window depicting the *Coronation of the Virgin* (above the central entrance); the Cappella Filippo Strozzi (to the right of the altar), containing late-15th-century frescoes and stained glass by Filippino Lippi; the *cappella maggiore* (the area around the high altar), displaying frescoes by Ghirlandaio; and the Cappella Gondi (to the left of the altar), containing Filippo Brunelleschi's famous wood crucifix, carved around 1410 and said to have so stunned the great Donatello when he first saw it that he dropped a basket of eggs. Of special interest for its great historical importance and beauty is Masaccio's *Trinity*, on the left-hand wall, almost halfway down the nave. Painted around 1426–27 (at the same time he was working on his frescoes in Santa Maria del Carmine), it unequivocally announced the arrival of the Renaissance. The realism of the figure of Christ was revolutionary in itself, but what was probably even more startling to contemporary Florentines was the barrel vault in the background. The mathematical rules for employing single-point perspective in painting had just been discovered (probably by Brunelleschi), and this was one of the first works of art to employ them with utterly convincing success. In the first cloister is a faded and damaged fresco cycle by Paolo Uccello depicting tales from Genesis, with a dramatic vision of the Deluge (at this writing, in restoration). Earlier and better-preserved frescoes painted in 1348–55 by Andrea da Firenze are in the chapter house, or the **Cappellone degli Spagnoli** (Spanish Chapel), off the cloister. ✉ *Piazza Santa Maria Novella 19, Florence* ☎ *055/219257 museo* ⊕ *www.smn.it/en* 🎫 *€7.50* ⊗ *Closed Tues.–Wed. and Sat.–Sun. Closed Thurs.–Fri. Apr.–Sept.*

Santa Trinita

CHURCH | Started in the 11th century by Vallombrosian monks and originally Romanesque in style, the church underwent a Gothic remodeling during the 14th century. (Remains of the Romanesque construction are visible on the interior front wall.) The major works are the fresco cycle and altarpiece in the Cappella Sassetti, the second to the high altar's right, painted by Ghirlandaio between 1480 and 1485. His work here possesses such graceful decorative appeal as well as a proud depiction of his native city (most of the cityscapes show 15th-century Florence in all her glory). The wall frescoes illustrate scenes from the life of St. Francis, and the altarpiece, depicting the *Adoration of the Shepherds*, veritably glows. ✉ *Piazza Santa Trinita, Santa Maria Novella* ⊗ *Closed Sun. 10:45–4.*

Meet the Medici

The Medici were the dominant family of Renaissance Florence, wielding political power and financing some of the world's greatest art. You'll see their names at every turn around the city. These are some of the more notable family members:

Cosimo il Vecchio (1389–1464), incredibly wealthy banker to the popes, was the first in the family line to act as de facto ruler of Florence. He was a great patron of the arts and architecture; he was the moving force behind the family palace and the Dominican complex of San Marco.

Lorenzo il Magnifico (1449–92), grandson of Cosimo il Vecchio, presided over a Florence largely at peace with her neighbors. A collector of cameos, a writer of sonnets, and a lover of ancient texts, he was the preeminent Renaissance man and, like his grandfather, the de facto ruler of Florence.

Leo X (1475–1521), also known as Giovanni de' Medici, became the first Medici pope, helping extend the family power base to include Rome and the Papal States. His reign was characterized by a host of problems, the biggest one being a former friar named Martin Luther.

Catherine de' Medici (1519–89) was married by her great uncle Pope Clement VII to Henry of Valois, who later became Henry II of France. Wife of one king and mother of three, she was the first Medici to marry into European royalty. Lorenzo il Magnifico, her great-grandfather, would have been thrilled.

Cosimo I (1537–74), the first grand duke of Tuscany, should not be confused with his ancestor Cosimo il Vecchio.

Restaurants

Cantinetta Antinori

$$$ | TUSCAN | After a morning of shopping on Via Tornabuoni, stop for lunch in this 15th-century palazzo in the company of Florentine ladies and men who come to see and be seen over lunch. The panache of the food matches its clientele: expect treats such as *tramezzino con pane di campagna al tartufo* (country pâté with truffles served on bread) and the *insalata di gamberoni e gamberetti con carciofi freschi* (crayfish and prawn salad with shaved raw artichokes). **Known for:** high prices to match the excellent food and wine; chic clientele; most ingredients come from the family farm. $ *Average main: €28* ⊠ *Piazza Antinori 3, Santa Maria Novella* ☎ *055/292234* ⊕ *www.cantinetta-antinori.com* ☉ *Closed Sun., 20 days in Aug., and Dec. 25–Jan. 6.*

La Spada

$ | ITALIAN | FAMILY | Near Santa Maria Novella is La Spada. Walk in and inhale the fragrant aromas of meats cooking in the wood-burning oven. **Known for:** aromatic pastas; adherence to Tuscan cuisine; grilled meats. $ *Average main: €11* ⊠ *Via della Spada 62/r, Santa Maria Novella* ☎ *055/218757.*

★ Mangiafoco

$$ | TUSCAN | Created by Francesco and Elisa in 2001, this small, brightly painted spot in the heart of the centro storico on a romantic medieval side street serves Tuscan classics *con fantasia* (with fantasy).

The menu changes daily, reflecting both what's in season and the whims of the chef. **Known for:** creative, seasonal menu changes daily; phenomenal wines by the glass and by the bottle; great service. [$] *Average main: €20* ✉ *Borgo Santi Apostoli 26/r, Santa Maria Novella* ☎ *055/2658170* 🌐 *www.mangiafoco.com.*

Obicà

$$ | **ITALIAN** | Mozzarella takes center stage at this sleek eatery on Florence's swankiest street. The cheese, along with its culinary cousin *burrata* (a fresh cheese filled with cream), arrives daily from southern Italy to become the centerpiece for various salads and pastas. **Known for:** outdoor seating in nice weather; mozzarella-laden menu; outstanding pizza and desserts. [$] *Average main: €20* ✉ *Via Tornabuoni 16, Santa Maria Novella* ☎ *055/2773526* 🌐 *www.obica.com.*

Osteria delle Belle Donne

$ | **TUSCAN** | Down the street from the church of Santa Maria Novella, this gaily decorated spot, always festooned with some sort of creative decoration (ropes of garlic and other vegetables have figured in the past) has an ever-changing menu and stellar service led by the irrepressible Giacinto. The menu offers Tuscan standards, but shakes things up with alternatives such as *sedani con bacon, verza, e uova* (thick noodles sauced with bacon, cabbage, and egg); when avocados are ripe, they're on the menu, too (either with cold boiled shrimp or expertly grilled chicken breast). **Known for:** dessert; many dishes not typical of Tuscany; seasonal ingredients. [$] *Average main: €13* ✉ *Via delle Belle Donne 16/r, Santa Maria Novella* ☎ *055/2382609* 🌐 *www.casatrattoria.com.*

★ **Procacci**

$$ | **ITALIAN** | At this classy Florentine institution dating to 1885, try one of the truffle panini and swish it down with a glass of prosecco. **Known for:** serene (but tiny) space; pane tartufato; excellent wines by the glass. [$] *Average main: €15* ✉ *Via Tornabuoni 64/r, Santa Maria Novella* ☎ *055/211656* 🌐 *www.procacci1885.it* ⏲ *Closed Sun.*

Vincanto

$$$ | **ITALIAN** | It opens at 11 am and closes at midnight: this is a rarity in Florentine dining. They do a little bit of everything here, including fine pastas, salads, pizzas, and even an American-style breakfast. **Known for:** outside terrace with views of a beautiful square; a wide-ranging menu; kitchen stays open. [$] *Average main: €28* ✉ *Piazza Santa Maria Novella 23/r, Santa Maria Novella* ☎ *055/2679300* 🌐 *www.ristorantevincanto.com.*

Hotels

Alessandra

$$ | **B&B/INN** | **FAMILY** | An aura of grandeur pervades these clean, ample rooms a block from the Ponte Vecchio. **Pros:** tiny terrace allows for solitude while sipping a glass of wine; several rooms have views of the Arno; the spacious suite is a bargain. **Cons:** two rooms do not have en suite baths; stairs to elevator; some street noise. [$] *Rooms from: €145* ✉ *Borgo Santi Apostoli 17, Santa Maria Novella* ☎ *055/283438* 🌐 *www.hotelalessandra.com* ⏲ *Closed Dec. 10–28* 🛏 *30 rooms* 🍴 *Free Breakfast.*

Antica Torre di Via Tornabuoni

$$$$ | **B&B/INN** | If you're looking for a room with a view you'll find it here, where just about every room looks out onto the awe-inspiring Duomo or the Arno (some even have small terraces). **Pros:** views of the Arno and Duomo; rooftop terrace with restaurant; tasteful decor. **Cons:** some street noise; books up very quickly; no staff after 7 pm. [$] *Rooms from: €395* ✉ *Via Tornabuoni 1, Santa Maria Novella* ☎ *055/2658161* 🌐 *www.tornabuoni1.com* 🛏 *24 rooms* 🍴 *Free Breakfast.*

Gallery Hotel Art

$$$$ | HOTEL | High design resides at this art showcase near the Ponte Vecchio, where sleek, uncluttered rooms are dressed mostly in neutrals and luxe touches, such as leather headboards and kimono robes, abound. **Pros:** artistic touches; the in-house Fusion Bar serves delightful cocktails; trendy atmosphere. **Cons:** might be too trendy for some; books up quickly; some street noise. $ *Rooms from: €350* ⊠ *Vicolo dell'Oro 5, Santa Maria Novella* 🕾 *055/27263* ⊕ *www.lungarnocollection.com* ⇋ *74 rooms* ⦿ *No Meals.*

Nuova Italia

$ | HOTEL | FAMILY | The genial Viti family oversees these clean and simple rooms near the train station and well within walking distance of the sights. **Pros:** great for those on a budget; reasonable rates; close to everything. **Cons:** the neighborhood is highly trafficked; no elevator; some street noise. $ *Rooms from: €54* ⊠ *Via Faenza 26, Santa Maria Novella* 🕾 *055/268430* ⊕ *www.hotel-nuovaitalia.com* ⦿ *Free Breakfast* ⊗ *Closed Dec. 20–Dec. 27* ⇋ *20 rooms.*

★ The Place Firenze

$$$$ | HOTEL | Hard to spot from the street, this sumptuous place provides all the comforts of a luxe home away from home—expect soothing earth tones in the guest rooms, free minibars, crisp linens, and room service offering organic dishes. **Pros:** private, intimate feel; small dogs allowed; stellar staff. **Cons:** breakfast at a shared table; books up quickly; might be too trendy for some. $ *Rooms from: €442* ⊠ *Piazza Santa Maria Novella 7, Florence* 🕾 *055/2645181* ⊕ *www.theplacefirenze.com* ⇋ *20 rooms* ⦿ *Free Breakfast.*

Torre Guelfa

$$ | B&B/INN | If you want a taste of medieval Florence, try one of these character-filled guest rooms—some with canopied beds, some with balconies—housed within a 13th-century tower. **Pros:** some family-friendly triple and quadruple rooms; rooftop terrace with tremendous views; wonderful staff. **Cons:** some street noise; 72 steps to get to the terrace; books up quickly. $ *Rooms from: €199* ⊠ *Borgo Santi Apostoli 8, Santa Maria Novella* 🕾 *055/2396338* ⊕ *www.hotel-torreguelfa.com* ⇋ *39 rooms* ⦿ *Free Breakfast.*

Performing Arts

Maggio Musicale Fiorentino

MUSIC | After some delay due to funding issues, a new music hall opened in 2014; the area is called the Parco della Musica (Music Park), and was designed by Paolo Desideri and associates. Maggio Musicale has taken up residence there, and continues to hold forth at the Teatro Comunale (Corso Italia 16, Lungarno North, 055/287222). Within Italy you can purchase tickets from late April through July directly at the box office or by phone (055/2779309). You can also buy them online. ⊠ *Via Alamanni 39, Florence* 🕾 *055/2001278* ⊕ *www.operadifirenze.it.*

Tuscany Hall

FESTIVALS | This large exhibition space, formerly Teatro Saschall, hosts many events throughout the year, including a big and boisterous Christmas bazaar run by the Red Cross, visiting rock stars, and trendy bands from all over Europe. ⊠ *Lungarno Aldo Moro 3, Santa Maria Novella* 🕾 *055/6504112* ⊕ *www.tuscanyhall.it.*

🛍 Shopping

Alberto Cozzi

STATIONERY | You'll find an extensive line of Florentine papers and paper products here. The artisans in the shop rebind and restore books and works on paper. Their hours are tricky, so it's best to call first before stopping by. ⊠ *Via del Parione 35/r, Santa Maria Novella* 🕾 *055/294968.*

★ Angela Caputi

JEWELRY & WATCHES | Angela Caputi wows Florentine cognoscenti with her highly creative, often outsize plastic jewelry. A small, but equally creative, collection of women's clothing made of fine fabrics is also on offer. ✉ *Borgo Santi Apostoli 44/46, Florence* ☎ *055/292 993* ⊕ *www.angelacaputi.com.*

Antica Officina del Farmacista Dr. Vranjes

PERFUME | Dr. Vranjes elevates aromatherapy to an art form with scents for the body and home. ✉ *Via della Vigna Nuova 30/r, Florence* ☎ *055/0945851* ⊕ *www.drvranjes.it.*

Cellerini

LEATHER GOODS | In a city where it seems just about everybody wears an expensive leather jacket, Cellerini is an institution. ✉ *Via del Sole 9/r, Santa Maria Novella* ☎ *055/282533* ⊕ *www.cellerini.it.*

Emilio Pucci

WOMEN'S CLOTHING | The aristocratic Marchese di Barsento, Emilio Pucci, became an international name in the late 1950s when the stretch ski clothes he designed for himself caught on with the *dolce vita* crowd—his pseudopsychedelic prints and "palazzo pajamas" became all the rage. ✉ *Via Tornabuoni 20–22/r, Santa Maria Novella* ☎ *055/2658082* ⊕ *www.emiliopucci.com.*

Ferragamo

LEATHER GOODS | This classy institution, in a 13th-century palazzo, displays designer clothing and accessories, though elegant footwear still underlies the Ferragamo success. ✉ *Via Tornabuoni 14/r, Santa Maria Novella* ☎ *055/292123* ⊕ *www.ferragamo.com.*

Gatto Bianco

JEWELRY & WATCHES | This contemporary jeweler has breathtakingly beautiful pieces worked in semiprecious and precious stones. ✉ *Borgo Santi Apostoli 12/r, Santa Maria Novella* ☎ *055/282989* ⊕ *www.gattobiancogioielli.com.*

Giotti

LEATHER GOODS | You'll find a full line of leather goods, including clothing. ✉ *Piazza Ognissanti 3–4/r, Lungarno North* ☎ *055/294265* ⊕ *www.bottegagiotti.com/collection.*

★ Loretta Caponi

MIXED CLOTHING | Synonymous with Florentine embroidery, the luxury lace, linens, and lingerie have earned the eponymous signora worldwide renown. There's also beautiful (and expensive) clothing for children. ✉ *Via delle Belle Donne 28/r, Santa Maria Novella* ☎ *055/213668* ⊕ *www.lorettacaponi.com.*

★ Officina Profumo Farmaceutica di Santa Maria Novella

PERFUME | The essence of a Florentine holiday is captured in the sachets of this art nouveau emporium of herbal cosmetics and soaps that are made following centuries-old recipes created by friars. It celebrated its 400th birthday in 2012. ✉ *Via della Scala 16, Santa Maria Novella* ☎ *055/216276* ⊕ *www.smnovella.it.*

★ Pineider

STATIONERY | Although it has shops throughout the world, Pineider started out in Florence in 1774 and still does all its printing here. Stationery and business cards are the mainstay, but the stores also sell fine-leather desk accessories as well as a less stuffy, more lighthearted line of products. ✉ *Piazza Rucellai 4/7/r, Santa Maria Novella* ☎ *055/284656* ⊕ *www.pineider.com.*

Principe

DEPARTMENT STORE | This Florentine institution sells casual clothes for men, women, and children at far-from-casual prices. It also has a great housewares department. ✉ *Via del Sole 2, Santa Maria Novella* ☎ *055/292843* ⊕ *www.principedifirenze.com.*

Tiffany

JEWELRY & WATCHES | One of Florence's oldest jewelers has supplied Italian (and other) royalty with finely crafted gems for centuries. Its selection of antique-looking classics has been updated with contemporary silver. ⊠ *Via Tornabuoni 37/r, Santa Maria Novella* ☎ *800/215506* ⊕ *www.tiffany.it.*

Santa Croce

The Santa Croce quarter, on the southeast fringe of the historic center, was built up in the Middle Ages outside the second set of medieval city walls. The centerpiece of the neighborhood was (and is) the basilica of Santa Croce, which could hold great numbers of worshippers; the vast piazza could accommodate any overflow and also served as a fairground and, allegedly since the middle of the 16th century, as a playing field for no-holds-barred soccer games. A center of leatherworking since the Middle Ages, the neighborhood is still packed with leatherworkers and leather shops.

 Sights

Casa Buonarroti

ART MUSEUM | If you really enjoy walking in the footsteps of the great genius, you may want to complete the picture by visiting the Buonarroti family home. Michelangelo lived here from 1516 to 1525, and later gave it to his nephew, whose son, called Michelangelo il Giovane (Michelangelo the Younger) turned it into a gallery dedicated to his great-uncle. The artist's descendants filled it with art treasures, some by Michelangelo himself. Two early marble works—the *Madonna of the Stairs* and *Battle of the Centaurs*—demonstrate his genius. ⊠ *Via Ghibellina 70, Santa Croce* ☎ *055/241752* ⊕ *www.casabuonarroti.it* ⊴ *€8* ⊙ *Closed Tues.*

Piazza Santa Croce

PLAZA/SQUARE | Originally outside the city's 12th-century walls, this piazza grew with the Franciscans, who used the large square for public preaching. During the Renaissance it was used for

giostre (jousts), including one sponsored by Lorenzo de' Medici. Lined with many palazzi dating from the 15th and 16th centuries, the square remains one of Florence's loveliest piazze and is a great place to people-watch. ⊠ *Florence.*

★ **Santa Croce**
CHURCH | Like the Duomo, this church is Gothic, but, like the Duomo, its facade dates from the 19th century. As a burial place, the church probably contains more skeletons of Renaissance celebrities than any other in Italy. The tomb of Michelangelo is on the right at the front of the basilica; he is said to have chosen this spot so that the first thing he would see on Judgment Day, when the graves of the dead fly open, would be Brunelleschi's dome through Santa Croce's open doors. The tomb of Galileo Galilei (1564–1642) is on the left wall; he was not granted a Christian burial until 100 years after his death because of his controversial contention that Earth was not the center of the universe. The tomb of Niccolò Machiavelli (1469–1527), the political theoretician whose brutally pragmatic philosophy so influenced the Medici, is halfway down the nave on the right. The grave of Lorenzo Ghiberti, creator of the Baptistery doors, is halfway down the nave on the left. Composer Gioachino Rossini (1792–1868) is buried at the end of the nave on the right. The monument to Dante Alighieri (1265–1321), the greatest Italian poet, is a memorial rather than a tomb (he is buried in Ravenna); it's on the right wall near the tomb of Michelangelo. The collection of art within the complex is by far the most important of any church in Florence. The most famous works are probably the Giotto frescoes in the two chapels immediately to the right of the high altar. They illustrate scenes from the lives of St. John the Evangelist and St. John the Baptist (in the right-hand chapel), as well as those from the life of St. Francis (in the left-hand chapel). Time has not been kind to these frescoes; through the centuries, wall tombs were

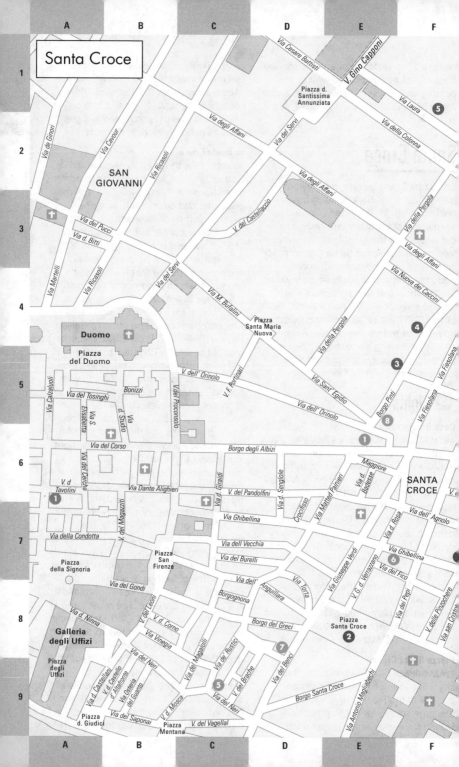

Sights ▼

1 Casa Buonarroti **F7**
2 Piazza Santa Croce................ **E8**
3 Santa Croce **H8**
4 Sinagoga........................... **H5**

Restaurants ▼

1 Antico Noe **E6**
2 Cibrèo **H6**
3 Cibrèo Trattoria **H6**
4 da Rocco........................... **I7**
5 Ditta Artigianale................... **C9**
6 Enoteca Pinchiorri................. **F7**
7 Kome **D8**
8 La Giostra.......................... **E5**

Quick Bites ▼

1 Perché No!...................... **A6**

Hotels ▼

1 The Four Seasons **H1**
2 Hotel Regency **J2**
3 Istituto Oblate
  dell'Assunzione **F5**
4 Monna Lisa......................... **F4**
5 Morandi alla Crocetta............. **F1**

placed in the middle of them, they were whitewashed and plastered over, and in the 19th century they suffered a clumsy restoration. But the reality that Giotto introduced into painting can still be seen. He did not paint beautifully stylized religious icons, as the Byzantine style that preceded him prescribed; he instead painted drama—St. Francis surrounded by grieving friars at the very moment of his death. This was a radical shift in emphasis: before Giotto, painting's role was to symbolize the attributes of God; after him, it was to imitate life. His work is indeed primitive compared with later painting, but in the early 14th century it caused a sensation that was not equaled for another 100 years. He was, for his time, the equal of both Masaccio and Michelangelo. Among the church's other highlights are Donatello's *Annunciation,* a moving expression of surprise (on the right wall two-thirds of the way down the nave); 14th-century frescoes by Taddeo Gaddi (circa 1300–66) illustrating scenes from the life of the Virgin Mary, clearly showing the influence of Giotto (in the chapel at the end of the right transept); and Donatello's *Crucifix,* criticized by Brunelleschi for making Christ look like a peasant (in the chapel at the end of the left transept). Outside the church proper, in the Museo dell'Opera di Santa Croce off the cloister, is the 13th-century *Triumphal Cross* by Cimabue (circa 1240–1302), badly damaged by the flood of 1966. A model of architectural geometry, the Cappella Pazzi, at the end of the cloister, is the work of Brunelleschi. ✉ *Piazza Santa Croce 16, Santa Croce* ☎ *055/2466105* 🌐 *www.santacroceopera.it* 🎫 *Church and museum €8* 🕒 *Closed Sun. morning and Tues.*

Sinagoga

SYNAGOGUE | Jews were well settled in Florence by the end of the 14th century, but by 1574 they were required to live within the large "ghetto" at the north side of today's Piazza della Repubblica, by decree of Cosimo I. Construction of the modern Moorish-style synagogue began in 1874 as a bequest of David Levi, who wished to endow a synagogue "worthy of the city." Falcini, Micheli, and Treves designed the building on a domed Greek cross plan with galleries in the transept and a roofline bearing three distinctive copper cupolas visible from all over Florence. The exterior has alternating bands of tan travertine and pink granite, reflecting an Islamic style repeated in Giovanni Panti's ornate interior. Of particular interest are the cast-iron gates by Pasquale Franci, the eternal light by Francesco Morini, and the Murano glass mosaics by Giacomo dal Medico. The gilded doors of the Moorish ark, which fronts the pulpit and is flanked by extravagant candelabra, are decorated with symbols of the ancient Temple of Jerusalem and bear bayonet marks from vandals. The synagogue was used as a garage by the Nazis, who failed to inflict much damage in spite of an attempt to blow up the place with dynamite. Only the columns on the left side were destroyed, and even then, the Women's Balcony above did not collapse. Note the Star of David in black and yellow marble inlay on the floor. The original capitals can be seen in the garden. ✉ *Via Farini 4, Santa Croce* ☎ *055/245253* 🌐 *www.jewishflorence.it* 🎫 *Synagogue and museum €6.50* 🕒 *Closed Sat. and Jewish holidays.*

🍴 Restaurants

Antico Noe

$$ | TUSCAN | The short menu at the one-room eatery relies heavily on seasonal ingredients picked up daily at the market. Although the secondi are good, the antipasti and primi really shine. **Known for:** artichoke dishes; porcini dishes; attention to seasonal vegetables. [$] *Average main: €20* ✉ *Volta di San Piero 6/r, Santa Croce* ☎ *055/2340838* 🕒 *No dinner Sun. Closed 2 wks in Aug.*

Continued on page 353

WHO'S WHO IN RENAISSANCE ART

Michelangelo. Leonardo da Vinci. Raphael. This heady triumvirate of the Italian Renaissance is synonymous with artistic genius. Yet they are only three of the remarkable cast of characters whose work defines the Renaissance, that extraordinary flourishing of art and culture in Italy, especially in Florence, as the Middle Ages drew to a close. The artists were visionaries, who redefined painting, sculpture, architecture, and even what it means to be an artist.

THE PIONEER. In the mid-14th century, a few artists began to move away the flat, two-dimensional painting of the Middle Ages. Giotto, who painted seemingly three-dimensional figures who show emotion, had a major impact on the artists of the next century.

THE GROUNDBREAKERS. The generations of Brunelleschi and Botticelli took center stage in the 15th century. Ghiberti, Masaccio, Donatello, Uccello, Fra Angelico, and Filippo Lippi were other major players. Part of the Renaissance (or "re-birth") was a renewed interest in classical sources—the texts, monuments, and sculpture of Ancient Greece and Rome. Perspective and the illusion of three-dimensional space in painting was another discovery of this era, known as the Early Renaissance. Suddenly the art appearing on the walls looked real, or more realistic than it used to.

Roman ruins were not the only thing to inspire these artists. There was an incredible exchange of ideas going on. In Santa Maria del Carmine, Filippo Lippi was inspired by the work of Masaccio, who in turn was a friend of Brunelleschi. Young artists also learned from the masters via the apprentice system. Ghiberti's workshop (bottega in Italian) included, at one time or another, Donatello, Masaccio, and Uccello. Botticelli was apprenticed to Filippo Lippi.

THE BIG THREE. The mathematical rationality and precision of 15th-century art gave way to what is known as the High Renaissance. Leonardo, Michelangelo, and Raphael were much more concerned with portraying the body in all its glory and with achieving harmony and grandeur in their work. Oil paint, used infrequently up until this time, became more widely employed: as a result, Leonardo's colors are deeper, more sensual, more alive. For one brief period, all three were in Florence at the same time. Michelangelo and Leonardo surely knew one another, as they were simultaneously working on frescoes (never completed) inside Palazzo Vecchio.

When Michelangelo left Florence for Rome in 1508, he began the slow drain of artistic exodus from Florence, which never really recovered her previous glory.

A RENAISSANCE TIMELINE

IN THE WORLD

Black Death in Europe kills one third of the population, 1347-50.

Joan of Arc burned at the stake, 1431.

IN FLORENCE

Dante, a native of Florence, writes *The Divine Comedy*, 1302-21.

Founding of the Medici bank, 1397.

Medici family made official papal bankers.

1434, Cosimo il Vecchio becomes de facto ruler of Florence. The Medici family will dominate the city until 1494.

1300

1400

IN ART

EARLY RENAISSANCE

Masaccio and Masolino fresco Santa Maria del Carmine, 1424-28.

GIOTTO (ca. 1267-1337)

Giotto fresoes in Santa Croce, 1320-25.

BRUNELLESCHI (1377-1446)

LORENZO GHIBERTI (ca. 1381-1455)

DONATELLO (ca. 1386-1466)

PAOLO UCCELLO (1397-1475)

FRA ANGELICO (ca. 1400-1455)

MASACCIO (1401-1428)

FILIPPO LIPPI (ca. 1406-1469

1334, 67-year-old Giotto is appointed chief architect of Santa Maria del Fiore, Florence's Duomo (below). He begins to work on the Campanile, which will be completed in 1359, after his death.

Donatello sculpts bronze *David*, ca. 14

Fra Angelico frescoes friars' cells in San Marco, 1438-45.

Uccello's Sir John Hawkwood, ca. 1436.

Ghiberti wins the competition for the Baptistery doors (above) in Florence, 1401.

Brunelleschi wins the competition for the Duomo' cupola (right), 1418.

Gutenberg Bible is
printed, 1455.

Columbus discovers
America, 1492.

Martin Luther posts his 95 theses on
the door at Wittenberg, kicking off the
Protestant Reformation, 1517.

Constantinople falls
to the Turks, 1453.

Machiavelli's *Prince*
appears, 1513.

Copernicus proves that the
earth is not the center of the
universe, 1530-43.

Lorenzo "il Magnifico"
(right), the Medici patron
of the arts, rules in
Florence, 1449-92.

Two Medici popes Leo X
(1513-21) and Clement VII
(1523-34) in Rome.

Catherine de'Medici
becomes Queen of
France, 1547.

1450　　　　　　**1500**　　　　　　**1550**

HIGH RENAISSANCE　　　MANNERISM

Fra Filippo Lippi's
Madonna and Child,
ca. 1452.

1508, Raphael begins
work on the chambers in
the Vatican, Rome.

Giorgio Vasari
publishes his first
edition of *Lives of
the Artists*, 1550.

1504, Michelangelo's
David is put on
display in Piazza della
Signoria, where it
remains until 1873.

Botticelli paints the *Birth
of Venus*, ca. 1482.

Michelangelo
begins to fresco
the Sistine Chapel
ceiling, 1508.

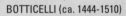

BOTTICELLI (ca. 1444-1510)

LEONARDO DA VINCI (1452-1519)

RAPHAEL (1483-1520)

MICHELANGELO (1475-1564)

Leonardo paints *The Last Supper* in Milan,
1495-98.

Giotto's *Nativity*

Donatello's *St. John the Baptist*

Ghiberti's *Gates of Paradise*

GIOTTO (CA. 1267-1337)
Painter/architect from a small town north of Florence.

He unequivocally set Italian painting on the course that led to the triumphs of the Renaissance masters. Unlike the rather flat, two-dimensional forms found in then prevailing Byzantine art, Giotto's figures have a fresh, life-like quality. The people in his paintings have bulk, and they show emotion, which you can see on their faces and in their gestures. This was something new in the late Middle Ages. Without Giotto, there wouldn't have been a Raphael.

In Florence: **Santa Croce; Uffizi; Campanile; Santa Maria Novella**
Elsewhere in Italy: **Scrovegni Chapel, Padua; Vatican Museums, Rome**

FILIPPO BRUNELLESCHI (1377-1446)
Architect/engineer from Florence.

If Brunelleschi had beaten Ghiberti in the Baptistery doors competition in Florence, the city's Duomo most likely would not have the striking appearance and authority that it has today. After his loss, he sulked off to Rome, where he studied the ancient Roman structures first-hand. Brunelleschi figured out how to vault the Duomo's dome, a structure unprecedented in its colossal size and great height. His Ospedale degli Innocenti employs classical elements in the creation of a stunning, new architectural statement; it is the first truly Renaissance structure.

In Florence: **Duomo; Ospedale degli Innocenti; San Lorenzo; Santo Spirito; Baptistery Doors Competition Entry, Bargello; Santa Croce**

LORENZO GHIBERTI (CA. 1381-1455)
Sculptor from Florence.

Ghiberti won a competition—besting his chief rival, Brunelleschi—to cast the gilded bronze North Doors of the Baptistery in Florence. These doors, and the East Doors that he subsequently executed, took up the next 50 years of his life. He created intricately worked figures that are more true-to-life than any since antiquity, and he was one of the first Renaissance sculptors to work in bronze. Ghiberti taught the next generation of artists; Donatello, Uccello, and Masaccio all passed through his studio.

In Florence: **Door Copies, Baptistery; Original Doors, Museo dell'Opera del Duomo; Baptistry Door Competition Entry, Bargello; Orsanmichele**

DONATELLO (CA. 1386-1466)
Sculptor from Florence.

Donatello was an innovator who, like his good friend Brunelleschi, spent most of his long life in Florence. Consumed with the science of optics, he used light and shadow to create the effects of nearness and distance. He made an essentially flat slab look like a three-dimensional scene. His bronze is probably the first free-standing male nude since antiquity. Not only technically brilliant, his work is also emotionally resonant; few sculptors are as expressive.

In Florence: *David*, **Bargello; St. Mark, Orsanmichele; Palazzo Vecchio; Museo dell'Opera del Duomo; San Lorenzo; Santa Croce**
Elsewhere in Italy: **Padua; Prato; Venice**

Fra Angelico's *The Deposition*   Masaccio's *Trinity*   Filippo Lippi's *Madonna and Child*

PAOLO UCCELLO (1397-1475)
Painter from Florence.
Renaissance chronicler Vasari once observed that had Uccello not been so obsessed with the mathematical problems posed by perspective, he would have been a very good painter. The struggle to master single-point perspective and to render motion in two dimensions is nowhere more apparent than in his battle scenes. His first major commission in Florence was the gargantuan fresco of the English mercenary Sir John Hawkwood (the Italians called him Giovanni Acuto) in Florence's Duomo.
In Florence: **Sir John Hawkwood, Duomo; Battle of San Romano, Uffizi; Santa Maria Novella**
Elsewhere in Italy: **Urbino, Prato**

FRA ANGELICO (CA. 1400-1455)
Painter from a small town north of Florence.
A Dominican friar, who eventually made his way to the convent of San Marco, Fra Angelico and his assistants painted frescoes for aid in prayer and meditation. He was known for his piety; Vasari wrote that Fra Angelico could never paint a crucifix without a tear running down his face. Perhaps no other painter so successfully translated the mysteries of faith and the sacred into painting. And yet his figures emote, his command of perspective is superb, and his use of color startles even today.
In Florence: **Museo di San Marco; Uffizi**
Elsewhere in Italy: **Vatican Museums, Rome; Fiesole; Cortona; Perugia; Orvieto**

MASACCIO (1401-1428)
Painter from San Giovanni Valdarno, southeast of Florence.
Masaccio and Masolino, a frequent collaborator, worked most famously together at Santa Maria del Carmine. Their frescoes of the life of St. Peter use light to mold figures in the painting by imitating the way light falls on figures in real life. Masaccio also pioneered the use of single-point perspective, masterfully rendered in his His friend Brunelleschi probably introduced him to the technique, yet another step forward in rendering things the way the eye sees them. Masaccio died young and under mysterious circumstances.
In Florence: **Santa Maria del Carmine; Trinity, Santa Maria Novella**

FILIPPO LIPPI (CA. 1406-1469)
Painter from Prato.
At a young age, Filippo Lippi entered the friary of Santa Maria del Carmine, where he was highly influenced by Masaccio and Masolino's frescoes. His religious vows appear to have made less of an impact; his affair with a young nun produced a son, Filippino (Little Philip, who later apprenticed with Botticelli), and a daughter. His religious paintings often have a playful, humorous note; some of his angels are downright impish and look directly out at the viewer. Lippi links the earlier painters of the 15th century with those who follow; Botticelli apprenticed with him.
In Florence: **Uffizi; Palazzo Medici Riccardi; San Lorenzo; Palazzo Pitti**
Elsewhere in Italy: **Prato**

Botticelli's *Primavera*

Leonardo's *Portrait of a Young Woman*

Raphael's *Madonna on the Meadow*

BOTTICELLI (CA. 1444–1510)

Painter from Florence.

Botticelli's work is characterized by stunning, elongated blondes, cherubic angels (something he undoubtedly learned from his time with Filippo Lippi), and tender Christs. Though he did many religious paintings, he also painted monumental, nonreligious panels—his *Birth of Venus* and *Primavera* being the two most famous of these. A brief sojourn took him to Rome, where he and a number of other artists frescoed the Sistine Chapel walls.

In Florence: **Birth of Venus, Primavera, Uffizi; Palazzo Pitti**
Elsewhere in Italy: **Vatican Museums, Rome**

LEONARDO DA VINCI (1452–1519)

Painter/sculptor/engineer from Anchiano, a small town outside Vinci.

Leonardo never lingered long in any place; his restless nature and his international reputation led to commissions throughout Italy, and took him to Milan, Vigevano, Pavia, Rome, and, ultimately, France. Though he is most famous for his mysterious *Mona Lisa* (at the Louvre in Paris), he painted other penetrating, psychological portraits in addition to his scientific experiments: his design for a flying machine (never built) predates Kitty Hawk by nearly 500 years. The greatest collection of Leonardo's work in Italy can be seen on one wall in the Uffizi.

In Florence: **Adoration of the Magi, Uffizi**
Elsewhere in Italy: **Last Supper, Santa Maria delle Grazie, Milan**

RAPHAEL (1483–1520)

Painter/architect from Urbino.

Raphael spent only four highly productive years of his short life in Florence, where he turned out made-to-order panel paintings of the *Madonna and Child* for a hungry public; he also executed a number of portraits of Florentine aristocrats. Perhaps no other artist had such a fine command of line and color, and could render it, seemingly effortlessly, in paint. His painting acquired new authority after he came up against Michelangelo toiling away on the Sistine ceiling. Raphael worked nearly next door in the Vatican, where his figures take on an epic, Michelangelesque scale.

In Florence: **Uffizi; Palazzo Pitti**
Elsewhere in Italy: **Vatican Museums, Rome**

MICHELANGELO (1475–1564)

Painter/sculptor/architect from Caprese.

Although Florentine and proud of it (he famously signed his St. Peter's *Pietà* to avoid confusion about where he was from), he spent most of his 89 years outside his native city. He painted and sculpted the male body on an epic scale and glorified it while doing so. Though he complained throughout the proceedings that he was really a sculptor, Michelangelo's Sistine Chapel ceiling is arguably the greatest fresco cycle ever painted (and the massive figures owe no small debt to Giotto).

In Florence: **David, Galleria dell'Accademia; Uffizi; Casa Buonarroti; Bargello**
Elsewhere in Italy: **St. Peter's Basilica, Vatican Museums, and Piazza del Campidoglio in Rome**

★ Cibrèo

$$$$ | TUSCAN | This upscale trattoria serves sumptuous options like the creamy crostini *di fegatini* (with a savory chicken-liver spread) and melt-in-your-mouth desserts. Many Florentines hail this as the city's best restaurant, and justifiably so: chef-owner Fabio Picchi knows Tuscan food better than anyone, and though there's not a pasta dish to be seen on the menu (he argues that Florence doesn't really have any native pasta dishes), his deep understanding of Tuscan food shines through. **Known for:** multilingual staff; authentic Tuscan food; no written menu. $ *Average main: €40* ✉ *Via A. del Verrocchio 8/r, Santa Croce* ☎ *055/2341100.*

Cibrèo Trattoria

$$ | TUSCAN | This intimate little trattoria, known to locals as Cibreino, shares its kitchen with the famed Florentine culinary institution from which it gets its name. It's the same kitchen, shorter menu, and is not nearly as expensive. **Known for:** go early to avoid a wait; excellent meal at a moderate price; clever riffs on classic dishes. $ *Average main: €15* ✉ *Via dei Macci 118, Santa Croce* ☎ *055/2341100* ✆ *Closed Sun., Mon., and July 25–Sept. 5.*

Da Rocco

$ | TUSCAN | At one of Florence's biggest markets you can grab lunch to go, or you can cram yourself into one of the booths and pour from the straw-cloaked flask (wine here is *da consumo,* which means they charge you for how much you drink). Food is abundant, Tuscan, and fast; locals pack in. **Known for:** takeout; tasty food at rock-bottom prices; ever-changing menu. $ *Average main: €7* ✉ *Mercato Sant'Ambrogio, Piazza Ghiberti, Santa Croce* ☎✆ *Closed Sun. No dinner.*

Ditta Artigianale

$ | ITALIAN | This place is always crowded with mostly young folk lingering over non-Italian cups of coffee. Light lunch and brunch are also on offer, and in between there's a steady supply of cakes, cookies, and croissants. **Known for:** long opening hours; non-Italian coffee; tasty food. $ *Average main: €12* ✉ *Via de'Neri 32, Santa Croce* ☎ *055/2741541* ⊕ *www.dittaartigianale.it.*

Enoteca Pinchiorri

$$$$ | ITALIAN | A sumptuous Renaissance palace with high frescoed ceilings and bouquets in silver vases provides the backdrop for this restaurant, one of the most expensive in Italy. Some consider it one of the best, and others consider it inauthentic as the cuisine extends far beyond Italian. **Known for:** exorbitantly high prices; wine cellar; creative food. $ *Average main: €103* ✉ *Via Ghibellina 87, Santa Croce* ☎ *055/242777* ⊕ *www.enotecapinchiorri.it* ✆ *Closed Sun., Mon., and Aug. No lunch* ⌂ *Jacket required.*

Kome

$$ | JAPANESE | If you're looking for a break from the ubiquitous ribollita, stop in at this eatery, which may be the only Japanese restaurant in the world to be housed in a 15th-century Renaissance palazzo. High, vaulted arches frame the kaiten sushi conveyor belt. **Known for:** ramen noodles; creative sushi; Japanese barbecue prepared table-side. $ *Average main: €16* ✉ *Via de' Benci 41/r, Santa Croce* ☎ *055/2008009* ⊕ *www.kome-firenze.it* ✆ *No lunch Sun.*

★ La Giostra

$$$ | ITALIAN | This clubby spot, whose name means "carousel" in Italian, was created by the late Prince Dimitri Kunz d'Asburgo Lorena and is now expertly run by Soldano and Dimitri, his friendly twin sons. The ever-changing menu almost always has vegetarian and vegan options. **Known for:** vegetarian and vegan options; sublime tiramisù and a wonderfully gooey Sacher torte; carefully curated wine list. $ *Average main: €34* ✉ *Borgo Pinti 12/r, Santa Croce* ☎ *055/241341* ⊕ *www.ristorantelagiostra.com.*

Coffee and Quick Bites

★ Perché No!
$ | **CAFÉ** | **FAMILY** | They've been making ice cream at this much-loved-by-Florentines place since 1939. Such continuity is the reason why this might be the best gelateria in the historic center. **Known for:** unusual flavors and vegan options; gelati made daily; one of the oldest gelaterias in the city. [$] *Average main: €3* ✉ *Via dei Tavolini 19r, Santa Croce* ☎ *055/2398969* 🌐 *www.percheno.firenze.it.*

Hotels

The Four Seasons
$$$$ | **HOTEL** | This 15th-century palazzo in Florence's center is perhaps the most luxurious show in town; many guest rooms have original 17th-century frescoes, while some face the garden and others face quiet interior courtyards. **Pros:** a Michelin-starred restaurant; pool and state-of-the-art spa; 11-acre garden. **Cons:** breakfast not included; small rooms; splashing children in the pool can be a nuisance for some. [$] *Rooms from: €850* ✉ *Borgo Pinti 99e, Santa Croce* ☎ *055/26261* 🌐 *www.fourseasons.com/florence* 🛏 *117 rooms* 🍴 *No Meals.*

Hotel Regency
$$$$ | **HOTEL** | Rooms dressed in richly colored fabrics and antique-style furniture remain faithful to the premises' 19th-century origins as a private mansion; meanwhile, the noise and crowds of Florence seem far from this stylish retreat in a residential district near the Sinagoga, though you're not more than 10 minutes from the Accademia and Michelangelo's *David.* Across the street is Piazza d'Azeglio, a small public park that somehow evokes 19th-century middle Europe. **Pros:** the lovely restaurant Il Relais le Jardin on-site; faces one of the few green parks in the center of Florence; quiet neighborhood. **Cons:** rooms facing the park can be noisy; somewhat removed from the city center; books up quickly. [$] *Rooms from: €350* ✉ *Piazza d'Azeglio 3, Santa Croce* ☎ *055/245247* 🌐 *www.regency-hotel.com* 🛏 *31 rooms* 🍴 *Free Breakfast.*

La Casa per Ferie Borgo Pinte delle Oblate dell'Assunzione
$ | **B&B/INN** | Nuns run this convent holiday house, minutes from the Duomo, with spotlessly clean, simple rooms; some have views of the cupola, and others look out onto a carefully tended garden where you are welcome to relax. **Pros:** a soothing, somewhat untended garden; great location and (mostly) quiet rooms; Mass held daily. **Cons:** rooms facing the street can be noisy; some have observed that there's hall noise; rooms are frugal. [$] *Rooms from: €90* ✉ *Borgo Pinti 15, Santa Croce* ☎ *055/2480582* 🌐 *www.oblate.it* 🛏 *40 rooms* 🍴 *Free Breakfast.*

★ Monna Lisa
$$ | **HOTEL** | Although some rooms are small, they are tastefully decorated, and best of all, housed in a 15th-century palazzo that retains some of its wood-coffered ceilings from the 1500s, as well as its original staircase. **Pros:** garden; lavish buffet breakfast; cheerful multilingual staff. **Cons:** street noise in some rooms; rooms in annex are less charming than those in palazzo; thin walls have been noted. [$] *Rooms from: €150* ✉ *Borgo Pinti 27, Santa Croce* ☎ *055/2479751* 🌐 *www.monnalisa.it* 🛏 *45 rooms* 🍴 *Free Breakfast.*

★ Morandi alla Crocetta
$$ | **B&B/INN** | You're made to feel like friends of the family at this charming and distinguished residence, furnished comfortably in the classic style of a gracious Florentine home and former convent. **Pros:** affable staff; historic touches like 17th-century fresco fragments; interesting, offbeat location near the sights. **Cons:** some say breakfast could be better; far from the "true" historical center; books up quickly. [$] *Rooms from: €170* ✉ *Via Laura 50, Santissima Annunziata*

☎ 055/2344747 ⊕ www.hotelmorandi.it
🛏 10 rooms ⫶◯⫶ Free Breakfast.

Nightlife

Jazz Club
DANCE CLUBS | Enjoy live music in this small basement club. ✉ Via Nuova de' Caccini 3, at Borgo Pinti, Santa Croce.

Rex
BARS | A trendy, artsy clientele frequents this bar at aperitivo time; around 10 pm, the place is packed with mostly young folks sipping artfully made cocktails. ✉ Via Fiesolana 23–25/r, Santa Croce ☎ 055/2480331 ⊕ www.rexfirenze.com.

Sant'Ambrogio Caffè
BARS | Come here when it's summer for outdoor seating with a view of an 11th-century church (Sant'Ambrogio) directly across the street. Come here when it's not for perfectly mixed drinks and a lively atmosphere filled with (mostly) locals. ✉ Piazza Sant'Ambrogio 7–8/r, Santa Croce ☎ 055/2477277.

Performing Arts

Amici della Musica
MUSIC | This organization sponsors classical and contemporary concerts at the Teatro della Pergola (Box office, Via delle Carceri 1, 055/210804). ✉ Via Pier Capponi 41, Florence ⊕ www.amicimusica.fi.it.

Orchestra della Toscana
MUSIC | The concert season of the Orchestra della Toscana runs from November to June. ✉ Via Ghibellina, Santa Croce ☎ 055/234 0710 ⊕ www.orchestradellatoscana.it.

Shopping

Mercato di Sant'Ambrogio
MARKET | FAMILY | It's possible to strike gold at this lively market, where clothing stalls abut the fruits and vegetables. ✉ Piazza Ghiberti, off Via dei Macci, Santa Croce.

Paolo Carandini
OTHER ACCESSORIES | Stop in here for exquisite leather objects such as picture frames, jewelry boxes, and desk accessories. ✉ Borgo Allegri 7/r, Santa Croce ☎ 055/3347355954 ⊕ www.paolocarandini.net.

★ Scuola del Cuoio
LEATHER GOODS | A consortium of leatherworkers ply their trade at Scuola del Cuoio (Leather School), in the former dormitory of the convent of Santa Croce; high-quality, fairly priced jackets, belts, and purses are sold here. ✉ Piazza Santa Croce 16, Florence ☎ 055/244533 ⊕ www.scuoladelcuoio.com.

The Oltrarno

A walk through the Oltrarno (literally "the other side of the Arno") takes in two very different aspects of Florence: the splendor of the Medici, manifest in the riches of the mammoth Palazzo Pitti and the gracious Giardino di Boboli; and the charm of the Oltrarno, a slightly gentrified but still fiercely proud working-class neighborhood with artisans' and antiques shops.

Farther east across the Arno, a series of ramps and stairs climb to Piazzale Michelangelo, where the city lies before you in all its glory (skip this trip if it's a hazy day). More stairs (behind La Loggia restaurant) lead to the church of San Miniato al Monte. You can avoid the long walk by taking Bus No. 12 or 13 at the west end of Ponte alle Grazie and getting off at Piazzale Michelangelo; you still have to climb the monumental stairs to and from San Miniato, but you can then take the bus from Piazzale Michelangelo back to the center of town. If you decide to take a bus, remember to buy your ticket before you board.

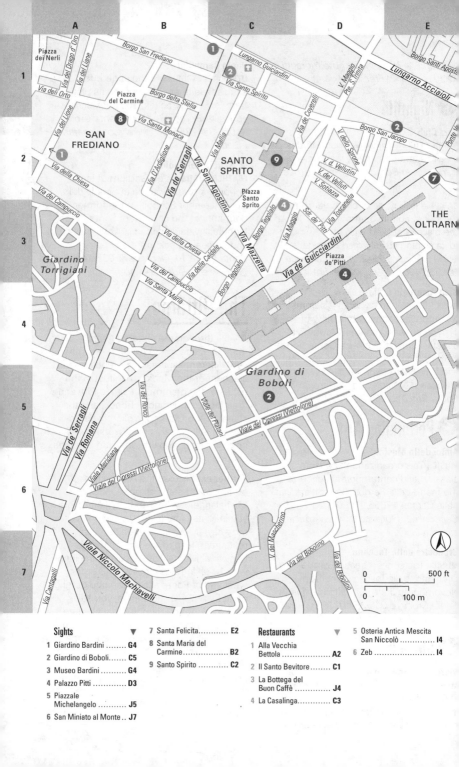

Sights ▼

1 Giardino Bardini **G4**
2 Giardino di Boboli **C5**
3 Museo Bardini **G4**
4 Palazzo Pitti **D3**
5 Piazzale
   Michelangelo **J5**
6 San Miniato al Monte .. **J7**

7 Santa Felicita **E2**
8 Santa Maria del
   Carmine **B2**
9 Santo Spirito **C2**

Restaurants ▼

1 Alla Vecchia
   Bettola **A2**
2 Il Santo Bevitore **C1**
3 La Bottega del
   Buon Caffè **J4**
4 La Casalinga **C3**

5 Osteria Antica Mescita
   San Niccolò **I4**
6 Zeb **I4**

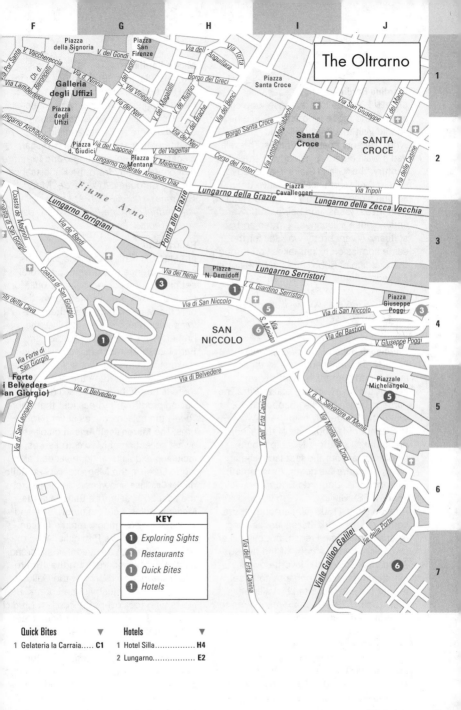

The Oltrarno

F | G | H | I | J

Piazza della Signoria
V. Vacchereccia
V. Por Santa Maria
Ch. d. Baroncelli
Via Lambertesca
Lungarno Archibusieri

Galleria degli Uffizi

Piazza degli Uffizi

V. del Gondi
V. d' Ninna
V. de' Leoni
Via de Leoni
Via del Neri
Via dei Neri
Via del Saponai
Piazza d. Giudici
Lungarno Generale Armando Diaz

Piazza San Firenze
Via dei Magalotti
V. de' Rustici
V. de' Bracche
Borgo del Greci
V. del Vagellai
V. Malenchini
Piazza Mentana

Via dell' Anguillara
Via Torta
Via dei Benci
Borgo Santa Croce
Corso dei Tintori
Via Antonio Magliabechi

Piazza Santa Croce

Santa Croce

SANTA CROCE

V. dei Macci
Via San Giuseppe
Via delle Canine

Fiume Arno

Lungarno Torrigiani

Via de Bardi

Coasta di Magnoli
Coasta di San Giorgio
Costa di San Giorgio
nto della Cava

Lungarno della Grazie

Piazza Cavalleggeri

Lungarno della Zecca Vecchia

Via Tripoli

Via dei Renai

Piazza N. Demidoff

Lungarno Serristori

V. d. Giardino Serristori

Via di San Niccolo

SAN NICCOLO

Via di Belvedere

Via Forte di San Giorgio

Forte i Belvedere San Giorgio)

Via di San Leonardo

Via di Belvedere

Piazza Giuseppe Poggi

Via di San Niccolo

Via del Bastioni

V. Giuseppe Poggi

Piazzale Michelangelo

V. d. S. Salvatore al Monte

V. dell' Erta Canina

Via del' Erta Canina

Viale Galileo Galilei

Via Monte alle Croci

Vie delle Porte

KEY

1 Exploring Sights
1 Restaurants
1 Quick Bites
1 Hotels

Quick Bites ▼

1 Gelateria la Carraia..... **C1**

Hotels ▼

1 Hotel Silla................ **H4**
2 Lungarno................. **E2**

Sights

Giardino Bardini

GARDEN | Garden lovers, those who crave a view, and those who enjoy a nice hike should visit this lovely villa and garden, whose history spans centuries. The villa had a walled garden as early as the 14th century; the "Grand Stairs"—a zigzag ascent well worth scaling—have been around since the 16th. The garden is filled with irises, roses, and heirloom flowers, and includes a Japanese garden and statuary. A very pretty walk (all for the same admission ticket) takes you through the Giardino di Boboli and past the Forte Belvedere to the upper entrance to the giardino. ⊠ *Via de'Bardini, San Niccolò* ☎ *055/2638599* ⊕ *www.villabardini. it* ⊠ *€10* ⊘ *Closed 1st and last Mon. of month.*

Giardino di Boboli (*Boboli Gardens*)

GARDEN | The main entrance to these landscaped gardens is from the right side of the courtyard of Palazzo Pitti. The gardens began to take shape in 1549, when the Pitti family sold the palazzo to Eleanor of Toledo, wife of the Medici grand duke Cosimo I. Niccolò Tribolo (1500–50) laid out the first landscaping plans, and after his death, Ammannati, Giambologna, Bernardo Buontalenti (circa 1536–1608), Giulio (1571–1635), and Alfonso Parigi (1606–56), among others, continued his work. Italian landscaping is less formal than French, but still full of sweeping drama. A copy of the famous *Morgante*, Cosimo I's favorite dwarf astride a particularly unhappy tortoise, is near the exit. Sculpted by Valerio Cioli (circa 1529–99), the work seems to illustrate the perils of culinary overindulgence. A visit here can be disappointing because the gardens are somewhat sparse, but the pleasant walk offers excellent views. ⊠ *Enter through Palazzo Pitti, Florence* ☎ *055/294883* ⊕ *www. polomuseale.firenze.it* ⊠ *€10 combined ticket, Giardino Bardini* ⊘ *Closed 1st and last Mon. of month.*

Museo Bardini

ART MUSEUM | The 19th-century collector and antiquarian Stefano Bardini turned his palace into his own private museum. Upon his death, the collection was turned over to the state and includes an interesting assortment of Etruscan pieces, sculpture, paintings, and furniture that dates mostly from the Renaissance and the Baroque. ⊠ *Piazza de' Mozzi 1, Florence* ☎ *055/2342427* ⊕ *museicivicifiorentini.comune.fi.it* ⊠ *€7* ⊘ *Closed Tues.–Thurs.*

Palazzo Pitti

ART MUSEUM | This enormous palace is one of Florence's largest architectural set pieces. The original palazzo, built for the Pitti family around 1460, comprised only the main entrance and the three windows on either side. In 1549, the property was sold to the Medici, and Bartolomeo Ammannati was called in to make substantial additions. Although he apparently operated on the principle that more is better, he succeeded only in producing proof that more is just that: more. Today, the palace houses several museums: The **Museo degli Argenti** displays a vast collection of Medici treasures, including exquisite antique vases belonging to Lorenzo the Magnificent. The **Galleria del Costume** showcases fashions from the past 300 years. The **Galleria d'Arte Moderna** holds a collection of 19th- and 20th-century paintings, mostly Tuscan. Most famous of the Pitti galleries is the **Galleria Palatina,** which contains a broad collection of paintings from the 15th to 17th century. The rooms of the Galleria Palatina remain much as the Lorena, the rulers who took over after the last Medici died in 1737, left them. Their floor-to-ceiling paintings are considered by some to be Italy's most egregious exercise in conspicuous consumption, aesthetic overkill, and trumpery. Still, the collection possesses high points, including a number of portraits by Titian and an unparalleled collection of paintings by Raphael. The price of admission to the Galleria

Palatina also allows you to explore the former **Appartamenti Reali,** containing furnishings from a remodeling done in the 19th century. ⊠ *Piazza Pitti, Florence* 🕾 *055/294883* ⊕ *www.polomuseale. firenze.it* 🎟 *From €16* 🕙 *Closed Mon.*

Piazzale Michelangelo

PLAZA/SQUARE | FAMILY | From this lookout you have a marvelous view of Florence and the hills around it, rivaling the vista from the Forte di Belvedere. A copy of Michelangelo's *David* overlooks outdoor cafés packed with tourists during the day and with Florentines in the evening. In May the **Giardino dell'Iris** (Iris Garden) off the piazza is abloom with more than 2,500 varieties of the flower. The **Giardino delle Rose** (Rose Garden) on the terraces below the piazza is also in full bloom in May and June. ⊠ *Florence.*

San Miniato al Monte

CHURCH | This church, like the Baptistery a fine example of Romanesque architecture, is one of the oldest churches in Florence, dating from the 11th century. A 12th-century mosaic topped by a gilt bronze eagle, emblem of San Miniato's sponsors, the Calimala (cloth merchants' guild), crowns the lovely green-and-white marble facade. Inside are a 13th-century inlaid-marble floor and apse mosaic. Artist Spinello Aretino (1350–1410) covered the walls of the Sagrestia with frescoes depicting scenes from the life of St. Benedict. The Cappella del Cardinale del Portogallo (Chapel of the Portuguese Cardinal) is one of the richest 15th-century Renaissance works in Florence. It contains the tomb of a young Portuguese cardinal, Prince James of Lusitania, who died in Florence in 1459. Its glorious ceiling is by Luca della Robbia, and the sculpted tomb by Antonio Rossellino (1427–79). Every day at 5:30 pm, the monks fill the church with the sounds of Gregorian chanting, and say Mass in Latin. ⊠ *Viale Galileo Galilei, Piazzale Michelangelo, Oltrarno* 🕾 *055/2342731* ⊕ *www.sanminiatoalmonte.it.*

Santa Felicita

CHURCH | This late Baroque church (its facade was remodeled between 1736 and 1739) contains the mannerist Jacopo Pontormo's *Deposition,* the centerpiece of the Cappella Capponi (executed 1525–28) and a masterpiece of 16th-century Florentine art. The remote figures, which transcend the realm of Renaissance classical form, are portrayed in tangled shapes and intense pastel colors (well preserved because of the low lights in the church), in a space and depth that defy reality. Note, too, the exquisitely frescoed *Annunciation,* also by Pontormo, at a right angle to the *Deposition.* The granite column in the piazza was erected in 1381 and marks a Christian cemetery. ⊠ *Piazza Santa Felicita, Via Guicciardini, Palazzo Pitti* 🕙 *Closed Sun.*

Santa Maria del Carmine

CHURCH | The Cappella Brancacci, at the end of the right transept of this church, houses a masterpiece of Renaissance painting: a fresco cycle that changed the course of Western art. Fire destroyed most of the church in the 18th century; miraculously, the Brancacci Chapel survived almost intact. The cycle is the work of three artists: Masaccio and Masolino (1383–circa 1447), who began it around 1424, and Filippino Lippi, who finished it some 50 years later, after a long interruption during which the sponsoring Brancacci family was exiled. It was Masaccio's work that opened a new frontier for painting, as he was among the first artists to employ single-point perspective; tragically, he died in 1428 at the age of 27, so he didn't live to experience the revolution his innovations caused. Masaccio collaborated with Masolino on several of the frescoes, but his style predominates in the *Tribute Money,* on the upper-left wall; *St. Peter Baptizing,* on the upper altar wall; the *Distribution of Goods,* on the lower altar wall; and the *Expulsion of Adam and Eve,* on the chapel's upper-left entrance pier. If you look closely at the last painting and compare it with some of the chapel's other works, you should see a pronounced difference. The figures of Adam and Eve possess a startling presence primarily thanks to the dramatic way in which their bodies seem to reflect light. Masaccio here shaded his figures consistently, so as to suggest a single, strong source of light within the world of the painting but outside its frame. In so doing, he succeeded in imitating with paint the real-world effect of light on mass, and he thereby imparted to his figures a sculptural reality unprecedented in his day. These matters have to do with technique, but with the *Expulsion of Adam and Eve* his skill went beyond mere technical innovation. In the faces of Adam and Eve, you see more than finely modeled figures; you see terrible shame and suffering depicted with a humanity rarely achieved in art. Reservations to see the chapel are mandatory, but can be booked on the same day. ✉ *Piazza del Carmine, Santo Spirito* ☎ *055/2768224 reservations* 🌐 *www.museicivicifiorentini.comune.fi.it* 🎫 *€4.50* 🕘 *Closed Tues.*

Santo Spirito

CHURCH | The plain, unfinished facade gives nothing away, but the interior, although it appears chilly compared with later churches, is one of the most important examples of Renaissance architecture in Italy. The interior is one of a pair designed in Florence by Filippo Brunelleschi in the early decades of the 15th century (the other is San Lorenzo). It was here that Brunelleschi supplied definitive solutions to the two major problems of interior Renaissance church design: how to build a cross-shape interior using classical architectural elements borrowed from antiquity and how to reflect in that interior the order and regularity that Renaissance scientists (among them Brunelleschi himself) were at the time discovering in the natural world around them. Brunelleschi's solution to the first problem was brilliantly simple: turn a Greek temple inside out. While ancient Greek temples were walled buildings surrounded by classical colonnades, Brunelleschi's churches were classical arcades surrounded by walled buildings. This brilliant architectural idea overthrew the previous era's religious taboo against pagan architecture once and for all, triumphantly claiming that architecture for Christian use. Brunelleschi's solution to the second problem—making the entire interior orderly and regular—was mathematically precise: he designed the ground plan of the church so that all its parts were proportionally related. The transepts and nave have exactly the same width; the side aisles are precisely half as wide as the nave; the little chapels off the side aisles are exactly half as deep as the side aisles; the chancel and transepts are exactly one-eighth the depth of the nave; and so on, with dizzying exactitude. For Brunelleschi, such a design technique was a matter of passionate conviction. Like most theoreticians of his day, he believed that mathematical regularity and aesthetic beauty were flip sides of the same coin, that one was not possible without the other. In the refectory, adjacent to the church, you can see Andrea Orcagna's highly damaged fresco of the Crucifixion. ✉ *Piazza Santo Spirito, Oltrarno* ☎ *055/210030* 🌐 *www.basilicasantospirito.it* 🕘 *Church closed Wed.*

🍴 Restaurants

Alla Vecchia Bettola

$$ | **TUSCAN** | The name doesn't exactly mean "old dive," but it comes pretty close. The recipes here come from "wise grandmothers" and celebrate Tuscan food in its glorious simplicity—prosciutto is sliced with a knife, portions of grilled meat are tender and ample, service is friendly, and the wine list is well priced and good. **Known for:** just outside the centro storico but worth the taxi ride; grilled meats; firmly Tuscan menu. [$] *Average main: €15* ✉ *Viale Vasco Pratolini, Oltrarno* ☎ *055/224158* 🕘 *Closed Sun. and Mon.*

★ Il Santo Bevitore

$$ | TUSCAN | Florentines and other lovers of good food flock to "The Holy Drinker" for tasty, well-priced dishes. Unpretentious white walls, dark wood furniture, and paper place mats provide the simple decor; start with the exceptional *verdure sott'olio* (vegetables in oil) or the *terrina di fegatini* (a creamy chicken-liver spread) before sampling any of the divine pastas. **Known for:** friendly waitstaff; pasta; verdure sott'olio. $ *Average main: €18* ✉ *Via Santo Spirito 64/66r, Santo Spirito* ☎ *055/211264* ⊕ *www.ilsantobevitore. com* ⊘ *No lunch Sun.*

La Bottega del Buon Caffè

$$$$ | MODERN ITALIAN | This restaurant is a symphony in gustatory pleasures in a room with exposed sandy brick walls and high, luminous windows. Executive chef Antonello Sardi is young and gifted, as is his ace brigade. **Known for:** stupendous wine list; farm to table; cutting-edge fare. $ *Average main: €44* ✉ *Lungarno, Cellini, 69/r, Oltrarno* ☎ *055/5535677* ⊕ *www. borgointhecity.com.*

★ La Casalinga

$ | TUSCAN | *Casalinga* means "housewife," and this place, which has been around since 1963, has the nostalgic charm of a mid-century kitchen with Tuscan comfort food to match. If you eat ribollita anywhere in Florence, eat it here—it couldn't be more authentic. **Known for:** often packed; ribollita; liver, Venetian style. $ *Average main: €13* ✉ *Via Michelozzi 9/r, Santo Spirito* ☎ *055/218624* ⊕ *www. trattorialacasalinga.it* ⊘ *Closed Sun.,1 wk at Christmas, and 3 wks in Aug.*

Osteria Antica Mescita San Niccolò

$ | TUSCAN | Always crowded, always good, and always inexpensive, the osteria is next to the church of San Niccolò, and, if you sit in the lower part, you'll find yourself in what was once a chapel dating from the 11th century. The subtle but dramatic background is a nice complement to the food, which is simple Tuscan at its best. **Known for:** delicious soup; outdoor seating in a small, lovely square; great, simple salads. $ *Average main: €11* ✉ *Via San Niccolò 60/r, San Niccolò* ☎ *055/2342836* ⊕ *www.osteriasanniccolo.it.*

Zeb

$ | TUSCAN | Incredibly tasty and gently priced, Zeb stands for *zuppa e bollito* (soup and boiled things) and nothing at this small *alimentari* (delicatessen) disappoints. It's home-style Tuscan cuisine at its very best, served in unpretentious, intimate surroundings: there's room for only about 15 guests. **Known for:** lovely wine list; fantastic soup; terrific pasta. $ *Average main: €13* ✉ *Via San Miniato 2, Oltrarno* ☎ *055/2342864* ⊕ *www. zebgastronomia.com* ⊘ *Closed Wed.*

Coffee and Quick Bites

Gelateria la Carraia

$ | ITALIAN | FAMILY | Although it's a bit of a haul to get here (it's at the foot of Ponte Carraia, two bridges down from the Ponte Vecchio), you'll be well rewarded for doing so. They do standard flavors, and then creative ones such as *limone con biscotti* (lemon sorbet with cookies), and they do both of these very well. **Known for:** every flavor is delicious; super-creamy gelato; generous €1 tasting cones. $ *Average main: €3* ✉ *Piazza Nazario Sauro 2, Santo Spirito* ☎ *055/280695* ⊕ *www. lacarraiagroup.eu.*

Hotels

Hotel Silla

$ | HOTEL | Rooms in this 15th-century palazzo, entered through a courtyard lined with potted plants and sculpture-filled niches, are simply furnished; some have views of the Arno, others have stuccoed ceilings. **Pros:** cordial, friendly staff; great breakfast; in the middle of everything except the crowds. **Cons:** could use an update; small rooms; street noise. $ *Rooms from: €92* ✉ *Via de' Renai 5, San Niccolò* ☎ *055/2342888*

⊕ *www.hotelsilla.it* ⇆ *39 rooms* ⊚*Ⓡ Free Breakfast.*

Lungarno

$$$$ | HOTEL | Many rooms and suites here have private terraces that jut out right over the Arno, granting stunning views of the Palazzo Vecchio and the Lungarno; a studio suite in a 13th-century tower preserves details like exposed stone walls and old archways, and looks over a little square with a medieval tower covered in jasmine. **Pros:** upscale without being stuffy; lovely views of the Arno; Borgo San Jacopo, its one-starred Michelin restaurant. **Cons:** street noise happens; walls can be thin; rooms without Arno views feel less special. Ⓢ *Rooms from: €472* ⊠ *Borgo San Jacopo 14, Oltrarno* ☎ *055/27261* ⊕ *www.lungarnocollection. com* ⇆ *63 rooms* ⊚*Ⓡ Free Breakfast.*

Nightlife

Montecarla

GATHERING PLACES | People sip cocktails against a backdrop of exotic flowers, leopard-print chairs and chintz, surrounded by red walls on the two crowded floors at Montecarla. ⊠ *Via de' Bardi 2, San Niccolò* ☎ *055/2480918.*

Zoe

GATHERING PLACES | Though it's called a *caffetteria,* and coffee is served (as well as terrific salads and burgers at lunchtime), Zoe's fine cocktails are the real draw for elegant Florentines who come here to see and be seen. ⊠ *Via de' Renai 13/r, San Niccolò* ☎ *055/243111* ⊕ *www. zoebar.it.*

Shopping

★ Giulio Giannini e Figlio

STATIONERY | One of Florence's oldest paper-goods stores is *the* place to buy the marbleized stock, which comes in many shapes and sizes, from flat sheets to boxes and even pencils. ⊠ *Piazza Pitti 37/r, Oltrarno* ☎ *055/212621* ⊕ *www. giuliogiannini.it.*

★ Il Torchio

STATIONERY | Photograph albums, frames, diaries, and other objects dressed in handmade paper are high quality, and the prices lower than usual. ⊠ *Via dei Bardi 17, San Niccolò* ☎ *055/2342862* ⊕ *www. legatoriailtorchio.com.*

Maçel

WOMEN'S CLOTHING | Browse collections by lesser-known Italian designers, many of whom use the same factories as the A-list, at this women's clothing shop. ⊠ *Via Guicciardini 128/r, Palazzo Pitti* ☎ *055/287355.*

★ Madova

HATS & GLOVES | Complete your winter wardrobe with a pair of high-quality leather gloves, available in a rainbow of colors and a choice of linings (silk, cashmere, and unlined), from Madova. They've been in business for 100 years. ⊠ *Via Guicciardini 1/r, Palazzo Pitti* ☎ *055/2396526* ⊕ *www.madova.com.*

Santo Spirito flea market

MARKET | FAMILY | The second Sunday of every month brings the Santo Spirito flea market. On the third Sunday of the month, vendors at the Fierucola organic fest sell such delectables as honeys, jams, spice mixes, and fresh vegetables. ⊠ *Santo Spirito, Florence.*

A Side Trip from Florence

Fiesole

A half-day excursion to Fiesole, in the hills 8 km (5 miles) above Florence, gives you a pleasant respite from museums and a wonderful view of the city. From here the view of the Duomo gives you a new appreciation for what the Renaissance accomplished. Fiesole began life as an ancient Etruscan and later Roman village that held some power until it succumbed to barbarian invasions. Eventually it gave up its independence in exchange for Florence's protection. The medieval cathedral, ancient Roman amphitheater, and lovely old villas behind garden walls are clustered on a series of hilltops. A walk around Fiesole can take from one to two or three hours, depending on how far you stroll from the main piazza.

GETTING HERE AND AROUND

The trip from Florence by car takes 20–30 minutes. Drive to Piazza Liberta and cross the Ponte Rosso heading in the direction of the SS65/SR65. Turn right on to Via Salviati and continue on to Via Roccettini. Make a left turn to Via Vecchia Fiesolana, which will take you directly to the center of town. There are several possible routes for the two-hour walk from central Florence to Fiesole. One route begins in a residential area of Florence called Salviatino (Via Barbacane, near Piazza Edison, on the No. 7 bus route), and after a short time, offers peeks over garden walls of beautiful villas, as well as the view over your shoulder at the panorama of Florence in the valley.

VISITOR INFORMATION

CONTACT Fiesole Tourism Office. ⊠ *Via Portigiani 3, Fiesole* ☎ *055/5961311* ⊕ *www.fiesoleforyou.it.*

Sights

Anfiteatro Romano (*Roman Amphitheater*)
RUINS | The beautifully preserved 2,000-seat Anfiteatro Romano, near the Duomo, dates from the 1st century BC and is still used for summer concerts. To the right of the amphitheater are the remains of the Terme Romani (Roman Baths), where you can see the gymnasium, hot and cold baths, and rectangular chamber where the water was heated. A beautifully designed Museo Archeologico,

its facade evoking an ancient Roman temple, is built amid the ruins and contains objects dating from as early as 2000 BC. The nearby Museo Bandini is filled with the private collection of Canon Angelo Maria Bandini (1726–1803); he fancied 13th- to 15th-century Florentine paintings, terra-cotta pieces, and wood sculpture, which he later bequeathed to the Diocese of Fiesole. ⊠ *Via Portigiani 1, Fiesole* ☎ *055/5961293* ⊕ *www.museidifiesole.it* ⊗ *Museo Bandini closed Mon.–Thurs.* ☒ *€12, includes access to archaeological park and museums.*

Badia Fiesolana

CHURCH | From the church of San Domenico it's a five-minute walk northwest to the Badia Fiesolana, which was Fiesole's original cathedral. Dating to the 11th century, it was first the home of the Camaldolese monks. Thanks to Cosimo il Vecchio, the complex was substantially restructured. The facade, never completed owing to Cosimo's death, contains elements of its original Romanesque decoration. ⊠ *Via della Badia dei Roccettini 11, Fiesole* ☎ *055/46851* ⊕ *www.eui.eu* ⊗ *Closed Sat. afternoon and Sun.*

Duomo

CHURCH | A stark medieval interior yields many masterpieces. In the raised presbytery, the **Cappella Salutati** was frescoed by 15th-century artist Cosimo Rosselli, but it was his contemporary, sculptor Mino da Fiesole (1430–84), who put the town on the artistic map. The Madonna on the altarpiece and the tomb of Bishop Salutati are fine examples of the artist's work. ⊠ *Piazza Mino da Fiesole, Fiesole.*

San Domenico

CHURCH | If you really want to stretch your legs, walk 4 km (2½ miles) toward the center of Florence along Via Vecchia Fiesolana, a narrow lane in use since Etruscan times, to the church of San Domenico. Sheltered in the church is the *Madonna and Child with Saints* by

Fra Angelico, who was a Dominican friar here before he moved to Florence. ✉ *Piazza San Domenico, off Via Giuseppe Mantellini, Fiesole* 🕓 *Closed Sun.*

San Francesco

CHURCH | This lovely hilltop church has a good view of Florence and the plain below from its terrace and benches. Off the little cloister is a small, eclectic museum containing, among other things, two Egyptian mummies. Halfway up the hill you'll see sloping steps to the right; they lead to a fragrant wooded park with trails that loop out and back to the church. ✉ *Fiesole.*

🍴 Restaurants

La Reggia degli Etruschi

$$ | **ITALIAN** | Located on a steep hill on the way up to the church of San Francesco, this lovely little eatery is certainly worth the trek. Indulge in inventive reworkings of Tuscan classics, like the *mezzaluna di pera a pecorino* (little half-moon pasta stuffed with pear and pecorino) sauced with Roquefort and poppy seeds. **Known for:** small terrace with outdoor seating; out-of-the-way location; good wine list and friendly service. [$] *Average main: €21* ✉ *Via San Francesco, Fiesole* ☎ *055/59385* 🌐 *www.lareggiadeglietruschi.com.*

🛏 Hotels

Villa San Michele

$$$$ | **HOTEL** | The cypress-lined driveway provides an elegant preamble to this incredibly gorgeous (and very expensive) hotel nestled in the hills of Fiesole. **Pros:** stunning views; exceptional convent conversion; shuttle bus makes frequent forays to and from Florence. **Cons:** you must either depend upon the shuttle bus or have a car; money must be no object; some rooms are small. [$] *Rooms from: €769* ✉ *Via Doccia 4, Fiesole* ☎ *055/5678200* 🌐 *www.belmond.com* 🛏 *45 rooms* 🍴 *Free Breakfast* 🕓 *Closed Nov.–Easter.*

Chapter 7

TUSCANY AND UMBRIA

7

Updated by
Liz Humphreys and
Patricia Rucidlo

◉ Sights	🍴 Restaurants	🛏 Hotels	🛍 Shopping	🍸 Nightlife
★★★★★	★★★★★	★★★★★	★★☆☆☆	★★☆☆☆

WELCOME TO TUSCANY AND UMBRIA

TOP REASONS TO GO

★ **Leaning Tower of Pisa:** It may be touristy, but it's still a whole lot of fun to climb to the top and admire the view.

★ **Wine tasting in Chianti:** Sample the fruits of the region's gorgeous vineyards, either at the wineries themselves or in the wine bars found in the towns.

★ **Piazza del Campo, Siena:** Sip a cappuccino or enjoy some gelato as you take in this spectacular shell-shape piazza.

★ **Assisi, shrine to St. Francis:** Recharge your soul in this rose-color hill town with a visit to the gentle saint's majestic basilica, adorned with great frescoes.

★ **Spoleto, Umbria's musical Mecca:** Crowds may descend and prices ascend here during summer's Festival dei Due Mondi, but Spoleto's hushed charm enchants year-round.

★ **Orvieto's Duomo:** Arresting visions of heaven and hell on the facade and brilliant frescoes within make this Gothic cathedral a dazzler.

A mix of forests, vineyards, olive groves, and poppy fields, the hill regions of central Italy add up to Italian countryside at its most beautiful. The hillside towns wear their history on their sleeves.

1 Lucca. Historic town with 99 churches.

2 Pisa. There's more than just its leaning tower.

3 Chianti. The heart of Italy's most famous wine region.

4 Volterra. Handicrafts made with alabaster can be purchased here.

5 San Gimignano. Hilltown with medieval "skyscrapers."

6 Siena. Charming medieval town.

7 Arezzo. Tuscany's third-largest city.

8 Cortona. This ancient stone town was made famous by the book *Under the Tuscan Sun.*

9 Perugia. Umbria's largest town.

10 Assisi. The city of St. Francis.

11 Spoleto. Come to see the Piazza del Duomo.

12 Orvieto. Carved out volcanic rock and known today for wine and shoe shopping.

EATING AND DRINKING WELL IN TUSCANY

The influence of the ancient Etruscans—who favored the use of fresh herbs—is still felt in Tuscan cuisine three millennia later. Simple and earthy, Tuscan food celebrates the seasons with fresh vegetable dishes, wonderful bread-based soups, and meats perfumed with sage, rosemary, and thyme.

Throughout Tuscany there are excellent upscale restaurants that serve elaborate dishes, but to get a real taste of the flavors of the region, head for the family-run trattorias found in every town. The service and setting are often basic, but the food can be memorable.

Few places serve lighter fare at midday, so expect substantial meals at lunch and dinner, especially in out-of-the-way towns. Dining hours are fairly standard: lunch between 12:30 and 2, dinner between 7:30 and 10.

HOLD THE SALT

Tuscan bread is famous for what it's missing: salt. That's because it's intended to pick up seasoning from the food it accompanies, not be eaten alone. That doesn't mean Tuscans don't like to start a meal with bread, but usually it's prepared in some way. It can be grilled and drizzled with olive oil (*fettunta*), covered with chicken liver spread (*crostino con fegatini*), or toasted, rubbed with garlic, and topped with tomatoes (*bruschetta*).

AFFETTATI MISTI

The name, roughly translated, means "mixed cold cuts," and it's something Tuscans do exceptionally well. A platter of cured meats, served as an antipasto, is sure to include *prosciutto crudo* (cured pork, cut paper-thin) and *salame* (dry sausage, prepared in dozens of ways—some spicy, some sweet). The most distinctly Tuscan affettati are made from *cinta senese* (a once nearly extinct pig found only in the heart of the region) and *cinghiale* (wild boar, which roam all over Italy). You can eat these delicious slices unadorned or layered on a piece of bread.

PASTA

Restaurants throughout Tuscany serve dishes similar to those in Florence, but they also have their own local specialties. Many recipes are from the *nonna* (grandmother) of the restaurant's owner, handed down over time but never written down.

Look in particular for pasta creations made with *pici* (a long, thick, hand-rolled spaghetti). *Pappardelle* (a long, ribbonlike pasta noodle) is frequently paired with sauces made with game, such as *lepre* (hare) or cinghiale. In the northwest, a specialty of Lucca is *tordelli di carne al ragù* (meat-stuffed pasta with a meat sauce).

MEAT

Bistecca fiorentina (a thick T-bone steak, grilled rare) is the classic meat dish of Tuscany, but there are other specialties as well. Many menus will include *tagliata di manzo* (thinly sliced, roasted beef, drizzled with olive oil), *arista di maiale* (roast pork with sage and rosemary), and *salsiccia e fagioli* (pork sausage and beans). In the southern part of the region, don't be surprised to find *piccione* (pigeon), which can be roasted, stuffed, or baked.

WINE

Grape cultivation here also dates from Etruscan times, and vineyards are abundant, particularly in Chianti. The resulting medium-body red wine is a staple on most tables; however, you can select from a multitude of other varieties, including such reds as Brunello di Montalcino and Vino Nobile di Montepulciano and such whites as vermentino and vernaccia.

Super Tuscans (a fanciful name given to a group of wines by American journalists) now command attention as some of the best produced in Italy; they have great depth and complexity. The dessert wine *vin santo* is made throughout the region, and is often sipped with *biscotti* (twice-baked almond cookies), perfect for dunking.

EATING AND DRINKING WELL IN UMBRIA AND THE MARCHES

Central Italy is mountainous, and its food is hearty and straightforward, with a stick-to-the-ribs quality that sees hardworking farmers and artisans through a long day's work and helps them make the steep climb home at night.

In restaurants here, as in much of Italy, you're rewarded for seeking out the local cuisines, and you'll often find better and cheaper food if you're willing to stray a few hundred yards from the main sights. Spoleto is noted for its good food and service, probably a result of high expectations from the international arts crowd. For gourmet food, however, it's hard to beat Spello, which has both excellent restaurants and first-rate wine merchants.

A rule of thumb for eating well throughout Umbria is to order what's in season; stroll through local markets to see what's for sale. A number of restaurants in the region offer *degustazione* (tasting) menus, which give you a chance to try different local specialties without breaking the bank.

TASTY TRUFFLES

More truffles are found in Umbria than anywhere else in Italy. Spoleto and Norcia are prime territory for the *tartufo nero* (reddish-black interior and fine white veins), prized for its extravagant flavor and intense aroma.

The mild summer truffle, *scorzone estivo* (black outside and beige inside), is in season from May through December. The *scorzone autunnale* (burnt brown color and visible veins inside) is found from October through December.

OLIVE OIL

Nearly everywhere you look in Umbria, olive trees grace the hillsides. The soil of the Apennines allows the olives to ripen slowly, guaranteeing low acidity, a cardinal virtue of fine oil. Look for restaurants that proudly display their own oil, often a sign that they care about their food.

Umbria's finest oil is found in Trevi, where the local product is intensely green and fruity. You can sample it in the town's wine bars, which often offer olive-oil tastings.

PORK PRODUCTS

Much of traditional Umbrian cuisine revolves around pork. It can be cooked in wood-fired stoves, sometimes basted with a rich sauce made from innards and red wine. The roasted pork known as *porchetta* is grilled on a spit and flavored with fennel and herbs, leaving a crisp outer sheen.

The art of pork processing has been handed down through generations in Norcia, so much so that charcuterie producers throughout Italy are often known as *norcini*. Don't miss *prosciutto di Norcia*, which is aged for two years.

LENTILS AND SOUPS

The town of Castelluccio di Norcia is particularly known for its lentils and its farro (an ancient grain used by

the Romans, similar to wheat), and for a variety of beans used in soups. Throughout Umbria, look for *imbrecciata,* a soup of beans and grains, delicately flavored with local herbs. Other ingredients that find their way into thick Umbrian soups are wild beet, sorrel, mushrooms, spelt, chickpeas, and the elusive, fragrant saffron, grown in nearby Cascia.

WINE

Sagrantino grapes are the star in Umbria's most notable red wines. For centuries they've been used in Sagrantino *passito,* a semisweet wine made by leaving the grapes to dry for a period after picking in order to intensify their sugar content. In recent decades, Montefalco Sagrantino *secco* (dry) has occupied the front stage. Both passito and secco have a deep red-ruby color, with a full body and rich flavor.

The abundance of *enotecas* (wineshops and wine bars) has made it easier to arrange wine tastings. Many also let you sample different olive oils on toasted bread, known as bruschetta. Some wine information centers, such as La Strada del Sagrantino in the town of Montefalco, will help set up appointments for tastings.

7

Tuscany and Umbria EATING AND DRINKING WELL IN UMBRIA AND THE MARCHES

No place better epitomizes the beauty and splendor of Italy than the central regions of Tuscany and Umbria. They are both characterized by midsize cities and small hilltop towns, each with its own rich history and art treasures. Highlights include the walled city of Lucca; Pisa and its Leaning Tower; Siena, home of the Palio; and Assisi, the city of St. Francis. In between, the gorgeous countryside produces some of Italy's finest wine.

The beauty of the landscape here proves the perfect foil for the regions abundance of outstanding art and architecture. Many of cities and towns in this region have retained the same fundemental character over the past 500 years. Civic rivalries that led to bloody battles centuries ago have given way to serious soccer rivalries.

MAJOR REGIONS

Nature outdid herself with **Tuscany**, the central Italian region that has Florence as its principal city. Descriptions and photographs can't do the landscape justice—the hills, draped with woods , vineyards and olive groves are magical. Assisi is famous for it's basilica, Lucca has 99 churches, Pisa's leaning tower is infamous, and the hilltop towns of Volterra, San Gimignano, Siena, Arezzo, and Cortona are magical. Take in panoramic views of the countryside in Chianti and shop **Umbria's** landscape is wilder, the valleys deeper, and the mountains higher. The trendy boutiques in Perugia are a pleasure and the towns of Spolenta, and Orvieto are good bases for exploration.

Planning

When to Go

Throughout Tuscany and Umbria, the best times to visit are spring and fall. Days are warm, nights are cool, and though there are still tourists, the crowds are smaller. In the countryside the scenery is gorgeous, with abundant greenery and flowers in spring, and burnished leaves in autumn.

July and August are the most popular times to visit. Note, though, that the heat is often oppressive and mosquitoes are prevalent. Try to start your days early and visit major sights first to beat the crowds and the midday sun. For relief from the heat, head to the mountains of the Garfagnana, where hiking is spectacular, or hit the beach at resort towns such as Forte dei Marmi and Viareggio, along the Maremma coast, on the island of Elba, or on the long, flat stretches of sandy beach on the east coast of the Marches.

November through March you might wonder who invented the term "sunny Italy." The panoramas are still beautiful, even with overcast skies, frequent rain, and occasional snow. In winter Florence benefits from shorter museum lines and less competition for restaurant tables. Outside the cities, though, many hotels and restaurants close for the season.

Planning Your Time

Central Italy isn't the place for a jam-packed itinerary. One of the greatest pleasures here is indulging in rustic hedonism, marked by long lunches and show-stopping sunsets. Whether by car, by bike, or on foot, you'll want to get out into the glorious landscape, but it's smart to keep your plans modest. Set a church or a hill town or an out-of-the-way restaurant as your destination, knowing that half the pleasure is in getting there—admiring as you go the stately palaces, the tidy geometry of row upon row of grapevines, the fields vibrant with red poppies, sunflowers, and yellow broom.

In Tuscany, you'll need to devise a strategy for seeing the sights. Take Siena: this beautiful, art-filled town simply can't be missed; it's compact enough that you can see the major sights on a day trip, and that's exactly what most people do. Spend the night, though, and you'll get to see the town breathe a sigh and relax on the day-trippers' departure. In Pisa, the famous tower and rest of the Camposanto are not only worth seeing but a must-see, a highlight of any trip to Italy. But nearby Lucca must not be overlooked either. In fact, this walled town has greater charms than Pisa does, making it a better choice for an overnight, so you should come up with a plan that takes in both places.

Umbria is a nicely compact collection of character-rich hill towns; you can settle in one, then explore the others, as well as the countryside and forest in between, on day trips. Perugia, Umbria's largest and liveliest city, is a logical choice for your base, particularly if you're arriving from the north. If you want something a little quieter, virtually any other town in the region will suit your purposes; even Assisi, which overflows with bus tours during the day, is delightfully quiet in the evening and early morning. Spoleto and Orvieto are the most developed towns to the south, but they're still of modest proportions.

GETTING HERE AND AROUND

Most flights to Tuscany originating in the United States stop either in Rome, London, Paris, or Frankfurt, and then connect to Florence's small **Aeroporto A. Vespucci** (commonly called Peretola), or to Pisa's **Aeroporto Galileo Galilei.** Delta currently has one seasonal direct flight from New York (JFK) to Pisa.

Alternatively, it's an hour by train or an hour and a half by car to reach the lovely town of Orvieto from Rome's **Aeroporto Leonardo da Vinci** (commonly called Fiumicino). Another option is to fly to Milan and pick up a connecting flight to Pisa, Florence, Perugia, or Ancona in the Marches.

Buses are a reliable but time-consuming means of getting around the region because they tend to stop in every town. Trains are a better option in virtually every respect when you're headed to Pisa, Lucca, Arezzo, and other cities with good rail service. But for most smaller towns, buses are the only option. Be aware that making arrangements for bus travel, particularly for a non-Italian speaker, can be a test of patience. Several direct daily trains run by the Italian state railway, **Trenitalia** (*892021, www.trenitalia.com*), link Florence and Rome with Perugia and Assisi, and local service to the same area is available from Terontola (on the

7

Tuscany and Umbria PLANNING

Rome–Florence line) and from Foligno (on the Rome–Ancona line). Intercity trains between Rome and Florence make stops in Orvieto, and the main Rome–Ancona line passes through Narni, Terni, Spoleto, and Foligno.

Driving is the only way (other than hiking or biking) to reach many of Central Italy's small towns and vineyards.

Restaurants

A meal in Central Italy traditionally consists of five courses, and every menu you enounter will be organized along this plan of antipasto, primo, secondo, contorno, and dolce. The crucial rule of restaurant dining is that you should order at least two courses. Otherwise, you'll likely end up with a lonely piece of meat and no sides.

Hotels

A visit to Central Italy is a trip into the country. There are plenty of good hotels in the larger towns, but the classic experience is to stay in one of the rural accommodations—often converted private homes, sometimes working farms or vineyards (known as *agriturismi*). Virtually every older town, no matter how small, has some kind of hotel. A trend, particularly around Gubbio, Orvieto, and Todi, is to convert old villas, farms, and monasteries into first-class hotels. The natural splendor of the countryside more than compensates for the distance from town—provided you have a car. Hotels in town tend to be simpler than their country cousins, with a few notable exceptions in Spoleto, Gubbio, and Perugia.

Although it's tempting to think you can stumble upon a little out-of-the-way hotel at the end of the day, you're better off not testing your luck. Make reservations before you go. If you don't have a reservation, you may be able to get help finding a room from the local tourist office.

Hotel reviews have been shortened. For full information, visit Fodors.com.

WHAT IT COSTS in Euros			
$	$$	$$$	$$$$
RESTAURANTS			
under €15	€15–€24	€25–€35	over €35
HOTELS			
under €125	€125–€200	€201–€300	over €300

Lucca

Ramparts built in the 16th and 17th centuries enclose a charming fortress town filled with churches (99 of them), terra-cotta–roofed buildings, and narrow cobblestone streets, along which locals maneuver bikes to do their daily shopping. Here Caesar, Pompey, and Crassus agreed to rule Rome as a triumvirate in 56 BC; Lucca was later the first Tuscan town to accept Christianity. The town still has a mind of its own, and when most of Tuscany was voting communist as a matter of course, Lucca's citizens rarely followed suit. The famous composer Giacomo Puccini (1858–1924) was born here; he is celebrated during the summer Opera Theater and Music Festival of Lucca. The ramparts circling the centro storico are the perfect place to stroll, bicycle, or just admire the view.

GETTING HERE AND AROUND

You can reach Lucca easily by train from Florence; the centro storico is a short walk from the station. If you're driving, take the A11/E76.

VISITOR INFORMATION

CONTACT Lucca Tourism Office. ✉ *Piazzale Verdi, Lucca* ☎ *0583/583150* ⊕ *www.luccaturismo.it.*

Sights

Duomo

CHURCH | The blind arches on the cathedral's facade are a fine example of the rigorously ordered Pisan Romanesque style, in this case happily enlivened by an extremely varied collection of small, carved columns. Take a closer look at the decoration of the facade and that of the portico below; they make this one of the most entertaining church exteriors in Tuscany. The Gothic interior contains a moving Byzantine crucifix—called the Volto Santo, or Holy Face—brought here, according to legend, in the 8th century (though it probably dates from between the 11th and early 13th century). The masterpiece of the Sienese sculptor Jacopo della Quercia (circa 1371–1438) is the marble *Tomb of Ilaria del Carretto* (1407–08). ⊠ *Piazza San Martino, Lucca* ☎ *0583/919175* ⊕ *www.museocattedrale-lucca.it* ☎ *€9.*

Museo Nazionale di Villa Guinigi

ART MUSEUM | On the eastern end of the historic center, this sadly overlooked museum has an extensive collection of local Etruscan, Roman, Romanesque, and Renaissance art. The museum represents an overview of Lucca's artistic traditions from Etruscan times until the 17th century, housed in the 15th-century former villa of the Guinigi family. ⊠ *Via della Quarquonia 4, Lucca* ☎ *0583/496033* ⊕ *www.polomusealetoscana.beniculturali.it* ☎ *€4* ☉ *Closed Mon., Wed., and Fri. morning. Closed Sat.–Sun.*

★ Passeggiata delle Mura

CITY PARK | **FAMILY** | Any time of day when the weather is nice, you can find the citizens of Lucca cycling, jogging, strolling, or kicking a soccer ball in this green, beautiful, and very large circular park—neither inside nor outside the city but rather right atop and around the ring of ramparts that defines Lucca. Sunlight streams through two rows of tall plane trees to dapple the *passeggiata delle mura* (walk on the walls), which is 4.2 km (2½ miles) in length. Ten bulwarks are topped with lawns, many with picnic tables and some with play equipment for children. Be aware at all times of where the edge is—there are no railings, and the drop to the ground outside the city is a precipitous 40 feet. ⊠ *Lucca.*

Piazza dell'Anfiteatro Romano

PLAZA/SQUARE | **FAMILY** | Here's where the ancient Roman amphitheater once stood; some of the medieval buildings built over the amphitheater retain its original oval shape and brick arches. ⊠ *Piazza Anfiteatro, Lucca.*

San Frediano

CHURCH | A 14th-century mosaic decorates the facade of this church just steps from the Anfiteatro. Inside are works by Jacopo della Quercia (circa 1371–1438) and Matteo Civitali (1436–1501), as well as the lace-clad mummy of St. Zita (circa 1218–78), the patron saint of household servants. ⊠ *Piazza San Frediano, Lucca* ☎ *3498440290* ⊕ *www.sanfredianolucca.com* ☎ *€3.*

San Michele in Foro

CHURCH | The facade here is even more fanciful than that of the Duomo. Its upper levels have nothing but air behind them (after the front of the church was built, there were no funds to raise the nave), and the winged Archangel Michael, who stands at the very top, seems precariously poised for flight. The facade, heavily restored in the 19th century, displays busts of such 19th-century Italian patriots as Garibaldi and Cavour. Check out the superb Filippino Lippi (1457/58–1504) panel painting of Saints Jerome, Sebastian, Rocco, and Helen in the right transept. ⊠ *Piazza San Michele, Lucca.*

Torre Guinigi

NOTABLE BUILDING | **FAMILY** | The tower of the medieval Palazzo Guinigi contains one of the city's most curious sights: a grove of ilex trees has grown at the top of the tower, and their roots have pushed

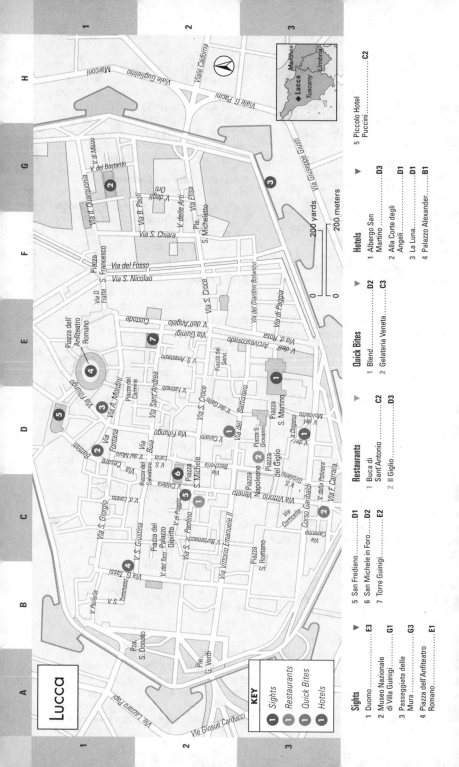

Lucca

KEY

1	Sights
1	Restaurants
1	Quick Bites
1	Hotels

Sights ▶

1	Duomo	D1
2	Museo Nazionale di Villa Guinigi	G1
3	Passeggiata delle Mura	G3
4	Piazza dell'Anfiteatro Romano	E1
5	San Frediano	D1
6	San Michele in Foro	D2
7	Torre Guinigi	E2

Restaurants ▶

| 1 | Buca di Sant'Antonio | C2 |
| 2 | Il Giglio | D3 |

Quick Bites ▶

| 1 | Blend | D2 |
| 2 | Gelateria Veneta | C3 |

Hotels ▶

1	Albergo San Martino	D3
2	Alla Corte degli Angeli	D1
3	La Luna	D1
4	Palazzo Alexander	B1
5	Piccolo Hotel Puccini	C2

Marches · Umbria · Lucca · Tuscany

0 ——— 200 yards

0 ——— 200 meters

heir way into the room below. From the op you have a magnificent view of the ity and the surrounding countryside. Only the tower is open to the public, not he palazzo.) ✉ *Via Sant'Andrea, Lucca* ☎ *0583/48090* 🎫 *€5.*

🍴 Restaurants

★ Buca di Sant'Antonio

$$ | **TUSCAN** | The staying power of Buca di Sant'Antonio—it's been around since 1782—is the result of superlative Tuscan ood brought to the table by waitstaff who don't miss a beat. The menu includes he simple but blissful *tortelli lucchesi al sugo* (meat-stuffed pasta with a tomato-and-meat sauce), as well as more daring dishes such as roast *capretto* (kid goat) with herbs. **Known for:** classy, family-run ambience; superlative pastas; excellent sommelier. [$] *Average main: €20* ✉ *Via della Cervia 3, Lucca* ☎ *0583/55881* 🌐 *www.bucadisantantonio.com* 🕒 *Closed Mon., 1 wk in Jan., and 1 wk in July. No dinner Sun.*

★ Il Giglio

$$$ | **TUSCAN** | Cutting-edge divine food along with Tuscan classics) are served n this one-room space; the roaring fire-place dominates. In the summer, there's seating outdoors on a pretty little piazza. **Known for:** fine service; creative menu and ingredients; the wine list, especially its selection of local wines. [$] *Average main: €28* ✉ *Piazza del Giglio 2, Lucca* ☎ *0583/494508* 🌐 *www.ristorantegiglio.com* 🕒 *Closed Wed. and 15 days in Nov. No dinner Tues.*

☕ Coffee and Quick Bites

Blend

$ | **ITALIAN** | If you're looking for a lovely spot to recharge, stop by this place (just around the corner from the Duomo), and have a fantastic sandwich, or a glass of wine, or a tasty salad, a coffee, or dessert. It's open from late morning to late in the evening. **Known for:** open late; near the Duomo; good salads. [$] *Average main: €7* ✉ *Piazza S. Giusto 8, Duomo.*

Gelateria Veneta

$ | **ITALIAN** | **FAMILY** | This place makes outstanding gelato, sorbet, and ices (some sugar-free). They prepare their confections three times a day, using the same recipes with which the brothers Arnoldo opened the place in 1927. **Known for:** delicious ices on a stick; longtime institution and a favorite with locals; sorbet-stuffed frozen fruits. [$] *Average main: €3* ✉ *Via V. Veneto 74, Lucca* ☎ *0583/467037* 🌐 *www.gelateriaveneta.net* 🕒 *Closed Nov.–Mar.*

🛏 Hotels

★ Albergo San Martino

$ | **B&B/INN** | **FAMILY** | The brocade bedspreads of this inn in the heart of the centro storico are fresh and crisp, the proprietor friendly, the breakfast, served in a cheerful apricot room, more than ample. **Pros:** friendly staff; comfortable beds; great breakfast, including homemade cakes and pastries. **Cons:** surroundings are pleasant and stylish though not luxurious; parking is difficult; slightly noisy during Lucca Music Festival. [$] *Rooms from: €89* ✉ *Via della Dogana 9, Lucca* ☎ *0583/469181* 🌐 *www.albergosanmartino.it* 🛏 *18 rooms* 🍴 *Free Breakfast.*

Alla Corte degli Angeli

$$ | **B&B/INN** | This charming hotel with a friendly staff is right off the main shopping drag, Via Fillungo. **Pros:** many rooms are connecting, making them good for families; fantastic on-site restaurant; great location. **Cons:** books up quickly; some rooms have tubs but no showers; not all rooms are created equal. [$] *Rooms from: €180* ✉ *Via degli Angeli 23, Lucca* ☎ *0583/469204, 0583/991989* 🌐 *www.allacortedegliangeli.it* 🛏 *21 rooms* 🍴 *Free Breakfast.*

La Luna

$$ | **B&B/INN** | On a quiet, airy courtyard close to the Piazza del Mercato, this hotel, run by the Barbieri family for more than four decades, occupies two renovated wings of an old building. **Pros:** central location; professional staff; the annex has wheelchair-accessible rooms. **Cons:** street noise can be a bit of a problem; some rooms feel dated; may be too central for some. [$] *Rooms from: €160* ✉ *Corte Compagni 12, at Via Fillungo, Lucca* ☎ *0583/493634, 0583/490021* 🌐 *www.hotellaluna.it* 🍴 *Free Breakfast* 🕒 *Closed Jan. 7–31* 🛏 *29 rooms.*

Palazzo Alexander

$$ | **HOTEL** | The building, dating from the 12th century, has been restructured to create the ease common to Lucchesi nobility: timbered ceilings, warm yellow walls, and brocaded chairs adorn the public rooms, and guest rooms have high ceilings and that same glorious damask. **Pros:** a short walk from San Michele in Foro; intimate feel; gracious staff. **Cons:** books up quickly; some complain of too-thin walls; might be too quiet for some. [$] *Rooms from: €160* ✉ *Via S. Giustina 48, Lucca* ☎ *0583/583571* 🌐 *www.hotelpalazzoalexander.it* 🛏 *13 rooms* 🍴 *Free Breakfast.*

Piccolo Hotel Puccini

$ | **HOTEL** | Steps away from the busy square and church of San Michele al Foro, this little hotel is quiet, calm, and affordable and a great deal: wallpaper, hardwood floors, and throw rugs are among the handsome decorations. **Pros:** quiet, central location; cheery, English-speaking staff; good value. **Cons:** some rooms are on the dark side; books up quickly; many wish the breakfast was more copious. [$] *Rooms from: €90* ✉ *Via di Poggio 9, Lucca* ☎ *0583/55421* 🌐 *www.hotelpuccini.com* 🛏 *14 rooms* 🍴 *Free Breakfast.*

Shopping

★ **Antica Bottega di Prospero**

FOOD | Stop by this shop for top-quality local food products, including farro, dried porcini mushrooms, olive oil, and wine. ✉ *Via San Lucia 13, Lucca* ☎ *0583/494875.*

★ **Caniparoli**

CHOCOLATE | Chocolate lovers will be pleased with the selection of artisanal chocolates, marzipan delights, and gorgeous cakes. Creations become even more fanciful during two big Christian holidays: Christmas and Easter. ✉ *Via San Paolino 44, Lucca* ☎ *0583/53456* 🌐 *www.caniparolicioccolateria.it.*

★ **Enoteca Vanni**

WINE/SPIRITS | A huge selection of wines, as well as an ancient cellar, make this place worth a stop. For the cost of the wine only, tastings can be organized through the shopkeepers and are held in the cellar or outside in a lovely little piazza. All of this can be paired with *affettati misti* (sliced cured meats) and cheeses of the highest caliber. ✉ *Piazza San Salvatore 7, Lucca* ☎ *0583/491902* 🌐 *www.enotecavanni.com.*

★ **Pasticceria Taddeucci**

FOOD | A particularly delicious version of *buccellato*—the sweet, anise-flavored bread with raisins that is a Luccan specialty—is baked at Pasticceria Taddeucci. ✉ *Piazza San Michele 34, Lucca* ☎ *0583/494933* 🌐 *www.buccellatotaddeucci.com.*

Activities

Poli Antonio Biciclette

BIKING | This is the best option for bicycle rental on the east side of town. ✉ *Piazza Santa Maria 42, Lucca East* ☎ *0583/493787* 🌐 *www.biciclettepoli.com.*

Pisa

If you can get beyond the kitsch of the stalls hawking cheap souvenirs around the Leaning Tower, you'll find that Pisa has much to offer. Its treasures aren't as abundant as those of Florence, to which it is inevitably compared, but the cathedral-baptistery-tower complex of Piazza del Duomo, known collectively as the Campo dei Miracoli (Field of Miracles), is among the most dramatic settings in Italy.

Pisa may have been inhabited as early as the Bronze Age. It was certainly populated by the Etruscans and, in turn, became part of the Roman Empire. In the early Middle Ages this city on the Arno River flourished as an economic powerhouse—along with Amalfi, Genoa, and Venice, it was one of the four maritime republics. The city's economic and political power ebbed in the early 15th century as it fell under Florence's domination, though it enjoyed a brief resurgence under Cosimo I de' Medici in the mid-16th century. Pisa sustained heavy damage during World War II, but the Duomo and the Leaning Tower were spared, along with some other grand Romanesque structures.

GETTING HERE AND AROUND

Pisa is an easy hour's train ride from Florence. By car it's a straight shot on the Firenze–Pisa–Livorno ("Fi-Pi-Li") autostrada. The Pisa–Lucca train runs frequently and takes about 30 minutes.

VISITOR INFORMATION

CONTACT Pisa Tourism Office. ✉ *Piazza del Duomo 7, Pisa* ☎ *050/550100* ⊕ *www. turismo.pisa.it.*

Sights

Battistero

NOTABLE BUILDING | This lovely Gothic baptistery, which stands across from the Duomo's facade, is best known for the pulpit carved by Nicola Pisano (circa 1220–84; father of Giovanni Pisano) in 1260. Every half hour, an employee will dramatically close the doors, then intone, thereby demonstrating how remarkable the acoustics are in the place. ✉ *Piazza del Duomo, Pisa* ☎ *050/835011* ⊕ *www. opapisa.it* ✉ *€5, discounts available if bought in combination with tickets for other monuments.*

Camposanto

CEMETERY | According to legend, the cemetery—a walled structure on the western side of the Piazza dei Miracoli—is filled with earth that returning Crusaders brought back from the Holy Land. Contained within are numerous frescoes, notably *The Drunkenness of Noah,* by Renaissance artist Benozzo Gozzoli (1422–97), and the disturbing *Triumph of Death* (14th century; artist uncertain), whose subject matter shows what was on people's minds in a century that saw the ravages of the Black Death. ✉ *Piazza del Duomo, Pisa* ☎ *050/835011* ⊕ *www. opapisa.it* ✉ *€5.*

Duomo

CHURCH | Pisa's cathedral brilliantly utilizes the horizontal marble-stripe motif (borrowed from Moorish architecture) that became common on Tuscan cathedrals. It is famous for the Romanesque panels on the transept door facing the tower that depict scenes from the life of Christ. The beautifully carved 14th-century pulpit is by Giovanni Pisano. ✉ *Piazza del Duomo, Pisa* ☎ *050/835011* ⊕ *www.opapisa.it.*

★ Leaning Tower (Torre Pendente)

NOTABLE BUILDING | Legend holds that Galileo conducted an experiment on the nature of gravity by dropping metal balls from the top of the 187-foot-high Leaning Tower of Pisa. Historians, however, say this legend has no basis in fact—which isn't quite to say that it's false. Work on this tower, built as a *campanile* (bell tower) for the Duomo, started in 1173: the lopsided settling began when construction reached the third story. The tower's architects attempted to compensate through such methods as making the

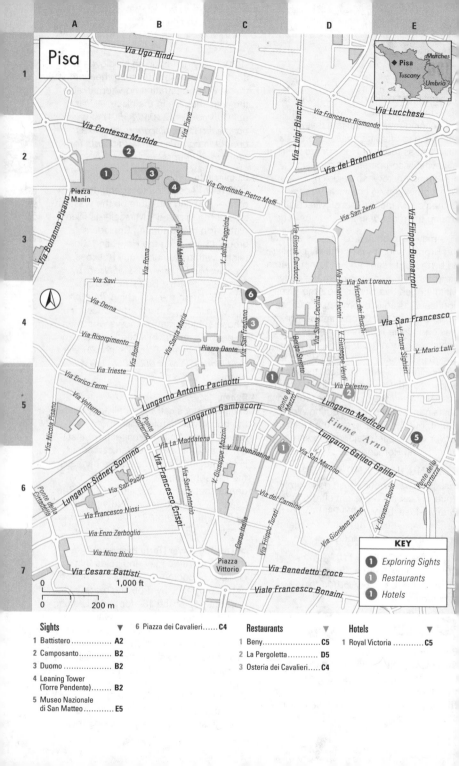

Pisa

Via Ugo Rindi

Via Contessa Matilde

Piazza Manin

KEY

① Exploring Sights
① Restaurants
① Hotels

0 — 1,000 ft
0 — 200 m

Sights ▼

1 Battistero **A2**
2 Camposanto **B2**
3 Duomo **B2**
4 Leaning Tower
(Torre Pendente)........ **B2**
5 Museo Nazionale
di San Matteo **E5**

6 Piazza dei Cavalieri...... **C4**

Restaurants ▼

1 Beny...................... **C5**
2 La Pergoletta **D5**
3 Osteria dei Cavalieri..... **C4**

Hotels ▼

1 Royal Victoria **C5**

emaining floors slightly taller on the eaning side, but the extra weight only made the problem worse. The settling continued, and by the late 20th century t had accelerated to such a point that many feared the tower would simply topple over, despite all efforts to prop it up. The structure has since been firmly anchored to the earth. The final phase to restore the tower to its original tilt of 300 years ago was launched in early 2000 and finished two years later. The last phase removed some 100 tons of earth from beneath the foundation. Reservations, which are essential, can be made online or by calling the Museo dell'Opera del Duomo; it's also possible to arrive at the ticket office and book for the same day. Note that children under eight years of age are not allowed to climb. ⊠ *Piazza del Duomo, Pisa* ☎ *050/835011* ⊕ *www. opapisa.it* ☒ *€18.*

Museo Nazionale di San Matteo

ART MUSEUM | On the north bank of the Arno, this museum contains some beautiful examples of local Romanesque and Gothic art. Here you'll find very few visitors, and stunning works by Donatello and Benozzo Gozzoli (among others). ⊠ *Piazza Matteo in Soarta 1, Pisa* ☎ *050/541865* ⊕ *www.polomusealetoscana.beniculturali.it* ☒ *€5* ⊙ *Closed Sun.*

Piazza dei Cavalieri

PLAZA/SQUARE | The piazza, with its fine Renaissance **Palazzo dei Cavalieri, Palazzo dell'Orologio,** and Chiesa di **Santo Stefano dei Cavalieri,** was laid out by Giorgio Vasari in about 1560. The square was the seat of the Ordine dei Cavalieri di San Stefano (Order of the Knights of St. Stephen), a military and religious institution meant to defend the coast from possible invasion by the Turks. Also in this square is the prestigious **Scuola Normale Superiore,** founded by Napoléon in 1810 on the French model. Here graduate students pursue doctorates in literature, philosophy, mathematics, and science. In front of the school is a large

statue of Ferdinando I de' Medici dating from 1596. On the extreme left is the tower where the hapless Ugolino della Gherardesca (died 1289) was imprisoned with his two sons and two grandsons—legend holds that he ate them. Dante immortalized him in Canto XXXIII of his *Inferno.* Duck into the **Church of Santo Stefano** (if you're lucky enough to find it open) and check out Bronzino's splendid *Nativity of Christ* (1564–65). ⊠ *Piazza dei Cavalieri, Pisa.*

🍴 Restaurants

★ Beny

$$$ | TUSCAN | Apricot walls hung with etchings of Pisa make this small, single-room restaurant warmly romantic. Husband and wife Damiano and Sandra Lazzerini have been running the place for two decades, and it shows in their obvious enthusiasm while talking about the menu (fish is a focus) and daily specials, which often astound. **Known for:** terrific wine list; superb fish dishes; gracious service. 💲 *Average main: €27* ⊠ *Piazza Gambacorti 22, Pisa* ☎ *050/25067* ⊙ *Closed Sun. and 2 wks in mid-Aug. No lunch Sat.*

La Pergoletta

$$ | TUSCAN | FAMILY | On an old town street named for its beautiful towers, this small, simple restaurant is in one such tower itself. It's a place where Pisans come to celebrate. **Known for:** gracious waitstaff; creative, inventive menu; festive atmosphere. 💲 *Average main: €16* ⊠ *Via delle Belle Torri 36, Pisa* ☎ *050/542458* ⊕ *www.ristorantelapergoletta.com* ⊙ *Closed Mon. and 1 wk in Aug. No lunch Sat.*

Osteria dei Cavalieri

$ | ITALIAN | This charming white-wall restaurant, a few steps from Piazza dei Cavalieri, is reason enough to come to Pisa. They can do it all here—serve up exquisitely grilled fish dishes, please vegetarians, and prepare tagliata for meat lovers. **Known for:** vegetable tasting menu; land tasting menu; sea tasting menu. $ *Average main: €14 ⊠ Via San Frediano 16, Pisa ☎ 050/580858 ⊕ www. osteriacavalieri.pisa.it ⊗ Closed Sun., 2 wks in Aug., and Dec. 29–Jan. 7. No lunch Sat.*

 ## Hotels

Royal Victoria
$ | **HOTEL** | In a pleasant palazzo facing the Arno, a 10-minute walk from the Campo dei Miracoli, the hotel has room styles that range from the 1800s, complete with frescoes, to the 1920s; the most charming are in the old tower. **Pros:** old-world charm; friendly staff; lovely views of the Arno from many rooms. **Cons:** rooms a little worn; rooms vary significantly in size; not all rooms have views of the Arno. $ *Rooms from: €60 ⊠ Lungarno Pacinotti 12, Pisa ☎ 050/940111 ⊕ www.royalvictoria.it ⇱ 38 rooms* ❑ *Free Breakfast.*

Performing Arts

Fondazione Teatro di Pisa
THEATER | Pisa has a lively performing-arts scene, most of which happens at the 19th-century Teatro Verdi. Music and dance performances are presented from September through May. Contact Fondazione Teatro di Pisa for schedules and information. ⊠ *Via Palestro 40, Lungarni ☎ 050/941111 ⊕ www.teatrodipisa.pi.it.*

Chianti

This is the heartland: both sides of the Strada Chiantigiana (SR222) are embraced by glorious panoramic views of vineyards, olive groves, and castle towers. Traveling south from Florence, you first reach the aptly named one-street town of Strada in Chianti. Farther south, the number of vineyards on either side of the road dramatically increases—as do the signs inviting you in for a free tasting. Beyond Strada lies Greve in Chianti, completely surrounded by wineries and filled with wineshops. There's art to be had as well: Passignano, west of Greve, has an abbey that shelters a 15th-century *Last Supper* by Domenico and Davide Ghirlandaio. Farther still, along the Strada Chiantigiana, are Panzano and Castellina in Chianti, both hill towns. It's from near Panzano and Castellina that branch roads head to the other main towns of eastern Chianti: Radda in Chianti, Gaiole in Chianti, and Castelnuovo Berardenga.

The Strada Chiantigiana gets crowded during the high season, but no one is in a hurry. The slow pace gives you time to soak up the beautiful scenery.

Greve in Chianti

40 km (25 miles) north of Siena, 28 km (17½ miles) south of Florence.

If there is a capital of Chianti, it is Greve, a friendly market town with no shortage of cafés, enoteche, and crafts shops lining its streets.

GETTING HERE AND AROUND
Driving from Florence or Siena, Greve is easily reached via the Strada Chiantigiana (SR222). SITA buses travel frequently between Florence and Greve. Tra-In and SITA buses connect Siena and Greve, but a direct trip is virtually impossible. There is no train service to Greve.

VISITOR INFORMATION
CONTACT Greve in Chianti Tourism Office. ⊠ *Piazza Matteotti 11 ☎ 055/8546299 ⊕ www.greve-in-chianti.info.*

 ## Sights

Montefioralle
TOWN | A tiny hilltop hamlet, about 2 km (1 mile) west of Greve in Chianti, Montefioralle is the ancestral home of Amerigo Vespucci (1454–1512), the mapmaker, navigator, and explorer who named

America. (His cousin-in-law Simonetta may have been the inspiration for Sandro Botticelli's *The Birth of Venus*, painted sometime in the 1480s.)

Piazza Matteotti

PLAZA/SQUARE | Greve's gently sloping and asymmetrical central piazza is surrounded by an attractive arcade with shops of all kinds. In the center stands a statue of the discoverer of New York harbor, Giovanni da Verrazzano (circa 1480–1527). Check out the lively market held here on Saturday morning. ✉ *Greve in Chianti.*

🍴 Restaurants

Da Padellina

$ | **TUSCAN** | Locals don't flock to this restaurant on the outskirts of Strada in Chianti for the art on the walls, some of it questionable, most of it kitsch, but instead for the bistecca fiorentina. As big as a breadboard and served rare, one of these justly renowned steaks is enough to feed a family of four, with doggie bags willingly provided if required. **Known for:** great grilled meats; large, diverse wine list; unpretentious local choice. [$] *Average main: €10* ✉ *Via Corso del Popolo 54, 10 km (6 miles) north of Greve, Greve in Chianti* ☎ *055/858388* ⏲ *Closed Thurs.*

Enoteca Fuoripiazza

$ | **TUSCAN** | Detour off Greve's flower-strewn main square for food that relies heavily on local ingredients (like cheese and salami produced nearby). The lengthy wine list provides a bewildering array of choices to pair with *affettati misti* (cured meats) or one of their primi—the *pici* (a thick, short noodle) are deftly prepared here. **Known for:** attentively prepared food; local cheese and salami; alfresco dining. [$] *Average main: €14* ✉ *Via I Maggio 2, Greve in Chianti* ☎ *055/8546313* 🌐 *www.enotecafuoripiazza.it* ⏲ *Closed Mon.*

★ **Ristoro di Lamole**

$$ | **TUSCAN** | Up a winding road lined with olive trees and vineyards, this place is worth the effort it takes to find. The view from the outdoor terrace is divine, as is the simple, exquisitely prepared Tuscan cuisine: start with the bruschetta drizzled with olive oil or the sublime *verdure sott'olio* (marinated vegetables) before moving on to any of the fine secondi. **Known for:** sweeping view from the terrace; your hosts Paolo and Filippo; *coniglio* (rabbit) is a specialty. [$] *Average main: €20* ✉ *Via di Lamole 6, Località Lamole, Greve in Chianti* ☎ *055/8547050* 🌐 *www.ristorodilamole.it* ⏲ *Closed Wed. and Nov.–Apr.*

🛏 Hotels

Albergo del Chianti

$$ | **B&B/INN** | **FAMILY** | Simple but pleasantly decorated bedrooms with plain modern cabinets and wardrobes and wrought-iron beds have views of the town square or out over the tile rooftops toward the surrounding hills. **Pros:** swimming pool; central location; best value in Greve. **Cons:** small bathrooms; rooms facing the piazza can be noisy; remote: a car is a necessity. [$] *Rooms from: €145* ✉ *Piazza Matteotti 86, Greve in Chianti* ☎ *055/853763* 🌐 *www.albergodelchianti.it* ⏲ *Closed Jan.–beginning Mar.* 🛏 *22 rooms* 🍴 *Free Breakfast.*

★ **Villa Bordoni**

$$$ | **B&B/INN** | Scottish expats David and Catherine Gardner transformed a ramshackle 16th-century villa into a stunning retreat where no two rooms are alike—all have stenciled walls; some have four-poster beds, others small mezzanines. **Pros:** wonderful hosts; splendidly isolated in the hills above Greve; beautiful decor. **Cons:** need a car to get around; on a long and bumpy dirt road; books up quickly. [$] *Rooms from: €235* ✉ *Via San Cresci 31/32, Greve in Chianti* ☎ *055/8546230* 🌐 *www.villabordoni.com* ⏲ *Closed Dec.–Feb.* 🛏 *11 rooms* 🍴 *Free Breakfast.*

Villa Il Poggiale

$ | B&B/INN | FAMILY | Renaissance gardens, beautiful rooms with high ceilings and elegant furnishings, a panoramic pool, and expert staff are just a few of the things that make a stay at this 16th-century villa memorable. **Pros:** exceptionally professional staff; beautiful gardens and panoramic setting; elegant historical building. **Cons:** some rooms face a country road and may be noisy during the day; private transportation necessary; it may be too isolated for some. $ *Rooms from: €142 ⊠ Via Empolese 69, 20 km (12 miles) northwest of Greve, San Casciano Val di Pesa, Greve in Chianti* ☎ *055/828311* ⊕ *www.villailpoggiale.it* ⊗ *Closed Jan. and Feb.* ⇆ *26 rooms* ⊙ *Free Breakfast.*

Panzano

7 km (4½ miles) south of Greve, 36 km (22 miles) south of Florence.

The magnificent views of the valleys of the Pesa and Greve Rivers easily make Panzano one of the prettiest stops in Chianti. The triangular Piazza Bucciarelli is the heart of the new town. A short stroll along Via Giovanni da Verrazzano brings you up to the old town, Panzano Alto, which is still partly surrounded by medieval walls. The town's 13th-century castle is now almost completely absorbed by later buildings (its central tower is now a private home).

GETTING HERE AND AROUND

From Florence or Siena, Panzano is easily reached by car along the Strada Chiantigiana (SR222). SITA buses travel frequently between Florence and Panzano. From Siena, the journey by bus is extremely difficult because SITA and Tra-In do not coordinate their schedules. There is no train service to Panzano.

 ## Sights

San Leolino

CHURCH | Ancient even by Chianti standards, this hilltop church probably dates from the 10th century, but was completely rebuilt in the Romanesque style sometime in the 13th century. It has a 14th-century cloister worth seeing. The 16th-century terra-cotta tabernacles are attributed to Giovanni della Robbia, and there's also a remarkable triptych (attributed to the Master of Panzano) that was executed sometime in the mid-14th century. Open days and hours are unpredictable; check with the tourist office in Greve in Chianti for the latest. ⊠ *Località San Leolino.*

Restaurants

★ Officina della Bistecca

$$ | ITALIAN | FAMILY | Local butcher and restaurateur Dario Cecchini has extended his empire of meat to include this space located directly above his butcher's shop. Here, you'll find only four items on the menu: the Dario DOC, a half-pound burger, without bun, served with roasted potatoes and onions; the Super Dario, the former with salad and beans added; the Welcome, with four different dishes of beef and pork served with fresh garden vegetables; and a vegetarian dish. **Known for:** enormously popular, especially in summer; the best burger in Italy; performing waitstaff. $ *Average main: €15 ⊠ Via XX Luglio 11, Panzano* ☎ *055/852020* ⊕ *www.dariocecchini.com* ⊗ *Closed Sun.*

 ## Hotels

★ Villa Le Barone

$$$ | B&B/INN | Once the home of the Viviani della Robbia family, this 16th-century villa in a grove of ancient cypress trees retains many aspects of a private country dwelling, complete with homey guest quarters. **Pros:** wonderful restaurant; great base for exploring the region;

beautiful location. **Cons:** a car is a must; some rooms are a bit small; 15-minute walk to nearest town. $ *Rooms from: €289* ✉ *Via San Leolino 19, Panzano* ☎ *055/852621* ⊕ *www.villalebarone.com* ℗ *Free Breakfast* ⊘ *Closed Oct..–Easter* ⇆ *28 rooms.*

Radda in Chianti

26 km (15 miles) southeast of Panzano, 55 km (34 miles) south of Florence.

Radda in Chianti sits on a ridge stretching between the Val di Pesa and Val d'Arbia. It is easily reached by following the SR429 from Castellina. It's another one of those tiny villages with steep streets for strolling; follow the signs that point you toward the *camminamento medioevale*, a covered 14th-century walkway that circles part of the city inside the walls.

GETTING HERE AND AROUND

Radda can be reached by car from either Siena or Florence along the SR222 (Strada Chiantigiana), and from the A1 autostrada. Three Tra-In buses make their way from Siena to Radda. One morning SITA bus travels from Florence to Radda. There is no train service convenient to Radda.

VISITOR INFORMATION

CONTACT Radda in Chianti Tourism Office.
✉ *Piazza Castello 6, Radda in Chianti* ☎ *0577/738494* ⊕ *www.chianti.com.*

Sights

Badia a Coltibuono

(Abbey of the Good Harvest)
GARDEN | This Romanesque abbey has been owned by internationally acclaimed cookbook author Lorenza de' Medici's family for more than a century and a half (the family isn't related to the Florentine Medici). Wine has been produced here since the abbey was founded by Vallombrosan monks in the 11th century.

Today the family continues the tradition, making wines, cold-pressed olive oil, and various flavored vinegars. Don't miss the jasmine-draped courtyard and the inner cloister with its antique well. ✉ *Località Badia a Coltibuono, 4 km (2½ miles) north of Gaiole, Gaiole in Chianti* ☎ *0577/74481 tours* ⊕ *www. coltibuono.com* ⊞ *Abbey €7* ⊘ *Closed Jan. 7–mid-Mar.*

★ Castello di Brolio

CASTLE/PALACE | If you have time for only one castle in Tuscany, this is it. At the end of the 12th century, when Florence conquered southern Chianti, Brolio became Florence's southernmost outpost, and it was often said, "When Brolio growls, all Siena trembles." It was built about AD 1000 and owned by the monks of the Badia Fiorentina. The "new" owners, the Ricasoli family, have been in possession since 1141. Bettino Ricasoli (1809–80), the so-called Iron Baron, was one of the founders of modern Italy and is said to have invented the original formula for Chianti wine. Brolio, one of Chianti's best-known labels, is still justifiably famous. The grounds are worth visiting, even though the 19th-century manor house is not open to the public. The entrance fee includes a wine tasting in the enoteca. A small museum, where the Ricasoli Collection is housed in a 12th-century tower, displays objects that relate the long history of the family and the origins of Chianti wine. There are two apartments here available for rent by the week. ✉ *Località Madonna a Brolio, 2 km (1 mile) southeast of Gaiole, Gaiole in Chianti* ☎ *0577/7301* ⊕ *www.ricasoli.com* ⊞ *€7.50 gardens* ⊘ *Closed Dec. Museum closed Mon.*

Palazzo del Podestà

GOVERNMENT BUILDING | Radda's town hall (aka Palazzo Comunale), in the middle of town, was built in the second half of the 14th century and has served the same function ever since. Fifty-one coats of arms (the largest is the Medici's) are nbedded in the facade, representing the ast governors of the town, but unless ou have official business, the building is losed to the public. ⊠ *Piazza Ferrucci 1, Radda in Chianti.*

Restaurants

Osteria Le Panzanelle

| **TUSCAN** | Silvia Bonechi's experience n the kitchen—with the help of a few precious recipes handed down from her grandmother—is one of the reasons for the success of this small restaurant in the tiny hamlet of Lucarelli; the other s the front-room hospitality of Nada Michelassi. These two *panzanelle* (women from Panzano) serve a short menu of tasty and authentic dishes at what the locals refer to as *il prezzo giusto* (the right price). **Known for:** unpretentious atmosphere; fine home cooking; good wine list. $ *Average main: €13* ⊠ *Località Lucarelli 29, 8 km (5 miles) northwest of Radda on the road to Panzano* ☎ *0577/733511* ⊕ *www.lepanzanelle.it* ☉ *Closed Mon. and Jan. and Feb.*

Hotels

La Bottega di Giovannino

$ | **B&B/INN** | This is a fantastic place for the budget-conscious traveler, as rooms are immaculate and most have a stunning view of the surrounding hills. **Pros:** super value; great location in the center of town; close to restaurants and shops. **Cons:** basic decor; books up quickly; some rooms are small. $ *Rooms from: €60* ⊠ *Via Roma 6–8, Radda in Chianti* ☎ *0577/735601* ⊕ *www.labottegadigiovannino.it* ⇆ *12 rooms* ❑ *Free Breakfast.*

★ La Locanda

$$$ | **B&B/INN** | At an altitude of more than 1,800 feet, this converted farmhouse is probably the loftiest luxury inn in Chianti. **Pros:** wonderful host; idyllic setting; panoramic views. **Cons:** isolated location; on a very rough gravel access road; need a car to get around. $ *Rooms from: €220*

⊠ *Località Montanino di Volpaia, off Via della Volpaia, 13 km (8 miles) northwest of Radda* ☎ *0577/738833* ⊕ *www.lalocanda.it* ⇆ *7 rooms* ❑ *Free Breakfast* ☉ *Closed mid-Oct.–mid-Apr.*

Palazzo San Niccolò

$ | **HOTEL** | The wood-beam ceilings, terra-cotta floors, and some of the original frescoes of a 19th-century town palace remain, but the marble bathrooms have all been updated, some with Jacuzzi tubs. **Pros:** pool (though a car is necessary to get there); central location; friendly staff. **Cons:** room sizes vary; some rooms face a main street; some street noise in some rooms. $ *Rooms from: €91* ⊠ *Via Roma 16, Radda in Chianti* ☎ *0577/735666* ⊕ *www.hotelsanniccolo. com* ☉ *Closed Nov.–Mar.* ⇆ *18 rooms* ❑ *Free Breakfast.*

★ Relais Fattoria Vignale

$$$ | **B&B/INN** | A refined and comfortable country house offers numerous sitting rooms with terra-cotta floors and attractive stonework, as well as wood-beamed guest rooms filled with simple wooden furnishings and handwoven rugs. **Pros:** intimate public spaces; nice grounds and pool; excellent restaurant. **Cons:** a car is necessary; annex across a busy road; single rooms are small. $ *Rooms from: €214* ⊠ *Via Pianigiani 9, Radda in Chianti* ☎ *0577/738300 hotel, 0577/738094 restaurant* ⊕ *www.vignale.it* ☉ *Closed Nov.–Mar.* ⇆ *41 rooms* ❑ *No Meals.*

Castellina in Chianti

13 km (8 miles) south of Panzano, 59 km (35 miles) south of Florence, 22 km (14 miles) north of Siena.

Castellina in Chianti—or simply Castellina—is on a ridge above three valleys: the Val di Pesa, Val d'Arbia, and Val d'Elsa. No matter what direction you turn, the panorama is bucolic. The strong 15th-century medieval walls and fortified town gate give a hint of the history of this village, which was an outpost during the continuing wars between Florence and Siena. In the main square, the Piazza del Comune, there's a 15th-century palace and a 15th-century fort constructed around a 13th-century tower. It now serves as the town hall.

GETTING HERE AND AROUND

As with all the towns along the Strada Chiantigiana (SR222), Castellina is an easy drive from either Siena or Florence. From Siena, Castellina is well served by the local Tra-In bus company. However, only one bus a day travels here from Florence. The closest train station is at Castellina Scalo, some 15 km (9 miles) away.

VISITOR INFORMATION

CONTACT Castellina in Chianti Tourism Office. ✉ *Via Ferruccio 40, Castellina in Chianti* ☎ *0577/741392.*

🍴 Restaurants

Albergaccio

$$$ | TUSCAN | The fact that the dining room can seat only 35 guests makes a meal here an intimate experience, and the ever-changing menu mixes traditional and creative dishes. In late September and October *zuppa di funghi e castagne* (mushroom and chestnut soup) is a treat; grilled meats and seafood are on the list throughout the year. **Known for:** marvelous waitstaff; creative menu; superb wine list. [$] *Average main: €25* ✉ *Via Fiorentina 63, Castellina in Chianti* ☎ *0577/741042* 🌐 *www.albergacciocast.com* 🕓 *Closed Sun.*

Ristorante Le Tre Porte

$$ | TUSCAN | Grilled meat dishes are the specialty at this popular restaurant, with a bistecca fiorentina (served very rare, as always) taking pride of place; paired with grilled fresh porcini mushrooms when in season (spring and fall), it's a heady dish. The panoramic terrace is a good choice for dining in summer. **Known for:** fine wine list with lots of local bottles; views from the terrace; their way with mushrooms. [$] *Average main: €17* ✉ *Via Trento e Trieste 4, Castellina in Chianti* ☎ *0577/741163* 🌐 *www.treporte.com.*

Sotto Le Volte

$$ | TUSCAN | As the name suggests, you'll find this small restaurant under the arches of Castellina's medieval walkway, and the eatery's vaulted ceilings make for a particularly romantic setting. The menu is short and eminently Tuscan, with typical soups and pasta dishes. **Known for:** unique setting; attentive waitstaff; flair for Tuscan classics. [$] *Average main: €17* ✉ *Via delle Volte 14–16, Castellina in Chianti* ☎ *0577/741299* 🌐 *www.ristorantesottolevolte.it* 🕓 *Closed Wed. and Jan.–Mar.*

🛏 Hotels

★ Palazzo Squarcialupi

$$ | B&B/INN | In this lovely 15th-century palace, spacious rooms have high ceilings, tile floors, and 18th-century furnishings, and many have views of the valley below. **Pros:** nice spa, pool, and grounds; great location in town center; elegant public spaces. **Cons:** across from a busy restaurant; on a street with no car access; rooms facing the street can experience some noise. [$] *Rooms from: €140* ✉ *Via Ferruccio 22, Castellina in Chianti* ☎ *0577/741186* 🌐 *www.squarcialupirelaxinchianti.com* 🕓 *Closed Nov.–Mar.* 🛏 *17 rooms* 🍴 *Free Breakfast.*

Volterra

30 km (18 miles) southwest of San Gimignano.

As you approach the town through bleak, rugged terrain, you can see that not all Tuscan hill towns rise above rolling green fields. Volterra stands mightily over Le Balze, a stunning series of gullied hills and valleys formed by erosion that has slowly eaten away at the foundation of

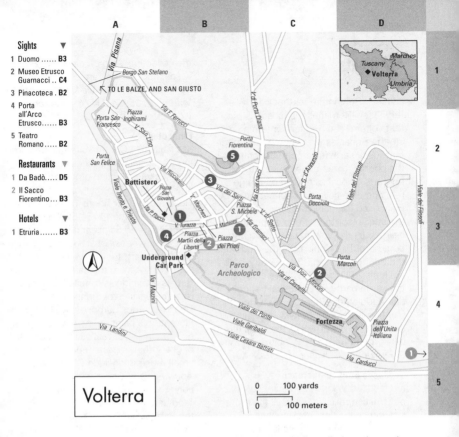

Volterra

the town—now considerably smaller than it was during its Etruscan glory days some 2000 years ago. The town began as the northernmost of the 12 cities that made up the Etruscan League, and excavations in the 18th century revealed a bounty of relics, which are on exhibit at the impressively overstocked Museo Etrusco Guarnacci. The Romans and later the Florentines laid siege to the town to secure its supply of minerals and stones, particularly alabaster, which is still worked into handicrafts on sale in many of the shops around town.

GETTING HERE AND AROUND

By car, the best route from San Gimignano follows the SP1 south to Castel San Gimignano and then the SS68 west to Volterra. Coming from the west, take the SS1, a coastal road to Cecina, then follow the SS68 east to Volterra. Either way,

there's a long, winding climb at the end of your trip. Traveling to Volterra by bus or train is complicated; avoid it if possible, especially if you have lots of luggage. From Florence or Siena the journey by public transit is best made by bus and involves a change in Colle di Val d'Elsa. From Rome or Pisa, it is best to take the train to Cecina and then take a bus to Volterra or a train to the Volterra-Saline station. The latter is 10 km (6 miles) from town.

VISITOR INFORMATION

CONTACT Volterra Tourism Office. ✉ *Piazza dei Priori 10, Volterra* ☎ *0588/86150* ⊕ *www.provolterra.it.*

Sights

Duomo

CHURCH | Behind the textbook 13th-century Pisan–Romanesque facade is proof that Volterra counted for something during the Renaissance, when many important Tuscan artists came to decorate the church. Three-dimensional stucco portraits of local saints are on the gold, red, and blue ceiling (1580) designed by Francesco Capriani, including St. Linus, the successor to St. Peter as pope and claimed by the Volterrans to have been born here. The highlight of the Duomo is the brightly painted, 13th-century, wooden, life-size *Deposition* in the chapel of the same name. The unusual Cappella dell'Addolorata (Chapel of the Grieved) has two terra-cotta Nativity scenes; the depiction of the arrival of the Magi has a background fresco by Benozzo Gozzoli. ✉ *Piazza San Giovanni, Volterra.*

★ Museo Etrusco Guarnacci

ART MUSEUM | An extraordinary collection of Etruscan relics is made all the more interesting by clear explanations in English. The bulk of the collection is comprised of roughly 700 carved funerary urns. The oldest, dating from the 7th century BC, were made from tufa (volcanic rock), a handful are made of terra-cotta, and the vast majority—from the 3rd to 1st century BC—are from alabaster. The urns are grouped by subject and taken together form a fascinating testimony about Etruscan life and death. Some illustrate domestic scenes, others the funeral procession of the deceased. Greek gods and mythology, adopted by the Etruscans, also figure prominently. The sculpted figures on many of the covers may have been made in the image of the deceased, reclining and often holding the cup of life overturned. Particularly well known is *Gli Sposi* (Husband and Wife), a haunting, elderly duo in terra-cotta. The *Ombra della Sera* (Evening Shadow)—an enigmatic bronze statue of an elongated, pencil-thin male nude—highlights

the collection. Also on display are Attic vases, bucchero ceramics, jewelry, and household items. ✉ *Via Don Minzoni 15, Volterra* ☎ *0588/86347* ⊕ *www.comune. volterra.pi.it* ✉ *From €8.*

Pinacoteca

ART MUSEUM | One of Volterra's best-looking Renaissance buildings contains an impressive collection of Tuscan paintings arranged chronologically on two floors. Head straight for Room 12, with Luca Signorelli's (circa 1445–1523) *Madonna and Child with Saints* and Rosso Fiorentino's later *Deposition*. Though painted just 30 years apart, they serve to illustrate the shift in style from the early 16th-century Renaissance ideals to full-blown mannerism: the balance of Signorelli's composition becomes purposefully skewed in Fiorentino's painting, where the colors go from vivid but realistic to emotively bright. Other important paintings in the small museum include Ghirlandaio's *Apotheosis of Christ with Saints* and a polyptych of the *Madonna and Saints* by Taddeo di Bartolo, which once hung in the Palazzo dei Priori. ✉ *Via dei Sarti 1, Volterra* ☎ *0588/87580* ⊕ *www.comune. volterra.pi.it* ✉ *From €8.*

Porta all'Arco Etrusco

RUINS | Even if a good portion of the arch was rebuilt by the Romans, three dark and weather-beaten 4th-century-BC heads (thought to represent Etruscan gods) still face outward to greet those who enter here. A plaque on the outer wall recalls the efforts of the locals who saved the arch from destruction by filling it with stones during the German withdrawal at the end of World War II. ✉ *Via Porta all'Arco, Volterra.*

Teatro Romano

RUINS | Just outside the walls past Porta Fiorentina are the ruins of the 1st-century-BC Roman theater, one of the best preserved in Italy, with adjacent remains of the Roman *terme* (baths). You can enjoy an excellent bird's-eye view of the theater from Via Lungo le Mura. ✉ *Viale*

Francesco Ferrucci, Volterra 🕾 ⊘ Closed weekdays Nov.–Mar. 🎟 From €5.

 Restaurants

Da Badò

$ | **TUSCAN** | This is the best place in town to eat traditional food elbow-to-elbow with the locals. Da Badò is family-run, with Lucia in the kitchen and her sons Giacomo and Michele waiting tables. **Known for:** local favorite; excellent traditional dishes; small menu. $ *Average main: €14* ⊠ *Borgo San Lazzaro 9, Volterra* 🕾 *0588/80402* ⊕ *www.trattoriadabado. com* ⊘ *Closed Wed.*

Il Sacco Fiorentino

$$ | **TUSCAN** | This lovely trattoria has been around for a long time, and with good reason. Here they turn out Tuscan classics, relying heavily on the local cheese (pecorino) and local meats (especially wild boar, among others). **Known for:** excellent wine list; inventive food; tranquil setting. $ *Average main: €15* ⊠ *Via Giusto Turazza 13, Volterra* 🕾 *0588/88537* ⊘ *Closed Wed.*

 Hotels

Etruria

$ | **B&B/INN** | The rooms are modest and there's no elevator, but the central location, the ample buffet breakfast, and the modest rates make this a good choice for those on a budget. **Pros:** great central location; tranquil garden with rooftop views; friendly staff. **Cons:** no elevator; books up quickly as it's good value; some rooms can be noisy during the day. $ *Rooms from: €83* ⊠ *Via Matteotti 32, Volterra* 🕾 *0588/87377* ⊕ *www.albergoetruria.it* ⏍ *Free Breakfast* ⊘ *Closed Jan. and Feb.* ⇨ *18 rooms.*

San Gimignano

14 km (9 miles) northwest of Colle di Val d'Elsa, 38 km (24 miles) northwest of Siena, 54 km (34 miles) southwest of Florence.

When you're on a hilltop surrounded by soaring medieval towers silhouetted against the sky, it's difficult not to fall under the spell of San Gimignano. Its tall walls and narrow streets are typical of Tuscan hill towns, but it's the medieval "skyscrapers" that set the town apart from its neighbors. Today 14 towers remain, but at the height of the Guelph–Ghibelline conflict there was a forest of more than 70, and it was possible to cross the town by rooftop rather than by road. The towers were built partly for defensive purposes—they were a safe refuge and useful for pouring boiling oil on attacking enemies—and partly for bolstering the egos of their owners, who competed with deadly seriousness to build the highest tower in town.

Today San Gimignano isn't much more than a gentrified walled city, touristy but still very much worth exploring because, despite the profusion of cheesy souvenir shops lining the main drag, there's some serious Renaissance art to be seen here. Tour groups arrive early and clog the wine-tasting rooms—San Gimignano is famous for its light, white *vernaccia*—and art galleries for much of the day, but most sights stay open through late afternoon, when all the tour groups have long since departed.

San Gimignano is particularly beautiful in the early morning. Take time to walk up to the *rocca* (castle), at the highest point of town. Here you can enjoy 360-degree views of the surrounding countryside. Apart from when it's used for summer outdoor film festivals, it's always open.

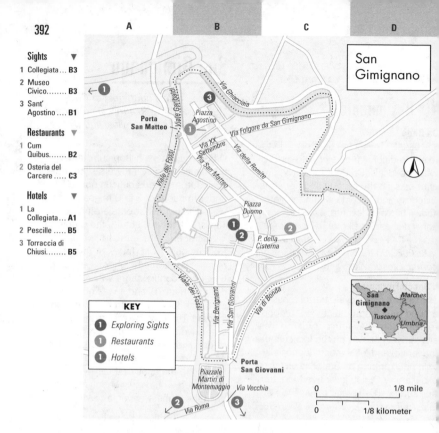

KEY

1 *Exploring Sights*
1 *Restaurants*
1 *Hotels*

GETTING HERE AND AROUND

You can reach San Gimignano by car from the Florence–Siena superstrada. Exit at Poggibonsi Nord and follow signs for San Gimignano. Although it involves changing buses in Poggibonsi, getting to San Gimignano by bus from Florence is a relatively straightforward affair. SITA operates the service between Siena or Florence and Poggibonsi. From Siena, Tra-In offers direct service to San Gimignano several times daily. You cannot reach San Gimignano by train.

VISITOR INFORMATION

CONTACT San Gimignano Tourism Office.
✉ *Piazza Duomo 1, San Gimignano* ☎ *0577/940008* ⊕ *www.sangimignano. com.*

◉ Sights

★ Collegiata

CHURCH | The town's main church is not officially a duomo (cathedral), because San Gimignano has no bishop. But behind the simple facade of the Romanesque Collegiata lies a treasure trove of fine frescoes, covering nearly every part of the interior. Bartolo di Fredi's 14th-century fresco cycle of Old Testament scenes extends along one wall. Their distinctly medieval feel, with misshapen bodies, buckets of spurting blood, and lack of perspective, contrasts with the much more reserved scenes from the *Life of Christ* (attributed to 14th-century artist Lippo Memmi) painted on the opposite wall just 14 years later. Taddeo di Bartolo's otherworldly *Last Judgment* (late 14th century), with its distorted and suffering nudes, reveals the great influence of Dante's horrifying imagery in *Inferno*. Proof that the town had more than one protector, Benozzo Gozzoli's arrow-riddled St. Sebastian was commissioned in gratitude after the locals prayed to the saint for relief from plague. The Cappella di Santa Fina is decorated with a fresco cycle by Domenico Ghirlandaio illustrating the life of St. Fina. ✉ *Piazza Pecori 1–2, entrance on left side of church, San Gimignano* ☎ *0577/286300* 🌐 *www.duomosangimignano.it* 🎟 *€3* 🕒 *Closed Thurs. and Jan. 1 and Dec. 25.*

Museo Civico

CASTLE/PALACE | The impressive civic museum occupies what was the "new" Palazzo del Popolo; the Torre Grossa is adjacent. Dante visited San Gimignano for only one day as a Guelph ambassador from Florence to ask the locals to join the Florentines in supporting the pope—just long enough to get the main council chamber, which now holds a 14th-century *Maestà* by Lippo Memmi, named after him. Off the stairway is a small room containing the racy frescoes by Memmo di Filippuccio (active 1288–1324), depicting the courtship, shared bath, and wedding of a young, androgynous-looking couple. That the space could have been a private room for the commune's chief magistrate may have something to do with the work's highly charged eroticism. Upstairs, paintings by famous Renaissance artists Pinturicchio (*Madonna Enthroned*) and Benozzo Gozzoli (*Madonna and Child*), and two large *tondi* (circular paintings) by Filippino Lippi (circa 1457–1504) attest to the importance and wealth of San Gimignano. Admission includes the steep climb to the top of the **Torre Grossa,** which on a clear day has spectacular views. ✉ *Piazza Duomo 2, San Gimignano* ☎ *0577/990312* 🌐 *www.sangimignanomusei.it* 🎟 *€9 cumulative ticket.*

Sant'Agostino

CHURCH | Make a beeline for Benozzo Gozzoli's superlative 15th-century fresco cycle depicting scenes from the life of St. Augustine. The saint's work was essential to the early development of church doctrine. As thoroughly discussed in his autobiographical *Confessions* (an acute dialogue with God), Augustine, like many saints, sinned considerably in his youth before finding God. But unlike the lives of other saints, where the story continues through a litany of deprivations, penitence, and often martyrdom, Augustine's life and work focused on philosophy and the reconciliation of faith and thought. Benozzo's 17 scenes on the choir wall depict Augustine as a man who traveled and taught extensively in the 4th and 5th centuries. The 15th-century altarpiece by Piero del Pollaiolo (1443–96) depicts *The Coronation of the Virgin* and the various protectors of the city. On your way out of Sant'Agostino, stop in at the **Cappella di San Bartolo,** with a sumptuously elaborate tomb by Benedetto da Maiano (1442–97). ✉ *Piazza Sant'Agostino 10, San Gimignano* 🌐 *www.sangimignano.com* 🎟 *Free.*

🍴 Restaurants

★ Cum Quibus

$$$ | **ITALIAN** | Without a doubt, this is among the most creative food happening in Tuscany. Lorenzo (in the front) has put together a menu that's Tuscan but not: it's rare to see bok choy incorporated into any dish, but here it's done with élan. **Known for:** two marvelous tasting menus; amazing wine list with prices to suit all budgets; incorporation of non-Tuscan ingredients into Tuscan food. [$] *Average main: €25* ✉ *Via San Martino 17, San Gimignano* ☎ *0577/943199* 🌐 *www.cumquibus.it* 🕒 *Closed Tues. and Jan.–Feb.*

Osteria del Carcere

$$ | **ITALIAN** | Although it calls itself an *osteria* (tavern), this place much more resembles a wine bar, with a bill of fare that includes several different types of pâtés and a short list of seasonal soups and salads. The sampler of goat cheeses, which can be paired with local wines, should not be missed. **Known for:** housed in a former jail; excellent chef-proprietor; inventive dishes. $ *Average main: €16* ✉ *Via del Castello 13 San Gimignano* ☎ *0577/941905* ⊘ *Closed Wed. and early Jan.–Mar. No lunch Thurs.*

Hotels

La Collegiata

$$$ | **HOTEL** | After serving as a Franciscan convent and then the residence of the noble Strozzi family, the Collegiata has been converted into a fine hotel, with no expense spared in the process. **Pros:** wonderful staff; gorgeous views from terrace; elegant rooms in main building. **Cons:** service can be impersonal; long walk into town; some rooms are dimly lit. $ *Rooms from: €220* ✉ *Località Strada 27, 1 km (½ mile) north of San Gimignano town center* ☎ *0577/943201* ⊕ *www.lacollegiata.it* ⊘ *Closed Nov.–Mar.* ⇆ *20 rooms* ⊚| *Free Breakfast.*

Pescille

$ | **B&B/INN** | A rambling farmhouse has been transformed into a handsome hotel with understated contemporary furniture in the bedrooms and country-classic motifs such as farm implements hanging on the walls in the bar. **Pros:** 10-minute walk to town; splendid views; quiet atmosphere. **Cons:** there's an elevator for luggage but not for guests; furnishings a bit austere; a vehicle is a must. $ *Rooms from: €89* ✉ *Località Pescille, 4 km (2½ miles) south of San Gimignano* ☎ *0577/940186* ⊕ *www.pescille.it* ⊘ *Closed mid-Oct.–Easter* ⇆ *38 rooms* ⊚| *Free Breakfast.*

Torraccia di Chiusi

$$ | **B&B/INN** | **FAMILY** | A perfect retreat for families, this tranquil hilltop *agriturismo* (farm stay) offers simple, comfortably decorated accommodations on extensive grounds 5 km (3 miles) from the hubbub of San Gimignano. **Pros:** delightful countryside view; great walking possibilities; family-run hospitality. **Cons:** 30 minutes from the nearest town on a winding gravel road; might be too remote for some; need a car to get here. $ *Rooms from: €160* ✉ *Località Montauto, San Gimignano* ☎ *0577/941972* ⊕ *www.torracciadichiusi.it* ⇆ *11 rooms* ⊚| *Free Breakfast.*

Siena

With its narrow streets and steep alleys, a Gothic Duomo, a bounty of early Renaissance art, and the glorious Palazzo Pubblico overlooking its magnificent Campo, Siena is often described as Italy's best-preserved medieval city. It is also remarkably modern: many shops sell clothes by up-and-coming designers. Make a point of catching the *passeggiata* (evening stroll), when locals throng the Via di Città, Banchi di Sopra, and Banchi di Sotto, the city's three main streets.

Victory over Florence in 1260 at Montaperti marked the beginning of Siena's golden age. Even though Florentines avenged the loss twenty-nine years later, Siena continued to prosper. During the following decades Siena erected its greatest buildings (including the Duomo); established a model city government presided over by the Council of Nine; and became a great art, textile, and trade center. All of these achievements came together in the decoration of the Sala della Pace in Palazzo Pubblico. It makes you wonder what greatness the city might have gone on to achieve had its fortunes been different, but in 1348 a plague decimated the population, brought an end to the Council of Nine, and left Siena economically vulnerable. Siena succumbed to Florentine rule in the mid-16th century, when a year-long siege virtually eliminated the native population. Ironically, it was precisely this decline that, along with Sienese pride, prevented further development, to which we owe the city's marvelous medieval condition today.

But although much looks as it did in the early 14th century, Siena is no museum. Walk through the streets and you can see that the medieval *contrade*—17 neighborhoods into which the city has been historically divided—are a vibrant part of modern life. You may see symbols of the *contrada* emblazoned on banners and engraved on building walls: Tartuca (turtle), Oca (goose), Istrice (porcupine), Torre (tower)—among others. The Sienese still strongly identify themselves with the contrada where they were born and raised; loyalty and rivalry run deep. At no time is this more visible than during the centuries-old Palio, a twice-yearly horse race held in the Piazza del Campo, but you need not visit then to come to know the rich culture of Siena, evident at every step.

GETTING HERE AND AROUND
From Florence, the quickest way to Siena is via the Florence–Siena superstrada. Otherwise, take the Via Cassia (SR2) for a scenic route. Coming from Rome, leave the A1 at Valdichiana, and follow the Siena–Bettole superstrada. SITA provides excellent bus service between Florence and Siena. Because buses are direct and speedy, they are preferable to the train, which sometimes involves a change in Empoli.

If you come by car, you're better off leaving it in one of the parking lots around the perimeter of town. Driving is difficult or impossible in most parts of the city center. Practically unchanged since medieval times, Siena is laid out in a "Y" over the slopes of several hills, dividing the city into *terzi* (thirds).

BUS CONTACT Tra-In. ☏ *0577/204111* ⊕ *www.trainspa.it*.

TIMING
It's a joy to walk in Siena—hills notwithstanding—as it's a rare opportunity to stroll through a medieval city rather than just a town. (There is quite a lot to explore, in contrast to tiny hill towns that can be crossed in minutes.) The walk can be done in as little as a day, with minimal stops at the sights. But stay longer and take time to tour the churches and museums, and to enjoy the streetscapes themselves. Many of the sites have reduced hours Sunday afternoon and Monday.

VISITOR INFORMATION
CONTACT Siena Tourism Office. ⊠ *Piazza del Duomo 2, Siena* ☏ *0577/280551* ⊕ *www.terresiena.it*.

 ## Sights

Battistero
RELIGIOUS BUILDING | The Duomo's 14th-century Gothic Baptistery was built to prop up the apse of the cathedral. There are frescoes throughout, but the highlight is a large bronze 15th-century baptismal font designed by Jacopo della Quercia (1374–1438). It's adorned with bas-reliefs by various artists, including two by Renaissance masters: the *Baptism of Christ* by Lorenzo Ghiberti (1378–1455) and the *Feast of Herod* by Donatello. ⊠ *Piazza San Giovanni, Città* ☏ *0577/286300* ⊕ *www.operaduomo.siena.it* ☜ *€20 combined ticket includes Duomo, Cripta, and Museo dell'Opera.*

★ Cripta
CEMETERY | After it had lain unseen for possibly 700 years, a crypt was rediscovered under the grand *pavimento* (floor) of the Duomo during routine excavation work and was opened to the public in 2003. An unknown master executed the breathtaking frescoes here sometime between 1270 and 1280. They retain their original colors and pack an emotional punch even with sporadic damage. The *Deposition/Lamentation* gives strong evidence that the Sienese school could paint emotion just as well as the Florentine school—and did it some 20 years before Giotto. ⊠ *Scale di San Giovanni, Città* ✛ *Down steps to right side of cathedral* ☏ *0577/286300* ⊕ *www.*

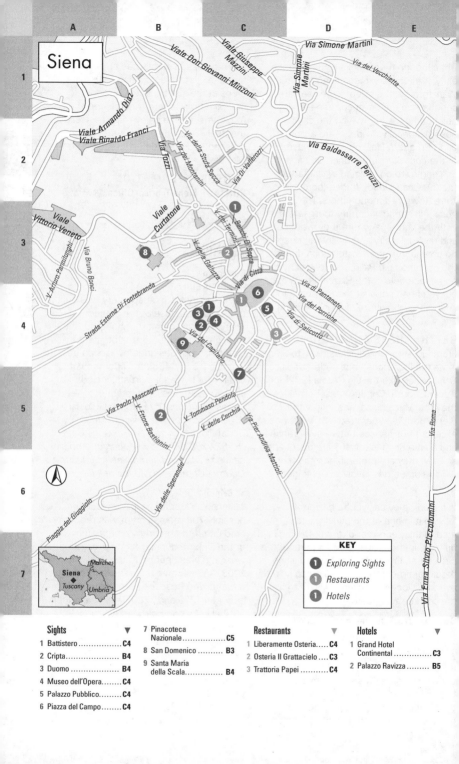

Siena

Sights ▼

1 Battistero **C4**
2 Cripta **B4**
3 Duomo **B4**
4 Museo dell'Opera **C4**
5 Palazzo Pubblico **C4**
6 Piazza del Campo **C4**

7 Pinacoteca
  Nazionale **C5**
8 San Domenico **B3**
9 Santa Maria
  della Scala **B4**

Restaurants ▼

1 Liberamente Osteria **C4**
2 Osteria Il Grattacielo **C3**
3 Trattoria Papei **C4**

Hotels ▼

1 Grand Hotel
  Continental **C3**
2 Palazzo Ravizza **B5**

KEY

1 *Exploring Sights*
1 *Restaurants*
1 *Hotels*

peraduomo.siena.it €20 combined ticket includes the Duomo, Battistero, and Museo dell'Opera.

★ **Duomo**

CHURCH | Siena's cathedral is beyond question one of the finest Gothic churches in Italy. The multicolor marbles and painted decoration are typical of the Italian approach to Gothic architecture—lighter and much less austere than the French. The amazingly detailed facade has few rivals. It was completed in two brief phases at the end of the 13th and 14th centuries. The statues and decorative work were designed by Nicola Pisano and his son Giovanni, although most of what we see today are copies, the originals having been removed to the nearby Museo dell'Opera. The gold mosaics are 18th-century restorations. The Campanile (no entry) is among central Italy's finest, the number of windows increasing with each level, a beautiful and ingenious way of reducing the weight of the structure as it climbs to the heavens. The Duomo's interior, with its dark green–and–white striping throughout and illusionistically coffered and gilded dome, is simply striking. Step in and look back up at a copy of Duccio's (circa 1255–1319) panels of stained glass that once filled the circular entrance window—the originals are now in the Museo dell'Opera Metropolitana. Finished in 1288, the window is the oldest example of stained glass in Italy. The Duomo is most famous for its unique and magnificent inlaid-marble floors, which took almost 200 years to complete. More than 40 artists contributed to the work, made up of 56 separate compositions depicting biblical scenes, allegories, religious symbols, and civic emblems. The floors are covered for most of the year for conservation purposes, but are unveiled during September and October. The Duomo's carousel pulpit, also much appreciated, was carved by Nicola Pisano (circa 1220–84) around 1265; the Life of Christ is depicted on the rostrum frieze.

In striking contrast to all the Gothic decoration in the nave are the magnificent Renaissance frescoes in the Biblioteca Piccolomini, off the left aisle. Painted by Pinturicchio (circa 1454–1513) and completed in 1509, they depict events from the life of Aeneas Sylvius Piccolomini (1405–64), who became Pope Pius II in 1458. The frescoes are in excellent condition, and have a freshness rarely seen in work so old. The Duomo is grand, but the medieval Sienese people had even bigger plans. They wanted to enlarge the building by using the existing church as a transept for a new church, with a new nave running toward the southeast, to make what would be the largest church in the world. But only the side wall and part of the new facade were completed when the Black Death struck in 1348, decimating Siena's population. The city fell into decline, funds dried up, and the plans were never carried out. (The dream of building the biggest church was actually doomed to failure from the start—subsequent attempts to get the project going revealed that the foundation was insufficient to bear the weight of the proposed structure.) The beginnings of the new nave, extending from the right side of the Duomo, were left unfinished, perhaps as a testament to unfulfilled dreams, and ultimately enclosed to house the adjacent Museo dell'Opera. The Cripta was discovered during routine preservation work on the church and has been opened to the public. The last entrance to the Duomo is 30 minutes before closing. ✉ Piazza del Duomo, Città ☎ 0577/286300 ⊕ www.operaduomo. siena.it €20 combined ticket includes Cripta, Battistero, and Museo dell'Opera.

★ **Museo dell'Opera**

ART MUSEUM | Part of the unfinished nave of what was to have been a new cathedral, the museum contains the Duomo's treasury and some of the original decoration from its facade and interior. The first room on the ground floor displays weather-beaten 13th-century sculptures by Giovanni Pisano (circa 1245–1318) that were brought inside for protection and replaced by copies, as was a tondo of the *Madonna and Child* (now attributed to Donatello) that once hung on the door to the south transept. The masterpiece is unquestionably Duccio's *Maestà*, one side with 26 panels depicting episodes from the Passion, the other side with a *Madonna and Child Enthroned*. Painted between 1308 and 1311 as the altarpiece for the Duomo (where it remained until 1505), its realistic elements, such as the lively depiction of the Christ child and the treatment of interior space, proved an enormous influence on later painters. The work originally decorated the Duomo's high altar, before being displaced by Duccio's *Maestà*. There is a fine view from the tower inside the museum. ✉ *Piazza del Duomo 8, Città* ☎ *0577/286300* ⊕ *www.operaduomo.siena.it* ✉ *€20 combined ticket includes the Duomo, Cripta, and Battistero.*

Palazzo Pubblico

GOVERNMENT BUILDING | The Gothic Palazzo Pubblico, the focal point of the Piazza del Campo, has served as Siena's town hall since the 1300s. It now also contains the Museo Civico, with walls covered in early Renaissance frescoes. The nine governors of Siena once met in the Sala della Pace, famous for Ambrogio Lorenzetti's frescoes called *Allegories of Good and Bad Government*, painted in the late 1330s to demonstrate the dangers of tyranny. The good government side depicts utopia, showing first the virtuous ruling council surrounded by angels and then scenes of a perfectly running city and countryside. Conversely, the bad government fresco tells a tale straight out of Dante. The evil ruler and his advisers have horns and fondle strange animals, and the town scene depicts the seven mortal sins in action. The **Torre del Mangia,** the palazzo's famous bell tower, is named after one of its first bell ringers, Giovanni di Duccio (called Mangiaguadagni, or earnings eater). The climb up to

the top is long and steep, but the view makes it worth every step. ✉ *Piazza del Campo 1, Città* ☎ *0577/292232* ⊕ *www. comune.siena.it* ✉ *Museum €10, ticket sales end 30 mins before closing; tower €10, ticket sales end 45 mins before closing.*

★ Piazza del Campo

PLAZA/SQUARE | The fan-shape Piazza del Campo, known simply as Il Campo (The Field), is one of the finest squares in Italy. Constructed toward the end of the 12th century on a market area unclaimed by any contrada, it's still the heart of town. The bricks of the Campo are patterned in nine different sections—representing each member of the medieval Government of Nine. At the top of the Campo is a copy of the early 15th-century **Fonte Gaia** by Siena's greatest sculptor, Jacopo della Quercia. The 13 sculpted reliefs of biblical events and virtues that line the fountain are 19th-century copies; the originals are in the museum complex of Santa Maria della Scala. On Palio horserace days (July 2 and August 16), the Campo and all its surrounding buildings are packed with cheering, frenzied locals and tourists craning their necks to take it all in. ✉ *Piazza del Campo, Città.*

Pinacoteca Nazionale

ART MUSEUM | The superb collection of five centuries of local painting in Siena's national picture gallery can easily convince you that the Renaissance was by no means just a Florentine thing. Accordingly, the most interesting section of the collection, chronologically arranged, has several important firsts. Room 1 contains a painting of the *Stories of the True Cross* (1215) by the so-called Master of Tressa, the earliest identified work by a painter of the Sienese school, and is followed in Room 2 by late-13th-century artist Guido da Siena's *Stories from the Life of Christ,* one of the first paintings ever made on canvas (earlier painters used wood panels). Rooms 3 and 4 are dedicated to Duccio, a student of Cimabue (circa 1240–1302) and considered to be the last of the proto-Renaissance painters. Ambrogio Lorenzetti's landscapes in Room 8 are among the first truly secular paintings in Western art. Among later works in the rooms on the floor above, keep an eye out for the preparatory sketches used by Domenico Beccafumi (1486–1551) for the 35 etched marble panels he made for the floor of the Duomo. ✉ *Via San Pietro 29, Città* ☎ *0577/286143* 🌐 *www.pinacotecanazionale.siena.it* 🎟 *€8* 🕓 *Closed Mon.*

San Domenico

CHURCH | Although the Duomo is celebrated as a triumph of 13th-century Gothic architecture, this church, built at about the same time, turned out to be an oversize, hulking brick box that never merited a finishing coat in marble, let alone a graceful facade. Named for the founder of the Dominican order, the church is now more closely associated with St. Catherine of Siena. Just to the right of the entrance is the chapel in which she received the stigmata. On the wall is the only known contemporary portrait of the saint, made in the late 14th century by Andrea Vanni (circa 1332–1414). Farther down is the famous **Cappella delle Santa Testa,** the church's official shrine. Catherine, or bits and pieces of her, was literally spread all over the country—a foot is in Venice, most of her body is in Rome, and only her head (kept in a reliquary on the chapel's altar) and her right thumb are here. She was revered throughout the country long before she was officially named a patron saint of Italy in 1939. On either side of the chapel are well-known frescoes by Sodoma (aka Giovanni Antonio Bazzi, 1477–1549) of *St. Catherine in Ecstasy.* Don't miss the view of the Duomo and town center from the apse-side terrace. ✉ *Piazza San Domenico, Camollìa* ☎ *0577/286848* 🌐 *www.basilicacateriniana.com.*

★ **Santa Maria della Scala**

HISTORIC SIGHT | For more than 1,000 years, this complex across from the Duomo was home to Siena's hospital, but now it serves as a museum to display some terrific frescoes and other Sienese Renaissance treasures. Restored 15th-century frescoes in the Sala del Pellegrinaio (once the emergency room) tell the history of the hospital, which was created to give refuge to passing pilgrims and to those in need, and to distribute charity to the poor. Incorporated into the complex is the church of the Santissima Annunziata, with a celebrated *Risen Christ* by Vecchietta (also known as Lorenzo di Pietro, circa 1412–80). Down in the dark, Cappella di Santa Caterina della Notte is where St. Catherine went to pray at night. The displays—including the *bucchero* (dark, reddish clay) ceramics, Roman coins, and tomb furnishings—are clearly marked and can serve as a good introduction to the history of regional excavations. Don't miss della Quercia's original sculpted reliefs in the subterranean archaeological museum, from the Fonte Gaia. Although the fountain has been faithfully copied for the Campo, there's something incomparably beautiful about the real thing. ✉ *Piazza del Duomo 2, Città* ☎ *0577/534511* 🌐 *www.santamariadellascala.com* 🎟 *€9.* 🕓 *Closed Tues.*

🍴 Restaurants

Liberamente Osteria

$ | **ITALIAN** | Though the food here is rather good, the real reasons to come are the exquisitely crafted cocktails and the view, which just happens to be of Il Campo, arguably the prettiest square in all of Italy. Tasty little nibbles accompany the generously proportioned aperitivi. **Known for:** facility with rum-based drinks; opens early (9 am) and closes late (2 am); variations on the spritz. [$] *Average main: €7* ✉ *Il Campo 27, Siena* ☎ *0577/274733* 🌐 *www.liberamenteosteria.it.*

Osteria Il Grattacielo
$ | **TUSCAN** | If you're wiped out from too much sightseeing, consider a meal at this hole-in-the-wall restaurant where locals congregate for a simple lunch over a glass of wine. There's a collection of *verdure sott'olio*, a wide selection of *affettati misti*, and various types of frittatas, and all of this can be washed down with the cheap, yet eminently drinkable, house red. **Known for:** usually filled with local men arguing about the Palio; simple, good-value food; earthy ambience. [$] *Average main: €10* ✉ *Via Pontani 8, Camollìa* ☎ *331/7422835.*

Trattoria Papei
$ | **TUSCAN** | The menu hasn't changed for years, and why should it? This place has been in the Papei family for three generations, and they know how to turn out Sienese specialties: their reasonable prices and fine, basic fare is what draws locals to the place. **Known for:** great place to sample local specialties; lively atmosphere; outdoor seating. [$] *Average main: €11* ✉ *Piazza del Mercato 6, Città* ☎ *0577/280894* 🌐 *www.anticatrattoriapapei.com.*

Hotels

Grand Hotel Continental
$$$ | **HOTEL** | Pope Alexander VII of the famed Sienese Chigi family gave this palace to his niece as a wedding present in 1600; through the centuries it has been a private family home as well as a grand hotel exuding elegance from the stately pillared entrance to the crisp-linen sheets. **Pros:** luxurious accommodations; first-rate concierge; great location on the main drag. **Cons:** breakfast costs extra; lots of noise if your room is street-side; sometimes stuffy atmosphere. [$] *Rooms from: €297* ✉ *Banchi di Sopra 85, Camollìa* ☎ *0577/56011* 🌐 *www.starhotelscollezione.com* 🛏 *51 rooms* 🍴 *No Meals.*

★ **Palazzo Ravizza**
$$ | **HOTEL** | This charming palazzo exudes a sense of an age gone by; its guest rooms have high ceilings, antique furnishings, and bathrooms decorated with hand-painted tiles. **Pros:** pleasant garden with a view beyond the city walls; professional staff; 10-minute walk to the center of town. **Cons:** somewhat removed from the center of things; some rooms are a little cramped; not all rooms have views. [$] *Rooms from: €139* ✉ *Piano dei Mantellini 34, Città* ☎ *0577/280462* 🌐 *www.palazzoravizza.it* 🛏 *41 rooms* 🍴 *Free Breakfast.*

Arezzo

63 km (39 miles) northeast of Siena, 81 km (50 miles) southeast of Florence.

Arezzo is best known for the magnificent Piero della Francesca frescoes in the church of San Francesco. It's also the birthplace of the poet Petrarch (1304–74), the Renaissance artist and art historian Giorgio Vasari, and Guido d'Arezzo (aka Guido Monaco), the inventor of contemporary musical notation. Arezzo dates from pre-Etruscan times, when around 1000 BC the first settlers erected a cluster of huts. Arezzo thrived as an Etruscan capital from the 7th to the 4th century BC, and was one of the most important cities in the Etruscans' anti-Roman 12-city federation, resisting Rome's rule to the last.

The city eventually fell and in turn flourished under the Romans. In 1248 Guglielmino degli Ubertini, a member of the powerful Ghibelline family, was elected bishop of Arezzo. This sent the city headlong into the enduring conflict between the Ghibellines (pro-emperor) and the Guelphs (pro-pope). In 1289 Florentine Guelphs defeated Arezzo in a famous battle at Campaldino. Among the Florentine soldiers was Dante Alighieri (1265–1321), who often referred to

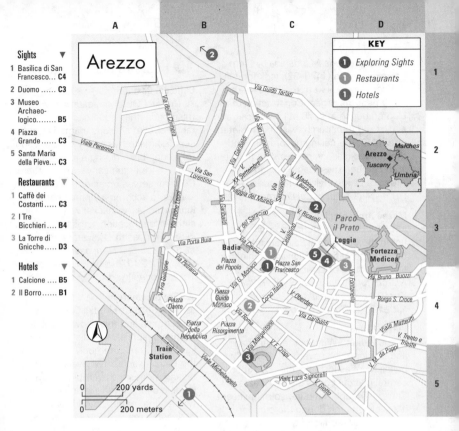

Arezzo

Sights ▼

1 Basilica di San Francesco... **C4**
2 Duomo **C3**
3 Museo Archaeologico........ **B5**
4 Piazza Grande...... **C3**
5 Santa Maria della Pieve... **C3**

Restaurants ▼

1 Caffè dei Costanti **C3**
2 I Tre Bicchieri **B4**
3 La Torre di Gnicche..... **D3**

Hotels ▼

1 Calcione **B5**
2 Il Borro **B1**

KEY

1 Exploring Sights
1 Restaurants
1 Hotels

Arezzo in his *Divine Comedy*. Guelph–Ghibelline wars continued to plague Arezzo until the end of the 14th century, when Arezzo lost its independence to Florence.

GETTING HERE AND AROUND

Arezzo is easily reached by car from the A1, the main highway running between Florence and Rome. Direct trains connect Arezzo with Rome (2½ hours) and Florence (1 hour). Direct bus service is available from Florence, but not from Rome.

VISITOR INFORMATION

CONTACT Arezzo Tourism Office. ⊠ Piazza Libertà 1, Arezzo ☎ 0575/377 678 ⊕ www.arezzointuscany.it.

◉ Sights

★ Basilica di San Francesco

CHURCH | The famous Piero della Francesca frescoes depicting *The Legend of the True Cross* (1452–66) were executed on the three walls of the Capella Bacci, the apse of this 14th-century church. What Sir Kenneth Clark called "the most perfect morning light in all Renaissance painting" may be seen in the lowest section of the right wall, where the troops of Emperor Maxentius flee before the sign of the cross. Reservations are recommended June through September. ⊠ Piazza San Francesco 2, Arezzo ☎ 0575/352727 ⊕ www.pierodellafrancesca-ticketoffice. it ⊠ €8.

Duomo

CHURCH | Arezzo's medieval cathedral at the top of the hill contains a fresco of a tender *Maria Maddalena* by Piero della Francesca (1420–92); look for it in the north aisle next to the large marble tomb near the organ. Construction of the Duomo began in 1278 but twice came to a halt, and the church wasn't completed until 1510. The ceiling decorations and the stained-glass windows date from the 16th century. The facade, designed by Arezzo's Dante Viviani, was added later (1901–14). ✉ *Piazza del Duomo 1, Arezzo.*

Museo Archeologico

ART MUSEUM | The Archaeological Museum in the **Convento di San Bernardo,** just outside the **Anfiteatro Romano,** exhibits a fine collection of Etruscan bronzes. ✉ *Via Margaritone 10, Arezzo* ☎ *0575/20882* 🌐 *www.polomusealetoscana.beniculturali.it* 🎫 *€6* 🕒 *Closed Wed. and Fri.–Sun.*

Piazza Grande

PLAZA/SQUARE | With its irregular shape and sloping brick pavement, framed by buildings of assorted centuries, Arezzo's central piazza echoes Siena's Piazza del Campo. Though not quite so magnificent, it's lively enough during the outdoor antiques fair the first weekend of the month and when the **Giostra del Saracino** (Saracen Joust), featuring medieval costumes and competition, is held here on the third Saturday of June and on the first Sunday of September. ✉ *Piazza Grande, Arezzo.*

Santa Maria della Pieve (*Church of Saint Mary of the Parish*)

CHURCH | The curving, tiered apse on Piazza Grande belongs to a fine Romanesque church that was originally an Early Christian structure, which had been constructed over the remains of a Roman temple. The church was rebuilt in Romanesque style in the 12th century. The splendid facade dates from the early 13th century but includes granite Roman columns. A magnificent polyptych, depicting the Madonna and Child with four saints, by Pietro Lorenzetti (circa 1290–1348), embellishes the high altar. ✉ *Corso Italia 7, Arezzo.*

🍴 Restaurants

Caffè dei Costanti

$ | **ITALIAN** | Outdoor seating on Arezzo's main pedestrian square and a tasty range of chef's salads (named after the servers) make this a very pleasant spot for a light lunch during a tour of town. If you're here in the early evening, the dei Costanti serves up an ample buffet of snacks to accompany predinner aperitifs. **Known for:** tasty snacks; very fine cappuccini; perfect location across from Basilica di San Francesco. [$] *Average main: €6* ✉ *Piazza San Francesco 19, Arezzo* ☎ *0575/1824075* 🌐 *www.caffedeicostanti.it* 🕒 *Closed Wed.*

★ **I Tre Bicchieri**

$$ | **SEAFOOD** | Chef Luigi Casotti hails from Amalfi and this shows through in his fine adaptations of dishes, notably seafood, more commonly served near the Bay of Naples. Two well-priced tasting menus are available. **Known for:** notable chef; creative menu including two tasting menus; superlative wine list. [$] *Average main: €19* ✉ *Piazzetta Sopra i Ponti 3–5, Arezzo* ☎ *0575/26557* 🌐 *www.ristoranteitrebicchieri.com* 🕒 *Closed Sun. (except 1st weekend of month).*

La Torre di Gnicche

$ | **ITALIAN** | Wine lovers shouldn't miss this wine bar/eatery, just off Piazza Grande, with more than 700 labels on the list. Seasonal dishes of traditional fare, such as *acquacotta del casentino* (porcini mushroom soup) and *baccalà in umido* (salt-cod stew), are served in the simply decorated, vaulted dining room. **Known for:** outdoor seating in warm weather; the extensive wine list, with many choices by the glass; an ever-changing menu. [$] *Average main: €9* ✉ *Piaggia San Martino 8, Arezzo* ☎ *0575/352035* 🌐 *www.latorredignicche.it* 🕒 *Closed Wed. and Jan.*

Hotels

Calcione

| **B&B/INN** | **FAMILY** | This six-century-old family estate (circa 1483) now houses sophisticated rustic lodgings; many of the apartments have open fireplaces, and the stone houses have a private pool (the rest share the estate pool). **Pros:** quiet, beautiful, remote setting; houses sleep up to 17; private lakes for fishing and windsurfing. **Cons:** no A/C; private transportation is a must—nearest village is 8 km (5 miles) away; minimum one-week stay in season. $ *Rooms from: €100* ⊠ *Località Il Calcione 102, 26 km (15 miles) southwest of Arezzo, Lucignano* ☎ *0575/837153* ⊕ *www.calcione.com* ⊘ *Closed Dec.–Feb.* ⤳ *30 rooms* ⦿ *No Meals.*

Il Borro

$$$$ | **HOTEL** | The location has been described as "heaven on earth," and a stay at this elegant Ferragamo estate, with a 10-bedroom villa (rented out as a single unit) that was once a luxurious hunting lodge, and nearby a medieval village is sure to bring similar descriptions to mind. **Pros:** unique setting and atmosphere; exceptional service; great location for exploring eastern Tuscany. **Cons:** not all suites have country views; off the beaten track, making private transport a must; very expensive. $ *Rooms from: €690* ⊠ *Località Il Borro 1, outside village of San Giustino Valdarno, 20 km (12 miles) northwest of Arezzo* ☎ *055/977053* ⊕ *www.ilborro.it* ⊘ *Closed Dec.–Mar.* ⤳ *61 rooms* ⦿ *Free Breakfast.*

Cortona

29 km (18 miles) south of Arezzo, 79 km (44 miles) east of Siena, 117 km (73 miles) southeast of Florence.

Brought into the limelight by Frances Mayes's book *Under the Tuscan Sun* and a subsequent movie, Cortona is no longer the destination of just a few specialist art historians and those seeking reprieve from busier tourist venues. The main street, Via Nazionale, is now lined with souvenir shops and fills with crowds during summer. Although the main sights of Cortona make braving the bustling center worthwhile, much of the town's charm lies in its maze of quiet backstreets. It's here that you will see laundry hanging from windows, find children playing, and catch the smell of simmering pasta sauce. Wander off the beaten track and you won't be disappointed.

GETTING HERE AND AROUND

Cortona is easily reached by car from the A1 autostrada: take the Valdichiana exit toward Perugia, then follow signs for Cortona. Regular bus service, provided by Etruria Mobilità, is available between Arezzo and Cortona (one hour). Train service to Cortona is made inconvenient by the location of the train station, in the valley 3 km (2 miles) steeply below the town itself. From there, you have to rely on bus or taxi service to get up to Cortona.

VISITOR INFORMATION

CONTACT Cortona Tourism Office. ⊠ *Piazza Signorelli 9, Cortona* ☎ *0575/637223* ⊕ *www.comunedicortona.it.*

Sights

Museo Diocesano

ART MUSEUM | Housed in part of the original cathedral structure, this nine-room museum houses an impressive number of large, splendid paintings by native son Luca Signorelli (1445–1523), as well as a beautiful *Annunciation* by Fra Angelico (1387/1400–55), which is a delightful surprise in this small town. The church was built between 1498 and 1505 and restructured by Giorgio Vasari in 1543. Frescoes depicting sacrifices from the Old Testament by Doceno (1508–56), based on designs by Vasari, line the walls. ⊠ *Piazza Duomo 1, Cortona* ☎ *0575/62830*

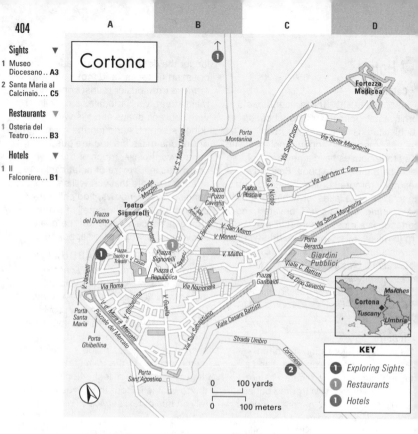

⊕ *www.cortonatuseibellezza.it* 🎫 *€6*
🕑 *Closed Mon.–Thurs. Nov.–Mar.*

Santa Maria al Calcinaio

CHURCH | Legend has it that the image of the Madonna appeared on a wall of a medieval *calcinaio* (lime pit used for curing leather), the site on which the church was then built between 1485 and 1513. The linear gray-and-white interior recalls Florence's Duomo. Sienese architect Francesco di Giorgio (1439–1502) most likely designed the sanctuary: the church is a terrific example of Renaissance architectural principles. ⊠ *Località Il Calcinaio 227, 3 km (2 miles) southeast of Cortona's center.*

🍴 Restaurants

Osteria del Teatro

$$ | TUSCAN | Photographs from theatrical productions spanning many years line the walls of this tavern off Cortona's large Piazza del Teatro. The food is simply delicious—try the *filetto al lardo di colonnata e prugne* (beef cooked with bacon and prunes); service is warm and friendly. **Known for:** pretty dining room; food that's in season; lively atmosphere. **$** *Average main: €18* ⊠ *Via Maffei 2, Cortona* ☎ *0575/630556* ⊕ *www.osteria-del-teatro.it* 🕑 *Closed Wed. and 2 wks in Nov.*

Hotels

★ Il Falconiere

$$$$ | B&B/INN | Accommodation options at this sumptuous property include rooms in an 18th-century villa, suites in the *chiesetta* (chapel, or little church), or for more seclusion, Le Vigne del Falco suites at the far end of the property. **Pros:** elegant, but relaxed; attractive setting in the valley beneath Cortona; excellent service. **Cons:** might be too isolated for some; a car is a must; some find rooms in main villa a little noisy. $ *Rooms from: €330* ⊠ *Località San Martino 370, 3 km (2 miles) north of Cortona* ☎ *0575/612679* ⊕ *www.ilfalconiere.it* ☉ *Closed Nov. 3– Mar. 27* ↬ *34 rooms* ❍| *Free Breakfast.*

Perugia

Perugia is a majestic, handsome, wealthy city, and with its trendy boutiques, refined cafés, and grandiose architecture, it doesn't try to hide its affluence. A student population of around 30,000 means that the city, with a permanent population of about 165,000, is abuzz with activity throughout the year. Umbria Jazz, one of the region's most important music festivals, attracts music lovers from around the world every July, and Eurochocolate, the international chocolate festival, is an irresistible draw each October for anyone with a sweet tooth.

GETTING HERE AND AROUND
The best approach to the city is by train. The area around the station doesn't attest to the rest of Perugia's elegance, but buses running from the station to Piazza d'Italia, the heart of the old town, are frequent. If you're in a hurry, take the *minimetro,* a one-line subway, to Stazione della Cupa. If you're driving to Perugia and your hotel doesn't have parking facilities, leave your car in one of the lots close to the center. Electronic displays indicate the location of lots and the number of spaces free. If you park in

the Piazza Partigiani, take the escalators that pass through the fascinating subterranean excavations of the Roman foundations of the city and lead to the town center.

 Sights

Collegio del Cambio (*Bankers' Guild Hall*)
HISTORIC SIGHT | These elaborate rooms, on the ground floor of the **Palazzo dei Priori,** served as the meeting hall and chapel of the guild of bankers and money changers. Most of the frescoes were completed by the most important Perugian painter of the Renaissance, Pietro Vannucci, better known as Perugino. He included a remarkably honest self-portrait on one of the pilasters. The iconography includes common religious themes, such as the Nativity and the Transfiguration seen on the end walls. On the left wall are female figures representing the virtues, and beneath them are the heroes and sages of antiquity. On the right wall are figures presumed to have been painted in part by Perugino's most famous pupil, Raphael. (His hand, experts say, is most apparent in the figure of Fortitude.) The *cappella* (chapel) of San Giovanni Battista has frescoes painted by Giannicola di Paolo, another student of Perugino's. ⊠ *Corso Vannucci 25, Perugia* ☎ *075/5728599* ⊕ *www.collegiodelcambio.it* ☉ *Closed Sun. afternoon, also Mon. afternoon Nov.–Mar.* ☑ *€4.50.*

Corso Vannucci
STREET | A string of elegantly connected palazzi expresses the artistic nature of this city center, the heart of which is concentrated along Corso Vannucci. Stately and broad, this pedestrian-only street runs from Piazza Italia to Piazza IV Novembre. Along the way, the entrances to many of Perugia's side streets might tempt you to wander off and explore. But don't stray too far as evening falls, when Corso Vannucci fills with Perugians out for their evening *passeggiata,* a pleasant predinner stroll that may include a pause

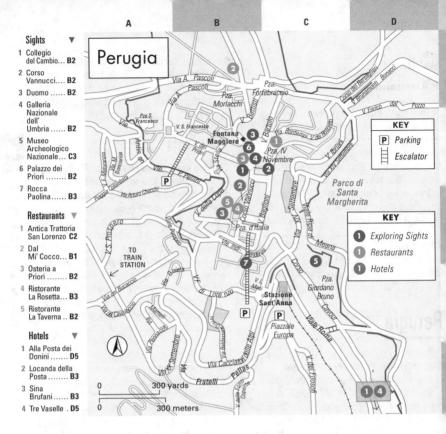

for an aperitif at one of the many bars that line the street. ⊠ *Perugia*.

Duomo

CHURCH | Severe yet mystical, the Cathedral of San Lorenzo is most famous for being the home of the wedding ring of the Virgin Mary, stolen by the Perugians in 1488 from the nearby town of Chiusi. The ring, kept high up in a red-curtained vault in the chapel immediately to the left of the entrance, is stored under lock and key—15 locks, to be precise—most of the year. It's shown to the .public on July 30 (the day it was brought to Perugia) and the second-to-last Sunday in January (Mary's wedding anniversary). The cathedral itself dates from the Middle Ages, and has many additions from the 15th and 16th centuries. The most visually interesting element is the altar to the Madonna of Grace; an elegant fresco on a column at the right of the entrance of the altar depicts La Madonna delle Grazie. Sections of the church may be closed to visitors during religious services. The **Museo Capitolare** displays a large array of precious objects associated with the cathedral, including vestments, vessels, and manuscripts. Outside the Duomo is the elaborate **Fontana Maggiore**, which dates from 1278. It's adorned with zodiac figures and symbols of the seven arts. ⊠ *Piazza IV Novembre, Perugia* ☎ *075/5723832* ⊕ *www.cattedrale.perugia.it* ⊠ *Museum €6* ⊗ *Museum closed Mon. Nov.–Mar.*

★ Galleria Nazionale dell'Umbria

ART MUSEUM | The region's most comprehensive art gallery is housed on the fourth floor of the **Palazzo dei Priori**. Enhanced by skillfully lit displays and computers that allow you to focus

Umbria Through the Ages

The earliest inhabitants of Umbria, the Umbri, were thought by the Romans to be the most ancient inhabitants of Italy. Little is known about them; with the coming of Etruscan culture the tribe fled into the mountains in the eastern portion of the region. The Etruscans, who founded some of the great cities of Umbria, were in turn supplanted by the Romans. Unlike Tuscany and other regions of central Italy, Umbria had few powerful medieval families to exert control over the cities in the Middle Ages—its proximity to Rome ensured that it would always be more or less under papal domination.

In the center of the country, Umbria has for much of its history been a battlefield where armies from north and south clashed. Hannibal destroyed a Roman army on the shores of Lake Trasimeno, and the bloody course of the interminable Guelph–Ghibelline conflict of the Middle Ages was played out here. Dante considered Umbria the most violent place in Italy. Trophies of war still decorate the Palazzo dei Priori in Perugia, and the little town of Gubbio continues a warlike rivalry begun in the Middle Ages—every year it challenges the Tuscan town of Sansepolcro to a cross-bow tournament. Today the bowmen shoot at targets, but neither side has forgotten that 500 years ago they were shooting at each other.

In spite of—or perhaps because of—this bloodshed, Umbria has produced more than its share of Christian saints. The most famous is St. Francis, the decidedly pacifist saint whose life shaped the Church of his time. His great shrine at Assisi is visited by hundreds of thousands of pilgrims each year. St. Clare, his devoted follower, was Umbria-born, as were St. Benedict, St. Rita of Cascia, and the patron saint of lovers, St. Valentine.

in the works' details and background information, the collection includes work by native artists—most notably Pintoricchio (1454–1513) and Perugino (circa 1450–1523)—and others of the Umbrian and Tuscan schools, among them Gentile la Fabriano (1370–1427), Duccio (circa 1255–1318), Fra Angelico (1387–1455), Fiorenzo di Lorenzo (1445–1525), and Piero della Francesca (1420–92). In addition to paintings, the gallery has frescoes, sculptures, and some superb examples of crucifixes from the 13th and 14th centuries. Some rooms are dedicated to Perugia itself, showing how the medieval city evolved. ⊠ Corso Vannucci 19, Perugia ☎ 075/58668415 ⊕ www.gallerianazionaledellumbria.it ☑ €8 ⊙ Closed Mon.

Museo Archeologico Nazionale

HISTORY MUSEUM | An excellent collection of Etruscan artifacts from throughout the region sheds light on Perugia as a flourishing Etruscan city long before it fell under Roman domination in 310 BC. Little else remains of Perugia's mysterious ancestors, although the Arco di Augusto, in Piazza Fortebraccio, the northern entrance to the city, is of Etruscan origin. ⊠ Piazza G. Bruno 10, Perugia ☎ 075/5727141 ⊕ www.polomusealeumbria.beniculturali.it ☑ €5 ⊙ Closed Mon.

Palazzo dei Priori (*Palace of the Priors*)
GOVERNMENT BUILDING | A series of elegant connected buildings, the palazzo serves as Perugia's city hall and houses three of the city's museums. The buildings string along Corso Vannucci and

wrap around the Piazza IV Novembre, where the original entrance is located. The steps here lead to the **Sala dei Notari** (Notaries' Hall). Other entrances lead to the **Galleria Nazionale dell'Umbria,** the **Collegio del Cambio,** and the **Collegio della Mercanzia.** The Sala dei Notari, which dates back to the 13th century and was the original meeting place of the town merchants, had become the seat of the notaries by the second half of the 15th century. Wood beams and an interesting array of frescoes attributed to Maestro di Farneto embellish the room. Coats of arms and crests line the back and right lateral walls; you can spot some famous figures from Aesop's *Fables* on the left wall. The palazzo facade is adorned with symbols of Perugia's pride and past power: the griffin is the city symbol, and the lion denotes Perugia's allegiance to the Guelph (or papal) cause. ✉ *Piazza IV Novembre 25, Perugia* 🎟 *Free.*

Rocca Paolina

CASTLE/PALACE | A labyrinth of little streets, alleys, and arches, this underground city was originally part of a fortress built at the behest of Pope Paul III between 1540 and 1543 to confirm papal dominion over the city. Parts of it were destroyed after the end of papal rule, but much still remains. Begin your visit by taking the escalators that descend through the subterranean ruins from Piazza Italia down to Via Masi. In the summer this is the coolest place in the city. ✉ *Piazza Italia, Perugia* 🎟 *Free.*

🍴 Restaurants

Antica Trattoria San Lorenzo

$$ | **UMBRIAN** | Both the food and the service are outstanding at this popular small, brick-vaulted eatery next to the Duomo. Particular attention is paid to adapting traditional Umbrian cuisine to the modern palate, and there's also a nice variety of seafood dishes on the menu—the *pacchero di Gragnano* (pasta with smoked eggplant, cod, clams, scampi, and prawns) is a real treat. **Known for:** good vegetarian choices; impeccable service; quality versions of local recipes [$] *Average main: €22* ✉ *Piazza Danti 19/ Perugia* ☎ *075/5721956* 🌐 *www.anticatrattoriasanlorenzo.com.*

Dal Mi' Cocco

$$ | **UMBRIAN** | A great favorite with Perugia's university students, it is fun, crowded, and inexpensive; you may find yourself seated at a long table with other diners, but some language help from your neighbors could come in handy—the menu is in pure Perugian dialect. Fixed-price meals change with the season, and each day of the week brings some new creation *dal cocco* (from the "coconut," or head) of the chef. **Known for:** abundant portions; honest prices; authentically casual feel. [$] *Average main: €15* ✉ *Corso Garibaldi 12, Perugia* ☎ *075/5732511* 🕓 *Closed Mon. and late July–mid-Aug.*

Ristorante La Rosetta

$$ | **ITALIAN** | The dining room of the hotel of the same name is a peaceful, elegant spot for travelers seeking to get away from the bustle of central Perugia; in winter you dine inside under medieval vaults and in summer, in the cool courtyard. The food is simple but reliable, and flawlessly served. **Known for:** elegant, old-fashioned setting; refined versions of local meat dishes; professional service. [$] *Average main: €18* ✉ *Piazza d'Italia 19, Perugia* ☎ *075/3747858* 🌐 *www.ristorantelarosettaperugia.com.*

Ristorante La Taverna

$$ | **UMBRIAN** | Medieval steps lead to a rustic two-story space where wine bottles and artful clutter decorate the walls. The regional menu features lots of delicious house-made pastas and grilled meats prepared by chef Claudio, served up in substantial portions, plus generous shavings of truffle in season. **Known for:** welcoming ambience; swift and efficient service; Umbrian specialties. [$] *Average main: €22* ✉ *Via delle Streghe 8, off*

Corso Vannucci, Perugia ☎ 075/5724128
⊕ www.ristorantelataverna.com.

Osteria a Priori

| **MODERN ITALIAN** | This charming
vine-and-olive-oil shop with a restaurant (with vaulted ceilings and exposed
brick) tucked into the back offers up
small plates using ingredients with a
"zero-kilometer" philosophy: everything
comes from local and artisanal Umbrian
producers. Regional cheeses, homemade
pastas, and slow-cooked meats steal the
show and, as might be expected, the
selection of wine is top-notch. **Known for:**
local, nontouristy atmosphere; knowledgeable servers; all Umbrian products.
$ *Average main: €12* ⊠ *Via dei Priori 39,
Perugia* ☎ 075/5727098 ⊕ www.oste-
riaapriori.it ⊗ *Closed Sun.*

🛏 Hotels

Alla Posta dei Donini

$ | **HOTEL** | Beguilingly comfortable guest
rooms are set on lovely grounds, where
gardeners go quietly about their business. **Pros:** great restaurant; plush atmosphere; a quiet and private getaway. **Cons:**
uninteresting village; outside Perugia; spa
sometimes overcrowded. $ *Rooms from:
€119* ⊠ *Via Deruta 43, 15 km (9 miles)
south of Perugia, San Martino in Campo*
☎ 075/609132 ⊕ www.postadonini.it
⇘ *48 rooms* ⊙ *No Meals.*

Locanda della Posta

$$ | **HOTEL** | Renovations have left the
lobby and other public areas rather bland,
but the rooms in this converted 18th-cen-
tury palazzo are soothingly decorated in
muted colors. **Pros:** exudes good taste
and refinement; some fine views; central
location. **Cons:** some small rooms; some
street noise; no public areas. $ *Rooms
from: €134* ⊠ *Corso Vannucci 97, Perugia*
☎ 075/5728925 ⊕ www.locandadellapos-
tahotel.it ⇘ *17 rooms* ⊙ *Free Breakfast.*

Sina Brufani

$$ | **HOTEL** | Though a tad old-fashioned,
this elegant centrally located hotel dating
from 1884 is the most upscale accommo-
dation in town. **Pros:** excellent views from
many rooms; wonderful location; unique
spa area. **Cons:** in-house restaurant not up
to par; could use a refresh; service can be
hit-or-miss. $ *Rooms from: €185* ⊠ *Piazza
Italia 12, Perugia* ☎ 075/5732541 ⊕ www.
sinahotels.com/en/h/sina-brufani-perugia
⇘ *94 rooms* ⊙ *No Meals.*

Tre Vaselle

$$ | **HOTEL** | Rooms spread throughout
four stone buildings are spacious and
graced with floors of typical red-clay Tus-
can tiles. **Pros:** nice pool; perfect for vis-
iting the Torgiano wine area and Deruta;
friendly staff. **Cons:** in center of uninspir-
ing village; somewhat far from Perugia;
service occasionally falters. $ *Rooms
from: €145* ⊠ *Via Garibaldi 48, Torgiano*
☎ 075/9880447 ⊕ www.3vaselle.it ⇘ *51
rooms* ⊙ *No Meals.*

Assisi

The small town of Assisi is one of the
Christian world's most important pilgrim-
age sites and home of the Basilica di
San Francesco—built to honor St. Francis
(1182–1226) and erected in swift order
after his death. The peace and serenity
of the town are a welcome respite after
the hustle and bustle of some of Italy's
major cities.

Like most other towns in the region, Assisi
began as an Umbri settlement in the 7th
century BC and was conquered by the
Romans 400 years later. The town was
Christianized by St. Rufino, its patron saint,
in the 3rd century, but it's the spirit of St.
Francis, a patron saint of Italy and founder
of the Franciscan monastic order, that's felt
throughout its narrow medieval streets.
The famous 13th-century basilica was dec-
orated by the greatest artists of the period.

Continued on page 414

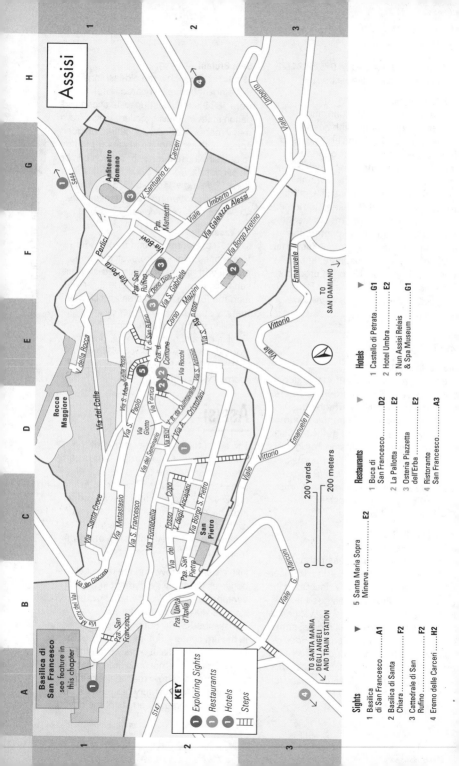

Assisi

Basilica di San Francesco
see feature in this chapter

Rocca Maggiore

Anfiteatro Romano

TO SANTA MARIA DEGLI ANGELI AND TRAIN STATION

TO SAN DAMIANO

200 yards
200 meters

KEY

- 1 Exploring Sights
- 1 Restaurants
- 1 Hotels
- Steps

Sights ▶

1 Basilica di San Francesco **A1**

2 Basilica di Santa Chiara **F2**

3 Cattedrale di San Rufino **F2**

4 Eremo delle Carceri **H2**

5 Santa Maria Sopra Minerva **E2**

Restaurants ▶

1 Buca di San Francesco..........**D2**

2 La Pallotta **E2**

3 Osteria Piazzetta dell'Erba **E2**

4 Ristorante San Francesco..........**A3**

Hotels ▶

1 Castello di Petrata.......**G1**

2 Hotel Umbra..........**E2**

3 Nun Assisi Relais & Spa Museum **G1**

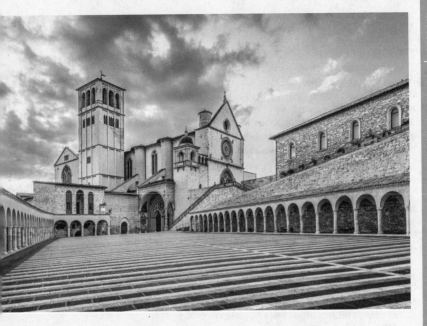

ASSISI'S BASILICA DI SAN FRANCESCO

The legacy of St. Francis, founder of the Franciscan monastic order, pervades Assisi. Each year the town hosts several million pilgrims, but the steady flow of visitors does nothing to diminish the singular beauty of one of Italy's most important religious centers. The pilgrims' ultimate destination is the massive Basilica di San Francesco, which sits halfway up Assisi's hill, supported by graceful arches.

The basilica is not one church but two. The Romanesque Lower Church came first; construction began in 1228, just two years after St. Francis's death, and was completed within a few years. The low ceilings and candlelit interior make an appropriately solemn setting for St. Francis's tomb, found in the crypt below the main altar. The Gothic Upper Church, built only half a century later, sits on top of the lower one, and is strikingly different, with soaring arches and tall stained-glass windows (the first in Italy). Inside, both churches are covered floor to ceiling with some of Europe's finest frescoes: the Lower Church is dim and full of candlelit shadows, and the Upper Church is bright and airy.

VISITING THE BASILICA

THE LOWER CHURCH

The most evocative way to experience the basilica is to begin with the dark Lower Church. As you enter, give your eyes a moment to adjust. Keep in mind that the artists at work here were conscious of the shadowy environment—they knew this was how their frescoes would be seen.

In the first chapel to the left, a superb fresco cycle by Simone Martini depicts scenes from the life of St. Martin. As you approach the main altar, the vaulting above you is decorated with the Three Virtues of St. Francis (poverty, chastity, and obedience) and St. Francis's Triumph, frescoes attributed to Giotto's followers. In the transept to your left, Pietro Lorenzetti's Madonna and Child with St. Francis and St. John sparkles when the sun hits it. Notice Mary's thumb; legend has it Jesus is asking which saint to bless, and Mary is pointing to Francis. Across the way in the right transept, Cimabue's Madonna Enthroned Among Angels and St. Francis is a famous portrait of the saint. Surrounding the portrait are painted scenes from the childhood of Christ, done by the assistants of Giotto. Nearby is a painting of the crucifixion attributed to Giotto himself.

You reach the crypt via stairs midway along the nave—on the crypt's altar, a stone coffin holds the saint's body. Steps up from the transepts lead to the cloister, where there's a gift shop, and the treasury, which contains holy objects.

THE UPPER CHURCH

The St. Francis fresco cycle is the highlight of the Upper Church. (See facing page.) Also worth special note is the 16th-century choir, with its remarkably delicate inlaid wood. When a 1997 earthquake rocked the basilica, the St. Francis cycle sustained little damage, but portions of the ceiling above the entrance and altar collapsed, reducing their frescoes (attributed to Cimabue and Giotto) to rubble. The painstaking restoration is ongoing. ⚠ The dress code is strictly enforced—no bare shoulders or bare knees.

FRANCIS, ITALY'S PATRON SAINT

St. Francis was born in Assisi in 1181, the son of a noblewoman and a well-to-do merchant. His troubled youth included a year in prison. He planned a military career, but after a long illness Francis heard the voice of God, renounced his father's wealth, and began a life of austerity. His mystical embrace of poverty, asceticism, and the beauty of man and nature struck a responsive chord in the medieval mind; he quickly attracted a vast number of followers. Francis was the first saint to receive the stigmata (wounds in his hands, feet, and side corresponding to those of Christ on the cross). He died on October 4, 1226, in the Porziuncola, the secluded chapel in the woods where he had first preached the virtue of poverty to his disciples. St. Francis was declared patron saint of Italy in 1939, and today the Franciscans make up the largest of the Catholic orders.

THE UPPER CHURCH'S ST. FRANCIS FRESCO CYCLE

The 28 frescoes in the Upper Church depicting the life of St. Francis are the most admired works in the entire basilica. They're also the subject of one of art history's biggest controversies. For centuries they thought to be by Giotto (1267-1337), the great early Renaissance innovator, but inconsistencies in style, both within this series and in comparison to later Giotto works, have thrown their origin into question. Some scholars now say Giotto was the brains behind the cycle, but that assistants helped with the execution; others claim he couldn't have been involved at all.

Two things are certain. First, the style is revolutionary—which argues for

Giotto's involvement. The tangible weight of the figures, the emotion they show, and the use of perspective all look familiar to modern eyes, but in the art of the time there was nothing like it. Second, these images have played a major part in shaping how the world sees St. Francis. In that respect, who painted them hardly matters.

Starting in the transept, the frescoes circle the church, showing events in the saint's life (and afterlife). Some of the best are grouped near the church's entrance—look for the nativity at Greccio, the miracle of the spring, the death of the knight at Celano, and, most famously, the sermon to the birds.

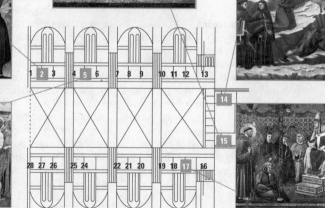

The St. Francis fresco cycle
1. Homage of a simple man
2. Giving cloak to a poor man
3. Dream of the palace
4. Hearing the voice of God
5. Rejection of worldly goods
6. Dream of Innocent III
7. Confirmation of the rules
8. Vision of flaming chariot
9. Vision of celestial thrones
10. Chasing devils from Arezzo
11. Before the sultan
12. Ecstasy of St. Francis
13. Nativity at Greccio
14. Miracle of the spring
15. Sermon to the birds
16. Death of knight at Celano
17. Preaching to Honorius III
18. Apparition at Arles
19. Receiving the stigmata
20. Death of St. Francis
21. Apparition before Bishop Guido and Fra Agostino
22. Verification of the stigmata
23. Mourning of St. Clare
24. Canonization
25. Apparition before Gregory IX
26. Healing of a devotee
27. Confession of a woman
28. Repentant heretic freed

GETTING HERE AND AROUND

Assisi lies on the Terontola–Foligno rail line, with almost hourly connections to Perugia and direct trains to Rome and Florence several times a day. The Stazione Centrale is 4 km (2½ miles) from town, with a bus service about every half hour. Assisi is easily reached from the A1 autostrada (Rome–Florence) and the S75b highway. The walled town is closed to traffic, so cars must be left in the parking lots at Porta San Pietro, near Porta Nuova, or beneath Piazza Matteotti. Pay your parking fee at the *cassa* (ticket booth) before you return to your car to get a ticket to insert in the machine that will allow you to exit. It's a short but sometimes steep walk into the center of town; frequent minibuses (buy tickets from a newsstand or tobacco shop near where you park your car) make the rounds for weary pilgrims.

Sights

★ Basilica di San Francesco

CHURCH | The basilica isn't one church but two: the Gothic church on the upper level, and the Romanesque church on the lower level. Work on this two-tiered monolith was begun in 1228. Both churches are magnificently decorated artistic treasure-houses, covered floor to ceiling with some of Europe's finest frescoes: the Lower Basilica is dim and full of candlelight shadows, while the Upper Basilica is bright and airy. In the **Upper Church,** the magnificent frescoes from 13th-century Italian painter Giotto, painted when he was only in his twenties, show that he was a pivotal artist in the development of Western painting. He broke away from the stiff, unnatural styles of earlier generations to move toward realism and three-dimensionality. The **Lower Church** features frescoes by celebrated Sienese painters Simone Martini and Pietro Lorenzetti, as well as by Giotto (or his assistants). The basilica's dress code is strictly enforced—no bare shoulders or bare knees are permitted. ⊠ *Piazza di San Francesco, Assisi* 🕾 *075/8190084* ⊕ *www.sanfrancescoassisi.org* 🎫 *Free.*

Basilica di Santa Chiara

CHURCH | The lovely, wide piazza in front of this church is reason enough to visit. The red-and-white-striped facade frames the piazza's panoramic view over the Umbrian plains. Santa Chiara is dedicated to St. Clare, one of the earliest and most fervent of St. Francis's followers and the founder of the order of the Poor Ladies—or Poor Clares—which was based on the Franciscan monastic order. The church contains Clare's body, and in the **Cappella del Crocifisso** (on the right) is the cross that spoke to St. Francis. A heavily veiled nun of the Poor Clares order is usually stationed before the cross in adoration of the image. ⊠ *Piazza Santa Chiara, Assisi* 🕾 *075/812216* ⊕ *www.assisisantachiara.it* 🎫 *Free.*

Cattedrale di San Rufino

CHURCH | St. Francis and St. Clare were among those baptized in Assisi's Cattedrale, which was the principal church in town until the 12th century. The baptismal font has since been redecorated, but it's possible to see the crypt of St. Rufino, the bishop who brought Christianity to Assisi and was martyred on August 11, 238 (or 236 by some accounts), as well as climb to the bell tower. Admission to the crypt includes the small Museo della Cattedrale, with its detached frescoes and artifacts. ⊠ *Piazza San Rufino, Assisi* 🕾 *075/812712* ⊕ *www.assisimuseodiocesano.it* 🎫 *Church free, Crypt and Museum €3.50, Bell Tower and Museum €4, Bell Tower €1.50* 🕙 *Bell tower closed Wed.*

Eremo delle Carceri

RELIGIOUS BUILDING | About 4 km (2½ miles) east of Assisi is a monastery set in a dense wood against Monte Subasio: the Hermitage of Prisons. This was the place where St. Francis and his followers went to "imprison" themselves in prayer. The only site in Assisi that remains essentially unchanged since St. Francis's time, the church and monastery are the kinds of tranquil places that St. Francis would have appreciated. The walk out from town is very pleasant, and many trails lead from here across the wooded hillside of Monte Subasio (now a protected forest), with beautiful vistas across the Umbrian countryside. True to their Franciscan heritage, the friars here are entirely dependent on alms from visitors. ✉ *Via Santuario delle Carceri, 4 km (2½ miles) east of Assisi* ☎ *075/812301* 🎫 *Donations accepted.*

Santa Maria Sopra Minerva

CHURCH | Dating from the time of the Emperor Augustus (27 BC–AD 14), this structure was originally dedicated to the Roman goddess of wisdom, and in later times it was used as a monastery and prison before being converted into a church in the 16th century. The expectations raised by the perfect classical facade are not met by the interior, which was subjected to a thorough Baroque transformation in the 17th century. ✉ *Piazza del Comune, Assisi* ☎ *075/812361* 🎫 *Free.*

🍴 Restaurants

Buca di San Francesco

$ | **UMBRIAN** | In summer, dine in a cool green garden; in winter, under the low brick arches of the cozy cellars. The unique settings and the first-rate fare make this central restaurant one of Assisi's busiest; try the namesake homemade spaghetti *alla buca,* served with a roasted mushroom sauce. **Known for:** warm and welcoming service; cozy atmosphere; historical surroundings. [$] *Average main: €14* ✉ *Via Eugenio Brizi 1, Assisi* ☎ *075/812204* 🌐 *buca-di-san-francesco.business.site* 🕒 *Closed Mon. and 10 days in late July.*

La Pallotta

$$ | **UMBRIAN** | At this homey, family-run trattoria with a crackling fireplace and stone walls, the women do the cooking and the men serve the food; try the *strangozzi alla pallotta* (thick spaghetti with a pesto of olives and mushrooms). Connected to the restaurant is an inn whose eight rooms have firm beds and some views across the rooftops of town. **Known for:** traditional local dishes; economical tourist menu; fast and courteous service. [$] *Average main: €15* ✉ *Vicolo della Volta Pinta 3, Assisi* ☎ *075/8155273* 🌐 *www.trattoriapallotta.it* 🕒 *Closed Tues.*

Osteria Piazzetta dell'Erba

$$ | **UMBRIAN** | Hip service and sophisticated presentations attract locals, who enjoy Italian cuisine with unusual twists (think porcini mushroom risotto with blue cheese and blueberries), a nice selection of salads—unusual for an Umbrian restaurant—and intriguing desserts. The enthusiastic young team keep things running smoothly and the energy high. **Known for:** intimate ambience; friendly staff; inventive dishes. [$] *Average main: €18* ✉ *Via San Gabriele dell'Addolorata 15/b, Assisi* ☎ *075/815352* 🌐 *www.osteriapiazzettadellerba.it/en* 🕒 *Closed Mon. and a few wks in Jan. or Feb.*

Ristorante San Francesco

$$ | **UMBRIAN** | An excellent view of the Basilica di San Francesco from the covered terrace is just one reason to enjoy this traditional restaurant, where Umbrian dishes are made with aromatic locally grown herbs. Menus change seasonally and include a fine selection of pastas and mains; appetizers and desserts are also especially good. **Known for:** pleasant staff; excellent location; pleasing desserts. [$] *Average main: €20* ✉ *Via di San Francesco 52, Assisi* ☎ *075/813302* 🌐 *www.ristorantesanfrancesco.com* 🕒 *Closed Wed. Nov.–Easter and 1–2 wks early July.*

Hotels

★ Castello di Petrata

$$ | HOTEL | Wood beams and sections of exposed medieval stonework add a lot of character to this fortress built in the 14th century, while comfortable couches turn each individually decorated room into a delightful retreat. **Pros:** peaceful pool; great views of town and countryside; medieval character. **Cons:** far from Assisi town center; slightly isolated; limited choices in restaurant. [$] *Rooms from: €171* ⊠ *Via Petrata 25, Località Petrata, Assisi* ☏ *075/815451* ⊕ *www.castellopetrata.it* ⊘ *Closed Sun.–Wed. Jan.–mid-Mar.* ⊅ *20 rooms* ⦿| *Free Breakfast.*

Hotel Umbra

$ | HOTEL | Rooms on the upper floors of this charming 16th-century town house near Piazza del Comune look out over the Assisi rooftops to the valley below, as does the sunny, vine-covered terrace. **Pros:** excellent valley views from some rooms; very central; pleasant small garden. **Cons:** some small rooms; difficult parking; uninspiring breakfasts. [$] *Rooms from: €100* ⊠ *Via degli Archi 6, Assisi* ☏ *075/812240* ⊕ *www.hotelumbra.it* ⊘ *Closed Nov.–late Mar.* ⊅ *24 rooms* ⦿| *Free Breakfast.*

★ Nun Assisi Relais & Spa Museum

$$$$ | HOTEL | A monastery built in 1275 has been converted into a thoroughly contemporary, high-end place to stay with a fabulous spa carved out of 2,000-year-old Roman baths and within walking distance of Assisi's restaurants and shops. **Pros:** wonderful place to relax; fantastic blend of the historic and modern; excellent restaurant. **Cons:** on-site parking costs extra; on the expensive side; split-level rooms with stairs difficult for those with mobility issues. [$] *Rooms from: €328* ⊠ *Via Eremo delle Carceri 1A, Assisi* ☏ *075/8155150* ⊕ *www.nunassisi.com* ⊅ *18 rooms* ⦿| *Free Breakfast.*

Spoleto

For most of the year, Spoleto is one more in a pleasant succession of sleepy hill towns, resting regally atop a mountain. But for three weeks every summer the town shifts into high gear for a turn in the international spotlight during the Festival dei Due Mondi (Festival of Two Worlds), an extravaganza of theater, opera, music, painting, and sculpture. As the world's top artists vie for honors, throngs of art aficionados vie for hotel rooms. If you plan to spend the night in Spoleto during the festival, make sure you have confirmed reservations, or you may find yourself scrambling at sunset.

Spoleto has plenty to lure you during the rest of the year as well: the final frescoes of Filippo Lippi, beautiful piazzas and streets with Roman and medieval attractions, and superb natural surroundings with rolling hills and a dramatic gorge. Spoleto makes a good base for exploring all of southern Umbria, as Assisi, Orvieto, and the towns in between are all within easy reach.

GETTING HERE AND AROUND

Spoleto is an hour's drive from Perugia. From the E45 highway, take the exit toward Assisi and Foligno, then merge onto the SS75 until you reach the Foligno Est exit. Merge onto the SS3, which leads to Spoleto. There are regular trains on the Perugia–Foligno line. From the train station it's a 15-minute uphill walk to the center, so you'll probably want to take a local bus or a taxi.

VISITOR INFORMATION

CONTACT Spoleto Tourism Office. ⊠ *Largo Ferrer 6, off Corso Mazzini, Spoleto* ☏ *0743/218620* ⊕ *www.comune.spoleto.pg.it/turismoecultura.*

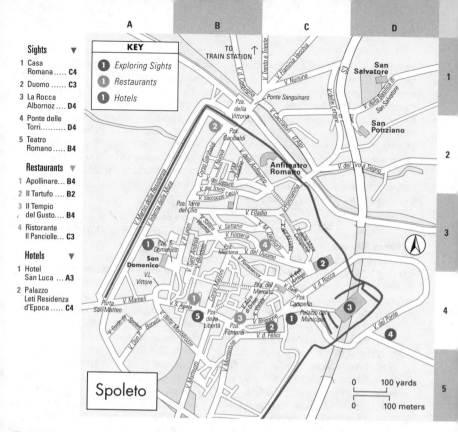

Spoleto

Sights ▼

1 Casa
  Romana..... **C4**
2 Duomo **C3**
3 La Rocca
  Albornoz **D4**
4 Ponte delle
  Torri.......... **D4**
5 Teatro
  Romano..... **B4**

Restaurants ▼

1 Apollinare... **B4**
2 Il Tartufo **B2**
3 Il Tempio
  del Gusto.... **B4**
4 Ristorante
  Il Panciolle... **C3**

Hotels ▼

1 Hotel
  San Luca ... **A3**
2 Palazzo
  Leti Residenza
  d'Epoca **C4**

 Sights

Casa Romana

RUINS | Spoleto became a Roman colony in the 3rd century BC, but the best excavated remains date from the 1st century AD. Best preserved among them is the Casa Romana. According to an inscription, it belonged to Vespasia Polla, the mother of Emperor Vespasian (one of the builders of the Colosseum and perhaps better known by the Romans for taxing them to install public toilets, later called "Vespasians"). The rooms, arranged around a large central atrium built over an *impluvium* (rain cistern), are decorated with black-and-white geometric mosaics. ⊠ *Palazzo del Municipio, Via Visiale 9, Spoleto* ☎ *0743/40255* ⊕ *www.spoleto-card.it* ⊠ *€3* ⊘ *Closed Mon.–Thu.*

★ Duomo

CHURCH | The 12th-century Romanesque facade received a Renaissance face-lift with the addition of a loggia in a rosy pink stone, creating a stunning contrast in styles. One of the finest cathedrals in the region is lit by eight rose windows that are especially dazzling in the late afternoon sun. The original floor tiles remain from an earlier church destroyed by Frederick I (circa 1123–90). Above the church's entrance is Bernini's bust of Pope Urban VIII (1568–1644), who had the church redecorated in 17th-century Baroque; fortunately he didn't touch the 15th-century frescoes painted in the apse by Fra Filippo Lippi (circa 1406–69) between 1466 and 1469. These immaculately restored masterpieces—the Annunciation, Nativity, and Dormition—tell the story of the life of the Virgin. The Coronation of the Virgin, adorning the half dome, is the literal and figurative high point. Portraits of Lippi and his assistants are on the right side of the central panel. The Florentine artist-priest, "whose colors expressed God's voice" (the words inscribed on his tomb), died shortly after completing the work. His tomb, which you can see in the right transept (note the artist's brushes and tools), was designed by his son, Filippino Lippi (circa 1457–1504). ⊠ *Piazza del Duomo, Spoleto* ☎ *0577/286300* ⊕ *www. duomospoleto.it* ☐ *Free.*

La Rocca Albornoz

CASTLE/PALACE | Built in the mid-14th century for Cardinal Egidio Albornoz, this massive fortress served as a seat for the local pontifical governors, a tangible sign of the restoration of the Church's power in the area when the pope was ruling from Avignon. Several popes spent time here, and one of them, Alexander VI, in 1499 sent his capable teenage daughter Lucrezia Borgia (1480–1519) to serve as governor for three months. The Gubbio-born architect Gattapone (14th century) used the ruins of a Roman acropolis as a foundation and took materials from many Roman-era sites, including the Teatro Romano. La Rocca's plan is long and rectangular, with six towers and two grand courtyards, an upper loggia, and inside some grand reception rooms. In the largest tower, Torre Maestà, you can visit an apartment with some interesting frescoes. The fortress also contains the Museo Nazionale del Ducato, 15 rooms dedicated to the art of the duchy of Spoleto during the Middle Ages. If you phone in advance, you may be able to secure an English-speaking guide. ⊠ *Piazza Campello, Spoleto* ☎ *0743/224952* ⊕ *www.asso-roccaspoleto.it* ⊙ *Closed Tue. and Wed.* ☐ *€7.50, including the Museo Nazionale del Ducato.*

★ Ponte delle Torri (*Bridge of the Towers*)

BRIDGE | Standing massive and graceful through the deep gorge that separates Spoleto from Monteluco, this 14th-century bridge is one of Umbria's most photographed monuments, and justifiably so. Built over the foundations of a Roman-era aqueduct, it soars 262 feet above the forested gorge—higher than the dome of St. Peter's in Rome. Sweeping views over the valley and a pleasant sense of vertigo make a walk across the bridge a must, particularly on a starry night. ⊠ *Via del Ponte, Spoleto* ☐ *Free.*

Teatro Romano

RUINS | The Romans who colonized the city in 241 BC constructed this small theater in the 1st century AD; for centuries afterward it was used as a quarry for building materials. The most intact portion is the hallway that passes under the *cavea* (stands). The rest was heavily restored in the early 1950s and serves as a venue for Spoleto's Festival dei Due Mondi. The theater was the site of a gruesome episode in Spoleto's history: during the medieval struggle between Guelph (papal) and Ghibelline (imperial) forces, Spoleto took the side of the Holy Roman Emperor. Afterward, 400 Guelph supporters were massacred in the theater, their bodies burned in an enormous pyre. In the end, the Guelphs were triumphant, and Spoleto was incorporated into the states of the Church in 1354. Through a door in the west portico of the adjoining building is the **Museo Archeologico,** with assorted artifacts found in excavations primarily around Spoleto and Norcia. The collection contains Bronze Age and Iron Age artifacts from Umbrian and pre-Roman eras. The highlight is the stone tablet inscribed on both sides with the Lex Spoletina (Spoleto Law). Dating from 315 BC, this legal document prohibited the desecration of the woods on the slopes of nearby Monteluco. ⊠ *Piazza della Libertà, Spoleto* ☎ *0743/223277* ⊕ *www.spoletocard.it* ☐ *€4* ⊙ *Closed Mon. and Tue.*

Restaurants

★ Apollinare

$$ | UMBRIAN | Low wooden ceilings and flickering candlelight make this monastery from the 10th and 11th centuries Spoleto's most romantic spot; in warm weather you can dine under a canopy on the piazza across from the archaeological museum. The kitchen serves sophisticated, innovative variations on local dishes, including long, slender *strengozzi* pasta with such toppings as cherry tomatoes, mint, and a touch of red pepper, or (in season) porcini mushrooms or truffles. **Known for:** impeccable service; modern versions of traditional Umbrian dishes; intimate and elegant setting. $ *Average main: €16* ✉ *Via Sant'Agata 14, Spoleto* ☎ *0743/223256* ⊕ *www.ristoranteapollinare.it* ⊗ *Closed Tues.*

Il Tartufo

$$ | UMBRIAN | As the name indicates, dishes prepared with truffles are the specialty here—don't miss the risotto al tartufo. Incorporating the ruins of a Roman villa, the surroundings are rustic on the ground floor and more modern upstairs; in summer, tables appear outdoors and the traditional fare is spiced up to appeal to the cosmopolitan crowd attending (or performing in) the Festival dei Due Mondi. **Known for:** abundant portions, well presented; recipes incorporating truffles; charming staff. $ *Average main: €18* ✉ *Piazza Garibaldi 24, Spoleto* ☎ *0743/40236* ⊕ *www.ristoranteiltartufo.it* ⊗ *Closed Mon. and early Jan.–early Feb. No dinner Sun.*

Il Tempio del Gusto

$ | UMBRIAN | In charming shabby-chic environs, this welcoming eatery near the Arco di Druso (ancient Roman arch) serves up Italian with a subtle twist. Along with an extensive selection of thoughtfully chosen Umbrian wines, you'll find lots of veggie options, mounds of truffles in season, and, to finish things off, a superlative version of Spoleto sponge cake. **Known for:** friendly atmosphere; flavorful Umbrian cuisine; quaint setting. $ *Average main: €14* ✉ *Via Arco di Druso 11, Spoleto* ☎ *0743/47121* ⊕ *www.iltempiodelgusto.com* ⊗ *Closed Thurs.*

Ristorante Il Panciolle

$ | UMBRIAN | A small garden filled with lemon trees in the heart of Spoleto's medieval quarter provides one of the most appealing settings you could wish for. Dishes change throughout the year, and may include pastas served with asparagus or mushrooms, as well as grilled meats; more expensive dishes prepared with fresh truffles are also available in season. **Known for:** panoramic terrace; affable staff; authentic local cuisine. $ *Average main: €14* ✉ *Via Duomo 3/5, Spoleto* ☎ *0743/45677* ⊕ *www.ilpanciolle.it* ⊗ *Closed Wed. Sept.–Mar.*

🛏 Hotels

★ Hotel San Luca

$ | HOTEL | Hand-painted friezes decorate the walls of the spacious guest rooms, and elegant comfort is the grace note throughout—you can sip afternoon tea in oversize armchairs by the fireplace, or take a walk in the sweet-smelling rose garden. **Pros:** very helpful staff; spacious rooms; close to escalators for exploring city. **Cons:** no restaurant; can feel soulless in winter; outside the town center. $ *Rooms from: €91* ✉ *Via Interna delle Mura 21, Spoleto* ☎ *0743/223399* ⊕ *www.hotelsanluca.com* 🛏 *35 rooms* ⦿ *Free Breakfast.*

★ Palazzo Leti Residenza d'Epoca

$ | HOTEL | Fabulously landscaped gardens, complete with fountains and sculptures, along with panoramic views provide a grand entrance to this late 13th-century residence turned charming hotel high up in Spoleto's old town. **Pros:** friendly owners happy to help; feels like a private hideaway; unbeatable views. **Cons:** often booked far in advance; reaching on-site parking can be tricky; few amenities (no restaurant, gym, or spa). $ *Rooms from: €109* ✉ *Via degli Eremiti 10, Spoleto* ☎ *0743/224930* ⊕ *www.palazzoleti.com* ➡ *12 rooms* ❑ *Free Breakfast.*

Orvieto

30 km (19 miles) southwest of Todi, 81 km (51 miles) west of Spoleto.

Carved out of an enormous plateau of volcanic rock high above a green valley, Orvieto has natural defenses that made the high walls seen in many Umbrian towns unnecessary. The Etruscans were the first to settle here, digging a honeycombed network of more than 1,200 wells and storage caves out of the soft stone. The Romans attacked, sacked, and destroyed the city in 283 BC; since then, it has grown up out of the rock into an enchanting maze of alleys and squares. Orvieto was solidly Guelph in the Middle Ages, and for several hundred years popes sought refuge in the city, at times needing protection from their enemies, at times seeking respite from the summer heat of Rome.

When painting his frescoes inside the Duomo, Luca Signorelli asked that part of his contract be paid in Orvietan wine, and he was neither the first nor the last to appreciate the region's popular white. In past times the caves carved underneath the town were used to ferment the Trebbiano grapes used in making Orvieto Classico; now local wine production has moved out to more traditional vineyards, but you can still while away the afternoon with tastings at any number of shops in town.

GETTING HERE AND AROUND
Orvieto is well connected by train to Rome, Florence, and Perugia. It's also adjacent to the A1 autostrada that runs between Florence and Rome. Parking areas in the upper town tend to be crowded. A better idea is to follow the signs for the Porta Orvetiana parking lot, then take the funicular that carries people up the hill.

VISITOR INFORMATION
The Carta Orvieto Unica (single ticket) is expensive but a great deal if you want to visit everything. For €20 you get admission to 11 museums and monuments, including the three major sights in town—Cappella di San Brizio (at the Duomo), Museo Etrusco Claudio Faina, and Orvieto Underground—along with entry to the Torre del Moro, with views of Orvieto, plus a bus and funicular pass.

CONTACT Orvieto Tourism Office. ✉ *Piazza del Duomo 24, Orvieto* ☎ *0763/341772* ⊕ *www.liveorvieto.com.*

Sights

★ Duomo
CHURCH | Orvieto's stunning cathedral was built to commemorate the Miracle at Bolsena. In 1263 a young priest who questioned the miracle of transubstantiation (in which the Communion bread and wine become the flesh and blood of Christ) was saying Mass at nearby Lago di Bolsena. A wafer he had just blessed suddenly started to drip blood, staining the linen covering the altar. Thirty years later, construction began on a duomo in Orvieto to celebrate the miracle and house the stained altar cloth. Inside, the cathedral is rather vast and empty; the major works are in the transepts. To the left is the **Cappella del Corporale**, where the square linen cloth (*corporale*) is kept in a golden reliquary that's modeled on the cathedral and inlaid with enamel scenes of the miracle. In the right transept is the **Cappella di San Brizio**, which holds one of Italy's greatest fresco cycles, notable for its influence on Michelangelo's *Last Judgment*, as well as for the extraordinary beauty of the figuration. In these works, a few by Fra Angelico and the majority by Luca Signorelli, the damned fall to hell, demons breathe fire and blood, and Christians are martyred. ✉ *Piazza del Duomo,*

Hiking the Umbrian Hills

Magnificent scenery makes the heart of Italy excellent walking, hiking, and mountaineering country. In Umbria, the area around Spoleto is particularly good; several pleasant, easy, and well-signed trails begin at the far end of the Ponte alle Torri bridge over Monteluco. From Cannara, an easy half-hour walk leads to the fields of Pian d'Arca, the site of St. Francis's sermon to the birds. For slightly more arduous walks, you can follow the saint's path, uphill from Assisi to the Eremo delle Carceri, and then continue along the trails that crisscross Monte Subasio. At 4,250 feet, the treeless summit affords views of Assisi, Perugia, far-off Gubbio, and the distant mountain ranges of Abruzzo.

For even more challenging hiking, the northern reaches of the Valnerina are exceptional; the mountains around Norcia should not be missed. Throughout Umbria and the Marches, you'll find that most recognized walking and hiking trails are marked with the distinctive red-and-white blazes of the Club Alpino Italiano. Tourist offices are a good source for walking and climbing itineraries to suit all ages and levels of ability, while bookstores, *tabacchi* (tobacconists), and *edicole* (newsstands) often have maps and hiking guides that detail the best routes in their area. Depending on the length and location of your walk, it can be important that you have comfortable walking shoes or boots, appropriate attire, and plenty of water to drink.

Orvieto ☎ 0763/342477 ⊕ www.opsm.it ✉ €5, including Cappella di San Brizio.

Museo Etrusco Claudio Faina

HISTORY MUSEUM | This superb private collection, beautifully arranged and presented, goes far beyond the usual museum offerings of a scattering of local remains. The collection is particularly rich in Greek- and Etruscan-era pottery, from large Attic amphorae (6th–4th century BC) to Attic black- and red-figure pieces to Etruscan *bucchero* (dark-reddish clay) vases. Other interesting pieces in the collection include a 6th-century sarcophagus and a substantial display of Roman-era coins. ✉ Piazza del Duomo 29, Orvieto ☎ 0763/341216 ⊕ www.museofaina.it ✉ €5 ⊗ Closed Mon.–Thurs.

Orvieto Underground

RUINS | More than just about any other town, Orvieto has grown from its own foundations. The Etruscans, the Romans, and those who followed dug into the tufa (the same soft volcanic rock from

which catacombs were made) to create more than 1,000 separate cisterns, caves, secret passages, storage areas, and production areas for wine and olive oil. Much of the tufa removed was used as building blocks for the city that exists today, and some was partly ground into *pozzolana*, which was made into mortar. You can see the labyrinth of dugout chambers beneath the city on the Orvieto Underground tour, which runs daily at 11, 12:15, 4, and 5:15 (more frequently in busy periods) from Piazza del Duomo 23. ✉ Orvieto ☎ 0763/344891 ⊕ www. orvietounderground.it ✉ Tours €7.

Pozzo della Cava

RUINS | If you're short on time but want a quick look at the cisterns and caves beneath the city, head for the Pozzo della Cava, an Etruscan well for spring water. ✉ Via della Cava 28, Orvieto ☎ 0763/342373 ⊕ www.pozzodellacava. it ✉ €4.

🍴 Restaurants

Le Grotte del Funaro

$ | **UMBRIAN** | Dine inside tufa caves under central Orvieto, where the two windows afford splendid views of the hilly countryside. The traditional Umbrian food is reliably good, with simple grilled meats and vegetables and pizzas—oddly, though, the food is outclassed by an extensive wine list, with top local and Italian labels and quite a few rare vintages. **Known for:** good choice of wines; unusual setting; crusty pizzas. [$] *Average main: €14* ✉ *Via Ripa Serancia 41, Orvieto* ☎ *0763/343276* 🌐 *www.grottedelfunaro.com* 🕒 *Closed Mon. and 10 days in July.*

Ristorante Maurizio

$$ | **UMBRIAN** | Off a busy pedestrian street near the Duomo, this welcoming family-owned restaurant has an uber-contemporary look, but is actually housed in a 14th-century medieval building with arched ceilings. The Martinelli family's own products, including balsamic vinegar, olive oil, and pasta, are used in their robustly flavored dishes, and you can also sample their own well-regarded Montefalco wines. **Known for:** local wines; traditional Umbrian dishes; complimentary balsamic vinegar tasting to start. [$] *Average main: €16* ✉ *Via del Duomo 78, Orvieto* ☎ *0763/341114, 0763/343212* 🌐 *www.ristorante-maurizio.com.*

Trattoria La Grotta

$$ | **UMBRIAN** | The vaulted, plant-filled dining area with white walls adorned with paintings, antique vases, and other knickknacks makes a congenial setting for this small, rustic-style trattoria that is lauded for its homemade pasta, perhaps with an artichoke, duck, or wild-boar sauce. Roast lamb, veal, and pork are all good, and the desserts are supplied by Orvieto's most eminent pasticceria. **Known for:** tasty homemade pastas; warm and welcoming service; fresh, local ingredients. [$] *Average main: €16* ✉ *Via Luca Signorelli 5, Orvieto* ☎ *0763/341348* 🌐 *www.trattorialagrottaorvieto.com* 🕒 *Closed Tues.*

🛏 Hotels

Hotel Palazzo Piccolomini

$ | **HOTEL** | This 16th-century family palazzo has been beautifully restored, with inviting public spaces and handsome guest quarters where contemporary surroundings are accented with old beams, vaulted ceilings, and other distinctive touches. **Pros:** good location; private parking; efficient staff. **Cons:** four-star category not completely justified; underwhelming breakfasts; some rooms and bathrooms are small. [$] *Rooms from: €120* ✉ *Piazza Ranieri 36, Orvieto* ☎ *0763/341743* 🌐 *www.palazzopiccolomini.it* 🛏 *33 rooms* 🍽 *Free Breakfast.*

★ **Locanda Palazzone**

$$$ | **HOTEL** | Spending the night in this 13th-century building just 5 km (3 miles) northwest of Orvieto is like staying in a sophisticated country home, with vineyard views, a private chef, and two-level rooms with modern furnishings. **Pros:** tasty meals served nightly; tranquil surroundings; extremely friendly owners and staff. **Cons:** limited public spaces to lounge in; no à la carte menus; split-level rooms can be difficult for those with mobility issues or young children. [$] *Rooms from: €234* ✉ *Località Rocca Ripesena 68, Orvieto* ☎ *0763/393614* 🌐 *www.locandapalazzone.it* 🛏 *7 rooms* 🍽 *Free Breakfast.*

Index

Photo Credits

Notes

Dear Captain Gossner,

Congratulations on your retirement! My husband and I are returning to the US after this, our second trip to Italy. We attended four wonderful concerts in Milan, Florence, Assissi, and Rome, in which our 12-year-old grandson sang with his choir from the Madeleine Choir School in Salt Lake City, Utah. The concert in Rome was in St. Peter's Basilica during Pope Francis's weekly Mass. Our memories of this wonderful week for our family represent all the memories you have enabled other families to share by your skill and expertise to transport us all safely away and back home again! We salute you, we thank you, and we wish you a retirement full of joy and adventure with your family!!
Bon Voyage!

M + J Siebels

Fodor's THE BEST OF ITALY

Publisher: Stephen Horowitz, *General Manager*

Editorial: Douglas Stallings, *Editorial Director*; Jill Fergus, Amanda Sadlowski, Caroline Trefler, *Senior Editors*; Kayla Becker, Alexis Kelly, *Editors;* Angelique Kennedy-Chavannes, *Assistant Editor*

Design: Tina Malaney, *Director of Design and Production*; Jessica Gonzalez, *Graphic Designer*

Production: Jennifer DePrima, *Editorial Production Manager*; Elyse Rozelle, *Senior Production Editor*; Monica White, *Production Editor*

Maps: Rebecca Baer, *Senior Map Editor*; David Lindroth, Mark Stroud (Moon Street Cartography), *Cartographers*

Photography: Viviane Teles, *Senior Photo Editor*; Namrata Aggarwal, Payal Gupta, Ashok Kumar, *Photo Editors*; Rebecca Rimmer, *Photo Production Associate*; Eddie Aldrete, *Photo Production Intern*

Business and Operations: Chuck Hoover, *Chief Marketing Officer*; Robert Ames, *Group General Manager*; Devin Duckworth, *Director of Print Publishing*

Public Relations and Marketing: Joe Ewaskiw, *Senior Director of Communications & Public Relations*

Fodors.com: Jeremy Tarr, *Editorial Director*; Rachael Levitt, *Managing Editor*

Technology: Jon Atkinson, *Director of Technology*; Rudresh Teotia, *Lead Developer*; Jacob Ashpis, *Content Operations Manager*

Writers: Nick Bruno, Liz Humphreys, Laura Itzkowitz, Fergal Kavanagh, Patricia Rucidlo, Liz Shemaria

Editor: Jill Fergus

Production Editor: Monica White

3rd Edition

ISBN 978-1-64097-419-7

ISSN 2476-0951

All details in this book are based on information supplied to us at press time. Always confirm information when it matters, especially if you're making a detour to visit a specific place. Fodor's expressly disclaims any liability, loss, or risk, personal or otherwise, that is incurred as a consequence of the use of any of the contents of this book.

SPECIAL SALES

This book is available at special discounts for bulk purchases for sales promotions or premiums. For more information, e-mail SpecialMarkets@fodors.com.

PRINTED IN CANADA

10 9 8 7 6 5 4 3 2 1

About Our Writers

Nick Bruno is an Italy specialist and frequent Fodor's contributor. As well as authoring and updating books and features, he makes radio packages for the BBC. A lifelong interest in history and Italian language has led to a project researching his paternal Italian family during the Il Ventennio Fascista period. For this edition, he contributed to the Experience and Northern Italy chapters. Follow him on Instagram and Twitter @nickjgbruno and barbruno.com.

Liz Humphreys is a transplant to Europe from New York City, where she spent a decade in editorial positions for media companies including Condé Nast and Time Inc. Since then she's written and edited for publications including *Condé Nast Traveler*, *Michelin Green Guides*, *Time Out*, *Forbes Travel*, and *Rough Guides*. Liz updated the Venice and Tuscany and Umbria chapters. Follow Liz on Instagram @winederlust_wanderings.

Laura Itzkowitz is a freelance writer and editor based in Rome with an MFA in creative writing and a passion for covering travel, arts and culture, lifestyle, design, food and wine. Her writing has appeared in *Travel + Leisure*, *Architectural Digest*, *Vogue*, *GQ*, *Departures*, *AFAR, and* others. Laura updated the Rome chapter. Follow her on Instagram and Twitter @ lauraitzkowitz.

Fergal Kavanagh travels extensively throughout Italy with his Tune Into English Roadshow, where he teaches English through pop music (tuneintoenglish.com). In his twenty five years in the country there is hardly a town square he has not passed through. He updated the Travel Smart chapter for this edition.

Patricia Rucidlo holds master's degrees in Italian Renaissance history and art history. She is also a licensed tour guide in Florence and also works in Lucca. When she's not extolling the virtues of a Pontormo masterpiece or angrily defending the Medici, you can find her leading food and wine tours in Florence and environs. Patricia updated the Florence, Tuscany and Umbria, and Northern Italy chapters.

Liz Shemaria is an award-winning journalist and third-generation Northern Californian who has trekked solo in Himalaya and interviewed artists in military-ruled Burma. Liz is a founding editor at Hidden Compass and has contributed to more than a dozen publications and organizations including *Human Rights Watch*, *BBC Travel*, *AFAR*, and *Roads & Kingdoms*. Liz lives in Italy and updated the Northern Italy chapter. Follow her on Instagram @lizshemaria.